Crime, Criminology,
and
Contemporary Society

THE DORSEY SERIES IN ANTHROPOLOGY AND SOCIOLOGY

EDITOR   ROBIN M. WILLIAMS, JR.   *Cornell University*

ANDERSON *Sociological Essays and Research: Introductory Readings*

BARNOUW *Culture and Personality*

BELL *Marriage and Family Interaction* rev. ed.

BELL & STUB (eds.) *The Sociology of Education: A Sourcebook* rev. ed.

BREER & LOCKE *Task Experience as a Source of Attitudes*

GAMSON *Power and Discontent*

GEORGES (ed.) *Studies on Mythology*

GOODMAN *The Individual and Culture*

GORDEN *Interviewing: Strategy, Techniques, and Tactics*

GOTTLIEB & RAMSEY *The American Adolescent*

HAGEN *On the Theory of Social Change: How Economic Growth Begins*

JACOBS *Pattern in Cultural Anthropology*

JOHNSON *Crime, Correction, and Society* rev. ed.

KNUDTEN *Crime, Criminology, and Contemporary Society*

KOHN *Class and Conformity: A Study in Values*

LeMASTERS *Parents in Modern America*

MARIS *Social Forces in Urban Suicide*

SALISBURY *Religion in American Culture: A Sociological Interpretation*

SHOSTAK (ed.) *Sociology in Action: Case Studies in Social Problems and Directed Social Change*

WARRINER *The Emergence of Society*

WILSON *Sociology: Rules, Roles, and Relationships*

Crime, Criminology, and Contemporary Society

Edited by

RICHARD D. KNUDTEN

Chairman, Department of Sociology
Valparaiso University

1970 | The
Dorsey
Press . HOMEWOOD, ILLINOIS
IRWIN-DORSEY LIMITED, GEORGETOWN, ONTARIO

Library of Congress Catalog Card No. 70-112829

Printed in the United States of America

To My Children
Stephen, David, Thomas, and *Susan,*
who are refreshingly oblivious of
modern crime anxieties

Preface

The increasing worldwide crime rate, especially noted since the middle 1940's, received attention during the 1968 presidential and even later elections. Defined as the problem of "crime in the streets," its debate largely reflected the fears and experiences of the growing urban population. Facing increasing challenges to the social order in attacks against the person and against property, rioting and civil disobedience, and even excessive police aggressiveness, the public served notice that it would demand a heightened war on crime at the same time that it would continue to seek economy in government. Nevertheless, the public continued to fear the effects of delinquency and crime. Even a change in political administrations could not quickly allay the fears of many urban dwellers: witness the 43 percent of a sample taken from high crime areas in two large cities who claimed in the mid-1960's that they do not walk on the streets at night, the 35 percent who do not speak to strangers, the 21 percent who use cars and cabs at night, and the 20 percent who would like to move to another neighborhood. When nearly one third of the American population feels it is unsafe to walk in their own neighborhoods after dark and more than one third argue that they need to keep arms to protect their person, they vividly suggest the problem and their plan for its solution.

In such a context of fear, charges and counter-charges are hurled quickly and emotionally. The police blame the courts for the current crime rise, while the courts suggest that the police are responsible for violation of basic constitutional rights. The public condones the aggressive police action at the Democratic National Convention, although a special commission on the Chicago violence accuses the police department of participating in a "police riot." Consequently, the bewildered public responds to news media reports with uncertainty and a demand that political leadership control the ambiguous situation. And yet, while the public is most afraid of violent crimes against the person, these are the most infrequent criminal acts. Conditioned by their fear of crime, the public fails to realize that crimes are much more frequent in the ghetto than in the suburban or rural areas and that organized crime involves greater social costs than many traditional crimes.

Crime is a product of human interaction. Adult crimes represent largely a continuity of juvenile delinquency; crime has continued to increase as the proportion of juveniles and young adults within the population has grown. As this younger portion of the population composes nearly one half of the

American total, the continuing growth in the volume of delinquent and criminal patterns is quite likely.

Since the problem of crime assumes many faces, it is not easily defined nor quickly comprehended. Despite this limitation, the editor has brought together in this volume of eight parts a wide spectrum of data concerning the nature and scope of the crime problem. Attempting to keep the analysis contemporary and well-integrated, he has introduced each part and each article within its basic criminological context. Throughout, however, the central focus continues to be crime, criminology, and contemporary American society.

In Part One, entitled Culture, Society and Criminology, the relationships of criminal law, general culture, public fears, and limitations of current data are examined. Part Two shifts to an overview of the many varied types of crime and the processes involved in criminal behavior. Special attention is paid to the youthful offender, the white-collar criminal, the defensive gang, organized crime, and the nature of violence. Based on the realization that crime is in part a product of socialization, Part Three introduces a discussion of school attendance, religious participation, and social roles in the delinquency–crime-producing process.

The relationships of social class and ethnic variables to crime are explored in Part Four, while the roles of the policeman receive special attention in Part Five. The focus on the system of justice, the topic of Part Six, includes insights into the administration of criminal justice, the problem of criminal responsibility, the relationship of the defense attorney to his client, the processes of the criminal jury, and the nature of juvenile justice. Part Seven offers a review of the context of Crime and Contemporary Corrections through presentation of five articles that discuss the sentencing and treatment of offenders, an overview of the correctional system, the divergent goals of the institutional and inmate social systems, an evaluation of the social meaning of prison homosexuality, and a probing of the alternatives to institutionalization. Finally, Part Eight concludes with the question of whether punishment is necessary, an evaluation of the future contributions of the sociology of law, a timely consideration of the Walker Report on the Chicago Democratic Convention disorders, and an overview of the crises of a society in ferment.

This volume is not intended to be all things to all people. It is designed to augment established criminology texts with contemporary data or to stand alone, as the instructor desires. Intended as a volume which brings the many disciplines in the field together in a coherent discussion, it nevertheless focuses on the interaction and conduct which occurs daily within the social system. Consequently, rather than establishing a special section on theories of causation, often deadly to student interest, theoretical contributions have been interspersed throughout in order to allow the student to see both the theory and its application in some problematic social context.

Crime, Criminology, and Contemporary Society possesses both strengths and weaknesses. It makes no pretenses of covering cross-cultural sources, because the current context of American criminology is filled with so many issues and the needs of both students and teachers suggest brevity. Of necessity, much meaningful data have been excluded. Rather than create a volume similar to those already on the market, the editor, too, has consciously attempted to avoid such duplication. Consequently, many favorite selections of potential users of this volume may have been omitted. However, this book has been created to introduce the student to the contemporary crime problem through the contributions of diverse authorities. The editor, therefore, is profoundly grateful to those who quickly granted him their permission to include their research within this volume. Special recognition must also be given to Linda Crowell, Sandra Spalding, Janet Thies, Barbara Gerken, Cheryl Buser, and Trudy Heinecke, who have assumed much of the clerical work involved in the production of this volume; and to my wife, Mary S. Knudten, who served as my editorial assistant. Any acknowledgments, however, would be incomplete without the recognition of the contributions of Moellering Librarian Carl Sachtleben, his staff, and the administration of Valparaiso University.

April, 1970   Richard D. Knudten

Contents

part EIGHT
Social Control and Social Change 385

part ONE

Culture, Society, and Criminology

Crime by definition is a violation of a criminal statute which either demands or prohibits specific conduct. Consequently, the criminal code is by nature diverse and inconsistent. On the federal level alone, there are more than 2,800 defined offenses. State laws and local ordinances prescribe an even larger number of misdemeanor or felony violations which range from prohibitions against harming another person, general or serious stealing, violations of public morals or public order, infringement of government revenue provisions, challenges to the nature of the regular economy, or participation in an activity which is hazardous to the public. The exact content of the law and the penalties to be inflicted for violation vary from jurisdiction to jurisdiction. While prostitution, a female crime, for example, may be largely ignored in some states, it may lead to a felony conviction in others. Even homicide, found in all areas of the United States but four to six times more common in the Southeast and Southwest than in the Northeast, can lead to a life sentence, which itself may be lessened by good behavior in prison, or to the infliction of the death penalty. In such cases, the content and process of legal disposition reflect the cultural and legal traditions of the legislature, the region, or the country.

For this reason, among others, the crime problem in any nation is not easily solved. Because criminal conduct is closely related to the nature and structure of society, crime control cannot be achieved by the mere application of force or the use of coercion. Ultimately, crime control depends upon the tacit and voluntary cooperation of the public and the reasoned use of police power (*see* Toby, Article 32). Most societies possess neither the manpower nor the facilities necessary to control the activities of all their members. Those that attempt total control, therefore, must enact a form of totalitarianism which consequently must radically restructure a democratic society in order to attain its closed-society control. Therefore, if such control could be accomplished, it is questionable whether it would be in the public interest.

Since crime, as Emile Durkheim noted decades ago, is a normal process of society, it cannot be interpreted as something abnormal within the social fabric. Undesirable, yes; fully abnormal, no. Crime often reflects the change of culture and calls attention to the structural and associational problems inherent in social change (*see* introduction to Article 7). While a society may inflict punishment upon the person, its use is authorized in order to bring about changes in individual and group conduct and to deter others through its example. The very use of punishment, therefore, assumes the continued existence of the criminal tendency and the need to control its practice. Crime, nevertheless, is a dynamic form of human behavior which both exists and is controlled by the society, which defines levels of acceptable and unacceptable conduct.

Contemporary statistics, despite the absence of fully comparable international crime data, tend to support the Durkheimian conception. Crime is worldwide. Although foreign crimes of violence follow no definite pattern, overseas property offense rates reflect the growth of modern urbanization and technology and continue to rise rapidly. International crimes of violence and offenses against property have been increasing at a rate somewhat greater than the population. Nevertheless, it is reasonable to assume that in most countries nearly all males and females believed to be "normal" citizens have committed some violations of the criminal code without detection, apprehension, trial, or conviction. In those nations marked by a rising technology and a growing middle class, white-collar crimes, largely undetected and unprosecuted, have become more common. However, organized crime, a European cultural form which found national root in the United States during Prohibition, has been largely ignored, as the focus has remained upon the traditional cultural and social crimes of homicide, aggravated assault, robbery, burglary, larceny, forcible rape, and auto theft (*see* Hawkins, Article 9). In any case, the definition and adjudication of the criminal code, whether nationally or internationally, reveal the cultural attitudes, values, and power groups operating within the existing political unit.

CRIME IN THE UNITED STATES

Crimes against the person comprise only 13 percent of the registered *Index Offenses* (7 most serious offenses) reported by the Federal Bureau of Investigation. The remaining 87 percent involve crimes against property, largely burglary and larceny, which are generally completed in secrecy. Nearly one half of all robberies, which involve both the theft of property and the use of force against the person, occur in the street. Slightly more than 50 percent of these acts include the use of weapons. Nearly 70 percent of all willful murders, approximately two thirds of all aggravated assaults, and a high percentage of forcible rapes are committed by family members, friends, or other persons previously known to their victims (*see* Schultz, Article 13). The probability of a serious attack against the person in any given year is about 1 in 550. However, because crime by its very nature is essentially secret, the exact volume of existing criminality is never fully known (*see* Quinney, Article 8).

The highest reported crime density occurs in urban and inner city areas. Urban crime rates tend to be three times the rate of rural areas. The greatest number of murders, forcible rapes, robberies, aggravated assaults, and burglaries occurs most frequently in large urban slums. The offenders and the victims tend to be the poorest, the most uneducated, and the most marginally employable of the national population. Consequently, the control of crime cannot be divorced from the human aspirations and conditions of the lower-class citizen (*see* Fannin and Clinard, Article 16; and Strecher, Article 17). Any meaningful analysis of the crime problem, therefore, cannot be divorced from an investigation of the relationship of the victim to the offender, the social psychology of the person, or the existing associational and cultural commitments of the offender.

Although the number of crimes reported to the police has increased each year, the contemporary crime concern has undoubtedly contributed to the recorded growth as the public has been sensitized to report observed or known criminal acts which they formerly ignored or failed to report to the police. However, changing variations in police practice, the rise in the use of insurance, the increasing trend toward urbanization, and the growth of economic affluence are also among the factors which influence the increase of the reported crime rate. The reported crime rate is affected by many other conditions: the density and size of the metropolitan population; the age, sex, and racial composition of the population; the economic status of the citizenry; the relative stability or mobility of the populace; seasonal weather conditions and climate; the educational, recreational, and religious characteristics of the population; the effective strength of the police force; standards governing appointments to the police force; policies of the prosecuting officials or the courts; attitudes of the public toward law enforcement problems; and the administrative and the investigative efficiency of the local law enforcement agency. Nevertheless, crime is a cultural product, defined in law and transmitted through socialization. It is related to the existing cultural practices and to the ambiguity resulting from cultural and normative conflicts. Crime, as Durkheim noted, is a consequential aspect of group existence.

Following this lead, Part One of this volume examines the crisis of overcriminalization and the influence of the general culture on crime definitions and criminal conduct. It also reviews the value of existing crime statistics, especially those concerning "race," and the future contribution of science and technology to data gathering and analysis. While Sanford H. Kadish, for example, examines the excessive use of law as a means of constraining human conduct, Donald R. Taft suggests that the general culture in effect aids the creation of crime patterns and stimulates criminal conduct. In a more specific vein, Gilbert Geis probes the relationship of racial factors and crime statistics, while Roland J. Chilton evaluates the value of a national center for crime statistics.

1. The Crisis of Overcriminalization*

SANFORD H. KADISH

The problem of determinism and indeterminism is a central issue in any study of crime. Ultimately, the problems of individual responsibility and guilt, pertinent to the definition of the crime, its eventual adjudication, and the treatment of criminal conduct, are inseparably bound to the philosophical argument posed by the determinist and the indeterminist. While the *indeterminist* suggests that each man's action is a product of his individual free will, the *determinist* argues that one's conduct is inseparably related to the conditions of his existence. Although Becarria and Lombroso posed the question in criminological terms in their Classical and Positivist theories of the 18th and 19th centuries, the issue continues to be a vital one in criminology even today.

Contemporary criminology generally assumes a determinist position and begins with the presupposition that crime is essentially a social product. The law, on the other hand, operates on the basic principle that each man must be held accountable for his own actions. While the criminal code recognizes the existence of gradations of individual responsibility, ranging from full premeditation to unintended accident, it nevertheless assumes that each man makes his decision to complete a particular act with full knowledge of its ultimate consequences. The criminologist's findings, however, are founded upon the presupposition that human beings do not always act upon adequate knowledge but may be stimulated by social interaction to complete those types of acts which they would not normally commit when left to themselves (*see* Hall, Article 23). Recognizing that the social self develops out of the interaction of innate biological, general socioenvironmental and mediating factors, the criminologist views crime as the product of human existence which is socially defined and socially acted out.

Criminal law is a product of the many historical attempts to justify the use of punishment in forcing the free will to stop criminal conduct (*see* Toby, Article 32). Although it originally presupposed a determinist viewpoint, the contemporary criminal code includes many indeterminist ideas within its formulations. As a result, criminal law seldom follows an integrated or coherent pattern in any country. Some laws represent universal prohibitions; others,

*Originally published in the *Annals*, Volume 374 (November, 1967), pp. 157-70. Reprinted by permission of the author and publisher, The American Academy of Political and Social Science.

however, are the clear creations of vested interest groups. Because laws are often merely pragmatic legislative solutions to difficult social questions, they generally include both deterministic and indeterministic elements, as witnessed, for example, in the legal demand for harsh punishment (indeterministic) and the humanist attempt to rehabilitate and remotivate the criminal offender (deterministic).

Data gathered by social scientists challenge the basic assumptions of the "pure" determinists. The recognition that the degree of choice in any act is often circumscribed by the emotion of the moment has forced the modification of the determinist's position in modern thought. The person's ability to resist delinquency and crime pressures varies in relationship to his age and experience, socioenvironmental conditions, and the existing opportunity, among other factors. Therefore, the attempt to reduce human behavior to the specificity assumed in criminal law is filled with many difficulties. Human conduct often cannot be defined as specifically as a law must be. The diversity of personality, cultural values, and human experience automatically extends conduct beyond the limits defined by the criminal code. Consequently, the attempt to constrain human behavior by an overuse of criminal law has created acute strains in modern urban societies. The dependence upon criminal law to enforce morals, provide social services, and eliminate legal restraints on law enforcement, Sanford H. Kadish believes, has created inefficient enforcement and lessened the actual realization of justice. The use of criminal code as an agency of suppression has often negated the specific purpose of the particular criminal law. Part of the modern crime problem, Kadish believes, is a produce of this overdependence upon law as a means by which to bring about desired behavioral responses (*see* Gibbs, Article 33).

Since the last war there have been striking achievements in reform of the substantive criminal law. Largely under the impetus of the American Law Institute's Model Penal Code, a number of states have completed revisions of their criminal codes, and still more are in the process. The importance of this reform for criminal justice cannot be overstated.

But there is a significant feature of substantive law-revision which these reforms have succeeded in reaching only in part. By and large, these efforts have dealt with offenses entailing substantial harm to persons, property, and the state, against which the criminal law is generally accepted as the last and necessary resort. But American criminal law typically has extended the criminal sanction well beyond these fundamental offenses to include very different kinds of behavior, kinds which threaten far less serious harms, or else highly intangible ones about which there is no genuine consensus, or even no harms at all. The existence of these crimes and attempts at their eradication raise problems of inestimable importance for the criminal law. . . .

The subjects raising the central issue of overcriminalization cut a wide swathe through the laws of most jurisdictions. In the process of revising the California criminal law, we encountered a mass of crimes outside the Penal Code, matching the Penal Code itself in volume, and authorizing criminal convictions for such offenses as failure by a school principal to use required textbooks,[1] failure of a teacher to carry first-aid kits on field trips,[2] gambling on the result of an election,[3] giving private commercial performances by a state-supported band,[4] and allowing waste of an artesian well by the landowner.[5] Then there are the criminal laws, enforced by state police forces, which have been the primary means used to deal with the death and injury toll of the automobile. Indications are that this response may ultimately do more harm than good by blocking off politically harder, but more likely, remedial alternatives.[6] Problematic also has been the use of criminal sanctions to enforce economic regulatory measures. . . . And there are other instances as well. In this piece I want to comment on the problems of overcriminalization in just three kinds of situations, in each of which the costs paid primarily affect the day-to-day business of law enforcement. These are the situations in which the criminal law is used: (1) to declare or enforce public standards of private morality, (2) as a means of providing social services in default of other public agencies, and (3) as a disingenuous means of permitting police to do indirectly what the law forbids them to do directly.

ENFORCEMENT OF MORALS

The use of the criminal law to prohibit moral deviancy among consenting adults has been a recurring subject of jurisprudential debate. Stephens in the last century[7] and Lord Devlin in this century have urged the legitimacy of criminal intervention on the ground that "society cannot ignore the morality of the individual any more than it can his loyalty; it flourishes on both and without either it dies."[8] The contrary view, vigorously espoused by John Stuart Mill in the nineteenth century,[9] and by H. L. A. Hart[10] and many others in recent years, is, in the words of the Wolfenden Report:

Unless a deliberate attempt is to be made by society, acting through the agency of the law, to equate the sphere of crime with that of sin, there

1/*Calif. Education Code* sec. 9255.
2/*Idem* at sec. 11955.
3/*Calif. Elections Code* sec. 29003.
4/*Calif. Government Code* sec. 6650.
5/*Calif. Water Code* sec. 307.
6/See the telling account of Moynihan, "The War Against the Automobile," *The Public Interest*, No. 3 (Spring 1966), especially at 21 *et seq.*
7/J. F. Stephens, *Liberty, Fraternity and Equality* (1873).
8/Devlin, *The Enforcement of Morals* 23 (1959).
9/J. S. Mill, *On Liberty* (1859).
10/H. L. A. Hart, *Law, Liberty and Morality* (1963).

must remain a realm of private morality and immorality which is, in brief and crude terms, not the law's business.[11]

It is not my purpose here to mediate or resolve that dispute. My objective is to call attention to matters of the hardest concreteness and practicality, which should be of as much concern in reaching final judgment to a Devlin as to the staunchest libertarian; namely, the adverse consequences to effective law enforcement of attempting to achieve conformity with private moral standards through use of the criminal law.

Sex Offenses

The classic instance of the use of the criminal law purely to enforce a moral code is the laws prohibiting extramarital and abnormal sexual intercourse between a man and a woman. Whether or not Kinsey's judgment is accurate that 95 per cent of the population are made potential criminals by these laws,[12] no one doubts that their standard of sexual conduct is not adhered to by vast numbers in the community, including the otherwise most respectable (and, most especially, the police themselves);[13] nor is it disputed that there is no effort to enforce these laws. . . . Thurman Arnold surely had it right when he observed that these laws "are unenforced because we want to continue our conduct, and unrepealed because we want to preserve our morals."[14]

But law enforcement pays a price for using the criminal law in this way. First, the moral message communicated by the law is contradicted by the total absence of enforcement; for while the public sees the conduct condemned in words, it also sees in the dramatic absence of prosecutions that it is not condemned in deed. Moral adjurations vulnerable to a charge of hypocrisy are self-defeating no less in law than elsewhere. Second, the spectacle of nullification of the legislature's solemn commands is an unhealthy influence on law enforcement generally. It tends to breed a cynicism and an indifference to the criminal-law processes which augment tendencies toward disrespect for those who make and enforce the law, a disrespect which is already widely in evidence. . . . Finally, these laws invite discriminatory enforcement against persons selected for prosecution on grounds unrelated to the evil against which these laws are purportedly addressed, whether those grounds be "the prodding of some reform group, a newspaper-generated hysteria over some local sex crime, a vice drive which is put on by the local authorities to distract attention from defects in their administration of the city government."[15]

The criminalization of consensual adult homosexuality represents another

11/Great Britain Committee on Homosexual Offenses and Prostitution, *Report, Command* No. 247 (1957) (Wolfenden Report), Paras. 61 and 62.

12/Kinsey, Pomeroy, and Martin, *Sexual Behavior in the Human Male* 392 (1948).

13/See Skolnik, *Justice without Trial* (1966), chap. iii.

14/Thurman Arnold, *Symbols of Government* 160 (1936).

15/Kinsey, Martin, and Gebhard, *Sexual Behavior in the Human Female* 392 (1953).

attempt to legislate private morality. It raises somewhat different problems from heterosexual offenses, in that there are some attempts at enforcement. The central questions are whether the criminal law is an effective way of discouraging this conduct and how wasteful or costly it is.

Despite the fact that homosexual practices are condemned as criminal in virtually all states, usually as a felony with substantial punishment, and despite sporadic efforts at enforcement in certain situations, there is little evidence that the criminal law has discouraged the practice to any substantial degree. . . . One major reason for the ineffectiveness of these laws is that the private and consensual nature of the conduct precludes the attainment of any substantial deterrent efficacy through law enforcement. . . . Another reason is the irrelevance of the threat of punishment. . . . Moreover, in view of the character of prison environments, putting the homosexual defendant into the prison system is, as observed recently by a United States District Court Judge, "a little like throwing Bre'r Rabbit into the briarpatch." [16]

On the other hand, the use of the criminal law has been attended by grave consequences. A commonly noted consequence is the enhanced opportunities created for extortionary threats of exposure and prosecution. . . . Only a small and insignificant manifestation of homosexuality is amenable to enforcement. This is that which takes place, either in the solicitation or the act, in public places. Even in these circumstances, it is not usual for persons to act openly. To obtain evidence, police are obliged to resort to behavior which tends to degrade and demean both themselves personally and law enforcement as an institution.[17] . . . Such conduct corrupts both citizenry and police and reduces the moral authority of the criminal law, especially among those portions of the citizenry—the poor and subcultural—who are particularly liable to be treated in an arbitrary fashion. . . .

The offense of prostitution creates similar problems. Although there are social harms beyond private immorality in commercialized sex—spread of venereal disease, exploitation of the young, and the affront of public solicitation, for example—the blunt use of the criminal prohibition has proven ineffective and costly. Prostitution has perdured in all civilizations; indeed, few institutions have proven as hardy. The inevitable conditions of social life unfailingly produce the supply to meet the ever-present demand. . . . The costs . . . of making the effort are similar to those entailed in enforcing the homosexual laws—diversion of police resources; encouragement of use of illegal means of police control (which, in the case of prostitution, take the form of knowingly unlawful harassment arrests to remove suspected prostitutes from the streets;[18] and various entrapment devices, usually the only means of obtaining

16/Chief Judge Craven in *Perkins v. North Carolina,* 234 F. Supp. 333, 339 (W.D.N.C. 1964).

17/See Project, "The Consenting Adult Homosexual and the Law: An Empirical Study of Enforcement in Los Angeles County," 13 *U.C.L.A. Law Rev.* 643 (1966).

18/LaFave, *Arrest: The Decision to Take a Suspect into Custody* 450 (1965).

convictions); degradation of the image of law enforcement; discriminatory enforcement against the poor; and official corruption.

To the extent that spread of venereal disease, corruption of the young, and public affront are the objects of prostitution controls, it would require little ingenuity to devise modes of social control short of the blanket criminalization of prostitution which would at the same time prove more effective and less costly for law enforcement. . . .

Abortion

The criminal prohibition of abortions is occasionally defended on the ground that it is necessary to protect the mother against the adverse physical and psychological effects of such operations. There seems little doubt, however, that these laws serve to augment rather than to reduce the danger. The criminal penalty has given rise to a black market of illegal abortionists who stand ready to run the risk of imprisonment in order to earn the high fees produced by the law's discouragement of legitimate physicians. . . . A relatively simple and nondangerous operation on patients strongly desirous of avoiding parenthood is therefore converted into a surreptitious, degrading, and traumatic experience in which the risk to the mental and physical well-being of the woman is many times increased. . . .

It is plain, therefore, that the primary force behind retention of the abortion laws is belief that it is immoral. One of the serious moral objections is based on the view that the unborn foetus, even in its early stages of development, has an independent claim to life equivalent to that of a developed human being. Even those holding this judgment, however, can scarcely ignore the hard fact that abortion laws do not work to stop abortion, except for those too poor and ignorant to avail themselves of black-market alternatives, and that the consequence of their retention is probably to sacrifice more lives of mothers than the total number of foetuses saved by the abortion laws.

. . . Among the factors responsible for [the] widespread nullification [of abortion prohibitions] , two appear to predominate. The first is that there is no general consensus on the legitimacy of the moral claim on behalf of the foetus. . . . Second, the demand for abortions, by both married and unmarried women, is urgent and widespread, arising out of natural and understandable motives manifesting no threat to other persons or property. . . .

Gambling and Narcotics

Laws against gambling and narcotics present serious problems for law enforcement. Despite arrests, prosecutions and convictions, and increasingly severe penalties, the conduct seems only to flourish. The irrepressible demand for gambling and drugs, like the demand for alcohol during Prohibition days, survives the condemnation of the criminal law. . . .

Nor have the laws and enforcement efforts suppressed sources of supply. . . . Risk of conviction, even of long terms of imprisonment, appears to have little effect. . . . [E]xperience has demonstrated that convictions are difficult to obtain against large, nonaddict, organized dealers.

Our indiscriminate policy of using the criminal law against selling what people insist on buying has spawned large-scale, organized systems, often of national scope, comprising an integration of the stages of production and distribution of the illicit product on a continuous and thoroughly business-like basis. Not only are these organizations especially difficult for law enforcement to deal with; they have the unpleasant quality of producing other crimes as well because, after the fashion of legitimate business, they tend to extend and diversify their operations. . . . To enhance their effectiveness, these organized systems engage in satellite forms of crime, of which bribery and corruption of local government are the most far-reaching in their consequences.[19] Hence the irony that, in some measure, crime is encouraged and successful modes of criminality are produced by the criminal law itself.

Another significant cost of our policy is that the intractable difficulties of enforcement, produced by the consensual character of the illegal conduct and the typically organized methods of operation, have driven enforcement agencies to excesses in pursuit of evidence. These are not only undesirable in themselves, but have evoked a counterreaction in the courts in the form of restrictions upon the use of evidence designed to discourage these police practices. . . . Legal restraints upon unlawful search and seizure have largely grown out of litigation over the last five decades concerning a variety of forms of physical intrusion by police in the course of obtaining evidence of violations of these same laws. The same is true with respect to the developing law of wire-tapping, bugging, and other forms of electronic interception. . . .

There is, finally, a cost of inestimable importance, one which tends to be a product of virtually all the misuses of the criminal law discussed in this paper. That is the substantial diversion of police, prosecutorial, and judicial time, personnel, and resources. . . . Indeed, in view of the minimal effectiveness of enforcement measures in dealing with vice crimes and the tangible costs and disadvantages of that effort, the case for this rediversion of resources to more profitable purposes becomes commanding. It seems fair to say that in few areas of the criminal law have we paid so much for so little.

One might, even so, quite reasonably take the position that gambling and narcotics are formidable social evils and that it would be dogmatic to insist that the criminal law should in no circumstances be used as one way, among others, of dealing with them. The exploitation of the weakness of vulnerable people, in the case of gambling, often results in economic loss and personal dislocations of

19/For a detailed description, see U.S. President's Commission on Law Enforcement and Administration of Justice, *Task Force Report: Organized Crime* (1967).

substantial proportions. And the major physical and emotional hardships imposed by narcotics addiction raise even more serious evils. Still, such a view would scarcely excuse perpetuating the pattern of indiscriminate criminalization. There are obvious ways at least to mitigate the problems described; for example, by narrowing the scope of criminality. In the case of gambling, there is an overwhelming case for abandoning the traditional approach of sweeping all forms of gambling within the scope of the prohibition, while relying on the discretion of police and prosecutor to exempt private gambling and charitable and religious fund-raising enterprises. . . . In the case of narcotics, our legislatures have tended indiscriminately to treat all narcotics as creative of the same dangers despite the strong evidence that some drugs, particularly marijuana, present evils of such limited character that elimination of the criminal prohibition is plainly indicated.[20] . . .

PROVISION OF SOCIAL SERVICES

In a number of instances which, taken together, consume a significant portion of law-enforcement resources, the criminal law is used neither to protect against serious misbehavior through the medium of crime and punishment nor to confirm standards of private morality, but rather to provide social services to needy segments of the community. The drunk, the deserted mother, and the creditor have been the chief beneficiaries. In each instance, the gains have been dubious in view of the toll exacted on effective law enforcement.

The Drunk

Using the criminal law to protect against offensive public behavior, whether by drunken or sober persons, is not the issue here. The trouble arises out of the use of laws against public drunkenness to deal with the inert, stuporous drunk in the public streets and alleyways, who constitutes a danger to himself and an ugly inconvenience to others. Staggering numbers of these drunks are fed daily into the criminal machinery. Indeed, more arrests are made for this offense than for any other—35 to 40 per cent of all reported arrests. Not only does the use of the criminal law, therefore, divert substantial law-enforcement resources away from genuinely threatening conduct, but the whole criminal-justice system is denigrated by the need to process massive numbers of pathetic and impoverished people through clumsy and inappropriate procedures. . . . Even if the social and personal problems of drunkenness were, in some measure, helped by this effort, these costs would make the investment doubtful. . . .

. . . .

20/See the review of the evidence in the papers of Messrs. Blum and Rosenthal in U.S. President's Commission on Law Enforcement and Administration of Justice, *Task Force Report: Narcotics and Drug Abuse* (1967), especially at pp. 24-26, 126-131.

The Creditor and the Deserted Mother

The bad-check laws and the family-nonsupport laws are two other instances in which the criminal law is used in practice to provide social services; in these cases, to assist a merchant in obtaining payment and to assist needy families in obtaining support from a deserting spouse. The issue for legislative choice is straightforward: Is it ultimately worth-while to employ the resources of police, prosecutors, and the criminal process generally in order to supplement civil remedies, even though such use entails a diversion of law-enforcement energies from more threatening criminal conduct?

Checks, of course, can be instruments of serious fraud for which it is proper to employ the sanctions of the criminal law. However, the typical bad-check laws provide for serious punishment as well for the person who draws a check on his account knowing that at the time it has insufficient funds to cover the check. Usually, the intent to defraud is presumed in these cases. Merchants, of course, are aware of the risk of accepting payment in checks, but expectedly prefer not to discourage sales. The effect of the insufficient-fund bad-check laws, therefore, is to enable them to make use of the resources of the criminal law to reduce what, in a sense, are voluntarily assumed business risks. . . .

The cost to law enforcement is, again, the diversion of resources from genuine threatening criminality. It is not clear that it is anything but habit which keeps states from narrowing their bad-check laws to exclude the occasional bad-check writer where there is no proof of intent to defraud. . . .

Nonsupport complaints by wives against deserting husbands are handled similarly. The objective of law-enforcement personnel—the probation officer, a deputy in the prosecutor's office, a welfare agency—is not to invoke the criminal process to punish or rehabilitate a wrongdoer, but to obtain needed support for the family. Instead, jailing the father is the least likely means of obtaining it. As in the bad-check cases, the chief effect on law-enforcement officers is that this duty amounts to still another diversion from their main business. Unlike the bad-check cases, however, here the criminal process is being used to provide a service which, indisputably, the state has an obligation to provide. It is apparent from the economic status of those usually involved that the service amounts to the equivalent of legal aid for needy families. . . .

AVOIDING RESTRAINTS ON LAW ENFORCEMENT

Another costly misuse of the substantive criminal law is exemplified in the disorderly conduct and vagrancy laws. These laws are not crimes which define serious misconduct which the law seeks to prevent through conviction and punishment. Instead, they function as delegations of discretion to the police to act in ways which formally we decline to extend to them because it would be inconsistent with certain fundamental principles with respect to the administration of criminal justice. The disorderly-conduct laws constitute, in effect, a grant of authority to the police to intervene in a great range of minor conduct, difficult or impossible legally to specify in advance, in which the police find it desirable to act. . . .

Disorderly-conduct statutes vary widely. They usually proscribe such conduct as riot, breach of the peace, unlawful assembly, disturbing the peace, and similar conduct in terms so general and imprecise as to offer the police a broad freedom to decide what conduct to treat as criminal. . . . In examining disorderly-conduct convictions, the Model Penal Code found that the statutes have been used to proscribe obscenity in a sermon, swearing in a public park, illicit sexual activity, picketing the home of a nonstriking employee, picketing the United Nations, obstructing law enforcement, shouting by a preacher whose "Amen" and "Glory Hallelujah" could be heard six blocks away, and talking back and otherwise using loud and offensive language to a policeman.[21] But the reported decisions give only a remote hint of the use of these laws since convictions are appealed only in a minute percentage of the cases.[22] . . .

Vagrancy-type laws define criminality in terms of a person's status or a set of circumstances. Often, no disorderly conduct need be committed at all. The usual components of the offense include living in idleness without employment and having no visible means of support; roaming, wandering or loitering; begging; being a common prostitute, drunkard, or gambler; and sleeping outdoors or in a residential building without permission. . . .

Both the disorderly-conduct and vagrancy laws, . . . constitute a powerful weapon in the hands of police in the day-to-day policing of urban communities. . . .

The chief vice of these laws is that they constitute wholesale abandonment of the basic principle of legality upon which law enforcement in a democratic community must rest—close control over the exercise of the delegated authority to employ official force through the medium of carefully defined laws and judicial and administrative accountability. . . .

The proper legislative task is to identify precisely the powers which we want the police to have and to provide by law that they shall have these powers in the circumstances defined. . . . Unfortunately, however, the future is not bright. Increasingly, in recent years, the Supreme Court has been imposing constitutional restraints upon powers which the police and most legislatures strongly believe the police should have. If anything, therefore, the temptation to invent subterfuge devices has increased. This is another of the unfortunate consequences of the tension between the police and the courts. But until law enforcement comes to yield less grudgingly to the law's restraints in the process of imposing its restraints upon others, the problem will long be with us.

CONCLUDING REMARKS

The plain sense that the criminal law is a highly specialized tool of social

---

21/*Model Penal Code,* sec. 250.1, Comments at 2 *et seq.* (Tent. Draft No. 13, 1961).

22/See Adlerberg and Chetow, "Disorderly Conduct in New York Penal Law Section 722," 25 *Brooklyn L. Rev.* 46 (1958).

control, useful for certain purposes but not for others; that when improperly used it is capable of producing more evil than good; that the decision to criminalize any particular behavior must follow only after an assessment and balancing of gains and losses—this obvious injunction of rationality has been noted widely for over 250 years, from Jeremy Bentham[23] to the National Crime Commission,[24] and by the moralistic philosophers[25] as well as the utilitarian ones.[26] And those whose daily business is the administration of the criminal law have, on occasion, exhibited acute awareness of the folly of departing from it.[27] The need for restraint seems to be recognized by those who deal with the criminal laws, but not by those who make them or by the general public which lives under them. . . .

Perhaps part of the explanation of the lack of success is the inherent limitation of any rational appeal against a course of conduct which is moved by powerful irrational drives. Explaining to legislatures why it does more harm than good to criminalize drunkenness or homosexuality, for example, has as little effect (and for the same reasons) as explaining to alcoholics or homosexuals that their behavior does them more harm than good. It may be that the best hope for the future lies in efforts to understand more subtly and comprehensively than we do now the dynamics of the legislative (and, it must be added, popular) drive to criminalize. The sociologists, the social psychologists, the political scientists, the survey research people, and, no doubt, others will have to be conscripted for any effort of this kind. A number of studies have already appeared which have revealed illuminating insights into the process of conversion of popular indignation into legislative designation of deviancy, the nature of the competitive struggles among rival moralities, and the use of the criminal law to solidify and manifest victory. We also have a degree of understanding of the effect of representative political processes on the choice of sanctions and the dynamics of law enforcement by the police. Perhaps by further substantial research along these lines—research which would put the process of overcriminalization by popularly elected legislators itself under the micro-scope—we will understand better the societal forces which have unfailingly produced it. Understanding, of course, is not control, and control may prove as hopeless with it as without it. But scientific progress over the past one hundred years has dramatized the control over the physical environment which comes from knowledge of its forces. It may prove possible to exert in like manner at least some measure of control over the social environment. It is an alternative worth pursuing.

23/Bentham, *Principles of Morals and Legislation* 281-288 (Harrison ed., 1948).
24/See *supra*, note 1.
25/Devlin, *The Enforcement of Morals* 17 (1959).
26/E.g., H. L. A. Hart, *The Morality of the Criminal Law,* chap. ii (1964).
27/See the quotation from the statement of a representative of the FBI before the National Crime Commission, U.S. President's Commission on Law Enforcement and Administration of Justice, *Task Force Report: The Courts,* 197 (1967).

2. Influence of the General Culture on Crime*

DONALD R. TAFT

The latter half of the 20th century has seen the attempt to define the meaning of individual and group rights within the growing mass society in the face of growing dependence upon law as a solution to social problems (*see* Kadish, Article 1). In several landmark decisions the U.S. Supreme Court has redefined the traditional relationships of the policeman to the alleged offender, the offender to his victim, and the attorney to his alleged offender-employer. While the landmark decisions have seemingly solved many of the issues in the enforcement-judicial systems, they represent only one step in the growing attempt to define what is normal and abnormal within the system of criminal law.

Federal institutional imperatives have come to overshadow the dual criminal sovereignity of the states. The content of a number of federal standards, either anticipated or rejected by the states in previous years, has now been required of the states. Consequently, states have been expected to provide counsel to the person financially unable to retain his own attorney upon accusation, exclude evidence seized in a manner which violates responsible police conduct and constitutional limitations, demand a higher standard of confession validity, and extend the rights accorded adults to adolescents in the juvenile court. The demand for judicial *fairness* has been added to the previous call for judicial *restraint*. In effect, the Court has focused upon the individual in the system of justice rather than upon the maintenance of the system itself. The arguments over the right to counsel, the limitations imposed on unlawful search and seizure, and juvenile court due process procedures are debates over the content of culture and the nature of law. Both laws and crimes are cultural products (*see* Kadish, Article 1; and Wolfgang, Article 7). Although crime usually occurs before the law defining the act or the crime is legislated, both reflect cultural patterns believed by a significant proportion of the population to be unacceptable within the normative social structure (*see* Hall, Article 23).

The object that is stolen is usually a culturally important object; even the attacked victim usually represents a culturally important choice. The infliction of punishment, too, usually occurs within the context of viable cultural alternatives. Even the basic codified law and the limitations imposed by the

*Reprinted from *Federal Probation*, Volume 30, Number 3 (September, 1966), pp. 16-23, with the permission of the author and editors.

courts are representations of cultural and social attitudes (*see* Kadish, Article 1). The periodic highjacking of American airplanes, for example, resulted in the extension of kidnapping laws. The resistance of students to the Vietnam war motivated a successful congressional drive to pass legislation placing overly severe penalties upon convicted draft-card burners. Both the acts and the penalties, however, were grounded within the social system. Products of reactions to social policy, they represent cultural and legislative responses to the problems facing contemporary society.

In an age of electronic Big Brothers, the fear of invasion of privacy is challenged by the demand to maintain surveillance of organized crime (*see* Hawkins, Article 9). The expectation of the police control of homicide, too, is counterbalanced by the cultural belief that the right to bear arms is almost an inalienable right or guarantee. Consequently, no finality exists in either law or culture. Because laws are collective responses to the problems of the day, the very process of social interaction causes the uneven emergence of the criminal code. While a number of citizens cry "we are a nation of laws," they fail to recognize conversely that law is a product of individual and group interaction, meant to express human concerns and to reach defined human goals. Both are related to and cannot be divorced from culture. In the following discussion criminologist Donald R. Taft suggests that American culture, as with any culture, is at the same time crime producing and crime preventing. Because each is related to and has its meaning in the other, any attempt to control undesired behavior through enactment of laws without consideration of the human situation (*see* Kadish, Article 1) will possess limited value.

.   .   .   .

As used in this article, the general culture is that contained in a very large group, the culture or set of cultures more or less characteristic of a country or nation or civilization—American culture specifically. Within our society many subgroups exist, each in some degree with its own value system. Perhaps it would be more accurate to speak of American cultures—the values and ways of life found among its peoples, perhaps common to all of its members but often varying as between subgroups. To call such a general culture "American" implies that certain of its characteristics are somewhat widespread, or, if more rare, are nevertheless often thought of as, in some slight degree at least, peculiar to our society. . . . But American characteristics, as we use the word, need not characterize all or even necessarily a majority of the citizens. The influence of such a culture might be thought of, not as uniform, but as a process in which varied elements are somehow combined.

American culture is in process of change so that it is unwise to think of it as having existed throughout our history. Our emphasis will be upon present or recent times. From any standpoint our society has many characteristics which are generally recognized as beneficial and some which no doubt operate to reduce, rather than to increase, our crime record. Yet, we must become accustomed to finding that bad crime may at times be produced by otherwise good elements in our society. Freer life for women no doubt is one of these. We want women free, but some aspects of their increased freedom have led both sexes into crime or into causes of crime.

Since we are concerned with general cultural influences on crime, we shall not be able wholly to avoid emphasis upon real but not necessarily wholly dominant characteristics we find to be criminogenic (crime-producing) aspects of our society. Our argument will not insist that ours is necessarily the "most criminal nation in the world," though such a statement has been made. . . . The very title of this article makes it evident that our explanations of crime will not be predominantly in terms of supposed "inherent" personalities of criminals. . . .

WHO IS A CRIMINAL?

Legally, the criminal differs from the noncriminal in that, known or unknown, he has violated the criminal law. In estimating the number of lawbreakers, to the *convicted* must be added the guilty but not convicted, the uncaught, the undiscovered and unknown. In the case of many serious felonies a court, in order to convict, must prove intent. Yet, unintentional injuries may sometimes be more harmful to society than some crimes which were deliberately planned. . . .

The concept of criminal as defined in the law clearly comprehends only a small proportion of those who might be included in the far broader category of "socially dangerous people." . . . These dangerous people are those who, not necessarily technically criminal themselves, nevertheless create conditions which result in crime or serve as examples consciously or unconsciously imitated by the potentially criminal. If our purpose is to solve the crime problem rather than simply to requite the individual criminal for his act, these "causers of the causes" of that problem are of basic importance. We cannot afford to stop short in our analyses with either the immediate people or the immediate conditions which are involved. We must examine the whole complex process within which social relations of both criminals and noncriminals have been found to be significant. This means that we must examine certain aspects of our society—of the general culture—which partly determine those relations.

DISCOVERY OF THE CAUSES OF CRIME

Criminologists have used one or more of the following three approaches or emphases in attempting to explain the causes of crime. These may be related to their several theories.

1. *Personality Characteristics.*—The investigation will sometimes be concerned with personality characteristics which seem immediately significant for a delinquent's behavior. Psychologists and psychiatrists, though dealing also with

objective conditions discovered in their analyses, are likely to stress especially more or less deviant personality traits. Such personal differences are not confined to the criminal population, however. . . .

Or the source of criminal behavior is explained as psychosomatic—the result of an emotional state associated with a physical disorder. No one has discovered or will discover a criminal type of personality common to all or most criminals or distinguishing them from the rest of us. Such elements in a criminal's personality are usually products of some elements in his life experience. A good investigator will, therefore, never stop short with labelling a personality. He will seek explanations of *why* a few delinquents have paranoid traits, *why* a larger number are more or less baffled or angry failures full of resentment at the achievements of the successful, and *why* others experience unusual emotional stress.

2. *Varying Life Experiences.*—Much more significant than the search for personality traits has been the investigation of a long list of varying life experiences which explain criminal behavior. Thousands of delinquents have lived in broken, strife-torn, or otherwise disorganized or inadequate homes. They have lived in a neighborhood slum known and despised as a seedbed of crime and populated by a collection of life's discards whose relative poverty and degredation labels them as failures in a period of great prosperity. The slum dweller may rebel or he may just accept his fate, too discouraged to object openly, and drifting into criminalistic patterns as the easiest reaction. Many young criminals have not been admitted to socially acceptable small primary groups which provide even an average degree of social acceptance and approval. Indeed, no human motivation seems to be more widespread than is yearning for the social status which such groups confer. American youths are dominated by their "desire to rate.". . .

Or the criminal has lived in a state of *anomie* with relative absence of approved moral standards. Other offenders have been members of an underprivileged class or minority group where they have experienced discrimination, exploitation, and frustration. Despite improvements in race relations, vast numbers of Negroes still live in a social world pertinently different from that of most of the dominant whites. Such partially differentiating life experiences are often analyzed separately by students without much effort to combine them into a social theory of crime. . . .

. . . .

3. *The General Culture.*—Every serious student of the crime problem will, of course, be interested in the two types of influence discussed above, namely, (1) pertinent aspects of the personalities of particular criminals and potential criminals, and (2) any significant social relationships or other experiences which are found to contribute to criminal behavior. But it is my contention that a third type of influence must be stressed if we are to cut the deeper roots of crime. We must analyze the effects on the crime problem of the very nature of our society—the general culture. More especially, these include certain values,

attitudes, and patterns of behavior which in different degrees characterize or at least are notable in the American society of which we all are a part. Such emphasis on the general culture is somewhat rare and very unpopular. . . . Most of us blame someone for crime and most of us do not blame ourselves. Restriction of our reactions to crime to this blaming and punishing is perhaps the most basic crime-producing characteristic of our society. We must, of course, find out "who done it" and "why." Sometimes we must punish.

Yet there are American patterns which tend to prevent crime. Probably a majority of Americans are friendly and reasonably considerate of others. Probably most of them contribute to some form of philanthropy. One or two of the values we list (for example, craving for status and the search for something for nothing) are almost universal in our country. Others (for example, competitive individualism and some degree of desire for individualistic advantages over others) seem to be characteristic of a majority. But many values which have resulted in serious crime (for example, tendency to practice or to approve violence) are by no means dominant among Americans. It follows that American culture is at the same time crime-producing and crime-preventing.

SYSTEMATIC RESEARCH ON RELATION
OF GENERAL CULTURE TO CRIME

. . . Why do some associate with criminals and quasi-criminals in the slum, while residents in the better type of city suburbs eschew relations with the cruder type of offenders but absorb perhaps unconsciously the more gentlemanly white-collar crimes or other forms of exploitative associations not defined as crimes?

The answer, we hold, is to be found in the differentiating and criminogenic characteristics of our society—the *general culture*. But the major sources of evidence and argument supporting our thesis [have] been found in investigations of specific social problems not necessarily dealing with the crime problem, or have been seen in efforts to characterize the American scene. . . . For example, urban renewal has been recognized as needed partly because of its hoped-for relationship to delinquency prevention. On the other hand, violations of our antimonopoly laws have not been looked upon or dealt with like "ordinary predatory crime." And there have been objections to consideration of white-collar crimes as crimes at all.[1]

To repeat, in studying differences between criminals and noncriminals, do we not need to know why those differences occur? Why family stresses? Why slums? Why gangs? Why our failures? Why handicapping personalities? Why both white-collar and blue-collar crimes? What also is the relationship of the former to the latter? Is it not logical, even if unusual, to reason from prevalent social

1/Cf. the late Paul W. Tappan's *Crime, Justice and Correction,* New York: McGraw-Hill Book Company, Inc., 1960.

injuries not usually thought of as crime to predatory criminal acts which are considered so and are punished? Will not the informed criminal stress their similarity? Will he not consider white-collar criminals and thousands of those who injure us in ways not punished as crime as blameworthy as he is?

CRIME-PREVENTING INFLUENCE OF AMERICAN CULTURE

The following are specific examples of the criminogenic influence of certain aspects of American culture:

1. Belief That Everyone Has a Racket

Many criminals, potential criminals, and others have the exaggerated belief that everyone has a racket, that in their dishonest behavior they have lots of company among noncriminals or those not popularly thought of as criminals. Even if the criminal has typical and illegal acts in mind, he has some alleged evidence in favor of his belief. Writers like Porterfield, and Wallerstein and Wylie,[2] have made studies tending to show that at some time "almost all persons have deliberately committed crimes." These have been said to include serious felonies. Even granting some exaggeration in such studies they properly underline a degree of truth in the beliefs of criminals. . . . If most of us are habitually honest, most of us are at times dishonest in some types of situations. There is not a little dishonesty in business. Our economy and competitive social and economic relations almost require us to take advantage of others. The strain to keep up with or get ahead of the Joneses creates tensions. Many become resentful if they do not succeed. Living in separation from the many socializing influences in our society, the experiences of criminals lead them to the view that "dog eat dog" is the slogan of our society.

2. Influence of Destitution or Relative Poverty

It is thought-provoking to raise the question: "If you were starving should you steal?" It is interesting, also, to note how many of the most morally upright among us reply in the affirmative. It is still probably true that the millions of petty offenses are statistically more prevalent in the slum—in areas of very low income, destitution, and dependency—than on the avenue. But a major recent trend in a period of prosperity has been the spread of serious crime into middle-class or upper-class families. Poverty is thus not absolute but relative. It

2/Austin L. Porterfield, "Delinquency and Its Outcome in Court and College," *American Journal of Sociology,* November 1953, pp. 199-208. James L. Wallerstein and Clement J. Wylie, "Our Law-Abiding Law-Breakers," *Probation,* March-April, 1947. Cf. also D. R. Cressey, *Other People's Money,* Glencoe: The Free Press, 1953; Paul Goodman, *Growing Up Absurd,* New York: Random House, 1960.

varies not only from class to class, from the financially successful to the unsuccessful, but also from time to time and from place to place. Its effects upon contentment are determined also by established expectations. Probation and parole officers must all know of a great many who are engaged in a constant struggle to maintain a very low standard of living, yet accept the situation without revolt or crime. We are exhorted to attend chiefly to the "hard core" of "real delinquents." These have been estimated at only 17 percent who presumably will be involved in crime before they are 18 years old.[3] This, in my judgment, is a basic error although that hard core calls for some special treatment. Relative failure involves tensions at all economic levels. Even the rich envy the richer. Do we not, then, have to modify our generalization to conclude that it is *relative poverty* rather than the sheer destitution on skid row that leads most toward crime? This seems to be what is left of the economic interpretation of the crime problem. . . . [I]t appears that it is social failure rather than economic failure alone which generates demoralization, resentment, and crime.

3. The Search for Something for Nothing

It seems clear that most criminals and potential criminals are gamblers. If we expand that term to include all search for or acceptance of gains based upon luck may we not say that substantially all Americans are gamblers? From our point of view, different types of gambling activities express similar attitudes of mind and motives of participants. Legal or illegal, commercialized or not, large or small-scale, the sport of playboys or the last desperate resort of the denizens of Skid Row, and even the small boy's crap-shooting group, all attract participants who hope that Lady Luck will favor them. But still more widespread and more significant in the crime problem is the well-nigh universal "search for something for nothing." That search and gambling itself are, of course, by no means peculiar to America. Yet many of our retail merchants build much of their hopes for larger profits upon this human weakness. The most prominently displayed advertisement in a big supermarket in my home community urges customers to participate in its Bingo game based wholly on luck plus large purchases. My automobile dealer recently tried to pressure me to be the single lucky individual in the whole country to win one of his cheaper cars. The chances of failure in that venture were probably some tens of thousands to one. . . .

Years ago the economist Henry George emphasized the hugeness of the unearned increment which some elements in our economy afforded especially in land and stock speculation. Whatever economists tell us of social benefits from such activities they may well appear to potential criminals as less deserved than

---

3/Cf. James Symington, Director of the President's Committee on Juvenile Delinquency, in *The Reporter* for February 24, 1966, pp. 41 ff.

the rewards of hard work. Criminals may rationalize their own unworked-for crime profits as somewhat similar. It seems not unexpected, then, that case histories of criminals indicate often a record of earlier gambling habits.

4. The Influence of Misrepresentation in Advertising

Some advertisements are socially useful as they simply record the prices of goods offered for sale or bring newer and better want satisfactions to our attention. But one can hardly turn on a commercialized television program without being importuned to purchase commodities the virtues of which are exaggerated and misrepresented while their possible ill effects are understated or omitted. . . . Misuse of the word "only" in such advertising is extremely frequent. It is said or implied that only one brand of cigarette will satisfy; only one lotion will make us beautiful or will disguise the wrinkles of old age; only one kind of deodorant will make us safe from offending. . . .

Another related form of dishonesty still prevails in many markets. Manufacturers of some brands of packaged goods label them "20 cents off" without any statement as to "off what." In stressing such examples of dishonesty we must not, of course, overlook the increased efforts of such organizations as the Federal Trade Commission, of the Federal Communications Commission, or even, in some degree, those of the Better Business Bureaus to expose and check such abuses. . . .

5. Influence of White-Collar Crime

Our Government advertises itself and the country as one of the homes of "free enterprise." Free enterprise implies equal opportunity to compete with other buyers and sellers. It also seems to imply relative absence of government ownership of industrial concerns and of limits set upon government controls of the economy. The preservation of open competition is held to be a major asset. Yet competition itself implies varying degrees of success and failure. The temptation to succeed in business by limiting competition through some form or degree of monopoly is naturally very great. Monopolies vary greatly from the local advantage which a single drugstore may possess to the wide market dominance of some of the largest corporations. . . .

A few years ago the business community and the public were shocked by the successful prosecution of a large number of big electrical corporations which had violated the Sherman Anti-Trust law or its amendments. This was big business—this was big crime. The resulting loss to customers or to the less well-organized competitors seems to have exceeded the loss from the biggest burglaries or robberies. A few employees of the guilty corporations were sent to prison for short terms. But their behavior had actually been in line with well-known business policies and practices. . . .

But from the point of view of our stress upon the influence of the general culture, the chief significance of such huge criminal activities is derived from attitudes toward such offenses. Even such well-known criminologists as the late Paul W. Tappan have argued that white-collar crimes should not be considered in the same category as the thefts, burglaries, and robberies of lower-class misdemeanants and felons. But, granting much popular indifference, it hardly seems that either the informed public or the potential criminal makes this distinction. Still, white-collar criminals of many types are the "respectable" offenders. They often are leaders in their communities, possessed of wealth, successful in business through great efficiency or through unusual advantages, supporters of the church, and engaged in important philanthropic activities.

In his exaggerated view that everyone has a racket, the typical predatory criminal may justly stress the fact that social acceptance and respectability by no means define the distinction between the criminal and the noncriminal, or that between the socially safe from the socially dangerous.

6. Preferential Loyalties

The teenage gang with its stand-by-the-bunch principle has properly been stressed as a prolific cause of delinquency. A special concern for groups like the family is, of course, a socially useful type of loyalty. But many restrictive loyalties involve intense emotional bonds within the group and produce fierce resentments on the part of outsiders who are discriminated against. Preferential loyalty in one's wider relations: to one's class, one's race, one's Rotary club or other prestige group, one's type of neighbors, even to one's religious group, and finally to one's little self. These are powerful forces in American society. They largely determine and limit one's relations with others. They may generate emotions extended from passionate affection to bitter hatred. They are widely accepted, expected, and even commanded. Each group requires that its members share common feelings, values, and interests if they are to be granted the status they crave. . . .

The gang did not invent the bond of limited loyalty and the practice of discrimination. It absorbed it from a society which reeks with it. The criminal class need not have had intimate association with prestige classes to have acquired their values and patterns of behavior. They are conscious of their prevalence in our society. Craving for status in some group is one of the most nearly universal among human motivations. Knowledge of this powerful need for status had been behind the use of the group approach in our best correctional programs. The apparent success of Alcoholics Anonymous, of halfway houses for those released from prison, and of various forms of counseling and discussion groups, work-release, etc., are notable.

7. Growing Acceptance of Violence

The crimes which shock us most today are those which take life or endanger life. There seems to be general agreement that violent crimes have increased in recent years, especially among teenagers, even if most teenagers are "good scouts." Many such physical attacks are personally motivated or are elements in gang warfare preceded by a long period of conflict. . . .

Our study also requires that we look for possible connections between American culture and violent acts of varied degrees and types. I believe that such a connection may be observed. For we are living in an age of violence and of considerable approval of some kinds of violence. . . .

It has not been too easy to eliminate the third degree on the part of our police. Actual surveys have shown that public opinion partially supports the practice. Such a largely cultural origin of the increase of violent crime may be maintained, and yet one may gladly grant that most of us do not habitually behave in a violent manner. Most do not approve of torture even on the battlefield. But we do live in a world and in a period when violence is clearly in the air. Our criminals seem to be urged toward violence, though in widely differing ways and degrees.

8. Discrimination against Minorities

Equality of opportunity for all is a widely cherished verbal American ideal. Its practice, as the civil rights movement spreads, has no doubt increased, if all too slowly. Race prejudice based on the color of the skin, the most superficial of all differences among men, is still in some areas, North as well as South, the least yielding of all separating and conflicting forces.

Current interracial tensions and riots since the United States Supreme Court Decision of 1954 have found the white[s] more often the aggressors than the Negroes. . . .

It remains to be seen how completely in both North and South discrimination in education, in residence, in the use of recreational facilities, in transportation, in employment, in court procedure will wholly cease. Of these, discrimination in place of residence has been the most difficult to eliminate.

Where educational handicaps have been nominally eliminated, continued location of schools in slum areas has often meant continued poor facilities for predominantly Negro pupils residing there. It should not be difficult to indicate that all such discriminations and attitudinal prejudices which underline them tend to increase crime.

9. Popular Reliance on Punishment as a Deterrent

When the criminal is in action, at least the "punishment" of capture is needed. Most of us will slow down if a police car is seen guarding a crossing or watching for speeders. In such simple cases the threat of punishment is evident and acts as a deterrent. With a few notable exceptions, the majority of our states retain the threat of capital punishment for deliberate murder. But even where the law provides for this the trend has been strongly toward the disuse of the death penalty in the United States (only 7 instances in 1965) and abroad except, perhaps, where there is fear of revolution or other serious political crimes. This trend has been based on research and logical argument demonstrating the ineffectiveness of capital punishment. The typical murderer reacts with intense emotion. He does not act rationally and calculate the possible consequences.

On the other hand, it is said that professional burglars or robbers expect that some of their gang members will be sent to prison. They charge that possibility off as a business cost much as an industrialist calculates his chances of failure. But most relatively thoughtful criminals expect to be lucky and believe that in each successive next crime they will avoid punishment. The point we stress here, however, is that the general public have by no means lost their faith in deterrence of crime through punishment. Most early Congressional investigations, even if recommending constructive preventive measures, have also urged that penalties be increased despite the fact that American punishments are more severe than those of most other countries. . . .

The great good news recently has been the increase of legislative provision for constructive treatment of adult prison inmates in the federal correctional system and in a number of our more progressive states. The Prisoner Rehabilitation Act of 1965 . . . is a milestone in the history of corrections. California and possibly a few other states have rivalled this federal development. But today an interesting test of the progressiveness of such activities is to report how far they have included the use of various successful group approaches. These important group programs include, among others, the following: the use of counseling and frank discussion groups in prisons; mutual aid as seen in Alcoholics Anonymous; furloughs from prison; work-release programs with return to the institution at night; chances to associate with constructive groups on the outside during or after incarceration; constructive use of inmate correspondence; similar use of relations between inmates and staff and visiting members of the inmates' families or even their friends; efforts to reduce the isolation of the institution and relate it to the people and the world outside; efforts to make the institution itself more nearly like a normal community.

CRITICISMS OF THE GENERAL CULTURAL "THEORY" OF CRIME

The general cultural "theory" of crime has been attacked on various grounds:

1. It has been said that if our society produces crime we should all be criminals. This is not true, because that society itself produces criminogenic experiences, but only for a part of us. It, for example, creates the gang, but most of us are not gangsters because we have not been exposed to the causes of gangs.

2. It has been said that stress on the general culture gives the criminal a quasi-excuse for his crimes. But if so this is equally true of explanations in terms of special types of life experiences. Moreover, an excuse or an explanation does not preclude punishment which may have a place when it can be proved to be absolutely essential to immediate protection of society.

3. It has been said that the deterministic philosophy implied undermines a needed sense of responsibility. Determinism merely implies that cause and effect operate in the field of human behavior. One who accepts a strictly deterministic philosophy might reply that socially minded noncriminals "cannot help" but engage in constructive activities because such activities are a major source of life satisfactions we enjoy and may learn to seek.

4. It has been said that we imply an idealistic and unattainable goal—a perfect society. This might be partly granted if one aims at a completely crimeless society. But reduction in crime may be obtained in an improved society which falls far short of perfection. Yet an implied program must indeed be broad and complex. And is it too idealistic to urge that we *enlist the help of our charges* in a program of social improvement to reduce crime and also to deal with even greater social dangers than that of crime? Experience has shown that participation in assistance to others has actually been successful in the rehabilitation of criminals. Get the criminal to enjoy helping you and you have won him. . . .

5. As noted earlier the connection between the general culture and crime has not been adequately studied. It appears, then, that the general cultural approach finds crime to be culturally stimulated in three ways: (1) By showing, in considerable degree, how logically a wide section of the so-called "noncriminal" population in America sets criminalistic patterns for delinquents and potential criminals; (2) by showing that behavior, often more socially dangerous than typical predatory crime, is widespread; and (3) by showing how family stresses, neighborhood disorganization, gang influences, and other more immediate causes of delinquency are themselves largely byproducts of the general culture; for example, we produce slums and gangs. Such a general cultural theory seems to be supported by much evidence and by logical analysis.

A more honest and socially minded society should produce less crime and less of the conditions which produce crimes. So let us be honest with the criminals we know. Let us use punishment as a deterrent when necessary, but only when absolutely necessary. Let us attack the more immediate causes of crime. Let us teach the probationer and prison inmate how he gets that way. Let us not make the criminal feel that he is the only or mayhap the chief danger to society. Let us increasingly utilize group methods which have proved especially successful. Let us join in every program designed to make our society less and less of a seedbed of crime. . . .

3. Statistics Concerning Race and Crime*

GILBERT GEIS

The measurement of the volume of crime, especially in the United States, is most difficult. The lack of comparable crime statistics in different cities, the failure to include many types of criminal activities and statistical reports within existing data, the impossibility of measurement of the total volume of undetected crime, and the variations apparent in statistical gathering procedures open the *Uniform Crime Report* of the Federal Bureau of Investigation to major criticism (*see* Empey and Erickson, Article 15; and Fox and Volakakis, Article 18). Because local police agencies provide the raw data, the FBI's *Uniform Crime Report* is only as good as the data gathering and responding procedures of the local law enforcement agency.

An attempt of the National Opinion Research Center to measure the volume of criminality through a nationwide sample offers some hope for a better future analysis of crime in the United States. The NORC study of 10,000 respondents concerning victimization and police contact disclosed that extensive slippage occurs between the known volume of initial victimization and the number of persons eventually arrested, charged, and tried. Of the 2,077 reporting that they had been victims during the previous year, only 49 percent reported the crime to the police. Of the 1,024 persons who were criminal victims, 23 percent reported that the police failed to pay attention to their complaint. Of the 787 who made successful personal contact with the police, 25 percent revealed that the police did not view their incident as a crime. Of the 593 remaining, only 20 percent were able to indicate that their complaint actually led to the arrest of the offender. Only 42 percent of the 120 who were eventually arrested, therefore, reached the point of trial. Of this 50-man group, only 52 percent, according to the victim, received a proper conviction. The NORC study revealed not only that an excessively high number of crimes never come to the attention of the police but also that the police choose to dismiss or ignore many incidents which the victims consider to be criminal acts. At the same time, however, the police received good or excellent ratings from more than two thirds of the adult sample.

Other statistical problems also exist. Nowhere is the difficulty in ascertaining the direction and meaning of criminal statistics greater than in the area of data

*Reprinted from *Crime and Delinquency*, Volume 11, Number 2 (April, 1965), pp. 142-50, with the permission of the author and editors.

concerning race and crime. While blacks, for example, constitute little more than 11 percent of the population, they are arrested for more than 30 percent of all crimes (*see* Strecher, Article 17). The excessive visibility of the black man, however, is a basic factor in the enumeration of his arrest, trial, sentencing, and imprisonment data (*see* Reiss, Article 21). And yet other factors are also involved. As Gilbert Geis reviews the statistics concerning race and crime, he also evaluates the context and value of current American crime statistics more generally.

Present statistics which pretend to report the criminal behavior of minority ethnic and racial groups both reflect and perpetrate a large number of errors and myths, which can be, in their most innocent form, misleading and, in their least innocent, both vicious and malevolent.

It is traditional for persons who have taken the time for even a cursory examination of the source and the meaning of the rather elaborate statistical documents periodically issued by the nation's police to deplore these documents as indicators of criminal activity. At the same time, it is traditional for the mass media, as well as other agencies and commentators, to ignore the patent inadequacies of such numerical data, to publicize the released figures, to moralize about their presumed meaning, and then to act upon them as if they were reliable.[1] . . .

. . . .

The most basic shortcoming in criminal statistics is that they can never hope to represent with accuracy the behavior that we are really interested in; that is, they cannot tell us the amount of criminal behavior taking place within a given jurisdiction. . . . The various indexes of criminal activity relied upon in statistical reports need not and do not bear any discernible relationship to this most basic item, the volume of criminal behavior itself.

Our best measure of actual criminal behavior is a category usually labeled *crimes known to the police*. Innumerable crimes, however, never become known to the police, and the numerical relationship between these and those which do come to the attention of the police has never been established beyond the point of sheer guesswork. Possibly one out of ten crimes committed becomes known to the police; maybe one out of twenty; perhaps one out of a hundred; or, if you would care to, you could easily defend the view that, for each 100,000 criminal acts committed, only one becomes known to the police. The New Jersey Commission on Habitual Sex Offenders once decided, to no one's surprise, that there are only twenty convictions for every sixty million homosexual acts performed.[2]

1/See for instance, "The Negro Crime Rate: A Failure in Integration," *Time*, April 21, 1958, p. 16.

2/P. Tappan (ed.), The New Jersey Commission on Habitual Sex Offenders, *Report*, 1949, pp. 18-19.

The reasons for these numerical gaps can be grouped under the major headings of *invisibility of the act* and *unwillingness to report it.* Crimes such as those involving concealed weapons will, almost by definition, become known to the police only with extreme infrequency; in the same fashion, sex and family offenses are very rarely reported to or discerned by law enforcement agencies. Many of these crimes, of course, are differentially engaged in by various racial and ethnic groups, and whether or not the acts enter into the official awareness of the police will have considerable bearing on the numerical portrait of these groups' criminal activity. Thus, white-collar crimes, such as embezzlement, committed primarily by whites, are severely underreported, as are several types of criminal acts which appear to be disproportionately committed by members of minority groups. . . .

SOME STATISTICAL CONTAMINANTS

Offenses known to the police may also be influenced by operating definitions, by the exercise of official discretion, and by the vagaries of the human animal. . . . So, too, the official exercise of discretion by the police, on grounds of overriding social importance or merely on the basis of momentary caprice, will be reflected in criminal statistics as will, also, the sometimes curious and always statistically variable tendencies of persons and social groups to report crimes. . . .

Crimes known to the police cannot, of course, be broken down by age, sex, or religious or ethnic identification of the perpetrators unless and until these persons are discovered. Thus, originally inadequate and inaccurate conglomerations of statistics become further distorted . . . by numerous idiosyncratic procedures. Before this stage, however, attempts sometimes are undertaken to establish some sort of rough indicator of criminal activities of divergent groups on the basis of the crimes known to the police category.

An illustration of one such approach is that found in the Statistical Digest prepared for 1961 by the Los Angeles Police Department.[3] On page 12 of this report we find a rather unique chart which lists, for five specified offenses (robbery, theft from person, murder, aggravated assault, and rape), the sex and the "descent" (i.e., Caucasian, Negro, Latin,[4] Japanese or Chinese, or "Others") of what are called "suspects observed." The report itself offers no help in overcoming the vagueness of the designation "suspects observed," though it is readily apparent that, if nothing else, these subjects are not routinely arrested. . . .

Whatever the table indicates, it certainly does not show any consistent

3/The Los Angeles Police Department stopped including race breakdowns in its annual statistical reports after 1961.

4/Latins, of course, are regarded as Caucasians in most classifications of the human tribe, and this matter is hardly resolved by use of the term "descent." What is the "descent," for instance, of a person born of a Negro mother and a Caucasian father?

relationship between itself and the figures for minority groups which appear in the arrest tabulations. . . .

STATISTICS IN CONTEXT

A number of interpretations can be brought to bear on these statistics. They may be telling us that there is an overreporting by minority groups of crimes among them, or that there is an overreporting of crimes allegedly committed by minority group members. The figures may also indicate a disinclination on the part of police to arrest minority group members as often as persons from other groups, or they may reflect a differential efficiency or effectiveness in resolving, by arrest, crimes committed by members of various subgroups in the society. It is noteworthy as well that the figures provide no clue regarding the involvement of the same person in a series of crimes, and the possible reporting of an individual several times as an observed suspect but only once as an arrested offender. If we accept any of these possible interpretations, or a combination of them, we must conclude that the tables tell us precious little about the criminal activity of the groups into which their numbers are broken down and that, as the tables stand, they represent little more than exercises in the use and abuse of the talents of an IBM tabulating machine.

. . . .

USE OF ARREST STATISTICS

Most statistical reports which attempt to convey a picture of the illegal behavior of different segments within a society employ *arrest* statistics for this purpose. . . . [T] here is a vast and almost totally unknown and unknowable gap between the reality of crimes committed and the residue involving those which come to the attention of the police. Patent statistical fallacies inevitably arise because of this gap, and these fallacies become even more exaggerated as we move farther away, in terms of procedure, from the behavior which we are trying to measure. Arrest statistics may indicate the efficiency or inefficiency of a police department as much as they may indicate the quantity of crime or the type of criminals within its jurisdiction. Arrest statistics do not, however, unless we resort to the most reckless kind of extrapolation, tell us very much about the criminal activity among minority groups.

. . . .

Arrest statistics reflect in myriad ways the procedures, paradoxes, and idiosyncrasies involved in the business of law enforcement. For instance, an efficient police force will often become aware of a greater number of offenses and will arrest a larger number of persons than will a less efficient police organization. Summary statistical reports, taken at face value (which is the way such reports are almost always taken), imply that a better agency is less effective in reducing crime than a less capable agency, a curious juxtaposition of the facts of the situation.

The same observation may apply in a different fashion to procedures involving minority groups. A belief, based on real or imagined information, that a particular minority group commits more crime than other groups will often lead to a greater saturation of this group's neighborhoods by police patrol. Such saturation will likely turn up more crime and produce a larger number of arrests of persons belonging to the group, though it will also often inhibit some kinds of criminal activity because of the increased likelihood of apprehension. But it is the police activity and not the behavior of the group itself which is conditioning the group's crime rates as they eventually appear in printed statistics.

ILLUSTRATIVE CASES

I was once walking downtown on Main Street when a patrolman stopped a Mexican boy, nudged him toward the side of the street, and requested that he roll up his sleeves so that it could be determined whether his arms had needle marks. The policeman may have recognized the boy as a possible addict, either through experience or perhaps by the way he walked.... Or perhaps the policeman was operating on the assumption that a Mexican boy on this street was much more likely to be a narcotics addict than, say, I was, with my tie and pressed suit. His assumption may have been correct, but it is obvious how readily it becomes self-fulfilling and inflates the "Latin" crime rate through procedural tactics. In the same manner, young Negro boys—and I have listened to them discuss the matter at length in college classes—driving a relatively new and expensive car in an area not populated with Negroes expect as a matter of course to be stopped by the police as potential auto thieves.... The procedure obviously serves to increase the number of apprehended and reported Negro car thieves, just as the road blockades during the Christmas season inevitably tend to inflate greatly the total of drunken drivers discovered and arrested.

... One of the few detailed studies of the nature of such distortion clearly documented how it might operate in the instance of an offense such as shoplifting. Examining the figures for three department stores in Philadelphia, Sellin found that the detectives there had knowledge of shoplifting offenses which exceeded in number the total of all thefts of all types for the entire city of Philadelphia; the shoplifting thefts were simply not reported, except occasionally, to the authorities.[5] And it is worth noting, further, that there was a distinct tendency for the detectives to report offenders to the police when they were Negroes and not to report them when they were not, possibly because they felt the Negro offenders were the most dangerous or were less likely to

5/T. Sellin, *Research Memorandum on Crime in the Depression* (New York: Social Science Research Council, 1937), p. 69.

initiate suits for false arrest, or possibly because they were prejudiced against Negroes. The impact of their policy on the racial components of the larceny statistics in Philadelphia is quite clear.

Nothing in all the foregoing material is meant to indicate that minority groups are either overrepresented or underrepresented in current statistics on their criminal activity. The point is only that they are *mis*represented and that the figures on them tell us little of value concerning an issue surrounded by much emotion and deeply involved in matters of social conscience and social policy. . . .

. . . .

CONCLUSIONS AND RECOMMENDATIONS

Statistical tabulations of the work of a public agency are usually undertaken to provide a reckoning for examination by the citizen taxpayer and to aid the agency itself in performing its job more effectively. Criminal statistics, as they now exist, perform neither of these tasks. The information they supply . . . is misleading and readily subject to misinterpretation. As guides to the most expeditious deployment of police resources, the figures hardly seem worth much, and even if they could be shown to be of some slight importance, an intramural awareness of their general content (in contrast to a public report) would be at least equally satisfactory.

. . . Statistics purporting to tell us something about the criminal activities of persons of divergent "descent," whatever dubious value they may possess as an item of social inventory, contain many deleterious aspects that render them of strong potential social harm. To defend themselves against charges of overpolicing certain groups, law enforcement agencies may make use of the figures, with all their shortcomings, though the figures themselves really neither lend support to nor contradict the necessity for the enforcement decisions.

The presence of such statistics also covertly indicates and reinforces a splintering of the society into so-called "descent" groups. Males and females will not likely find it discriminatory if their crime rates are singled out for attention, but minority groups have historically sound reasons to believe, correctly or incorrectly, that something invidious is intended by such distinctions. These fears should not be fed unless there are compelling reasons to do so. . . .

The elimination of racial classifications from public criminal statistical reports would probably do much good and little harm. It might allow issues between law enforcement agencies and minority groups to be resolved on grounds more substantial than those provided by rather specious statistics. . . .

There is already enough antagonism between law enforcement agencies and minority groups. . . . Some of this antagonism may be unavoidable, but it will not do to play into its hands—and the statistics we have been examining seem to tend toward this end—unless strong reasons exist for such a policy. We should not imitate the ways of the person who, as described by Andrew Lang, a

Scottish writer, "uses statistics as a drunken man uses lampposts—for support rather than for illumination."

4. The Potential Contribution of Science and Technology to Better Crime Statistics*

ROLAND J. CHILTON

The Westchester Misdemeanant Survey of the nine tenths of those minor crimes which are generally submerged and little noticed disclosed that neither the police nor the courts maintain enough adequate records to enable any accurate enumeration or analysis of petty crimes. The court, the study revealed, is neither organized nor equipped to adjudicate or to dispose of misdemeanor cases adequately. Of the 88 judges manning the 44 courts trying misdemeanor cases in Westchester County, 10 were not even lawyers. Although their positions ranged from part-time to full-time judgeships, many had had no experience as defense counsel in criminal matters and had been chiefly concerned with civil cases. City courts disposed of 48 percent of their misdemeanor cases within three days; corresponding figures were 32 percent in towns and 37 percent in villages. While cities processed another 30 percent within one month, the towns completed 43 percent and the villages 75 percent. Most strikingly, city judges ordered 42 percent of all convicted to the state or county penitentiary, while towns committed only 9 percent and villages 21 percent. Only 19 of the 113 persons eligible for sentencing under the Youth Offender Act in the 693 cases surveyed were allowed the use of its provisions. Probation was granted to only 2.4 percent of the 458 convicted. In summary, the committee concluded that too many arrests for minor misdemeanors were being completed; much greater use should be made of release with minimal security pending trial; prosecution of misdemeanors should be conducted routinely by the district attorney's office; greater coordination of the 39 police forces in Westchester County should be established; and clearer, more legible, and certainly more accurate records and statistics should be kept in order to gain a valid insight into the extent of the misdemeanor problem.

The need for new and meaningful data concerning the crime problem is clearly evident to persons familiar with the limitations of existing data (*see* Geis, Article 3). Social researcher Roland J. Chilton believes that scientists and

*Paper given at the Second National Symposium on Law Enforcement, Science and Technology, April 16, 1968.

engineers with an interest in the field of crime data can make important contributions to more accurate and useful crime statistics by recognizing and calling attention to the need for better data, by noting and publicizing the distinction between enforcement and judicial agency statistics and large collections of dossiers, and by working with social scientists and legal scholars to develop new programs for improving crime data gathering.

Recent attempts by physical scientists and engineers to apply modern technology to problems of law enforcement and the administration of justice have produced results which suggest that the approach can be of great value, as well as results which illustrate some of its shortcomings and some of the problems to be overcome if future applications are to be more useful.[1] In particular, these early efforts by scientists and engineers have been weak in their approach to, and treatment of, crime statistics. The discussion which follows attempts to call attention to the contribution which science and technology might make in the improvement of crime statistics, and it attempts to do this by examining the ways in which previous efforts by scientists and engineers have fallen short of their potential.

One of the most important early efforts of this type was a project funded by the State of California and undertaken by the Space-General Corporation in 1965. The results of the study were sufficiently interesting for the Ford Foundation to convene a distinguished panel of experts to evaluate it. . . . In 1966 the President's Commission on Law Enforcement and Administration of Justice . . . recognized the potential value of this approach with the establishment of a science and technology task force and the appointment of an advisory panel for it. Despite the fact that the advisory panel of the task force was extremely critical of the quality of the data which were available to, and which were of necessity being used by, the staff, the task force report recommended very little which would improve crime statistics. . . .

Both the National Crime Commission's science and technology task force and the Space-General Corporation's research staff underrated the importance of crime statistics in that they avoided making suggestions for general improvements in the existing system and accepted and made more or less extensive use of the statistical information which was available to them. In part because of their general unfamiliarity with the history and fallibility of currently available crime data, there was a tendency to accept shaky data, execute rather sophisticated analyses of it, and produce questionable results. In both projects considerable emphasis was placed upon the utility of systems analysis and

1/Space-General Corporation, *Prevention and Control of Crime and Delinquency in California, Final Report,* July, 1965; The President's Commission on Law Enforcement and Administration of Justice, *Task Force Report: Science and Technology* (Washington, D.C.: U.S. Government Printing Office, 1967).

information storage and retrieval, while crime statistics programs were generally neglected.

.   .   .   .

Crime statistics, as such, represent an attempt to provide periodic quantitative estimates of the amount of crime occurring during a given period of time in specific areas as well as counts of the number of persons arrested, detained, released, prosecuted, convicted, acquitted, incarcerated, or placed on probation or parole. Other information uniformly compiled from reports about persons brought into contact with the system may also be included under the heading of crime statistics. But, in general, crime statistics represent an attempt to answer questions about the number of offenses which have occurred, the number of persons who have been the victims of crimes, the number of and characteristics of persons engaged by the system, and the kinds of outcomes which have resulted from such contact.

To understand why an expanded and computerized system of directories and registries[2] will not adequately replace current crime statistics programs it is necessary for us to recognize that such lists simply provide information about individuals who have encountered the system of justice at some point in time, while crime statistics provide an indication of agency work load and a very crude estimate of the number of crimes which have occurred in specified geographic areas during standard periods of time. While it is possible for a computerized data system to include counts of offenses known to the police, directories and registries *per se* do not provide such information. When fully developed, they can be expected to provide better information about persons taken into custody by the police than is currently available. But they would be of little help in attempts to answer such crucial questions as: (1) how much crime occurs, (2) what appears to be the trend for particular types of crime, and (3) what appear to be the pressures toward or away from specific types of criminal activity.

Crime statistics are also distinguished from systems containing information about individuals by their potential as measures of agency activity and efficiency. Accurate accounts of the amount and type of crime occurring in particular jurisdictions may quite reasonably be perceived as a threat to the police agencies assigned to provide protection for the area, while increases in the number of entries in directories and registries do not provide the same possibilities for evaluation.[3]

Since the collection of information about individual suspects and offenders will be less threatening to official agencies, although quite possibly more threatening to individual citizens, we may anticipate little resistance to its

2/A directory is a file of persons who have been arrested which contains information about each individual's prior arrests and dispositions. A registry is a file which contains more detailed background information about each individual than a directory.

3/For detailed discussion of this point see R. J. Chilton, "Persistent Problems of Crime Statistics," in W. C. Reckless and S. Dinitz (eds.), *Critical Issues in the Study of Crime* (Boston: Little, Brown & Co., 1968).

acceptance by police agencies. Moreover, since it is technically simpler than the development of accurate and timely information about amounts and types of criminal activity, we will probably find that scientists and engineers will more frequently work to develop systems which compile information about individuals than they will to develop systems which provide better estimates of the amounts and kinds of criminal activity in specified areas. The attempts of the National Crime Commission and Space-General Corporation to use the knowledge and skills of scientists and engineers have followed this pattern.

The characteristics of these approaches of science and technology to crime data ... suggest a number of ways in which scientists and engineers could make important contributions to more accurate and useful crime statistics. The most important single step in this direction would involve calling attention to the need for better data and suggesting ways in which it might be improved. Rather than accept whatever is available for use in tests of sophisticated new techniques, scientists could make an invaluable contribution by clearly stating the limitations of available data and accurately describing the kind of information which must be obtained for the most efficient use of the new techniques.

They could also make an important contribution to better crime statistics by recognizing the distinction between crime statistics and dossier operations. Continued failure to acknowledge this difference may result in the development of extensive files on persons contacted by social control agencies and decreasing knowledge of the amount and kinds of offenses being committed. Although there is now considerable doubt that offenses known to the police are as useful as early proponents of this kind of indicator thought they might be,[4] any systematic attempts to identify factors which appear to increase or decrease crime or to estimate the effectiveness of crime prevention programs require improved information about the amount of crime which is occurring, not less information or more questionable information.

In addition to making more forceful statements about the need for better data and recognizing the distinction between dossiers and crime reporting systems, scientists and engineers could make important contributions to more informative crime statistics by insisting that the quantitative information obtained by government agencies be made available to independent investigators. They could also make a worthwhile contribution by avoiding euphemisms and technical jargon which tend to conceal questions of decency and fairness and tend to mislead the public about the nature of the system which they are suggesting. . . .

One of the most promising possibilities for better crime statistics suggested by the science and technology task group of the National Crime Commission was the recommendation that federally supported regional research centers be established which would bring together research specialists from the physical and

---

4/R. H. Beattie, *Crime in the United States—1965*, California Bureau of Criminal Statistics, 1966; The President's Commission on Law Enforcement and Administration of Justice, *Task Force Report: Assessment of Crime* (Washington, D.C.: U.S. Government Printing Office, 1967), chap. 2.

social sciences as well as legal scholars. This may be one of the most effective ways to overcome the limitations of science and technology which are discussed above. It would permit scientists and technicians to test new techniques while utilizing the knowledge and experience of persons trained in law and social science. In undertaking the measurement of crime and the study of factors related to it, such an organization would be forced to participate in the development of better crime data. To be efficient and effective, however, the research teams in such an institute would have to be truly interdisciplinary and would have to operate so that there would be genuine interchange among the scientists, the social scientists, and practitioners in the system of justice. Even agreement on the identification of worthwhile problems would be difficult without the mutual respect which comes with the realization that both scientists and nonscientists have knowledge, information, and techniques which may be of value in a joint endeavor.

Perhaps an even more promising recommendation of the National Crime Commission was the suggestion that a National Center for Crime Statistics be established which would be responsible for the collection, analysis, and dissemination of data on crime and the systems response to it as well as the study of information about individuals contacted by social control agencies and officially included in one or more of the files maintained by federal agencies. [5] The success of such a center would depend in large measure upon the cooperation it received from state and local agencies, but its potential for improving current information about crime is probably even greater than that of the federally supported research institute—especially if its staff and list of consultants included scientists and appropriately trained technicians.

Such a center would be charged with the responsibility of developing and maintaining a comprehensive system of crime statistics as well as the task of analyzing and interpreting the information obtained. It might also develop additional independent indicators of the amount and kinds of crime which have occurred and provide technical assistance to local and state statistical centers. . . .

The potential impact of science and technology upon the development of crime statistics is impressive. If a number of physical scientists and engineers will first examine the efforts of those who have been working with existing data on crime and criminals as well as make a thorough study of existing data systems, they will be able to call attention to the need for better data and they will be in a position to specify the kinds of information needed. Moreover, they will be less likely to recommend the development of extensive files on individual suspects and offenders at the expense of more accurate information about the number and kinds of criminal events experienced by specific populations.

5/The agency recommended was actually described as a National Criminal Justice Statistical Center but the name National Center for Crime Statistics parallels the names of agencies with similar functions such as the National Center for Health Statistics and the National Center for Education Statistics.

part TWO

Criminal Processes and Organization

Criminal associations, like other groups, follow basic social procedures, manifest primary and secondary relations, identify with other reference groups or reference group members, and interact with the various elements in their existing or presumed environment. Often operating as in-groups, criminal associations define others as out-group members. Although such groups reveal differential levels of trust, commitment, friendliness, loyalty, and cooperation, both delinquent gangs and organized criminals evidence in-group solidarity. Bound by ties of common fate, self-interest, sympathy, obligation, and affection, in-group members seek to advance common security or financial goals. Distrustful of out-group members, the criminal in-group exaggerates its member's virtues and degrades those of its enemies.

In-group and out-group discrimination represents a form of status conflict. The juvenile who joins a gang to secure his neighborhood or to oppose law enforcement authorities, the organized criminal who participates in a syndicate in order to gain excessive monetary and status rewards, and the youthful offender who commits a single crime in order to achieve a particular personal goal reveal class- and competition-conflict influences. Offering a spontaneous or reasoned answer to his particular situation or goal in his action, each ignores general socioethical norms as he responds to norms of his reference or associational group.

While an individual is socialized throughout his life to become a complete male or female role participant, the two roles are further differentiated into various subtypes. Because roles are associated with statuses, every man, woman, or child shares in a combination of differentiated ascribed or achieved social roles and statuses. Inasmuch as each role also contains particular rights, privileges, and responsibilities which vary from place to place and time to time, the individual's roles tend to influence the form and context of his criminality. The bank clerk or accountant who embezzles, for example, does so because his role involves him in the opportunity to embezzle. The laborer who steals copper tubing from his job to sell for a profit engages in this activity in relationship to

39

his current construction employment. Crime patterns, therefore, are influenced by the roles and the statuses which one assumes throughout his life. Because greater value is attached to some statuses and roles and not to others, each role or status encourages peculiar standards of behavior. Not only do they provide the role recipient with specific opportunities to relate to other persons of similar class but they also define the general location of the person's future, if any, recorded criminality (*see* Empey and Erickson, Article 15).

Because some crimes especially reflect patterns of class competition or conflict, government works to accommodate conflicting interests either through redefinition of legal harms or through control of deviant elements. Since social coercion is generally regarded as undesirable in a democracy, the process of accommodation, designed to enable opposing individuals and groups to resolve their differences, assumes added importance (*see* Kadish, Article 1; and Taft, Article 2). Labor-management conflict of the 19th century, for example, was redefined from a criminal to an administrative violation. While the rise of the labor union was met by many early management attempts to break unions through the use of "goon" squads, unions responded with a similar use of force. Both union and management committed criminal acts. However, management-sponsored violations were largely ignored by enforcement officials, since corporate legislative power at the time exceeded that of the union member. Only as the conflict of management and labor was resolved through the recognition of union bargaining rights and the transference of union-management disagreements from the criminal court to the National Labor Relations Board was the conflict lessened. While periodic violence or use of force occurs infrequently in modern strikes, this form of union activity is generally no longer processed as a criminal offense.

Organized crime has also become partially assimilated into modern society. As the many syndicates have succeeded financially, its leaders have moved to assume airs of respectability. Consequently, members of each syndicate hierarchy have moved to suburban communities while continuing to serve as members of the organized crime corporate board. Viewing violence as bad public relations, syndicate operators and leaders continue to seek profits through monopolistic enterprise control, while minimizing any public recognition of their parasitic activities (*see* Hawkins, Article 9).

Criminal organization takes many forms. While the Cosa Nostra, probably the largest and most important single American syndicate organization, is an outstanding example of the nature of organized crime, all criminal syndicates are not so extensive or so well organized. The Cosa Nostra, composed of 24 "families" located primarily in large metropolitan areas, possesses an estimated single family membership of 20 to 700 men. Organized in hierarchical form, each family possesses a *boss* and an *underboss*. The *counselor (consiglieri),* often an elder family member, advises the boss and the underboss and serves as a respected syndicate advisor. The *lieutenant (caporegime)* serves as a buffer between top family members and lower echelon workers. The *soldiers (sodati),* the lowest level members of the family, generally operate an illicit enterprise on behalf of the syndicate. Although other workers are eventually recruited for the operation, they do not share in family membership. Each family is largely autonomous; the families, however, are coordinated through the activities of the *commission (commissione),* composed of 9 to 12 family representatives.

Not all criminal forms are this pervasive. Delinquent gangs, for example, generally lack the stability and economic resources of the syndicate. Nevertheless, delinquent gangs, composites of individuals and groups, assume many forms. Hyman Rodman and Paul Grams suggest that delinquency may be categorized into eight basic types which they define as (1) adjusted-occasional-gang delinquency, (2) adjusted-habitual-gang delinquency, (3) adjusted-occasional-lone delinquency, (4) adjusted-habitual-lone delinquency, (5) maladjusted-occasional-gang delinquency, (6) maladjusted-habitual-gang delinquency, (7) maladjusted-occasional-lone delinquency, and (8) maladjusted-habitual-lone delinquency. But this is only one illustrative typology.

Delinquent and criminal behavior is a diverse form of human behavior, making any attempt to define deviance causes and to control deviant conduct highly difficult. Nowhere is the problem more difficult than in the area of the youthful offender who is above the age of defined delinquency but is often a legal minor under 21. Milton Luger probes the importance of this concept and the problems which the youthful offender faces and evaluates his potential for rehabilitation in the first article of Part Two. Next, Thomas M. Gannon analyzes the growth and characteristics of the defensive gang, and Marvin E. Wolfgang follows with an evaluation of the place of violence in the delinquency-crime system. Richard Quinney turns to the problem of the white-collar offender, whose offenses are frequently legitimated or ignored by the criminal code because of his influence in the legislative process. Finally, Gordon Hawkins examines the functions and operations of the Mafia, a term often used to refer to the highly publicized Cosa Nostra ("Our Thing").

5. The Youthful Offender*

MILTON LUGER

The development of juvenile court philosophy involved an attempt to overcome the harshness of punishment applied to juveniles in the former system of punishment (*see* Toby, Article 32). Recognizing that juveniles may not have reached an adult level of socialization or of normative conduct, juvenile court

*Reprinted from the *Juvenile Delinquency and Youth Crime* Task Force Report of the President's Commission on Law Enforcement and the Administration of Justice.

philosophy ultimately assumed that delinquents should be treated in a manner different from adults. Therefore, this view represented a marked humanitarian advance, for it negated the centuries-old philosophy that all persons, whether child, juvenile, or adult, should pay the same penalty when convicted for the same act.

Although the juvenile court was created in Chicago in 1899, it has never fully realized its full promise (*see* Lemert, Article 26). The 1967 *Kent* and *Gault* decisions of the Federal District and United States Supreme courts, for example, recognized that the juvenile receives the worst of two worlds: neither the solicitous care promised the youth by juvenile court philosophy nor the guarantees accorded adults by the Constitution. However, despite the shortcomings of the juvenile court and its inability to realize fully the goals of juvenile court philosophy, few persons are eager to return to the former system of harsh or brutal treatment of inadequately socialized delinquents, although the contemporary *Gault* decision has limited court flexibility in serious delinquency cases.

While law assumes that a child below the age of seven (or slightly older in other nations) is unable to form the *intent* (as opposed to accident) necessary to define his act as a specific crime worthy of judicial action, it is illogical to assume that every child is suddenly able to distinguish among all aspects of right and wrong at the moment of his seventh birthday (*see* Hall, Article 23). Likewise, it is presumptuous to maintain that an individual below 16 or 18, depending upon the definition in a particular state, is less juvenile than the person who has suddenly reached the age separating juvenile delinquency and adult crime (*see* also Empey and Erickson, Article 15).

Large numbers of youthful defenders (youths between the upper delinquency age limit, usually 16-18 and 24) reveal many of the basic personality needs which are common to juvenile delinquents. In the ensuing discussion Milton Luger notes that youthful offenders generally possess deep-seated feelings of self-worthlessness which are often expressed in compensatory antisocial behavior (*see* Fannin and Clinard, Article 16). The rehabilitation of the youthful offender, Luger believes, will not be accomplished until a heightened sense of ego-worth replaces the youth's earlier tendencies to self-destructive conduct.

THE YOUTHFUL OFFENDER: HIS UNIQUE CHARACTERISTICS

It is obvious that the term youthful offender connotes different things to different people. For some it indicates a legal definition involving specialized judicial procedures; for others, a chronological age grouping of offenders evidencing developmental needs; behavioral characteristics are stressed by still others seeking reasons to treat this group with measures ranging from stringent security handling, because of their seemingly aggressive, volatile proclivities, to those advocating benign, protective techniques which shield them from contamination from older criminals. Others think of youthful offender as synonymous with juvenile delinquent. There are strong arguments to treat this group as a definable entity, even though there is a wide range of needs, potential, and development within the youthful offender group. Admittedly some are vicious and require intensive security measures for the community's protection, while some are passive, immature scapegoats who need to be protected from their peers. Some would be far better off if they were not apprehended for their illegal activity. Too many youths deteriorate in our care, rather than receiving the vital treatment they require. Since many antisocial activities are unplanned outbursts of childhood and adolescent frustration, many offenders will mature to productive adulthood, if they are not labeled as delinquent and stigmatized by correctional processes.

In this paper, the term youthful offenders is used to mean those individuals enmeshed in the judicial and correctional process through illegal activities on their part, who are older than their own State's children's or juvenile court's jurisdiction and who have not reached the age of 24. . . .

In his review of current practices and programs for the young adult offender, Dr. Albert G. Hess[1] summarizes the arguments against differential treatment of this group:

a) It has been argued that the establishment of age categories for offenders contradicts one of the most important principles of modern corrective theories, that of the individualization of treatment in accordance with the specific needs of each offender.

b) There is the argument that grouping may, if inappropriately handled, lead to increased standardization rather than the individualization of treatment. This has happened, for example, in those older penal codes under which youth was made the criterion for an automatic reduction in the length of sentence.

c) Another important argument concerns the question of responsibility. The creation of a young adult offender group, it is held, unjustifiably allows young criminals to evade full responsibility for their offenses. In this connection it is argued that the young adult, who, in most parts of the world, handles complicated occupational responsibilities and is permitted to marry and to vote, certainly understands the basic provisions of the penal codes.

d) It has been objected that the delimitation of a category of young adults on the basis of fixed age limits would be as arbitrary and as little related to the realities involved as the admittedly arbitrary borderline which now separates juveniles and adults.

. . . .

1/Albert G. Hess (ed.), "The Young Adult Offender," United Nations, New York, 1965.

FIGURE 1

The Younger a Prisoner Was When First Arrested, the More Likely He Is to Return to Prison
(post-release failure rate* of federal prisoners, in relation to age of first arrest)

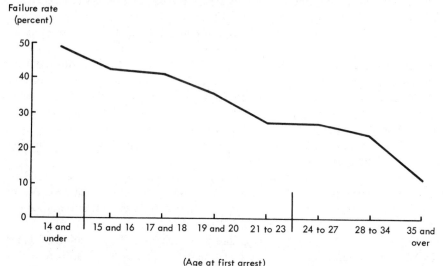

(Age at first arrest)

*Return to a correctional institution for violation of parole or commission of a new offense.

Source: U.S. Department of Labor, Manpower Administration, Office of Manpower Policy, Evaluation, and Research, based on a study by Daniel Glaser of 1,015 Federal prisoners released in 1956, reported in *The Effectiveness of a Prison and Parole System* (New York: Bobbs-Merrill Co., Inc., 1964).

STATUTORY AND JUDICIAL TREATMENT OF THE YOUTHFUL OFFENDER

We are here concerned with current laws, procedures, and programs that distinguish youthful offenders, defined as the postjuvenile court group, ages 16 to 23, from the juvenile offender and the adult criminal groups.

The Young Offender under the Criminal Law

Youths under the statutory maximum age for juvenile delinquency, varying among most States from 15 to 19, are generally the wards of juvenile courts. But persons still minors, yet over the juvenile age, who are in trouble with the law are usually accorded the traditional procedural safeguards and subjected to the penalties of the criminal law and the criminal courts. By and large, for detention and pretrial custody, they are generally relegated to police lockups and local jails; for punishment or correctional care, committed to adult prisons, reformatories, county jails, and penitentiaries. Criminal laws and courts, with few exceptions, do not distinguish between youthful and adult offenders. It is true that some courts and correctional authorities apply special procedures for youthful offenders before and after adjudication, ranging from pretrial investigation and separate youth detention to privacy of proceedings, preferential probation treatment, and specialized youth institutions and parole programs. But the vast majority of jurisdictions make no provision whatever for such young offenders. Forty-four of the 50 States and the Commonwealth of Puerto Rico[2] have no separate procedures or protections for the handling of law-violating minors above the juvenile court age limit. Most youthful offenders bear the same stigma and suffer the same legal disabilities and handicapping criminal record as the convicted adult criminal.

Convicted adults are in many States prohibited by law from voting, foreclosed from obtaining licenses to enter certain businesses and most licensed professions, disabled from seeking or filling public office, barred from the civil service, and, in certain cities, compelled to officially register their criminal records when seeking employment. The domestic relations laws and judicial decisions in some of the 50 States hold that concealment of prior adult criminal conviction is grounds for annulment of marriage. There is evidence that a substantial proportion of applications for executive clemency (pardons, certificates of good conduct, and other forms of legal amelioration of the consequences of criminal adjudication) is sought for convictions which occurred when the applicant was still under 21 years of age. Applications for removal of criminal statutory disabilities incurred before age 20 constituted over 40 percent of requests for the New York State parole board's certificate of good conduct, which requires discharge from parole and proof of 5 years of satisfactory good behavior in the community after conviction, suspended sentence, or unrevoked release from an institution.[3]

Treating the youth as an adult offender is puzzlingly inconsistent in light of the special protections given minors under civil law. Minors are granted immunity from certain types of civil liabilities and court suits and their obligations under contracts are controlled and supervised. Their property rights are safeguarded by a complex network of special laws and courts.

The adult criminal procedure fails to differentiate among vastly differing problems of criminality. The youth who takes a car for a joyride will bear the same label as an older, assaultive, dangerous offender. Penal codes distinguish among defendants by the nature of the offense rather than the nature of the offender. By this distinction, an 18-year-old first offender may be sentenced to prison while another youth of the same age goes to jail for 90 days, simply because the object stolen was valued at less than the legal definition of a felony. The first is stigmatized with a felony record with the consequent high price to be paid. The second is deprived of needed correctional guidance, training, and

2/National Council on Crime & Delinquency, "National Survey on Youthful Offenders," February 1966.

3/N.Y.S. Division of Parole, "Communication from Executive Clemency Bureau," June 1966.

supervision—almost invariably absent in local jail programs—because he did not steal enough. The problem is one of devising and using procedures appropriate to the offender. The malleability and immaturity of the preadult group and its need for specialized rehabilitative effort are largely ignored in codes governing criminal procedure.

The Quest for Flexibility in Precourt and Court Procedure for Youths

Law enforcement and judicial officials have sought to achieve flexibility and individualized dispositions of preadult offenders by using alternative procedures within the framework of criminal practice.

The criminal court seeking appropriate handling and sentencing of youth may be compelled to strain the language of the criminal statutes governing the offense. It may borrow dispositions and proceedings designed for entirely different situations. Thus, where probation supervision is lacking, the court may substitute wayward minor proceedings for a substantive criminal charge and discharge on own recognizance (release during good behavior with the open charge remaining on the books as a Sword of Damocles) in lieu of jail sentence. Common is the bargain of accepting the plea to a lesser offense to permit placement on probation otherwise interdicted for the higher degree of crime; or allowing suspended sentence, fine, or shorter commitment, which may, in turn, backfire by denying the offender a needed correctional program that might help him avoid a future criminal record, long confinement, and permanent legal disabilities. Some of these expedients come very close to vitiating due process of law, as has recently been shown in New York State: to eliminate abuses of long pretrial confinement during probation investigation and treatment efforts, the outcome of which would determine later adjudication and disposition, jurisdiction over female persons in need of supervision was raised to age 18 and vested exclusively in the family court. The latter is required to hold a detention hearing within 72 hours and to accord other procedural protections. In other instances as well, ludicrous contradictions often arise. Defense counsel may plead his client incapable of rehabilitation, for example, to insure a short definite penal sentence rather than a longer one with correctional treatment and parole provisions. This is a frequent product of a system where youths may be tried and disposed of under one of several alternative adult or youth statutes at judicial discretion rather than through uniform coordinated provisions for this offender class.

Among the more successful of flexible court procedures for modifying the severity of the criminal process for youths and providing more adequate treatment methods are the following:

1. *Deferred Prosecution or Disposition.* The Federal Courts have utilized a system of deferred prosecution in criminal cases for many years. Under this plan, formal proceedings in juvenile cases presented to Federal courts may be

postponed pending satisfactory adjustments through informal probation, special placement, or treatment. Consent of defendant and counsel is required. On the reaching of a satisfactory solution, the court may dismiss the complaint.

A similar arrangement, termed deferred disposition, is employed in Chicago boys' court (a misdemeanor court for 17- to 21-year-olds).[4] Selected youths are placed under supervision, with their consent. Successful supervision avoids conviction. Selection is made on the basis of social investigation by court social workers. In some cases, the judge may release the youthful defendant on his own recognizance or in the care of his parents pending outcome of the investigation.

2. *Baltimore City Court Plan.*[5] This is primarily a special probation procedure similar in effect to the Chicago boys' court method but taking place after a hearing on the charge and a preliminary finding of fact. When a defendant completes successfully the probation period, there is a formal hearing to confirm the preliminary finding of fact, but no verdict is entered against him (similar to the New York State youthful offender statute, under which youths are adjudicated youthful offenders but the original indictment or information is sealed). Violation of probation results in trial.

3. *Detroit Recorder's Court Plan.* This is patterned after Baltimore, for youths 15 to 22, but probation is granted only after conviction. Probation may include placement of youths under 22 in the Michigan Department of Corrections Probation Camp for up to 1 year. Upon successfully completing probation the youthful offender may apply for a new trial, usually under the rubric of a claim of newly discovered evidence, and his adjustment on probation may be the basis for acquittal. One or two other Michigan courts use this arrangement.

4. *The New York City Youth Council Bureau* is an adjunct of the district attorney's office.[6] Youths 16 to 21 are interviewed after arrest but before arraignment. The bureau's findings aid the district attorney and the judge in determining whether proceedings and disposition other than prosecution under the penal statute should be brought. These may include substitution of wayward minor procedure, deferment of official action during good behavior and subsequent request for dismissal of the charges, release on bail or recognizance, transfer to an adolescent court for youthful offender proceedings, or vacating of the charge.

Casework services are provided to youths on long-term parole to the district attorney's office (a form of deferred prosecution) or, on a voluntary basis, after youths have been discharged by the court on their own recognizance.

5. *Wayward Minor Proceedings.* Wayward minor procedures seek to extend definitions of misbehavior, disobedience, incorrigibility from juveniles to older

4/Professional Social Service Committee of Boys' Court, "Meaning of Supervision in Boys' Court," May 1956.

5/City of Baltimore, "Baltimore City Court Plan," 1960.

6/National Council on Crime & Delinquency, "A Study of the Youth Counsel Bureau of N.Y.C.," May 1963.

minors, usually 16 to 21. The condition of waywardness is more a legal status attached to the individual than an offense. It is sometimes termed a civil offense. The conduct subject to complaint generally includes truancy; habitual running away from home; failure to obey lawful commands of parents or guardians; habitual association with thieves, pimps, procurers, dissolute persons; being found in a house of prostitution, or deporting oneself as to wilfully injure or endanger personal morals or health; being morally depraved or in danger of becoming so.

In some jurisdictions, such as New York, the wayward minor is tried in adult court but given special correctional treatment including preadjudication investigation, not necessarily with a requirement of his consent (as parents are usually the complainants). In Michigan wayward minor petitions limited to ages 17 to 19 are generally heard in juvenile court. The New York Wayward Minor Act of 1923,[7] limited to magistrates courts, applies to youths 16 to 21 whose conduct may lead to crime. Some persons so adjudicated are commitable to the State department of correction reception center. Wayward minor proceedings may be substituted for criminal (misdemeanor or less) charges for youths who have no prior record and who do not deny the criminal charge, but this is a practice sanctioned by the courts as a means of avoiding full criminal treatment, not a legislative provision. Adjudication as a wayward minor is not denominated as a conviction of crime and does not result in disqualification for public office or licensure nor forfeiture of any legal right or privilege. Probation up to 2 years is the preferred, prescribed correctional treatment where practicable, but, if the youth is deemed not a fit subject, commitment for up to 3 years to a religious, charitable, or reformative institution authorized to accept persons over 16 is the alternative.

In Michigan[8] the law grants concurrent jurisdiction over wayward minors (17 and 18 years old) to the juvenile court. If the juvenile court judges the youth a wayward minor, he can be either placed on probation or committed to the adult corrections department. The department must keep him separate from persons committed by the criminal courts.

For helping young offenders, the wayward minor provisions are virtually useless. The grounds for adjudication are narrow and specialized, designed more to reinforce parental control of minors over the juvenile age through the adult courts than to prevent or treat. . . .

YOUTH CORRECTIONS LEGISLATION

Inspired by dramatic examples of the impropriety of treating youths as criminals and by the advances in youth reformation technology, the American Law Institute focused attention on the problems of the 16-21 age group and

7/New York Code of Criminal Procedure, sec. 913 A.
8/State of Michigan, Criminal Law, sec. 712 A, 1948.

formulated the Model Youth Corrections Authority Act.[9] The model act did not alter existing court structure, juvenile or adult, but was concerned only with sentencing procedures and correctional practice. Another model act—the proposed youth court act—was drafted but never promulgated, as the drafters of the Youth Corrections Authority Act believed the necessary changes in procedure could be accomplished within the structure of existing criminal law. In 1956, New York enacted a Statewide youth court similar to that proposed by the American Law Institute. It was withdrawn, despite approval in two referendums, after considerable opposition from courts which opposed loss of criminal jurisdiction over youth to a specialized tribunal; from probation departments and youth care institutions which deplored the expected tremendous increase in concentrated youth caseloads; and from the press, which uniformly opposed the privacy of proceedings features and the "coddling of vicious youth" at a time of great public concern over youthful lawbreaking.

The salient features of the Model Youth Corrections Authority Act include:

1. Removal of sentencing power from the court to a central administrative authority.
2. Establishment of central diagnostic facilities.
3. Power to assign to and transfer among institutions.
4. Determination of release with no minimum sentence required.

California adopted major provisions of the act in 1943, but included juvenile procedures and institutions as well as those for the 16-21 range. Prevention and precourt community treatment were included in California youth authority functions. Minnesota and the Federal Government followed (the latter, however, left its independent procedures for juvenile delinquents intact). California and Minnesota also have instituted adult authorities and have combined the two authorities in a department of corrections. In most other jurisdictions which have applied the authority principle, the emphasis has been shifted to correctional resources for the juvenile delinquent. . . .

.   .   .   .

THE TREATMENT OF YOUTHFUL OFFENDERS

.   .   .   .

. . . No matter which specific type of administrative structure is employed to deal with youthful offenders, it is vital that the personnel and agency have status and respect within the governmental structure. In order to be accountable for its progress and programs, the selected governmental unit must have the power to coordinate the individual State's efforts on behalf of this target population. It must have at its disposal hard data on which to base its policy decisions. This can come about only through the support of important, innovative research programs and statistical survey units which continually gather and evaluate

9/American Law Institute, Youth Corrections Authority Act, Philadelphia, 1940.

significant material. The dearth of valid statistics concerned with youthful offenders is appalling. Very often statistics are blurred because of overlapping age categories used by different inquiring bodies. It is important that the State unit differentiate between mere statistics and evaluative studies. What they are doing and how well they are doing are important questions to be answered, but why programs are succeeding or failing is basic. . . . The need to experiment and research at the same time is recognized by correctional leaders more than it is satisfied. This need implies the creation of a laboratory atmosphere within facilities for experimental purposes. Ex-Commissioner Anna M. Kross of the New York City Department of Correction has long advocated this approach and has formalized it in a proposed Institute of Behavioral Sciences.[10] This ambitious undertaking would include close cooperation with universities and related professional agencies and the establishment of correctional curricula. The dual aims of this institute are:

1. to integrate the contributions of all disciplines concerned with the treatment and prevention of crime, and train qualified graduate students in their application; and
2. to encourage interdisciplinary research within a major correctional system in order to discover and explore new approaches to crime prevention and treatment.

In implementing this program, all of the physical facilities of her correctional system were offered for training and research purposes.

Within any system of correctional programing, it is basic to recognize the necessity for diversified facilities. While sheer numbers dictate the necessity of some mass congregate institutions, the thrust should be toward smaller, more intensive intervention to deal with young offenders. It is true that some large facilities offer enriched programs. Exciting and innovative approaches for youthful offenders are being tried in Texas, Alabama, New York, California, and other States. There is increasingly closer liaison, through Federal funding, between labor officials and correctional administrators, as evidenced by the MDTA programs inaugurated since 1962.

An MDTA experimental and demonstration project at Draper Correctional Center in Elmore, Ala., for instance, is concerned with the training and placement of youthful inmates. Vocational training is being offered for jobs as combination welder, small electric appliance repairman, and technical writer. Intensive counseling and both school and basic education courses are complementing vocational training.

This project is exploring whether:

1. Intensive vocational and personal counseling can alleviate the behavioral problems of these inmates, enabling them to become working members of our

10/New York City Department of Correction, "Progress Through Crisis," 1966.

society who are capable of adjusting to the demands placed upon them.
2. Direct family counseling can effect an easier transition from the prison to the home and also increase the community's acceptance of the individual.
3. Volunteers can be recruited from the surrounding communities to assist in the prerelease program.
4. The community can be induced to establish local committees to sponsor individual inmates who will be paroled to the community.

In the Nation's capital, one experimental and demonstration project which the Department of Labor is supporting in cooperation with a private research foundation and other Government agencies provides services for approximately 1,000 released youthful misdemeanants and felony offenders. The project is designed to (1) test, select, counsel, provide work experience, evaluate, and refer the youthful subjects to training, and (2) emphasize the development of new jobs in service occupations and new methods of opening up to disadvantaged youth existing but previously unobtainable jobs in the Washington, D.C., area.

In Pennsylvania in January 1965, a pilot project was initiated at the youth development center at Canonsburg, using MDTA funds. The purpose of the project was to establish a suitable vocational-remedial education level for delinquent youth, age 16 and above. Courses for boys included agriculture, meatcutting, food service, clerical work, auto repair, and furniture repair and refinishing. Classes for girls included food service and seamstress, clerical, and greenhouse work. In addition to the vocational areas, remedial education classes were instituted. The academic portion of the MDTA program is handled under the county school board, with the project being set up under joint auspices of the Department of Labor and Industry, including the Bureau of Employment Security, the Department of Public Instruction, the county school board, and the Department of Public Welfare. A thorough screening for each youngster is provided by the employment service, which also provides a follow-up program upon release.

. . . .

The impact of the program on the institution has been quite positive, with both boys and girls responding favorably to the coeducational parts of the program and to the improved level of instruction and the higher achievement expectation.

. . . .

. . . In New York State all 16- to 21-year-olds who are committed to the department of correction are processed through the Elmira Reception Center. Departmental officials determine, after 2 months of intensive orientation, observation, testing, and interviewing, which of 21 diversified institutions the offender should be transferred to for control and treatment. The diagnostic study record accompanies each young offender. The facilities vary in program and focus from small conservation work camps to vocational training centers to reformatory and medium security installations to centers for the defective and criminally insane and, as a last resort, to maximum security prisons. High school diplomas received by over 8,000 prisoners and nearly $5 million worth of goods produced through industrial programs indicate the attempts being made to utilize the talents and potential of the offenders.

Other States have established meaningful programs as well, but where diversification has not been implemented because of lack of fiscal resources or unimaginative administration, the situation is far from satisfactory.

Small residential resources must be established for the many young offenders who have to be removed from their own homes but who do not require custodial handling. These facilities must attract skilled directors who are willing to invest a considerable portion of their own and their family's lives. These directors, living with the offenders, can derive an immense satisfaction from significantly influencing the lives of their charges. Their compensations, however, must be in keeping with the around-the-clock responsibility they have assumed. For example, the Ford Foundation has sponsored a program in Newark, N.J., under which it paid a skilled therapist over $14,000 yearly and provided a free home for him to counsel 20 youths, on an outpatient basis. States should experiment with varying arrangements in this area. A home with a professional director and up to 20 youths could be one alternative. Another approach might establish three homes within the same neighborhood, each housing seven youths under the daily care of mature houseparents, with one professional director responsible for all operations. In the latter arrangement, rented apartments or small private homes might be utilized which would eliminate costly capital investments and renovations. Hopeful steps are being made in some States in this direction.

The utilization of professionals' own homes or inexpensive store fronts should be explored for the establishment of nonresidential treatment units. These would provide intensive therapy sessions with small groups of troubled youth who would be required to meet during the evenings, after working during the day on private jobs, attending school, or working on a crew in some State-owned facility. The professional therapist might view utilizing his own basement for the therapy meetings as a distinct tax advantage.

There are other distinct advantages to the operation of small, intensive facilities, if they are managed by sensitive, skillful staff. Some youths would be better off if we did not probe their personalities and psyche but instead gave them a pressure-free opportunity to mature under stable adult images. Other youths require a more intensive "ego battering" confrontation approach. In the small institution, youths can receive the individual attention, so difficult to achieve in a mass congregate facility. They can be known to the limited number of staff members available as individuals, for whom program planning is detailed and individualized. In a small institution, because of the numbers of staff members involved, employee roles and functioning become meaningfully blurred. The aura of specialization is diminished and a youth begins to understand that individuals can be flexible to meet changing exigencies. He recognizes that false status needs are not a sign of security or manliness. He begins to understand that interchangeability of roles among staff is a beneficial problem-solving approach, unlike that of large institutions where correction officer, psychologist, cook, etc., trod parallel, unintegrated paths. He may realize that a realistic work situation after his discharge may demand of him the performance of a variety of duties and that the important thing is to get the job done rather than to argue about who is to do it. In a small facility the youth has a better chance of being involved in meaningful work and not being forced into the usual pattern of overspecialization and made-work prevalent in massive installations. Correctional administrators recognize the detrimental effects of having 40 mops polishing and repolishing a prison corridor, when there is really need for just two or three. With limited numbers of youth workers, the administrators of a small unit can seek more interesting and diversified job assignments, demanding a realistic pace and accomplishment similar to that of the regular employment market. In a small unit, the director can be much more flexible in his decisionmaking and in his interpretation of these decisions to the youths in program. This is virtually impossible in large facilities, where there is neither time nor communication facilities for explaining why certain policies were established. Indeed, in a smaller unit there is the potential for involving youths much more in the decisionmaking process itself, so that they will feel responsibility for implementing the decision that the small group has made. Vital to the treatment process is the realization on the part of youths that they have direct access to and contact with the decisionmakers in the institution. The curse of large facilities is that the so-called treatment people (mental health specialist, teachers, etc.) have little influence over the administrative policies established by the correctional hierarchy. In a small facility, the decisionmaker is a person who is usually director, administrator, and chief counselor all at once. Youths must interact with him constantly. Since he has a direct voice in the decision to release or to continue youths in program, he becomes a high status person in their eyes and the interaction with him takes on a much more important, meaningful tone. The reason to manipulate the traditional dichotomy between treatment and control staffs is gone, because these roles are blended within existing staff members.

An exciting innovation in working with adolescents and young adults is the fuller utilization of small group processes for therapy or counseling. As a treatment approach it holds rich promise, not because of false economy but because of the inherent nature of the young offender. . . .

As one example of smaller facility planning, the current movement toward the establishment of group homes for youthful offenders in local neighborhoods offers exciting promise but demands sensitive planning. Small group residences could effectively be utilized in diversifying any agency's offerings.

Group homes seem especially helpful for:

1. the young offender who can not respond within traditional probation or parole caseloads but who, it is felt, did not require isolation or secure custody;

2. the older adolescent who has outgrown foster home placement with all of its demands for intense emotional interaction with substitute parents;
3. for the young person who possesses sufficient stability and skill to take advantage of community resources but whose own home and family have deleterious effects;
4. for the youth returning from an institutional experience who has no home to which to return, yet is not mature enough for independent living.

There are other categories of youths under the jurisdiction of probation, correction, and parole agencies who could benefit from this approach, which has been utilized by private child-care agencies for years. Why have authorities moved so slowly into this area?

1. Our knowledge of typology of youthful offenders has been severely limited and we have not been able to program intelligent alternatives with confidence. We have not been able to define in specific and sure terms the personal and behavioral characteristics of those who could be referred to a group home resource. Hence our motivation to create such resources has not been great.
2. We have been cautious because opposition stiffens as we approach local citizenry with problem youth. . . .
3. When attempts to establish racially integrated group residences have been launched, fear of depressed realty values has brought opposition. . . .
4. Local zoning restrictions have been established to thwart group home undertakings. . . .
5. In most States, child care standards have been promulgated by welfare officials. . . .
6. Many agencies have not experimented with group homes for young offenders, because they believed staffing and operating costs would far exceed those of the more traditional prisons and training schools. . . .

    As far as capital costs are concerned, community and group home beds can be established at approximately half the cost of congregate facilities requiring greater emphasis upon security features. As far as operating costs are concerned, small group home expenditures are two-thirds those of training schools which attempt to establish on-campus educational programs, but usually one-third higher than maximum security prisons. Intelligent utilization of community resources not only keeps those in program in contact with the "real" world to which they must ultimately adjust, but curtails costs for the operating agency.

Diversification of facilities provides additional resources to correctional administrators but demands the intelligent utilization of these alternatives. It is wasteful to have varying treatment interventions at one's disposal and then to employ them indiscriminately. For example, the establishment and use of open facilities such as conservation camps, community group homes, etc., for youthful offenders only after these individuals have been subjected to a regular prison experience is a prostitution of the minimum security concept. While it is reasonable to expect many young inmates to graduate to the less stringent, controlling atmosphere of open institutions after they have exhibited sufficient impulse control and positive personal adjustment to warrant such transfer, the fullest potential for these facilities rests in their complete substitution for maximum security programing. Giving young inmates a taste of the big house, so that they will appreciate and better adjust to the open units is an administrative rationalization. Correctional administrators have to become skilled enough to fit the right inmate into the right program and spare him the deleterious wrong program. This fact must be understood, as well, by the naive administrator who advocates minimum or no controls for a youth literally crying out for structure in his present state of development.

While many of these alternate open approaches were pioneered in the juvenile field, an increasing number of States are experimenting with these programs for the older adolescent and young adult. This is especially true with forestry camps, begun in 1934 in California for juvenile court cases. In New York State, for example, the department of correction places inmates as old as 25 in its camps.

Work release programs constitute another approach rich in potential for youthful offenders. Such States as Wisconsin and Maryland as well as others have established meaningful patterns of operation in this area. These are far removed from the convict labor exploitations previously practiced in the name of economy by some States. The Federal Bureau of Prisons also is experimenting with the concept. Although it is not limited exclusively to youthful offenders, the Prisoner Rehabilitation Act, signed into law in September 1965, authorizes unescorted furloughs to Federal prisoners for a variety of purposes and allows selected inmates work releases for employment or study in the community with continuing residence in the institutions. In a preliminary progress report, Federal Bureau of Prisons Director Myrl E. Alexander said[11] that "the beginning has been modest but vigorous," and that "no single development in many, many years has had the impact and great promise for future innovation in the intervention in criminal careers.". . .

STAFF DEVELOPMENT

. . . .

Frequently in this field, workers exhibit conscientious efforts in their endeavors, but find it almost impossible to communicate fully with young offenders, because they come from and possess different cultural backgrounds, value systems, and aspirations than their clients. Ironically enough, one of the most valuable sources of rich staff recruitment has been almost totally ignored

11/*Washington Bulletin,* Social Legislation Information Service, Washington, D.C., June 27, 1966, vol. 19, No. 46, p. 215.

by most treatment agencies. That source is the youth who has been through a rehabilitative process himself. Not only are the skills and understandings of the rehabilitated offender not employed, but the frustrations he encounters and blocked opportunities he experiences after discharge increase the likelihood of his recidivism. He requires a chance to earn a livelihood at work which will be challenging, satisfying, and important to him. The reality of the situation is that many of the technical skills required in today's industrial labor market will not be acquired in the foreseeable future by many offenders, because of their severe retardation in formal communication and functioning. Research by Bernstein,[12] Deutsch,[13] Reissman,[14] May,[15] and Harrington[16] indicates the handicaps which lower class and deprived youths suffer in traditional communication skills. Their ability to conquer abstractions and technical terminology is limited at the present time and requires massive educational intervention which the Government, in programs such as Operation Headstart, is just beginning to undertake. A recently completed program in a large urban penitentiary, which attempted to train youthful offenders in the area of key punch and computer operation, indicated that placement in these vocations did not result in sustained employment for these youths. For rebellious, antisocial adolescents, the type of employment characterized by the computer age is termed women's work and unrewarding. . . .

. . . .

The utilization of ex-offenders does not, of course, lessen the need for competent professionals. Indeed, it enhances the position of the professional worker, because he has the additional responsibility of training, as well as treating. He must act as the supervisor of the nonprofessional staff member rather than a competitor of his. It is becoming increasingly clear, however, through the findings of Clyde Sullivan,[17] Marguerite Warren,[18] Ted Palmer,[19] and others, that different types of young offenders require differing treatment approaches. These approaches cannot be implemented by one discipline or one treatment ideology. Thus, a practical blending of individual and group approaches, dependent upon maturity levels and prior experiences of youth, is

12/Basil Bernstein, "A Public Language: Some Sociological Implications of a Linguistic Form," *British Journal of Sociology*, 1959, pp. 311-327.

13/Martin Deutsch, "Minority Group & Class Status as Related to Social & Personality Factors in Scholastic Achievement," Monograph No. 2, 1960, Social Science Institute, Washington University, St. Louis, Mo.

14/Frank Reissman, "The Culturally Deprived Child," 1962, Harper & Bros., Inc., New York.

15/Edgar May, "The Wasted Americans," New York, Harper & Row, 1964.

16/Michael Harrington, "The Other America: Poverty in the U.S.," 1962, The Macmillan Co., New York.

17/Clyde Sullivan, M. Grant, and D. J. Grant, "The Development of Interpersonal Maturity: Applications to Delinquency," *Psychiatry,* Journal for the Study of Interpersonal Processes, vol. 20, No. 4, 1957.

18/M. Q. Warren, "Implications of a Typology of Delinquents for Measures of Behavior Changes," *California Youth Authority Quarterly,* 1965, No. 3, pp. 6-13.

19/T. Palmer, "Types of Treators and Types of Juvenile Offenders," *California Youth Authority Quarterly,* 1965, No. 3, pp. 14-23.

indicated. The Youth Study Center at Howard University,[20] with Federal funding, demonstrated methods of establishing treatment teams ranging from a psychiatrist to delinquent youth recreation leaders for implementing professional programs in troubled areas. Their mutuality of concern transcended the individual training and background of each member of the team while work with difficult, antisocial adolescents was undertaken.

The Joint Commission on Correctional Manpower and Training has launched a massive and intensive inquiry into the types, functions and development of personnel in this vital area. New roles for youth workers will be explored and the utilization of professional and indigenous leaders is being analyzed.

A CLOSING NOTE

In the final analysis we are far from knowing what amount of what program ingredient is necessary to insure youthful offender rehabilitation. We can offer the usual treatment components such as clean, wholesome quarters, the latest educational materials, costly vocational equipment, inspired chaplaincy services, active recreational outlets, individual and group counseling, and even, in many instances, an interested, involved citizenry. Why don't they automatically add up to rehabilitation? Of course the most obvious answer is that these approaches are not coordinated effectively in one continuum of service. But the answer goes deeper than that. What we have missed is the ability to impart to the young offender in a consistent fashion the notion that we do care about what happens to him. Hard-nosed correction officials and antiseptic clinicians may scoff at this notion, but this writer sincerely believes that all the program offerings we can bring to bear will be wasted unless this understanding is internalized and believed by the youthful offender. The deep-seated feelings of lack of self-worth and the concomitant antisocial compensations on the part of the young offender can be affected only by this realization. We might incarcerate him until he burns out; we might adequately interpret his past experiences through therapy, and make him understand why he acted the way he did; we might keep him occupied for some time through an enriched activity program; we might raise his reading level or teach him to operate a drill press; we might even provide the opportunity for him to begin to utilize his new-found skills and insights. But we must provide him with the desire to put to consistent practice what he might have gained. He will do this to please himself and to prove to significant others that their trust and interest were well-founded. This desire to prove himself to another and to emulate another he respects are the forerunners of more permanent personal change. Once modest indices of success are achieved through this motivation, inner satisfactions leading to heightened feelings of ego-worth will result in socially acceptable rather than self-destructive conduct. This is the true essence of rehabilitation.

20/Center for Youth & Community Studies, "Community Apprentice Program," Howard University, Washington, D.C., 1965.

6. Emergence of the "Defensive" Gang*

THOMAS M. GANNON

Delinquency and criminality, whether by youthful (*see* Luger, Article 5) or younger juvenile offenders, may be expressed in either individual or congregate (group) forms. Some crimes take the form of violence by one person against another, although violence may be committed on behalf of a peer organization or a syndicate (*see* Wolfgang, Article 7). Others involve clearly identifiable gang action or organized criminality (*see* Hawkins, Article 9). Because delinquency and crime cover such a wide variety of types and organizational forms, they are hard to classify and to categorize absolutely. The more than 15 typologies which attempt to coordinate the various forms of juvenile delinquency reveal the difficulty of the problem (*see* introduction to Part Two). While one typology focuses upon the loyalty of delinquent pairs to the norms of the larger society, another category deals with individual reactions to the delinquent subculture.

John W. Kinch believes that delinquents may be categorized most effectively in the three categories of prosocial, antisocial, and asocial delinquents. While the *prosocial delinquent* identifies with the larger society, the *antisocial delinquent* fails to relate to the relevant parts of the value system of the larger society and uses delinquent groups as reference sources. The *asocial delinquent,* however, uses neither normative nor nonnormative reference groups as sources for his values and attitudes. Therefore, any understanding of delinquency, Kinch concludes, must include adequate knowledge concerning delinquent offense patterns, self-concepts, and reference group relationships. The study of offense patterns should encompass the investigation of that type of behavior which brings the delinquent to the attention of a police agency. Research into the delinquent's self-concept will ultimately reveal what type of delinquency pattern they express and represent. The study of the delinquent's reference groups, Kinch concludes, will also offer insight into the nature of delinquent conduct.

Since these variables are interrelated, any attempt to categorize the processes of delinquent and criminal organizations is subject to potential error. However, any investigation of causative factors cannot overlook the influence of social class, racial, familial, or role variables (*see* Empey and Erickson, Article 15; Fanin and Clinard, Article 16; Strecher, Article 17; and Fox and Volakakis,

*Reprinted from *Federal Probation*, Volume 30, Number 4 (December, 1966), pp. 44-48, with the permission of the author and editors.

Article 18). Not only do social class factors account for many attitudinal and procedural differences in delinquent and nondelinquent juvenile arrest and disposition, but they also play a large part in class-conflict-based delinquency. The influence of family life is underscored by evidence which suggests that the kinds of treatment, training, and attitudes that the child experiences in the home play a crucial part in the types of behavior which he will reveal in his later life. Because delinquency involves role playing, role definitions assume added importance.

These processes are also apparent in delinquent gang activity. Thomas M. Gannon notes that although gangs have been traditionally distinguished in terms of the corner group, the social club, the conflict group, or the thoroughly delinquent and pathological group, the *defensive gang* attempts to maintain its identity without initiating open conflict or hostility. Preferring to settle provocations through peaceful procedures, the defensive group uses violence only as a means of retaliation to the most severe violations (*see* Wolfgang, Article 7). The recent overall shift in gang patterns, Gannon concludes, necessitates greater opportunities for gang members to play constructive roles in their community.

... Recent research into the types of groups serviced by the street club workers of the New York City Youth Board clearly points to the beginnings of a more sophisticated type of delinquent group, the "defensive" gang. The structure of these groups has been taking shape almost imperceptibly over the past several years in New York City, and deserves explicit recognition and closer observation from those concerned with problems of youth and their prevention. The following analysis is based on actual observation of the groups in their natural habitat, discussions with the boys themselves and with the street workers attached to them, as well as on questionnaires submitted to the street club staff as part of a research project at the Youth Board during the summer of 1965.

A TYPOLOGY OF THE DELINQUENT GANG

Before going further, it would be helpful to delineate the various types of New York gangs. Traditionally, the Youth Board has distinguished four types of adolescent groups with whom it has come in contact.[1]

1. The *corner group* which develops from a particular spot, usually grows up together, and continues to hang around as a group, talking or engaging in some joint activity. Together they normally display little antisocial behavior.

2. The *social club* almost always organizes around some common interest (e.g., baseball, basketball, jazz) and, like the corner group, is seldom involved in any serious group delinquency.

1/*Reaching the Fighting Gang*, ed. Donald J. Merwin (N.Y.: New York City Youth Board, 1960), pp. 14-16.

3. The *conflict group* might begin either as a corner or social group, but has become involved in serious conflict with other groups. This conflict may result from the need for protection or be due to the desire for aggression; as a rule the group has weapons and an organizational structure designed to carry out its conflict orientation.

4. The *thoroughly delinquent and pathological group* totally committed to continuous violent and often criminal activity. This last category closely resembles what Short has called the "hustling" group organized for the purpose of economic gain through nonlegitimate means, or Cloward and Ohlin's "criminal" gang whose primary activities are centered around rational, systematic, economically motivated criminal activity.

Most of the Youth Board's concern since the initiation of the street club project in 1950 has understandably focused on the conflict group. But fighting potential varies not only in degree from one gang to another, but also in the form of conflict itself. Thus the Youth Board came to distinguish between the fighting gang, strictly so called, and the *defensive* group as subtypes of the more general conflict group.

A fighting gang is involved in considerable aggressive conflict with rival gangs, in reputation and status-seeking, in protection of its own "turf," in initiating violence. It often boasts of arsenals that include tire irons, knives, guns, dynamite, and acid. The group is tightly organized with a clearly defined leadership structure (president, war counselors, etc.).

A *defensive* group, on the other hand, seeks to maintain its identity without initiating such conflict. It will usually prefer settling provocations through peaceful means, employing violent retaliation only for the most severe situations. Even this retaliation will frequently be carried out without weapons and may be followed by increased self-isolation from other gangs in the community.

This distinction between fighting gangs and defensive groups has become increasingly important. At the present time, over half of the Youth Board's street workers (53.8 percent) now describe their groups as defensive, less than one-sixth (15.0 percent) as fighting gangs, and almost one-third (31.2 percent) as corner or social groups. These findings collected in 1965 substantiate the results of a similar 1964 survey of the Street Club Project which found that, in the worker's judgment, over three-fourths of the approximately 300 groups now serviced by the Youth Board are organized and structured to meet needs other than aggression. Of course, all aggressive behavior is not excluded from the defensive, corner, and social groups; but fighting does not constitute their main activity.

CHARACTERISTICS OF THE DEFENSIVE GROUP

Generally, these defensive groups contain about 35 members, 10 of whom can be classified as "hard core." The group ranges in age from 13 to 19 years old, is either Puerto Rican or Negro, displays a rather loosely knit structure, informal leadership, and some relationship to an older or allied group.

The key to understanding the defensive group, however, is to grasp the shift in its patterns of aggression. In the traditional fighting gang, aggression generally falls into three categories.[2] The first is a planned battle, often called "bopping" by the boys, a "rumble" by the press. In this kind of warfare the decision to fight is made by the rival clubs, and the time and place for battle is set in advance. Here some kind of weapons often will be used, especially when one or both groups come with the idea that the rival group will be well armed. Before fighting actually begins the opposing war counselors meet with their supporting forces drawn up behind them. When negotiations break down (e.g., when one counselor fails to give in after the other has recounted the "reps" of the various "warriors" present), conflict results.

A second type of gang fighting might be called "wolf packing," or "rat packing." Wolf packing generally consists of raids into enemy or neutral territory with the object of ambushing enemy forces. As a variation, the group may beat up any person they encounter on the street, just for the fun of it. As one of the boys told me, "Sure, we've done *some* of those things—beating people up, stealing, tearing up a house. But not night after night! Them other cats—they make a business out of it. That's a *rat pack*. They *mean* to be ornery. They're looking for trouble. My group's not like that. Guys don't go out, man, and just look for a fight. If they've been drinking, if they run into trouble, sure, they'll fight. But, man, they don't beg for it."

Finally, many gang fights result from the accidental confrontation of groups from rival clubs. Most of the boys refer to all kinds of fights as "jitterbugging" or "bopping." Usually this means deliberate raiding of another group. "Japping" refers to deliberate raiding of several members of one group by a small band from a rival club. Accidental fighting in this third category has no special designation. It often occurs as an accumulation of previous events and is frequently carried out along ethnic lines.

The defensive group seldom seems to engage in any of these kinds of conflict. Almost three-fourths of the street workers reported that their groups were involved in an average of four or five serious incidents over the past year, a decrease of almost 40 percent in the past 4 years. In comparison with the fighting gangs, the defensive groups encountered half as many serious incidents with rival groups and one-fourth less incidents with other people not involved with a gang. Actually, the corner and social groups tend to become involved in more conflicts with nongang youths than either intragroup or intergroup conflicts.

The most common form of conflict for the defensive group includes individual skirmishes, spontaneous fighting, and japping. Planned "rumbles" rank fifth as one of the least common forms of group violence. . . .

. . . .

2/Cf. R. Lincoln Keiser, "The Teen Age Gang," *Briefs,* September 1965, published by the Social Service Department, Municipal Court of Chicago.

In the defensive group, fighting skills continue to run high as a status symbol. But with the decrease in gang warfare, a member's reputation tends to rest on his fighting *potential* rather than on his proved victories. Also, with more of the boys interested in getting jobs, staying in school, and "getting ahead," status begins to be measured in terms of a boy's job, weekly salary, future plans, and his involvement with the larger society. Given the fact that all these boys come from the lower class culture where toughness is virtually connatural with social prestige, aggression, and a certain amount of violence will continue to be a motivating factor. What is more surprising is the emergence of the desire to get ahead, to have a stake in society; this trend, which is reflected in all our data of the defensive group, runs a bit counter to the fatalism and lack of concern with legitimate achievement predicated of the lower class boy.[3]

The emergence of the defensive group poses many questions to those interested in understanding the teenage gang. . . . Why has fighting declined in importance for these groups? What prognosis follows from our analysis of the defensive gang? And what are the implications of this phenomenon for social workers, police, and parole officers? As yet there have been no satisfactory answers to these questions. It is possible, however, to indicate certain factors and find some clues that shed some light on the problem.

THE DECREASE IN CONFLICT

In discussing the roots of the gang, Thrasher observed that "the gang represents the spontaneous effort of boys to create a society for themselves where none adequate to their needs exists."[4] Indirectly Thrasher took the position that the various agencies responsible for the socialization of the child (the family, church, and school) failed in fulfilling the needs of these youngsters; hence their involvement in their own associations. "The gang functions with reference to these conditions in two ways; it offers a substitute for what society fails to give; and it provides a relief from suppression and distasteful behavior. It fills a gap and affords an escape."[5]

Recent research like the Flint Youth Study and Short and Strodtbeck's investigations into 16 Chicago gangs[6] suggests that disadvantaged youngsters do not become alienated; that even if the gang ethic is not one of reaction-formation *against* widely shared values in society, nevertheless peer groups in the lower class often come to serve important *status functions* for youngsters who are unable to "make it" according to the success criteria of the

3/W. B. Miller, "Lower Class Culture as a Generating Milieu of Gang Delinquency," *Journal of Social Issues,* Volume 14 (1958), pp. 5-14, or Arthur Pearl, "Youth in Lower Class Settings," in Muzafer and Carolyn Sherif, *Problems of Youth* (Chicago: Aldine, 1965), pp. 89-109.

4/Frederick M. Thrasher, *The Gang* (Chicago: University of Chicago Press, 1963), p. 32.

5/*Ibid.,* p. 33.

6/James F. Short and Fred L. Strodtbeck, *Group Processes and Gang Delinquency* (Chicago: University of Chicago Press, 1965).

larger society. But there is also evidence that the gang offers far less solidarity and satisfaction to its members than might be imagined. Thus it would seem that the lack of "social assurance" which Whyte attributed to his "corner boys" is just as true for all delinquent gangs.[7]

Given this status function of the gang, plus the precariousness of gang life and the lack of social assurance and social abilities among these youngsters, violence clearly functions as a significant status symbol precisely when these boys have no real stake in society or any hope in their own possibilities for success. Random violence, and certainly systematic violence, are consistently discouraged among middle-class youngsters because these boys are taught that their present decisions and behavior are inextricably linked with long-run consequences and their future well-being. But for most gang boys, the absence of these values and realistic achievement opportunities leaves a kind of vacuum which becomes occupied with other time-filling expenditures of energy centered around success and satisfaction in the gang.

. . . .

As these youngsters are given a hope for succeeding in society, as their stake in the adult work appears more tangible, fighting loses its appeal. With due account taken of cultural differences, the emerging defensive groups often seem to resemble their middle-class counterparts who also will fight to protect themselves or take retaliation against those who threaten their reputations or opportunities, even if in less violent fashion.

WHAT IS THE PROGNOSIS?

Short has suggested that "the gang's failure to deal satisfactorily with the very real concerns and problems of its members (i.e., status insecurity and social disability) contributes to the instability of most gangs. It also contributes to the fact that the direct influence of gang norms on gang boys' behavior appears to be limited to situations directly involving other gang boys."[8] Thus, to the extent that a group is characterized by social disabilities, it will also be characterized by attempts to create symbols and situations that will allow the expression of the members' dependency needs and the achievement of interpersonal gratifications. In the defensive group, violence still serves as such a symbol, but to a lesser extent than it once did. If this trend is to continue, the larger society must become ever more concerned to provide these youths with real opportunities for gratification and success outside the limits of the gang. As the present research indicates, once the youngsters are given some access to legitimate social gain and a stake in the future, there is every reason to expect that they will perceive their gang experiences less as the source of stability and continuity and more in terms

7/William F. Whyte, *Street Corner Society* (Chicago: University of Chicago Press, 1955), pp. 256-264.
8/Short, "Social Structure and Group Processes in Gang Delinquency," in Sherif and Sherif, *Problems of Youth*, p. 183.

of short-run satisfaction. But only the larger society can finally ring down the curtain on the West Side Story.

IMPLICATIONS FOR DELINQUENCY CONTROL

This prognosis is closely tied to the implications of the emerging defensive gangs for society's agencies of delinquency prevention and control. For the Youth Board the most profound ramifications of its study were felt in the street club project.[9] In the past, the street worker was an individual, often with some social work orientation, who was assigned to one or more fighting gangs. His aim was to redirect their behavior especially by averting gang conflict. As the fighting began to decline, the worker has been called upon to serve more as liaison between the boys and the larger community. This involves much more than establishing personal relationships or mediating warfare. It demands contact with the institutional structure of the community. In the Youth Board's opinion, its street work will continue to be effective only if the workers can create clear-cut channels to training for increased skills and provide legitimate job opportunities, direct the youngsters to them, and provide follow-up guidance along the way.

. . . .

If the Youth Board findings about the defensive gang have relevance for street workers, they also have importance for the police. To treat all delinquent groups as if they were fighting gangs is simply to misread the situation, and to run the risk of needlessly heightening antipolice feelings. One can no longer assume that breaking up the cohesiveness of the group by splitting apart the hard-core members from the rest is an unqualified good. Yablonsky has observed that there is little hope of helping the group until this core has been broken away and dealt with severely.[10] Few would question this approach to the traditional fighting gang.[11] If the group's cohesiveness naturally decreases, is it fair to assume that the remaining structure must be split in order to maintain control and reduce violence? As delinquent groups turn further away from systematic aggression, is there not added reason for planning and cooperation between social agencies and police intervention policies? These and similar questions need not remain the subject of speculation or untested assumptions. They can be answered with data. Once responsible enforcement and social agencies consider together the shifting styles of the delinquent groups under their surveillance, greater strides can be made in developing empirically based programs for handling these boys.

. . . .

9/Gannon, "The Changing Role of the Street Worker," Mimeographed Report, New York City Youth Board, 1966.

10/Leon Yablonsky, *The Violent Gang* (N.Y.: Macmillan, 1962).

11/See, Harry Gottesfeld, "Evaluating Professional Methods with Delinquents," *Social Problems,* Volume 13 (Summer 1965), pp. 45-58.

7. A Preface to Violence*

MARVIN E. WOLFGANG

The apparent increase in urban violence in the United States has become a major public concern. Urban ghetto rioting, together with the alleged American increase in homicide and in acts of simple and aggravated assault, have caused many to fear that the stability of society is being suddenly undermined (*see* Lohman, Article 35). Is violence, however, as dysfunctional as the public believes, or does it serve to open alternate channels for achievement success? Sociologist Louis Coser argues that violence may indeed serve as an alternate road to potential achievement, since violence demands little skill and is a class equalizer. Ascribed status differentials, he notes, are irrelevant in violence. The wilderness of the city, as the wilderness of the frontier, is equalized by the gun. Many gangs, therefore, arise to guarantee the stability of the "turf" and to offer its members a general status and reputation (*see* Gannon, Article 6).

The potential of violence is not limited to the ghetto member or the juvenile gang. Southern (and Northern) police officers (*see* Reiss, Article 21) and self-proclaimed extremists of the left and right have periodically invoked violence in order to attain defined group goals. Violence, therefore, is well known to American cultural history. What is new, however, is the major news media's disclosure of violent activity to the public. As middle- and upper-class citizens have become aware of the threat of the existing violent situation to their own interests, they have moved to minimize or resolve these challenges as quickly as possible. Consequently, the exercise of violence, often symptomatic of public attitudes in the past, now produces, Coser notes, public indignation rather than public tolerance. The assassinations of John F. Kennedy (1963) and Martin Luther King, Jr., and Robert F. Kennedy (1968), which especially focused public attention upon the threat of violence to the community and to the nation, made middle-class ignorance of the problem of violence impossible any longer. Nevertheless, while violence serves to signal the dangers inherent in the existing society, its application, Coser notes, is likely to alienate those who might be potential recruits to its cause.

The use of violence is central to the maintenance of organized crime (*see* Hawkins, Article 9). The role of the syndicate enforcer, Donald Cressey suggests, is similar to the maintenance role of the judge and the legitimate policeman. However, while the enforcer works illegitimately, the police officer operates

*Reprinted from the *Annals*, Volume 364 (March, 1966), pp. 1-7, with the permission of the author and the publisher, The American Academy of Political and Social Science.

within the legitimate structure of the enforcement and judicial systems. The enforcer, therefore, is a participant in a system of institutionalized violence designed to maximize economic goals while minimizing risks and economic interference. Although organized crime has recently developed more subtle and legitimate manipulative techniques which have lessened the observable violence of the enforcer, it still maintains organizational stability and power through the threat and the fulfillment of periodic violence in mugging, beating, bombing, or homicide.

While violence may be apparent in many forms of social conflict, whether in ghetto rioting, political assaults, or organized crime, it is ultimately a form of physical injury inflicted upon some person. Sociologist-criminologist Marvin E. Wolfgang theorizes that the dominant middle class morally denounces violence in order to maintain political order and to secure its own self-interest. However, a subculture of violence, he notes, may normatively support violent acts. The violent act, therefore, may serve to legitimate the violent actor within his own subcultural group or community (see Gannon, Article 6; Luger, Article 5; and Lohman, Article 35).

Violence is a generic term that may include many forms of overt, and often noxious, expressions, ranging from internal physiological changes in the organism to external behavior that directly impinges upon the safety and security of other organisms. Hostility, psychological and physical aggression, anger, and rage are all terms that have been associated with the meaning of violent responses to stimuli. The terms are not synonymous, and the experimental psychologist in laboratory settings still seeks to distinguish their behavioral differences. Discord, conflict, protest, and even revolution do not necessarily involve violence, as the history of nonviolent opposition to established polity and policy has shown. We even use the term "war" in a way that does not invariably mean bloodshed when we speak of a "war on crime," a "war against disease," or a "war on poverty," and refer to our mounting a massive collective attack on a social problem.

It is probably safe to assert, however, that violence is generally perceived as the display of behavior which inflicts physical injury. Although suicide may fall within this more delimited definition, there appears to be more public concern with violence which results in injury inflicted by others. Not all violence transgresses legal norms, but legal sanctions proscribing many types of violence reflect a general societal opposition to violence, the historical concern with it, and the need to regulate its expression. Murder, rape, aggravated assault, armed robbery, and kidnapping are obvious examples of criminal violence. Labor riots, race riots, lynching mobs, fights among delinquent gangs, and attacks by organized criminal syndicates are all forms of collective violence that have punctuated the history of social change.

Together, these types of individual and collective violence comprise the concern of this volume. The authors have addressed themselves to the existence of violence in American culture, that is, violence as part of our normal social functioning, as an element in our literary history, our current fiction, and our mass media, as a cultural expression of the masculine role, and as a psychologically analyzable phenomenon socially transmitted through child-rearing in different social classes.

The President's Commission on Law Enforcement and the Administration of Justice is much concerned with the public fear of criminal violence. Several of our authors have analyzed national trends in aggressive crimes, the existence of violence in organized crime, the extent of violence among juvenile gangs, and the amount of violence among prisoners.

We recognize, however, that the use of physical violence is not confined to common-law criminals. The police and other institutional representatives of legitimized activity use violence to express their disdain of, and to control, opposing forces. Labor groups have both used and suffered from violence in their conflicts with the managerial forces of production. Political groups on the far left and on the extreme right of the Establishment call for violence in their ideologies or have actually engaged in collective aggression. These forms of violence are discussed in factual detail and in theoretical style in this volume. (See * note above.)

In the usual fashion of the compendium of the sort represented by *The Annals,* each author was asked to focus his paper on a relatively specific topic; there was no interaction among the authors except through the structure provided by the editor. Yet, there are some clearly related themes emerging from this collection of expertise.

1. There is considerable public fear that there has been a great increase of violence in American culture.
2. Contrary to this rise in public fear, crimes of violence are not significantly increasing.
3. The high-volume content of fantasy violence in American literature and in mass media like television has not been shown to be correlated with changes in the extent of real violence.
4. In its institutional mode of in-group control and accommodation to the legitimate culture, organized crime has shifted from blatant violence to financial fighting and only an occasional subterranean resort to physical force.
5. Even juvenile gangs, selected for their reputation of "toughness," whose actions have been carefully observed and documented over long stretches of time, engage more in verbal violence than in violent behavior, and the amount of the latter is described as surprisingly low.
6. Legal regulations and past violent victories in labor disputes have reduced violence in this arena to the point where it can be declared that no one has been slain in labor disputes in this country since the 1950's.

7. If aggressively violent actors are rewarded, in the laboratory, in fantasy, or in the real world, they may readily be imitated as role models; if they are punished, the probability of imitation is considerably decreased.

8. There appears to be no set of personality variables sufficiently correlated with aggressive behavior to permit valid predictions of which individuals will engage in violence.

9. The social system may generate violence by the labels of virtue it attaches to legitimized violence in efforts to maintain social control: for example, through the police, prison guards, the masculine role, and international relations, including the use of military force in war.

10. Despite the middle-class antipathy to certain kinds of violence that are viewed as "messy" (that is, crime, riots, and other attacks on the social order), there may be a functional role for properly controlled violence and the use of a language of violence.

To survive, a political culture must maintain a dominant thesis of nonviolence. If the group possessing power to enforce its value system is to retain power, subduing enemies from without or within is really subsidiary to the necessity to promote nonviolence. To be a functioning social system, even a totalitarian society ruled by fear and force must ultimately have the behavioral obedience of the masses, which, in effect, means nonviolent conformity. The power elite of a democracy, as of any other particular governmental form, similarly relies upon the virtue of nonviolence within its borders.

One of the functions of a moral denunciation of violence is to deter direct attacks against the Establishment, to prevent the dethroned and the weak from using violent methods, like revolution, to usurp positions of power. Death is the ultimate weapon of force, as is capital punishment for crime; and with a paucity of alternatives to this weapon, expressions of violence leading to death will be used both by those groups with the maximum means of control and by those with the minimum of power. Of course, a group, like slaves, whose demands do not rise to the level of conscious and collective desire to share the position and power of the entrenched masters, will adhere to the twin principles of successful systems of slavery: nonviolence and submission.

In general, however, there is probably an inverse relation between the number of legitimately alternative means to achieve status and power, on the one hand, and the amount of violence expressed by a group consciously seeking those ends.

Even if one is opposed to the use of violence, it should be possible to examine violence from the viewpoint of functionalism and with considerable ethical detachment. The sociology of violence still needs to be written, but certainly one of the modern starting points should be Georges Sorel's *Réflexions sur la violence,* which first appeared in 1906.[1] Speaking for the revolutionary

---

1/Georges Sorel, *Réflexions sur la violence* (Paris: M. Riviere, 1936). The earlier "conflict school" of sociology would, of course, have to be examined as part of a sociology of violence.

syndicalist wing of the labor movement, Sorel focused in his theoretical writings on the struggle for social power. He saw a positive function for violence (but not brutality) in social conflicts and the desirability of an open recognition of the necessity of violence. With a worn and weak analogy, it could be claimed that a doctor's denial of germs or death does not reduce either, and denying the social role of violence does not reduce the amount of violence. Such denial, Sorel said, is the means which controllers of existing institutions use to prevent threats from proletarian violence. . . .

In view of the comments by several authors of this volume that violence is not increasing, or is even decreasing, among persons involved in organized crime, it is interesting to note that Sorel suggests that reduction of overt acts of violence in social relations is correlated with an increase in fraud and corruption, that fraud comes to replace violence as the road to success and privilege. Those more adept at fraud than at force, adds James Burnham, cling to humanitarian ideals.[2] Crimes of fraud are not so morally reprehensible as are crimes of violence, as Sutherland, echoing Sorel, made analytically clear to criminologists.[3] What Sorel called "cunning" in his references to co-operation, arbitration, and "social peace" has come to replace the use of violence in many aspects of the social struggle for power. Manipulation of persons and things, especially through economic institutions and the impersonalized relationships represented by money (so well analyzed by Simmel),[4] increasingly is substituted for force. Men become interchangeable, alienation accumulates, and minds are raped in subtle ways. Like other groups in the midst of growth and in the struggle for success and power, adolescents, thinks Edgar Friedenberg, cope more readily with force than manipulation.[5] His notion is that more firm and forceful treatment may be easier for adolescents to respond to than the psychologizing management by teachers and counselors.

But the traumas resulting from bureaucratic and professional manipulation have not been adequately catalogued, so that we cannot yet determine whether this functional equivalence of violence is beneficial or deleterious to society. . . . Hence, it should follow that the greater the participation which members of society have in its maintenance, control, and direction, the less vulnerable that society will be to the emergence of collective violence designed to alter or overthrow it.

Except for violent acts due to idiosyncratic psychopathologies, crimes of violence in interpersonal relations are of a different order and require a slightly altered theoretical formulation. In another context, the sociological notion of subculture has been used to analyze what some of us have called a "subculture of violence."[6]

2/James Burnham, *The Machiavellians* (Chicago: Henry Regnery, 1963), p. 140.
3/Edwin Sutherland, *White Collar Crime* (New York: Holt, Rinehart & Winston, 1949).
4/Georg Simmel, *Philosophie des Geldes* (Leipzig: Duncker und Humblot, 1900).
5/Edgar Z. Friedenberg, *The Vanishing Adolescent* (New York: Dell, 1962).
6/Marvin E. Wolfgang, *Patterns in Criminal Homicide* (Philadelphia: University of Pennsylvania Press, 1958).

We find no physiological evidence of any spontaneous stimuli for fighting arising within the body of a normal organism. This lack of evidence leads to an important consideration: the chain of causation of overt aggression traces back to the outside of the organism, and although there may be individual differences in the reactivity to external stimuli evoking aggression, these inner characteristics do not, by themselves, explain aggressive behavior. We are therefore directed to the external social environment as the area where the causative key to aggression must presently be found.[7] It is claimed that the use of force or violence, either in interpersonal relationships or in group interactions such as delinquent gangs, is to be viewed as a reflection of basic values that stand apart from the dominant, central, or parent culture. The theory suggests that this overt and often illicit expression of violence is part of a subcultural normative system.

Now it is obvious that no subculture can be totally different from or totally in conflict with the society of which it is a part. Even a subculture of violence is not entirely an expression of violence, for there must be interlocking value elements shared with the dominant culture. It is not even necessary that violent aggression be the predominant mode of expression in order to contend that the value system is set apart as subcultural. When violence occurs in the dominant culture, it usually is legitimized, as in the case of war, but most often is vicarious and a part of fantasy, although it is not farfetched to suggest that an entire political entity may become a culture of violence when engaging in war.

Subcultural variations may be viewed as quantitative and relative. The extent of differences from the larger culture and the degree of intensity which they possess are variables that could be measured by known sociopsychological techniques. At present we are required to rely almost entirely upon expressions of violence and conduct in various forms—parent-child relationships, parental discipline, domestic quarrels, street fights, delinquent-conflict gangs, criminal records of assaultive behavior, criminal homicides, and the like—for descriptions of the extent of these subcultural variations.

The subcultural normative system designates that in some types of social interaction a violent and physically aggressive response is either expected or required by all members sharing in that system of values. That the actors' behavior expectations occur in more than one situation is obvious. There is, for example, a variety of circumstances in which homicide occurs, and the high frequency of prior aggressive crimes, both among victims and offenders, attests to the multisituational use of violence. Obviously, persons living in a subcultural milieu designated as a subculture of violence cannot and do not engage in violence continuously. Otherwise normal social functioning would be virtually impossible. It is only suggested that such things as ready access to weapons in this milieu may become essential to protection against others who respond in similarly violent ways in certain situations, and that the carrying of knives or other protective devices becomes a common symbol of willingness to participate in violence, to expect violence, and to be ready for its retaliation.

7/There is an abundant literature supporting this position.

The subcultural ethos of violence may be shared by all ages in a subsociety, but this ethos is most prominent in a limited age group, ranging from late adolescence to middle age. It is not suggested that all persons in a particular ethnic, sex, or age group share in common the use of potential threats of violence. But the known empirical distribution of conduct, which expresses the sharing of this violence theme, shows greatest localization, incidence, and frequency in limited subgroups and reflects differences in learning about violence as a problem-solving mechanism.

As Parsons[8] and others have suggested, every norm has its counternorm. In the case of the subculture of violence, the counternorm is nonviolence. That is, violation of expected and required violence is most likely to result in a sanction such as ostracism from the group. Alienation of some kind, depending on the range of violence expectations that are unmet, seems to be a form of punitive action most feasible for this subculture. The juvenile who fails to live up to the conflict gang's requirements is pushed outside the group. The adult male who does not defend his honor or his female companion may be socially emasculated. The "coward" is forced to move out of the territory to find new friends and make new alliances. Membership is lost in the subsociety sharing the cluster of attitudes positively associated with violence. If forced withdrawal or voluntary retreat are not acceptable modes of response to engaging in the counternorm, then execution, as it is reputed to occur in organized crime, may be used as the extreme punitive measure.

The use of violence in a subculture is not necessarily viewed as illicit conduct, and the users therefore do not have to deal with feelings of guilt about their aggression. Violence can become a part of the life style, the theme for solving difficult problems. It should be stressed that the problems and situations to which this thesis refers arise mostly within the subculture, for violence is used primarily between persons and groups who themselves rely upon the same supportive values and norms. A carrier and user of violence will not be burdened by conscious guilt, then, not only because he generally is not attacking the representatives of the nonviolent culture, but also because the recipient of his violence shares in the same subculture and is from similar class, occupation, residence, age, and other attribute categories which characterize the subuniverse of persons sharing in the subculture of violence. . . . Thus, when the attacked see their assaulters as agents of the same kind of aggression that they themselves represent, violent retaliation is readily legitimized for them by a situationally specific rationale, as well as by the generally normative supports for violence.

The major thrust of the thesis of a subculture of violence is related to assaultive offenses, but the thesis is intimately connected to our earlier discussion of the dominant culture, its moral denouncement of violence, its demands for conformity to what is in many Western countries the middle-class value system. The thesis remains viable also in terms of the lack of appropriate

8/Talcott Parsons, *The Social System* (Glencoe, Ill.: Free Press, 1951), chap. 7 ("Deviant Behavior and The Mechanisms of Social Control"), pp. 249-325.

alternatives for solving problems arising from interpersonal relations and the relation of self to the larger life arena. When the repertoire of response to the demands of social life is limited, violence may become a modal reaction and part of a normal system.

.   .   .   .

8. The Study of White Collar Crime: Toward a Reorientation in Theory and Research*

RICHARD QUINNEY

When Edwin H. Sutherland first defined the concept of white-collar crime as a crime committed by a person of respectability and high social status in the course of his occupational role, he opened up a debate in criminological circles which still continues. White-collar crime, Sutherland argues, does not follow traditional lines but is the type of crime which takes such forms as restraint of trade, misrepresentation in advertising, infringement of patents, unfair labor practices, financial fraud, unethical or illegal rebating, and violations of trust. Among medical professionals white-collar crimes take the form of illegal sales of narcotics and alcohol, abortion, fraudulent accident reports, income tax fraud, fake specializations, fee splitting, unnecessary treatment or surgical operations, or illegal services to criminals. Although many of these acts are not legally defined as crimes in the criminal code, they are functionally similar to many of those acts, committed by lower-class members, which have been defined as legal violations. However, the relatively high status of the professional or the businessman, the trend away from punishment, and the relatively unorganized resentment of the public against white-collar crimes, Sutherland hypothesizes, undoubtedly protect the white-collar criminal from general prosecution. Even if prosecuted, his case is more likely to be handled by an administrative rather than a judicial agency. The common cultural and social bonds between legislators and those engaging in white-collar criminality make it difficult, Sutherland believes, to prosecute the white-collar offender (*see* Empey and Erickson, Article 15).

Although the concept of white-collar crime has been attacked by Paul W. Tappan as an overextension of the crime concept to any form of dubious behavior, the role of the middle- and upper-class person in criminal deviation

*Reprinted with special permission from the *Journal of Criminal Law, Criminology and Police Science*, Copyright © 1964 by the Northwestern University School of Law, Volume 55, No. 2.

cannot be denied. However, responding to Tappan's criticism, Sutherland argues that the fact that an unlawful act is *punishable* is much more important than the fact that it is *actually punished (see* Toby, Article 32). While white-collar crimes may not be tried in criminal courts, they are nevertheless harmful to society and challenge civil stability.

As the debate continues, the sociologist-criminologist Richard Quinney suggests that homogeneous units within the white-collar crime concept must be delineated for study. The need to evaluate varieties of social conduct in relationship to occupational as well as general social norms is of critical importance for the future.

White collar crime as a unique form of illegal behavior has received a great deal of attention since Sutherland introduced the concept in his 1939 presidential address to the American Sociological Society.[1] White collar crime—the violation of criminal law by a person of high socio-economic status in the course of occupational activity—has been focused upon in several ways. For instance, a number of research studies of white collar crime have been initiated;[2] the legal character of the violations has been questioned;[3] the sociological relevance of the concept has been doubted;[4] the theoretical and research significance of the concept has been indicated;[5] critiques and summaries have been written;[6] and in most criminology textbooks considerable space has been devoted to a discussion of white collar crime.[7] Most important to the field of criminology, use of the concept of white collar crime has led to the reexamination of the grounds on which generalizations about crime and criminals are made. Although controversy still occurs, the majority of criminologists regard white collar crime as a legitimate subject for criminological research.

Because the validity of white collar crime as a form of crime has been a subject of severe controversy, the question of conceptual clarity has largely been ignored. Today, as a result, the meaning of the concept is not always clear. In addition to the lack of conceptual clarity, a satisfactory explanation of the

1/Sutherland, "White Collar Criminality," 5 *Am. Soc. Rev.* 1 (1940).

2/Significant studies are those of Clinard, *The Black Market* (1952); Cressey, *Other People's Money* (1953); Hartung, "White Collar Offenses in the Wholesale Meat Industry in Detroit," 56 *Am. J. Sociology* 25 (1950); Sutherland, *White Collar Crime* (1949).

3/Caldwell, "A Reexamination of the Concept of White Collar Crime," 22 *Fed. Prob.* 30 (March, 1958); and Tappan, "Who Is the Criminal?" 12 *Am. Soc. Rev.* 96 (1947).

4/Burgess, "Comment" on Hartung, "White Collar Offenses in the Wholesale Meat Industry in Detroit," 56 *Am. J. Sociology* 32 (1950).

5/Hartung, "White Collar Crime: Its Significance for Theory and Practice," 17 *Fed. Prob.* 31 (June, 1953).

6/Newman, "White Collar Crime," 23 *Law & Contemp. Prob.* 735 (1958); Vold, *Theoretical Criminology* 243-61 (1958).

7/*E.g.*, Barnes & Teeters, *New Horizons in Criminology* 3-57 (1959); Bloch & Geis, *Man, Crime, and Society* 379-404 (1962); Reckless, *The Crime Problem* 207-29 (1961); Taft, *Criminology* 250-56 (1956).

diverse behaviors subsumed under the concept does not exist. These difficulties are to be expected since the search for a causative theory of white collar crime has been hampered by a number of problems which have also impeded the study of other forms of crime. Two principal problems have been (1) unit of analysis, and (2) level of explanation. A discussion of these problems as they apply particularly to the study of white collar crime will aid to clarify the concept of white collar crime and also will provide suggestions for a reorientation in theory and research.

UNIT OF ANALYSIS

The first problem stems from the fact that the legal category of crime includes many different kinds of behavior, and it follows that it is unlikely that the different behaviors are subject to a common explanation. Several writers have attempted to correct this difficulty by delineating various behaviors within the legal definition of criminal behavior. Law violators have been placed into behavior units that are more homogeneous than those provided in the legal definitions.

Arguments for the delineation of types of white collar crime have been made on several occasions. Aubert noted a few years ago that, similar to the concept of crime, white collar crime probably covers a range of behaviors and each type of behavior may need a different causal explanation.[8] Recently, Bloch and Geis in their criminology textbook, which concentrates on behavior systems in crime, noted in regard to white collar crime that the concept has come to cover a vast array of illegal behaviors and that "it is apparent that more rigid procedures to distinguish categories of white collar offenses will have to be undertaken to render the classification of maximum scientific worth."[9] As a starting point in delineating types of white collar crime, Bloch and Geis suggested that it might be desirable to separate white collar crimes committed (1) by individuals as individuals (e.g., lawyers, doctors), (2) by employees against the corporation (e.g., embezzlers), and (3) by policy-making officials for the corporation (as in the recent antitrust cases).

In a somewhat different manner, Geis in a recent article, after recommending that white collar crimes be grouped into forms of behaviors that analytically resemble one another both in their manifestation and in terms of the ingredients which appear to enter into their origin, suggested that the concept of white collar crime be restricted to "corporate violations." He concluded that "unless the concept of white collar crime is restricted, in line with the above or similar ideas, it will continue to remain prey to the legitimate criticisms of numerous scholars . . . , and it will continue to be so broad and indefinite as to fall into inevitable desuetude."[10]

8/Aubert, "White Collar Crime and Social Structure," *Am. J. Sociology* 270 (1952).
9/Bloch & Geis, *op. cit. supra* note 7, at 379.
10/Geis, "Toward a Delineation of White Collar Offenses," 32 *Sociological Inquiry* 171 (1962).

It is apparent, then, that such efforts to distinguish categories of white collar crime, or to restrict the definition of white collar crime itself, must be undertaken in order to give the concept any scientific utility. Various principles of classification should be considered. Possible classifications could include such factors as a more elaborate indication of the kind of occupation and the source of employment, the position of the occupation in the occupational structure, the occupational role or roles of the offender, and the institutional nature of the occupation or organization (political, business, industrial, medical, etc.). Also, classifications could be based on the nature and recency of the law itself and the relation of the offense to societal values. An additional consideration is the possibility of a multi-dimensional classification.[11]

However, before white collar typologies can be developed, a more pressing problem must be faced and that is that the concept of white collar crime today rather indiscriminately covers a diverse, wide, and oftentimes uncertain and inconsistent range of behaviors. The result is that we are not entirely certain what behaviors constitute white collar crime. This is due in part to Sutherland's definition and to his own subsequent use of the concept.[12] The research and writing of others on the subject have done little to clarify the concept. We remain uncertain as to (1) the importance of the social status of the offender, (2) the exact meaning of occupational activity, and (3) the possibility of including deviant behaviors which are not strictly legal violations.

Social Status of the Offender

Sutherland conceptually limited white collar crime to violation of the criminal laws regulating occupations by persons who are "respectable" or of the "upper socioeconomic class." His reason for emphasizing social status was primarily for the purpose of illustrating that persons of high status commit crimes and may be included in the study of criminal behavior—thus altering the picture of crime as well as the usual conception of the pathological criminal. While the limitation of white collar crime to a particular status group may be of historical significance in the reformulation of criminological theory, it appears to have little theoretical merit today, except to point to procedural differences in the administration of justice. Newman, in his critique of white collar crime, suggested that "farmers, repairmen, and others in essentially non-white collar occupations, could through such illegalities as watering milk for public consumption, making unnecessary 'repairs' on television sets, and so forth, be classified as white collar violators."[13] Such an expansion of the concept to include all violations that occur in the course of occupational activity—regardless of the offender's social status—would increase the utility of the concept. It would then be advisable to change the term to *occupational crime.*

11/For a multi-dimensional classification in regard to juvenile delinquency see Gibbons, "Prospects and Problems of Delinquent Typology," 32 *Sociological Inquiry* 235 (1962).

12/See Cressey, "Foreward" to Sutherland, *White Collar Crime* vii (5th ed. 1961); and Geis, *supra* note 10, at 160-61.

13/Newman, *supra* note 6, at 737. See also Bloch & Geis, *op. cit. supra* note 7, at 402.

Occupational Activity

The exact meaning of occupational activity is drawn into question when one reviews the writings on white collar crime. One cannot quarrel with the fact that the study of such offenses as embezzlement, price fixing, over-pricing in time of war, misrepresentation in advertising, unfair labor practices, and medical fee-splitting involve behaviors that occur directly in the course of one's occupational activities. It is another thing, however, to include certain forms of such acts as income tax evasion, rent control violation, and violation of welfare compensation laws in the category of occupational crime. These latter behaviors usually do not strictly occur in the course of occupational activity, except, for example, in the case of income tax evasion which is carried out for a corporation or in the case of rent control violation when it can be established that one pursues renting as an occupation. The important point here is that the behavior must be directly related to the violator's occupational activities if it is to be included in white collar crime or occupational crime. Such precision will reduce conceptual problems in future theory and research.

Crime and Deviant Behavior

Those who have argued against the inclusion of white collar crime in criminology have stressed that the violations are not crimes because they are not in violation of the traditional criminal code and, what is more, that the violations are not crimes because the offenders are not usually convicted in a court of criminal law.[14] The advocates of the concept of white collar crime have argued that the behaviors are nevertheless in violation of laws and regulations which contain provisions for punishment. They also argue that the fact that cases are usually processed differently is of no scientific interest, at least for the purpose of explanation.[15]

Although the controversy no longer seems to be of primary concern, ambiguities arise because some writers on white collar crime, Sutherland included, have been interested in behaviors which are not punishable by law, for example, "sharp" business practices and contract violation. It is important that only behaviors which are punishable by law be included in the concept of white collar crime (or occupational crime). On the other hand, the student of occupational crime could gain much by focusing on any deviations in occupational activity, be they criminal or not. It would be valuable, then, to employ the concept of *occupational deviation.* In keeping with recent conceptualization of deviant behavior in general, occupational deviation represents departures from expectations that are shared and recognized as legitimate within an occupation.[16] Occupational deviation includes all

14/Caldwell, *supra* note 3; and Tappan, *supra* note 3.
15/See Sutherland, "Is 'White Collar Crime' Crime?" 10 *Am. Soc. Rev.* 132 (1945).
16/Cohen, "The Study of Social Disorganization and Deviant Behavior," in *Sociology Today* 461-84 (Merton, Broom, & Cottrell eds. 1959).

occupational behavior that violates the institutionalized expectations of an occupation, that is, deviant behavior that occurs in the course of occupational activity. It should be made explicit at all times, however, whether or not the behavior in question is criminal as well as a deviation from occupational norms.

By thus expanding the concept beyond the limits set by legal definitions, but still noting if the behaviors are illegal or not, it would be possible to handle the heretofore unmanageable fact that violations of the legal norms are not necessarily violations of other (non-legal) norms. Because many of the white collar crimes are in violation of laws and regulations recently enacted, they may not yet be a part of the normative structure of the occupation. These laws and regulations are often opposed by outsiders and thus are not necessarily held as binding by the occupational incumbents themselves. Although the violation of the laws and regulations is defined as crime, it is often the case that an occupational norm is not broken. In fact, the white collar offender is likely at most to regard himself as a lawbreaker rather than a criminal.[17] Even the public is unlikely to regard the violation of such laws as crime. These laws do not have their basis in other norms, occupational or otherwise, and the offenses are only bad because they are prohibited (*mala prohibita* rather than *mala in se*).[18]

Therefore, a shift to the concept of occupational violation would allow researchers to investigate actual departures from occupational norms without having to rely upon the otherwise necessary inference that violations of legal norms are also deviations from occupational norms. It would also be possible to study occupational deviations that have not been formalized into law. A range of other problems would be opened by the use of the concept, such as the relationship between law-making and law-breaking, the acceptance of legal norms and the process by which they are incorporated into the occupation, resistance to laws by particular occupational members and the factors associated with resistance, competing occupational norms, redefinition of occupational roles, and occupational change.

In addition to occupational crime and deviation, there are several different orders of behavior which are made obvious when both the violation of legal norms and deviation from occupational norms are considered together and in relation to occupational behavior in general. Each type of behavior presents the researcher with a different set of problems for investigation. Figure 1 is an attempt at a graphic presentation of the relationship between the violation of legal norms and deviation from occupational norms in the larger framework of occupational behavior. It should be kept in mind, however, that the circles representing occupational deviation and occupational crime could assume varying positions in the diagram and are likely to do so in reality. There is the possibility, for example, that the circles could be either mutually exclusive or equivalent, as well as vary in the degree of overlap. Also, either circle could

17/Clinard, *Sociology of Deviant Behavior* 263-65 (1963); and Clinard, *The Black Market* 236 (1952).

18/See the classical article by Fuller, "Morals and the Criminal Law," 32 *J. Crim. L. & C.* 624 (1942). Also Clinard, *Sociology of Deviant Behavior* 152-53 (1963).

FIGURE 1
Relationship Between Occupational Behavior,
Occupational Crime, and Occupational Deviation

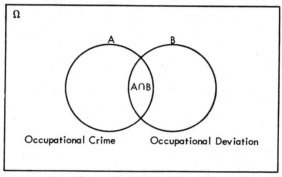

Occupational Behavior

contain the other, or one or both circles could be nonexistent. The circles can, of course, vary in size in relation to the universe of discourse. Nevertheless, the diagram as shown probably presents the most common situation. The circle A represents behavior in violation of laws and regulations governing an occupation (occupational crime). The behaviors in B are the deviations from occupational norms (occupational deviation). The intersection of A and B represents criminal violations which are also deviations from occupational norms (or those occupational deviations which have also been defined as crime)—possibly called *criminal occupational deviation.* Other combinations could also be of theoretical interest. For example, in notation form, AUB represents all behaviors which are either in violation of a criminal law or a deviation from an occupational norm; A − (A ∩ B) includes behaviors which are in violation of the law but do not deviate from an occupational norm; similarly, B − (A ∩ B) includes deviations from occupational norms which have not been defined as crime; Ω − B (or c [B]) represents behaviors that do not deviate from occupational norms, while Ω − A (or c [A]) represents behaviors which are not in violation of laws regulating the occupation; and Ω − (AUB) (or c [AUB]) includes behaviors that do not depart from either criminal laws or occupational norms. Such distinctions could continue until the possibilities are exhausted. The important point is that there are a number of different orders of behavior in reference to the combination of criminal violation and deviation from occupational norms. It follows that researchers must always make clear what order of behavior they are trying to describe and explain. The theories in turn will vary according to the particular behavior (or unit of analysis) in question.

Another interesting observation arises when the criminologist views the relationship between legal norms and occupational norms. There is the special case in which most of the occupational behaviors are defined as criminal by persons outside of the occupation. To the incumbents, however, the behaviors may be legitimate according to their own standards, yet there are entirely different behaviors which they regard as occupational deviations.[19] These are the illegitimate (and usually illegal) occupations which are organized around criminal activity. Crime is pursued by the members as a career and as a regular day-by-day means of livelihood, as in the case of professional theft and the various forms of organized crime.[20] These criminal occupations are known to have their own norms and deviations. The criminal code, for example, presents the professional criminal with the rules that one criminal should not inform on another and that there should be an honest division of the loot with partners in crime. The study of occupational crime and occupational deviation among these illegitimate occupations would certainly present the researcher with two separate and distinct behaviors. Of course, it is not unlikely that the criminal behaviors of illegitimate occupations are also supported by some legitimate occupations.[21]

There is also the fact that in some occupations deviations become institutionalized for certain segments of the occupation or even for most members in particular situations. There may be cases in which there are patterned evasions of occupational norms. Alternative norms may exist which are followed by some members.[22] Also, it is known that certain occupational behaviors which are usually regarded as deviant are legitimate in certain situations.[23] There is, in addition, the fact that occupations are in a constant process of change, and occupational deviation (and sometimes crime) is a necessary concomitant of occupational change. The deviant or criminal is often an innovator. Occupational deviation and crime can be an indication of the development of new occupational norms.[24] It can therefore be seen that in the process of occupational change, definitions of both occupational deviation and occupational crime change, as does the relationship between occupational deviation and occupational crime.

Thus, because the concept of white collar crime does not accurately purport what criminologists always desire to study, it is suggested that rather than restrict the area of investigations to a narrow range of illegal behavior, the various orders of behavior should be specified. Such specification is necessary in order to assure future progress in both theory and research. Particularly valuable for study is the behavior noted in the concept of occupational deviation which

19/A discussion of the norms of deviant groups is found in Lemert, *Social Pathology* 49-51 (1951).

20/Sutherland, *The Professional Thief* 1937); Clinard, *Sociology of Deviant Behavior* 257-91 (1963); and Reckless, *The Crime Problem*, 153-206 (1961).

21/See Vold, *op. cit. supra* note 6, at 220-42.

22/A discussion of alternative norms and patterned evasion of norms in general is found in Williams, *American Society* (1960), especially chapter 10.

23/Bensman & Gerver, "Crime and Punishment in the Factory: The Function of Deviancy in Maintaining the Social System," 28 *Am. Soc. Rev.* 588 (1963).

24/Coser, "Some Functions of Deviant Behavior and Normative Flexibility," 68 *Am. J. Sociology* 172 (1962); Menzel, "Innovation, Integration, and Marginality," 25 *Am. Soc. Rev.* 704 (1960); and Merton, *Social Theory and Social Structure* 131-94 (1957).

includes all deviant behaviors committed in the course of occupational activity, yet at the same time the legal status of the specific deviations should be considered. Distinguishing the different orders of behavior is a step in the delineation of homogeneous behavioral units for the purpose of explanation. It is likely, in reference to the problem which follows, that the level of explanation employed will depend upon the particular behavioral unit under study.

LEVEL OF EXPLANATION

The problem of level of explanation has caused a great deal of confusion in criminology. Theories have differed from one another not only because some have been valid and others have not been, but because they have merely been on different levels. Cressey, in the introduction to his study of embezzlement, identified two levels in the sociological explanation of crime: "The first kind of theory deals with social learning. The data are the specific behaviors of persons, and the task is to identify the process or processes by which a person becomes a criminal. In the other type of theory the data are the social statistics of crime, and the aim is to account for variations in crime rates." [25]

Sutherland, on the same occasion that he introduced the concept of white collar crime, offered his theory of differential association as an explanation of the process by which a person becomes a white collar criminal. Since that time most of the studies of white collar crime have employed differential association as an explanation of the behavior. The theory, however, has been only partially successful in explaining white collar criminality. For example, even though Clinard in his study of the black market concluded that most of the violations appeared to have their origins in behavior learned in association with others, he noted that the theory was limited because it could not adequately explain why some individuals who are familiar with the techniques of violation and also frequently associate with persons familiar with techniques of violation do not engage in such practices. In addition, Clinard noted that the theory did not consider the variety of roles played by the individual, the early associations, the independent invention of a complex technique for violations which are extraordinarily simple, nor the individual's personality pattern. [26]

Also critical of differential association, Cressey in his study of embezzlement seriously questioned the usefulness of the theory in explaining some types of crime. It was found that contacts with criminal behavior patterns were not necessary for the learning of techniques of trust violation and that the specific sources of rationalizations for trust violation could not be identified precisely. Cressey found it necessary to conclude that "it is doubtful that it can be shown empirically that the differential association theory applies or does not apply to crimes of financial trust violation or even to other kinds of criminal behavior." [27]

25/Cressey, *Other People's Money* 11-12 (1953).
26/Clinard, "Criminological Theories of Violations of Wartime Regulations," 11 *Am. Soc. Rev.* 258 (1946).
27/Cressey, "Application and Verification of the Differential Association Theory," 43 *J. Crim. L., C. & P.S.* 52 (1952).

It remains questionable then, whether or not differential association as utilized thus far can state precisely the process by which a person becomes a criminal. Further refinement of this level of explanation, however, might be attempted in future studies of specific types of occupational crime and deviation.

Sutherland originally presented his theory of differential association in nine propositions on two pages of the 1939 Third Edition of his well-established textbook in criminology. Only slight modifications, primarily in terminology, were made in subsequent editions.[28] As Cressey has recently pointed out, numerous errors have arisen in the interpretation of the theory because readers have not understood what Sutherland apparently was trying to say.[29] An important interpretative error, according to Cressy, is that of assuming that Sutherland's theory deals only with the process by which a person becomes a criminal. However, an examination of Sutherland's writing clearly indicates that he was greatly, if not primarily, concerned with organizing and integrating the factual information about crime rates.[30] This conclusion is supported by the fact that Sutherland proposed the concept of "differential social organization" or "differential group organization" as a complementary concept to differential association in order to account for variations in rates of crime. The essential idea in differential social organization is that in a multi-group or heterogeneous type of social organization, alternative and likely inconsistent standards of conduct are possessed by the various segments.[31] The conception that crime (or deviant behavior in general) is structured and that there are strains for crime in a social organization is also found in another sociological tradition, that of functionalism.[32] Both approaches attempt to account for variations in rates of crime between or within social organizations.

Consideration should be given to the explanation of rates of criminal behavior in occupations, a level of analysis which has been ignored in the study of white collar crime. However, even given this level, it is likely that the orientation will be so general that it can serve only as an organizing principle, as seems to be the case with differential association. In fact, it may be suggested that differential social organization be employed as a general orientation. It would thus turn research in the direction of attempting to account for variations in rates of crime among different occupations or among segments within an occupation. The particular social organization of the occupation in question would determine the further specification of the theory.[33]

A glaring omission in criminology is the failure to use a level of explanation

28/Sutherland & Cressey, *Principles of Criminology* 74-81 (6th ed. 1960).

29/Cressey, "Epidemiology and Individual Conduct: A Case from Criminology," 3 *Pacific Sociological Rev.* 37 (1960).

30/As particularly seen in Sutherland, "Development of the Theory," in *The Sutherland Papers* 13-29 (Cohen, Lindesmith & Schuessler eds. 1956).

31/Sutherland & Cressey, *op. cit. supra* note 28, at 79-80, 82-85.

32/See especially Merton, "Social Structure and Anomie," 3 *Am. Soc. Rev.* 672 (1938); and Parsons, *The Social System* 249 (1951).

33/This strategy was taken in my own recent research, Quinney, "Occupational Structure and Criminal Behavior: Prescription Violation by Retail Pharmacists," 11 *Social Problems* 179 (1963).

based on the criminal law itself. The study of white collar crime, however, has forced some criminologists to realize that the criminal law should be considered as well as the behavior in violation of the law. As Aubert has noted in reference to white collar crime, "The recent concern among social scientists with white collar crime tends to bring long-neglected relationships between criminal behavior, criminal law, penal sanctions, and social structure into focus. The unexpected and somehow deviant nature of many recent laws defining white collar crimes has made it natural to ask for an explanation of the norms themselves and not only of their infringements. As soon as this happens new theoretical vistas are immediately opened."[34] It seems obvious, then, that an urgent need in the study of occupational crime, and crime in general, is research that explicitly takes the nature of particular criminal laws into consideration in the explanation of specific types of crime. The discussion above, and accompanying diagram, in reference to the relationship between criminal law and occupational norms could provide a framework for the formulation of such a research problem.

The idea that criminal law is important in the study of crime was noted some time ago by Michael and Adler. They forcefully stated at one point that "if crime is merely an instance of conduct which is proscribed by the criminal code it follows that the criminal law is the formal cause of crime."[35] It is only the criminal law that gives any behavior its quality and criminality. And, as Jeffery has been arguing more recently, attention must be turned to the study of criminal law, not the criminal, in order to determine why a particular behavior is defined as crime.[36] The study of the conditions in society by which certain behaviors become defined as criminal may be important in explanation of the resulting criminal behaviors. It is probably the case, for example, that in some occupations certain behaviors have been a part (possibly deviant) of the occupation for some time, but the fact that for some reason a law was established suddenly made the behaviors criminal. The point is that the relationship between social structure, criminal law, occupational norms, and criminal behavior should be given further consideration. This level of analysis, as well as others, should be attempted in future study of the specific orders of behavior that are related to violations of the criminal law and deviations from occupational norms.

CONCLUSION

Although there has been considerable interest and activity in the study of white collar crime, the development of the area has been hampered by a number

34/Aubert, *supra* note 8, at 264.
35/Michael & Adler, *Crime, Law, and Social Science* 5 (1933).
36/Stated in several places by Jeffery, especially in "The Structure of American Criminological Thinking," 46 *J. Crim. L., C. & P.S.* 658 (1956). A similar idea is found in Vold, "Some Basic Problems in Criminological Research," 17 *Fed. Prob.* 37 (March 1953).

of problems that have not been made explicit. The concept has remained unclear because criminologists have subsumed different behaviors under the term. In addition, writers have varied on the amount of emphasis given to the social status of the offender, have employed different meanings of occupational activity, and have lacked consistency in designating the illegal nature of the offenses. Because the concept includes a wide range of behaviors, it becomes necessary to delineate more homogeneous units for the purpose of explanation. Several distinct orders of behavior become evident when the relationship between criminal behavior and occupational deviation is considered. Finally, it is important that different levels of explanation be employed in future studies of occupational crime and deviation.

9. God and the Mafia*

GORDON HAWKINS

Although organized crime in the United States is structured in the form of many close-knit and cooperating syndicates which attempt to minimize conflict and maximize income through illegal means, its workers have succeeded in infiltrating a few labor unions and legitimate businesses which they dominate by force. Bribing, corrupting, and intimidating law enforcement officials, legislators, and judges, syndicate operators support and attempt to elect officials favorable to their interests. The high costs of political candidacy make public officials highly susceptible to syndicate influences. Offering gambling, drugs, prostitution, and illegal liquor, among other goods or services, organized crime operates in the marginal or fringe areas of public morality, which is nowhere more clearly illustrated than in the popular attitude toward gambling which allows governments to sponsor state lotteries for the advancement of education and in the interests of lower taxes while disallowing the more extensive and popular poor man's gambling in the numbers and *bolita* operations which the syndicate provides.

Following the organizational form of the traditional corporation, the syndicate bureaucracy invests capital in physical plants, secures managerial personnel, and employs various other workers in order to enhance its capitalistic return. Although the illegal business enterprise is essentially similar to a legitimate corporation, the central difference between the legal and illegal organization, Thorsten Sellin finds, rests in the illicit nature of organized crime which creates problems that are necessarily solved only by the use of other illegal means or techniques (e.g., threats, murder) that are prohibited within

*Reprinted from *The Public Interest*, Number 14 (Winter, 1969), pp. 24-51.

legitimate business practice. Both, however, seek operational survival and continuity in a competitive capitalistic situation (*see* also Quinney, Article 8).

The actual economic impact of organized crime is poorly understood by the public. The bureaucracy of organized crime, however, is a new economic and political power in American urban society. Possessing deep roots within American culture (*see* Taft, Article 2), organized crime has become an economy within the economy and a government behind the government. Its development, Gus Tyler hypothesizes, is caused by the revolutionary American tradition which stimulated an undue emphasis upon extreme individualism and allowed the individual on the *old* frontier to take as he was able to take. The *new* frontier of the urban metropolis, which has replaced the old, has become the location in which members of deprived, alienated, and often-aspiring subcultures challenge the established order first in the form of gang activity (*see* Gannon, Article 6) and later through organized crime. The American Puritan heritage, superimposed on a materialistic pragmatism, has created, Tyler believes, a widespread hypocrisy which allows Americans to outlaw collectively many of the practices in which they privately indulge and to fall victim to organized crime without knowledge of its costs. Although organized crime has largely moved from violence to diplomacy and the gangster from hood to statesman, the organization continues to recruit delinquent and alienated youth to its organizational system (*see* Wolfgang, Article 7), just as legitimate business recruits trainees from local campuses.

While the existence of organized crime and the Cosa Nostra cannot be challenged, its exact scope and influence are yet unclear. Placing current knowledge concerning organized crime in perspective, Gordon Hawkins in the following article pleads for an intensive investigation of its operation by the social sciences "without too many preconceptions."

A perplexing and elusive problem confronts the student seeking information about organized crime. It concerns the concept "organized crime" itself. For a curious feature characterizes almost all the literature on the subject, up to and including the Task Force Report on this topic published in 1967 by the President's Commission on Law Enforcement and Administration of Justice. This is that a large proportion of what has been written seems not to be dealing with an empirical matter at all. It is almost as though what is referred to as organized crime belonged to the realm of metaphysics or theology.

.   .   .   .

Take first the question of the existence of organized crime, a matter about which, like the existence of God, doubts have been expressed. On this subject Estes Kefauver, in his *Crime in America,* which is based on testimony taken at the hearings before, and upon reports of, the Senate Crime Committee between 1950 and 1951, writes as follows:

A nationwide crime syndicate does exist in the United States of America, despite the protestations of a strangely assorted company of criminals, self-serving politicians, plain blind fools, and others who may be honestly misguided, that there is no such combine. .... The national crime syndicate as it exists today is an elusive and furtive but nonetheless tangible thing. Its organization and machinations are not always easy to pinpoint. ... However, by patient digging and by putting together little pieces of a huge and widely scattered puzzle, the picture emerges. ... Behind the local mobs which make up the national crime syndicate is a shadowy, international criminal organization known as the Mafia, so fantastic that most Americans find it hard to believe it really exists.

Now, apart from the bizarre nature of its content, one of the most remarkable facts about this quite categorical statement, which occurs in the first chapter of Kefauver's book, is that the evidence necessary to substantiate it is never produced. Indeed Daniel Bell in his *The End of Ideology* comments as follows:

Unfortunately for a good story—and the existence of the Mafia would be a whale of a story—neither the Senate Crime Committee in its testimony, nor Kefauver in his book, presented any real evidence that the Mafia exists as a functioning organization. One finds public officials asserting before the Kefauver committee their *belief* in the Mafia; the Narcotic Bureau *thinks* that a world-wide dope ring allegedly run by Luciano is part of the Mafia: but the only other "evidence" presented—aside from the incredulous responses both of Senator Kefauver and Rudolph Halley when nearly all the Italian gangsters asserted that they didn't know about the Mafia—is that certain crimes bear "the earmarks of the Mafia." (Author's italics.)

Others have been equally skeptical. Thus, Burton B. Turkus, in *Murder Incorporated,* writing at the time when the Senate Crime Investigating Committee was publishing its findings, said:

If one such unit had all crime in this country under its power, is it not reasonable to assume that somewhere along the line, some law agency—federal, state, county or municipal—would have tripped it up long before this? No single man or group ever was so clever, so completely genius, as to foil all of them forever. ... In fact, as a factor of power in national crime, Mafia has been virtually extinct for two decades.

Gus Tyler, editor of *Organized Crime in America,* prefaces the section devoted to the Mafia with an essay in which he says that the Mafia "whose existence is assumed by some government agencies" is "a still unproven fact." He adds, however, that "while the existence of the Mafia is still legally conjectural, theories of its existence cannot be ignored."

But the "theories of its existence" prove on examination to consist of little more than a series of dogmatic assertions. Thus, the Final Report of the California Special Crime Study Commission on Organized Crime (1953) speaks of The Mafia, which it says is "now known as L'Unione Siciliana," as "the most sinister and powerful criminal organization in the world (with) headquarters on at least two continents." But after giving a somewhat desultory account of a variety of "illegal enterprises," and making further reference to "a criminal organization extending all over the world," the report falls back on the argument that "The study of these crimes over the years shows a definite pattern, the repetition of which in case after case cannot be laid to coincidence." This incidentally bears an extraordinary resemblance to one of the best known arguments for the existence of God: that is "the argument from design" in the form in which it was used by the eighteenth- and nineteenth-century rationalist theologians. But it is neither probative nor particularly persuasive.

DIVINE ATTRIBUTES

Another respect in which assertions about the existence of organized crime in general, and a Mafia in particular, resemble statements about the existence of God is that in neither case is it clear what would be regarded as constituting significant counterevidence. Thus, in the Third Interim Report of the Special Committee to Investigate Organized Crime in Interstate Commerce (i.e., the Senate Crime Committee, or the Kefauver Committee), it is said that "Almost all the witnesses who appeared before the committee and who were suspected of Mafia membership, either denied that they had ever heard of the Mafia, which is patently absurd, or denied membership in the Mafia."

The only exception to this which stood up under cross examination was a witness who said "that the Mafia was freely discussed in his home when he was a child." It is not at all clear what the significance of this childhood reminiscence is supposed to be. What is perfectly clear however is that *whatever* witnesses had said would have been construed as evidence *for* the existence of Mafia. . . .

But even when organized crime is not identified with a Mafia it is still referred to in terms that imply divine attributes, such as invisibility, immateriality, eternity, omnipresence, and omnipotence. Thus, in the President's Commission Task Force Report on Organized Crime, it is said that "organized crime affects the lives of millions of Americans, but . . . preserves its *invisibility*." Again, organized crime is said to have its own discipline, but "the laws and regulations they obey, the procedures they use, are private and secret ones that they devise themselves, change when they see fit, and administer summarily and *invisibly*." Moreover, "Agents and employees . . . cannot implicate the highest level figures, since frequently they have neither spoken to *nor even seen them*." Another Task Force Report, "Assessment of Crime," states that "Organized crime thrives on *invisibility*. . . . No one knows whether it is getting bigger or smaller. . . ." And

F. J. Cook, in *The Secret Rulers,* speaks of "a secret organization, an *invisible* government of crime." (My italics.)

As for immateriality, we are also told by the President's Commission:

> But to discuss the impact of organized crime in terms of whatever direct, personal, everyday effect it has on individuals is to miss most of the point. Most individuals are not affected in this sense, very much. . . . Sometimes organized crime's activities do not directly affect individuals at all.

And one writer, "the former attorney for an illicit New York organization," is quoted as speaking in mystical terms of "a mysterious, all pervasive reality."

The Task Force Report also emphasizes the perpetually enduring nature of organized crime. "[O]rganized crime maintains a coherent, efficient organization with a *permanency of form that survives changes* in working and leadership personnel." And Gus Tyler, in an article on "The Roots of Organized Crime," speaks of ". . . its *eternal life* . . . an institutional longevity extending far beyond the natural life span of its more mortal leadership." (My italics in both cases.)

With regard to omnipresence and omnipotence, Robert F. Kennedy said that "The insidious influence of organized crime can reach into almost every facet of our life, corrupting and undermining our society." The Task Force Report goes further and states that "Organized criminal groups are known to operate in all sections of the Nation." Professor D. R. Cressey writing of "the American confederation of criminals," in his paper on "The Functions and Structure of Criminal Syndicates," which is printed as an appendix to the Task Force Report, says that "while organized criminals do not yet have control of all the legitimate economic and political activities in any metropolitan or other geographic area of America," they have started "to undermine basic economic and political traditions."

As with the Deity, moreover, direct knowledge of this phenomenon is apparently not vouchsafed to us. "While law-enforcement officials now have detailed information about the criminal activities of individual men," Professor Cressey writes, "knowledge of the structure of their confederation remains fragmentary and impressionistic." He goes on to say that "Our knowledge of the structure that makes 'organized crime' organized is somewhat comparable to the knowledge of Standard Oil that could be gleaned from interviews with gasoline station attendants." But there is nothing tentative about his explicit statement that "in the United States, criminals have managed to organize a nationwide illicit cartel and confederation." And in a lengthy chapter beginning, "The structure of the nationwide cartel and confederation which today operates the principal illicit businesses in America, and which is now striking at the foundations of legitimate business and government as well came into being in

1931," sufficient baroque detail is provided to suggest that interviews with gasoline station attendants may not be totally uninformative for those with ears to hear.

THE CODE OF THE UNDERWORLD

Yet, as Professor Cressey acknowledges, "some officials, and some plain citizens, remain unconvinced." And, although he regards skepticism as "misplaced," he does not, like Senator Kefauver, define unbelievers as criminals, self-servers, blind fools, and so on. This is, in the circumstances, prudent. For when only "fragmentary and impressionistic" data about an "elusive and furtive" phenomenon are available for judgment, it is unwise to assume that doubt must be disingenuous or perverse.

Thus, as an instance of the sort of thing that might occasion doubt on the part of a plain citizen, consider the tenets of the code that Professor Cressey says "form the foundation of the legal order of the confederation." He states frankly that he was "unable to locate even a summary statement of the code" and that his statement of it is based only on "the snippets of information we have been able to obtain." Yet, on this presumably exiguous basis, he constructs a code that, in regard to form and content, compares favorably with more easily accessible examples of such systems of general rules regarding conduct.

The sinister underworld code that "gives the leaders exploitative authoritarian power over everyone in the organization," reads like the product of collaboration between Rudyard Kipling and Emily Post. Most of it would not appear incongruous if embroidered on a sampler. Organized criminals are enjoined to "be loyal members of the organization," to "be a member of the team," to "be independent," and yet not to "rock the boat." At the same time, they are told to "be a man of honor" and to "respect womanhood and your elders."

The organized criminal "is to be cool and calm at all times"; "is not to use narcotics . . . not to be drunk on duty . . . not to get into fights. . . ." "He does not whine or complain in the face of adversity." "The world seen by organized criminals is a world of graft, fraud, and corruption, and they are concerned with their own honesty and manliness as compared with the hypocrisy of corrupt policemen and corrupt political figures."

In a world of corrupt police and politicians, it must be difficult to preserve these standards. But Professor Cressey explains that, by a "process of recruitment and indoctrination," the leaders of organized crime "have some degree of success" in inculcating "a sense of decency and morality—a sense of honor—so deep that there will be absolute obedience." It is no surprise when we are told that Mr. Vito Genovese, who is said to have been, in 1957, leader of the "All-American 'Commission'" which is "the highest ruling body in the confederation," was "invested with charismatic qualities by his followers. He was almost revered, while at the same time being feared, like an Old Testament divine. Even his name had a somewhat sacred quality. . . ."

The truth is that this sounds very much like what Gus Tyler calls "the fantasy of the Mafia," and Daniel Bell refers to as the "myth of an omnipotent Mafia" all over again. Indeed, Professor Bell, in a subsequent article entitled, "The Myth of Cosa Nostra" (*The New Leader,* 1963), seems to have been one of the few persons to have remained unpersuaded by the later evidence that we shall examine critically in some detail. For others, however, the same sparsity of data supports an equally grandiose inferential superstructure. "Since we know so little," Professor Cressey says, "it is easy to make the assumption that there is nothing to know anything about." But the scarcity of "hard facts" does not appear to constrict him unduly. And although some of what he says sounds plausible in a nonderogatory sense, when it comes to the question of the *existence* of "the American confederation of criminals" he uses a form of argument that comes close to what one might call logical legerdemain.

The argument is worth examining briefly. Under the heading, "The Structural Skeleton," Professor Cressey provides an outline of the "authority structure" or " 'organizational chart' of the American confederation." Twenty-four criminal "families," each with its "boss," are said to operate under the "commission" that "serves as a combination board of business directors, legislature, supreme court and arbitration board." After giving some details of "the formal structure of the organization," Professor Cressey deals briefly with street-level operations and more informal functions. He then concludes briskly:

[T]he skeleton has more bones than those we have described, as our discussion of informal positions and roles indicates. *The structure outlined is sufficient to demonstrate, however, that a confederation of "families" exists.* (My italics.)

It scarcely seems necessary to point out that if "to demonstrate" here means "to prove by reasoning" or "to establish as true," the existence of the confederation cannot be said to have been demonstrated.

. . . .

But we come now to what must in this context and in the present state of knowledge be crucial questions. The first of these concerns what may be called the mythopeic factors that operate in this field. For it is important to recognize that, quite apart from the evidence available, the notion that behind the diverse phenomena of crime there exists a single mysterious omnipotent organization that is responsible for much of it is one that has long exerted a powerful influence on the minds not only of journalists, but also of law enforcement agents and serious students of crime. The second question which we have to ask is, leaving aside nonevidential and irrational considerations, what kinds of evidence may be regarded as providing a means of ascertaining the truth in this matter. . . .

FOLKLORE AND MYTH

With regard to the first question, it is evident that there is a considerable *folklore* relating to organized crime. Much of the literature on the subject consists of myths and folktales. The point is made in Earl Johnson's article, "Organized Crime: Challenge to the American Legal System" that: "America has a new folklore. This folklore has grown up around—organized crime. . . ."

The significance of this development has nowhere been fully analyzed, but in the light of the functionalist interpretation of myth made by anthropologists, it would be unwise to dismiss it as of little account. Bronislaw Malinowski, for example, holds that "Myth fulfills in primitive culture an indispensable function: it expresses, enhances and codifies belief; it safeguards and enforces morality; . . ." In regard to our own society, Ruth Benedict has pointed out that "the fundamental opposition of good and evil is a trait of occidental folklore that is expressed equally in Grimms' fairy tales and in the *Arabian Nights.* . . ."

It is probable that a large part of the appeal of such television series as "The Untouchables," "Target: The Corrupters," and "The F.B.I." is that they dramatize the struggle against organized crime in terms of this fundamental myth. In this, too, it seems likely lies some of the appeal of televised and reported congressional investigations, newspaper accounts of "crusades" against organized crime, and a vast literature. . . .

Another function of mythology, however, is that it provides an *explanation,* in that it helps to introduce some intelligible order into the bewildering diversity of phenomena surrounding us. . . .

Yet, something more than a demand for simplicity and order is involved. In this connection, the way in which anger and distress lead to a demand for the identification of a responsible individual or group, which is brought out by Professor Allport in his discussion of the psychological process of "scapegoating," is directly relevant to our discussion. "The common use of the orphaned pronoun 'they,' " says Allport, "teaches us that people often want and need to designate out-groups—usually for the purpose of venting hostility. . . ." And Daniel Bell attributes part of the attractiveness of the

> theory of a Mafia and national crime syndicate to the fact that there is in the American temper, a feeling that "somewhere," "somebody" is pulling all the complicated strings to which this jumbled world dances. In politics the labor image is "Wall Street" or "Big Business"; while the business stereotype was the "New Dealers."

In the field of crime, the national crime syndicate provides a specific focus or target for fear and discontent.

· ·

WHAT IS "ORGANIZED CRIME"?

When the existence of some social phenomenon or complex of phenomena is asserted, it is reasonable to ask, "What difference does it make?" For, however elusive and invisible and impalpable a social phenomenon may be, the assertion that it exists must, if it is to be regarded as significant, imply the occurrence of some concrete conditions, some specific actions, events, or series of events present in our society that constitute evidence for it. Otherwise, one is entitled, in the present context, to ask a question, analogous to the sort of question posed by skeptics in theological discussions: How does this elusive, invisible, impalpable organization differ from an imaginary organization or from no organization at all? What would count as evidence *against* the assertion that an All-American crime syndicate exists? What would constitute disproof of, or be regarded as sufficient reason for withdrawing, that assertion? Is there anything that might conceivably count against it and, if so, what?

At this point, it is necessary to define the question at issue a little more precisely than has been done so far. In the first place, there is no doubt that small groups of criminals organized for carrying out particular kinds of crime have existed for centuries. . . .

. . . .

It should be clear, however, that the concept of organized crime with which we are dealing here relates to something of different character. . . . We are here concerned with what Sutherland and Cressey call the "organization of the vices.". . .

. . . .

The question we are considering is whether in addition to "large-scale continuing firms" located in various parts of the country, there is a national syndicate that dominates organized crime throughout the country—one large nationwide criminal organization that controls the majority, if not all, of the local undertakings. For the concept of organized crime that was presented in the evidence given by Attorney General Robert F. Kennedy before the Permanent Subcommittee on Investigations of the Committee on Government Operations (McClellan Committee) in 1963 involves

a private government of organized crime, a government with an annual income of billions—run by a commission (which) makes major policy decisions for the organization, settles disputes among the families and allocates territories of criminal operation within the organizations.

ENTER VALACHI

Clearly a crucial question in this context concerns the evidence on which the Attorney General based his contention that such a government and such an organization existed. The nature of that evidence became clear as the McClellan Committee Hearings proceeded. For, at those Hearings, as Senator McClellan himself put it: "For the first time a member of the secret underworld government, Cosa Nostra, testified under oath describing the operations of that criminal organization, and the misguided and dedicated loyalty of its members."

The witness referred to was Joseph Valachi, a sixty-year-old man with a long criminal record, at that time serving a life sentence for murder and a twenty-year sentence for a narcotics offense.

Of the significance attached to Valachi's evidence there seems to be no doubt. The Attorney General described his disclosures as "the biggest intelligence breakthrough yet in combating organized crime and racketeering in the United States." William George Hundley, head of the Justice Department's Organized Crime Section, was even more revealing. He said:

> Before Valachi came along *we had no tangible evidence that anything like this actually existed.* He's the first to talk openly and specifically about the organization. In the past we've heard that so-and-so was a "syndicate man" and that was all. Frankly I always thought it was a lot of hogwash. But Valachi named names. He showed us what the structure is and how it operates. . . . (My italics.)

It becomes necessary therefore to examine Valachi's testimony critically. In this connection, it has to be remembered that, prior to his giving evidence, Valachi, who had the year before (June 1962) murdered a fellow prisoner, was, according to his own statements, in fear of his life. He claimed that his former criminal associates intended to kill him. His feelings for them were no less inimical. When asked why he had decided to cooperate with the Department of Justice, he replied: "The main answer to that is very simple. Number one: It is to destroy them." With such an objective in view, the witness could not be regarded as totally disinterested. Moreover, on his own evidence, he clearly did not regard veracity as always obligatory when speaking to law enforcement agencies.

In the circumstances, it is understandable that Senator McClellan attached importance to securing some corroboration for Valachi's testimony. Thus, in opening the Hearings, he said: "We believe a substantial part of his testimony can and will be corroborated." And, in closing them, he said: "The corroboration furnished by law enforcement officers makes Valachi's testimony more credible and important."

We may ask therefore how far that verdict is borne out. For in such a case as this, the corroborative process assumes unusual significance.

COSA NOSTRA OR MAFIA?

Let us take first a point of detail that has already attracted some comment. What was the name of the organization about which Valachi testified? According to Valachi, it was "Cosa Nostra." He was asked if the organization was "anything like the Mafia, or is it part of the Mafia, or is it the Mafia?" He replied:

> Senator, as long as I belong to this Cosa Nostra, all I can tell you is that

they never express it as a Mafia. When I was speaking, I just spoke what I knew. . . . I know this thing existed a long time, but in my time I have been with this Cosa Nostra and that is the way it was called. . . .

On this, F. J. Cook, in his *The Secret Rulers*, comments that:

there is a consensus among the nation's best investigators, men with the most intimate knowledge of the underworld and its rackets that they had never heard the name before Valachi used it. . . . This has cast some doubt upon the validity of Valachi's story.

It is not a doubt that troubles Mr. Cook however. "Regardless of name," he says, "the vital fact remains: the criminal organization exists. . . . The name itself is secondary. What matters is the reality of a secret organization, an invisible government of crime. . . ." Yet for those more skeptical than Mr. Cook, and concerned about the *corroboration* of Valachi's testimony, it is not a matter that can be passed over so lightly. For the fact is that on this point Valachi's evidence was *never* corroborated, although a large number of expert witnesses were examined on this subject. . . .

. . . It seems a little surprising that out of all those who appeared before the commission not one person was found to confirm Valachi's evidence on this matter.

INITIATION RITES

But if the question of nomenclature is regarded as of no great significance, there are what may be seen as more substantial matters about which the state of the evidence is equally unsatisfactory. Take, for example, the question of initiation rites, about which a great deal has been written in the literature. The Attorney General told the McClellan Commission: "They literally take an oath and they have the bloodletting. I think it will be described to you before the committee, but those who are members of this organization, take the oath."

When he testified on this, Valachi described a ceremony at which thirty-five or forty persons were present in the course of which he took an oath ("I repeated some words they told me, but I couldn't explain what he meant."); burnt a piece of paper ("Well then he gave me a piece of paper, and I was to burn it."); had his finger pricked ("With a needle and he makes a little blood come out."); and repeated some more words ("I never asked what it meant.").

Now the purpose of this meeting, according to Valachi, was "to make new members and *to meet all of them.*" Yet later, when questioned, Valachi, although he claimed to have proposed others for membership, twice stated that he couldn't remember being "invited to participate at any other initiation ceremony." No member of the committee thought to ask him how it was that subsequently—from 1930 onward—no new member was ever to meet *him* at an initiation ceremony. . . .

THE GENOVESE "FAMILY"

We come now, however, to what is unquestionably a matter of substance, to that part of Valachi's testimony that dealt with the membership and organizational structure of the Vito Genovese "family" in New York to which he belonged. It was in this connection that his evidence was said to be most valuable and reliable. John F. Shanley, Deputy Chief Inspector in the Central Investigations Bureau, which is the intelligence unit concerned with organized crime in the New York City Police Department, stated, "His strength is in the Genovese chart, his greatest strength. . . ."; the chart referred to being one prepared by the Central Investigations Bureau showing details of the Vito Genovese "family." It is important, therefore, to see how far Valachi's evidence was corroborated by the police. In this connection, the evidence given by Deputy Chief Shanley reveals that the information given by Valachi coincided with that put forward by the police in a number of respects. Yet an examination of the record reveals other facts which also make it clear that:

1. It would have been very surprising indeed if the police evidence had not agreed with that of Valachi, and,
2. To talk of the police evidence as *corroborating* Valachi's testimony is to totally misrepresent the situation.

In order to demonstrate this point, it is only necessary to reproduce two brief passages from Deputy Chief Inspector Shanley's testimony. The first passage is taken from the beginning of that testimony:

The Chairman: Have you gone over the information that the committee has obtained and conferred with the staff regarding it, and also with this witness, Joe Valachi?

Mr. Shanley: I haven't conferred with the witness.

The Chairman: You never conferred with the witness?

Mr. Shanley: No, sir.

The Chairman: So, what you are going to testify here is not a result of any conference you have had with Valachi?

Mr. Shanley: No, sir.

The Chairman: Very well, you may proceed.

The second passage occurs toward the end of Deputy Chief Inspector Shanley's evidence, after he had produced the chart referred to above and testified about the Genovese "family." It runs as follows:

The Chairman: Senator Muskie, you have a question?

Senator Muskie: You testified earlier, Inspector Shanley, that you had not personally talked to Mr Valachi.

Mr. Shanley: That is right.

Senator Muskie: Yet these charts are based heavily on his information, am I correct?

Mr. Shanley: That is correct.

Senator Muskie: What was the source of your access to his information?

Mr. Shanley: The Committee.

Senator Muskie: These hearings?

Mr. Shanley: Yes, sir. We received the information prior to the hearings.

Senator Muskie: Would it have been possible for you to reconstruct these charts without his testimony?

Mr. Shanley: No, sir.

Senator Mundt: Mr. Chairman.

The Chairman: Senator Mundt.

Senator Mundt: While we are talking about the value of the charts, you have been in the hearing room, I think, Inspector, since the very beginning of the Valachi testimony. Is that right?

Mr. Shanley: Yes, sir.

It is only necessary to add that sedulous reproduction is not the same thing as substantiation. Nor is it sufficient merely to assert, as Mr. Shanley did, that Valachi's information possessed "an apparent authenticity that is hard to doubt.". . .

.   .   .   .

THE CASE OF ABE RELES

There is, however, one example in the transcript of the McClellan Committee Hearings which throws some light on the credibility of Valachi's evidence, and the reliability of the sources from which he derived his information. That is the case of Abe Reles. Early in the hearings, Valachi cited Reles' death as an example of the way in which "the organization" was able "to kill somebody when they are in prison if they want to." He testified as follows:

Mr. Valachi: There was another one, Abe Reles. He was also supposed to testify. He fell out of the window.

Senator Brewster: How did he fall out of the window, do you know?

Mr. Valachi: They threw him out.

Later in the hearings, the committee returned to this point. Senator Javits read out the passage quoted above and then asked:

Senator Javits: Who threw him out?

Mr. Valachi: That was the rumor that they threw him out.

Senator Javits: Who is "they"? You used the word.

Mr. Valachi: Let us put it this way, whoever was in charge.

Senator Javits: That is on the gang side; is that right: What was the rumor, as you knew it?

Mr. Valachi: That the police threw him out.

Senator Javits: That was the rumor as you knew it?

Mr. Valachi: Yes.

Senator Javits: Do you know any more about it?

Mr. Valachi: No; that is all.

Senator Javits: Did you hear that confirmed in prison or in any way?

Mr. Valachi: The boys talked about it; that is good enough for me.

Senator Javits: The boys in prison?

Mr. Valachi: No; the boys outside.

Senator Javits: The boys in your gang, is that right?

Mr. Valachi: Yes.

Senator Javits: Any particular boy?

Mr. Valachi: Well, now, I would say in general conversation here and there. When you have a conversation, it is pretty solid.

Senator Javits: You believed it?

Mr. Valachi: Yes, anything I hear.

Eight days later, the committee was to hear more about the death of Abe Reles. Picturesque stories about "the organization" were one thing; allegations against the police were a different matter. Deputy Chief Inspector Shanley, who had been so impressed by the "apparent authenticity" of Valachi's information, reappeared, speaking in a somewhat different vein.

The Chairman: Very well. Is there anything further?

Mr. Adlerman: I think that Inspector Shanley has something that he would like to put into the record, a statement he would like to make.

Mr. Shanley: I have here a grand jury presentment in the matter of the investigation of the circumstances surrounding the death of Abe Reles on November 12, 1941. . . .

Shanley then read a statement to the effect that the grand jury, after examining 86 witnesses, viewing 127 exhibits, and hearing scientific reports from the FBI, had concluded:

That Abe Reles met his death while trying to escape, by means of a knotted sheet which was attached to a wire, which wire was in turn attached to the radiator in his room. He fell to his death, while suspended from or supporting himself in this sheet, when the wire parted as a result of the strain of his weight on it. We find that Reles did not meet with foul play and that he did not die by suicide.

ORGANIZATIONAL DISCIPLINE

We turn now from "the corroboration furnished by law enforcement officers [that] makes Valachi's testimony more credible and important," to what, in the circumstances, is the only other criterion of validity available, that is, the internal consistency of the evidence. Here there are a variety of matters that might be considered. In view, however, of the great emphasis that is always placed, in the literature, on the strictness of organizational discipline, and the obvious necessity for this if such an organization is to cohere and continue to exist, it is interesting to examine first the evidence on this topic.

In this connection, Senator McClellan spoke in his opening address of "the strict discipline imposed upon the members." He said: "This tightly knit association of professional criminals demands and gets *complete dedication and unquestioned obedience* by its members to orders, instructions and commands from the ruling authority or boss or bosses thereof." Subsequently, many witnesses were to refer to this. Thus, William H. Schneider, commissioner of police of Buffalo, spoke of the syndicate as "a multibillion dollar syndicate which depends on brutal assault and murder as its means of *cold, dispassionate discipline.*" (My italics.) Valachi was asked about this by Senator McClellan.

> *The Chairman:* [T]hat (i.e., Cosa Nostra) is an organization, is it that requires *absolute obedience and conformity* to its policy as handed down by those in authority? (My italics again.)
> *Mr. Valachi:* Yes, sir.
>
> .   .   .   .
>
> *The Chairman:* Is that correct?
> *Mr. Valachi:* Yes, sir.

It is interesting to compare these statements with some passages in Valachi's later testimony. It appears that, because of "the heat of the narcotics prosecutions, and the investigations and the publicity" in 1957, "those in authority" decreed that there was to be no more dealing in narcotics among members of Cosa Nostra. As Valachi put it: "No narcotics. You are in serious trouble if you were arrested for narcotics. You had to prove to them—you have another trial after having a trial with the government." His examination on this topic ran as follows:

> *Mr. Valachi:* After Anastasia died in 1957, all families were notified—no narcotics.
> *Mr. Adlerman:* Who laid down that rule?
> *Mr. Valachi:* That was a rule that was discussed by the bosses themselves.
> *Mr. Adlerman:* Was that the consigliere and the bosses themselves made that rule?
> *Mr. Valachi:* That is right; that covered all families.

It is instructive to read what came next:

> *Mr. Adlerman:* Was the narcotics trade one of the principal moneymakers for the members of the Cosa Nostra?
> *Mr. Valachi:* Yes, it was.
> *Mr. Adlerman:* And was this rule disregarded to a large extent?
> *Mr. Valachi:* You mean there were lots of people in business?
> *Mr. Adlerman:* That is right.
> *Mr. Valachi:* Yes, sir.

Valachi went on to say that even some of "the bosses" violated the rule and he was then asked:

> *Mr. Adlerman:* What was the reason why the members, the soldiers and so forth, and even some of the bosses disregarded the rule?
>
> *Mr. Valachi:* Because of the moneymaking, the profit in it.
>
> *Mr. Adlerman:* There was big money?
>
> *Mr. Valachi:* They would chance their own lives.
>
> *Mr. Adlerman:* And there was a conflict between the desire to make money and the desire to obey the rules; is that right?
>
> *Mr. Valachi:* Well, they just defied the rules.
>
> *Mr. Adlerman:* They defied the rules?
>
> *Mr. Valachi:* That is the way I can explain it that way.

In the light of what had been said earlier about "complete dedication and unquestioned obedience," it was not an entirely satisfactory explanation. But then no explanation, however ingenious, could encompass the logically impossible task of reconciling the development described with the concept of a ruthless, unquestionable authority imposing "cold, dispassionate discipline" and securing "absolute obedience and conformity.". . .

MUTUAL AID?

It is, in fact, extremely difficult to understand what membership of the organization was supposed to entail either in the way of rights or duties. When Valachi was describing his initiation, he was asked:

> *Senator Mundt:* In executive session you said when you had your hands all clasped together and repeated some words in Italian or Sicilian, that what it meant was "One for all and all for one."
>
> *Mr. Valachi:* Yes; that is the way I explained it.
>
> *Senator Mundt:* One for all and all for one.
>
> *Mr. Valachi:* That is right. But I didn't know the words, Senator. You remember, I didn't know the words.
>
> *Senator Mundt:* That is right, but you said that is the reaction you got.
>
> *Mr. Valachi:* That is correct.
>
> *Senator Mundt:* All right, then you became there a full-fledged member.
>
> *Mr. Valachi:* Yes, sir.

It would seem reasonable to assume that the slogan, assuming that Valachi understood it correctly, implied some kind of mutual aid and protection. Certainly Senator McClellan had told the committee that "The benefits of membership . . . are a share in its illicit gains from criminal activities and protection from prosecution and the penalties of the law. . . ." Later Valachi was asked:

Senator Mundt: I want to ask you a couple of questions dealing with the first part of your testimony. You belonged to Cosa Nostra for about 30 years?

Mr. Valachi: Since 1930.

Senator Mundt: What was your average income from your criminal contacts during those 30 years, your average annual income?

Mr. Valachi: Senator, I wouldn't be able to tell you. Sometimes I was doing bad, sometimes I was doing good.

Senator Mundt: What I am trying to establish is that you were working as a soldier in this family, I am trying to determine what your income was as a soldier working for Genovese.

Mr. Valachi: You don't get any salary, Senator.

Senator Mundt: Well, you get a cut then.

Mr. Valachi: You get nothing, only what you earn yourself. Do you understand? . . .

Senator Mundt: You say the only thing you got out of your membership and for carrying out your assignments that Genovese gave you was protection?

Mr. Valachi: Yes. . . .

So much then for Senator McClellan's "share in its illicit gains." What about "protection from prosecution and the penalties of the law"? Deputy Chief Inspector Shanley had told the Committee that "[T]he family will help with lawyers, bail bondsmen, *et cetera,* if anything goes wrong."

The following passages are relevant here:

Senator Javits: Were you represented, for example, by lawyers in that time when you were picked up?

Mr. Valachi: When you are picked up, sometimes yes; sometimes no. Sometimes you don't even require a lawyer.

Senator Javits: How did you seek the help of your family when you were picked up?

Mr. Valachi: I used to get my own help. What family do you mean?

Senator Javits: The family to which you belonged, the Genovese family.

Mr. Valachi: I never bothered them. If I got picked up, I got myself out, I got my own lawyers.

Senator Javits: Did they give you any protection in the 35 years?

Mr. Valachi: No.

Senator Javits: They did not furnish lawyers?

Mr. Valachi: Never.

Senator Javits: Or bondsmen?

Mr. Valachi: Never, I got my own bondsmen, my own lawyers.

Senator Javits: Do you attribute the fact that you were not convicted of a crime for 35 years to your membership in this family? Do you connect the two at all?

Mr. Valachi: No.

Senator Javits: You were just lucky?

Mr. Valachi: That is right.

Senator Javits: And you changed the nature of activities?

Mr. Valachi: Put it that way.

Senator Javits: So your membership in the family had nothing to do, in your opinion . . .

Mr. Valachi: I was never in a position, if I was I would tell you, Senator, I was never in a position where the family helped me.

In his evidence before the McClellan Committee, the Attorney General spoke of the commission ("We know that Cosa Nostra is run by a commission. . . .") as a body that "makes major policy decisions for the organization, settles disputes among families and allocates territories of criminal operation within the organizations." It sounds a very businesslike and efficient operation on the part of men about whom the committee were later told "frequently they don't make out in the legitimate business" because they are "not very smart businessmen." But it is hardly consistent with Valachi's testimony. He was asked:

> *Senator Curtis:* In that connection, did they divide up the territory? Even though you operated on your own, you knew where you could operate?
>
> *Mr. Valachi:* No, you see, Senator, you take Harlem, for instance. We have about four families all mixed up there. *There isn't any territory.* You find Brooklyn gangs in New York and New York into Brooklyn. They get along very well. If anything, you have in Brooklyn, in fact they help protect it for you. *I would not say it is territories.* You take for instance in Harlem, we have about three families bumping onto one another. You have the Gambino family, the Lucchese family, and you have the Genovese family right in Harlem. . . . You have three families right there. You have members there from all different groups. (My italics.)

PRECEPTS AND RULES

We may deal briefly with one other matter and then leave the McClellan Committee. Senator McClellan told members that "The penalty for disloyalty or any serious deviation from the precepts, rules and dictates of the order is usually death.". . . What did Joseph Valachi have to say on the subject? He stated that at the time of his initiation he was told that he must never divulge the secrets of the initiation ceremony or of the organization. On this point, he said:

> As to what I am telling you now, I need go no further to say nothing else but this here, what I am telling you, what I am exposing to you and the press and everybody. This is my doom. This is the promise I am

breaking. Even if I talked, I should never talk about this, and I am doing so. That is my best way to explain it.

His examination continued as follows:

The Chairman: . . . Were any of the rules explained to you there, or were they explained to you later?
Mr. Valachi: Just two rules at this time.
The Chairman: Just two at that time?
Mr. Valachi: At this time.
The Chairman: What were they?
Mr. Valachi: One was the secret which I was just telling you about, and the other rule was, for instance, a wife, if you violate the law of another member's wife, or sister, or daughter, these two rules were told; in other words, you had no defense.
The Chairman: You had no defense?
Mr. Valachi: These two main rules. If you give away the secret or you violate—at this time that is all of the rules I was told.
The Chairman: Those two.
Mr. Valachi: At this time.
The Chairman: If you violated the family relationship of a husband and his wife, and if they were members of Cosa Nostra; is that all?
Mr. Valachi: If they were members. If they were members of Cosa Nostra.
The Chairman: You were prohibited from violating the rules of family relationship.
Mr. Valachi: That is right.
The Chairman: Those two at that time.
Mr. Valachi: That is right.

But, although Valachi testified that later on he "learned the rules," the only other example he gave was, "For instance you can't hit another member with your fist." He admitted having broken this rule himself when he found his partner "was stealing most of the profit." Senator McClellan seems to have scented another rule at this point, for he asked: "Was that against your code, to steal from each other?" But Valachi's reply was somewhat equivocal. "Well yes," he said, "against my code it was." And that was all the committee learnt about "the code" which, according to the President's Commission Task Force Report on Organized Crime "gives the leaders exploitative authoritarian power over everyone in the organization."

Of the three rules he mentioned, Valachi had avowedly broken two. Was he unusual in this? He was certainly not unique in becoming an informer. . . . Over two years later, J. Edgar Hoover told a House of Representatives Appropriations Subcommittee that *"all the Valachi information* . . . had been obtained from informants of the Bureau" prior to the McClellan committee hearings. But, apart from this sort of disloyalty, did the chivalric code of "One for all and all for one" otherwise prevail? . . . Valachi's testimony suggests the opposite. He spoke of vicious power struggles and murderous internecine conflicts like the Masseria-Maranzano war and the Gallo-Profaci feud. . . . He portrayed Professor Cressey's "almost revered" Vito Genovese as mean, murderous, and megalomaniacal. If there existed anywhere amongst organized criminals that "sense of decency and morality—a sense of honor," which Professor Cressey remarks as characteristic of them, it seems to have escaped Joseph Valachi's notice.

In sum then, what can be said about the Valachi evidence? . . .

. . . .

Despite what Senator McClellan said about his evidence being corroborated, it was not corroborated on any points essential to the hypothesis we are considering. It was neither consistent with itself nor with other evidence that was presented to the Committee. Valachi both contradicted himself and was contradicted by others. Moreover, what the Attorney General called "the biggest intelligence breakthrough yet" appears to have produced nothing in the way of tangible results.

Two and a half years after Valachi testified, J. Edgar Hoover was asked before the House of Representatives Appropriations Subcommittee mentioned earlier:

> *Mr. Rooney (Chairman):* Has Valachi been of any assistance to the Bureau in the prosecution of any criminal as a result of which there has been a conviction?
>
> *Mr. Hoover:* There has been no person convicted as a direct result of any information furnished by Valachi.

And four years later, the President's Commission Task Force Report on Organized Crime described the situation regarding organized crime in precisely the same terms as those used by the Attorney General before the McClellan Committee. . . .

APALACHIN

There is one other piece of "evidence" which should be mentioned here before we conclude. This relates to what J. Edgar Hoover called the "meeting of hoodlums at Apalachin, N.Y.," which has been referred to somewhat more grandly by others as the "Crime Convention at Apalachin" and the "historic rally of the Mafia at Apalachin.". . .

. . . .

There seems to be general agreement that on November 14, 1957 a number of individuals, most of whom "had criminal records relating to the kind of offense customarily called 'organized crime,' " gathered at the home of Joseph Barbara in Apalachin, N.Y., and that the gathering was interrupted by the police. But, beyond that point, the evidence becomes extraordinarily confused. Indeed, even such basic information as how many persons were present at the gathering is lacking. . . .

Where such discrepancies exist about a matter that is, at least in principle, subject to quantitative measurement, it is not surprising that there is disagreement about less objective features. . . .

. . . .

Consider, for instance, the question of the nature of the gathering at Apalachin. John T. Cusack, District Supervisor for the Federal Bureau of Narcotics, testified before the New York State Legislative Committee that "the meeting at Apalachin, New York, should be considered a meeting of the Grand Council" of "the Mafia Society." Attorney General Robert Kennedy, in his evidence to the McClellan Committee, cited "the meeting at Apalachin" as an example of a meeting of the commission that runs Cosa Nostra and "makes major policy decisions for the organization." But he also testified that "membership in the commission varies between 9 and 12 active members." He made no attempt to reconcile this evidence with his earlier statement that "more than a hundred top racketeers" were present at Apalachin. Senator McClellan allowed himself a rhetorical flourish. "The meeting of the delegates to the Apalachin convention," he said, "suggests a lawless and clandestine army . . . at war with the government and the people of the United States." He failed to mention, however, that not one of these lawless warriors was armed, and that only one (a parole violator from New Jersey who should not have left the state) was wanted anywhere by the police.

. . . .

. . . When, subsequently, twenty of those present at Apalachin were charged with "conspiring to obstruct justice and commit perjury," the government frankly admitted at the outset of the trial "that it would not be able to show what was going on at the meeting." Regarding this trial, the *Task Force Report: Organized Crime* says: "In 1957, twenty of organized crime's top leaders were convicted (later reversed on appeal) of a criminal charge arising from a meeting at Apalachin, N.Y." It is characteristic of the inconsequential way in which the whole subject is treated in both official and unofficial reports that the defendants are said to have been convicted in 1957 of charges on which they were not even indicted until May 1959. But the report is accurate in stating that all the convictions were reversed on appeal.

. . . One thing is certain: the information available about Apalachin provides no serious evidence that "a single national crime syndicate" dominates organized crime in America; nor does it make this seem probable.

AN ARTICLE OF FAITH

Yet if the evidence for the existence of an All-American crime confederation or syndicate is both suspect and tenuous to the point of nullity, it is clear that for the believer there is nothing that could count decisively against the assertion that it exists. Indeed, precisely those features that in ordinary discourse about human affairs might be regarded as evidence in rebuttal are instantly assimilated as further strengthening the case *for* the hypothesis. The absence of direct evidence, apart from Valachi's uninhibited garrulity (and other unspecified informants), merely demonstrates "the fear instilled in them by the code of nondisclosure." Thus, denials of membership in, or knowledge of, the syndicate can not only be dismissed as self-evidently false, but also adduced as evidence of what they deny. If there is gang warfare, this indicates that "an internal struggle for dominance over the entire organization" is going on; and also provides "a somber illustration of how cruel and calculating the underworld continues to be." If peace prevails this may be taken either as evidence of the power of the syndicate leadership and the fear in which it is held; or alternatively as reflecting the development of "the sophisticated and polished control of rackets that now characterize that organization."

It is said that "practically all" the members of the organization "are of Sicilian birth or ancestry." Professor Cressey, for example, speaks of "the Italian-Sicilian apparatus [that] continues to dominate organized crime in America." But counterevidence relating to the activities of those from other ethnic backgrounds (e.g., Meyer Lansky, said by J. Edgar Hoover to be "generally recognized as one of the most powerful racketeers in this country"), can easily be accommodated as illustrating the "characteristic Mafia method of utilizing non-Sicilian associates where it serves its criminal objectives." In the end, it is difficult to resist the conclusion that one is not dealing with an empirical phenomenon at all, but with an article of faith, transcending the contingent particularity of everyday experience and logically unassailable; one of those reassuring popular demonologies that, William Buckley has remarked, the successful politician has to cherish and preserve and may, in the end, come to believe.

In conclusion, two things can be said. First, here as elsewhere, it may be salutary to bear in mind the principle expressed in the celebrated scholastic dictum that has become known as Occam's Razor: *entia non sunt multiplicanda praeter necessitatem* (entities ought not to be multiplied except out of necessity). For it seems likely that what Laplace found in the sphere of cosmology will also obtain in the more mundane field of criminology: there are hypotheses that we do not need. Second, it is inherently improbable that organized crime is for the most part in the hands of a monolithic nationwide crime syndicate controlled by a single "commission." As Thomas C. Schelling says in his "Economic Analysis and Organized Crime," which is printed as an appendix to the President's Commission Task Force Report, "A large part of organized crime involves selling commodities and services contrary to law." But, "not all businesses lend themselves to centralized organization," and "the inducements to expansion and the advantages of large-scale over small are especially present in some markets rather than others." It is conceivable, of course, that the economy of the underworld is totally different from that of legitimate business. But it seems reasonable to assume that, as Professor Schelling says,

> a good many economic and business principles that operate in the "upperworld" must, with suitable modification for change in environment, operate in the underworld as well, just as a good many economic principles that operate in an advanced competitive economy operate as well in a Socialist or a primitive economy.

In other words, the assumption that, despite the diversity of the activities involved and the absence or presence of the market characteristics that would be likely to determine whether or not, or to what degree, organization would be likely to occur, one vast criminal monopoly has developed with the profits pouring into "the treasury of the Cosa Nostra"—this assumption seems extraordinarily fanciful. But it is true that we do not have the data that would enable us to reject it. What is needed—and here the Task Force Report is unexceptionable—is that the "relevant disciplines such as economics, political science, sociology and operations research" should "begin to study organized crime intensively," and preferably without too many preconceptions.

part THREE
Socialization and Criminal Roles

Criminal behavior is essentially learned behavior. Whether delinquent or criminal, the participant in illegal conduct ultimately learns what objects to steal or attack as well as what method to use to reach his goals from other people within his culture. Even though a school boy may drop out as he reacts to "normal" learning demands (*see* Elliott, Article 10), he, too, must learn the techniques for committing delinquency and later criminal behavior through general familial, peer, or community socialization. Consequently, socialization takes place in both normative and nonnormative processes. In either instance the individual is socialized to particular ends in relationship to his mental and emotional capacity, his familial and ecological situation, his potential employment or unemployment, or other diverse factors.

Although the specific causes of delinquency or crime have not been validated scientifically, these factors are diverse and exist in different combinations in each criminal act. Because every human being is both a psychic individual and a member of multiple social groups, he represents a composite of human needs, biological satisfactions, and symbolic and group interactions. His patterns are part of cultural patterns; his behavior is part of cultural behavior. Although his acts in some societies may not be defined as criminal violations, in others they may be severely prosecuted. Because the nature of criminal law differs from nation to nation and culture to culture, it reflects the ideological, political, and socioenvironmental response of power groups to existing social systems.

Criminal conduct does not take place in a vacuum. Instead, it represents an illicit adjustment to various forces and pressures which impinge upon the individual person or his group. Because most crime occurs in relationship to other deviant members, the interactional dimension of criminality should not be minimized. Certain types of crime, for example, are primarily products of victim-offender interaction and occur as spontaneous (and sometimes planned) responses (*see* Schultz, Article 13).

Former family and neighborhood interactional relationships have been redefined because of the growth of urban life. Psychological and social needs have been redirected, extensive social competition has created greater personal tension, and the individual's potential for employment has been affected by the demand for greater working skills. Each individual, however, must respond to these situations in relationship to his level of socialization. Consequently, some may express hostility and war with society, while others may withdraw from competition by redefining existing reality and fleeing from its consequences. A few turn to violence; others find meaning in other systems and values which reduce the tension caused by existing dissonance. As society changes, those ill-equipped to respond to these changes, therefore, find themselves increasingly becoming marginal men who turn to crime, which itself is a greater social equalizer.

Single companions, friends, and heroes exert important influence upon one's tendencies towards delinquency or criminality. While membership in passive groups may do little to offset delinquency pressures, vital and intense commitments to other interactional associations and group members may stimulate the crime-learning and crime-producing process (*see* introduction to Article 10). While role models are undoubtedly important in both crime participation or crime rejection, the exact processes to be followed in reaching these ends is not easily traced.

Although many suppose that the juvenile gang provides the basic source of later criminality, mere group membership alone does not guarantee the juvenile's future criminal participation. Membership in the Boy Scouts, YMCA, or other youth programs may or may not encourage conforming behavior. Many delinquent gangs likewise evidence highly diverse conduct patterns. While personality deficiencies, family tensions, and ganging patterns are highly influential in delinquency and criminality formation, they are often only the by-products of deeper social influences and tensions. Even though the public believes that a disproportionate number of delinquents and criminals coming from the lower class are products of poverty, unemployment, poor health, and ineffectual education, scientific data fail to support this assumption. Although lower-class members tend to engage in those activities which are more likely to be defined as traditional crimes, much of their deviance reflects their ambiguous subcultural existence (*see* Gannon, Article 6; and Wolfgang, Article 7).

Human behavior is heavily influenced by the roles which the individual assumes. The role of the delinquent, the sex offender, the robber, or the organized criminal are acquired as one is socialized to these role expectations and techniques. Each role teaches a method and offers a status to the role recipient. However, when role aspirations do not coincide with role potentials, alternate goals and roles assume increased importance. Whether one is a gang leader or a syndicate enforcer, he is completing a particular role within a socially deviant, but for him a highly normative, system.

Examining the dimensions of socialization and criminal roles in Part Three, Delbert S. Elliott probes the relationships of student roles, school attendance, and juvenile delinquency. Thomas M. Gannon examines the degree of association between religious socialization and delinquency. Julian B. Roebuck and Ronald C. Johnson view the role characteristics of the "short con" man. While LeRoy G. Schultz investigates the effect of the victim-offender role relationship, Peter G. Garabedian discusses the importance of each inmate role for prison socialization and organization.

10. Delinquency, School Attendance, and Dropout*

DELBERT S. ELLIOTT

When Edwin H. Sutherland first presented the seven propositions in his formal statement of the Differential Association Theory of crime causation in 1939, he offered a new insight into the nature of criminal process. Although he later expanded the seven propositions to nine, they have remained largely unchanged since the 1947 edition of his basic criminology text. Sutherland suggests that:

1. Criminal behavior is learned.
2. Criminal behavior is learned in interaction with other persons in a process of communication.
3. The principal part of the learning of criminal behavior occurs within intimate personal groups.
4. When criminal behavior is learned, it includes the learning of techniques to commit the crime and the specific direction of motives, drives, rationalizations, and attitudes in relation to the crime to be committed.
5. Specific direction of motives and drives is learned from definitions of the legal codes as favorable or unfavorable.
6. A person becomes delinquent because definitions favorable to violation of the law overshadow definitions unfavorable to violations of the law.
7. The relationships in the differential associations may vary in frequency, duration, and intensity.
8. The process of learning criminal behavior involves all the mechanisms that are involved in any other learning.
9. While criminal behavior is an expression of general needs and values, it is not to be explained by those general needs and values since noncriminal behavior is an expression of the same needs and values.

*Reprinted from *Social Problems*, journal of the Society for the Study of Social Problems, Volume 13, Number 3 (Winter, 1966), pp. 307-14, with permission of the editors and author.

Sutherland, in effect, assumes that criminality is learned as the individual relates to particular types of delinquent or nondelinquent groups which either support or reject delinquency or criminality (*see* Gannon, Article 11). Arguing that delinquency and crime are cultural products (*see* Taft, Article 2), Sutherland maintains that crime is rooted in learning processes and associational conduct.

Disagreeing with Sutherland, Daniel Glaser refuses to accept the totality of Sutherland's belief. Instead, Glaser argues that a person pursues criminal behavior to the extent that he *identifies* with real or imaginary persons whose perspectives he believes to be acceptable. Placing greater emphasis upon differential identifications and anticipations, Glaser places less emphasis upon mere association and pays greater attention to the implications of social interaction as the person selects models for his own behavior. Because most individuals, Glaser recognizes, identify with both criminal and noncriminal persons in the course of their lives, they may act out patterns which vary in relationship to their model commitments. Individual offenders oscillate "between criminal and non-criminal pursuits, persisting in each alternative," Glaser believes, "according to the gratifications that they come to *anticipate* there." Despite their other differences in interpretation, both Sutherland and Glaser suggest, however, that the individual's environment plays a large part in the final determination of the person's character.

While studies of the relationship of school failure and delinquency show that many delinquencies seemingly due to school maladjustment are symptoms of emotional problems, they fail to prove that the school is the direct cause of delinquency. Their findings, however, tend to support the assumption that a high percentage of juvenile delinquents generally dislike school and that a high correlation exists between truancy and repeated delinquency. While delinquency is not the only alternative available to juveniles who experience status separation in school, many delinquent and nondelinquent youth use the dropout technique to escape the frustrations of the school milieu. However, Delbert S. Elliott finds that, contrary to general belief, the rate of delinquency referral is greater for boys when *in* school than when *out* of school.

Theoretical explanations of delinquent behavior have come to place increasing emphasis upon some form of "status deprivation" as the motivational source of lower-class delinquency.[1] According to these views, the socialization of lower-class boys does not adequately prepare them to compete effectively for status rewards in middle-class dominated institutions. The intense frustration

1/See David J. Bordua, "Sociological Theories and Their Implications for Juvenile Delinquency: A Report of a Children's Bureau Conference," U.S. Department of Health, Education, and Welfare, 1960; Albert K. Cohen, *Delinquent Boys,* Glencoe, Ill.: The Free Press, 1955; and Richard Cloward and Lloyd Ohlin, *Delinquency and Opportunity,* Glencoe, Ill.: The Free Press, 1960.

experienced by these boys consequently motivates them toward delinquent patterns of behavior in an attempt to recoup their loss of self-esteem.

Albert Cohen in *Delinquent Boys* suggests that the school in particular awards status upon the basis of middle-class standards. Here, lower- and middle-class youths compete for status in terms of the same set of middle-class criteria, with the result that lower-class youths are relegated to the lowest status positions. As a result of the unequal competition, lower-class youths develop feelings of insecurity, become frustrated, and begin to search for some solution to their status problem.[2]

Delinquency is thus viewed as a by-product of the unequal competition at school. Youth who are denied opportunities to achieve higher status positions because of their lower-class socialization are consequently "provoked" to engage in delinquent behavior in an attempt to avail themselves of illegitimate means to reach legitimate goals[3] or to express their rejection and disdain for middle-class goals which are not available to them.[4]

Delinquency is not the only alternative open to youth who experienced status deprivation in school. Dropping out of school also offers a solution to this problem and is not confined to those lacking intellectual ability. Studies of school dropouts suggest that capable youth are leaving school prior to graduation to escape a condition similar to that described by Cohen and Cloward and Ohlin. For example, Lichter and his associates concluded that the capable dropout leaves school because of his desire to escape frustrations encountered in the school milieu. . . .

One significant point regarding the decision to drop out of school as an alternative to the status frustration experienced in school is that it should reduce the motivational stimulus to engage in delinquent behavior. The individual who drops out is no longer involved in the competition with middle-class youth at school, and the adjustment problem described by Cohen as the motivational source of delinquency is at least partially resolved.[5] If status deprivation experienced at school is causally related to delinquency, it follows that the probability of engaging in delinquent behavior is less for out-of-school youth than for in-school youth.[6] This proposition is examined in this study in the form of two specific hypotheses:

2/Cohen, *op. cit.,* pp. 112-119.

3/Cloward and Ohlin maintain that some communities have both conventional and criminal opportunity structures. This solution is essentially that described by Merton as an innovating mode of adaptation. Robert K. Merton, *Social Theory and Social Structure,* Glencoe, Ill.: The Free Press, 1957, pp. 141-149.

4/Cohen, on the other hand, maintains that the delinquent subculture engages in behavior which expresses rejection and derogation of middle-class norms and goals.

5/It is possible, however, that the individual has merely traded the status frustrations encountered at school for those encountered in our economic institutions.

6/The hypothesis that delinquency is related to frustrations encountered in the school milieu and that leaving this milieu reduces the motivation for delinquent behavior appears consistent with the fact that offense rates in the U.S. drop significantly after 17, when most lower-class American youth leave school and enter the labor force.

1. The rate of delinquency is greater for boys while in than while out of school.[7]
2. Delinquents who drop out have a higher delinquency rate while in than while out of school.

THE STUDY DESIGN

The study population is composed of 743 tenth grade boys who entered the two largest high schools in a large western city in September, 1959.[8] In this *ex post facto* design, data were gathered on this group of boys for a three year period beginning with their entrance into high school in September, 1959 and ending with their class graduation in June of 1962.[9] The research design specified a comparison of the delinquency rates of these boys while in and out of school. The "in-school" and "out-of-school" distinction requires that each boy be classified as a graduate or dropout. Boys who graduated in June, 1962 or were in school throughout the entire study period were classified as graduates. All those who left school (during the three years) were classified as dropouts. The dropout category thus includes those who were "pushed" out of school for disciplinary problems as well as those who left voluntarily. Those who left to move to another geographical area were excluded from the analysis.[10] All boys classified as graduates were in school during the entire study period and consequently contributed *only* to the in-school delinquency rate. Boys classified as dropouts were in school for some part of the study period and out of school for the remainder of the period, contributing to *both* the in-school and out-of-school delinquency rates.[11] Of the 743 boys in the study, 182 were classified as dropouts and 561 were classified as graduates.

The comparison of in- and out-of-school delinquency rates also required that these rates be calculated upon a common base. Consequently, it was necessary to determine the actual number of days graduates and dropouts were attending school and the number of days the dropouts were out of school. The number of in-school days for graduates was constant. The number of in-school days for dropouts varied, depending upon the date they left school. School records were examined to determine this date, and an attempt was made to contact each dropout during September and October of 1962 to determine the number of days he was out of school and in the study area. This information was secured

7/It is recognized that leaving school may not reduce the likelihood of a boy who is already delinquent committing another delinquent act.

8/The total number of males entering these two schools in 1959 was 821.

9/Police contacts during the summer months of 1960 and 1961 were not considered in this analysis. Almost all of the subjects were out of school during this period of time and there was no practical way of determining how many subjects left the area and for what periods of time.

10/This was determined by a "request for transcript" received by the school of origin. In several cases boys indicated they were moving but no request for transcript was received.

11/There were two boys who dropped out of school for a period of time and then re-entered school.

for 132 or 73 per cent of the 182 dropouts. For the remainder, an estimate of their out-of-school time in the area was made after examining all available records. The latest date the subject was *known* to be in the area was used to calculate the length of time this subject was out-of-school and in the study area. The estimate of the number of out-of-school days is therefore a conservative one.[12]

Official contact reports by police, sheriff, and other law enforcement agencies constitute the measure of delinquency. The date and nature of each offense, as stated on the contact report (referral), were recorded.[13] The use of official statistics as a measure of delinquent behavior has been questioned by many.[14] Certainly a direct measure of actual behavior which violates legal statuses would provide a more adequate test of the hypothesis. Short and Nye have suggested the use of a self-reported measure of delinquency to more closely approximate a direct measure of delinquent behavior, but the nature of this study precluded the use of such a measure of delinquency.[15] However, an indirect assessment of delinquent behavior can be obtained from official referrals of law enforcement agencies. The definition of a delinquent act in terms of official referrals is comprised of two essential elements: (1) it involves behavior which violates legal statutes and (2) it involves the initiation of official proceedings by law enforcement agencies.[16] While the legal definition includes an illegal behavior component, official records are an inaccurate measure of this behavior since the second component requires that the illegal act be known officially and that some action be initiated against the offender. When an official definition of delinquency is used, therefore, any differences in rates of delinquency noted may be attributed to (1) differences in actual behavior, (2) differences in the knowledge or reaction of official agencies to the offender, or (3) both of these elements. If the design of the study permits the investigator to rule out the second possibility, then tests of theoretically derived hypotheses will not be biased by the use of an official definition of delinquency. The crucial question, therefore, is what determines the behavior of official agents and how will these factors affect the tests of these hypotheses.

Since the comparison is between dropouts and graduates there are some

12/A conservative estimate works against the hypothesis in this case, since it maximized the out-of-school delinquency rate.

13/Kobrin asserts that police "complaint records" or contact reports are probably the most inclusive measure of delinquency obtainable though he recognizes that they are not an accurate measure of delinquent behavior. Solomon Kobrin, "The Conflict of Values in Delinquency Areas," *The American Sociological Review*, 16, 1951, pp. 652-661.

14/Thorsten Sellin, "The Significance of Records of Crime," *The Law Quarterly Review*, 67, 1951, pp. 489-504; and "Culture Conflict and Crime," *Social Science Research Council*, Bulletin 41, 1938, pp. 17-32; James F. Short, Jr. and F. Ivan Nye, "Reported Behavior as a Criterion of Deviant Behavior," *Social Problems*, 5, 1957, pp. 207-213; John I. Kitsuse and Aaron V. Cicourel, "A Note on the Use of Statistics," *Social Problems*, 11, 1963, pp. 131-139.

15/Short and Nye, *op. cit.*, p. 48.

16/Cloward and Ohlin, *op. cit.*, p. 3; Kitsuse & Cicourel, *op. cit.*, pp. 131-137.

logical grounds for assuming that, to the extent differences in knowledge or reaction of official agencies are operating, they would work *against* the hypothesis being tested, i.e., the effect of these biases would be to increase the magnitude of the *out-of-school* delinquency rate. On the basis of available research evidence, it would appear that a major factor influencing the action of official agents is the social class of the offender. Not only is the surveillance likely to be greater in lower-class neighborhoods, but the risk of formal action after detection appears to be greater for those living in these neighborhoods.[17] Since the research evidence also indicates that dropouts come disproportionately from lower-class neighborhoods, the effect of this type of official bias on a comparison of in- and out-of-school delinquency rates would be to accentuate the out-of-school rate and increase the likelihood of rejecting the hypothesis.[18]

It might be argued that those in school are more "visible" to law enforcement agents than are those out of school. One way the police may learn about delinquent behavior is through reports from school officials. To the extent schools make such reports to law enforcement agencies, the delinquent acts of those in school are more visible than are those of out-of-school youth. In connection with another study, contact reports filed in the county during 1963 and 1964 were reviewed to determine the source of each referral.[19] After excluding truancy offenses, it was found that less than one half of one per cent of the referrals identified the school as the source of the referral. Clearly the school is not a significant source for delinquency referrals in this community.

One other factor which might account for a different response on the part of law enforcement agents is the offense. If offenses committed while in school are characteristically different from those committed while out of school, this could account for a differential response on the part of law enforcement agents and a higher in-school delinquency rate. The relatively small number of offenses involved in this study precluded the use of a detailed offense breakdown, but the in- and out-of-school offense patterns were compared with respect to (1) property offenses, (2) offenses against persons, and (3) control offenses.[20] The proportions of in- and out-of-school offenses falling into these three categories were as follows: property offenses, 48 per cent compared to 50 per cent;

17/Clifford R. Shaw and Henry D. McKay, *Juvenile Delinquency and Urban Areas,* Chicago: The University of Chicago Press, 1942.

18/R. A. Tesseneer and L. M. Tesseneer, "Review of the Literature on School Dropouts," *Bulletin of the National Association of Secondary School Principals* (May, 1958), pp. 141-153.

19/These data were gathered in connection with a five year longitudinal study on delinquency and dropout supported by a Public Health Service Research Grant No. MH 07173 from the National Institute of Mental Health.

20/The offenses as listed on the police contact report were classified as follows: (1) Property Offenses—Auto Theft, Burglary, Petty Theft, Other Theft, Vandalism; (2) Offenses against Persons—Sex Offenses, Assault and Battery; and (3) Control Offenses—Runaway, Dangerous Drugs, Drunkenness and Possession of Alcohol, Incorrigible, Beyond Control, & Curfew. Other offenses were classified as miscellaneous. Twelve per cent of the in-school and 25 per cent of the out-of-school offenses were classified as miscellaneous.

offenses against persons, 4 per cent and 0 per cent; control offenses, 36 per cent and 25 per cent. The major difference noted was in the control offenses where the greater in-school proportion was due to a relatively greater number of curfew offenses. In terms of seriousness of offense, a greater proportion of out-of-school than in-school offenses would be classified as felonies. If there are differences in reactions of officials based on the seriousness of the offense, this would tend to operate against the hypotheses in this study. In general, the observed differences in offense patterns do not appear great enough to evoke a systematic difference in response on the part of law enforcement agents.

In the light of the above discussion, it is argued that the use of official referrals as a measure of delinquency should result in a conservative test of the hypotheses since the kinds of distortions or biases introduced by the knowledge and reaction of official agents would tend to work against the hypotheses. If the rates of actual delinquent behavior among boys in and out of school were in fact equal, the most probable effect of using official police contacts to measure these rates would be to overestimate the out-of-school delinquency rate among the dropouts who are more likely to be drawn from a lower-class background.

FINDINGS

The comparison of the in- and out-of-school delinquency referral rates is presented in Table 1. The overall in-school referral rate is 4.95 compared to an out-of-school rate of 2.75. This difference is substantial and in the direction hypothesized. Table 1 also presents the in-school delinquency rates for both graduates and future dropouts and for those residing in lower and higher socioeconomic (SES) neighborhoods. The highest delinquency rate was observed among lower SES dropouts prior to their leaving school. It is quite possible that their involvement in this kind of activity was responsible for some of them being pushed out of school. What is surprising is that this same group of boys had the lowest referral rate after dropping out of school. Their out-of-school rate is less than one-third their in-school rate. These data clearly support the hypothesis.

Cohen's explanation of delinquency applies specifically to working class boys, and the status deprivation variable automatically incorporated the class variable.

TABLE 1
Delinquent Referral Rate* among Boys In and Out of School

SES Areas	In School			Out of School Dropouts†
	Graduates	Dropouts†	Sub-total	
Lower	4.13	8.70	4.96	2.42
Higher	4.92	4.95	4.92	4.63
Total	4.34	8.03	4.95	2.75

*Number of referrals per 10,000 in- or out-of-school days.
†These are the same individuals during two different time periods.

Since there was no attempt to obtain a measure of this independent variable in this study, it seemed important to calculate separate rates for those from lower and higher SES areas. While the in-school rate for boys from higher SES areas is greater than their out-of-school rate, the difference is quite small and may be of little substantive significance. In fact, there appears to be little difference in any of the rates shown for boys from higher SES areas. The in-school rates for dropouts and graduates are almost identical and are only slightly greater than the out-of-school rates. It would appear that leaving school does not have the same impact on boys from higher SES areas as it does on those from lower SES areas. One might expect that leaving school would affect boys from these two SES areas differently. While leaving school should help to eliminate the status frustration of boys from lower-class areas, it would not necessarily solve the adjustment problem of those from middle- and upper-class areas. Boys from lower-class areas can retreat into the lower-class community where they may seek employment in the unskilled or semi-skilled occupations which are available to them. Their parents and other adult members of their community are willing to accept these occupations as legitimate endeavors for young men.

Boys from middle-class areas who leave school subsequently find themselves limited to lower-class occupations while their parents and other adult members of their community continue to hold middle-class expectations for them. They are unable or unwilling to meet the formal expectations of school and are equally unable to meet the expectations of their parents if they drop out of school.

A separate but related issue involves the effect of leaving school on the referral rate of boys who were known officially as delinquents while in school. Although the rate of delinquent referral is less for boys while out of school than while in school, it does not necessarily follow that those who have official referrals while in school will have fewer referrals after leaving school. To test the hypothesis that delinquents who drop out have a higher referral rate while in school, in- and out-of-school referral rates were calculated for this group (Table 2).

The data in Table 2 supports this hypothesis. The in-school referral rate for delinquents is almost twice their out-of-school referral rate. This relationship holds for delinquents from both lower and higher SES areas. The rates in Table 2

TABLE 2
Offense Rates* for Delinquent Dropouts
Before and After Leaving School

SES Areas	Before	After
Lower	64.96	34.52
Higher	40.12	23.75
Total	60.78	31.01

*Number of delinquent referrals per 10,000 student-days.

also suggest that delinquents from lower SES neighborhoods have a higher referral rate than do delinquents from higher SES neighborhoods. This is particularly interesting since there is little difference in the proportions (.112 and .118) of boys from each of these two areas who are delinquent, i.e., who had one or more official referrals on file. It appears that delinquents from lower SES neighborhoods are more frequent offenders than are those from higher SES areas.

CONCLUSION

Cohen suggests that delinquency on the part of lower-class boys is a response to the unequal competition encountered at school. Delinquency is thus associated with frustration and failure particularly experienced in school, for it is in this milieu that youth from disparate cultural backgrounds are forced to compete for middle-class success goals.

There are several alternatives available to those who experience frustration at school. They may remain in school and attempt to deal with their frustration by attacking the system of norms and values which they believe to be the source of their difficulties. Delinquent behavior may thus be viewed as an expression of their resentment toward this system and those who attempt to enforce its norms. On the other hand, those experiencing failure may leave school making a "retreatist" adaptation in an effort to escape from the situation which produces the frustrations. No longer frustrated by the unequal competition at school, there is little or no need to attack the school or the normative system it represents.

It was hypothesized, therefore, that (1) the rate of delinquency referral is greater for boys while in school than while out of school; and (2) delinquents who drop out have a higher referral rate while in school than while out of school. The data supported both hypotheses. The small difference between in- and out-of-school offense rates for boys from higher SES neighborhoods suggests that dropping out of school may not constitute a solution to problems of status deprivation for boys from higher SES areas. One might infer that dropout is a satisfactory solution for those from lower SES areas, for the delinquency rate of such youth is lower after leaving school than it was while they were in school.

11. Religious Control and Delinquent Behavior*

THOMAS M. GANNON

Early studies of criminal deviance and religious commitment singly examined the relationship of delinquency or crime and church attendance. Presupposing that religion offers its members new aspirations, life ideals, and motivation for action, early research simply assumed that religious participation obviously guaranteed right conduct. Various early studies suggested that the prison population was equally if not more religious than the general population. Consequently, the need to devise means by which to measure religiousity assumed paramount importance.

In later years several studies offered conflicting evidence concerning the importance of religion in delinquency prevention. While William C. Kvaraceus reported that 92 percent of the delinquents in a study at Passaic (N.J.) claimed religious affiliation, only 54 percent were regular church attenders. Although Kvaraceus found that the proportion of delinquents regularly attending church was not significantly different from that proportion of the state's population similarly constant in church attendance, the research of Sheldon and Eleanor Glueck and of William Healy and Augusta F. Bonner revealed that delinquents are less likely to attend church regularly than nondelinquents. While many other researchers have challenged the reliability of church attendance or institutional affiliation as a meaningful index of religious conviction, few additional attempts have been made to measure the importance of religion in delinquency and crime causation or prevention.

Religious behavior is too well integrated into character traits to be defined in simple categories. Neither regularity in Sunday school attendance nor length of time in Sunday school attendance, Hugh Hartshorne and Mark May found, seem to influence the juvenile's tendency to deceive. Deceit and honesty, they discovered, are specific functions of life situations rather than unified character traits. An unpublished 1968 study of 64 convicted forcible rapists at a midwest prison by William L. Vincent in cooperation with Richard D. Knudten disclosed that religious value orientations based upon doctrinal beliefs possess less importance for the rape offender than for the general population. The rape offenders exhibited a high degree of doubt and confusion about their beliefs in the Christian diety. Contrary to the expected hypothesis, they disclosed a consistently liberal religious attitude which was often directly opposed to a

*Reprinted from *Sociology and Social Research,* Volume 51, Number 4 (July, 1967), pp. 418-32, with permission of the author and editors.

fundamentalist conception of sin. The rape offenders continually fell short of the percentage of fundamentalist responses reported in the study of denominationalism by Charles Y. Glock and Rodney Stark. These feelings about sin, Vincent concluded, may possibly be explained in terms of guilt feelings concerning their earlier acts which reflect a self-imposed social judgment rather than an expression of religious doctrine. While nearly 38 percent of the incarcerated rapists indicated that they never attended church in prison, their nonparticipation was partially due to their antagonism against the parole board, which considered church attendance as a central factor for parole eligibility.

The exact relationship of religion and delinquency or crime, however, still remains unclear. Thomas M. Gannon, reporting in the following article, finds that while delinquent Catholic boys evidence a high degree of doctrinal and ethical knowledge and a limited degree of religious commitment, the group's stated beliefs and values, in effect, neutralize the formal influence of religion (*see* introductions to Article 10 and Article 12).

The examination of the effects of religion on individuals and groups as well as the specific relationship of religion to delinquency and crime has long intrigued social scientists. . . . Unfortunately, these discussions have shed little light on what the impact of religion is or can be in rehabilitating the offender or in preventing deviance. Part of the difficulty, as Martin and Fitzpatrick indicate, is a lack of agreement in defining religion.[1] Is religion to be identified by church affiliation or by observable religious practice, or does not religion penetrate beyond mere statements of membership or attendance into intensity of a person's commitment to religious belief and practice as they relate to his behavior?[2] There is also the dispute whether religion transcends society defining what society's ultimate values are, or whether, as Durkheim thought, religion is simply the projection onto the plane of the sacred of the natural values already inherent in society.[3]

In terms of the relationship between religion and delinquent behavior, some writers have asserted that religion is the most vital influence in developing the character of youth and, if delinquency takes place, the most effective means for reforming the young offender.[4] Other sociologists have taken the position that because of the insincerity of church leaders, stringent laws imposed by the

1/John M. Martin and Joseph P. Fitzpatrick, *Delinquent Behavior* (New York: Random House, 1964), 91. See also, Thomas F. O'Dea, *The Sociology of Religion* (Englewood Cliffs, New Jersey: Prentice-Hall, Inc., 1966), 11-12.

2/Cf. Gordon W. Allport, *The Nature of Prejudice* (Garden City, New York: Doubleday and Co., Inc., 1958), 420-25.

3/Cf. Emile Durkheim, *The Elementary Forms of Religious Life* (New York: Collier Books, 1961); also *Moral Education* (New York: The Free Press, a Division of the Macmillan Co., 1961), 102.

4/For example, E. J. Cooley, *Probation and Delinquency* (New York: Thomas Nelson and Sons, 1927), 14; John E. Coogan, "Religion and the Criminologist," *American Catholic Sociological Review*, 6 (October, 1945), 154-59; "The Myth Mind in an Engineer's World," *Federal Probation*, 16 (March, 1952), 26-30.

church, the ethnocentrism that evolves from denominationalism, and the identification of the church with the power structure of society, religion provokes and facilitates delinquent behavior.[5]

A major factor hindering the resolution of these controversies has been the lack of empirical evidence. What is needed are studies which discriminate between religion and such variables as social class or cultural background, and studies which attempt to detail the quality of a person's religious commitment, his religious practice in matters other than mere Church attendance, and his religious values as these relate to his everyday behavior.

METHOD

The present study focuses on this second area of religious commitment and values in the attitudes and behavior of a group of officially labelled, but not institutionalized, delinquents. The findings are based on questionnaires and interviews with a random sample of Catholic boys drawn from among those processed by the Intake Department of the juvenile detention home in Cook County, Illinois (the Chicago area).[6]

Given the paucity of available data, the study design involved an essentially exploratory analysis of religious influence patterns. The research aims were threefold: (1) to select a sample of boys who had been officially judged delinquent but not yet formally placed in a correctional setting; (2) to relate patterns of religious influence to the group's attitudes and behavior; (3) to gain insight into the ways in which religion exercised or did not exercise influence.

The study was concerned with specific attitudes, values, and religious practices, not merely with general religious orientation; thus, the sample was restricted to a single religious denomination, and it was decided to select a group of more serious offenders.[7] The Intake Department was chosen as the location of the study because it offered an accessible group which would include the more serious delinquents, and at the same time, provide a minimally institutionalized setting. The boys were interviewed on the day of their arrival before any decision was made either to release them to parental custody or to retain them in the adjacent detention home to await a delinquency hearing in the Family Court.

It was impossible to interview all the delinquent Catholic boys received during the period allotted for the study. . . . Thus, the sample was limited to

5/For example, Cesare Lombroso, *Crime: Its Causes and Remedies* (Boston: Little, Brown, and Co., 1918), 144; Walter C. Reckless and Napheus Smith, *Juvenile Delinquency* (New York: McGraw-Hill Book Co., 1932), 151.

6/As a result of the over-crowded conditions at the detention home, the county established the Intake Department in 1937 for the explicit purpose of screening each child's need for detention, and whenever possible, of providing alternatives to detention.

7/It seemed desirable to focus attention on the more serious delinquent in order to obtain a group that, in terms of their public behavior, most clearly cuts against both the expectations of the larger society and their church.

Catholic boys, fourteen to sixteen years old; every second boy, as the names appeared on the admission list, was interviewed, comprising a random sample of 150 delinquents out of 290 cases admitted during the same period (51.7 per cent).

... [T]he final questionnaire involved items dealing with the delinquent's social and religious background, religious beliefs, values, and practices, related attitudes toward stealing, sex, fighting, and peer-group values, as well as L. L. Thurstone's standardized "Scale of Attitudes Toward God—Form *D*." The administration of the questionnaire was followed by an in-depth interview lasting about one hour....

FINDINGS

Family and Environmental Control

The majority of the delinquents studied (67.3 per cent) came from the lower socioeconomic strata as measured by Hollingshead's "Two-Factor Index of Social Position." Half of them (50.7 per cent) were intermediate children in medium-sized families, while 25.3 per cent were the oldest children. The theory that there is a close association between physically or legally broken homes and delinquency was supported not by its incidence within the sample (41.3 per cent), but by the almost doubled proportion of broken homes as compared with the national average.[8] The number of employed mothers (53.3 per cent) was also higher than the national average.

On the level of internal family relationships, the delinquents felt that their parents were generally happy, fair in their regulations and discipline—except with regard to choice of companions. Correlatively, the parents' regulations on companions, as reported by the group, were less strict than those regarding curfew and church attendance. The data reveal that the boys seldom sought advice or information from their parents, especially in religious matters. Still, over half the group (52.4 per cent) felt that their parents knew a great deal about religion. The point seems to be that the delinquent rarely thought about religion or, when he did, he did not feel there was any need to question or discuss it.

Since the entire sample was within the required school age, virtually all the boys attended school during the academic year. Almost one-third of them (32.7 per cent), however, were enrolled in one of the "continuation" schools in the city demanding only one day of attendance per week.... More to the point within the context of social control, almost half of the group (47 per cent)

8/See, Gordon H. Barker, "Family Factors in the Sociology of Juvenile Delinquency," *Journal of Criminal Law and Criminology*, 30 (January-February, 1940), 681-91; Sheldon and Eleanor Glueck, *Unraveling Juvenile Delinquency* (New York: Commonwealth Fund, 1950), 123-25; F. Ivan Nye, *Family Relationships and Delinquent Behavior* (New York: John Wiley and Sons, 1958).

reported they had attended school in three to five communities; over a third (34.7 per cent) reported attendance in more than five communities. Over three-fourths of the boys (77 per cent) had received some formal Catholic education, and 47.2 per cent had attended a total of three to five different schools. . . .

Most of the delinquents had at least three contacts with the police in terms of station arrests; 43.2 per cent had previously been processed by the Intake Department, and about one-third (32.2 per cent) had experience in a correctional institution.

Religious Control Factors

. . . For Catholic adolescents, regular attendance at Sunday Mass is probably most directly related to their religious behavior, especially in view of the strict rule of the church regarding it. Parents and other adults provide the models in this instance, and when control is exercised, one would expect it to be in the direction of conformity to the church's regulation. [See Table 1.]

TABLE 1
Parental and Personal Church Attendance as Reported by the Delinquents

Frequency of Church Attendance	Per Cent Attending		
	Mothers (N = 120)	Fathers (N = 101)	Delinquents (N = 150)
Never	10.7	25.3	12.2
Once or twice a year	14.6	17.4	8.0
Once or twice a month	26.7	28.0	52.7
Every Sunday	48.0	29.3	27.1

More crucial than attendance figures would be whether or not the values generated in the delinquent by his parents' regulations are more influential than their conduct. In this connection we find that among the delinquents who attended church every week 63 per cent have parents who were equally faithful to their obligations, while among the delinquents who seldom or never went to church only one-third had parents who set this example. Yet in both instances, the majority of parents (91.2 per cent and 82.5 per cent, respectively) told their children that they ought to attend church. Interestingly, over three-fourths of the boys themselves (77.2 per cent) felt they also should attend church every Sunday; 13.8 per cent were uncertain, and only nine per cent felt they should not attend.

Second only to church attendance as a basic indicator of Catholic worship and belief is the reception of Holy Communion. Over a third of the group (38.7 per cent) reported that they received Communion about every two or three months, with a slightly larger number (41.3 per cent) seldom, if ever, receiving. Generally, a lower frequency of Eucharistic reception was expected; as other studies have shown, the normal communion rate among practicing Catholics is usually less than their rate of church attendance.[9]

When asked how often they prayed, 40.1 per cent said they prayed often, and only four boys reported that they never prayed. The reason given for praying by most of the group (59.3 per cent) was the need they felt for help and guidance. The second reason, lagging far behind the first, was the desire for forgiveness (20.7 per cent). As would be expected, more boys prayed since they had gotten into trouble than before. Probing to test the intensity of the delinquent's experience of prayer, the question was asked whether they ever made up their own prayers, ever just "talked things over" with God. The largest number (48.3 per cent) said they did so every now and then, while about the same number of boys reported they often prayed spontaneously as the number saying they never prayed (24.5 per cent and 27.2 per cent). The fact that over half the group indicated they were not taught to pray at home supports the pattern beginning to emerge that these boys had parents who felt strongly that their children should go to church on Sundays, but this was practically all the religion they taught them.

.   .   .   .

To probe the delinquent's idea of God further we employed the Thurstone scale for measuring one's sense of the reality of God. According to the usages of the scale, a favorable attitude is indicated by a low numerical score. As Table 2 indicates, the majority of the present sample (69 per cent) showed positive attitudes toward God, 12 per cent were noncommital, while 19 per cent revealed

TABLE 2
The Delinquents' Attitude toward God

Attitude Score		(N = 150) (Per Cent)
0-2.9	(Strong religious attitude toward God)	32.0
3.0-3.9	(Definite recognition of God affecting conduct)	20.0
4.0-4.9	(Slightly affected by idea of God)	17.3
5.0-5.9	(Noncommital, neutral, or agnostic attitude)	12.0
6.0-6.9	(Disbelief but attitude not yet strongly set)	8.0
7.0-7.9	(Definite denial of God influencing conduct)	2.7
8.0-11.0	(Strong atheistic attitude)	8.0

9/Cf. Joseph H. Fichter, "The Marginal Catholic," *Social Forces,* 32 (1953), 167-73; Joseph B. Schuyler, *Northern Parish* (Chicago: Loyola University Press, 1960), 197-215, 230.

a negative attitude. The mean score of the group was 4.2, meaning that, as a whole, the group was "slightly affected by the idea of God," only one level above the noncommital.[10]

Religious Attitudes in Practice

Given the level of religious commitment described above, it is important to ask how the delinquents scored on other questions of belief and what their response was to attitude and behavior questions related to religious commitment. Four specific areas were investigated; sex, stealing, fighting, and peer-group relations.

None of the boys in the present study showed that they were ignorant of the church's position on sex; of the total number, 63.4 per cent agreed with the church's regulations, while over one-third (36.6 per cent) thought the church's position was too strict. A slightly different pattern emerges, however, when we compare the boys' attitude toward sex and their reported sexual practices. The most common practice is masturbation, with well over half the group (60.7 per cent) admitting frequent masturbation, even despite their apparently negative attitudes towards the practice (58.7 per cent strongly negative, 28.7 per cent mostly negative). Formal homosexuality and "gang sex parties" were more infrequent, with 83.5 per cent reporting they had never participated in them. Sexual intercourse was more widespread, with over half the group (54.2 per cent) saying they had performed the act at least twice, although habitual intercourse was low in comparison with masturbation.

Table 3 illustrates the lack of consistency between moral attitudes and sexual practices. . . .

The second item tested was the delinquent's attitude toward stealing. Only a small fraction of the group felt that stealing was all right, and the majority showed little hesitation in establishing the rightness or wrongness of the act. But

TABLE 3
Sexual Attitudes and Practices Reported by the Delinquents

Specific Sexual Practice	Those Who "Mostly" or "Completely" Disagreed with the Specific Practice (N = 150) (Per Cent)	The Reported Practice of Those Whose Attitudes Were Strongly Negative toward the Practice		
		Never (Per Cent)	A Few Times (Per Cent)	A Number of Times (Per Cent)
Homosexuality	93.1	90.3	6.0	4.0
Masturbation	92.0	16.3	24.6	59.1
Illicit intercourse	62.6	53.2	20.3	26.5

10/Cf. Albert K. Cohen, *Delinquent Boys* (New York: The Free Press, a Division of the Macmillan Co., 1955), 127-37; James F. Short, Jr. and Fred L. Strodtbeck, *Group Processes and Gang Delinquency* (Chicago: University of Chicago Press, 1965), 47-76.

when reporting actual stealing experiences, most of the group (68.7 per cent) indicated they had stolen items on several occasions, ranging in value from $5 to $50. This inconsistency becomes clearer when we select those who "mostly" or "totally" disapproved of stealing and compare these attitudes with their practice. . . .

The question of gang fighting presents a more complicated phenomenon in view of the differing patterns of legitimate and imagined defensive fighting and sheer aggressive warfare. . . . The reported attitude of the delinquents here followed the trend of the sex and stealing attitudes. Over three-fourths of the boys said it was certainly wrong to fight or to beat someone up if "you wanted to get something" or "just wanted to get even." Understandably, most of the group felt it was all right to fight to defend oneself or the group. . . .

The last item concerned the relationship between values operating within the delinquent's own peer group and his own value judgments. Interestingly, the boys felt that their group was generally indifferent to whether they attended church or not and would not make fun of them for participating in church activities. The same thing cannot be said for the group's invitation to delinquency. Here the boys' response shows a stronger commitment to the group and its expectations than to any moral or religious values. While almost three-fourths (72.3 per cent) stated that if the group wanted them to go along with something they knew was wrong or sinful they would always or usually refuse, still almost half the boys (48.4 per cent) usually or always had gone along when the group went stealing, fighting, or causing general disorder. Table 4 provides illustration of some specific patterns of attitude and behavior inconsistency. . . .

TABLE 4
Sample Items Regarding Attitudes of the Group versus Individual Response

Attitude Statement (N = 150)	Always (Per Cent)	Usually (Per Cent)	Seldom (Per Cent)	Never (Per Cent)
Have you ever stopped doing something/refused that you knew was wrong or was a sin? . . .	24.0	37.0	30.8	8.2
If the fellows wanted you to go along with them in doing something wrong, would you refuse?	24.3	47.0	23.0	4.7
Have you ever gone against your group because they wanted you to do something wrong or "sinful"?	10.7	33.3	38.7	17.3
If the fellows wanted you to go stealing with them, would you refuse?	9.4	17.0	63.6	11.0
If the fellows wanted you to go fighting with them, would you go along?	38.4	42.0	12.6	7.0

DISCUSSION

. . . .

Even if it is fair to assume that delinquency is the result of a breakdown or absence of social controls, it is simply false to say that these boys have no interest in religion. Over half the group attended church; frequently they attended more often than their parents, although parental example is still the most important element in frequent attendance. Most of the group felt they ought to go to church every Sunday.

The scores on the Thurstone scale show a slight, marginal commitment to religious belief and values. In this the delinquents share the same attitudes they report for their comrades, and, it would seem, show little difference from nondelinquents in their attitude toward God.[11] In terms of religious practice, there seems to be no conflict arising from a type of "dual allegiance" of the boy to his own group and the church. The data suggest, in other words, that religious commitment as expressed by this group has controlling influence only if supported by other factors more immediately crucial to the delinquent.

Nevertheless, with the exception of car-theft, the delinquents have no doubt about the morality of their actions, the sin factor involved, and the apparent betrayal of their religious values. On tests of religious and moral orthodoxy the group revealed a basic theoretical knowledge of the doctrines of their faith, except for their lack of awareness of God as a person who is interested in them individually.[12]

Regarding the inconsistency revealed in the data between the boys' reported religious values and related behavior, what is most striking is that this inconsistency did not appear as such to the delinquent. In many ways this lack of tension, or inner conflict, could be seen as a logical consequence of what Becker has termed "commitment by default."[13] . . .

. . . In addition to the delinquent's marginal commitment, the data show that the group associates with adolescents equally apathetic toward religion and is surrounded by generally noncensuring, related outsiders—parents who provide ineffectual conformity models and no priests, religious, or religiously-oriented adults with whom the delinquents have identified.

A final factor involved in this failure to transpose a commitment by default

11/Using a similar Thurstone scale, Middleton and Wright found in studying a delinquent and nondelinquent group that both samples showed a positive belief in God—two levels above a neutral attitude on the scale. Cf. Warren C. Middleton and Robert R. Wright, "A Comparison of a Group of Ninth and Tenth Grade Delinquents and Non-Delinquent Boys and Girls on Certain Attitude Scales," *Journal of Genetic Psychology,* 58 (March, 1941), 149.

12/These findings resemble those found in studying another group of delinquents regarding religious attitude and behavior change. Cf. Thomas M. Gannon, S.J., "Religious Attitude and Behavior Changes of Institutional Delinquents," *Sociological Analysis,* forthcoming.

13/Howard S. Becker, "Notes on the Concept of Commitment," *American Journal of Sociology,* 66 (July, 1960), 38.

into personal decision would seem to arise from the nature of religious control. Religion exerts its strongest influence by means of the religious experience—the personal, felt, relation of the individual with God. The data reveals no such personally experienced relationship. In a way this is to be expected from ambiguous parental influence, limited formal Catholic education, and negligence in regular religious practice. But what appears missing in the delinquent's attitudes is precisely what is lacking in his total religious orientation. . . . And, as the data show, the group's commitment by default was not entirely a matter of "not caring" what the demands of the church were.

The sermon outlines used in the churches during this time, the catechism approach to religion used in the primary grades when the delinquents were in them or later in religious instruction classes—all these stressed an intellectualistic grasp of creed and moral principles. It was almost as if the church were telling these youngsters that once the truth and inevitability of a doctrinal or ethical proposition were grasped, conformity would follow automatically. Any doubts about these dogmatic propositions were temptations against the faith; deviations from the code, sinful. Although the methods of pulpit and classroom have shifted in very recent years, the attitudes of the delinquents reflect, more accurately than was expected, this previous approach.

At the same time, it would seem that many of the delinquents interviewed tended to conform to the demands of the church insofar as these did not threaten their social role or their self-image. . . .

.   .   .   .

CONCLUSIONS

The principal difficulty in assessing the relation between religion and delinquency is similar to that encountered in evaluating any institutional factor. What we are really studying is the problem of human motivation in its relationship to social structure. The futility of mere correlation of statistics is indicated by the tendency to establish relationships between such items as church attendance or religious affiliation and the extent of delinquency.

But the effectiveness of religion depends upon the internalization of standards during the critical formative years of childhood and is developed through close identification with parents, family members, and other significant primary groups. Much of this control is exercised unconsciously and depends largely upon behavioral examples and religious experience rather than on precept. Only later does it reach the level of conscious decision and personal commitment.

If other supporting controlling agencies are missing, this simply means that the church has encountered a difficulty in coping with factors in modern life that tend to neutralize the fundamental tenets of religious teaching. It also means that the church will have to develop a new dimension to its teaching, particularly for the lower class youngster, and that it will have to assume wider community responsibility in communicating its message.

Our findings suggest that if religion is only one instrument of social control, as Martin and Fitzpatrick have pointed out, it is not a necessary one if other techniques can be used to prevent delinquency or to cure it.[14] This is not to say that religion is of little importance. But as long as it is perceived within the context of social control, the relationship of religion to delinquency will not be very different from any other source of motivation and control.

12. The "Short Con" Man*

JULIAN B. ROEBUCK and RONALD C. JOHNSON

The roles which men are encouraged to seek within society usually encompass culturally defined goals and relate to the social structure which delineates and regulates the acceptable procedures by which these goals and interests may be realized. Actual roles, therefore, depend upon cultural characteristics and the potential for realization of one's aspirations (see Kadish, Article 1; and Taft, Article 2). Because institutionalized norms and goals may vary independently of one another, the individual aspiring to a particular end may at times find himself in direct opposition to the structural regulations of the society. If goals and institutionalized norms are poorly integrated, the extraordinary stress placed upon goal completion may actually undermine existing social structures. Goal striving without an adequate recognition of the structural means by which to accomplish acceptable goals may indeed undermine the nature of social control (see Toby, Article 32; Violence in Chicago, Article 34; and Lohman, Article 35). The attempt to complete a college degree, for example, may lead some to cheat on a final exam. Should they do so, they are, in effect, seeking goal fulfillment while undermining the structural means by which such goals are usually achieved. If, on the other hand, excessive emphasis is placed upon conformity to norms, goal seeking may likewise be undermined and initiative be stifled.

Explaining the situation in contemporary America, Robert K. Merton maintains that the American society is anomic because it emphasizes success goals without an equivalent emphasis upon institutionalized conduct norms. The imperfect integration of the two, therefore, does not allow every member of society to possess equal access to culturally defined goals. Although opportunity

14/Martin and Fitzpatrick, 93.

*Reprinted from *Crime and Delinquency*, Volume 10, Number 3 (July, 1964), pp. 235 ff., with the permission of the author and editors.

structures (see introduction to Article 16) are differentially available to class and ethnic groups, the frustrations between aspirations and the structural potential to achieve culturally defined goals vary widely. Consequently, certain classes of individuals are encouraged to participate in deviant conduct by the differentially closed character of the structural system. The syndicate "soldier" who serves as a functionary in a bookie operation may in fact be responding to an achievement ethos without investing years of time and effort in educational programs which would allow him to enter an occupation at a similar income level. The black youth who riots may similarly be protesting against the structural system which limits his full development as a person.

In order to overcome the limitations and frustrations introduced by the disparity of culturally defined goals and structural opportunities for achieving these ends, individuals, Merton suggests, adapt to disjunctive situations through either conformity, innovation, ritualism, retreatism, or rebellion. If the person conforms, he may realign his aspirations to comply with existing achievement potentials. On the other hand, he may innovate and seek his aspirational goals by deviant or illegitimate means. While ritualism and retreatism may lead the possible deviant either to mask or to retreat from the limitations existing in society, rebellion may cause him to seek overt changes in the role- and status-limiting social structure.

The short con men, described in the following article by Julian B. Roebuck and Ronald C. Johnson, are a group of innovative black men interviewed as part of a larger sample of 400 offenders at the District of Columbia Reformatory in Lorton, Virginia. From the time that they were four to eight years of age, these men, Roebuck and Johnson found, used deceit as a major tool by which to overcome the structural limitations placed upon their aspirations.

Though they do not always agree on his etiology, sociologists and psychologists generally consider the confidence man to be a professional criminal who has high prestige in the underworld.[1] Confidence men are described in the literature as smooth, adroit, convincing talkers who live by their wits and their ability to manipulate people. Their criminal activity, a form of "grift," is nonviolent. Victims give their money or property to con men voluntarily because of the confidence they place in them and their own desire to get something for nothing. The con man, in short, plays upon the gullibility and the latent larceny of his victim, who is generally willing to engage in an illegal act for profit. . . .

1/H. A. Bloch and G. Geis, *Man, Crime, and Society* (New York: Random House, 1962), pp. 199-202; D. W. Maurer, *The Big Con: The Story of the Confidence Man and the Confidence Game* (Bobbs-Merrill, 1940), p. 201; E. M. Schur, "Sociological Analysis of Confidence Swindling," *Journal of Criminal Law, Criminology and Police Science,* September-October, 1948, pp. 296-304; R. L. Jenkins, *Breaking Patterns of Defeat—The Effective Readjustment of the Sick Personality* (Philadelphia: J. B. Lippincott, 1954), pp. 148-158.

The elaborateness of the build-up, the period of time spent in "setting up" the victim and "trimming" him, the number of confidence operators involved in the swindle, and the amount of money taken from the victim determine whether a given confidence game or trick falls into the category of "big con" (sometimes called "long con") or "short con."[2] The "big con" game includes numerous accomplices and props. Through prearranged stages, several operators (each one assuming a specific post) work at luring the victim into getting all the money he possesses or can command to put into a transaction they have devised. The proper build-up and subsequent "trimming" in the big-con game require weeks of planning and at least four contact positions. First in line is the "steerer" or "roper," an operator who selects the victim, introduces him to the scheme, and leads him to the second contact, the "build-up man." The latter gradually sounds out the victim regarding his resources, funds, and gullibility. The third contact stimulates his confidence. When the victim is ripe, the fourth contact relieves him of his money and "shakes him off." Together the contacts form an apparently casual chain of occurrences, but each gives some signal for an operator to appear and take his part in the conspiracy.[3] Often the victim of the big con is "cooled off" rather than "shaken off" in order to prevent him from making a complaint to the police. In the "shake off" the con man reminds the victim that if he reports the swindle he may also go to jail because of his own participation in an illegal act. He reminds him, in addition, that short of a jail sentence, the victim risks exposure, ridicule, and contempt from his friends and the police if he reports his loss. In the "cooling off" process, the con operator does not force the victim to realize he was just another "easy mark"; rather, he consoles him and attempts to redeem the ruse in a way that will make it easier for the victim to accept the inevitable and retain his self-respect. Cooling off represents a process of adjusting the victim to an impossible situation.[4]

Short-con games require fewer actors and props, less preparation, and less finesse and originality. They are geared toward smaller "scores" than the big-con games and the "take" is usually limited to the amount of money the mark has in his possession at the time. The method of operation is much quicker than in the big-con game; the operator must "hook the sucker and get rid of him fast." The short-con man usually works for brief periods in various cities, striking a location suddenly and then moving quickly in order to avoid contacts with his victim and the police.[5]

2/J. C. R. MacDonald, *Crime Is a Business: Buncos, Rackets, Confidence Schemes* (Stanford, Calif.: Stanford University Press, 1938), pp. 1-10.

3/For an overview of the *modus operandi* used in various con games see: W. Dienstein, *Techniques for Crime Investigation* (Springfield, Ill.: Charles C. Thomas, 1956), pp. 70-80; and C. E. O'Hara, *Fundamentals of Criminal Investigation* (Springfield, Ill.: Charles C. Thomas, 1956), pp. 290-294.

4/E. Goffman, "On Cooling the Mark Out: Some Aspects of Adaptation to Failure," *Psychiatry*, November 1952, pp. 451-463. Also on cooling off the mark, see M. J. Fitzgerald, *Handbook of Criminal Investigation* (New York: Greenberg Publishers, 1951), pp. 173-190.

5/MacDonald, *op. cit. supra* note 2, pp. 2-3.

According to Maurer's researches, most of the long-con operators have been recruited from the short-con men. They entered the confidence game when young and had the benefit of early training from skilled operators.[6] Confidence men may be placed along a continuum ranging from the unsuccessful, bungling, frequently arrested short-con man (flimflammer), whose modus operandi is dated and pitched at a low level, to the highly successful, accomplished big-con man who is infrequently arrested and whose modus operandi is original and pitched at a high level.

. . . .

This paper consists of a description of ten Negro short-con men who were part of a larger sample of 400 offenders interviewed and tested at the District of Columbia Reformatory (actually a penitentiary) at Lorton, Va.[7] The 400 male prisoners were divided into offender types according to arrest history.[8] It was hypothesized that specific patterns of criminality result from rather specific sets of social and psychological background factors and that the background factors common to a particular pattern of criminality would be found to vary significantly from those common to other offender types. This appears to be the case.[9]

. . . .

CHARACTERISTICS OF THE CON MEN

The ten con men shared a number of characteristics.[10] They were of average ability (mean I.Q. 100) as compared with the general population and were considerably superior to the mean score of the remainder of the offender group (mean I.Q. 85). They had a median grade level of 6.4 on the Stanford Achievement Test, as compared with the 5.2 grade level of the remainder of the sample. They were older men, aged 30 and over (mean age 38), as compared with the remainder of the sample (mean age 30.4). At least eight of the ten were reared in slums in metropolitan areas (population 500,000 and over) and came

6/Maurer, op. cit. supra note 1; pp. 175-178.

7/J. Roebuck, "A Tentative Criminal Typology of 400 Negro Felons," an unpublished study conducted in 1958 for the Institute for Criminological Research, District of Columbia Department of Corrections, Washington, D.C.

8/An analysis of the configuration of each offender's total known arrests by criminal charge made it possible to assign individual offenders to criminal-pattern categories.

9/See J. Roebuck and M. L. Cadwallader, "The Negro Armed Robber as a Criminal Type: The Construction and Application of a Typology," Pacific Sociological Review, Spring 1961, pp. 21-26; Roebuck and Johnson, "The Jack-of-All-Trades Offender," Crime and Delinquency, April 1962, pp. 172-181; Roebuck, "The Drug Addict as an Offender Type," The Journal of Criminal Law, Criminology and Police Science, March 1962, pp. 36-43.

10/In order to be included in the confidence game criminal category, the men had to have the following arrest record: four arrests throughout the arrest history had to be on confidence game charges; 33 per cent of all charges occurring in the last two-thirds of the arrest history had to be confidence game charges; at least one confidence game charge had to appear in the last third of the arrest history.

from homes that were demoralized, criminalistic, in continuous conflict, dominated by the mother, or on relief. Not one was reared in a rural area. Their criminal tutelage started early. All had delinquent companions before age ten, and eight belonged, in a loose sort of way, to delinquent gangs. All had police contacts, and eight had criminal companions before reaching eighteen years of age. The major difference between the delinquencies of this group and those of most of the offenders in the rest of the sample was the avoidance of violence. The con men had not been involved in fighting at home, at school, or with neighborhood peer groups. They did not destroy property and did not participate in mugging or purse snatching. None carried weapons. . . .

Probably the most significant factor in the development of these men was their early reliance, from four to eight years of age, on deceit as a major tool of life. As we shall soon see, their early childhood experiences approved and rewarded deceit and made the practice of deception necessary.[11] . . .

Coupled with this early practice of deceit was the dictum that violence doesn't pay. . . .

Three of the men were reared in homes where, when their passive fathers were absent, the mothers would entertain paramours for money. . . .

In three cases the mothers were small-time bootleggers who sold to clients in need of whiskey during hours when the liquor stores were closed. . . . In two of these three cases, the mothers also intermittently operated a poker game and the sons would serve drinks to the customers and help their mothers "cut the pot.". . .

In one of the cases the mother was a check passer and a shoplifter, and her son would accompany her in some of her illegal activities. . . .

In two cases a pattern of stealing, lying, and disobedience at home and at school was evident at age eight. . . .

In the remaining case the mother was known in the community as the "root woman." She removed warts and treated headaches, rheumatism, and other somatic ills with magic words and the use of herbs. With the help of her son she also made sacred candles that were supposed to insure health and happiness in the homes in which they were lighted.

Not one of these ten men closed on pimping, bootlegging, gambling, check passing, shoplifting, or fake healing as a criminal career. What they learned in childhood was not so much a set of criminal techniques but rather a principle—the principle of deceit and nonviolence.

COMPARISON WITH THE NUMBERS MAN

Though there were differences, the criminal offenses of the con men were most similar to the offenses of those involved in the numbers racket; both types

11/Jenkins, *op. cit. supra* note 1, cites grift as an example of motivation behavior of a highly adaptive sort. He theorized that early childhood experiences which make deceit necessary and reward it make for a "budding grifter."

of crime were nonviolent and required planning and organizational talent. [12] Despite other ostensible similarities—their high mental ability as compared with most other offenders under study and their distaste for violence—the numbers men and the con men were remarkably different in background and personality type. While the con men were upwardly mobile persons from slum environments who identified themselves with the underworld, the numbers men, despite their illegal activities, were products of, and identified with, the Negro middle class. . . . The numbers man was found to be a well-integrated personality, whereas the con man approximated the sociopath. [13] Thus, despite a certain similarity in the offenses of the con men and the numbers men, quite different factors entered into their development and the consequences (in terms of influence on the life styles of the offenders) of these two varieties of offense were equally disparate.

The con men were most similar in social background to the least specialized and least competent of all groups, the "Jack-of-all-trades offender," in that both were products of the slums and were reared in economically and emotionally deprived homes. [14]. . . . Throughout their lives they were talkers, not fighters, and neatness ranked high among their values. . . .

FINDING A "NICHE"

A well-dressed young man with a ready tongue, fair intelligence, and an aversion to foolish fighting might be expected to find a niche in society. These con men began seeking their niches early in life. By the age of eight, each of them had begun a long career of running away. When they ran, they ran far, hitching rides up and down the Eastern seaboard, covering all of the Northeast coast while still in their teens. While on these expeditions, each of the offenders found his mentor, an experienced con man looking for an apprentice. A teamwork approach is required in most games rigged to con a mark. One man sets up the mark and the other "knocks him off." Thus, the experienced con man is benefited by having a bright young apprentice who is not in the position to demand an equal division of the loot. The apprentice is benefited by learning a trade that requires no hard work, can be profitable, is reasonably safe, and is never short of customers. . . .

. . . [E]ach of the ten offenders entered an apprenticeship with an older con

12/See Roebuck, "The Negro Numbers Man as an Offender Type," *The Journal of Criminal Law, Criminology and Police Science*, in which a group of sixteen highly successful professional criminals is analyzed.

13/An inspection of the Minnesota Multiphasic Personality Inventory profiles for the group of numbers men revealed no more deviation than one would find among profiles constituting the norm group.

14/See Roebuck and Johnson, *op. cit. supra* note 9, in which seventy-one criminals with long arrest histories that revealed no pattern or concentration on a specific variety of crime were analyzed.

man, and after they learned their tutor's techniques, they moved out on their own....

These men were not marked successes at their vocation. Even so, their reference group consisted only of con men. They had broken home ties early, were wanderers who had developed no permanent relationship with women, and had few if any close friends. They were acquainted with many other con men since, as noted above, many con games require cooperative efforts. Their favorite term for anyone who acted impulsively or who employed violence in the pursuit of money was "fool." All con men respect one another as not being fools. To be "smart" is to have a "rep" as an ingenious con man who has made much money and suffered few busts (arrests). Much jockeying for position occurred within the group as each told anecdotes of previous victories aimed at "putting down" his rivals and showing himself off as "smart." The true criterion of success was money, and all else was forgiven the "money man."

.   .   .   .

THE CON GAMES

Here are some of the more common games used by these offenders in conning "marks":

High Dice

High Dice is a game based on the mark's desire to be recognized as an important person in his community, a man to whom others will look for advice and help. This bunko requires two operators.

A well-dressed and friendly stranger appears at a station prior to the arrival of an incoming train from the South. He selects as his victim a well-dressed Negro man or woman who appears to have resources. The operator enters into conversation with the victim by inquiring about hotels, names of persons, and the location of the Negro community.

While talking, both observe a Negro man (Operator 2) leaving the train in apparent bewilderment. He seems lost, and his dress and general demeanor classify him as a yokel. Operator 1 explains to the victim that he will talk to the stranger and see whether he can be of some help. He has a lengthy conversation with the yokel. He then walks back to the waiting victim and explains that the simple fellow is a farm laborer who has saved all of his last year's wages and has come to the big town to spend it on a good time. He wishes to meet an honest person who will give him lodging and take care of his money. He will pay well for this kind attention. The con man elaborates upon the evident simplicity of this yokel and how a smart person could obtain most of his money without great effort. He then suggests that the victim board this yokel at his home. Why should he not secure the yokel's money for himself? The victim agrees to meet the yokel and have a talk with him.

Operator 1 calls the yokel over to the victim, introduces them, explains that the victim has become interested in him and is willing to board him and show him the town. The yokel appears impressed by this kindness. He explains that he has $600, is frightened of the big city, and is afraid that city slickers will rob him of his hard-earned money. He shows his money to the victim, expressing a desire that the victim take care of it for him, and asks whether the victim knows how to handle big money. He desires some proof that the victim will be careful and not lose it. Has he (the victim) any money? If he has some money of his own, the yokel will gladly let him take care of his.

At this point, Operator 1 expresses amazement that anyone would carry so much money on his person. He turns to the victim and asks whether he would carry so much money on his person and also inquires where he keeps his money. Although the yokel has a fear of banks, he is willing to bank his money if the victim will withdraw his own and place it with his. Then the victim can place both lots in any safe place that he wishes. If the victim can take his money out of the bank, then the yokel is sure that his money will be safe.

. . . .

Now Operator 1 suggests that the victim humor the yokel and not let all of that good money stray away from him. The yokel is too dumb to make a "kick" to the law and, after all, the victim will have continuous possession of his own money in addition to the yokel's roll. The victim weakens at this point and goes to the bank, accompanied by Operator 1, in order to prove to the yokel how easy it is to withdraw money. The yokel awaits their return. The victim, having been coached by Operator 1, shows his withdrawn money to the yokel. Although the yokel is surprised at the ease with which the victim can withdraw his money from the bank, he still is concerned about the way his money and the victim's ought to be wrapped for safety. He tries to describe the method used by his "boss man" and holds up his hands as if measuring small distances. Suddenly Operator 1 understands and says: "It's one of those large brown envelopes!" He leaves to obtain one. During his absence the yokel holds his money in his hands, giving the victim a "big eyeful" (generally a dummy roll). Operator 1 returns with a large brown envelope which the yokel recognizes as the kind used by his boss man. Operator 1 takes the yokel's money and places both rolls in the large brown envelope. As the yokel (Operator 2) engages the victim in animated conversation, Operator 1 deftly makes a switch, placing the envelope with the two rolls of money in his breast pocket and handing the victim a similar envelope containing folded paper. The yokel now expresses himself as fully satisfied. He wishes to know where the victim lives, is given the name and address, and promises to come to the victim's house within an hour or two. Each operator walks away in a different direction. The victim hurries away, his mind filled with the desire to open the package and look at his money.

The operators meet at a prearranged spot to divide the victim's money.

Pigeon Drop

Pigeon Drop is an ancient game whose exact origin is unknown. Reportedly introduced into this country by Chinese immigrants early in the nineteenth century, it was later adopted by whites and still later by Negroes predominantly. Endless varieties of this swindle prevail; but in all its modifications, certain basics must go into it, not the least of which is the "vic's" (victim's) own greed. Two players are active in this game (also known as "The Slip" and "The Drag"); sometimes—in a cruder form barely distinguishable from a polite robbery known simply as "stuff"—it is played by only one man.

The game consists of a story in three parts. The first part is enacted by the "catch man," who approaches the vic with a plausible but dramatic tale designed to win sympathy and show trust. The second part is executed by the "hit partner," who moves into the conversation on signal to report some "found money," usually described as a bookie's receipts. Through several ruses which may employ a "switch" (sleight-of-hand transference of the vic's money) or a direction to a fictional "boss," the money which the victim is asked to "show" as evidence of "good faith" or "financial responsibility" comes into the possession of the players. In the "blowoff," the third part of this bold drama, the vic is given some final instructions which allow the players to leave his presence before he discovers he has been mulcted.

Spanish Prisoner Game

Many variations of the *Spanish Prisoner Game* have evolved in the past thirty years. The props common to each consist of a worthless but impressive negotiable paper for a large sum of money, a purported smuggled letter from a dejected prisoner (customarily a Latin American), and a picture of the prisoner's "charming" daughter. For whatever arbitrary reason the operator may choose, the prisoner's letter promises the marked Galahad his daughter's hand and a sizable portion of his estate (or some secret treasure, or whatever else the mark has been prepared to find enticing), if a certain sum of money is given to a certain courier to effect his daughter's escape from "this villainous country." One may easily imagine the infinite variety of themes that may be used in this stock drama to fit the times and the breed of persons being tricked. The "Spanish Prisoner" is now occasionally the "American Prisoner," a wealthy businessman in jail for income tax evasion. But all the features of the game—the beautiful young daughter and hidden funds that require some bribery or "grease" before they can be brought into use (with the victim providing the grease)—remain substantially the same.

Three Card Monte

Three Card Monte, which requires two operators (one to rope in the mark and one to manipulate the cards) is, theoretically, a game of chance, requiring the use of three ordinary playing cards, two of a black suit and one of a red suit. The "sucker" is inveigled into believing how easy it would be to capitalize on the fantastic odds (purely illusory) and witlessness (equally imaginary) of the operator, who promises to double the bet if the sucker can put his finger on the "red card," which the operator deftly proceeds to manipulate in various positions face down.

The Greasy Pig

The Greasy Pig is worked in much the same fashion as Three Card Monte, except that three nut shells are used and a pea-shaped object becomes the elusive goal in the game to claim the stakes. The pea is shifted from one cover to another by a few quick movements of the hands and resides as often as not under the operator's fingernails instead of under the shell. No matter how devilishly simple these proposals may seem to the guileless person, once he gives in to the temptation to lay hold of this easy money, the fever to beat the confounding game is unrelenting. Never does it seem to occur to the mark's own larcenous bent of mind that a man's game rarely, if ever, gives away any odds other than to himself.

The ten con men also practiced, in addition to these games, the "Badger Game" (in which a prostitute lures a mark to her room and a con man, posing as a jealous husband, breaks in on them in the midst of their activities and is ultimately paid off by the mark) and the "Murphy Game" (in which the con man poses as a pimp, is paid by a mark to procure a prostitute, and then runs off with the money). "A long con man" would not usually resort to these low-level techniques.

LACK OF INGENUITY

Occasionally a con man would show ingenuity. One, for example, was proud of having sold two lions and an elephant to a remarkably gullible circus owner in Chicago via telephone, receiving a cashier's check for the not yet delivered, nonexistent animals. Most of the games, however, were old (the Spanish Prisoner Game can be traced back to the defeat of the Armada) and crude. Although the con man prides himself on being smart, these short cons were markedly lacking in creativity. They were not "money men"; their careers were full of short scores and many "busts." In manipulating their victims, they depended on sudden attack and speed and on quick exits from the city of their operations. They seldom used careful planning or long-con techniques such as "cooling off" the mark. Their failure as successful criminals may perhaps be explained by this obvious lack of finesse. . . . [T]hey showed little insight into the cause of their failures, but rather naïvely attributed failure to fate or, as they often put it, "Kismet.". . .

They lived in cheap furnished rooms, waiting to make a score. . . .

.   .   .   .

The arrest histories of these men were lengthy (mean arrests per man—18, and at least four workhouse sentences and two felonies in every arrest history) and the charges ranged from petty theft up to grand larceny. In most cases, however, once a confidence game charge is noted, the other types of charges rarely appear afterward. This lends some credence to their own belief (shared by the police): "Once a con man always a con man."[15] Charges for violent crimes against the person were practically nonexistent.

The district attorney's reports showed that these men operated at a rather low criminal level. Usually the marks were "set up" for a loss of not more than $250. Whether operating alone or in pairs, these con men did not have tight organization, leadership, timing, or careful planning. At times they were conned out of the take by their own confederates and various women companions. They, too, were marks. Yet, despite the fact that their stories and the institutional records showed this to be the case, they were reluctant to admit being conned by others. . . .

The idea that "all you got to do is know what to say with your mouth" did not disappear as a result of getting "busted." Once inside the penitentiary the cons shifted operations and became "jail house lawyers," attempting to gain release through appeals. Nine of the ten mentioned technicalities in the law which they believed should have precluded their arrest. Eight of the ten were writing writs for fellow inmates for which they were "paid off" in cigarettes, although none of the writs composed during previous periods of incarceration had proven effective. Their attempts at "conning" were even less effective inside than outside the penitentiary.

As a group these men seemed in the interviews to be older than their chronological age. They had many different kinds of physical complaints and did not appear to be strong.[16] All of them reacted to the interviewer in an apparently friendly and cooperative manner. They spoke softly in a breezy, chatty way, and their verbal expression seemed to be better than their educational levels indicated. They were prone to "projection" in that they attempted to express their opinions as if they were the opinions of the interviewer. They expressed few warm ties of affection with others and seemed to be shrewd, calculating, and interested in others only for what they could get out of them. . . .

A qualitative assessment of the personality characteristics of these Negro con men indicates a sociopathic trend.[17] They divided humanity into two groups, con men and marks. They definitely committed themselves to the ranks of the con men, felt superior to the marks, and rationalized their socially disapproved

15/Fitzgerald, *op. cit. supra* note 4, p. 187, notes that the confidence man follows his trade despite the number of times he is arrested and he rarely engages in other types of crimes.

16/The medical records showed that two were organically sound, three were partially crippled in the legs, one had a stiff left arm, one suffered from myopia, one was a diabetic, and two had heart murmurs.

17/The above personality assessment was in part validated by inspection of the MMPI scale 4 scores (Pd.), which showed that all of these con men had T scores above 75.

behavior by insisting that all people have larceny in their hearts and "you have to take others before they take you." Their interpersonal relationships were defective in that they expressed few if any emotional ties and evinced little interest in other people, except in terms of exploitation. When they did make a "score," they exhibited an inability to forgo immediate pleasures for future gains and long-range goals. Hedonistic, they lived in the present without consideration of the past or future. They demonstrated a lack of insight into the causes of their behavior, were unable to profit from their mistakes, and attributed failure to fate.

While certainly not among the most expert of con men, they had developed a rather high degree of proficiency as compared with most of the offenders in the remainder of the sample (390 cases).[18] Their reference group was that of con men, and they judged themselves (and others) according to the degree to which behavior was consonant with the values of con men. Since status depended on success, and they were in jail and thus seemingly unsuccessful, they blamed fate for their incarceration and continued to operate as con men in prison—in this case, attempting to con their way out to freedom. With this set of values, the con men's likelihood of making any marked change in their behavior patterns is questionable, but because of the small size of the sample and the type of data utilized, the findings are tentative and replications with larger samples are necessary.

13. The Victim-Offender Relationship*

LEROY G. SCHULTZ

The role of the criminal victim has received increased attention in the past 10 years in the work of Stephen Schafer and LeRoy G. Schultz. Other empirical studies additionally reveal that not only are the highest rates of victimization found among the lower income groups but the risks of victimization from forcible rape, robbery, and burglary are concentrated in the lowest income groups and tend to decrease steadily at the higher income levels. While the 1967 President's Crime Commission Report revealed that nonwhites are disproportionately victimized, they also documented the finding that serious offenses

18/The modus operandi of the sixteen numbers men, organized professional criminals, was pitched at a much higher level than that of these ten con men.

*Reprinted from *Crime and Delinquency,* Volume 14, Number 2 (April, 1968), pp. 135-41, with the permission of the author and editors.

against men are nearly three times as great as those against women. An earlier study by the District of Columbia Crime Commission, too, indicated that nearly two thirds of the 151 rape victims surveyed were attacked by persons who were at least casual acquaintances. Nearly 20 percent of the examined aggravated assaults involved a victim and an offender who had faced each other previously in troubled situations. A study of the Chicago Police Department similarly disclosed that the Chicago Negro male is a victim nearly six times as often as is the white male, a Negro woman nearly eight times as often as is a white female. Of all serious crimes involving violence, whites were victimized most often by Negroes in the crime of robbery.

The interactional roles of the victim and the offender are probably most clearly evident in homicide. John Gillin found in his study of murder and murderers at the Wisconsin state prison at Waupan that the act of murder could be categorized into several broad types, including those committed (1) as an outcome of a quarrel, marital discord dispute, or argument, (2) while drinking or gambling, (3) at the climax of a long-standing quarrel, and (4) in connection with another crime (i.e., robbery, sex offense, or resisting arrest). Although the greater number of murders fell into the first two categories, most were acts of passion.

What is the relationship of the three-time loser to the murder of a pursuing policeman? How is the conduct of the threatened businessman related to the harm inflicted against his person by an armed robber? Social worker LeRoy G. Schultz recognizes that the victim may intentionally or unintentionally stimulate his own victimization. Since consent may vary by degree and a major degree of consent negates or reduces the severity of the offense, the victim-offender relationship, Schultz concludes, must receive greater attention in the presentence investigation if justice is to be served (*see* Wolfgang, Article 7). In addition, the role of the offender, he argues, cannot be presumed without understanding the personality of the victim.

The presentence investigation has become the keystone of the sentencing structure. Courts are beginning to demand professionally prepared, well-rounded reports before sentencing.[1] Some permit the defendant or his counsel to read and challenge the validity of the presentence investigation report and to cite errors and omissions.[2]

.   .   .   .

"Victimology"—the study of the degree and type of participation of the victim in the genesis or development of the offense, and an evaluation of what is

[1]/For the development of this pattern, *see* Rubin, "Developments in Correctional Law," 8-12 *Crime and Delinquency* 80-90 (1960), 64-74 (1961), 65-73 (1962), 189-98 (1963), 172-85 (1964), 192-99 (1965).

[2]/Higgins, "Confidentiality of Presentence Reports," 28 *Albany L. Rev.* 12-45 (1964).

just and proper for the victim's welfare—is a relevant consideration in many professional presentence investigation reports. Just as we stress individualizing the offender and his sentence, so we should also individualize the offense and the victim. A good presentence investigation report will direct the attention of the sentencing judge to factors of aggravation and mitigation where relevant.

Since the victim-offender relationship is significant and a prime factor affecting sentencing,[3] the judge and the probation officer must be thoroughly acquainted with it. The American Law Institute's Model Penal Code states that a prime consideration for granting probation is that "the victim of the defendant's criminal conduct induced or facilitated its commission."[4] In general, consent of the victim nullifies an offense against that person. There are varying degrees of consent. In many cases, the victim-offender relationship will determine the question of guilt and the type and degree of penalty. . . .

VICTIM'S ROLE

Although the study of "victimology" is rarely stressed in this country, . . . every experienced probation officer is familiar with offenses in which the victim invited, initiated, and worked diligently toward the success of the offense. Typical instances are criminal abortion, where the female hunts for and pays the abortionist;[5] prostitution, where the male seeks out the prostitute to contract for illegal sexual behavior;[6] and various "con games," where the victim's larcenous impulse is exploited by the criminal.[7] At the same time, we are all experienced with cases in which the victim was totally innocent of any involvement in victimogenesis.[8] We are not concerned here with the latter.

Many types of crimes have two partners: the offender and the victim. . . . A careful investigation of many offenses reveals a psychological interaction between offender and victim that makes one indistinguishable from the other.[9] The concepts of aggressor and victim are not always absolutely opposite; the aggressor is not always guilty, and the victim is not always innocent. The terms "victim" and "aggressor" are sometimes interchangeable; the victim and the offender (referred to in Europe as the "penal couple") are not always antagonistic to each other. The personality of the victim as a cause of the offense is sometimes more significant than that of the offender.

3/HMSO, *Royal Comm. on Capital Punishment, Report 1949-1953* 45-53; *Model Penal Code* sec. 7.01 (Proposed Official Draft, 1962); Hentig, *The Criminal and His Victim* 384 (1948).

4/*Model Penal Code, supra* note 3.

5/Bates & Zawadski, *Criminal Abortion* (1964).

6/Winick, "Prostitutes' Clients' Perception of the Prostitutes and of Themselves," 8 *Int'l J. Soc. Psych.* 289-97 (1962).

7/Maurer, *The Big Con* (1949); R. Glaser, "The Confidence Game," *Fed. Prob.,* Dec. 1963, pp. 47-54.

8/Schultz, *How Many More Victims?* (1966).

9/Ellenberger, "Psychological Relationships between the Criminal and His Victim," 2 *Arch. Crim. Psycho.* 257-90 (1955).

A victim can contribute to the offense and facilitate its execution in the following ways: (1) By provoking or initiating a hostile reaction in the offender; e.g., during a heated argument one party hands the other a gun and, knowing full well the other's hostile mood, accuses him of not having "the guts to shoot." (2) By direct invitation or incitation; e.g., a female engages in heavy petting and mutual sexual preludes and, at the last moment, begins to resist the man's advances that are, by that time, uncontrollable. (3) By omission of normal preventive measures; e.g., the auto-theft victim parks his unlocked car with the engine running while he does some shopping. (4) By unconsciously inviting the offense through his emotional pathology; e.g., a wife has masochistic needs that are gratified by her assaultive husband.

[Hans] Von Hentig has described four psychological types of victims: (1) victims who desire the injury; (2) victims whose injury may be the price of a greater gain; (3) victims who bring about the detrimental result partly by their own concurrent effort; (4) victims who provoke or instigate the offense. He further divided victim attitudes as (1) apathetic or lethargic, (2) submitting or conniving, (3) cooperative or contributory, and (4) provocative, instigative, or soliciting. To view each offense as Cain v. Abel is oversimplification.[10]

The victimology factors that should be included in the presentence investigation may be gathered from a close review of the police report of the offense, the prosecution file, the notes of the grand jury, and a series of interviews with the offender and his victim. In crimes of violence and sex offenses, the *victim's* police record should be checked and his reputation should be determined as a matter of routine. Knowledge of victimology may become a new element in understanding criminal dynamics.

Each of two types of victims reveals a common background and pattern. These two groups consist of certain victims of sex offenses and victims of certain types of assault and homicide.

SEX-VICTIM TYPOLOGY

In sex-offense studies, victims have been described as "collaborative" in 8 per cent of 330 offenses,[11] as "non-objecting" in 40 per cent of 1,994 offenses,[12] as "participating" in 60 per cent of 73 offenses,[13] and as "seductive" in 21 per cent of 185 offenses.[14] The conclusion is that, of all types of crime, the sex offense requires the closest investigation and evaluation of the actual offender-victim relationship if the true dynamics of each offense are to be fully comprehended. These studies further indicate that victims may trigger the offense, be

10/Hentig, *supra* note 3. For the European contribution to victimology, *see* 1-3 *Int'l. Biblio. on Crime & Delin.* (1963-1965).

11/Gagnon, "Female Child Victims of Sex-Offenses," 13 *Soc. Prob.* 176-92 (1965).

12/Radzinowicz, *Sexual Offenses* 83-109 (1957).

13/Weiss et al., "A Study of Girl Sex Victims," 29 *Psych. Q.* 1-29 (1955).

14/*Final Report* (Research Project for the Study and Treatment of Persons Convicted of Crimes Involving Sexual Aberrations) 296 (Glueck ed. 1956).

unnecessarily cooperative, invite the offense, simulate resistence, or act as the aggressor. . . .

In sex offenses, what oftentimes appears, on the surface, to be a convincing story is often pure fabrication.[15]. . . A woman's sexual need can lead to the unconscious desire for the aggressive act, the coercion serving to avoid guilt feelings which may arise against willing participation. The presumption that all young women lack the capacity to comprehend the nature and implication of the sexual act is a legal fiction, another example of institutional lag.[16] Evidence that the victim understood the significance of the sexual act[17] should be allowed—if not at the trial or arraignment, then certainly in the presentence report. Many victims are nothing more than aiders and abettors, if not offenders themselves, and should be examined psychiatrically along with the offender.[18]

Most sex offenders are acquainted with their victims prior to the crime, and the overt act is not directed against a sexual object selected by chance alone. The victim must be regarded as a clue to the behavior of the offender. . . .

Two studies of sex-offenders' young victims[19] hold that they have the following personality traits in common: they are very attractive, charming, appealing, submissive, and seductive; they attempt to win adults over by being masochistic; they make adult contacts easily; they want pity and demand proof of affection. They use the sex act to defy their parents (who encourage them to be "sexy" and allow them to watch sexual intercourse at home), to generate a feeling of independence, and to satisfy their urge for approval and attention. . . .

ASSAULT-HOMICIDAL VICTIM TYPOLOGY

Assault and homicide are treated together since the dynamics are similar. In some instances, the difference between the offenses depends on how quickly the victims receive medical attention.

The concept of victim provocation as a mitigating factor has been long accepted in the legal history of homicide,[20] and the importance of the role played by the victim's personality and conduct is established in crimes of violence more than in any other type of crime. . . .

The motive to assault or kill not only is indicative of the offender but, in many cases, points to a distinct relationship with his victim, understood only by

15/Machtinger, "Psychiatric Testimony for the Impeachment of Witnesses in Sex Cases," 39 *J. Crim. L., C. & P.S.* 750-54 (1949).

16/Ehrmann, *Premarital Dating Behavior* (1960); Sherwin, "Sex Expression and the Law of Rape," 4 *Inter. J. Sex* 206-10 (1951).

17/Note, "Forcible and Statutory Rape: An Exploraton of the Operation and Objective of the Consent Standard," 62 *Yale L. J.* 55-84 (1952).

18/Orenstein, "The Sex Offender," *NPPA Yearbook* 201 (1950). Switzerland has such a law.

19/Bender & Blau, "Reaction of Children to Sexual Relations with Adults," 7 *Am. J. Ortho.* 500-18 (1937); Bender, "Offended and Offender Children" in *Sexual Behavior and the Law* 687-703 (Slovenko ed. 1965); Weiss *supra* note 13.

20/HMSO, *supra* note 3.

the play of motive-forming and inhibition-removing interactions. Some take sadistic delight in finding out the limits of the offender's "cool" by teasing, baiting, tormenting, or overchallenging his manhood self-concept. . . .

The provocative and precipitating factors may be overt or covert, psychological or physical, and over a long or a short period of time. In some homicides, the victim's behavior is so provocative that it must be assumed he is using the killer as an instrument of suicide.[21] Wolfgang found that many victims had the characteristics of offenders, that 54 per cent of the victims had arrests for crimes of violence, and that, in many of the relationships, chance determines which of the pair will be the victim and which the offender.[22]

The victims of many assaults and homicides have what may be called an aggressive-tyrannical personality and engage in acts with the offender which invite or excite assaultive response.[23] The victim is usually emotionally involved with the offender—a spouse, parent, or lover.[24] The assaulters and killers can be described as submissive and passive, desiring to avoid conflict whenever possible, particularly if playing the masochistic role results in gaining them affection.[25]. . .

INTERVIEWING THE VICTIM

In many offenses, the victim must be interviewed. The emphasis by police and the prosecutor is primarily on the *if* and *when* of the alleged offense, but the probation officer will also be concerned with the *how* and *why*. . . . This allows the probation officer to assess the type and degree of victim-offender relationship and its bearing on the offense. Typically the victim feels that, once the state completes the prosecution, he is forgotten. This attitude could be corrected by an interview with a sympathetic court official, who would encourage him to express his hurt and outrage and who could refer him to a wide range of social, medical, or psychiatric agencies, depending on his needs.[26]

. . . .

CORRECTIONAL RESTITUTION

England, New Zealand, and California have established victim-compensation

21/Wolfgang, "Suicide by Means of Victim-Precipitated Homicide," 20 *Q.R. Psych. & Neur.* 335-49 (1959); Gold, "Invitation to Homicide," 10 *J. For. Sci.* 415-21 (1965).

22/Wolfgang, *Patterns of Criminal Homicide* ch. 3 (1958).

23/Mendelsohn, "Origin of the Doctrine of Victimology," 3 *Excerpta Crim.* 239-42 (1963).

24/Schultz, "The Spouse Assaulter," 6 *J. Soc. Ther.* 103-11 (1960); Cormier, "Psycho-Dynamics of Homicide Committed in a Marital Relationship," 8 *J. Soc. Ther.* 111-18 (1962); Sargent, "Children Who Kill—A Family Conspiracy?" 7 *Soc. Work* 35-43 (1962); Snell et al., "The Wife Beater's Wife," 11 *Arch. Gen. Psych.* 107-12 (1964).

25/Megargee, "Undercontrolled and Overcontrolled Personality Types in Extreme Antisocial Aggression" (unpublished Ph.D. dissertation, U. Calif. 1965); MacDonald, "The Threat to Kill," 120 *Am. J. Psych.* 125-30 (1963).

26/Halleck, "Emotional Effects of Victimization," in Slovenko, *op. cit. supra* note 19, 673-86.

programs.[27] A recent White Paper in England suggested that society has concentrated so much on the rehabilitation of the offender that it has lost sight of the equally important concern for the victim's welfare.[28] The tendency is to see the offender's personality primarily in terms of society's needs rather than those of the victim, and the reformative potential of the requirement of restitution has been given only secondary emphasis.[29] Restitution is generally ordered as a condition of probation only if it does not hinder the offender's rehabilitation and never in an amount greater than the victim's loss.[30] It should not be so high as to jeopardize the security of the offender's family, who may be devoid of any direct responsibility for the offense.

Many probation officers feel that extracting large amounts of restitution unduly strains the traditional relationship, even with its authority overtones, and interferes with treatment; others feel that the probation office should not be a collection agency; while still others have strong negative feelings about revoking probation for nonpayment of restitution, a practice that finds the probationer sentenced to a "debtor's prison."

After assessment of the victim's loss and the offender's ability to pay, a payment plan, subject to fluctuating economic circumstances in the future, can be worked out in agreement with the victim.

CONCLUSION

Two aspects of victimology are important for the probation officer. The first is an understanding of the specific role the victim plays in the offense; the second, an understanding of the factors affecting the victim's welfare after sentencing. Where a degree of consent to the offense was present, or the victim "induced or facilitated its commission," the use of probation is indicated.[31] The presentence investigation report should be so conclusive in dealing with factors of victimology that it can serve as the determining document in state victim-compensation eligibility.[32]

27/Schultz, "The Violated: A Proposal to Compensate Victims of Violent Crime," 10 *St. Louis U.L.J.* 238-50 (1965).

28/HMSO C.P., 645 *Penal Practice in a Changing Society* 7 (1959).

29/Schafer, "Restitution to Victims of Crime—An Old Correctional Aim Modernized," 50 *Minn. L. Rev.* 243-55 (1965).

30/Rubin, *The Law of Criminal Correction* 198-202 (1963).

31/*Model Penal Code* art. 7, sec. 7.01; Hughes, "Two Views of Consent in Criminal Law," 26 *Mod. L.R.,* 233-48 (1963).

32/The New Zealand Victim Compensation Commission requires receipt of a presentence investigation report in each case of victim application. Act. 134. 1963.

14. Social Roles in a Correctional Community*

PETER G. GARABEDIAN

Although Robert K. Merton finds the potential delinquent adapting to the lack of integration between culturally defined goals and social structures which provide the means for reaching these goals, through conformity, innovation, ritualism, retreatism, or rebellion (*see* introduction to Article 12), David Matza views deviant behavior as a product of neutralization and drift. Because individuals operate on a continuum between freedom and restraint, the roles which a delinquent accepts are products of the individual's fluctuating responses to these polar alternatives. Flirting at one time with freedom and at another with restraint, the delinquent may subsequently postpone commitment and avoid making a decision, thereby drifting between criminal and conventional action. Much delinquency, Matza contends, is a product of this drift, which, however, does not necessarily lead one into an adult criminal career. Because a delinquency subculture includes both conventional and delinquent cultural elements, it is delicately balanced between conventional and criminal expectations. Through neutralization, which may negate a sense of responsibility and justice or an injury done to others, drift occurs. As the restraints of convention and law are removed, infractions not only are made possible but also become permissible. Drift, therefore, may be directed, Matza contends, to a particular end when the person becomes motivated to commit crime. Consequently, the *Drift Hypothesis* holds that neutralization facilitates drift which may be activated or directed to a delinquent goal through the activation of the will.

In many respects the process of neutralization and drift is not limited to the delinquent subculture, although Matza does not extend its operation further. The challenge to follow the normative system, defined by conventional society and represented in the prison community by penal administrators, or to respond to the norms of the inmate subculture represents two polar conditions (*see* Berk, Article 29) which cause neutralization and drift within the prison setting. While the prison-entering inmate is directed toward four major role alternatives, his actual response in the correctional community may fluctuate periodically

*Reprinted with special permission from the *Journal of Criminal Law, Criminology and Police Science,* Copyright © 1964 by the Northwestern University School of Law, Volume 55, No. 3.

between the conventional-correctional and inmate-subcultural normative systems. Although David Matza has not extended his Drift Hypothesis to the prison community, many of its processes found in the delinquent subculture also operate in the prison setting. Each inmate role, Peter G. Garabedian writes in the following article, represents a potentially alternative inmate response to issues or concerns that are centrally important to the prisoner group. While institutional restraints encourage inmate conformity, some inmates drift between the normative demands of the institutional and the inmate social systems.

The traditional conception of our maximum custody prisons assumes the existence of two normative systems that are in point for point opposition to each other. The first system represents standards of behavior that are defined and sanctioned by conventional society and by prison administrations as representatives of that society. Legitimate norms are embodied in the formal rules and regulations of the institution and represent standards of appropriate behavior which the inmate is to use in his relationships with prison officials and with other prisoners. Ideally, no inmate is exempt from employing these formal standards. In theory, the prison's administration demands that all inmates conform to these norms. . . .

The second normative system is part of the inmate subculture and is also assumed to prescribe appropriate behavior for the inmate. Behavior prescribed by this system, however, is assumed to be contrary and opposed to behavior prescribed by the formal authority system. These illegitimate behavior prescriptions are embodied in the prisoners' code which emphasizes loyalty to the inmate community.[1] Unlike the norms of the prison's administration, however, illegitimate prescriptions do not demand uniformity of behavior. . . .

The present study directs its attention to an investigation of four major role alternatives that are available to inmates as they enter maximum custody prisons. Specifically, the purpose of this paper is to construct an empirical typology of inmate role types that have been identified by a number of investigators and to examine variations among the types with respect to (a) criminal careers, (b) institutional behavior, and (c) normative orientations.

SOCIAL ROLES IN PRISON

Inmate roles are differentiated and integrated around such focal issues as "doing time" in prison, loyalty attachments, food, sex, health, etc. The inmate learns the importance of these issues early in his institutional career while being

---

1/Earlier accounts of the prisoners' code are described in Clemmer, *The Prison Community* esp. 152 (1958); Ohlin, *Sociology and the Field of Corrections* 28-29 (1956). A more recent discussion may be found in Sykes & Messinger, "The Inmate Social System," in *Theoretical Studies in Social Organization of the Prison* 5 (Cloward, Grosser, McCleery, Ohlin, Sykes & Messinger eds. 1960).

exposed to processes of mortification.[2] His mode of adaptation, both actions and verbalizations, with respect to focal issues is observed and assessed informally by other inmates, and through a process of mutual agreement they assign the inmate to a given role. Consider for example the issue of "doing time" in prison. There are two major alternatives available to prisoners with respect to this issue. The first involves inmates who are constantly aware of their sentences and, in the language of the prisoners, they do "tough time." Inmates occupying the second alternative absorb themselves into the affairs of the prison community and are characterized as doing "easy time."[3]

Another focal concern in prison is sex. The prison is a uni-sexual community, and as such as devoid of many of the affectional relations commonly derived from heterosexual contacts. . . . Although behavior with respect to this issue varies widely among prisoners, there are a variety of alternatives that are generally recognized by staff and inmates. Some inmates occupy a role alternative consisting of behavior characteristic of the female role in the free community. According to the inmate argot, these role incumbents are *fairies* or *queens,* since they employ female gestures and mannerisms to seduce other inmates. Techniques of seduction employed by this role type, however, are generally of a non-violent kind. On the other hand, inmates recognize another role alternative with respect to the issue of sex. Recognized as a *wolf* or *jocker,* this role type also seeks to seduce other inmates, but techniques of seduction are likely to be of a violent type, using force or the threat of force to exploit weaker inmates. *Wolves* are likely to be active homosexuals, while *fairies* are of the passive type. A third major behavior alternative recognized is the *punk.* The term *punk* generally refers to the inmate who allows himself to be seduced by either of the above two types, and thus may be active or passive. Finally, many inmates refrain completely from homosexual behavior, or engage in this practice only periodically. These inmates for the most part are called *normals.*[4]

.   .   .   .

The set of role alternatives that concerns us in this paper is organized around the issues of "doing time" in prison, loyalty attachments, relations with inmates, and contacts with staff members. From the language of prisoners, it is possible to relate five major role types to these focal concerns. . . .

The first role in the set is defined in terms of doing "tough time" while incarcerated in the institution. Affective attachments are oriented toward legitimate norms and standards, and thus loyalties are anchored in conventional groups in the free community and with the prison's administration. Relations with staff members, therefore, are generally good, involving a high degree of contact, but contacts with other inmates are generally limited to those with

2/Goffman, "Characteristics of Total Institutions," in *Walter Reed Army Institute of Research, Symposium on Preventive and Social Psychiatry* 43 (1957).
3/Schrag, "Social Role, Social Position, and Prison Social Structure," 1959 *Proceedings of the American Correctional Association* 178.
4/Schrag, "Social Types in a Prison Community," 48-49 (unpublished Master's Thesis, University of Washington, 1944).

similar affective attachments. Thus there is a lack of intensive involvement in informal inmate activities, and as a result the occupant of this role remains naïve about much of the prison culture. Inmates at the prison studied refer to this alternative as *Square John* behavior.

In contrast to the *Square John* role, a second major behavior alternative is defined in terms of doing "easy time" while in the institution. Affective attachments are oriented toward illegitimate norms, and thus loyalties are anchored with criminal persons and groups. This alternative involves strict conformity to the principles of the prisoner's code. Relations with other inmates are generally good, involving a high degree of contact with them, while contacts with staff members are minimized and avoided if possible. Deep involvement in prison rackets and other informal inmate activities also characterize this role. Although a variety of labels are used to identify the incumbent of this role, the most frequent label used in the prison studied is *Right Guy*.

The third alternative in the set is also characterized by doing "easy time" in the institution. But unlike either of the first two alternatives, this role involves affective neutrality with respect to conventional or illegitimate behavior prescriptions. Contacts with staff and inmates are extensive, but members of both these groups are manipulated for the promotion of personal goals. Manipulation involves a high degree of role-taking skill, with normative perspectives rapidly shifting to accommodate the exigencies of the situation. Frequent contacts with staff members and involvement in informal inmate activities result in a storehouse of knowledge regarding prisoner and official affairs. A familiar label used to identify the behavior alternative is *Con Politician*.

The fourth role in the set involves doing "tough time" in the institution primarily because of prolonged difficulties of adjustment to the authoritarian climate characteristic of prison life. Similar to the role of the *Con Politician,* this alternative involves rejection of the two major normative systems, and the manipulation of staff and inmates. But unlike the *Politician* role, manipulation in this case takes the form of direct physical aggression or the threat of force, and as a result, the incumbent of this role isolates himself from both staff and inmate contacts. The alternative therefore involves self-oriented behavior, expressive violence, and deficient role-taking skills. Notwithstanding isolation, inmates adopting this mode of adjustment become deeply involved in prison rackets, make frequent attempts at escape, and rise to positions of temporary leadership during times of general strikes and prison riots. Inmates at the prison studied employed the label of *Outlaw* to identify this role alternative.

. . . .

There is an increasing amount of informal observational evidence that these behavior alternatives exist in many of our maximum security prisons.[5] Although

5/In addition to Schrag's works cited above, see the following works by Sykes: "Men, Merchants, and Toughs," 4 *Social Problems* 130 (1956); *The Society of Captives* 85-108 (1955); and Sykes & Messinger, "The Inmate Social System," in Cloward, *et al., op. cit.*

different labels may be used by inmates in various institutions throughout the United States, their behavioral referents nevertheless remain fairly stable. The prison argot, then, reflects the organization of the inmate social system. It defines the interrelationships between the various inmate roles. . . . The prisoner society, then, is conceptualized in terms of spontaneously emerging networks of social relationships structured around important institutional problems.

METHODOLOGY

The data to be reported were collected from a maximum security prison in a Western state. At the time of the study there were approximately 1,700 convicted adult felons housed in the institution. From this population, a random sample of 345 inmates was selected to be included in the study. Inmates in the sample were asked to complete an anonymous questionnaire. The questionnaire was also administered to a sample of 141 members of the custodial staff.

The method of identifying incumbents of the four roles described above consisted of obtaining responses of the inmates in the sample to a set of 12 items included in the questionnaire. The items, which dealt with attitudes toward self, others, and philosophy of life, are listed below:

1. You've got to have confidence in yourself if you're going to be successful.
2. I generally feel guilty whenever I do wrong.
3. "Might is right" and "every man for himself" are the main rules of living, regardless of what people say.
4. The biggest criminals are protected by society and rarely get to prison.
5. There's a little larceny in everybody, if you're really honest about it.
6. The only criminals I really know are the ones here in the institution.
7. You have to take care of yourself because nobody else is going to take care of you.
8. Inmates can trust me to be honest and loyal in my dealings with them.
9. Who you know is more important than what you know, and brains are more important than brawn.
10. Most people try to be law abiding and true.
11. It makes me sore to have people tell me what to do.
12. Police, judges, prosecutors, and politicians are just as crooked as most of the people they send to prison.

Each of the above types is assumed to reflect a component of the attitudinal organization of a given role type. . . .

Inmates responded to the items by checking one of four response categories for each statement: strongly agree, agree, disagree, and strongly disagree. Weights of plus two, plus one, minus one, and minus two were assigned, respectively, to

---

supra note 1, at 5. See also Korn & McCorkle, *Criminology and Penology,* ch. 22 (1959); and Kinch, "Self Conceptions of Types of Delinquents," 32 *Sociological Inquiry* 228 (1962).

each of the above response categories. The weights for the four sets of three items were then algebraically summed for each inmate. Thus, a given inmate was represented by a set of four scores, with each score having a possible range of plus six to minus six and indicating his status on the five role types mentioned above.

Ideally, the occupant of a given role should endorse (strongly agree or agree) the three items designed to tap his attitudes, and should not endorse the remaining nine items. That is, an inmate who has been assigned a given role in the prisoner society should exhibit a high positive score with respect to the items characterizing the role type and should exhibit low positive or negative scores on items characterizing the other role types. The highest positive score shown by an inmate on any one set of items determined his classification.[6] On this basis, an empirical typology was constructed classifying 227, or 66 per cent, of the inmate sample as incumbents of one of the four roles. The 227 inmates comprise the sample on which the data to be presented in this paper are based.

ROLE TYPES AND CRIMINAL CAREERS

In this section three aspects of criminal career are selected for investigation. First, the extent of juvenile delinquency in the offender's background; second, the degree of participation in adult crime in the background of the individual; and third, the offense for which the inmate is currently committed. Delinquency is defined in terms of being arrested for the first time before the age of 18 plus prior experience in a juvenile training school. Adult crime is defined in terms of having three or more prior arrests and prior experience in an adult correctional institution.

Square Johns

Compared with the other role types, Square Johns show the least amount of juvenile delinquency and participation in adult crime in their backgrounds. It is also seen that these incumbents are committed, more frequently than the other role types, for the crime of homicide and to a lesser extent for forgery and non-violent sex offenses. These findings support the notion that Square Johns have not had an extensive delinquent and criminal career, but may become involved in a serious personal offense, probably due to a set of extenuating circumstances. Moreover, Square Johns may become involved in writing "rubber checks" usually against their own bank accounts, and often while drinking. Investigators have called this type the "naive check forger" in that highly developed and specialized techniques of professional forgery are not used. Naive

---

6/Inmates whose highest score on any of the four sets of items was three or less were not considered in the classification.

check writers conceive of themselves not as criminals, but as individuals laboring under a burden of personal problems for which checkwriting seemed to be an appropriate solution.[7]

.   .   .   .

Right Guys

Compared with Square Johns, inmates occupying the antisocial role in the prisoner society have had early contact with delinquent traditions and continued participation in adult crime. Tables 1 and 2 show that Right Guys are

TABLE 1
Juvenile Delinquency among Role Types

Role Type	Per Cent Delinquent	N*
Square John	17	36
Politician	21	77
Right Guy	24	73
Outlaw	35	38

*In this and most of the following tables, N refers to the number of cases on which the percentage is based. For example, 21 per cent of the 77 politicians are classified as having been delinquents.

TABLE 2
Involvement in Adult Crime among Role Types

Role Type	Per Cent Involved in Adult Crime	N
Square John	16	37
Right Guy	30	72
Politician	41	78
Outlaw	51	37

considerably more likely than Square Johns to have been delinquent, with subsequent participation in adult crime. The Right Guy type most frequently comes from an economically underprivileged family residing in the disorganized sections of large cities making possible early contact and association with delinquent traditions and peers.[8] Table 3 shows that compared with the other

7/Gibbons & Garrity, "Some Suggestions for the Development of Etiological and Treatment Theory in Criminology," 38 *Social Forces* 51 (1959).
    8/*Id.* at 56.

TABLE 3
Offenses among Role Types

Role Types	Assault, Robbery		Burglary, Auto Theft		Forgery		Homicide		Non-Violent Sex		Total	
	%	N	%	N	%	N	%	N	%	N	%	N
Square John	9	3	29	10	31	11	20	7	11	4	100	35
Politician	15	10	41	27	30	20	8	5	6	4	100	66
Right Guy	30	21	41	28	13	9	9	6	7	5	100	69
Outlaw	24	8	50	17	14	5	6	2	6	2	100	34

role types, Right Guys are committed more frequently for the traditional property offenses, such as robbery, burglary, and auto theft, in addition to assault. The data suggest that the Right Guy may be a nonprofessional property offender who attempts to make a career out of crime, albeit an unsuccessful one.[9]

Con Politicians

Contrasted with Right Guys, Con Politicians show slightly less evidence of juvenile delinquency in their background, but more evidence of involvement in adult crime. In addition, they are more likely than Right Guys and Outlaws to be committed for forgery and grand larceny by check. That these crimes are easily detected and frequently lead to arrest and prosecution may be a partial explanation of the Politicians' position in Table 2. Lemert's study of the systematic forger tends to corroborate the latter point, in that he found his sample of forgers were very likely to be detected, and further were highly recidivistic.[10]

A significant feature differentiating Politicians from Right Guys and Outlaws may be seen by considering the role of the victim in the commission of offenses. Right Guys and Outlaws are likely to commit offenses involving little or no manipulation of the victim. When the victim is manipulated, as in the case of robbery, it tends to be direct, unsophisticated, and involves the threat of force. Con Politicians, however, tend to commit offenses involving a high degree of role-playing skill, where the victim is manipulated by words.

Outlaws

From the data shown in Tables 1 and 2, Outlaws appear to have had the most prolonged career in delinquency and crime. Notwithstanding the fact that

9/*Ibid.*
10/Lemert, "The Systematic Check Forger," 6 *Social Problems* 141 (1958).

Outlaws, like Right Guys, also tend to be committed for the traditional property crimes, they are nevertheless much more likely to be detected for these offenses. This may provide some indication of the relative degree of skill used by each type in the commission of these crimes. Outlaws are likely to commit crimes on impulse with little or no thought given to planning prior to their commission.

ROLE TYPES AND INSTITUTIONAL BEHAVIOR

Investigators have observed the institutional behavior of inmates to vary widely. Clemmer, for example, found that some inmates were involved in primary relationships with other inmates, while others were relatively isolated from any close friendship ties.[11] Again, some inmates were more prone to break institutional rules than others.[12] Because he lacked a systematic conceptual framework of the inmate role system within which to interpret his findings, Clemmer was forced to conclude that the prisoner community was an atomistic society which lacked consensus and solidarity.[13]

We feel that much of the seemingly divergent inmate behavior can be accounted for in terms of the theoretical framework presented above such that the conduct, contact, and communication of inmates are importantly related to the role occupied within the inmate social system. Thus although inmate behavior may vary widely, we should generally expect uniform behavior among incumbents occupying the same role within the informal social structure. Social role, then, regulates behavior within the institution.

Participation in Formal Institutional Programs

If this general proposition is valid, then we should expect participation in formal staff-sponsored programs to be distributed differentially among the role types in two important respects. First, the rate or extensiveness of formal participation should be related to role type. Some inmates will take an active interest in the programs offered by the prison's administration and take advantage of as many of these activities as possible. Other inmates, however, will not be motivated to participate. Second, role type should be related to participation in the *types* of programs offered by the staff. For example, some of the activities included in the total program of many prisons are aimed directly at changing or modifying attitudes and values. These activities are *therapeutic* in their orientation. Other programs are aimed at improving the moral character of the inmate and are *religious* in their orientation. Still others do not have any specific underlying rationale, but exist primarily to expend the inmate's excess energy, or help the inmate pass his time. These activities are *neutral* in their

11/Clemmer, *op. cit. supra* note 1, ch. 5.
12/*Id.* at 122.
13/*Id.* at 322.

orientation. Thus, the two aspects of formal participation are defined in terms of extensiveness and type of program involvement.

The data presented in Table 4 show the percentage of the four role types who actively participate in at least one staff-sponsored program. These data show fairly clearly that Square Johns are the most active, followed by Politicians, Right Guys and Outlaws in that order. Since the Square John alternative represents "pro-social" behavior, it is reasonable to assume that this incumbent will be relatively isolated from many of the informal inmate activities and thus will direct more of his energies toward formal staff-sponsored activities which are open to all inmates regardless of informal social status.

Table 5 presents evidence regarding type of program involvement. Although the numbers are small, the trends are nevertheless evident and supportive of the

TABLE 4
Extensiveness of Participation in Staff-Sponsored Programs among Role Types

Role Type	Per Cent in at Least One Program	N
Square John	84	37
Politician	71	79
Right Guy	63	73
Outlaw	62	38

TABLE 5
Type of Program Involvement among Role Types*

Role Type	Therapeutic		Religious		Neutral		Total	
	%	N	%	N	%	N	%	N
Square John	55	6	27	3	18	2	100	11
Politician	29	8	7	2	64	18	100	28
Right Guy	23	4	23	4	54	9	100	17
Outlaw	33	4	17	2	50	6	100	12

*The small size N in this table reflects the mode of analysis. Thus of the Square Johns, six participated in *only* therapeutic programs, three in *only* religious activities, etc.

general hypothesis. Square Johns are much more likely than other role types to participate in programs geared specifically at therapy, while Politicians, Right Guys, and Outlaws in that order are more likely to participate in neutral programs. These data suggest that those inmates who are least likely to be affectively attached to illegitimate norms are most likely to become involved in instrumental therapy programs. Thus it may be that many of the therapy programs that exist in correctional institutions have the function of supporting and *reinforcing* conventional affective orientations rather than being vehicles of change.[14]

Institutional Adjustment

An index commonly used by prison classification committees and parole boards to evaluate an inmate's adjustment in prison is the number of rule or conduct infractions incurred by the inmate. Inmates were asked to note the number of times they had been referred to the adjustment committee for rule infractions and violations. Table 6 shows that rule infraction is systematically related to role type. . . .

TABLE 6
Serious Conduct Infractions among Role Types

Role Type	Per Cent with Three or More Infractions	N
Square John	00	37
Politician	14	79
Right Guy	16	73
Outlaw	22	27

Reported Social Contacts

Studies by Clemmer, Wheeler, and others have shown the importance of informal social contacts and involvement to the attitudes and values of inmates. . . . In our investigations, we had the opportunity to examine the relationship between role type and social contact. Although we do not have at the present time direct measures on the actual number and types of contacts an inmate has, we do have evidence on the *reported* frequency and types of contacts inmates claim they have. The sample of inmates was asked to report whether they had more or less contacts with staff members and inmates as compared with the average inmate. The data are reported in Table 7.

The findings appear to be consistent with the evidence presented in the previous tables and suggest that the amount and kind of contacts an inmate reports are in fact associated with the role he occupies in the informal social system. . . . Apparently, involvement with prison officials generally implies involvement with inmates as well.

14/Prison therapy programs may also be vehicles of change, especially when they are devised and regulated within the inmate community.

TABLE 7
Reported Social Contacts among Role Types

Role Type	Hi Staff-Hi Inmate		Hi Staff-Lo Inmate		Lo Staff-Hi Inmate		Lo Staff-Lo Inmate		Total	
	%	N	%	N	%	N	%	N	%	N
Square John ..	38	14	3	1	13	5	46	17	100	37
Politician	27	21	3	2	24	18	46	37	100	78
Right Guy ...	16	12	8	6	35	25	41	30	100	73
Outlaw	13	5	3	1	29	11	55	21	100	38

Communication

Investigators have also noted the existence of a "grapevine" in our prisons, which refers to the rapidity with which a bit of information circulates through the inmate population.[15] However, the pervasiveness and effectiveness of the grapevine as a means of informing inmates of events and conditions within the institution has not been submitted to empirical test. It is very likely that all

TABLE 8
Knowledge of Therapy Group among Role Types

Role Type	Per Cent with Knowledge of Therapy Group	N
Square John	68	37
Politician	52	79
Right Guy	44	73
Outlaw	37	38

inmates in a given prison do not possess an equal amount of information, nor are the kinds of information possessed likely to be distributed in an equitable or random fashion. Moreover, possession of information and knowledge enables inmates to understand and interpret events in the institution. A lack of information may lead many inmates to employ the "rat" concept as a basis for interpreting events or changes that take place in an institution.[16] Since the data suggest that social contacts are associated with role types, we should also expect that some degree of communication would take place during these contacts and

15/Clemmer, *op. cit. supra* note 1, at 97. See also McCleery, "Communication Patterns as Bases of Systems of Authority," in Cloward, *et al., op. cit. supra* note 1, at 49.
16/McCleery, "The Strange Journey," 1953 *University of North Carolina Extension Bulletin.*

thus varying degrees of cognitive knowledge should be possessed by the incumbents.

Just prior to the time of our study, several inmates obtained official sanction to initiate a therapy group. In an effort to determine whether cognitive knowledge varied with role incumbency, the sample of inmates was asked whether they had heard of a therapy group recently organized in the institution. The results presented in Table 8 show that knowledge of the therapy group varies systematically with role type. . . .

ROLE TYPES AND AFFECTIVE ATTACHMENTS

The data presented in the previous sections suggest that there are fairly uniform and distinct variations in the criminal careers and in the institutional behavior of the various role types. This section directs its attention to the final problem of normative orientations.

In order to examine this relationship, the 141 staff members, along with the sample of inmates, were asked to evaluate a series of five contrived situations referring to life in prison. . . . Staff responses to this and the other four items were overwhelmingly in agreement. That is, there was a high degree of consensus among staff with respect to the action taken in the five hypothetical situations. On the other hand, little consensus was observed to exist among inmate responses to the five items. . . .

The data shown in Table 9 are clear. The per cent of conformists to staff norms decreases systematically with role type. Square Johns rank highest,

TABLE 9
Conformity to Staff Norms among Role Types

Role Type	Per Cent Conforming to Staff Norms	N
Square John	46	37
Politician	37	79
Right Guy	23	73
Outlaw	16	38

followed by Politicians, Right Guys, and Outlaws respectively. The fact that Square Johns evaluate problematic situations in terms of legitimate standards suggests that these types identify with noncriminal persons and groups. The opposite is true of Right Guys. Were it possible to construct an index of conformity to deviant or illegitimate norms, we should expect to find a larger per cent of Right Guys among the high conformists as compared with Square

Johns.[17] Similarly, while Politicians rank second only to Square Johns on the conformity index, they should also rank high in conformity to illegitimate norms. Finally, Outlaws should rank low on both indices.

CONCLUSIONS

Once an inmate occupies a given role, much of his behavior in the institution is predictable. By virtue of his location in the social structure, the inmate will have access to a variety of social and cultural resources that will make it possible for him to employ certain means for goal attainment. Square Johns, for example, have access to a variety of social resources making it possible for these types to employ legitimate alternatives for goal achievement. By the same token, however, they generally do not have access to resources making possible the use of illegitimate means. In short, the role is a mechanism regulating conduct, contact, and communication within the inmate social system.

... Systematic linkages were found to exist between the criminal careers, institutional behavior, and normative orientations of inmates identified as Square Johns, Right Guys, Politicians, or Outlaws. The evidence suggests that the typology may be a fruitful and parsimonious method enabling researchers to approximate the complex network of social relationships actually maintained by inmates.

17/For a logical presentation of the cognitive and affective orientations of the role types, see Schrag, "Some Foundations for a Theory of Correction," in *The Prison: Studies in Institutional Organization and Change* 309 (Cressey ed. 1961).

part FOUR

Stratification, Minorities, and Criminal Conduct

Although existing crime data clearly suggest that *known* delinquents and criminals are disproportionately drawn from the lower classes, the data are misleading. White-collar (*see* Quinney, Article 8) and organized (*see* Hawkins, Article 9) crime are generally neglected in crime-reporting procedures. Handled procedurally, if at all, by administrative boards, these crimes less frequently result in criminal adjudication. However, this does not mean that they do not exist. Rather, it suggests that society has chosen to ignore or minimize their consequences. Nevertheless, recent delinquency studies indicate that middle- and upper-class violations tend to be great in number and often more serious acts than the presumed delinquency of the lower classes. The overemphasis upon individual crimes, for example, has allowed the false advertiser to act with impunity. However, the growing recognition that crime can no longer be merely defined as abnormal behavior but must be viewed more explicitly as illegal conduct in which a large part of the population participates at some period in its life has challenged some of the stated "facts" concerning crime.

Although pioneer criminologists attempted to relate crime to lower socioeconomic status caused by poverty or depression, later researchers failed to validate their presuppositions. Neither current American nor European research, for example, discloses a direct relationship between general and/or nonviolent crimes and economic depressions. While some studies suggest that robbery or other property crimes increase with the growth of unemployment, most research reveals that the greater crime increases occur not in depression but in prosperity. Crime, criminologists find, is more likely to be reflected in dissatisfaction due to blocked ambitions and aspirations rather than to economic hardship (*see* introduction to Fannin and Clinard, Article 16; and Strecher, Article 17). Status goals, therefore, may actually possess a greater importance than many would normally assume (*see* Empey and Erickson, Article 15). Economic depressions affect not only one's income but potentially one's social roles and achieved community status.

The economic and status problem is most acute among minority members who have not shared proportionately in the general socioeconomic advance. Disproportionately restricted to lower income occupations, faced with limited educational potentials, unreinforced by family or community stability, and confronted by police-minority group tensions, minority members evidence higher delinquency and criminality rates than members of similar age groups within the population. However, differentiated minority group data reveal that Japanese-American and Chinese-American crime patterns remain rather insignificant. Negro and Puerto Rican delinquency and crime rates, on the other hand, exceed the normal levels found in most suburban and rural communities. Since policemen are disproportionately assigned to enforcement in minority communities, they readily believe, especially if prejudiced themselves, that the majority of minority members are potential criminal threats (*see* Strecher, Article 17; Reiss, Article 21; and Lohman, Article 35).

Nevertheless, the common belief that crime is a product of evil people has been challenged by the discovery that crime participants come from all classes, occupations, locations, and educational groups. LaMar T. Empey and Maynard L. Erickson, in the first article of Part Four, find that status differentials play a large role in the type of offense committed. Leon F. Fannin and Marshall B. Clinard examine the impact of one's concept of self upon his conduct, and Victor G. Strecher points out the importance of the subculture in continuing minority group-police conflict. Finally, Vernon Fox and Joann Volakakis take a closer look at the offenses and problems of the Negro offender in industrial Michigan.

A. Stratification and Criminality

15. Hidden Delinquency and Social Status*

LAMAR T. EMPEY and MAYNARD L. ERICKSON

The few existing studies of delinquency and social class imply that middle-class delinquent conduct may actually be more serious than lower-class delinquent behavior (*see* Taft, Article 2; Luger, Article 5; and Gannon, Article 6). One study of suburban secondary school students identified a subgroup of

*Reprinted from *Social Forces*, Volume 44, Number 4 (June, 1966), pp. 546-54, with the permission of the authors and the publisher, The University of North Carolina Press.

aggressive middle- and upper-class delinquents whose patterns of police contact were generally comparable to those of delinquents in lower-class neighborhoods. Seventy-seven percent of the suburban delinquent group, Fred J. Shanley found, had two or more, 43 percent four or more, and 16 percent seven or more police contacts. Of the police contacts among a sample of Negro delinquents in the Los Angeles metropolitan area, 72 percent had had two or more contacts with the police, 41 percent had four or more contacts, and 22 percent had seven or more police contacts. A consequent comparison of juvenile court petitions of the aggressive middle- and upper-class delinquent with the Negro delinquent group similarly disclosed that 56 percent of the middle-class group had one or more petitions filed, 27 percent had two or more, and 9 percent four or more. Among the Negro delinquent group, corresponding percentages were 60 percent, 38 percent and 10 percent. As a result of his research Shanley concluded that the distributions for the two groups offer striking evidence of the seriousness of a police record for this particular group of middle-class adolescents.

A second study of law violation patterns by Herbert H. Herskovitz, Murray Levene, and George Spivack further stipulated that the offenses most frequently committed by institutionalized middle- and upper-class delinquents are auto theft, other thefts, vandalism, sexual offenses, breaking and entering, and physical assault (see Fannin and Clinard, Article 16). Consequently, with rare exceptions, the authors concluded, few differences exist among lower- and middle- or upper-class delinquents in the nature of the crimes committed. With the exception of burglary and auto theft, delinquency, they believed, seems to be delinquency, "irrespective of slums or suburbs, material advantages or underprivilege, gangs or no" (see Gannon, Article 6).

In the following study, LaMar T. Empey and Maynard L. Erickson discovered that middle-status boys, in contrast with lower- and upper-status boys, commit the most serious offenses, including such crimes as forgery, breaking and entering, destroying property, and arson. Low-status respondents, on the other hand, are more inclined to smoke regularly, skip school, fight, and use narcotics. Although the respondents reported a large number of undetected violations, the number of violations varied insignificantly from one status level to another. Upper-status respondents, however, appeared to be slightly less often delinquent.

Available data regarding the relationship of social status to delinquency are limited and contradictory. On one hand, almost all official statistics report the incidence of delinquency to be concentrated most heavily among lower-status juveniles.[1] The evidence has been sufficiently persuasive as to lead to a large

1/For examples see: Ernest W. Burgess, "The Economic Factor in Juvenile Delinquency," *Journal of Criminal Law, Criminology and Police Science*, 43 (May-June 1952), pp. 29-42; Cletus Dirksen, *Economic Factors in Delinquency* (Milwaukee: Bruce Publishing Co., 1948); Joseph W. Eaton and Kenneth Polk, *Measuring Delinquency: A Study of Probation Department Referrals* (Pittsburgh: University of Pittsburgh Press, 1961), p. 4; and Albert K. Cohen's analysis of several studies in *Delinquent Boys: The Culture of the Gang* (Glencoe, Illinois: The Free Press, 1955), pp. 37-44.

body of theory designed to explain it: Merton,[2] Cohen,[3] Cloward and Ohlin,[4] Miller,[5] and others.

Yet, there have always been those who argue that the supporting evidence is nothing more than a statistical artifact. Warner and Lunt,[6] Porterfield,[7] Barron[8] and Kvaraceus[9] have all concluded that the reason some juveniles are officially charged while others are not is a function of social status. But is their conclusion based on fact or what Cohen calls "egalitarian proclivities and sentimental humanitarianism?"[10]

The answer is not easy to find. On one hand, the empirical findings of Nye, Short and Olsen support Porterfield's pioneer studies which suggested that there is no direct association between delinquency and social status.[11] On the other hand, Gold reported a statistically reliable relationship between white, low-status boys and delinquency.[12] Meanwhile, a recent conference involving investigators who had been concerned with studying hidden delinquency ended up in some disagreement over the matter,[13] some contending there were differences among status levels, others questioning it.

The same kinds of disagreement exist with respect to the *kinds* of delinquent acts which young people from different status levels commit. Ohlin maintains, for example, that middle-status delinquency is "petty" in comparison with low-status delinquency. The latter is more deeply ingrained and possesses a much greater potential for the development of a criminal career.[14] Myerhoff and

---

2/Robert K. Merton, *Social Theory and Social Structure* (Glencoe, Illinois: The Free Press, 1957), chapts. 4-5.

3/Cohen, *op. cit.*

4/Richard A. Cloward and Lloyd E. Ohlin, *Delinquency and Opportunity: A Theory of Delinquent Gangs* (Glencoe, Illinois: The Free Press, 1960).

5/Walter B. Miller, "Lower Class Culture as a Generating Milieu of Gang Delinquency," *The Journal of Social Issues,* 14 (1958), pp. 5-19.

6/Lloyd Warner and Paul S. Lunt, *The Social Life of a Modern Community* (New Haven: Yale University Press, 1941), p. 427.

7/"Delinquency and Its Outcome in Court and College," *American Journal of Sociology,* 49 (1943), pp. 199-204; "The Complainant in the Juvenile Court," *Sociology and Social Research,* 28 (January-February 1944), pp. 171-181; and *Youth in Trouble* (Ft. Worth, Texas: The Leo Potishman Foundation, 1946).

8/Milton A. Barron, *The Juvenile in Delinquent Society* (New York: Alfred A. Knopf, 1956), p. 32.

9/William C. Kvaraceus, *What Research Says to the Teacher: Juvenile Delinquency* (Washington, D.C.: National Education Association, August, 1958), pp. 331-332.

10/Cohen, *op. cit.,* p. 42.

11/F. Ivan Nye, James Short, and V. J. Olsen, "Socio-Economic Status and Delinquent Behavior," *American Journal of Sociology,* 63 (January 1958), pp. 318-389.

12/Martin Gold, "Socio-Economic Distributions of Juvenile Delinquency," University of Michigan, Institute for Social Research paper presented at the annual meeting of the American Psychological Association, Los Angeles, September, 1964.

13/Robert H. Hardt and George E. Bodine, *Development of Self-Report Instruments in Delinquency Research,* A Conference Report (Syracuse, New York: Syracuse University, Youth Development Center, 1965), pp. 12-13.

14/Lloyd E. Ohlin, *The Development of Opportunities for Youth* (Syracuse, New York: Syracuse University, Youth Development Center, 1960), pp. 8-9.

Myerhoff agree. In their observations of deviant, middle-class youth, they conclude that the violations of these groups were more often capricious and manipulative than violent.[15]

Karacki and Toby, on the other hand, found fighting gangs that did not come from economically deprived homes. These gangs placed emphasis upon many of the characteristics traditionally associated with lower-class delinquent groups: physical aggression, loyalty to delinquent peers and a search for immediate gratification.[16] Shanley located a similar group of middle- and upper-class boys in the suburbs of Los Angeles. This small minority had patterns of police contact which were every bit as extensive and serious as samples of adjudicated delinquents from lower-class neighborhoods.[17] Herskovitz *et al.,* found likewise. They noted that, among incarcerated offenders, there were comparatively few differences in the nature of offenses committed by middle- and upper- as contrasted to low-status juveniles.[18]

THIS STUDY

This study is concerned with a rather comprehensive analysis of the subject. It utilizes *self-reported* data on delinquency as a means for examining both the *amounts* and *kinds* of delinquent acts which juveniles from different status levels have committed.

The sample was drawn in Utah and included only white males, ages 15-17 years. Negro and Mexican boys were excluded for two reasons: (1) because they constitute a very small minority in Utah; and (2) because their exclusion permitted ethnic status to be eliminated as a contributing influence. The overall sample was made up of four subsamples:

1. *Fifty randomly selected high school boys who had never been to court;*

2. *Thirty randomly selected boys who had been to court once* (responses for this group have been inflated as though N = 50 in order to make them equal with other subsamples);[19]

3. *Fifty randomly selected offenders who were on probation* (these respondents were all repeaters and all had been assigned to the Provo

15/Howard L. Myerhoff and Barbara G. Myerhoff, "Field Observations of Middle-Class Groups," *Social Forces,* 42 (March 1964), pp. 328-336.

16/Larry Karacki and Jackson Toby, "The Uncommitted Adolescent: Candidates for Gang Socialization," *Sociological Inquiry,* 32 (Spring 1962), pp. 203-215.

17/Fred J. Shanley, "Middle-class Delinquency as a Social Problem," paper presented at the annual meeting of the Pacific Sociological Association, Salt Lake City, April, 1965, p. 2.

18/Herbert H. Herskovitz, Murray Leven, and George Spivak, "Anti-Social Behavior of Adolescents from Higher Socio-Economic Groups," *Journal of Nervous and Mental Diseases,* 125 (November 1959), pp. 1-9.

19/It is impossible to assess any increase in error which might have resulted from this inflation. If there is bias in the sample of 30, it will have been magnified. If not, the change in sample size is not especially significant since both (N = 30 and N = 50) are very small proportions of the total population of one-time offenders.

Experiment in Delinquency Rehabilitation, a special community treatment program.[20] If the program had not existed, 32 percent of these offenders would have been incarcerated, and 68 percent on regular probation); and

4. *Fifty randomly selected, incarcerated offenders.*

Subsamples 1, 2, and 3 were drawn from a county population of 110,000 people. Subsample 4 was drawn from a statewide population of incarcerated offenders.

Data Collection

All respondents were contacted in person by the authors. Data were gathered by means of a detailed interview which was conducted as follows:[21] (1) each of 22 different offenses was defined in detail; (2) the respondent was asked if he had ever committed the offense; (3) how many times he had done so; (4) if he had ever been caught, arrested, or brought to court for the offense; and (5) if so, how many times he had been detected, arrested, or brought to court.

The names of all respondents were checked through court records as a means of testing response validity. The findings confirmed those of both Short and Nye[22] and Gold[23] that the majority of respondents seemed to be telling the truth about their offenses. However, the problem of determining both validity and reliability is a great one and any conclusions must consider that fact.[24]

Measurement of Social Status

The occupational status of the father or guardian was used as the criterion for defining the status level for each respondent. It was measured by means of an occupational prestige scale which was formed by combining the Hatt-North[25] and Smith[26] scales.[27]

This scale ranks occupations from *0* to *100* in terms of prestige. However, for

20/LaMar T. Empey and Jerome Rabow, "The Provo Experiment in Delinquency Rehabilitation," *American Sociological Review,* 26 (October 1961), pp. 679-696.

21/For greater detail on data collection and methodological problems, see Maynard L. Erickson and LaMar T. Empey, "Court Records, Undetected Delinquency and Decision-making," *The Journal of Criminal Law, Criminology and Police Science,* 54 (December 1963), pp. 456-469.

22/James F. Short and Ivan Nye, "Reported Behavior as a Criterion of Deviant Behavior," *Social Problems,* 5 (Winter 1957-1958), pp. 207-213.

23/Gold, *op. cit.,* pp. 8-10.

24/For an analysis of the subject see Hardt and Bodine, *op. cit.*

25/Paul K. Hatt and C. C. North, "Jobs and Occupations; A Popular Evaluation," in *Class, Status and Power* (ed.), R. Bendix and S. M. Lipset (Glencoe, Illinois: The Free Press, 1953), pp. 411-426.

26/Mapheus Smith, "An Empirical Scale of Prestige of Occupations," *American Sociological Review,* 8 (April 1943), pp. 185-192.

27/For greater detail on this combination, see LaMar T. Empey, "Social Class and Occupational Aspiration: A Comparison of Absolute and Relative Measurement," *American Sociological Review,* 21 (December 1956), pp. 705-706.

purposes of this analysis it was collapsed into three main categories based upon the occupations located in the lower, middle and upper thirds of the scale.

Twenty-nine percent of the respondents were located in the *lower* category which was made up primarily of unskilled or semiskilled occupations. Fifty-five percent were located in the *middle* category. It included skilled occupations, owners of small businesses and a variety of white-collar jobs. Finally, 16 percent were located in the *upper* category, which included most professions, a variety of business positions, scientists, and artists.

No attempt is made to assess the accuracy of equating these three status categories with the "lower," "middle" and "upper" classes. That complex problem cannot be solved here. Instead the scale is simply one way of ordering respondents empirically through the use of occupation as perhaps the most important single measure of status.[28]

FINDINGS

Overall, the 180 respondents reported a tremendous number of violations, running into the thousands on all but a few serious offenses such as arson, selling and using narcotics, forgery and armed robbery. Furthermore, the large number of violations reported by them was not restricted to a minority. Virtually all respondents reported having committed not one but a variety of different offenses. More than nine times out of ten, they said, these offenses went undetected and unacted upon.[29]

So striking were their reports that one was reminded of the 20-year-old statement of Murphy, Shirley and Witmer who, in noting similar figures, concluded that "even a moderate increase in the amount of attention paid to [them] by law enforcement authorities could create a semblance of a 'delinquency wave' without there being the slightest change in adolescent behavior."[30] One wonders to what extent the current "delinquency wave" is a function of this very phenomenon and, whether, if attention were focused elsewhere, it might also result in a "crime wave" among white-collar and other segments of adult society.

STATUS AND DELINQUENCY

This sample is of limited utility in comparing the delinquency of different status levels, both because it is small and because it relies heavily on data from *official* delinquents. However, there are factors which compensate for these

28/W. Lloyd Warner, M. Meeker and K. Eells, *Social Class in America* (Chicago: Social Science Research Associates, 1949), pp. 167-168; and Leona Tyler, *The Psychology of Human Differences* (New York: Appleton-Century-Crofts, 1947), pp. 145-146.

29/For a great deal of detail on both the numbers of violations and the proportions of respondents involved, see Erickson and Empey, *op. cit.*

30/Fred J. Murphy, M. M. Shirley, and Helen L. Witmer, "The Incidence of Hidden Delinquency," *American Journal of Orthopsychiatry*, 16 (October 1946), pp. 686-696.

problems and suggest that some confidence can be placed in the findings: (1) because tests of significance were used in such a way as to provide a conservative and stringent test of differences, and (2) because the findings were so consistent throughout, both in (officially) delinquent and non-delinquent subsamples, that there is undoubtedly some reliability in the directions noted here.

Despite the finding that these adolescents reported having committed a great number of violations, the data provided little support for the notion that there are status differences. Most respondents on one status level were no more nor no less delinquent than most respondents on another. If, and when, status differences did occur, they occurred because of the excessive violations of a small minority, not because of the general activities of one whole group versus another.

This conclusion was reached on the basis of two kinds of statistical analyses. The first utilized *chi square* in such a way as to provide a stringent examination of possible differences. Instead of lumping all respondents from each status level together and making gross comparisons between total groups, respondents were ordered according to the number of times they reported having committed each offense (i.e., 0, 1-3 times, 4-6 times, etc.). The *chi square* test was then run comparing the number of respondents from each subsample who were found in each of these categories. This test had the effect of eliminating gross differences because it ruled out the possible impact of a large number of offenses which might have been committed by only a few individuals and presented, instead, a more accurate picture of all respondents. It permitted a much better comparison of all individuals in one group with all individuals in another because it controlled for excesses on the extremes.

This comparison revealed very few differences among low- and middle-status respondents. The delinquency patterns for boys on these two status levels were not only similar but each of them also tended to be somewhat more delinquent than upper-status respondents on exactly the same offenses. For example, low- and middle-status boys were significantly more inclined ($P < .05$ or greater) than upper-status boys to have stolen items worth \$2.00-\$50.00, stolen autos, skipped school, smoked regularly and drank more. But even so, the most important consideration is that, out of 22 items, only these few differences were statistically significant among the three status levels.

Second, a correlation analysis was used as a means of analyzing the data in another way. Instead of relating status position to each of the 22 offenses, attempts were made to construct scales which would combine several offenses into unidimensional patterns to see if these patterns were related in some way to status. Three Guttman scales were developed:

1. A *general theft* scale made up of dichotomous items and including theft of articles or money valued at less than \$2.00, theft of articles or money valued from \$2.00-\$50.00 and theft of articles worth more than \$50.00. The coefficient of reproducibility for the scale is .91.
2. A *serious theft* scale made up of dichotomous items and including theft of

articles or money worth more than $50.00, auto theft, and theft involving breaking and entering. The coefficient of reproducibility for this scale was .93.

3. A *common delinquency* scale made up of dichotomous items and including illegal drinking, petty theft, open defiance of people in authority, skipping school and fighting. The coefficient of reproducibility was .91.[31]

When the single scores from each of these scales were correlated with status position, a slight, positive correlation was found between low-status and a greater amount of delinquency: .20 for *general theft,* .17 for *serious theft,* and .17 for *common delinquency.* But, when analysis of variance was used to trace down the source of the variation, it was found to exist, not between low-status respondents and the other two, but between upper-status respondents and the other two. On all three delinquency scales, low- and middle-status respondents did not differ significantly from each other while both differed from upper-status respondents. Thus, the slight correlation that was discovered was due more to the lower amount of delinquency on the extreme upper end of the status ladder than to a high concentration solely on the lower end.

The important thing to remember, therefore, is that the predictive efficiency of status position for this sample is extremely poor, explaining only four percent of the variance on *general theft* and only three percent on both *serious theft* and *common delinquency.* This finding stands out because it is so different from that which came to light when, instead of social status, respondents were compared in terms of their official designation as delinquent or non-delinquent.

Delinquency and Official Position

It will be recalled that the overall sample included respondents in four subsamples who, in *official* terms, were non-delinquent, one-time offenders, serious offenders on probation and incarcerated offenders. A comparison of these groups, using *chi square,* revealed that, while *non and one-time* offenders did not differ significantly from each other, both of them differed significantly on virtually every offense from *serious offenders* who were on probation or were incarcerated. The likelihood was less than one in a thousand that the differences between them could have occurred by chance. Boys whose official position placed them on probation or in an institution reported having been far more delinquent. On many offenses their reported violations exceeded those of non- and one-time offenders by thousands.

Thus, while these findings tended to support the Porterfield thesis that differences do not exist between adolescents from different status levels, they did not support his thesis that nondelinquents have committed as many offenses as official delinquents who are on probation or incarcerated. It would be a

---

31/For details on these scales see Maynard L. Erickson and LaMar T. Empey, "Class, Peers and Delinquency," *Sociology and Social Research,* 49 (April 1965), pp. 268-282.

mistake, therefore, to assume, as he did, that official standing is a function entirely of social status. However, since these findings are based on self-reported data, it could be argued that differences are due to non-official offenders who wish to hide their delinquency and serious offenders who wish to advertise it. But this hardly seems to be the case.

It is not as though non- and one-time offenders did not reveal incriminating evidence. They did. It was just by comparison with officially serious offenders that they seemed to be less delinquent. Meanwhile, it could be argued that offenders who are already in the toils of the law would have much to lose by revealing incriminating evidence. Yet, they did.

It seems, therefore, that actual involvement in more delinquency seems to have been a major reason why some boys were labeled as serious offenders and others were not. What the process was that led to their excessive delinquency, the data do not reveal; that is, whether they were excessively delinquent *prior* to becoming labeled as delinquent or whether the label was self-fulfilling in some way. It would be extremely important, therefore, for subsequent studies to pursue this issue, to determine whether official attention seems to precede excessive delinquency, or whether excessive delinquency precedes official attention.

Kinds of Delinquency

Despite the failure to locate strong differences according to amount of delinquency, there were hints that there were some differences among status levels with respect to *kinds* of delinquency, especially among the minority of respondents who have been the most delinquent. These hints were confirmed when a different series of statistical tests were run.

In order to concentrate upon offense patterns, as contrasted to individuals, a study was made of the cases in which the proportion of violations committed by each status group, on each offense, may have exceeded the proportions of respondents contributed by that status level to the total sample. For example, the middle-status group, with 55 percent of the respondents, committed 90 percent of the forgeries. Obviously, middle-status respondents, *as a group,* had been significantly more involved in forgeries than the other two. A *chi square* test on the significance of differences among proportions confirmed the conclusion.[32] Thus, despite the fact that most individuals in that group had not committed any more or less forgeries than *most* individuals in the others, those few who did commit such offenses tended almost always to be from the middle-status.

In the simplest sense, therefore, more detail was sought through comparing groups, rather than individuals within groups, saying nothing about whether the

32/For an example of the test used, see Helen M. Walker and Joseph Lev, *Statistical Inference* (New York, Henry Holt & Co., 1953), pp. 94-95.

violations of each group were contributed by a large number or only a few individuals within it. The findings were these:

Upper-Status Delinquency. The upper-status group constituted *16 percent* of the total sample but contributed only nine percent of the total violations. Compared to the other two, in terms of both volume and seriousness, it was considerably less delinquent.

Among respondents who were on probation or incarcerated, upper-status boys contributed only six percent of all offenses even though they comprised nine percent of the two subsamples. Thus, even though these boys were in serious trouble—i.e., on probation or incarcerated—they had contributed, as a group, significantly fewer than their share of violations. They exceeded the other two status groups on only one offense: defying parents (P < .001). Apparently parent-child tensions for the upper-status group constitute an important source of difficulty. Defying parents was more strongly associated with being labeled a serious offender among upper-status than low- or middle-status boys.

Middle-Status Delinquency. The middle-status group constituted *55 percent* of the total sample and contributed 59 percent of the total violations. The significant thing about its delinquency, however, is the type and extent of certain violations, not its overall violation rate.

Looking at the total sample, this group was inclined to exceed others in five major areas: (1) general traffic (63 percent of the violations); (2) theft in general, including forgery (90%); (3) defying people other than parents (83%); (4) property violations of all types including breaking and entering (67%), destroying property (70%) and arson (84%); and (5) armed robbery (87%). These items and the extent to which observed differences are real, when the middle is compared separately with each of the other two status groups, are displayed in Table 1.

Many of the violations in Table 1 are notable for their seriousness: felony thefts, forgery, breaking and entering, arson and armed robbery. The fact that the middle-status group was high on these items is important. As shown in Table 2, they reported having committed over *two-thirds* of the *serious* violations in both the non- and one-time offender, and the probation and incarcerated, groups. The primary mitigating factor was that most of the serious offenses were apparently committed by those boys who had already been officially designated as persistent offenders. All non- and one-time offenders reported only 173 serious violations, most of which were for breaking and entering, as contrasted to 1,628 for respondents in the persistent category. Even so, it is notable that the proportionate rate of serious violations for the middle-status group remains significantly high throughout. Thus, even though there may be a large number of differences among the various delinquent and non-delinquent subsamples in the study, this particular one remained consistent throughout.

Overall, then, the middle-status group was more inclined to activities of a destructive and serious quality. However, the fact that this tendency did not

TABLE 1
Comparison of Middle-Status Delinquency with Others

Offense	Middle (55% of Sample) % of Violations	Lower (29% of Sample) % of Violations	Significant Level	Upper (16% of Sample) % of Violations	Significant Level
Traffic					
General traffic	63	22	.001	15	.05
Theft					
Articles less than $2.00	61	29	.001	10	.001
Articles, $2.00					
to $50.00	69	26	.001	5	.001
Articles more					
than $50.00	59	33	N.S.	8	.05
Forgery	90	9	.001	1	.001
Defiance					
Defying people other					
than parents	83	16	.001	1	.001
Property violations					
Breaking and entering	67	24	.001	8	.001
Destroying property	70	22	.001	8	.001
Arson	85	10	.05	5	.05
Retreatist					
Running away	85	12	.001	3	.001
Offenses against person					
Armed robbery	88	12	.10	0	...

TABLE 2
Percent of Serious Offenses Committed
by Different Status Groups

Status	Non- and One-Time Offenders N	%	Probation and Incarcerated Offenders N	%
Lower	8	5	521	32
Middle	124	72	1055	65
Upper	41	23	52	3
Total	173	100	1628	100

show up quite so strongly in the previous analysis, when tests were designed to maximize individual, rather than group differences, implies the existence of a group among middle-status respondents which, when it becomes delinquent, is excessively delinquent. This implication was further confirmed by the finding that among respondents who were on probation or incarcerated, the middle-status group had committed significantly (P < .005 or greater) more violations than the upper-status group on all but four items (theft of more than $50.00, defying parents, arson and smoking habitually) and more than the low-status group on all but six items (buying alcohol, using narcotics, defying parents, skipping school, fighting and smoking habitually). Consequently, this group, rather than middle-status respondents across the board, seems to have contributed to the disproportionate number of serious and destructive offenses reported by the middle-status group.

Low-Status Delinquency. The pattern of offenses for low-status respondents is displayed in Table 3. With 29 percent of the total sample, they reported 32

TABLE 3
Comparison of Low-Status Delinquency with Others

Offense	Lower (29% of Sample) % of Violations	Middle (55% of Sample) % of Violations	Significant Level	Upper (16% of Sample) % of Violations	Significant Level
Traffic					
Driving without a license	44	51	.001	4	.001
Theft					
Articles more than $50.00	33	59	N.S.	8	.01
Auto theft	38	60	.05	2	.001
Alcohol and narcotics					
Buying alcohol	58	37	.001	5	.001
Drinking alcohol	33	59	.05	8	.001
Using narcotics	64	36	.005	0	...*
Defiance					
Defying parents	41	39	.001	19	.005
Retreatist					
Skipping school	46	47	.001	7	.001
Offenses against person					
Fighting and assault	52	45	.001	2	.001
Others					
Smoking regularly	39	52	N.S.	9	N.S.

percent of the total violations and were disproportionately high on the following offenses: driving without a license (44 percent of total violations), stealing articles worth more than $50.00 (33%), auto theft (38%), buying alcohol (58%), drinking alcohol (33%), using narcotics (64%), defying parents (39%), skipping school (46%), and fighting and assault (52%).

They differed significantly from the other two status groups on all these offenses except for stealing articles worth more than $50.00 where the differences between them and middle-status respondents was not great enough.

They also tended to smoke regularly more often than the other two but differences were not significant.

This pattern for low-status respondents might have been more predictable than for the middle-status group. For example, it is common to assume that skipping school, using narcotics, or fighting is more characteristic of low- than middle- or upper-status juveniles.

Even the findings with respect to traffic violations seem consistent with previous preconceptions; namely, that, while low-status juveniles may be less inclined than the other two groups to violate traffic laws in general, probably because they do not have means to drive as much, they are *more* inclined to steal autos and drive without a license. One could speculate that, with lower literacy skills and less legitimate access to a car, they would be more likely to commit these offenses.

However, when the low-status respondents in the *non- and one-time* offender category were compared with those in the *probation and incarcerated* category, some interesting things came to light. Low-status respondents in the first category constituted only *17* percent of the sample but reported *24* percent of the offenses. The pattern of offenses just described was the one most pronounced.

But in the *probation and incarcerated* category, some marked changes occurred. Low-status boys constituted a much heavier proportion of the total number of respondents (41%) but contributed a much smaller proportion of the total violations (34%). The differences between them and upper-status respondents tended to persist but compared to middle-status respondents, their contribution to the total number of violations declined heavily. They remained significantly higher than middle-status respondents only on the offenses of buying alcohol, using narcotics, fighting and defying parents. Otherwise, as mentioned earlier, middle-status boys who eventually became probation violators, or were incarcerated, were the ones who seemed to have been extremely delinquent.

IMPLICATIONS

One can only speculate as to the reasons for these findings. The need for qualification is always present. The size of the sample is one limitation; it inhibits generalization. But it also points to the problems of gathering valid data on a subject such as this. In this particular study, sample size had to be limited because of the time consumed in locating, obtaining cooperation from, and interviewing respondents. And, as it turned out, the sheer quantity of violations that were recorded became a difficult matter for description and display.

A second problem was the geographic location of the study. Perhaps the influences responsible for the findings were inherent in the relatively small Utah cities from which the respondents came. The same study, conducted in a large, urban center may have resulted in an entirely different picture. But, again, it may be an oversimplification to assume that conditions of poverty, ethnicity and class in metropolitan centers would result in distinctions among status levels of the kind which did not appear here.

One important factor to be remembered is that the prevailing subculture in which these data were gathered was Mormon. It is generally believed that this subculture retains a traditional belief system emphasizing obedience to parents, hard work, and observance of the law even more than our large cities. Yet, if familial and community controls are ineffective in this setting, then one might expect even less control in large metropolitan centers. It could be hypothesized, therefore, that the amount of delinquency for all status levels would be greater there. We cannot know until more data such as these are gathered on *actual* rather than *official* delinquency.

The data on both the amount and kinds of hidden delinquency committed by these respondents imply that official records provide information only on the tip, not on the entire iceberg, of delinquency. If this is the case, they suggest why so much difficulty has been encountered in pinpointing important variables. Adequate information has not been available.

The lack of information has been qualitative as well as quantitative. For example, even though in this study we met daily for a period of months with many of the respondents from the probations and incarcerated subsamples, we formed incorrect impressions about them. It was our impression that virtually all of these officially serious respondents had low-status roots. They wore clothes, used language, and had hairdos which were alike and which, generally, are associated with low-status. Yet, it was not until we gathered objective data on their backgrounds that we discovered that we were wrong. The regular "uniform" was being worn by middle- as well as low-status boys. Only upper-status boys were exceptional. We concluded, therefore, that the uniform was a symbol of a life-style, as much the result of membership in a delinquent subsystem as of membership in a low social stratum. The implication is that, if different patterns of delinquency have important significance for the administration of justice, for prevention and treatment strategies and for research purposes, then far more data are needed on hidden delinquency. They are needed to determine the shape of the total iceberg.

16. Differences in the Conception of Self as a Male among Lower and Middle Class Delinquents*

LEON F. FANNIN and MARSHALL B. CLINARD

Albert K. Cohen suggests that delinquent subcultures in working-class areas of American cities exemplify behavior which is nonutilitarian, malicious, and negativistic. Characterized by short-run hedonism, the gang, therefore, serves as a proponent of group autonomy which guarantees one's status in the existing community (*see* Gannon, Article 6). Because the delinquent subculture, Cohen believes, represents a solution to the shared problem of low status evidenced among working-class youth, the values of the group become operating norms which the youth shares and understands. Since a working-class boy has been inadequately socialized to the norms of his middle-class teachers, he is at a competitive disadvantage in the classroom and in other social areas where he competes for recognition with other middle-class youth and adults (*see* Elliott, Article 10). The delinquent subculture, therefore, arises in order to bring about an adjustment in the tension between stated goals and status potentials.

Richard A. Cloward and Lloyd E. Ohlin, on the other hand, modify Cohen's assumptions in their hypothesis that the working-class gang delinquent subculture shares a value commitment to success but is at a competitive disadvantage in reaching success goals. Because the delinquent gang member does not possess access to the legitimate or conventional means by which these success goals are reached, or because he believes his chances of reaching these goals are limited, the working-class gang delinquent revises his aspirations downward in order to resolve his frustrations and potentially shares in a criminalistic, conflict, or retreatist subculture which offers some structural support for his own concept of self. Existing *opportunity structures,* Cloward and Ohlin believe, largely determine the future direction of juvenile conduct.

The differences in lower- and middle-class delinquent self-conceptions are undoubtedly a result of this adaptation process. Although, as Leon F. Fannin and Marshall B. Clinard argue, the lower-class and lower-middle-class delinquents share similar concepts of self, lower-class boys view themselves as being tougher and more fearless, powerful, fierce, and dangerous (image of the tough guy). On

*Reprinted from *Social Problems,* journal of The Society for the Study of Social Problems, Volume 13, Number 2 (Fall, 1965), pp. 205-14, with permission of the editors and authors.

the other hand, middle-class boys feel more clever, smart, smooth, bad, and loyal (image of the loyal and daring comrade). These self-conceptions, Fannin and Clinard believe, are related to specific types of eventual behavior (*see* Gannon, Article 6; Elliott, Article 10; Roebuck and Johnson, Article 12; and Garabedian, Article 14).

This study investigated differences between lower and lower-middle class white delinquents in conception of self as a male, and behavioral correlates of such differences.

. . . .

Some self-conceptions may have greater importance than others because they are more generalized and thus function in a wider variety of social actions. Self-conceptions related to many occupational roles, such as those ascribed to the military elite, high level business executives, or confidence man, would appear to be of this nature.[1]

Another such generalized self-conception, and the subject of this study, is that attached to sex status. Indeed, of all self-conceptions this may be one of the most decisive, as there are relatively few actions in which the participants conceive of themselves as sexless, or are so conceived by others. A "proper" sex self-conception may thus sharply limit approved behavioral alternatives.

The present study focused upon possible differences in the degree to which certain "masculine" traits were held by delinquents from the lower and middle classes. . . . It seemed reasonable to hypothesize that: (1) lower class males would conceive of themselves as tougher, harder, more powerful, and dangerous, and place greater value upon physical prowess and aggression than middle class males; consequently, (2) they probably would be involved more often in physically violent offenses, and define and act with less verbal sophistication and dexterity, but more physical aggression, in dating and sexual behavior.

RESEARCH PROCEDURES

Characteristics of the Samples. Data to test these hypotheses were collected from random samples of lower and lower-middle class white delinquents committed to a training school in a mid-western state. All boys present at the school during the summer of 1962 who were 16 or 17 years old, and who had resided in urban areas of at least 300,000 population, were given a class rank on the basis of their fathers' or guardians' levels of occupation and education. The distribution of these ranks was then differentiated into lower, working, and lower-middle class levels.

1/See Morris Janowitz, *The Professional Soldier*, Glencoe, Ill.: The Free Press, 1960, pp. 228-229; Charles H. Coates and Roland J. Pellegrin, "Executives and Supervisors: Contrasting Self-Conceptions and Conceptions of Each Other," *American Sociological Review*, 22 (1957), pp. 217-220.

Delinquents from the working class were eliminated to obtain class levels as disparate as possible. Class levels higher than the lower-middle[2] were desired but only one boy represented a higher level. The lower and middle classes were treated as separate statistical populations, and 25 cases were randomly selected from each; the sampling fractions were 23.4% and 75.8%, respectively. . . .

Data Collection. Depth interviewing and self-conception scales elicited the most crucial information, with official records used to determine class affiliation and reported delinquent histories. The interviews were structured. . . .

Operationally, self-conception as a male was defined by the relative intensity of specific traits which the delinquents felt characterized them when they were placed, verbally, in varying situations that made them explicitly aware of their sex status. Their responses to these situations were then elicited through intensive probing by open-ended questions and by forced-choice scales.

These scales were constructed on the basis of a technique developed by Bennett,[3] whereby the respondent selects traits, three at a time from a list of 15 until none remain, which are ranked "most" or "least" descriptive of himself, or of others, or of situations, and so on. . . .

Each list of 15 traits was administered three times, with the situation under which the respondents selected traits varied each time. They were asked to rank the traits contained in each list according to: (1) how they felt the traits *actually* described them as males (actual, or perceived, self); (2) how they *would like* to be as males (ideal self); and (3) how they felt *other people in general* believed them to be as males (generalized looking-glass self). These selections were scored from zero to four points for each trait, so that those which the boys felt described them most closely had the highest values.

SELF-CONCEPTIONS AND SOCIAL CLASS

The findings indicate that while the male self-conception is very similar across class lines, there are a few crucial differences which apparently are related to a diverse range of behavior patterns.

A partial test of the first hypothesis, stating in the null form that *there is no significant difference in the conception of self as a male held by lower and middle class delinquents,* is provided by analysis of the delinquents' responses to the Trait Lists (see Tables 1 and 2). . . .

Tough Guys and Loyal Comrades. Lower class boys felt themselves to be (actual self) tougher, more powerful, fierce, fearless, and dangerous than middle class boys. It was unexpected, however, that they did not feel themselves to be significantly more violent, hard, and pugilistic. Middle class delinquents, on the other hand, conceived of themselves as being more loyal, clever, smart, smooth,

2/To avoid repetition, lower-middle class will be referred to hereafter as middle class.
3/Edward Bennett, *Personality Assessment and Diagnosis,* New York: The Ronald Press, 1961, pp. v, 69-80, 173-187, 253-270.

TABLE 1
Social Class Comparison of Item Means from Trait Lists I and II
for Actual, Ideal, and Generalized Looking-Glass Selves

Trait Lists	Actual Self		Ideal Self		Generalized Looking-Glass Self	
	Lower Class	Middle Class	Lower Class	Middle Class	Lower Class	Middle Class
List I						
Fearless	1.89*	1.52*	1.37	1.81	1.74	2.00
Loyal	3.05*	3.71*	2.63*	3.71*	2.21*	3.16*
Brave	2.58	2.49	2.79	2.76	3.00	3.00
Strong	2.26	2.33	2.47	2.62	2.37	2.21
Active	2.79	3.29	2.64	2.71	2.16	2.89
Tough	1.88*	1.45*	1.63*	.91*	1.74	1.79
Athletic	2.47	2.52	3.05	2.90	2.18	2.42
Hard	1.42	1.29	1.47*	1.05*	1.88*	1.42*
Reckless	1.11	1.00	.84	.71	1.00	1.05
Courageous	2.59	2.90	3.05	3.19	2.89	3.05
Loud	1.40	1.24	1.16	1.00	1.68*	.89*
Powerful	2.04*	1.50*	1.90	1.91	2.42*	1.63*
Rough	1.68	1.14	1.05	1.24	1.21	1.60
Smart	1.89*	2.86*	3.00	3.19	2.20	2.42
Violent	.95	.76	.95*	.29*	1.32*	.47*
List II						
Clever	1.95*	2.95*	3.00	2.38	2.53	2.89
Cruel	1.21	.95	.89	1.05	1.42*	.63*
Lucky	2.32	2.05	2.89*	3.62*	2.47	2.63
Fierce	2.58*	1.05*	1.95	1.67	1.47	1.42
Bad	1.14*	1.57*	.84	1.05	1.32*	1.74*
Wild	1.05	1.19	1.16	.81	1.53	1.21
Proud	3.11	3.71	3.47*	3.06*	2.74*	3.21*
Dangerous	1.11*	.57*	.95	.67	.54*	1.00*
Bold	2.21	2.24	2.21	2.14	2.37*	1.74*
Firm	2.16	2.52	2.79*	3.14*	2.42	2.78
Shrewd	2.11	2.05	1.42	1.76	1.88*	1.69*
Cunning	2.79	2.14	1.95	1.90	2.00	1.74
Stern	2.32	2.81	2.74	2.71	2.68	2.26
Smooth	2.26*	2.72*	2.53	2.71	2.79	2.63
Fighter	1.68	1.48	1.21	1.33	1.84*	2.53*

*Differences between means for lower and middle classes are significant at the .05 level (Student's test). The range for any mean is 0 to 4.

and bad. This greater stress upon loyalty by the middle class is surprising,[4] even though the lower class also ranked it very high.

When responses depicting the ideal self and the generalized looking-glass self are studied, essentially the same traits separate the class levels, with some

4/Walter B. Miller, "Lower Class Culture as a Generating Milieu of Gang Delinquency," *Journal of Social Issues,* 14 (1958), pp. 5-19.

TABLE 2
Social Class Comparison of Item Means from Trait Lists III and IV
for Actual, Ideal, and Generalized Looking-Glass Selves

Trait Lists	Actual Self		Ideal Self		Generalized Looking-Glass Self	
	Lower Class	Middle Class	Lower Class	Middle Class	Lower Class	Middle Class
List III						
Proper	1.63	1.33	1.69	1.48	1.42	1.32
Loving	2.26	2.43	2.74	3.00	1.75*	2.63*
Graceful	1.58	1.24	2.00	1.95	1.92	1.42
Modest	1.58	1.57	1.89*	.95*	1.69	1.47
Respectable	2.63	2.43	3.00*	3.62*	2.63	2.37
Shy	1.74	2.10	.53	.19	1.42	1.16
Sympathetic	1.53*	2.57*	1.32	1.81	1.79	2.21
Gentle	1.95	1.86	2.68*	2.02*	2.11	2.26
Courteous	2.26	2.10	2.05	2.33	2.42	2.32
Peaceful	2.68	2.43	2.58	2.51	2.37	2.58
Friendly	2.84*	3.52*	3.05	3.10	3.16	3.68
Soft	.96	.86	1.05	.67	1.21	.74
Neat	2.78*	2.14*	2.57*	3.05*	2.68	2.89
Affectionate	2.05	2.14	1.53*	2.05*	1.69	1.95
Tender	1.53	1.28	1.32	1.27	1.74*	1.00*
List IV						
False	.95	.71	.79	.71	1.32*	.68*
Kind	2.89*	3.33*	3.21	3.29	3.32	3.37
Sweet	1.79	1.88	2.53	2.68	2.32	2.78
Upright	2.32	2.71	2.78	2.95	2.21	2.37
Sensitive	2.74	2.62	2.37	2.52	2.11*	2.78*
Feeble	.63	.62	.37*	.85*	1.11*	.47*
Delicate	1.84	1.52	1.84	1.95	1.85	1.53
Helpless	1.17	1.14	.89	.76	1.44*	.89*
Safe	2.89	2.81	2.68	3.05	2.68	3.07
Timid	1.89	1.95	1.79	1.62	1.89	1.58
Afraid	1.37	1.71	1.11	1.14	.95	1.32
Fearful	1.84	1.62	2.11*	1.23*	2.32	2.21
Quiet	3.68	3.10	3.21	2.97	3.11	2.84
Loved	2.58*	3.33*	3.74	3.66	2.32*	3.11*
Weak	1.42*	.95*	.58	.62	1.05	1.00

*Differences between means for lower and middle classes are significant at the .05 level (Student's test). The range for any mean is 0 to 4.

interesting exceptions. The lower class would like to be (ideal self) tougher, harder, and more violent than the middle class, while the latter would like to be more loyal, lucky, and firm. When their interpretations of how other people in general view them are analyzed (generalized looking-glass self), approximately the same findings hold, except that the middle class felt others believed them to be more dangerous, bad, and pugilistic. It would seem to be quite clear that the norms from which these delinquents believed others evaluated them were sharply different, because the lower class had been actually involved in more assaults, robberies, fights, and other delinquencies (see above) than the middle class and yet the latter felt others believed them to be more "dangerous" and "bad."

The more negatively connoted traits used in Lists III and IV were far less discriminatory except for a sharp difference in responses to "love" and related traits. Middle class boys felt they were loved to a significantly greater degree and felt others also believed them to be more loving. In addition, they conceived of themselves as being more friendly, sympathetic, and kind.

These differences were strongly supported and supplemented by the results gained from informal interviewing. . . .

An additional trait which appeared to more adequately characterize the lower class boys was a greater degree of callousness in their relations with others, particularly in regard to "enemies" (which may reflect a relative lack of propathic role taking). . . .

While exciting exploits and incredulous adventures were highly evaluated by members of both class levels, it appeared that middle class boys conceived of themselves as more daring. They liked to take risks and regale others with their fascinating tales. . . .

From an over-all perspective, then, it would appear these classes differ chiefly in that significantly more lower class delinquents feel themselves to be "tough guys," while more middle class delinquents feel themselves to be "loyal and daring comrades."

. . . .

The degree to which these boys conceived of themselves as tough guys, . . . varied within the class levels. . . .

. . . .

SELF-CONCEPTIONS RELATED TO BEHAVIOR

It had been hypothesized that if these differences in self-conceptions by class had meaning, this would probably be reflected in behavioral differences, such as frequency of physical violence, occupational aspiration, and attitudes toward sexuality. To a large extent these expectations were fulfilled. Six statistical tests were made and five allowed rejection of the null hypothesis.

Physical Violence. One of the more important of the tests was a comparison of the frequency with which reported and unreported robberies and assaults were committed by members of the two class levels. The vast majority of all lower class delinquents, 84%, had committed at least one such offense compared to 28% of the middle class ($p < .01$); 28% of the lower and 8% of the middle class had committed 10 or more violent offenses.

Class level was also related to the frequency of fighting with other boys. Lower class delinquents fought singly and in groups significantly more often ($p < .05$) than middle class delinquents, with 20% of them averaging five or more fights per month compared to 4.0%. The possibly greater lack of propathic role taking characteristic of lower class boys also appeared in their techniques of fighting. More of them used weapons, and more advocated "stomping" (kicking a fallen opponent, particularly in the face). . . .

Lower class boys also regularly carried weapons on their persons significantly more often than middle class boys ($p < .02$); 80% usually carried a knife, gun, or "knuckles," compared to 48% of the middle class. The most frequent reason given for having a weapon close at hand was self protection.

One factor which ran counter to the expectations was the similarity in the frequency of forcible rape committed by boys of both classes ($p > .05$); the proportions having done this were 12% in the lower and 16% in the middle classes, but differences in class definitions of "rape" may have been an important obscuring variable.

Occupational Aspirations. While occupational aspirations are influenced by a wide variety of factors, it was anticipated that one which might help to explain the different aspirations of the lower class would be their orientation toward certain categories of work as related to their male self-conceptions.

Eighty per cent of the lower class boys wanted a type of adult occupation in which they could work with their hands, while only 36% of the middle class desired this ($p < .01$). . . .

Sexuality. Masculinity was also expressed differently by members of the two class levels in their orientation and behavior toward adolescent females.[5] Toughness, callousness, and physical prowess appeared to be dominant for the lower class, while sophistication, dexterity, and verbal manipulation seemed prominent for the middle class.

Dating was viewed by the lower class, for example, primarily as the *means* to an end (sexual intercourse) while the middle class stressed dating as an *end* in itself (the fun element in going out). . . .

For the lower class boy, sexual intercourse was to be achieved by the raw force of his masculinity; he would not "seduce" his date so much as he would "conquer" her. The aura of his maleness should be enough for the girl, without stooping to demean himself by clever, witty, and manipulative verbal "propaganda." The female should surrender herself to this image of the "all man" rather than be converted to willingness by gentle and smoothly coined phrases. . . .

· · · · · · · · · · · · · · · · · ·

DISCUSSION

. . . The data suggest that a significant proportion of offenses involving physical violence may be committed by delinquents who stress certain

5/See Clark E. Vincent, "Ego Involvement in Sexual Relations: Implications for Research on Illegitimacy," *American Journal of Sociology,* 65 (November, 1959), pp. 287-295.

"masculine" traits in their self-conceptions as males, which help channel and legitimize such violence. Self-conception may act as a closure factor,[6] restricting the possibilities of behavior to a narrowed universe. In terms of rehabilitating violent offenders, consequently, it would seem feasible that a highly selective program directed toward the limited ends of changing this aspect of the self-conception might prove more helpful than a global effort at pervasive personality change, or other current techniques. . . .

Another implication of the findings is that this tough guy self-conception may be related to a wide range of other types of behavior, deviant and nondeviant, including drinking patterns, leisure habits, divorce and desertion, illegitimacy, and so on. . . .

Finally, empirically oriented analyses of the components of social interaction may help to better understand deviant and nondeviant behavior; this refers not only to further studies of the types and interrelation of self-conceptions, but also to analyses of the various aspects of role taking, the relationship between role taking and role playing, the internalization of significant and generalized others and their specific influence upon behavior, and the complex interrelationships of these factors within the "social self."

SUMMARY

. . . While self-conceptions were found to be quite similar, lower class boys did conceive of themselves as being tougher, more fearless, powerful, fierce, and dangerous, while middle class boys felt they were more clever, smart, smooth, bad, and loyal. Descriptively, these were labeled as "tough guy" and "loyal and daring comrade" self-conceptions.

These self-conceptions were then found to be related to specific types of behavior. The "tough guys" significantly more often committed violent offenses, fought more often and with harsher means, carried weapons, had lower occupational aspirations, and stressed toughness and related traits in the reputation they desired and in sexual behavior.

Rehabilitative and preventive efforts to decrease violent offenses might be more profitable if focused upon this aspect of the offender's social self. The possible relation of the tough guy self-conception, and other types of self-conceptions, to varying types of behavior was also pointed out.

6/Edwin M. Lemert, "An Isolation and Closure Theory of Naive Check Forgery," *Journal of Criminal Law, Criminology and Police Science,* 44 (1953), pp. 296-307.

B. Minorities and Criminality

17. When Subcultures Meet: Police-Negro Relations*

VICTOR G. STRECHER

Taking issue with the Delinquent Subculture Theory of Albert K. Cohen (*see* introduction to Article 16), Walter B. Miller suggests that the structure of lower class life plays a concomitant dominant role in the creation of gang delinquency. Delinquency, Miller stipulates, is the product of a long-established and durable lower-class cultural tradition and is not the result of conflict responses to middle-class values. Because lower-class individuals have little hope of ascending to a higher status, they are limited to a culture context which possesses peculiar structural elements and a complex pattern of *focal concerns.*

Dominated by the female-based household, mother and daughters assume multiple roles as they provide economic support to the family and discharge general household and affectional duties. Because they may be involved in the practice of *serial monogamy* (repetitive sequences of mate-finding, legal or common-law marriage, and divorce or male desertion), they are sequentially involved in a search for masculine commitment. Consequently, the children in the family may have been born to the same mother but possess different and potentially unknown fathers. Attempting to overcome his anxieties about sex-role identification, the male child, therefore, learns to identify and to deal with such focal concerns as trouble, toughness, smartness, excitement, fate, and autonomy. These broad themes, Miller argues, condition the specific acts of lower-class persons and become the source of their differential relations to the police or other enforcement agencies (*see* Fox and Volakakis, Article 18).

From a second point of view, David Matza and Gresham M. Sykes, who believe that middle-class culture stresses ascetic devotion to thrift and hard labor in order to fulfill a calling or similar goal assumed in a one-sided Protestant ethic, emphasize the functional importance of *subterranean values* in delinquency. Other respectable but subterranean or unpublicized values in such forms as a search for fun or for tolerance of particular types of violence or aggression, they assume, command the commitment of large numbers of conventional citizens.

*Reprinted from *Law Enforcement, Science and Technology,* ed. by S. A. Yefsky, 1967, pp. 701-707.

The delinquent's lack of work desire, search for kicks, hope for the "big score," and tendencies towards toughness and aggressiveness, Matza and Sykes hypothesize, are exaggerated and immature versions of several middle-class values. Juveniles alienated from schools or lacking adult role preparation, therefore, find positive meaning in such subterranean value expressions (*see* Elliott, Article 10).

Whatever the hypothesis or reason, the problem of lower-class minority group and police conflict reached challenging proportions during the late 1960's. Because the arresting officer possesses his own cultural or subcultural attitudes and coinmitments, which he often reveals in his arrest patterns (*see* Reiss, Article 21) and the minority member has assumed a new aggressiveness, subcultural and interracial conflicts have reached a greater frequency. The vast majority of urban riots in America have been triggered by an initial police-minority member confrontation within an emotional setting in which subcultural attitudes of the police and the Negro have found release. That police brutality and minority hatred for the police exist cannot be denied (*see* Reiss, Article 21). Their effects upon arrest patterns and prison incarcerations, however, are only now coming to light. While the problem is not new, its dimensions have been realigned by the changes in the dominant minority group relations in the years following the 1954 U.S. Supreme Court decision which declared racial segregation unconstitutional.

The existing subcultural conflict evident in police-minority tensions, Victor G. Strecher believes, is a product of Negro migration and adaptation to urban life, the characteristics of the lower-class Negro subculture, the nature of the police subculture, the problems involved in cognitive dissonance and culture shock, and the nature of police-Negro interaction.

INTRODUCTION

Relations between the police and lower class Negro residents of large urban areas of the northern and western United States have become increasingly discordant in recent years. Ironically, this has occurred during a period of growing technical competence in law enforcement, and burgeoning police sensitivity to community reaction. Police and Negro explanations of the conflict have tended to obscure the real issues, and have done little to secure a mutually satisfactory relationship.

. . . .

... The hypothesis is offered that most police-Negro encounters are predisposed to mutual hostility even prior to the moment of occurrence as a consequence of ... larger social forces. ... Main sections of this preliminary report are the following.

1. Migration of Negroes from the rural South to large urban areas of the North and West; patterns and implications of social adaptation to urban life.

2. The lower class Negro subculture.
3. The police subculture.
4. Cognitive Dissonance: the theory.
5. Culture Shock: a foreign service conceptualization.
6. Police-Negro interaction analyzed in terms of antecedent subcultural variables, cognitive dissonance, and culture shock.

The Negro Exodus from the South

Between 1910 and 1963 more than 5,000,000 Negroes are estimated to have migrated from the Deep South,[1] mostly to the large cities of the North and the West, in two distinctive patterns. Between 1910 and 1940, about 1,750,000 migrants moved straight northward to the large cities directly in their paths ". . . from South Carolina to New York, from Georgia to Philadelphia, from Alabama to Detroit, and from Mississippi to Chicago."[2]

Between 1940 and 1963 most of the 3,300,000 Negroes who left the South migrated to the western as well as northern cities. Negro population outside of the South has grown from 5 per cent in 1860 to 10 per cent in 1910, 24 per cent in 1950, and 40 per cent in 1960.[3] Only 54 per cent of the Negro population of this country now resides in the southern states.[4]

Reasons for moving have more often been a desire to leave the South rather than a specific attraction of the destination. . . .

.   .   .   .

The Lower Class Negro Subculture

Culture has been defined by Oscar Lewis, in the tradition of Ruth Benedict, as a ". . . design for living which is passed down from generation to generation."[5] This intergenerational design for living consists of behavior, goals, values, attitudes, personality patterns and achievement levels, and is a direct consequence of patterns of child-rearing and family life-style.[6]

The idea that a "culture of poverty" exists has been with us since 1961 when Oscar Lewis used the phrase.[7] Catherine Chilman feels that ". . . it would probably be more accurate to talk about the *sub*-cultures of poverty . . . because

1/G. Myrdal, *An American Dilemma,* Harper and Brothers, New York, pp. 183, 1229; 1944.

2/U.S. Department of Labor, *The Negroes in the United States,* U.S. Government Printing Office, Washington, D.C., p. 1; 1966.

3/R. Thomlinson, *Population Dynamics,* Random House, New York, pp. 219-220; 1965.
4/*Ibid.,* pp. 444-445.

5/C. S. Chilman, *Growing up Poor,* U.S. Department of Health, Education, and Welfare, Washington, D.C., p. 5; 1966.

6/*Ibid.*
7/*Ibid.,* p. 5.

most of our poor would seem to subscribe to the 'middle-class American way' as
... a cultural ideal which most would accept, in theory and fantasy."[8]. . .
[Rainwater] [9] suggests that a more viable approach to the issue is Hyman
Rodman's concept of a "lower class value stretch," [10] which permits the lower
class person to scale down a set of values to an operable level without
abandoning the conventional middle-class values of society. . . .

. . . .

Chilman notes that "it is now generally recognized that lower-class and
middle-class families tend to raise their children and conduct their family
relationships in quite different styles."[11]. . .

Frazier calls attention to the pattern of family desertion by Negro men, and
estimates that women head the households in 10 to 30 per cent of northern
urban Negro families.[12] He calls this pattern an "inevitable consequence of the
impact of urban life on the simple family organization and folk culture which
the Negro has evolved in the rural South."[13]

Rainwater explores the view that scaled-down values and norms constitute
"legitimate cultural alternatives" to conventional norms, in the lower class
subculture. His analysis centers on heterosexual behavior—particularly
pre-marital sexual intercourse, extra-marital intercourse, and illegitimacy—of
lower class Negroes, and compares the *normative* expressions of housing project
residents—"how things ought to be"—with their *existential* views—"how things
are.". . .

Boone Hammond has described "a 'contest system' which serves as a survival
technique in the Negro lower-class subculture."[14] This system is one of
nonphysical competition, in which the actors seek, through strategies of
manipulation, to obtain the scarce goods of others. It is described as a
"zero-sum" game, in that one person gains only that which another loses. The
two prime scarce objects in this system are money and women, although women
often represent another means of getting more money. . . . Hammond's major
findings are that "the contest system causes an overriding atmosphere of
skepticism and distrust; where an act of friendliness is construed to be a prelude
to subsequent manipulation; the methods of contestants are at variance with
conventional social norms; the contest system is pervasive, and prevents

8/*Ibid.*, p. 6.

9/L. Rainwater, "The Problem of Lower-class Culture," unpublished Pruitt-Igo
Occasional Paper No. 8, Washington University, Saint Louis; 1966.

10/H. Rodman, "The Lower-Class Value Stretch," *Planning for a Nation of Cities,*
Cambridge: M.I.T. Press, 1966.

11/Chilman, *op. cit.,* p. 5.

12/E. F. Frazier, *The Negro Family in the United States,* University of Chicago Press, p.
246; 1966.

13/*Ibid.*, p. 225.

14/B. E. Hammond, "The Contest System: A Survival Technique," unpublished essay,
Department of Sociology and Anthropology, Washington University, Saint Louis, p. 1;
1965.

development of stable interpersonal relations in every phase of life—and inevitably between husbands and wives . . . deferred gratifications are not seen to be of any utility. . . ."

The Police Subculture

.   .   .   .

It is important to point out here that the generalized pattern of racial segregation on the national scene ensures that social groups from which policemen are drawn know little more about the lower class Negro subculture than they know about many foreign cultures. . . .

Beyond childhood and adolescent socialization, the police officer undergoes a process of occupational socialization, through which he becomes identified by himself and his associates as a policeman, and begins to share all the police perspectives relevant to the police role.[15]

The hypothesis of the police subculture will be based explicitly on the theoretical paradigm of occupational subculture presented in Becker, Geer, Hughes and Strauss's *Boys in White*.[16] So directly does this conceptual model of medical student subculture accept the materials relating to the police subculture hypothesis, that a literal use of Becker's text will be made, changed only by the substitution of appropriate police-oriented phrases.

> . . . we often have occasion to use the term *police subculture*. By this we mean the body of collective understandings among *policemen* about matters related to their roles as *officers*. Our use of this phrase has several connotations.
>
> In the first place, we mean to indicate that there is a substantial element of coherence and consistency among the perspectives we describe as making up *police subculture*. In speaking of a group's culture, social scientists ordinarily mean to indicate that there is some such degree of coherence and consistency between the parts which make it up.
>
> The term *police subculture* carries a second connotation as well. It is meant to emphasize that the perspectives held by the *police officers* are related very much to the fact that these people occupy the position of *policeman* in an institution known as a *police department*. . . . The opportunities and disabilities of the *police role* are decisive in shaping the perspectives *policemen* hold.
>
> Likewise, by using the term *police subculture,* we mean to indicate that *policemen* do not simply apply those perspectives which they bring with them from their previous experience in other institutional positions. Put another way, this is to say that elements in the *police officers'*

15/H. S. Becker, B. Geer, E. C. Hughes and A. L. Strauss, *Boys in White,* University of Chicago Press, adapted from p. 47; 1961.
16/*Ibid.*

backgrounds do not exert any decisive influence on how *policemen* behave on the job. Such background factors may have indirect influence in many ways, but the problems of the *police officer* are so pressing and the *policemen's* initial perspectives so similar that the perspectives developed are much more apt to reflect the pressures of the immediate *law enforcement* situation than of ideas associated with prior roles and experiences.

We use police subculture, then, as a kind of shorthand term for the organized sum of *police perspectives* relevant to the *police role.*[17]

Becker describes a number of medical student perspectives toward medical practice and patients, drawn from medical culture. These perspectives, each followed by an appropriate transformation, provide a second part of the subculture model applicable to the police occupation: [18]

> ... the concept of medical responsibility pictures a world in which patients may be in danger of losing their lives and identifies the true work of the physician as saving those endangered lives. Further, where the physician's work does not afford (at least in some symbolic sense) the possibility of saving a life or restoring health through skillful practice ... the physician himself lacks some of the essence of physicianhood.

Transformation of this passage for applicability to the police occupation reads:

> ... the concept of police responsibility pictures a world in which the acts and intended acts of criminals threaten the lives or well-being of victims, and the security of their property. The true work of the police officer is the protection of life and property by intervention in, and solution of criminal acts. Further, where the policeman's work does not afford (at least in some symbolic sense) the possibility of protecting life or property by intervening in criminal acts, the police officer himself lacks some of the essence of police identity.

> Those patients who can be cured are better than those who cannot.
> Those cases which can be solved are better than those which cannot.

> "Crocks" ... are not physically ill and ... are not regarded as worthwhile patients because nothing can be done for them.
> Chronic neighborhood complainants are not worth taking seriously because there is no substance to their complaints, and nothing can be done for them.

> Students worry about the dangers to their own health involved in seeing a steady stream of unscreened patients, some of whom may have communicable diseases.

17/*Ibid.*, pp. 46-47.
18/*Ibid.*, pp. 316-320.

Policemen worry about dangers to their own safety involved in approaching a steady stream of unknown persons, some of whom may have serious behavioral problems, and intentions of causing them injury or even death, because of circumstances unknown to the policemen.

The most interesting and applicable medical perspective—one that echoes in the police world—is the following:

"Perhaps the most difficult scenes come about when patients have no respect for the doctor's authority. Physicians resent this immensely." [19]

The transformation is left to you.

There is one police subcultural perspective that deserves mention on its own; this is the perspective that certain criminal problems must be dealt with through extra-legal means, because some of these criminal activities are organized specifically for evasion of legally normative enforcement procedures. Among these are: organized crime, inter-criminal incidents, meetings of "known hoodlums," and certain vice operations. This is an interesting counterpart to the scaled-down, Negro subculture alternatives of conventional social norms, instituted to solve the problems of living with inconsistent, ambiguous, idealistic and unreachable values of the larger society. It is not surprising that police officers express ambivalence toward these pragmatic but socially unacceptable alternatives, as do Negroes toward their adaptations.

.   .   .   .

Cognitive Dissonance: The Theory

The *Theory of Cognitive Dissonance,* first published by Leon Festinger in 1957, and elaborated in 1962 by Brehm and Cohen, is based on the "notion that the human organism tries to establish internal harmony, consistency, or congruity among his opinions, attitudes, knowledge, and values. That is, there is a drive toward consonance among cognitions." [20] He goes on to say that the relations between pairs of cognitive elements can be *irrelevant*—that is, have nothing to do with each other—*dissonant*—the obverse of one element follows from the other—or *consonant*—one element follows from the other. Dissonance, then, refers to the strain or tension existing between two bits of knowledge, two attitudes, opinions, or values. . . .

.   .   .   .

The central hypothesis of the Theory of Cognitive Dissonance is that "the presence of dissonance gives rise to pressures to reduce that dissonance," [21] and that the pressure to reduce dissonance is related to the magnitude of the dissonance.

19/*Ibid.,* pp. 320-321.
20/L. Festinger, *A Theory of Cognitive Dissonance,* Stanford University Press, p. 260; 1957.
21/*Ibid.,* p. 263.

The ways of reducing dissonance consist of changing one of the dissonant elements of knowledge, opinion, attitude, or value; addition of new, consonant elements to support the decision taken, or; decreasing the importance of the dissonant elements of knowledge, opinion, attitude, or value.

The direct significance of this body of theory for police-Negro relations will be considered in the final section of the paper.

Culture Shock: A Foreign Service Conceptualization

Personnel recruited for overseas programs conducted by or through the United States Government generally undergo training at the Foreign Service Institute, just outside Washington, D.C. This training is designed to facilitate the socio-psychological adjustment of new personnel to life in a foreign culture.

. . . .

Culture shock has been called ". . . an occupational disease of people who have been suddenly transplanted abroad. Like most ailments it has its own etiology, symptoms, and cure." [22] It is attributable to the loss of the innumerable cultural cues—words, gestures, facial expression, customs or norms—which are indispensable to peace of mind and efficiency in conducting the ordinary affairs of daily life. Entry into a strange culture eliminates these long-standing props, and precipitates a reaction of anxiety and frustration, followed by rejection of the environment which causes the discomfort. Some of the symptoms of culture shock are dislike or fear of physical contact with the local population, fits of anger over minor frustrations, excessive fear of being cheated, robbed or injured, longing to talk to people who really make sense, desire for dependence on associates who have long experience in the strange culture.

There are four discernible stages in the culture shock syndrome. [23] The first is a kind of honeymoon period, lasting anywhere from a few days to several months depending on circumstances, during which the individual is fascinated by the novelty of the strange culture. He remains polite, friendly, and perhaps a bit self-effacing. The second stage begins when the individual settles down to a long-run confrontation with the real conditions of life in the strange culture, and the need for him to function effectively there. He becomes hostile and aggressive toward the culture and its people. He criticizes their way of life, and attributes his difficulties to deliberate troublemaking on their part; he seeks out others suffering from culture shock and, with them, develops elaborate stereotypical caricatures of the local people. This is a critical period. A few personnel never do adjust to the strange culture, and either leave the environment—voluntarily or involuntarily—or suffer debilitating emotional problems, and consequently ineffective relations with the local population. In the third stage the individual is beginning to open a way into the new cultural environment. He may take a

22/Michigan State University, *Vietnam Project Briefing Information,* East Lansing, p. 59; 1958.

23/Myrdal, *op. cit.,* pp. 59-64.

superior attitude to the local people, but he will joke about their behavior rather than bitterly criticize it. He is on his way to recovery. In the fourth stage the individual's adjustment is about as complete as it can be. He accepts the customs of the other culture as just another way of living.[24]

What is perhaps most significant in all of this, is that culture shock is recognized, expected, prepared for, and ameliorated by more or less systematic—if informal—means. Underlying this pattern is a basic assumption that culture shock is a form of sociopsychological maladjustment which is susceptible to treatment, and a transition to satisfactory adjustment, and effective cross-cultural relationships.

Police Interaction with Lower Class Negroes

First, to summarize: The exodus of approximately 5,000,000 Negroes from the rural South and their migration largely into the metropolitan areas of the North and West resulted in patterns of social adaptation unlike either their own previous folk culture of rural, southern life, or pre-existing urban, northern Negro life of the receiving areas. The social adaptations—sometimes called "survival techniques" in this paper—which rendered Negro life at least functionally possible in urban slums produced behavior patterns within the Negro community which are clearly at variance with the conventional norms of the larger society, conventional norms expressed by lower class Negro residents as "how things ought to be." . . .

Cognitive dissonance exists in the lower class Negro's simultaneous awareness of the conventional social norms of behavior, and the substituted norms by which he lives. There is also cognitive dissonance in his knowledge that this subcultural behavior does not work out nearly as well as most residents say it does. The means of reducing this cognitive dissonance are to reject the conventional cultural goals and legitimate means of accomplishing them, and to attach allegiance to other goals and means which bring behavior and norms into consonance. This, however, is a tensely balanced solution for the lower class Negro.

Enter the policeman, who has problems of his own. He is recruited from the middle and working classes, and as a result of historical racial segregation patterns, knows almost nothing of the Negro poverty subculture. His occupational socialization produces a self-conception centered upon crime-fighting and life-protection, and a set of subcultural perspectives which tend to reject all roles dissonant with this self-conception. The police officer assigned in any part of the community discovers that his radio assignments break down to approximately 85 per cent minor regulatory functions or service calls, 15 per cent serious crimes. In the latter cases, he is quickly supplanted by investigative personnel, so that he can return to radio service for additional service calls. The

24/Michigan State University, *op. cit.*

policeman who is assigned to work in predominantly lower-class Negro neighborhoods, in addition to the initial dissonance of function, experiences a culture shock reaction to the social strangeness, loss of familiar cues and symbols, and his inability to interact spontaneously with the Negro residents. He is anxious and frustrated upon discovering that his 21 or more years of social experience and the added perspectives of his new role utterly fail his needs in the first few encounters with lower class Negro behavior and problems. It is natural for him to react to this uncomfortable experience aggressively.

At the moment of police-Negro interaction, the officer is expecting something unpleasant—generally dissonant with his concept of police work, and the requirement that he maintain an orderly beat—in the form of infra-cultural, alien behavior. What comes across clearly to the lower-class Negro is a harsh, moralistic indictment of his way of life. For him, the result is a reactivation and intensification of the dissonance between conventional and lower class norms, between his community's ambivalent adherence to these lower-class norms and the hostile, superior reaction from institutionalized middle-class morality—the policeman.

. . . As far as it is recognized in the average police department, culture shock in young policemen appears to be considered a coming of age, in which the new officer is learning the proper way to regard the behavior of lower-class Negroes. Emotional support from contemporaries is offered, not so much to sensitize the young officer, but to toughen him to the problems of dealing with lower class behavior, and to crystallize this toughness.

It is of more serious consequence that the very adaptations, subcultural perspectives and behaviors which both the police and lower-class Negroes have developed as solutions to their problems, are the cognitive elements which are placed in severe dissonance, each by the other. Lower-class Negro behavior is dissonant with the police view of social order, morality and propriety; the implicitly moralistic evaluation of lower-class Negro life-style by policemen reactivates for the Negro dissonance between behavior and conventional ideals, up to then reduced by his subcultural solution.

If this linkage of concepts has any validity, it suggests that a genuine ameliorative intervention in the strained police-Negro relationship is not to be found at the level of discussion presently found in police-community relations programming, except insofar as this discussion is a phase of transition toward a restructuring of subcultural norms and behavior patterns. This kind of restructuring, almost by definition, cannot be initiated and sustained from within the subcultures because it presents a threat to painfully wrought solutions to the most pressing problems of those subcultures. It is equally clear that the admittance of instruments of change from outside these groups will require first of all some demonstration to both subcultures that change will indeed be progress.

18. The Negro Offender in a Northern Industrial Area*

VERNON FOX and JOANN VOLAKAKIS

The exact importance of the "racial" variable in crime causation is hidden by the many sociocultural factors which make the specific comparison of race and criminality extremely difficult. While most crime statistics reveal that Negro criminality far exceeds the "normal" volume of crimes of the non-Negro population, the disproportionate lower-class locus of the black population, where arrests are traditionally greater, enhances its arrest potential (*see* Strecher, Article 17). Even higher Negro prison commitment rates may reflect the lack of community facilities and specialized institutions for minority members rather than excessive minority criminality, as generally believed. Because the socially undesired may be quickly isolated from those who make this judgment by the imposition of a prison sentence, high black imprisonment rates may represent social problems which have been ignored rather than met in the past (*see* Bennett, Article 27). Even in cases involving the sexual deviant, the alcoholic, the mentally defective, the psychotic or the irresponsible parent, the jail or prison has frequently become a substitute facility for the community which has failed to provide treatment institutions (*see* National Profile, Article 28; and Stark, Article 31). A study of the significance of the racial factor in the length of prison sentences, for example, led Henry A. Bullock to conclude that "those who enforce the law conform to the norms of their local society concerning racial prejudice thus denying equality before the law." Even Negro juvenile offenders on the average tend to be less frequently placed on probation and more often institutionalized for less serious offenses.

While whites generally record higher crime rates for automobile theft, driving while intoxicated, embezzlement, fraud, forgery, counterfeiting, and sex offenses (other than rape), blacks reveal higher involvement in gambling, aggravated assault, illegal use of weapons, and robbery. Interestingly, the disproportionate involvement of white juveniles in auto theft, Wattenberg and Balistrieri believe, is due to the greater tendency of white than Negro delinquents to define the automobile as a prestige symbol within their peer groups. Consequently, criminal statistics, in effect, reflect the prejudices, social

*Reprinted with special permission from the *Journal of Criminal Law, Criminology and Police Science*, Copyright © 1956 by the Northwestern University School of Law, Volume 46, No. 5.

customs, and values of the community (*see* Kadish, Article 1; Taft, Article 2; Geis, Article 3; and Chilton, Article 4).

In the following selection Vernon Fox and Joann Volakakis quantitatively examine the characteristics and offenses of the Negro offender in the state of Michigan and find that he tends more often to commit larceny and certain crimes of violence. While a large proportion of the Negro violators are migrants from the South, their prison experience does not disillusion them sufficiently to encourage their return to that region.

Negroes are sentenced to prison in Michigan, a northern industrial State, with significantly greater frequency in proportion to the total population than are whites. The reason for the higher proportion of delinquency among Negroes in that state, according to Wiers, is that Negro migrants to Michigan had settled in cities which had already established a high rate of delinquency to which the newcomers merely conformed.[1] Taft generalizes that urbanization makes for crime, and the urbanization rate for Negroes has recently exceeded that of whites.[2] Reckless believes that the Negro has greater problems of adjustment in the United States than do whites and hence, has greater difficulty in conforming to law.[3]

Another phenomenon was observed in Michigan. In 1940, the population of the State of Michigan was 5,256,106, of which approximately four percent was Negro. With four percent Negro in its general population, the state had twenty percent Negro in its prison population. In 1950, the population of the State of Michigan was 6,371,766, with seven percent Negro in the general population and the proportion of Negroes in its prison population had risen to forty percent. While the proportion of Negroes in the prison population was rising appreciably in Michigan more rapidly than the whites, States like Missouri, Mississippi, Alabama, Georgia, and Florida held a rather constant proportion of Negroes in their prisons as compared with the proportion in the general populations of these States. With approximately twenty percent Negroes in its general population, for instance, they were but twenty-seven percent in the prison population in 1950. Other southern States showed similar figures. While the explanations and generalizations in the literature undoubtedly apply, further explanation is needed to account for Michigan's significant rise in proportion of Negroes in its prison population. One hypothesis may be that the Negro in contemporary American culture constitutes an entirely separate social group which, when transported to an unfamiliar socio-economic milieu, finds difficulty in adjusting.

This situation presented problems of administrative importance to corrections in northern industrial Michigan. With a general population of only seven percent

1/Paul Wiers, *Economic Factors in Michigan Delinquency*, New York, 1944; p. 37.
2/Donald R. Taft, *Criminology*, New York, 1947; p. 100.
3/Walter C. Reckless, *Criminal Behavior*, New York, 1940; p. 115.

Negro in 1950, the prison population was forty percent Negro. Should the emphasis in the prison program be shifted to accommodate a different cultural group on a permanent basis? If so, how should the shifts be made? ...

In order to determine some of the social, psychological, and occupational differences between Negroes and whites in the prison population, one thousand whites and one thousand Negroes were selected at random from the population of the State Prison of Southern Michigan at Jackson in May, 1951. All had arrived at the prison during the years 1949 and 1950. Tabulations were made on each group as to (1) offenses, (2) county of residence, (3) place of birth, (4) intelligence quotient, (5) grade claimed to have completed in school, (6) occupation, (7) marital status, (8) number of children, (9) religious preference, and (10) age. To determine the significance of the differences, critical ratios were computed on intelligence quotients, grades claimed completed in school, number of children, and age. The chi-square method was used in determining the significance of the differences in the other factors. In order to determine whether or not Negro in-migrants intended to remain in Michigan, one hundred Negroes who came to Michigan from other States during the period from 1940 to 1949, inclusive, were interviewed for another study in 1949 and 1950. Reasons for their coming to Michigan and whether or not they expected to remain were recorded.

RESULTS

The results of this study showed a statistically significant difference in the types of crimes for which the Negroes and whites were sentenced. The comparisons of the offenses are shown in Table 1. The Negroes tended to commit more (1) homicide, (2) assault, (3) larceny, and (4) narcotics violations. The last consisted mostly in possession of marijuana. Whites tended to commit more (1) burglary, (2) forgery, (3) embezzlement, and (4) drunk and disorderly offenses. ...

... Significantly more Negroes were sentenced from Detroit and Wayne County, and the other industrial areas of southeastern Michigan. Significantly more whites were sentenced from the industrial areas of western Michigan and in the rural and other areas of northern Michigan [Table 2]. ... Of the 1,000 Negroes in the sample, 801 came from Detroit, with the rest of Michigan contributing only 199. Twelve Negroes came from agricultural counties, one from the up-state cut-over area, and none from the upper peninsula. Of the 186 Negroes who came from the industrial areas, the large majority came from industrial areas near Detroit. Significantly more whites came from industrial areas other than Detroit and from all other socio-economic areas.

More than half of the whites were natives of Michigan, while less than a quarter of the Negroes were natives of the state. ... This shows a considerable shift from the prewar, wartime, and early postwar periods when the number of

TABLE 1
Offenses for Which Negroes and Whites Were Sentenced

Offenses	Whites		Negroes		Total
	Observed	Expected	Observed	Expected	
Homicide	21	41.0	61	41.0	82
Rape	45	35.5	26	35.5	71
Robbery	132	137.5	143	137.5	275
Aggravated assault	21	45.5	69	45.5	90
Other assault	7	7.0	7	7.0	14
Burglary	289	246.5	204	246.5	493
Larceny	120	157.5	195	157.5	315
Auto theft	61	67.0	73	67.0	134
Property offenses	2	5.0	8	5.0	10
Forgery	72	54.0	37	54.0	109
Embezzlement	57	44.5	32	44.5	89
Carrying weapons	12	18.0	24	18.0	36
Marriage laws	3	3.5	4	3.5	7
Sex offenses	55	51.0	47	51.0	102
Offenses against family	24	19.0	14	19.0	38
Drug laws	2	18.0	34	18.0	36
Traffic violations	3	2.5	2	2.5	5
Liquor laws	0	1.5	3	1.5	3
Drunk and disorderly	13	7.5	2	7.5	15
Gambling	10	7.5	5	7.5	15
Other major offenses	10	5.5	1	5.5	11
Miscellaneous	41	25.0	9	25.0	50

TABLE 2
Negroes and Whites Sentenced from Various Socio-Economic Areas

Area	Whites		Negroes		Total
	Observed	Expected	Observed	Expected	
Upper peninsula	1	0.5	0	0.5	1
Upstate cutover	65	33.0	1	33.0	66
Agricultural	125	68.5	12	68.5	137
Industrial	446	316.0	186	316.0	632
Wayne	363	583	801	582.0	1,164

southern Negroes sentenced to Michigan's prisons significantly exceeded both the whites and the Michigan-born Negroes. . . .

It is suspected that two factors may account for this shift. First, the same processes of culture conflict and its attendant disorganization by which second generation immigrants manifest higher crime rates than the immigrants themselves or the third generation, may be at work in the cases of northern-born

Negro children to southern-born parents. . . . Second, the Negro boys who were arriving in prison in 1949-50 had gone through middle and late adolescence during the time when Detroit was the "Arsenal of Democracy" with the highest wages in the land, where southern Negroes were experiencing northern freedom, and social values were shifting to the extent that the famous Detroit race riot broke out in June, 1943. That this race riot was part of the shifting social values is illustrated by the fact that the men arrested and sentenced to prison on charges growing out of that race riot were primarily southern Negroes and southern whites. These two in-migrant groups were trying to settle their conflicts in a northern industrial area where the southern institutionalized racial controls to which each group had become accustomed were absent. . . .

Interviews with 100 in-migrant Negroes in 1949-50 indicated that 92 intended to remain in Michigan for the rest of their lives, three intended to return "home" and five were undecided or did not want to commit themselves to permanent residence. All objected to the winters in Michigan, which they considered to be severe, but the majority considered the economic opportunity and greater social freedom worth enduring the winter. . . .

The mean age for the whites was 36.6, as compared with 34.0 for the Negroes. . . .

The marital status of the whites differed significantly from that of the Negroes [Table 3]. . . . The greatest difference was the large number of

TABLE 3
Marital Status of Negro and White Prisoners

Marital Status	Whites		Negroes		Total
	Observed	Expected	Observed	Expected	
Single	354	340.5	327	340.5	681
Married	305	267.0	229	267.0	534
Separated	74	125.0	176	125.0	250
Common law	28	84.5	141	84.5	169
Divorced	207	146.5	86	146.5	293
Widowed	32	36.5	41	36.5	73

common-law relationships among the Negroes. A fifth of the whites were divorced while less than a tenth of the Negroes were divorced. A greater number of Negroes was separated. Whites and Negroes were single with approximately similar frequency, 354 and 327, respectively. The pattern was one of greater fluidity in marital status among the Negroes, with less regard for ceremonial marriage. The average number of children in both groups was 1.7, with no difference indicated.

. . . More whites were in the skilled, the agricultural, and the clerical and sales occupations. More Negroes were in the unskilled industrial and the service occupations [Table 4].

Comparison of religious preferences shows significant differences in all demoninations, as listed in Table 5. One-tenth of the whites and only half that proportion of Negroes claimed atheism. Most of the Negroes, but little more than half the whites were Protestants. One-tenth of the Negroes were Catholic

TABLE 4
Occupational Classifications of Incarcerated Negroes and Whites

Occupational Classification	Whites		Negroes		Total
	Observed	Expected	Observed	Expected	
Professional and managerial	46	38.5	31	38.5	77
Clerical and sales	74	48.5	23	48.5	97
Service occupations	79	113.5	148	113.5	227
Agriculture	137	92.0	47	92.0	184
Skilled	140	101.0	62	101.0	202
Semi-skilled	341	360.5	380	360.5	721
Unskilled	183	246.0	309	246.0	492

TABLE 5
Religions of Incarcerated Whites and Negroes

Religion	Whites		Negroes		Totals
	Observed	Expected	Observed	Expected	
Protestant	533	698.5	844	698.5	1,397
Catholic	330	213.0	96	213.0	426
Mohammedan	0	4.0	8	4.0	8
Jewish	13	6.5	0	6.5	13
Atheism	104	78.0	52	78.0	156

and one percent of the Negroes claimed Mohammedanism. Thirteen Jewish persons were among the whites. . . .

Differences in intelligence between Negroes and whites were significant as tested by the Bregman (1941) revision of the Army Alpha. The I.Q.'s of the whites averaged 96.6, while the mean I.Q. for the Negroes was 83.4. A critical ratio of 39.0 indicates that this difference is highly significant. The whites claimed to have completed 8.6 grades in school (unverified) and the Negroes claimed to have completed 8.0 grades in school (unverified). Because of the value the Negroes seemed to place on education, the unverified claims of the grades they completed in school must be accepted with some reservation. It is noted that on the New Stanford Achievement Test, the whites averaged 7.6 grades retained while the Negroes averaged 5.2 grades in 1949.

At any rate, it is obvious that the Negro offender in Michigan differs considerably from the white prisoner in terms of types of crime committed; he is concentrated in and around Detroit; type of marital behavior; occupations; and intelligence as measured by pencil-and-paper test. Some differences can be shown in religious preferences and southern or out-of-state nativity. While only a few years ago, the vast majority of Negro prisoners in Michigan were from Georgia, Alabama, Tennessee, Mississippi, and Arkansas, by 1949-50, the number of Michigan-born Negroes had increased so that the out-of-state Negroes, while still in the majority, had dropped below the level of statistical significance in proportion to the native and out-of-state whites.

CONCLUSIONS

The Negro offender in a northern industrial area tends to commit more assaultive and larceny offenses. The Negro prisoner is generally sentenced from industrial Detroit or the industrial areas around Detroit. While a large proportion of the Negro offenders was born in Georgia, Alabama, Tennessee, Mississippi, and Arkansas, the sons of migrants from the South, the Michigan-born Negro offenders, were beginning to reduce the formerly overwhelming significance of the original in-migrant group. . . .

As a group, the Negro offenders tended to be nearly three years younger than the whites. Their marital status showed greater fluidity and less regard for ceremonial marriage, although the proportion of single men and the number of children in the Negro and white groups were similar. Religious differences were present, with Protestantism prevalent in 53 percent of the whites and 84 percent of the Negroes. The Negroes reported less atheism, Judaism, and Catholicism, and more Mohammedanism. The Negroes scored considerably below the white group on paper-and-pencil tests of intelligence.

From the practical administrative viewpoint, it was obvious that the Negro group had come to industrial Michigan to stay, and a program had to be devised to effect the greatest benefit for the group. Plans had to be made to expand industrial trade training and on-the-job vocational training in the areas most selected by Negroes. This meant an expansion of the technical foundry program and the welding school, two areas in which the parole officers in Detroit had found most success in placing Negro parolees. The agricultural program was not expanded for the Negro group because they were not interested in it, and they were not going to be placed in agriculture after parole. The elementary school had to be expanded because of the limited education the Negroes showed on tests and the value they placed on academic achievement. An important phase of the program pointed out by this study was group discussions which had to be planned at the same elementary educational level for these adult southern Negroes or Michigan-born sons of southern Negroes. Some assistance had to be afforded them in gaining sufficient insight into cultural differences and changes from living with institutionalized prejudices to living with competitive prejudices in a northern industrial area so that adjustment in and around Detroit would present fewer problems.

The migration of the southern Negro to Michigan for permanent residence, then, had its influence in shifting the prison program to meet a changing need. No need for shifts in basic therapeutic program was discovered. The shift was in expansion of educational facilities already present in the direction of need as shown by a minority group which had grown to constitute 40 percent of the prison population where that minority group constituted only 7 percent of the State's total population. A further new program to be instituted as a result of this study was the examining in group discussion of cultural changes and compromises necessary for social adjustment when a new group with different social characteristics and values moves into a northern industrial area.

part FIVE

Law Enforcement

The modern police mission has become extremely complex and in many instances highly hazardous (*see* Wolfgang, Article 7). Because police work by its very nature demands police and citizen contact under tense and emotional conditions, the policeman is always subject to overt attempts to harm his person. However, the greatest number of offenders coming into contact with the police do not disclose violence patterns. The most frequent police-citizen contacts occur in traffic violations, drunkenness arrests, delinquency apprehensions, or simply attempts to quell family disorder (*see* Kadish, Article 1). The delicate nature of modern police work, however, demands especially qualified and highly competent enforcement officers. Police who are at war with society are often as much of a social threat as the criminal who is warring against the public.

Much of the fundamental conflict is related to enforcement philosophy which is expressed in views ranging between the concept of full or total enforcement and a mere police presence in order to maintain law and order. Full enforcement, with its ensuing prosecution of offenders, however, leads to totalitarian police control; the mere presence of the police without use of arrest powers, on the other hand, may cause a form of community anarchy. The police, therefore, are continually under the injunction to represent law and order and still to represent the public at large. While police power is used ineffectively in some social situations (*see* Violence in Chicago, Article 34), it has been neutralized by political interference in others.

Although law enforcement standards have been rising during the past three decades, the courts have been demanding even greater progress (*see* Bilek, Article 22). The problems posed by unreasonable searches and seizures, student and other demonstrations, station-house detention, methods of questioning, and questionable use of enforcement powers have come under increasing attack in the post World War II years. Constitutional guarantees of due process, right to counsel, probable cause, privilege against self-incrimination, prompt court action, and free speech and peaceful assembly have been increasingly defined as the courts have attempted to delineate individual rights in a mass society which demands greater conformity and tends to limit individuality.

The development of the electronic and communications industries has forced a reevaluation of the traditional constitutional guarantees. However, the *Escobedo* judgment, which made criminal lawyers available to persons charged for serious crimes, and the *Miranda* decision, which held that all arrested persons must be informed of their rights before the police begin an interrogation, were immediately denounced by the police as an intrusion into their activities at the same time enforcement officials were demanding the right to use electronic eavesdropping and wire-tapping techniques in order to fight the war against crime. But the crime problem is not enforcement's private conflict and will never be controlled until a correct emphasis is placed upon the basic nature of the crime problem. While the 1968 crime bill signed by the President modified many of these restrictions and served to lessen antagonism, it did little to solve the basic problem inherent in the lack of offender detection.

Because police power can either order or coerce a society, its consequences are mighty. An unrestrained use of power makes the loss of individual rights inevitable. However, the minimization of the police potential allows the unhindered continuity of criminal activity. And yet the average ratio of 1.7 policemen per thousand citizens reveals the limited number of enforcement officials available for any type of police task. Although the 1967 President's Crime Commission suggested that police functions should be divided among three officer types, termed the community service officer, the police officer, and the police agent, traditional systems have been slow to accept this suggestion. Under these provisions, the *community service officer,* a young man typically between 17 and 21 with the necessary aptitude, integrity, and stability to perform police work, would work as an apprentice policeman. Replacing the present police cadet, he would engage in street surveillance under the supervision and in close cooperation with the police officer and police agent. Although he would not possess full enforcement powers or carry arms, he would operate within the community, performing service duties which would bring needy persons into contact with community or city agencies. While the *police officer* would perform the normal police duties of law enforcement and crime investigation, he would be of lesser rank than the police agent. The officer would respond to selected called-for services, perform routine patrol, enforce traffic regulations, render emergency service, and investigate traffic accidents. The *police agent,* on the other hand, would enter the enforcement process with at least two years of college work and preferably a baccalaureate degree in the liberal arts or social sciences. He would assume responsibility for the most complicated, demanding, or sensitive jobs, working as a juvenile officer, community-relations officer, or a career specialist in narcotics, robbery, or homicide investigation. Although he might be assigned other staff or investigative duties, he would represent the most knowledgeable element of the police team and would guide and advise community service officers in their enforcement function.

The questions of law enforcement are not restricted to these levels, however.

While William Dienstein examines the sociology of law enforcement in a paper presented to the Second National Symposium of Law Enforcement Science and Technology, Elaine and Ian Cumming and Laura Edell evaluate the roles of the policeman as philosopher, guide, and friend. But these are not their only roles. Albert J. Reiss, Jr. suggests that the police also have another role facet which is largely unknown to middle- and upper-class citizens. Police brutality, a dimension of the misuse of police power, may also be evidenced in the police role (*also see* Strecher, Article 17).

19. Sociology of Law Enforcement*

WILLIAM DIENSTEIN

The proper nature of the police role is a central question in the sociology of law enforcement. What role should the police play in fashioning and implementing a meaningful law enforcement policy in their community? Since the police possess the power both to aid and to coerce, many persons are loathe to allow the police a policy-making position in community affairs. On the other hand, because the police are centrally located within the functioning community system, they are able to offer particular insights into specific community problems which others may overlook. Police, however, are too often denied the status, training, and resources necessary to complete their most difficult enforcement tasks. Although American society has continuously attempted to keep police power under civilian control, the growing need to integrate law enforcement agencies into a coherent program of community organization and development can no longer be denied.

Because the resources made available to law enforcement are insufficient, it is impossible to enforce all criminal laws. Even if adequate resources were provided, the full enforcement of criminal law would create a form of enforcement totalitarianism, leading to the arrest of those persons who violate less serious criminal statutes but whose normal action is not serious enough to subject them to the full impact of the criminal process. The overdependence upon law as a means of encouraging social conformity (*see* Kadish, Article 1; and Lohman, Article 35) leads to the definition of more behavior as criminal than is necessary, desirable, or even controllable. Where this does occur, it is due, Frank J. Remington suggests, to the overgeneralization of criminal statutes, evident, for example, in the extension of gambling laws to the citizen's home in the attempt to limit the activity of the professional gambler and his floating "crap game."

*Portions of a paper presented at the Second National Symposium on Law Enforcement Science and Technology, April 16, 1968.

The tendency to use criminal law to reflect class aspirations rather than actual achievable community goals, too, is ultimately involved in the overextension process (*see* Empey and Erickson, Article 15).

To prohibit the police from sharing in policy-making decisions only serves to further aggravate many current law enforcement problems (*see* Cumming, Cumming, and Edell, Article 20). Recent Supreme Court decisions designed to control police malpractice through the exclusion of illegally seized evidence from the criminal trial merely focus upon law enforcement weaknesses without redressing their shortcomings. The cry that the Supreme Court is handcuffing the police merely camouflages the fact that law enforcement in recent years has been progressively failing to apprehend both property and personal offenders. By default, the Supreme Court has been forced to demand changes in policy, which police and community authorities have neglected, by refusal to accept evidence gained in violation of the constitution as valid evidence in criminal trials. Government officials, too, have been required to coordinate enforcement functions and responsibilities with the needs and interests of the total community (*see* Reiss, Article 21).

If a court decision fails to reflect the legitimate needs of the enforcement agency, the police often react by asserting that the courts should remain free of the enforcement business. Such an assumption, however, is not only unrealistic but may actually be harmful to future society. The courts must continue to act as societal representatives to determine whether a governmental agency has abused the rights of the individual or its own prescribed power. In like manner, however, the courts must also decide at what point the individual has violated the legitimate functions of law and order as represented by the police. Such questions should not be the exclusive concerns of either law enforcement or the courts but properly involve a dialogue of the society and the two agencies involved. Government emerges from the people; law enforcement and the courts are products of the human group. When either fails to fulfill its allotted social responsibilities and preempts a domain of power for its own vested interests, the interests of neither the agencies nor the society are fulfilled.

The sociology of law enforcement, William Dienstein argues, must investigate the functions and roles of the police officer. Law enforcement is not only a form of human interaction but also the social conscience of the people in operation. If it becomes mere force, social organization passes from a *policed society* to a *police state.*

The basic premise of sociology is the assumption that human behavior is the result of indentifiable processes and forces. Therefore the sociologist seeks to identify some of these forces and processes.

As we are able to identify these processes and forces we can predict behavior. To the degree we are able to control these forces we can influence behavior.

There are numerous obstacles in the study of human behavior. Four significant obstacles are:

1. Cherished beliefs (emotionally held beliefs).
2. Unwillingness to accept the verifiable and valid findings of sociological or other research.
3. Inability to accept conclusions based upon research findings.
4. Inability to think in generalizations.

Let us consider one of these obstacles, cherished beliefs. Often these emotionally held beliefs appear to be insurmountable, since they are accepted as self-evident "truths." These "truths" are proved throughout one's lifetime by means of selective observation. We observe only those occurrences which support our beliefs and fail to register those occurrences which deny our beliefs.

Our cherished beliefs are basic to a social process which is called the "self-fulfilling prophecy." On the basis of these beliefs we falsely define a situation as real. We act on the false definition. The consequences of our action are real. We use the consequences to prove the original false definition.

For example, when a society interprets darkness of skin as a sign that an individual is mentally inferior, lazy, incompetent, and irresponsible, that society automatically sets up forces and processes that will make its interpretations (predictions) come true.

The social definition of the physical characteristic possessed by an individual is negative. The expectations triggered by the negative definition set into operation social and institutional forces that enforce behavioral conformity to the social definition. The victim is trapped by the definition, succumbs to it, acts out the expectations, and "proves" the social definition.

. . . When a person has been identified as a member of a particular group, then no matter what he does, it can be used against him through another social process called "moral transmutation."

Cherished beliefs make up our social climate. We seldom question them since they are transmitted informally through daily interaction from childhood. As a consequence, our personalities tend to be structured around them. Too often a cherished belief becomes a keystone of personality. When it does, questioning the validity of the belief violently threatens the person. He cannot allow himself to be intimidated by the facts.

All of this relates to law enforcement. Law enforcement functions to control the behavior of people. Its purpose is to maintain order by applying the laws of the society to the actions of its members. Law enforcement is human interaction.

In contemporary urban society law enforcement is much more than the exercise of procedures and the application of technology to the problem of crime control.

Law enforcement in the contemporary urban society is the social conscience of the people in operation. Therein lies the source of many of the difficulties in law enforcement.

The police operate under the law. Laws are enacted by legislative bodies. Laws are restrictions on behavior by demanding compliance to prohibitions or prescriptions.

There tends to be agreement on actions which injure others or destroy property. But there is less than agreement on laws which prohibit actions where there are no victims, other than the doer. These are known as sumptuary laws and are designed to regulate behaviors primarily on moral or religious grounds and are traditionally regarded as justified under the police power of the state.

Such behaviors as alcoholism, drug addiction, use and abuse of dangerous drugs and narcotics, suicide, sexual activities between consenting adults, and pornography illustrate the category of sumptuary laws.

Most police recognize these sumptuary laws as "unenforceable laws." These laws attempt to achieve a religious or moral consensus in a heterogeneous society through criminal punishment.

When there is lack of consensus about the validity of a law, the enforcement becomes a matter of discretion which can be interpreted as unequal treatment.

Since most action of the police is reactive, that is, responding to a complaint, the requirement of sumptuary laws is different. Action on sumptuary laws requires discovery of violation which requires moving into areas where violations may occur. This aggressive action by enforcement invites enforcement behaviors that challenge some of our basic political ideology—invasions of privacy by various means.

The point is that law enforcement does not operate in a vacuum. It is an integral part of a complex web of behaviors. That web is as broad as the American society and all that it implies.

American society is a heterogeneous composite of people and activities. Its people are stratified on economic levels and differentiated on occupational, educational, religious, ethnic, racial, and a multitude of other factors. Because of these differences, groups and categories so classified develop points of view. These points of view reflect the way in which self and society are perceived by its members. The way in which the self and society are perceived is determined by what has happened to the person—his life experiences.

The operation of the self-fulfilling prophecy may be applied here and is not limited to physical characteristics. It operates in relation to *any* characteristic, be it physical, social, or fictional. When these characteristics are ascribed to a person, they influence his life from the moment of birth.

We do have an open-ended social system, and people do move up and down the economic ladder. Even with movement, previous experiences remain and influence what is done and how it is done. However, findings do indicate various life styles—the poor learn to behave differently than do the affluent. Life chances vary with category of parent. A person born into a poverty family in a rural area of black parents will have life chances much different from a person born into an affluent family in an urban area of white, Protestant parents. These are the facts of society, however we may respond to them.

Governments are instituted among men for the purpose of setting up a structure that will permit the interaction of numerous divergent and complementary activities necessary to aggregate living.

Basic to governments are political ideals, sometimes articulated in documents. These provide the guidelines for goals. The United States Constitution sets the goals for American society in general terms and specifies limitations on the manner of achievement. The United States Constitution implies that means and ends must be consistent and one is as important as the other. We cannot justify how we do in terms of what we seek. Yet this has become a fragment of the American dilemma. Do goals justify means?

American political ideology encourages the availability of legitimate avenues for the redress of grievances; for every "beef" there is an acceptable way for making it known and getting action.

When legitimate ways of expressing grievances are unknown to the aggrieved, or blocked, then illegitimate ways may be utilized to direct the attention of the society to the conditions which are basic to the grievance.

When illegitimate avenues are utilized to redress grievances (real or alleged), then the issue changes from what it is that creates the disaffection, disenchantment, frustration, or strain, to what is being done.

When what is being done to call attention to the grievances is in violation of the law, then the police are utilized to "maintain order."

The confrontation between the aggrieved and the police may be interpreted in various ways.

The aggrieved may view the police as *the* device used by the power structure or establishment to prevent them from their rightful expression and achievement. The police may view the aggrieved as violators who are disrupting the social system.

The police view the disorder as a hostile outburst requiring immediate reaction. They are not concerned at the moment about the history of the development of the conditions that made the outburst probable.

The aggrieved view the police as the "cause" of their grievances. The immediacy of the confrontation changes the issue from one of expressing accumulated grievances to overcoming the immediate obstacle, the police.

At this point let us consider another approach.

In a rural-oriented society (and somehow many wish for the return to ruralism), the police function was interpreted in terms of interpersonal interaction on a one-to-one basis: the policeman and the violator. The policeman in a rural society was a neighbor. He knew the community and its members. He was recognized as a human being. He recognized the violator as a human being. He personified the social conscience of the community and was accepted as such. His authority lay in his badge of office and the community's acceptance of him.

When Officer Johns picked up a juvenile offender, he knew the youth, the parents, their background. Disposition was made on the basis of familiarity. Seldom did the parents question the facts of the allegation against the juvenile. Officer Johns said so; therefore it was so. After all, they had known Officer Johns as a boy.

In frontier communities, police authority when challenged was supported by force. Modern mass media of communication are replete with "Westerners" reflecting the personalization of the law into the body of the sheriff, or marshal, or deputy. The theme revolves about the good guy versus the bad guy, the white hat against the black hat. (It is most interesting to note that the good guys have to be identified by headgear.)

With this indoctrination the consequence that policemen may view their function as a personal one, that is, the good guys versus the bad guys, should be expected. A policeman's activity is confrontation with the violators who must be overcome. From this develops the attitude that may be labeled the "personalization of offenders and offenses."

The violators' actions are interpreted as a violation not only against society, but also against the policeman. A subtle transmutation occurs. The violator becomes a personal antagonist. The consequence is a battle between the policeman and the offender.

On the other hand, the violator interprets the policeman's action as an attack on his person. The violator sees the policeman as a personal antagonist. The battle is between the violator and the policeman.

When this transmutation occurs, gone is the reality that the violator has harmed society by his behavior. The social implications of violation and enforcement are suppressed and removed by conversion to personal combat.

The policeman who represents an official governmental agency, can justify his attitude and behavior in the name of the community. How he acts is justified on the one hand by his protecting the community (social) and on the other hand by punishing an evil-doer (personal) who deserves no better.

The violator views the policeman as an obstacle to his achievement as a representative of the establishment (social) and as a person to be defeated (personal).

As a consequence of this attitudinal transmutation of violation from social to personal, law enforcement in the American society is looked upon all too often as a game—competition between two persons or two groups.

Interpreting law enforcement as a game between policeman and violator is a delusion modern urban society can no longer support.

We must recognize that good guys and bad guys do not spring full blown from the environment. They develop within the environment and are molded by the force and processes that are permitted to prevail.

Law enforcement must encourage the kinds of studies and changes that will make it a viable, interdependent, effective function. The police must reevaluate their functions and roles. They must call upon the assistance of the social

sciences as well as the physical sciences in this reevaluation. Perhaps the police are required to engage in contradictory behaviors. Perhaps functions should be redefined. Can police prevent and enforce in the traditional sense? Should police be a political police and a morals police as well as a criminal police?

Much research must be done to discover what happens between and among personnel in law enforcement and between law enforcement personnel and offenders and nonoffenders.

Let me close with one observation: It seems to be impossible financially for any modern metropolis to provide enough policemen to control a significant segment of its population that engages in a hostile outburst.

Recent disturbances and riots illustrate that no community will have enough policemen to control mass hostilities.

Society must be made aware that laws are not operational. They are merely commands or prohibitions which must be enforced. To the police has been delegated the task of implementing laws by enforcement. But delegation of enforcement cannot bring about compliance with law unless there is positive community involvement. Control does not and cannot lie with law enforcement alone.

When social control depends entirely on force, we have converted from a *policed* society to a *police state.*

20. Policeman as Philosopher, Guide, and Friend*

ELAINE CUMMING, IAN CUMMING, and LAURA EDELL

The modern crisis in law enforcement has been created by the metropolitan distribution of the population, the changing characteristics of urban areas, the nature of the urban police mission, the tendencies of the public to develop polar and antagonistic positions toward the police, the changing character of urban power groups, and the large-scale development of police bureaucratization. Mere advancements in training, equipment, and police administration, Gordon E. Misner suggests, are insufficient responses to the changing character of the police mission. While the modern police are better trained, equipped, and administered than at any time in previous history, they have not reached a level of full effectiveness. Although standard police duties continue to include such

*Reprinted from *Social Problems,* journal of The Society for the Study of Social Problems, Volume 12, Number 3 (Winter, 1965), pp. 276-86, with permission of the editors and authors.

responsibilities as crime prevention, repression, apprehension, and investigation; public service; maintenance of peace and security; regulation of noncriminal conduct; traffic regulation and control; and additional provisions for emergency services, traditional police training and structures, Misner argues, are no longer adequate. Because the policeman on duty may spend up to 90 percent of his time in activities which are noncriminal in orientation, much of his potential daily effort in the community is unused. This minimal use of the so-called "dead time," when the officer is available for assignment to duties other than the investigation of a criminal offense, suggests that traditional policing methods fail to consider the need for adjustments in primary and secondary police-community relationships. While automotive patrol, for example, represents mobile police presence within the community, it fails to develop strong community-police commitments. Although such a "conspicuous" patrol serves a preventive function, the actual effectiveness of this method is uncertain. The tendency to evaluate effective law enforcement in terms of the volume of crime reported to the police and completed arrests fails to consider the "exchange" and "hostility" costs which ensue to the police as a result of their added "effectiveness."

Nowhere is the reputational cost more apparent than among minority groups (see Strecher, Article 17). Existing police-community tensions make it largely impossible to reduce violent crime substantially in minority areas (see Fox and Volakakis, Article 18; and Reiss, Article 21). The unwillingness of minority groups to accept previous status limitations, the frequent police physical and verbal abuse of citizens, and the nature of police activity make such tensions difficult to resolve. Mere professionalization of the policeman is not enough. Ultimately involved is a new concept of police activity which will bring policemen to a new conception of the enforcement function and personal role commitments. The service role of the police must balance the more coercive enforcement function. Elaine and Ian Cumming and Laura Edell suggest that the policeman must expand his role to include the roles of philosopher, guide, and friend.

This is the fourth report from a group of studies designed to throw some light upon the division of labor among the social agents whose central role is concerned with maintaining social integration by controlling various forms of deviant behavior.[1]

In earlier reports, we have adopted the convention of looking at social agents and agencies in terms of their relatively supportive or relatively controlling

[1]/Earlier reports include: Elaine Cumming, "Phase Movement in the Support and Control of the Psychiatric Patient," *Journal of Health and Human Behavior,* 3 (Winter, 1962), pp. 235-241; Isabel McCaffrey, Elaine Cumming and Claire Rudolph, "Mental Disorders in Socially Defined Populations," *American Journal of Public Health,* 53 (July, 1963), pp. 1025-1030; Elaine Cumming and Charles Harrington, "Clergyman as Counselor," *American Journal of Sociology,* LXIX (November, 1963), pp. 234-243.

character. We have assumed that it is difficult for an agent to exercise both support and control at the same time and that any agent tends, therefore, to specialize in one or the other aspect of the integrative process.[2] Even when he is specialized, such an agent may be considered controlling when he is compared with some agents, and supportive when compared with others. Thus, the probation officer is more on the client's side, that is, supportive to him, than the policeman, but less so than the psychiatrist. Furthermore, the agent may be seen as supportive by the layman but experienced as controlling by the client, and *vice versa.* For example, the prisoner remanded by the court for psychiatric treatment may well experience his hospitalization as incarceration. Conversely, a chronic alcoholic may be grateful, in mid-winter, for a night in prison.

There is another aspect to this duality in the handling of deviance. While it is probably impossible to perform acts of support and control simultaneously, support without control is overprotection and invites passivity and dependency, while control without support is tyranny and invites rebellion. While the agent may specialize in one aspect of social control of deviance, the other must, nevertheless, be part of his repertoire.[3] Thus while physicians and clergymen are generally supportive of people in pain or trouble, such people are expected, in return, to perform appropriately the role of patient or parishioner. The support is overt, the control is latent. In general, the agent's training and professional ethics focus on the skills needed for the overt part of his role; the latent aspects are derived from and governed by general norms and values. Role conflict can be avoided in part by keeping the "contradictory" side of a role latent.

The policeman's role in an integrative system is, by definition and by law, explicitly concerned with control—keeping the law from being broken and apprehending those who break it—and only latently with support. For example, if you break the law, you can expect to be arrested, but if you go along quietly, you can, unless there is a special circumstance, expect to be treated reasonably.[4] In the course of controlling one member of society, moreover, the policeman often provides indirect support to another. For example, when he apprehends, and thus controls a wife-beating husband, he supports the wife, just as, in a reverse situation, the doctor controls the behavior of those attending a patient when he prescribes rest and sympathy. Finally, besides latent support, the policeman often gives direct help to people in certain kinds of trouble. When he does this, the balance between support and control has shifted, and he is acting

2/This assumption is derived in part from studies of the division of labor in small groups (see, for example, Bales' "The Equilibrium Problem in Small Groups," in T. Parsons and R. F. Bales, *Working Papers in the Theory of Action,* Glencoe: The Free Press, 1953), and upon theories of role conflict [see, for example, W. J. Goode, "A Theory of Role Strain," *American Sociological Review,* 25 (August, 1960), pp. 483-495.]

3/Certain highly skilled agents, such as psychoanalysts, may be able to phase their activities so that they are supportive in certain phases of the treatment and controlling in others.

4/For an excellent discussion of the many problems inherent in the controlling function of the police, see ed. Claude R. Sowle, *Police Power and Individual Freedom,* Chicago: Aldine, 1962.

overtly as a supportive agent and only latently in his controlling role. He has, at the same time, changed from a professional to an amateur. This paper reports a study of the requests for help received by a city police department and the policeman's response to them, with special attention to what is assumed here to be the latent side of his role.

METHOD OF STUDY

Because there seems to be no systematic account of the day-to-day activities of policemen, two specific questions were posed: (1) What kinds of calls for help do policemen get, and (2) How do they answer them? Two kinds of data were collected. First, a total of 801 incoming telephone calls at the police complaint desk in a metropolitan police department were observed over a total of 82 hours. These hours were not evenly distributed around the 24 hours, for reasons connected with the field worker, not with the Police Department. As each complaint was received and disposed of, a description was dictated into a tape recorder. Fourteen selected prowl car calls were then observed. At the end of this phase of the study, the worker submitted field notes concerned with the general culture of the police station. Secondly, interviews were conducted with detectives concerning their special assignments. A formulation of the nature of the policeman's supporting role was then constructed from these data.

RESULTS

The Complaint Desk. Figure 1 shows that the hourly distribution of police calls in the first part of the week from the last part of the week. The daily peak activity is between the evening hours of seven and eight o'clock excepting for Thursday, Friday and Saturday when it is between nine and ten. (Because of the gaps in the data, there is a possibility that there is a peak at about noon in the first part of the week, but on both theoretical and common-sense grounds, it seems unlikely.) The last part of the week also shows a greater volume of calls than the first. In general, the high rate of calls in the evening and on weekends suggests that problems arise when the social pulse is beating fast—when people are coming and going, regrouping, and, of course, engaging in informal rather than formal activities.

In order to interpret these rhythms further, the 801 calls were classified according to their content, as Table 1 shows. One hundred and forty-nine, or 18.6 per cent of the calls, were excluded from analysis; 88 of these were call-backs on earlier complaints, 33 were requests for information only, and 28 were outside this police department's jurisdiction.[5] The remaining 652 calls were for service within the purview of these police. They are treated as independent,

---

5/The latter two groups (61 calls) were excluded because there was no chance of a car being sent, and therefore they could not be compared with the remainder.

FIGURE 1
Average Police Calls per Hour, First Part of the Week (6 a.m. Sunday-5 a.m. Thursday)
and Second Part of the Week (6 a.m. Thursday-5 a.m. Sunday)

NUMBER OF CALLS
PER HOUR

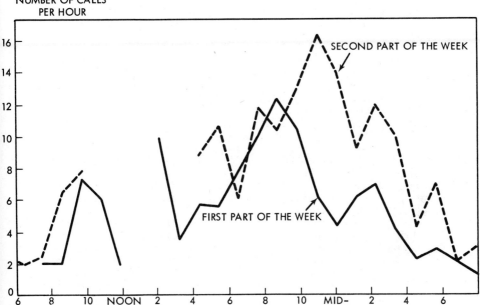

but the unit of analyses is the call, and not the caller, and results must be interpreted with this in mind.

The 652 calls included in the study were divided into two major groups: the first included calls for service in connection with things or possessions, while the second included calls for support or assistance with regard to problems of health, safety or interpersonal relationships.[6]

The first (nearly one-third of the total of 801 calls) include traffic violations, reports of losses or thefts, calls about unlocked doors, fallen power wires and so on. These are part of the regular controlling function of the police and are not the main focus of this paper. The second major group (about one-half of all calls) is concerned with personal problems and therefore may reasonably be expected to include the need or desire for some form of support. These calls were subdivided into two types: (1) persistent problems occurring throughout the week; and (2) periodic problems occurring mainly on the weekend.

As Table 1 shows, the first type comprises 230 calls, of which about one-third are requests for health services, that is, ambulance escorts, investigation of

6/It was surprisingly easy to classify the calls on these two major dimensions and coders had no trouble getting over 90% agreement. Differences were reconciled in conferences.

TABLE 1
Classification of Calls to the Complaint Desk of a Metropolitan Police
Department during 82 Selected Hours in June and July 1961

Type of Call	Number of Calls	Per Cent of Total
Total	801	100.0
Calls included in analysis	652	81.4
1. Calls about "things"	255	31.8
2. Calls for support	397	49.6
Persistent personal problems	230	28.7
a. Health services	81	10.1
b. Children's problems	83	10.4
c. Incapacitated people	33	4.1
d. Nuisances	33	4.1
Periodic personal problems	167	20.9
a. Disputes	63	7.9
b. Violence	43	5.4
c. Protection	29	3.6
d. Missing persons	11	1.4
e. Youths' behavior	21	2.6
Calls excluded from analysis	149	18.6
Information only	33	4.1
Not police business	28	3.5
Feedback calls	88	11.0

accidents, suicide attempts, and so on; another third are children's problems, usually complaints about trespassing, or destructive behavior; and the remainder are divided equally between incapacitated people, usually described over the phone as drunk or "psycho," and nuisances, usually noisy behavior.

Periodic problems comprise 167 calls of which more than a third are about disputes and quarrels of all kinds, both in families and among unrelated people. Almost half are concerned with violence or protection from potential violence[7] and the remainder are about missing persons or gangs of youths and hot-rodders.

Table 2 shows the distribution of the calls, by type, through the days of the week and the period of the day. It now appears that the heaping up of calls in the last part of the week is made up of two effects: first, routine police business and persistent interpersonal calls occur most frequently on Thursday, while periodic interpersonal problems heap up on Friday night. The meaning of this finding is not clear, but it may be that the tensions associated with the instrumental activity of the working week are increasing by Thursday and are then let go on Friday—payday—and on the weekend, when formal constraints are fewer. Because fewer of the other agents are available at these times, the

7/Most "protection" calls are for a "clothing escort," that is, for a policeman to accompany a person who has left his home, or been thrown out of it, into the house to get his clothing.

TABLE 2
Number of Calls to the Complaint Desk of a Metropolitan Police Department by
Type of Problem,* Day of Week, Time of Day, and Hours of Observation
during 82 Selected Hours in June and July 1961

Time of Day, Hours of Observation, and Type of Call	Total	Sun.	Mon.	Tue.	Wed.	Thur.	Fri.	Sat.
All calls	652	50	69	55	76	95	54	253
(hours observed)	(82)	(8)	(14)	(9)	(9)	(9)	(6)	(27)
12:01 a.m.-5:00 a.m.	91	16	18					57
(hours observed)	(14)	(2)	(5)	(0)	(0)	(0)	(0)	(7)
Routine	28	4	8					16
Persistent	21	4	4					13
Periodic	42	8	6					28
5:01 a.m.-noon	52		9	19		17		7
(hours observed)	(13)	(0)	(4)	(3)	(0)	(3)	(0)	(3)
Routine	36		6	11		15		4
Persistent	10		2	4		2		2
Periodic	6		1	4		0		1
12:01 p.m.-6:00 p.m.	187	18		36	38	38	31	26
(hours observed)	(26)	(4)	(0)	(6)	(5)	(3)	(4)	(4)
Routine	88	9		12	18	18	16	15
Persistent	68	6		17	11	16	12	6
Periodic	31	3		7	9	4	3	5
6:01 p.m.-midnight	322	16	42		38	40	23	163
(hours observed)	(29)	(2)	(5)	(0)	(4)	(3)	(2)	(13)
Routine	103	4	13		17	15	2	52
Persistent	131	5	22		18	17	7	62
Periodic	88	7	7		3	8	14	49

*Departures from uniformity:

1. Periodic interpersonal calls occur more often than chance would indicate on Friday evening ($\chi^2 = 24.1$, df. = 5, $P < .01$) and the early hours of Saturday ($\chi^2 = 8.4$, d.f. = 2, $P = .02$).

2. Both routine police calls and persistent interpersonal calls occur more frequently than chance would indicate on Thursday, the former in the morning ($\chi^2 = 12.3$, d.f. = 3, $P < .01$) and the latter in the afternoon ($\chi^2 = 13.1$, d.f. = 5, $P = .05$).

policeman takes over many emergency health and welfare services, a kind of division of labor through time.

Almost three quarters of all 652 calls were answered by dispatch of a patrolman in a squad car to the scene, while about eight per cent received various kinds of advice or information, and about four-and-one-half per cent were referred to another source of help. Of the 29 referrals, one was to a medical service, one to a social service, 19 to other legal services and the remaining eight to commercial concerns, such as the Telephone Company. Almost 15 per cent of the calls were terminated—that is, service was withheld for reasons not determined, occasionally because no car was available.

In Table 3, we see that the probability of a car being sent out is inversely

TABLE 3
Per Cent of Calls to Which Cars Sent by Hours of the Day, Days of the Week and
Type of Call, and Number of Calls Received per Hour
(82 selected hours at the complaint desk of a metropolitan
police department, June and July 1961)

Time of Day, Type of Call, and Calls/Hr.	Total		Sun.-Wed.*		Thursday		Fri.-Sat.*	
	No. of Calls	% to Which Car Sent	No. of Calls	% to Which Car Sent	No. of Calls	% to Which Car Sent	No. of Calls	% to Which Car Sent
Total calls	652	72.1	250	72.8	95	71.6	307	70.0
(Total/hr.)	(8.0)		(6.3)		(10.6)		(9.3)	
12:01 a.m.-								
5:00 a.m.	91	80.2	34	85.3			57	77.2
(calls/hour)	(6.5)		(4.9)				(8.1)	
Routine	28	85.7	12	91.7			16	81.3
Persistent	21	71.4	8	87.5			13	61.5
Periodic	42	81.0	14	78.6			28	82.1
5:01 a.m.-noon	52	86.5	28	89.3	17	88.2	7	71.4
(calls/hour)	(4.0)		(4.0)		(5.7)		(2.3)	
Routine	36	88.9	17	94.1	15	86.7	4	75.0
Persistent	10	90.0	6	83.3	2	100.0	2	100.0
Periodic	6	66.7	5	80.0	0	. . .	1	. . .
12:01 p.m.-								
6:00 p.m.	187	73.8	92	70.7	38	71.0	57	80.7
(calls/hour)	(7.2)		(6.1)		(12.7)		(7.1)	
Routine	88	69.3	39	66.7	18	66.7	31	74.2
Persistent	68	80.9	34	76.5	16	75.0	18	94.4
Periodic	31	71.0	19	68.4	4	75.0	8	75.0
6:01 p.m.-								
midnight	322	66.5	96	65.6	40	65.0	186	67.2
(calls/hour)	(11.1)		(8.7)		(13.3)		(12.4)	
Routine	103	60.2	34	58.8	15	40.0	54	66.7
Persistent	131	72.5	45	73.3	17	76.4	69	71.0
Periodic	88	64.8	17	58.8	8	87.5	63	57.1

*Calls grouped because of similar distribution.

related to the rate at which calls are coming in. During the six time periods in which a total of 235 calls were received at a rate of fewer than eight calls per hour, 78 per cent of them were responded to with cars. During the five time periods in which 417 calls were received at a rate of more than eight calls per hour, cars were sent only 68 per cent of the time. This difference is highly significant ($\chi^2 = 7.54$, d.f. = 1), and suggests that cars are sent on a simple supply-and-demand basis. Furthermore, there is no difference among the three major categories with regard to the likelihood of a car being sent. Nevertheless, certain sub-categories of complaint are more likely to get service than others. As Table 4 shows, calls regarding violence (control), children and youths (support

TABLE 4
Disposition of 397 Calls to the Complaint Desk of a Metropolitan Police Department
Regarding Interpersonal Problems, by Sub-Category of Complaint
(82 selected hours in June and July 1961)

Type of Call	Total Calls	Per Cent Car Sent
Total calls	397	76.8
Persistent problems	230	79.1
a. Health services	81	86.4
b. Children's problems	83	85.5
c. Incapacitated people	33	75.8
d. Nuisances	33	48.5
Periodic problems	167	73.7
a. Disputes	63	50.8
b. Violence	43	95.3
c. Protection	29	79.3
d. Missing persons	11	81.8
e. Youths' behavior	21	85.7

and control), and illness (support) are the most likely to be responded to with a car, although the likelihood of the law being broken—which defines the police mandate—is greater for some of these complaints than for others.

When the complainant reports a nuisance or a dispute, he has only one chance in two of getting more than advice—albeit philosophical advice. Thus, a man calls to say that he has had a fight with his girl and she hasn't come to see him, although he knows she is off duty from the hospital; the policeman says he can't make her come to his house—perhaps she doesn't want to—and goes on to advise the man that that's the way life is sometimes.

It is possible that some of the calls about violence are later stages of these unanswered dispute calls. For example, to one complaint, "My boy friend is mad at me and is going to beat me up," the answer was, "Call us again when he does."[8]

It is quite apparent that the policeman must often exercise a kind of clinical judgement about these complaints, and that this judgement reflects his own values. The field notes suggest, for example, that policemen are sincerely, if sentimentally, concerned about children, and that negligent parents are likely to find the police at their most truculent. The following example is taken from the notes:

A call came from a very kindly-sounding Italian man at about 11 o'clock in the evening. He was reporting that he had found a little boy from next door wandering in the street . . . and he thought the police ought to know about the situation. A car was dispatched and reported that

8/Police Chief Murphy describes this entry as "poor police practice."

there was nobody home, and in fact, there were three smaller children in the house. . . . The captain dispatched a camera crew, child placement was notified and the children were immediately placed in a temporary placement home. A stake-out was set for the parents. Meanwhile the pictures had been developed and they showed four under-nourished, under-clothed little children lying in their own feces on a mattress on the floor. The refrigerator contained two cans of condensed milk and some rotten vegetables; the place was filthy and unheated. As the time went by, anger began to rise and when at about four o'clock in the morning the parents were brought in to the station everybody was in an ugly mood. . . . Had they been the least bit smart, glib, or said almost anything other than "yes" or "no" while they were issued tickets, they would have gotten poked.

All-out support for the children is accompanied by the barest minimum of support to the parents in the form of approval for appropriately docile behavior.

The Squad Car. Certain calls are considered serious enough to warrant a captain following the squad car to the scene.[9] The following thumb-nail summaries represent 14 calls made by the captains in a 23-hour period. Half of them were not considered serious, but the field worker asked the captain to go to the scene.

1. A man, reported by his ex-wife as dangerous and perhaps mentally ill, is found asleep; his ex-wife and her mother are in an agitated state. They report that when the ex-wife came to the home the husband shook his fist under her nose and said, "I have divorced you, I want you out of this goddam house by morning." The police officer woke up the man who once again threatened his ex-wife, and the officer then told her that since it was his house and she was legally divorced from him, she and her mother should "please leave, and not cause any more trouble."

2. A car accident severely injures a woman and the police supervise her removal to hospital.

3. A bartender asks for, and receives, help in closing up so that there will be no problems—a routine "preventive" police service usually given by the car on the beat.

4. A man has beaten up his female neighbor earlier in the day and she has called the police and preferred charges. At the time of this call, the man's wife had threatened this woman with a knife. All are drunk and are taken to the station for further investigation.

5. A call from a woman about neighborhood children bullying a small boy who wears glasses. The field notes read, "There was a lot of argument and a lot of screaming back and forth, nothing was particularly

9/The field worker could not go with the regular prowl car owing to a rule forbidding the officers to carry passengers. It is also possible that the captain did not want the field worker to see episodes that he did not himself monitor.

accomplished, the three policemen (captain and two officers from a squad car) stood around for awhile, questioned people, did a little shouting, got shouted at, then the whole thing sort of dissolved and was resolved in a manner that I don't understand."

6. A woman complains that her husband doesn't bring home enough of his money to feed the kids. She is advised to go to Children's Court.

7. Field notes read: "Husband destroying property at his house. He's drunk and he and his wife got in an argument over the children . . . the wife smashed the gift he had given her for Mothers' Day. This set the incident off. He fought the officers, they handcuffed him, and is taken to the station—a psycho."

8. A slightly drunk man is an unwelcome visitor in his ex-wife's home. Police send him home in a cab.

9. An ex-patient from a mental hospital is missing from her relative's home. They will broadcast a missing persons call.

10. A drunk man claims he has been slugged, but cannot amplify so no action is taken. "This is a low IQ street," says the policeman.

11. A woman in her pajamas and covered with mud says her husband threw her out. He is at home drunk with the children. As he has a police record, two cars are dispatched, one with a tear-gas gun. The house is found in a shambles. The wife is taken to hospital, children to a shelter, and the husband is booked for investigation and possible psychiatric treatment.

12. Fight in a third floor apartment between a man and his wife. Policeman settles it in some undiscernible fashion.

13. A man has "gone out of his mind over a girl" and has gone beserk with a gun. The man is shipped to hospital and witnesses are taken in because the gun makes the affair a felony.

14. The call is "see if an ambulance is needed." A young Negro in a filthy, crowded house appears to be in agony. Police examine him for knife wounds and being satisfied that he has not been stabbed, and that no further investigation is needed, send him to hospital in an ambulance.

There seem to be three types of cases here. In the first, the police act as guides or conveyors to the courts and hospitals, giving indirect support meanwhile. In the second, they appear to resolve problems by giving concrete information and guidance about what is and is not possible under the law. Here both indirect and overt support are given. In the third type, they appear to settle problems through some consensual method based on mutual understanding between the police and the people involved. Here support is fairly overt but control is, of course, latent because of the policeman's representation of law and order. Occasionally, the police give outright friendly support, as in the following incident from the field notes:

Sitting in the police station is an old man, a citizen wanderer who is on his way to Oregon, and has become dissatisfied with the Rescue Mission and walked out. He's going to spend the night out of the rain until the morning when he's going over to the Salvation Army.

It is, of course, not possible to say what proportion of the policeman's responses to citizens fall into these three types, nor indeed, to know what other types there may be, because of the method of selecting the squad car calls.

Detectives. Four detectives of the twenty in the department, selected only because they were on duty at the time of the field worker's visit, were asked to describe their ten most recent cases. It was felt that they might be assigned the more "professional" and hence controlling tasks. Two of them were specialists in theft and forgery and so their cases were, indeed, of this character. However, fifteen out of twenty cases described by the two general detectives fell into our two personal-problem categories, and were similar to the complaint calls except that they were being further investigated because of more serious breaches of the law.

Another detective, in charge of services to alcoholics, reported that in 1956 the police department sent him to Yale for training in the handling of alcoholics. He says, "As a police officer I saw people being arrested for drunk and re-arrested for drunk and I thought it was a pretty medieval way of going about trying to help a person with a basic problem and illness that the public was just kicking in the corner and that's how I wound up here." This officer handles about 900 alcoholics a year. Of these, he takes about 150 charged persons on suspended sentence from the court and tries to arrange for some agency to carry them—an outright supportive service.

Missing Persons: The sergeant in charge of this service estimates that he locates about 600 missing people from this area in a year, about half of them children. He further estimates that from three to five per cent are mentally disturbed adults. This particular officer says that he sometimes counsels with children that he has traced after they have been returned home. At the same time, he complains to the interviewer that children don't respect police officers the way they did when he was young.

Detectives in charge of homicide and those on duty with the vice squad were not interviewed, so it is impossible to say what proportion of all detective work is supportive. These data suggest that it is similar to the patrolman's.

Police Culture. The field worker reports several impressions that are relevant to our interests. Although they cannot be demonstrated from these data, some of them are similar to findings from other studies. First, poor, uneducated people appear to use the police in the way that middle-class people use family doctors and clergymen—that is, as the first port of call in time of trouble. Second, the policeman must often enforce unpopular laws among these poor people at the same time that he sees these laws being flouted by those in positions of power.[10] Third, many policemen are themselves recruited from, and

10/This seems to be most true of the vice squad and it was not covered here. Nevertheless, a lot of police station conversation was on this topic.

sympathetic to, the class of people from whom most of the "interpersonal" calls for assistance come.[11]

Fourth, the police have little knowledge of, and liaison with, social or even medical agencies, and seem to feel that these agencies' activities are irrelevant to the problems they, themselves, face.

Fifth, the police appear to have a concern not only for children but also for those they define as disturbed and ill. They are tolerant, for example, about many crank calls, and will, if a car is available, help a paranoid old lady search her house for the malignant intruder she feels sure is hiding there. Nevertheless, it is possible to see, both in episodes of prejudice against minorities, and in less dramatic ways, how their own values transcend the individual's rights. A field note says, for example, "A woman wants protection from her doctor who is trying to commit her to a mental institution; the officer replies, 'That's not police business, lady. The police cannot go against any doctor.' "[12]

Finally, many policemen are bitter about their low pay, the label "punitive" applied to them in a world that values "warmth," the conflicting demands of their jobs, and the ingratitude of the public. This bitterness is reflected, in this police force, in a catch phrase, "I hate citizens."[13]

SUMMARY AND DISCUSSION

We return now to our starting questions: What calls are made on the police and how do they respond? More than one-half of the calls coming routinely to the police complaint desk, and perhaps to detectives, appear to involve calls for help and some form of support for personal or interpersonal problems. To about three-quarters of these appeals, a car is sent. When the policeman reaches the scene, the data suggest that he either guides the complainant to someone who can solve his problem or tries to solve it himself. To do this, he must often provide support, either by friendly sympathy, by feeding authoritative information into the troubled situation, or by helping consensual resolution to take place. We started with the assumption that these activities belonged to the latent aspect of his role, and he is certainly an amateur—these policemen have no training for this kind of service. Why, then, are they called upon to exercise their amateur talents half of the time?

The reasons are probably complex. First, the policeman has to do much of what he does because he is on duty at times of the day when no other agent is available. Second, he deals with the problems of a group of people—the poor and the ignorant—that studies of our own and others have shown no other agent to

11/This becomes less true, of course, as the police department becomes more professionalized, and is probably less true of this department now than it was in 1961 when these data were collected.

12/This attitude is, of course, construed by some as a denial of the basic rights of the mentally ill person. See, in this regard, Thomas Szasz, *The Myth of Mental Illness,* New York: Harper, 1961.

13/It may be that the higher respect for policemen in England is related to the higher value on order and the lower value on warmth.

be anxious to serve [14] and, third, he has knowledge of, and access to, very few other agents. In other words, he is part of an integrative system in which the labor is divided not so much on the basis of function as on the basis of the time of day and the nature of the target population. All citizens can count on emergency help from the police when there is sudden illness at night, but only a certain kind of citizen takes his marital troubles to them.

The policeman's supportive acts are not only the latent and hence amateur part of his role, they are also latent in not being recognized and legitimated by the other agents in the integrative system. These others, our own studies show, prefer to recognize the policeman's professional controlling function, which they both need and often call upon. [15] Thus, it is as an agent of control that the policeman participates in a divided labor with social workers, doctors, clergymen, lawyers and teachers in maintaining social integration. The problems he faces appear to be a *failure of integration within the integrative system,* so that he cannot mobilize the other agents when he needs them.

Some modern advocates of "professionalization" of police work recognize that the policeman on the beat spends about half his time as an amateur social worker and they hope, instead of improving the referral process, to equip him with the skills of a professional. The policeman will then have a role containing both overtly supportive and overtly controlling elements. If our assumption that these are incompatible activities is correct, this development would lead to a division of labor within police work that would tend once more to segregate these elements. This, in turn, would result in a basic shift in the relationship of the police to the rest of the integrative system. All of this might remove the policeman's present reasons for hating citizens, but it would not guarantee that they would not be replaced with others.

14/See, for a discussion of this problem in this community, Claire Rudolph and John Cumming, "Where are Psychiatric Services Most Needed?" *Social Work,* 7 (July, 1962), pp. 15-20.

15/There is reason to believe that most social workers, clergymen, and doctors have no conception of the amount of support policemen give during a day's work.

21. Police Brutality—Answers to Key Questions*

ALBERT J. REISS, JR.

Any attempt to revise the police function or image faces a multitude of cultural and subcultural difficulties. The socialization of the policeman usually takes place within the enforcement agency and, therefore, every assumed value and norm of the existing police system is transmitted through differential association and learning procedures to the rookie policeman. If the officer is criticized by the press, degraded by the public, hated by the poor, obstructed by the courts, and underpaid by the politicians, he is likely to develop a general distrust of civilians, whether on review boards or in general life (*see* Dienstein, Article 19). Politically sensitive, he recognizes that his future rests with his allegience to the existing political system. Emerging within a system which has known graft, corruption, and the partisan use of power, he finds it difficult to act in an unprejudiced, fully scientific, and consistent manner as he relates to persons from varying social classes. Often identified with the reactionary elements of society, the policeman may become defensive and highly negativistic. Disproportionately involved in the discovery and apprehension of crime and criminals, he is subject to the easy belief that each person he approaches is his potential murderer. Seeking justice in order to fight the criminal he has discovered, he periodically assumes illegal powers in the name of justice. In one instance, for example, a policeman shot and killed a robber he had wounded earlier out of his own fear that the injured man would take revenge upon the policeman's family.

If the police officer becomes apprehender, judge, juror, and sentence inflictor, he assumes responsibilities which are neither constitutionally delegated nor socially desirable. His ultimate actions are largely determined by his self-conception and perceived attitudes toward the community. Faced with social ambivalence, he, too, is socially ambivalent. Recruited primarily from the lower working classes, he often treats the middle- and upper-class member with special deference. Reflecting cultural prejudice, the policeman often degrades a group of citizens whom he has personally defined as nonpersons or persons of lesser stature. Having become the agent of the middle class, he is oftentimes disowned by his own lower-class community. Committed to existing values, he becomes automatically distrustful of the unconventional. Hated by some, he finds it difficult not to hate in return. Trained to assume the initiative, he often aggressively violates the rights of the individual (*see* Cumming, Cumming, and Edell, Article 20).

The policeman's lot is not an easy one. He occupies a central but not readily reconciled position in modern society. While he is a force for moderation and constraint and is the representative of what is seemingly the best in the general culture, the police officer is expected to act as men generally do not act, to be what many men are unable to be. Called upon to use his authority in the public interest, he often finds that he is criticized for the misuse of power, excessive zeal, or mistaken judgment. The continuing cries of police brutality suggest that the problem has not yet been solved (*see* Strecher, Article 17). Albert J. Reiss, Jr., reports that police brutality in three large cities is "far from rare," and the lower class of either race is its most likely victim.

"For three years, there has been through the courts and the streets a dreary procession of citizens with broken heads and bruised bodies against few of whom was violence needed to effect an arrest. Many of them had done nothing to deserve an arrest. In a majority of such cases, no complaint was made. If the victim complains, his charge is generally dismissed. The police are practically above the law."

This statement was published in 1903, and its author was the Hon. Frank Moss, a former police commissioner of New York City. Clearly, today's charges of police brutality and mistreatment of citizens have a precedent in American history—but never before has the issue of police brutality assumed the public urgency it has today. In Newark, in Detroit, in Watts, in Harlem, and, in fact, in practically every city that has had a civil disturbance, "deep hostility between police and ghetto" was, reports the Kerner Commission, "a primary cause of the riots."

Whether or not the police accept the words "police brutality," the public now wants some plain answers to some plain questions. How widespread is police mistreatment of citizens? Is it on the increase? Why do policemen mistreat citizens? Do the police mistreat Negroes more than whites?

To find some answers, 36 people working for the Center of Research on Social Organization observed police-citizen encounters in the cities of Boston, Chicago, and Washington, D.C. For seven days a week, for seven weeks during the summer of 1966, these observers, with police permission, sat in patrol cars and monitored booking and lockup procedures in high-crime precincts.

. . . .

THE MEANING OF BRUTALITY

What citizens mean by police brutality covers the full range of police practices. These practices, contrary to the impression of many civil-rights activists, are not newly devised to deal with Negroes in our urban ghettos. They are ways in which the police have traditionally behaved in dealing with certain citizens, particularly those in the lower classes. The most common of these practices are:

The use of profane and abusive language.

Commands to move on or get home.

Stopping and questioning people on the street or searching them and their cars.

Threats to use force if not obeyed.

Prodding with a nightstick or approaching with a pistol.

The actual use of physical force or violence itself.

Citizens and the police do not always agree on what constitutes proper police practice. What is "proper," or what is "brutal," it need hardly be pointed out, is more a matter of judgment about what someone did than a description of what police do. What is important is not the practice itself but what it means to the citizen. What citizens object to and call "police brutality" is really the judgment that they have not been treated with the full rights and dignity owing citizens in a democratic society. Any practice that degrades their status, that restricts their freedom, that annoys or harasses them, or that uses physical force is frequently seen as unnecessary and unwarranted. More often than not, they are probably right.

Many police practices serve only to degrade the citizen's sense of himself and his status. This is particularly true with regard to the way the police use language. Most citizens who have contact with the police object less to their use of four-letter words than to *how* the policeman talks to them. Particularly objectionable is the habit policemen have of "talking down" to citizens, of calling them names that deprecate them in their own eyes and those of others. More than one Negro citizen has complained: "They talk down to me as if I had no name—like 'boy' or 'man' or whatever, or they call me 'Jack' or by my first name. They don't show me no respect."

Members of minority groups and those seen as nonconformists, for whatever reason, are the most likely targets of status degradation. Someone who has been drinking may be told he is a "bum" or a "shitty wino." A woman walking alone may be called a "whore." And a man who doesn't happen to meet a policeman's standard of how one should look or dress may be met with the remark, "What's the matter, you a queer?" A white migrant from the South may be called a "hillbilly" or "shitkicker"; a Puerto Rican, a "pork chop"; a young boy, a "punk kid." When the policeman does not use words of status degradation, his manner may be degrading. Citizens want to be treated as people, not as "nonpersons" who are talked about as if they were not present.

That many Negroes believe that the police have degraded their status is clear from surveys in Watts, Newark, and Detroit. One out of every five Negroes in our center's post-riot survey in Detroit reports that the police have "talked down to him." More than one in ten says a policeman has "called me a bad name."

To be treated as "suspicious" is not only degrading, but is also a form of harassment and a restriction on the right to move freely. The harassing tactics of the police—dispersing social street-gatherings, the indiscriminate stopping of Negroes on foot or in cars, and commands to move on or go home—are particularly common in ghetto areas.

Young people are the most likely targets of harassing orders to disperse or move on. . . . Given the inadequacy of their housing and the absence of community facilities, the street corner is often their social center. As the police cruise the busy streets of the ghetto, they frequently shout at groups of teenagers to "get going" or "get home." Our observations of police practices show that *white as well as Negro youths* are often harassed in this way.

Frequently the policeman may leave the car and threaten or force youths to move on. . . . Such tactics can only intensify resentment toward the police.

Police harassment is not confined to youth. One in every four adult Negroes in Detroit claims he has been stopped and questioned by the police without good reason. The same proportion claim they have been stopped in their cars. One in five says he has been searched unnecessarily; and one in six says that his car was searched for no good reason. The members of an interracial couple, particularly a Negro man accompanying a white woman, are perhaps the most vulnerable to harassment.

What citizens regard as police brutality many policemen consider necessary for law enforcement. While degrading epithets and abusive language may no longer be considered proper by either police commanders or citizens, they often disagree about other practices related to law enforcement. For example, although many citizens see "stop and question" or "stop and frisk" procedures as harassment, police commanders usually regard them merely as "aggressive prevention" to curb crime.

PHYSICAL FORCE—OR SELF-DEFENSE?

The nub of the police-brutality issue seems to lie in police use of physical force. By law, the police have the right to use such force if necessary to make an arrest, to keep the peace, or to maintain public order. But just how much force is necessary or proper?

This was the crucial problem we attempted to answer by placing observers in the patrol cars and in the precincts. Our 36 observers, divided equally between Chicago, Boston, and Washington, were responsible for reporting the details of all situations where police used physical force against a citizen. To ensure the observation of a large number of encounters, two high-crime police precincts were monitored in Boston and Chicago; four in Washington. At least one precinct was composed of primarily Negro residents, another primarily of whites. Where possible, we also tried to select precincts with considerable variation in social-class composition. Given the criterion of a high-crime rate, however, people of low socio-economic status predominated in most of the areas surveyed.

The law fails to provide simple rules about what—and how much—force that policemen can properly use. The American Bar Foundation's study *Arrest,* by Wayne La Fave, put the matter rather well, stating that the courts of all states would undoubtedly agree that in making an arrest a policeman should use only that amount of force he reasonably believes necessary. But La Fave also pointed out that there is no agreement on the question of when it is better to let the suspect escape than to employ "deadly" force.

Even in those states where the use of deadly force is limited by law, the kinds of physical force a policeman may use are not clearly defined. No kind of force is categorically denied a policeman, since he is always permitted to use deadly force in self-defense.

This right to protect himself often leads the policeman to argue self-defense whenever he uses force. We found that many policemen, whether or not the facts justify it, regularly follow their use of force with the charge that the citizen was assaulting a policeman or resisting arrest. Our observers also found that some policemen even carry pistols and knives that they have confiscated while searching citizens; they carry them so they may be placed at a scene should it be necessary to establish a case of self-defense.

Of course, not all cases of force involve the use of *unnecessary* force. Each instance of force reported by our observers was examined and judged to be either necessary or unnecessary. Cases involving simple restraint—holding a man by the arm—were deliberately excluded from consideration, even though a policeman's right to do so can, in many instances, be challenged. In judging when police force is "unwarranted," "unreasonable," or "undue," we rather deliberately selected only those cases in which a policeman struck the citizen with his hands, fist, feet, or body, or where he used a weapon of some kind—such as a nightstick or a pistol. In these cases, had the policeman been found to have used physical force improperly, he could have been arrested on complaint and, like any other citizen, charged with a simple or aggravated assault. A physical assault on a citizen was judged to be "improper" or "unnecessary" only if force was used in one or more of the following ways:

If a policeman physically assaulted a citizen and then failed to make an arrest; proper use involves an arrest.

If the citizen being arrested did not, by word or deed, resist the policeman; force should be used only if it is necessary to make the arrest.

If the policeman, even though there was resistance to the arrest, could easily have restrained the citizen in other ways.

If a large number of policemen were present and could have assisted in subduing the citizen in the station, in lockup, and in the interrogation rooms.

If an offender was handcuffed and made no attempt to flee or offer violent resistance.

If the citizen resisted arrest, but the use of force continued even after the citizen was subdued.

In the seven-week period, we found 37 cases in which force was used improperly. In all, 44 citizens had been assaulted. In 15 of these cases, no one was arrested. Of these, 8 had offered no verbal or physical resistance whatsoever, while 7 had.

An arrest was made in 22 of the cases. In 13, force was exercised in the station house when at least four other policemen were present. . . .

Just how serious was the improper use of force in these 44 cases? Naturally there were differences in degree of injury. In about one-half of the cases, the citizen appeared little more than physically bruised; in three cases, the amount of force was so great that the citizen had to be hospitalized. . . .

OBSERVING ON PATROL

In the following two cases, the citizens offered no physical or verbal resistance, and the two white policemen made no arrest. It is the only instance in which the observers saw the same two policemen using force improperly more than once.

The police precinct in which these incidents occurred is typical of those found in some of our larger cities, where the patrolmen move routinely from gold coast to slum. There are little islands of the rich and poor, of old Americans and new, of recent migrants and old settlers. One moves from high-rise areas of middle- and upper-income whites through an area of the really old Americans—Indians—to an enclave of the recently arrived. The recently arrived are primarily those the policemen call "hillbillies" (migrants from Kentucky and Tennessee) and "porkchops" (Puerto Ricans). There are ethnic islands of Germans and Swedes. Although there is a small area where Negroes live, it is principally a precinct of whites. The police in the district are, with one exception, white.

On a Friday in the middle of July, the observer arrived for the 4 to 12 midnight watch. The beat car that had been randomly chosen carried two white patrolmen—one with 14 years of experience in the precinct, the other with three.

The watch began rather routinely as the policemen cruised the district. Their first radio dispatch came at about 5:30 P.M. They were told to investigate two drunks in a cemetery. On arriving they found two white men "sleeping one off." Without questioning the men, the older policeman began to search one of them, ripping his shirt and hitting him in the groin with a nightstick. The younger policeman, as he searched the second, ripped away the seat of his trousers, exposing his buttocks. The policemen then prodded the men toward the cemetery fence and forced them to climb it, laughing at the plight of the drunk with the exposed buttocks. As the drunks went over the fence, one policemen shouted, "I ought to run you fuckers in!" The other remarked to the observer, "Those assholes won't be back; a bunch of shitty winos."

Not long after they returned to their car, the policemen stopped a woman who had made a left turn improperly. She was treated very politely, and the younger policeman, who wrote the ticket, later commented to the observer, "Nice lady." At 7:30 they were dispatched to check a suspicious auto. After a quick check, the car was marked abandoned.

Shortly after a 30-minute break for a 7:30 "lunch," the two policemen received a dispatch to take a burglary report. Arriving at a slum walkup, the police entered a room where an obviously drunk white man in his late 40s insisted that someone had entered and stolen his food and liquor. He kept insisting that it had been taken and that he had been forced to borrow money to buy beer. The younger policeman, who took the report, kept harassing the man, alternating between mocking and badgering him [with] rhetorical questions. "You say your name is Half-A-Wit [for Hathaway]? Do you sleep with niggers? How did you vote on the bond issue? Are you sure that's all that's missing? Are you a virgin yet?" The man responded to all of this with the seeming vagueness and joviality of the intoxicated, expressing gratitude for the policemen's help as they left. The older policeman remarked to the observer as they left, "Ain't drunks funny?"

For the next hour little happened, but as the two were moving across the precinct shortly after 10 P.M., a white man and a woman in their 50s flagged them down. Since they were obviously "substantial" middle-class citizens of the district, the policemen listened to their complaints that a Negro man was causing trouble inside the public-transport station from which they had just emerged. The woman said that he had sworn at her. The older policeman remarked, "What's a nigger doing up here? He should be down on Franklin Road!"

With that, they ran into the station and grabbed the Negro man who was inside. Without questioning him, they shoved him into a phone booth and began beating him with their fists and a flashlight. They also hit him in the groin. Then they dragged him out and kept him on his knees. He pleaded that he had just been released from a mental hospital that day and, begging not to be hit again, asked them to let him return to the hospital. One policeman said: "Don't you like us, nigger? I like to beat niggers and rip out their eyes." They took him outside to their patrol car. Then they decided to put him on a bus, telling him that he was returning to the hospital; they deliberately put him on a bus going in the opposite direction. Just before the Negro boarded the bus, he said, "You police just like to shoot and beat people." The first policeman replied, "Get moving, nigger, or I'll shoot you." The man was crying and bleeding as he was put on the bus. Leaving the scene, the younger policeman commented, "He won't be back."

For the rest of the evening, the two policemen kept looking for drunks and harassing any they found. They concluded the evening by being dispatched to an address where, they were told, a man was being held for the police. No one answered their knock. They left.

.   .   .   .

BACKSTAGE AT THE STATION

The police station, ... is more than just a series of cubicles called interrogation rooms. There are other rooms and usually a lockup as well. Many of these are also hidden from public view. It is not surprising, then, that one-third of all the observations of the undue use of force occurred within the station.

.   .   .   .

Force is used unnecessarily at many different points and places in the station. The citizen who is not cooperative during the booking process may be pushed or shoved, have his handcuffs twisted with a nightstick, have his foot stomped, or be pulled by the hair. All of these practices were reported by policemen as ways of obtaining "cooperation." But it was clear that the booking could have been completed without any of this harassment.

The lockup was the scene of some of the most severe applications of force. Two of the three cases requiring hospitalization came about when an offender was "worked over" in the lockup. To be sure, the arrested are not always cooperative when they get in the lockup, and force may be necessary to place them in a cell. But the amount of force observed hardly seemed necessary.

One evening an observer was present in the lockup when two white policemen came in with a white man. The suspect had been handcuffed and brought to the station because he had proved obstreperous after being arrested for a traffic violation. Apparently he had been drinking. While waiting in the lockup, the man began to urinate on the floor. In response, the policemen began to beat the man. They jumped him, knocked him down, and beat his head against the concrete floor. He required emergency treatment at a nearby hospital.

At times a policeman may be involved in a kind of escalation of force. Using force appropriately for an arrest in the field seemingly sets the stage for its later use, improperly, in the station. . . .

.   .   .   .

Cases where the offender resists an arrest provide perhaps the most difficulty in judging the legitimacy of the force applied. An encounter that began as a dispatch to a disturbance at a private residence was one case about which there could be honest difference in judgment. On arrival, the policemen—one white, the other Negro—met a white woman who claimed that her husband, who was in the back yard and drunk, had beaten her. She asked the policemen to "take him in." The observer reported that the police found the man in the house. When they attempted to take him, he resisted by placing his hands between the door jamb. Both policemen then grabbed him. The Negro policeman said, "We're going to have trouble, so let's finish it right here." He grabbed the offender and knocked him down. Both policemen then wrestled with the man, handcuffed him, and took him to the station. As they did so, one of the policemen remarked, "These sons of bitches want to fight, so you have to break them quick."

A MINIMAL PICTURE?

The reader, as well as most police administrators, may be skeptical about reports that policemen used force in the presence of observers. . . .

There were and are a number of reasons why our observers were able to see policemen behaving improperly. We entered each department with the full cooperation of the top administrators. So far as the men in the line were concerned, our chief interest was in how citizens behave toward the police, a main object of our study. Many policemen, given their strong feelings against citizens, fail to see that their own behavior is equally open to observation. Furthermore, our observers are trained to fit into a role of trust—one that is genuine, since most observers are actually sympathetic to the plight of the policeman, if not to his behavior.

Finally, and this is a fact all too easily forgotten, people cannot change their behavior in the presence of others as easily as many think. This is particularly true when people become deeply involved in certain situations. The policeman not only comes to "trust" the observer in the law-enforcement situation—regarding him as a source of additional help if necessary—but, when he becomes involved in a dispute with a citizen, he easily forgets that an observer is present. Partly because he does not know what else to do, in such situations the policeman behaves "normally." But should one cling to the notion that most policemen modify their behavior in the presence of outsiders, one is left with the uncomfortable conclusion that our cases represent a minimal picture of actual misbehavior.

Superficially it might seem that the use of an excessive amount of force against citizens is low. In only 37 of 3826 encounters observed did the police use undue force. Of the 4604 white citizens in these encounters, 27 experienced an excessive amount of force—a rate of 5.9 for every 1000 citizens involved. The comparable rate for 5960 Negroes, of whom 17 experienced an excessive amount of force, is 2.8. Thus, whether one considers these rates high or low, the fact is that the *rate of excessive force for all white citizens in encounters with the police is twice that for Negro citizens.*

A rate depends, however, upon selecting a population that is logically the target of force. What we have just given is a rate for *all* citizens involved in encounters with the police. But many of these citizens are not logical targets of force. Many, for example, simply call the police to complain about crimes against themselves or their property. And others are merely witnesses to crimes.

The more logical target population consists of citizens whom the police allege to be offenders—a population of suspects. In our study, there were 643 white suspects, 27 of whom experienced undue use of force. This yields an abuse rate of 41.9 per 1000 white suspects. The comparable rate for 751 Negro suspects, of whom 17 experienced undue use of force, is 22.6 per 1000. If one accepts these rates as reasonably reliable estimates of the undue force against suspects, then there should be little doubt that in major metropolitan areas the sort of behavior commonly called "police brutality" is far from rare.

Popular impression casts police brutality as a racial matter—white police mistreating Negro citizens. The fact is that white suspects are more liable to being treated improperly by the police than Negro suspects are. This, however, should not be confused with the chances a citizen takes of being mistreated. In two of the cities we studied, Negroes are a minority. The chances, then, that any Negro has of being treated improperly are, perhaps, more nearly comparable to that for whites. If the rates are comparable, then one might say that the application of force unnecessarily by the police operates without respect to the race of an offender.

Many people believe that the race of the policeman must affect his use of force, particularly since many white policemen express prejudice against Negroes. Our own work shows that in the police precincts made up largely of Negro citizens, over three-fourths of the policemen express prejudice against Negroes. Only 1 percent express sympathetic attitudes. But as sociologists and social psychologists have often shown, prejudice and attitudes do not necessarily carry over into discriminatory actions.

Our findings show that there is little difference between the rate of force used by white and by Negro policemen. Of the 54 policemen observed using too much force, 45 were white and 9 were Negro. For every 100 white policemen, 8.7 will use force; for every 100 Negro policemen, 9.8 will. What this really means, though, is that about one in every 10 policemen in high-crime rate areas of cities sometimes uses force unnecessarily.

. . . Policemen, both Negro and white, are most likely to exercise force against members of their *own* race:

67 percent of the citizens victimized by white policemen were white.
71 percent of the citizens victimized by Negro policemen were Negro.

To interpret these statistics correctly, however, one should take into account the differences in opportunity policemen have to use force against members of their own and other races. Negro policemen, in the three cities we studied, were far *less* less likely to police white citizens than white policemen were to police Negroes. Negro policemen usually policed other Negroes, while white policemen policed both whites and Negroes about equally. In total numbers, then, more white policemen than Negro policemen used force against Negroes. But this is explained by the fact that whites make up 85 percent of the police force, and more than 50 percent of all policemen policing Negroes.

The disparity between our findings and the public's sense that Negroes are the main victims of police brutality can easily be resolved if one asks how the public becomes aware of the police misusing force.

LACK OF INFORMATION

Police chiefs are notoriously reluctant to disclose information that would allow us to assess the nature and volume of complaints against the police. Only a few departments have begun to report something about citizen complaints. And these give us very little information.

Consider, for example, the 1966 Annual Report released by the New Orleans Police Department. It tells us that there were 208 cases of "alleged police misconduct on which action was taken.". . . Of the 208 cases the department considered "disciplinary matters," the report tells us that no disciplinary action was taken in 106 cases. There were 11 cases that resulted in 14 dismissals; 56 cases that resulted in 72 suspensions, fines, or loss of days; and 35 cases involving 52 written or verbal "reprimands" or "cautionings."

The failure of the report to tell us the charge against the policeman is a significant omission. We cannot tell how many of these allegations involved improper use of force, how many involved verbal abuse or harassment, how many involved police felonies or misdemeanors, and so on. In such reports, the defensive posture of the nation's police departments is all too apparent. . . .

Many responsible people believe that the use of physical brutality by the police is on the wane. . . . Whether or not the policeman's "sense of justice" and his use of unnecessary force have changed remains an open question. Forms may change while practices go on. To move misuse from the street to the station house, or from the interrogation room to the lockup, changes the place but not the practice itself.

THE VICTIMS AND THE TURF

Fifty years ago, the immigrants to our cities—Eastern and Southern Europeans such as the Poles and the Italians—complained about police brutality. Today the new immigrants to our cities—mostly Negroes from the rural South—raise their voices through the civil-rights movement, through black-nationalist and other race-conscious organizations. There is no comparable voice for white citizens since, except for the Puerto Ricans, they now lack the nationality organizations that were once formed to promote and protect the interests of their immigrant forbears.

Although policemen do not seem to select their victims according to race, two facts stand out. All victims were offenders, and all were from the lower class. Concentrating as we did on high-crime rate areas of cities, we do not have a representative sample of residents in any city. Nonetheless, we observed a sizable minority of middle- and upper-status citizens, some of whom were offenders.

But since no middle- or upper-class offender, white or Negro, was the victim of an excessive amount of force, it appears that the lower class bears the brunt of victimization by the police.

The most likely victim of excessive force is a lower-class man of either race. No white woman and only two Negro women were victimized. The difference between the risk assumed by white and by Negro women can be accounted for by the fact that far more Negro women are processed as suspects or offenders.

Whether or not a policeman uses force unnecessarily depends upon the social setting in which the encounter takes place. Of the 37 instances of excessive force, 37 percent took place in police-controlled settings, such as the patrol car or the precinct station. Public places, usually streets, accounted for 41 percent, and 16 percent took place in a private residence. The remaining 6 percent occurred in commercial settings. This is not, of course, a random sample of settings where the police encounter suspects.

What is most obvious, and most disturbing, is that the police are very likely to use force in settings that they control. Although only 18 percent of all situations involving suspects ever ended up at the station house, 32 percent of all situations where an excessive amount of force was used took place in the police station.

No one who accepts the fact that the police sometimes use an excessive amount of force should be surprised by our finding that they often select their own turf. What should be apparent to the nation's police administrators, however, is that these settings are under their command and control. Controlling the police in the field, where the policeman is away from direct supervision, is understandably difficult. But the station house is the police administrator's domain. The fact that one in three instances of excessive force took place in settings that can be directly controlled should cause concern among police officials.

The presence of citizens who might serve as witnesses against a policeman should deter him from undue use of force. . . .

In most situations involving the use of excessive force, there were witnesses. In our 37 cases, there were bystanders present three-fourths of the time. But in only one situation did the group present sympathize with the citizen and threaten to report the policeman. A complaint was filed on that incident—the only one of the 37 observed instances of undue force in which a formal complaint was filed.

All in all, the situations where excessive force was used were devoid of bystanders who did not have a stake in being "against" the offender. Generally, they were fellow policemen, or fellow offenders whose truthfulness could be easily challenged. When a policeman uses undue force, then, he usually does not risk a complaint against himself or testimony from witnesses who favor the complainant against the policeman. This, as much as anything, probably accounts for the low rate of formal complaints against policemen who use force unnecessarily.

A striking fact is that in more than one-half of all instances of undue coercion, at least one other policeman was present who did not participate in the use of force. This shows that, for the most part, the police do not restrain their fellow policemen. On the contrary, there were times when their very presence encouraged the use of force. One man brought into the lockup for threatening a policeman with a pistol was so severely beaten by this policeman that he required hospitalization. During the beating, some fellow policemen propped the man up, while others shouted encouragement. Though the official police code does not legitimate this practice, police culture does.

VICTIMS—DEFIANT OR DEVIANT

Now, are there characteristics of the offender or his behavior that precipitate the use of excessive force by the police? Superficially, yes. Almost one-half of the cases involved open defiance of police authority (39 percent) or resisting arrest (9 percent). Open defiance of police authority, however, is what the policeman defines as *his* authority, not necessarily "official" authority. Indeed in 40 percent of the cases that the police considered open defiance, the policeman never executed an arrest—a somewhat surprising fact for those who assume that policemen generally "cover" improper use of force with a "bona-fide" arrest and a charge of resisting arrest.

But it is still of interest to know what a policeman *sees* as defiance. Often he seems threatened by a simple refusal to acquiesce to his own authority. A policeman beat a handcuffed offender because, when told to sit, the offender did not sit down. One Negro woman was soundly slapped for her refusal to approach the police car and identify herself.

Important as the threat to his authority may appear to the policeman, there were many more of these instances in which the policeman did *not* respond with the use of force. The important issue seems to be whether the policeman manages to assert his authority despite the threat to it. I suspect that policemen are more likely to respond with excessive force when they define the situation as one in which there remains a question as to who is "in charge."

Similarly, some evidence indicates that harassment of deviants plays a role in the undue use of force. Incidents involving drunks made up 27 percent of all incidents of improper use of force; an additional 5 percent involved homosexuals or narcotics users. Since deviants generally remain silent victims to avoid public exposure of their deviance, they are particularly susceptible to the use of excessive force.

It is clear, though, that the police encounter many situations involving deviants where no force is used. Generally they respond to them routinely. What is surprising, then, is that the police do not mistreat deviants more than they do. The explanation may lie in the kind of relationships the police have with deviants. Many are valuable to the police because they serve as informers. To mistreat them severely would be to cut off a major source of police intelligence. At the same time, deviants are easily controlled by harassment.

Clearly, we have seen that police mistreatment of citizens exists. Is it, however, on the increase?

Citizen complaints against the police are common, and allegations that the police use force improperly are frequent. There is evidence that physical brutality exists today. But there is also evidence, from the history of our cities, that the police have long engaged in the use of unnecessary physical force. No one can say with confidence whether there is more or less of it today than there was at the turn of the century.

What we lack is evidence that would permit us to calculate comparative rates of police misuse of force for different periods of American history. Only recently have we begun to count and report the volume of complaints against the police. And the research reported in this article represents the only attempt to estimate the amount of police mistreatment by actual observation of what the police do to citizens.

part SIX
The Courts and the Public

Law enforcement and correctional effectiveness largely depend upon the judicial system. Representing the concept of justice and serving as a public countervailing force to prevent the misuse of power and law while seeking the social goals of stability and crime control, the courts decide the delicate balance between crime control and social coercion, effective jurisprudence and excessive harshness, a respect for law and social alienation. Because law emanates from the interaction of representatives of private interests, precedents, pressure groups, abstract ideas, national or local emergencies, and general fears or anxieties, to name a few sources, the courts must interpret the meaning of a law on behalf of the public. A criminal violation is simply an act which is either completed or not completed in violation of legislative prohibitions or demands, and the courts must ultimately decide the validity of the criminal charge. Inasmuch as the criminal court must decide questions of guilt or innocence, it is always placed in the position of having to determine the actual context and meaning of the specific criminal act (*see* introduction to Article 24). Based upon the concepts of due process, the courts guarantee the rights of the individual in the state whose powers may overwhelm the person in any moment of his life. In the American adversary system the defense lawyer represents the accused (*see* Blumberg, Article 24); the courts begin with the assumption that the accused is innocent until proven guilty in a court of law, usually by a jury of peers (*see* Kalven and Zeisel, Article 25). Following procedural rules for the admission of evidence, the courts theoretically offer the same judicial safeguards to *all* alleged violators regardless of the serious or minor nature of their crimes.

While these presuppositions have represented American constitutional ideals, their intent has not been adequately realized. The American system of justice, too, has failed to keep pace with population change. Pluralistic mores and multiple ethical systems have caused legislative bodies increasingly to enact laws designed to unify human behavior. The statutes and ordinances that compose substantive criminal law, therefore, have grown at a rate which has outrun the court's capacity to adjudicate the issues in question. Part of the reason is the still largely rural orientation of the American judicial system. Designed for smaller socioecological units, it has faced severe burdens with the increase in the urban population. Consequently, inadequate organization, funding, and personnel assignment have encouraged treadmill justice (*see* Bilek, Article 22).

The overuse of criminal law in order to control deviant behavior has further compounded the problem (*see* Kadish, Article 1). In most states both the system of criminal law and the courts require major revision. While court overcrowding has led to an overdependence upon the negotiated guilty plea as a means to speed up criminal prosecution, many voices are now asking whether such a procedure enhances or detracts from a meaningful system of theoretical and functional justice (*see* Blumberg, Article 24). When court action is tied to police, prosecutor, or judicial collusion, the convicted offender's respect for law or justice is often muted. In addition, an overemphasis upon the easy conviction leads to a decline in the quality of justice accorded the lesser offender who commits the greatest volume of criminal offenses.

The quantity of misdemeanor (minor) offenses coming before the lower courts poses the greatest challenge to the existing system of justice. Whether an act is criminal or not is often a matter of degree (*see* Hall, Article 23). The man who runs the stop sign may commit a minor misdemeanor. If, however, he strikes a passing car after running the stop sign, killing one of its occupants, the "less serious" misdemeanor may well become a "more serious" felony. Even the distinction between a simple and an aggravated assault is largely a distinction between the severity of the harm. In both instances similar violent behavior is inflicted but with differing degree of physical contact and ensuing consequence.

Because misdemeanor courts usually receive the offender at a critical point in his life, their procedures are of critical importance to the eventual control of more serious crimes. Inasmuch as most felony (serious) offenders have previously been tried for less serious offenses, what is or is not done in misdemeanant corrections largely determines the offender's future. However, the weaknesses of the system of justice are paradoxically most apparent in the lower court. Assembly-line justice is not unknown. The four judges of the District of Columbia Court of General Sessions, for example, processed the preliminary stages of more than 1,500 felony and 7,500 serious misdemeanor cases, 38,000 petty offenses, and an equal number of traffic violations in a single year. The mere volume of cases caused the judges to focus upon the simple movement of cases through the court. Because most lower courts have also become the testing ground of judges who aspire to higher court positions, the quality of the lower court judiciary is uneven. Inasmuch as promotions from a lower to felony court carry a similar rise in status, many of the more competent justices spend little time in the lower courts.

The need for court reforms is readily apparent. The 1967 Report of the President's Commission suggests that all misdemeanant and felony courts, including their prosecution, defense, and probation services, should be unified; lower court judicial manpower should be increased; greater and better physical facilities should be provided; the states and the federal government should abolish or overhaul the justice of the peace and U.S. commissioner systems; each state should enact comprehensive bail reform legislation on the pattern set by the Federal Bail Reform Act of 1966; and each community should establish procedures in appropriate cases to enable and encourage police departments to release as many arrested persons as possible "promptly after arrest upon issuance of a citation of summons requiring subsequent appearance."

Because court effectiveness depends upon the quality of the presentation of evidence supporting the charge, prosecutors, the Commission recommends, should make discriminating charge decisions in order to ensure that sentenced offenders are not released because of technicalities. While prosecutors should define explicit policies for the informal disposition or dismissal of cases involving marginal offenders, the explicit terms of the negotiated guilty plea agreement should be stated in writing.

Greater prosecutor and defense counsel evidence sharing, the Commission suggests, should be encouraged in order to accomplish the aim of justice and to hasten early case disposition. Standards and regulations concerning the types of information properly released to news media should be defined by the police, prosecutors, bar associations, and courts in order to guarantee the true expression of criminal justice. Even sentencing procedures, the Commission believes, should be reexamined with the view of simplifying the gradation of offenses, removing mandatory minimum prison terms, and eliminating other limitations upon the use of probation and parole (*see* Stark, Article 31). The legislature, it encourages, should give the judge greater discretionary power in order to allow the greater use of individualized sentences (*see* Toby, Article 32).

Calling for regular judicial conferences and institutes to inform judges of court interpretations, programs, or procedures, the Commission further urges all states to recognize that the issues of modern life have become so complex that the modern judge must engage in a program of continuing education throughout his life. While the judiciary should be isolated from political pressures, the state should also designate appropriate provisions to guarantee a retirement of judges at a predetermined age. However, even these provisions, the Commission notes, will not solve the total judicial problem.

Five authors suggest the dimensions of the problem of the courts and the public in Part Six. Arthur J. Bilek sets the scene in his analysis of the current state of the administration of criminal justice. Jerome Hall notes the problem of determining responsibility for one's actions and urges the repair rather than the replacement of the M'Naghten Rule. Abraham S. Blumberg points out that legal aid in the future may not be meaningful legal aid but rather manipulation toward the guilty plea. Harry Kalven, Jr., and Hans Zeisel examine the dynamics of the American jury in a death penalty situation. Finally, Edwin M. Lemert evaluates the real context of juvenile justice.

22. State of the Art: The Administration of Criminal Justice*

ARTHUR J. BILEK

Although the arrest of a suspected offender is merely the first step in the judicial process, many intervening steps and variables may lead to the modification of a so-called "known" conviction. Once the arrest has been completed, the prosecuting attorney must decide whether to process the charge against the individual in court. In instances of business misconduct, the failure to fulfill family obligations or other minor borderline disturbances, out-of-court settlement rather than prosecution is usually attempted. Using his vast discretionary power, the prosecuting attorney determines whether the evidence justifies the anticipated charge and whether to prosecute the accused for one or all committed offenses, either singly or successively. Oftentimes, the charge and even the sentence are determined by the offender's willingness to plead guilty (see Blumberg, Article 24).

Court action is usually initiated after a private complaint or after a police officer has signed a sworn complaint charging the alleged violator with a criminal violation. Although suspects must be promptly brought before the magistrate or equivalent to hear charges placed against them, minor offenses which may be tried in a magistrate's or comparable court are often summarily processed. If the suspected offender desires bail, a preliminary examination is often scheduled in the more serious cases. In some instances the grand jury assumes a similar function as it evaluates whether the evidence presented to its attention by the prosecuting or district attorney justifies a formal indictment. If probable cause is believed evident in either the preliminary examination or the grand jury consideration, the suspect is bound over to the trial court for eventual case adjudication.

Because the adjudication process has necessarily involved the close cooperation of the police, the prosecutor, and even the trial judge, recent attempts to protect the neutrality of the judiciary have resulted in a major vacuum between the police and the trial court. The problems of scheduling court business, negotiating the release of arrested persons pending their appearance in

*From a paper presented at the Second National Symposium on Law Enforcement Science and Technology, April 16, 1968.

court, and issuing of arrest and search warrants make enforcement, prosecution, and judicial coordination mandatory. At the same time, however, the trial judge must maintain his position of neutrality in order to review and control effectively police practices within the limits of the inclusionary rules which restrict the admission of evidence gained illegally from the trial process.

Whatever the situation, the American legal system is undergoing extensive changes as it faces the extreme tensions brought about by major urban growth and the lack of state legislative response to the needs of the judiciary. Nearly all American state court systems stand in need of reform. Even the President's Task Force on the Courts, in effect, questioned whether justice can truly be justice under current conditions. In the continuing discussion Arthur J. Bilek examines the philosophical foundation of criminal justice, suggests the scope of the problem, and delineates the probable direction for the resolution of existing conflicts.

The administration of criminal justice is a contemporary and continuing synthesis of the process of criminal jurisprudence, an idea as old as man.

Primitive man, confronted with the fact of his individuality, formed tribal communities from which developed man's two basic rights; the right to self-preservation and the right to own property. Evolving from these rights are the complex and sophisticated laws of modern society.

As the public and private relationships of man grew in number and complexity, criminal law slowly emerged. During the early food-gathering periods, public offenses were limited to primitive concepts of incest, murder by magic, and various sacral offenses.[1] Homicide, assault, and theft were personal wrongs to be settled by the individuals involved. These personal wrongs were beyond tribal concern or action unless they threatened the peace of the entire community.[2]

Even in later periods, when intertribal battles over hunting grounds, questions relating to land possession, and blood feuds came into being and folkways were becoming more numerous and definitive, there still existed a sharp distinction between public and private offenses. Several thousand years elapsed before offenses against the individual, such as assault and theft, became offenses against the state as well.

The advent of the theocratic governments around 3000 B.C. introduced the ethical concepts of religion into legal customs.[3]

For hundreds of thousand years, rulemaking and adjudication were accomplished by the unwritten rule of the reigning clan and tribe elders. While there may have been earlier systems of jurisprudence and compilation of written laws prior to the reign of Hammurabi (1750 B.C.), no detailed physical evidence

1/A. S. Diamond, *The Evolution of Law and Order* (Watts & Co., London, 1951), p. 21.
2/*Ibid.*
3/*Ibid.*, pp. 67-166, *passim.*

remains of such antecedents. Thereafter, more sophisticated codifications, digests, and compilations of laws into single documents appear at irregular intervals. Thus, the folkways of early man became customs of the first tribes and thence the laws of the emerging nations, until the eventual evolution of the unique system of justice, laws, and jurisprudence of Western man.

PHILOSOPHY OF JUSTICE

Plato believed that the human mind was capable of ascertaining absolute truth and further that reason enabled such truth to be used as a guide for action and decision in life. His pupil Aristotle believed strongly in the concept of government by law and not by men. He urged that a natural law—based on the nature of man—was the foundation of all law. From this concept, Aristotle evolved the philosophy of human rights in which each man was guaranteed certain rights. He saw justice as the balance by which every man received his fair due.[4]

The democratic government of the Greek city-states and the highly structured Roman government embodying complex legal systems, countless governmental officers, and laws, codes, and edicts tumbled before the invading hordes from the North. But the spark of justice and law was kept glowing in the monasteries and later through the efforts of the university faculties.

Many types of law and justice filled the European Continent during the Middle Ages, including personal, feudal, customary, manor, city, and ecclesiastical law. Gradually, the Norman feudal law and the Anglo-Saxon tribal law fused into one to become the English legal system.

Through all these developments, justice is perhaps the most enduring concept in legal and political thought. In *The Republic,* Plato states that justice cannot be defined merely as obedience to law—it is obedience to law, provided law is understood to be that which binds man together in political association. Plato's doctrine stipulates that justice is a part of human virtue and is therefore synonymous with morality.[5]

The particular identification of law and justice is made by Cicero, who defines natural law as a single system of laws governing the entire universe, to which all natural things have an obligation to conform. Ulpian depicts justice as "the fixed and perpetual will to give to everyone his due." St. Augustine adds the thought that justice is incomplete if it is not based upon Christian law as well as the law of nature.[6] In the 13th century, St. Thomas Aquinas applied a more moderate interpretation to the rigid Augustinian views. He sees human law as

4/G. Del Vecchio, *Justice: An Historical and Philosophical Essay,* ed. by A. H. Campbell (Edinburgh at the University Press, Scotland, 1956), pp. 13-26, *passim;* C. J. Friedrich, *The Philosophy of Law in Historical Perspective* (The University of Chicago Press, Chicago, 1963), 2nd edition.

5/W. S. Carpenter, *Foundations of Modern Jurisprudence* (Appleton-Century-Crofts, Inc., New York, 1958), p. 30.

6/Friedrich, "The Philosophy of the Law," pp. 27-34, *passim.*

springing from eternal law, with human laws being made for the common good promulgated by the legitimate rulers of the community. In the quest for justice, St. Thomas saw man as promoting peace and order on earth for human happiness. The legal philosophers of the Middle Ages gave way to the social reformers and finally to the framers of the Constitution of the United States. The men who wrote the Constitution believed that the main objective of the state was the maintenance of justice. In *The Federalist,* it was declared that "justice is the end of government." The framers felt that the realization of justice involved the task of subordinating the selfish interests of each part of the people to the permanent interest of the whole society. Central to this theme was the concept that achieving justice was not based on the maintenance of equality but upon the preservation of liberty.[7]

ADMINISTRATION OF CRIMINAL JUSTICE

Each generation, each culture, each nation, and each civilization left its mark on the 500,000-year development of the administration of criminal justice as it now is practiced in the United States. From caveman to hunter, food-gatherer, farmer, and fisherman, to novice nations with first crude and then complex religious involvements, and finally to empires with sophisticated governmental structures, law was nurtured and developed. Additions were made by the Jews as well as the Christians, the Greeks and Romans, the Barbarians, the monks and the priests, the philosophers and the emperors.

While some basic rudiments of the administration of criminal justice may predate 500,000 B.C., others such as the police began as late as 1829. A critical examination of the criminal justice spectrum reveals that while many of the individual parts have been carefully refined over the centuries, the overall system remains in need of further study and improvement.

The origin of criminal justice arises from the need of man to live in harmony with other men. Even in the smallest family group, it is quickly apparent that such harmony is not automatic and that friction and contention cannot be totally avoided. In the simplest society, the elder made all the rules and the clan obeyed or suffered his wrath. As tribes developed, it became necessary to have tribal councils composed of the elders of all of the leading clans. These councils served the twofold purpose of setting rules and administering justice. When nations replaced tribes, more sophisticated and complex lawmaking and justice-dispensing systems were needed. When the group could no longer police itself or force obedience to its rules, various types of enforcement agencies developed throughout the centuries.

Today, while the cast has changed and the structure has become increasingly complex, the schematic remains essentially the same. People within a village, city, county, state, or nation indicate that a rule is needed to ensure compliance

7/R. A. Wormser, *The Story of the Law* (Simon and Schuster, New York, 1962), revised edition.

to a desired norm. This need is translated into law by the city councils, county boards, state assemblies, and federal legislature. To provide meaning to the law, enforcement is necessary on the part of the police. Officials such as the village attorney, corporation counsel, coroner, county attorney, district attorney, attorney general and the grand jury serve the function of initiating prosecution and provide legal guidance attendant to arrest and search warrants as well as the placing of appropriate criminal charges.

Adjudication to determine guilt or innocence is carried out by justices of the peace, municipal court judges, and circuit, county, and criminal court judges. Sanctions are applied by the judges in the form of supervision, fines, probation, incarceration, and the death penalty. A final legal stage is accomplished by the appellate and review courts who have the ultimate responsibility to determine if the criminal laws are in themselves constitutional and if the criminal process was validly and licitly carried out with due regard for the rights of the defendant. The final units in the spectrum are the correctional and rehabilitative agencies, such as jails, prisons, penitentiaries, reformatories, training schools, work farms, and work camps.

The goal of the administration of criminal justice is to secure justice for all men in the area of criminal behavior, while at the same time providing for and promoting peace and safety within the community. Neither goal can be subordinated to reasons of momentary importance or current interest. The concept of justice involves a confluence of the rights of the individual, the virtue of man, and the good and preservation of the society.[8]

CRIMINAL JUSTICE PROBLEMS

A brief review of where the nation now stands in the administration of criminal justice would indicate three major problems:

1. Personnel is grossly inadequate in number and skill.
2. Agencies are woefully archaic in structure and operation.
3. There is little or no regard for the totality of the system by the participating agencies and their personnel.

Each of the shortcomings within the administration of justice poses significant dangers to the protection of liberty and the preservation of peace in this society.

Inadequate Personnel

There is little doubt and in fact there is sizable evidence that, across the United States, a critical need for additional police in the many undermanned law

8/P. B. Weston and K. M. Wells, *The Administration of Justice* (Prentice-Hall, Inc., Englewood Cliffs, N.J., 1967); A. C. Germann, *et al., Introduction to Law Enforcement and Criminal Justice* (Charles C. Thomas, Springfield, Ill., 1962), revised 6th ptng.

enforcement agencies exists.[9] It is apparent that the number of police has not kept pace with the relocation of the population and the attendant increases in crime. But even more universal than the lack of police has been the need for improved quality of police officers.

There is clearly an insufficient number of court personnel—judges, prosecutors, defense attorneys, and legal aides—to handle the present volume of criminal cases in any fashion resembling justice and due process. In some states the lower courts still do not require that their judges be attorneys. Many a county or city prosecutor holds the position on a part-time basis, juggling it between his regular business.

In corrections, thousands of additional staff are required now to achieve even minimum standards for effective treatment and control. Over 100 years after the appearance of probation and parole as effective devices for assisting defendant rehabilitation, it appears that almost one third of the United States either do not have such services or have them only in token quantities.

Archaic Structure

In the area of agency structure, administration, and operation, there are but a handful of really excellent police departments, prosecutors' offices, local-county-state court systems, detention and incarceration facilities, and probation and parole services. The age-old complaints of politics, too little money, public apathy, insufficient personnel, overly rigid civil service versus "spoils system," political appointment, and lack of community support, continue to be heard.

Faculty System Conceptualization

Lastly, the conceptualization of the administration of criminal justice as a system or process in which there is an essential need for coordination and consolidation to best secure the ends of justice is an approach that can be found in only a handful of situations in the entire United States. Little or no coordination and rapport exist between police, the prosecutors, the judges, the correctional personnel, and the probation and parole officers. Each agency continues to build his "Chinese Wall" and consider the organizations to either side as staffed by individuals who appear to be corrupt, stupid, or lazy and at the least, woefully inefficient.

Further elaboration of this problem would serve no useful purpose. It is sufficient to state that the administration of criminal justice does not exist as a systematized process. It is a continuum only for the offender, not for the agencies and staffs involved.

9/U.S., President, Remarks upon signing Executive Order 11296, *Federal Law Enforcement and Crime Prevention Programs,* Weekly Compilation of Presidential Documents (Feb. 12, 1968, Vol. IV, No. 6, U.S. Government Printing Office, Washington, D.C.), p. 230.

RECENT DEVELOPMENTS

Such are three of the main areas of crisis affecting the process of criminal justice in America today. What are the indications that can be observed on the positive side? What are the innovations? What are the recent developments in each of the fields?

Legal Proceedings

No useful projection of possible future developments in the administration of criminal justice can be made without taking into consideration the role of laws and legal decisions. Following the lead of Illinois and a few other states, a number of states are currently reviewing their entire criminal codes and statutes relating to crime with the thought of consolidation, updating, and codification.[10]

At the federal level, the National Commission on Reform of Federal Criminal Laws was created by Congress to develop and recommend legislation which will modernize and improve the federal system of criminal justice and revise and codify the federal criminal laws.

A number of states, agencies, and organizations are researching laws that will meaningfully apply to specific antisocial behavior involving the so-called "crimes without victims." Recent enactment of state statutes dealing with syndicated gambling and other organized crime activities have been the outgrowth of purposeful collaboration between forward-thinking law enforcement personnel, prosecutors, and legislators—sometimes with a helping hand from private crime commissions.[11]

This is not to suggest that hysteria legislation does not continue to pass through state legislatures and city councils. The immature belief that "passing a law" will somehow bring a particular practice to a halt continues to be nurtured by many officeholders and legislators, as well as the general public.

Court Decisions

From the landmark case of *Mapp v. Ohio* [12] to the present, the United States Supreme Court has taken an increasingly active role in shaping state criminal trials and law enforcement operations and procedures. With the recognition that state courts may not use unlawfully seized evidence or confessions that do not meet appropriate due process tests, there has been an increase in the emphasis placed on the definition of legality as applied to the collection of various types of evidence for use in criminal cases.

10/*Illinois Proposed Code of Criminal Procedures,* Illinois State Bar Association and The Chicago Bar Association, Chicago, 1962.

11/*Illinois Criminal Law and Procedure, Revised statutes, Chap. 38, as amended to December 31, 1967* (Burdette Smith Co., Chicago, 1966).

12/*Mapp v. Ohio,* 367 U.S. 643 (1961).

Following the *Miranda*[13] decision, which was based on the ever-widening constitutional doctrine of exclusion, the Supreme Court and the state courts have been steadily expanding the limits of the lateral application of this rule. Important decisions dealing with lineups, handwriting samples, blood tests for intoxication, and other police procedures have forced law enforcement agencies across the country to critically evaluate their operational techniques and tools.[14] Many further interpretations of criminal investigation procedures will need to be made before the investigator clearly understands the boundaries and "no-man's-land" of his work. The Supreme Court has acted in the area of eavesdropping and wiretapping,[15] eliminating the old, safe criteria of nontrespassitory eavesdropping and replacing it with broadened concepts of an individual's rights to privacy. However, the Supreme Court strongly suggested that it would allow eavesdropping warrants paralleling standard search warrant concepts.

In another subject area, the remodeling job on agency practices which must now take place following the *Gault* case in the area of juvenile hearings has barely begun to take effect.[16] The *parens patria* philosophy which supposedly controlled juvenile courts has been seriously cut away and replaced with structured procedural safeguards akin to that utilized in regular criminal trials.

Law Enforcement

Securing enforcement of criminal laws in the United States are some 420,000 people working for approximately 40,000 separate police agencies.[17] The quantity of change and action within the police is greater at the present moment than at any time in the profession's brief history. From the use of helicopters in routine police patrol operations in Los Angeles County,[18] and the development of a model to predict crime occurrences in Philadelphia,[19] to the New Jersey legislation requiring statewide mandatory recordkeeping and reporting of criminal activity by police departments,[20] widely varied developmental activity can be observed in every corner of the nation.

Interesting paradoxes have also appeared. The most striking and well-attended

13/*Miranda v. Arizona,* 384 U.S. 436 (1966).

14/*United States v. Wade,* 388 U.S. 218 (1967); *Gilbert v. California,* 388 U.S. 263 (1967); *Schmerber v. California,* 384 U.S. 764.

15/*Berger v. New York,* 388 U.S. 41 (1967); *Katz v. U.S.,* 36 Law Week 4080.

16/*In re Gault,* 387 U.S. 1 (1967).

17/The President's Commission on Law Enforcement and Administration of Justice, *Task Force Report: The Police* (U.S. Government Printing Office, Washington, D.C., 1967), p. 1.

18/C. R. Guthrie and P. M. Whisenand, "The Use of Helicopters in Routine Police Patrol Operations" (Paper presented at the 2nd National Symposium on Law Enforcement Science and Technology, Chicago, April 16-18, 1968).

19/D. P. Stein, J. Crawshaw, and J. C. Herron, "Crime Prediction by Computer—Does It Work and Is It Useful?" (Paper, 2nd National Symposium).

20/Society of Professional Investigators, *The Bulletin* (Feb. 1968, Winter Ed., New York).

displays at the 1967 International Association of Chiefs of Police Annual Conference in Kansas City dealt with tanks, armored personnel carriers, and new types of rifles and semiautomatic weapons.[21] At the same time, numerous police departments were experimenting with wide-ranging community service programs, with officers in overalls repairing slum housing and operating out of store-front police stations.

In the area of police administration, the Management Institute for Police Chiefs held at Harvard University Graduate School of Business Administration in 1966 gave birth to dozens of similar programs on other campuses. Such programs demonstrated conclusively that police administrators could profit from campus programs taught by competent professionals in business management who might not have had any prior experience with law enforcement.

Early in 1968, another series of management conferences was initiated, this time at Airlie House in Warrenton, Virginia. Fifteen conferences, all dealing with civil disorder, were scheduled for 1968 in a variety of locations around the country.[22] There seems to be little question that the fourfold approach of restoring order, maintaining order, planning, and developing community concern and resources discussed at the conference was a contributing factor to the considerably improved police procedures employed during the disturbances and rioting of April 5, 6, 7, and 8, 1968. An interesting sidelight to the recent disorders is that it is now apparent that the police themselves are not the central problem in America's racial crisis and that the "professional blame-placers" will have to look elsewhere for scapegoats.

The most significant development in American policing in the last few years has been the steadily increasing number of states which are assuming their appropriate responsibility in assuring that certain minimum levels of police service and quality are present everywhere within their boundaries.[23]

Other areas of significant progress in policing include the development of a variety of statewide programs such as the many and varied approaches being used in New York and California. In California, along with the newly developed Council on Criminal Justice and Crime Technological Research Foundation, the Peace Officers Standards and Training Commission has been given the authority to establish statewide programs in the area of police management, executive development, and technical and advanced courses.[24]

Other areas of significant progress in policing include: the development of research and planning units; improved applications of science and technology to police problems, particularly in the areas of system analysis[25] and information and communication systems; and the development of local, regional, statewide

21/"Armored Vehicles," *Law and Order,* 15, 44 (1967).
22/"Civil Disorders" (International Association of Chiefs of Police, Washington, D.C., 1968).
23/N. C. Kassoff, "State Laws on Police Training Standards," *The Police Chief,* 33, 10 (1966).
24/Letter from Gene S. Muehleisen, Executive Officer, Commission on Peace Officer Standards and Training, Dept. of Justice, State of California, Sacramento, March 6, 1968.
25/Illinois Academy of Criminology, Archivist's Report (Chicago, Jan. 17, 1968).

and national information and data bank systems dealing with wanted persons, missing persons, stolen autos, and stolen and recovered property. Much of this activity has been initiated by three sources: the Office of Law Enforcement Assistance of the U.S. Department of Justice, the *Reports* of the President's Commission on Law Enforcement and the Administration of Justice, and the National Symposium on Science and Technology in Law Enforcement.[26]

The inauguration of the National Crime Information Center operated by the Federal Bureau of Investigation on a coast-to-coast basis[27] and the New York State Identification and Intelligence System covering all criminal justice agencies on a statewide basis are prime examples of two modern information networks.[28]

Prosecution and Adjudication

In prosecution and adjudication, the progress has not been as visibly dramatic, due to the somewhat unyielding nature of legal structures and institutions and the centuries of slow developmental tradition. The highly controversial Reardon Report which was recently approved by the American Bar Association establishes new guidelines dealing with the relationship between free press and a fair trial.[29] The ABA Special Committee on Minimal Standards for the Administration of Criminal Justice, headed by Chairman J. Edward Lumbard, continues to develop forward-looking recommendations in areas such as sentencing alternatives and procedures.[30] At the national level, President Johnson signed a bill designed to modernize and expedite procedures in the federal court system by establishing the Federal Judicial Training Center, which conducts research and training programs.[31]

Three sessions, in Michigan, Colorado, and New York, of a nationwide institute on the far-reaching implication of the *Gault* decision are being given by the Institute of Continuing Legal Education.[32] Significant advances continue to be made in bail reform practices. In addition, there has been some modest streamlining and revamping of courts to meet the volume of today's criminal cases.

Corrections

In corrections, the amount of change and activity appears to equal that in law enforcement. It would be impossible to list all of the many developments that

---

26/S. A. Yefsky, ed., *Law Enforcement Science and Technology* (Academic Press, London, England, 1967), *passim.*

27/"NCIC Progress Report," *F.B.I. Law Enforcement Bulletin,* 36, 2 (1967).

28/Bureau of Public Information, New York State Identification and Intelligence System, "NYSIIS Against Crime" (Albany, N.Y., 1967).

29/*Chicago Daily News,* Feb. 17, 1968, article by Roger Doughty, p. 5.

30/*Sentencing Alternatives and Procedures* (Tentative Draft), American Bar Association (1967).

31/*NCCD News,* 47, 1 (1968).

32/*Ibid.,* p. 2.

are taking place. Several of the more significant and representative programs are:

1. The development of incentives as a device for motivating prisoner behavior.[33]
2. The presentation by Southern Illinois University of a series of eight-week training courses for personnel of state correctional systems across the nation.[34]
3. The continuing program of research into all facets of manpower needs in corrections being conducted by the Joint Commission on Correctional Manpower and Training.[35]
4. The application of electric data processing techniques to the Bucks County, Pennsylvania, jail by a team composed of a correctional institution official, an academician, and a systems analyst.[36]
5. Continued expansion of the work-release program at the Federal Bureau of Prisons, which has included 3,900 participants since October, 1965.[37]
6. The utilization in 24 states of some form of work-release program for adult felons, such as the one pioneered by North Carolina in 1959.[38]
7. A plan to provide for statewide organization and coordination of correctional services dealing with the control and treatment of crime and delinquency for the entire state of California.[39]
8. The opening in 1967 of the first community treatment centers in the federal prison system which were designed to house selected adult inmates during the weeks preceding their discharge from prison and provide them with employment services, counseling, and other programs prepared to assist the participants in achieving a stable life in the community.[40]

Many of the changes within the correctional field are occurring in probation and parole services. Some of the more promising developments include:

1. Expansion of the use of volunteers in tasks ranging from "friends" of offenders to supervisors of work projects and group therapy by courts dealing with misdemeanors in cities across the country.[41]
2. The presentation of the National Council on Crime and Delinquency of Probation Management Institutes during 1967 and 1968 designed to enhance the decision-making skills of key probation administrators.[42]

33/The Pennsylvania Prison Society, *The Prison Journal* (1967), pp. 4-58, *passim.*
34/*Chicago Tribune,* March 29, 1968, p. 57.
35/R. M. Gutekunst, Jr., "Research as the Basis for a National Action Strategy in Corrections" (Paper, 2nd National Symposium).
36/R. Sheeder and C. L. Newman, "Systems Analysis of an Information System for a County Jail" (Paper, 2nd National Symposium).
37/Letter from Harry W. Schloetter, Deputy Director of Training, Federal Probation Training Center, Chicago, April 8, 1968.
38/Letter from Schloetter and F.B.I. news release, Dec. 11, 1967.
39/The Organization of State Correctional Services in the Control and Treatment of Crime and Delinquency, State of California, May, 1967, pp. 152-227, *passim.*
40/*NCCD News,* 46, 3 (1967).
41/*NCCD News,* 47, 4 (1968).
42/*NCCD News,* 46, 5 (1967).

Federal Government

The missions of the federal government in the field of criminal justice are many and varied. Within the Department of Justice alone, activities ranging from the civil rights investigations to the local law enforcement training activities of the Federal Bureau of Investigation are evidence of a serious concern for the improvement of American criminal justice.

Established in 1965, the Office of Law Enforcement Assistance over the past three years awarded $16,800,807 for 300 projects in six categories dealing with law enforcement, courts, and corrections: [43]

1. Law enforcement—education and training.
2. Law enforcement—operations improvement.
3. Corrections—probation, parole, and institutions.
4. Criminal justice—courts and prosecution.
5. General studies and crime prevention.
6. Special programs.
   a) State planning committees in criminal administration.
   b) Police science degree development.
   c) State law enforcement standards and training systems.
   d) Police-community relations planning and development.
   e) Statewide, in-service training for correctional personnel.
   f) Technical assistance, dissemination, etc.[44]

Many programs and projects included in this report are funded through OLEA.[45] The total effect of OLEA's funding appears to be both sizable and notable even at this early date.

Academic Interest

A field that has not been mentioned thus far is the appearance of the universities and colleges in criminal justice programs. The role of the so-called "hard" sciences is well covered in the various sessions of this symposium. Exploration of the use of the computer as it relates to the administration of criminal justice is being pursued on a multiuniversity basis.[46] The role of the social and behavioral sciences is less spectacular and less widely heralded but equally as vigorous. Research, education, and comment on a wide variety of subjects are taking place in America's institutions of higher learning.[47] Studies

43/*OLEA Grants and Contracts,* Office of Law Enforcement Assistance, U.S. Dept. of Justice, Fiscal 1966, 67, p. vii.
44/*Ibid.,* p. iii.
45/*Ibid.,* pp. 1-73, *passim.*
46/"The Computer and the Administration of Justice," Bulletin of Inter-University Communications Council (EDUCOM), Pittsburgh, 2, 4 (1967).
47/*Law and Society Review,* 2, 227 (1968).

dealing with the criminal victim, the cost of crime, the relationships between social problems and crime, deviant behavior, crime reporting and crime statistics, typology of criminality, and the role of the police exemplify the types of projects that are underway.[48]

The number of two- and four-year institutions granting college degrees in police science, police administration, criminology, criminalistics, and criminal justice rose during 1967 to 184.[49]

FUTURE IN CRIMINAL JUSTICE

A survey of the state-of-the-art in criminal justice must include more than a brief philosophical and historical résumé of what has happened and what is current. It is just as essential to review what is ahead—what are the emerging trends, the potential crises, and the possible developments.

In the all-important area of community support for criminal justice, there are faint but encouraging signs on several fronts:

1. On February 7, 1968, President Lyndon B. Johnson for the third year sent a State of the Union Message to Congress on "Meeting the Challenge of Crime in the United States." The President proposed a long list of measures to deal with crime, rioting, drug traffic, and the entire system of law enforcement and justice. Foremost was his plea for passage of the year-old Safe Streets and Crime Control Bill with a budget of $100 million for the first year.[50]
2. A substantial number of states have now, by executive order or legislation, established statutes and councils dealing with minimum standards for police in training and recruitment, statewide information systems, crime commissions, and various other criminal justice activities on a state level.
3. The National Council on Crime and Delinquency has embarked on a massive program to develop community and business support for effective action in crime prevention. The use of group methods by businessmen and trade associations to fight the infiltration of organized crime into legitimate business is one example of this attack involving NCCD's National Emergency Committee. The Committee was formed in response to the recommendations of the President's Commission on Law Enforcement and the Administration of Justice.[51]
4. An Associated Press survey among members of Congress on voter attitudes towards issues of national interest found that concern about crime and riot in America runs a close second to the war in Vietnam.[52]

48/Simon Dinitz, Ed. and W. C. Reckless, Ed., *Critical Issues in the Study of Crime* (Little, Brown and Co., Boston, 1968).

49/International Association of Chiefs of Police, *Police Science Programs* (Washington, D.C., 1967), p. 2.

50/U.S., President, "Remarks," pp. 230-232.

51/*NCCD News,* 47, 1 (1968).

52/*Ibid.,* p. 3.

Each of these developments indicates a mounting concern on the part of government, business, and the public over crime and criminal justice in this country.

What lies ahead in criminal justice?

In the crucial problem of dealing with rioting in America's urban communities, all of the administrations of criminal justice agencies will need to increase their efficiency and effectiveness by:

1. Working to identify and remove the intermediate and proximate causes of rioting.
2. Developing effective techniques of response and control by the police and the community.
3. Providing humane detention facilities for the large influx of arrestees.
4. Establishing emergency judicial processing, including the setting of reasonable bail, prompt arraignment and hearing, and providing public legal aid whenever needed.

In law, the role of the United States Supreme Court in bringing the operations of the administration of criminal justice team into conformity with the Constitution and the Bill of Rights will continue.

Law enforcement can look for decisions in the areas of: questioning and frisking of suspects, reasonable bail, release on recognizance,[53] and legal representation for all persons in all courts. Sentencing, probation, and parole practices will have to conform to strict due process standards. Recodifications of state statutes will increase, with the deviant behavior crimes such as alcoholism, sexual perversion, drug addiction, attempted suicide, and mental illness being generally excluded as criminal offenses.

The national crime rate will continue to ascend and accelerate until public pressure and professional operation of the administration of the criminal justice system combine meaningfully to stay the constant advance.

The law enforcement agencies stand on a most significant threshold. A strong and vital decision will need to be made as to the precise role of the police in answer to the question: Should police function solely as controllers of crime or should they include broad prevention programs within their operational policies?

As unrealistic as it may seem now to some, minimum entry educational standards for police must and will become first, a two-year degree, and shortly thereafter, a four-year college degree. Specialists, middle management personnel, and chiefs will be able to move horizontally from agency to agency, and entry of nonpolice types into the first and third groups will be allowed. The recent spiraling "arms race" will halt as the point of no return is reached. The "team" concept, using a multidisciplinary attack on delinquency problems, will be applied to police youth work.[54]

53/Editorial, *Chicago Daily News,* April 11, 1968, p. 10.
54/"Treatment Teams in Delinquency Prevention," *Police,* 12, 26-31 (1968), *passim.*

Prosecutive officials presently form the weakest link in the administration of criminal justice system. They undergo the least specialized training for their particular duty and engage in the least in-service training programs. Positive changes can be anticipated in these areas. The days of the hack political prosecutor as well as those of the nonprofessional coroner are numbered. Plea-bargaining, recognized neither by law nor rule of court, will be the subject of close scrutiny by the American Bar Association as well as the Supreme Court. Pretrial discovery of both prosecution and defense evidence will reduce the adversary nature of court proceedings without damage to the defendant's rights.

The treadmill circus of abortive justice involving unprofessional magistrates, justices of the peace, and municipal court judges will come to an end with their absorption into centralized court systems.

Additional judges and other legal officials, including more grand juries, clerks, public defenders, and prosecutors, will be added to court staffs. Full due process will be accorded in every court on every charge to every defendant.

Certainly, the Supreme Court decision which substantially nullified the federal wagering tax stamp and the federal firearms registration statutes will open the way for new attacks on other federal registration and reporting provisions as well as local registration and reporting statutes and ordinances.[55]

In view of the estimate by Attorney General Ramsey Clark that 50 percent of today's prison inmates do not belong in jail, the trend in corrections will be to remove this group from their "cages." Such action will allow for a greater concentration of services on the 15 percent of inmates who are dangerous or unreformable and need to be incarcerated.[56]

Despite the current pleas of certain elements of the public for the construction of more and bigger prisons, the old giant jails will come tumbling down. The urban-centered community treatment facility will replace the majority of penitentiaries across the United States.

While adequate diagnostic and treatment personnel for all American penal institutions may never be available, there will be substantial increases in the number of educated and skilled rehabilitative workers assigned to the institutions. Work-release, study-release, half-way houses and other innovative treatment projects will be commonplace within just a few short years.

The reintegration of the offender into the community at an earlier time than in the past will be the probable direction of the correction system. Probation and parole will undertake far wider functions than are now generally conceived within their casework-oriented programs. The probation officer will function more skillfully as a counselor than did his predecessor. Group therapy and group counseling, which have long been used in some correctional institutions, will be adopted by probation and parole agencies.[57]

Certainly, we can anticipate ever-increasing participation by all branches of

55/*NCCD News,* 47, 1 (1968).
56/"Criminals Should be Cured Not Caged," *Time,* March 29, 1968, p. 41.
57/O. T. Irwin, "Group Therapy with Juvenile Probationers," *Federal Probation,* 31, 57-63 (1967).

the academic community. Particularly, we can expect the behavioral sciences to show an ever-broadening interest in the areas of crime causation, criminal careers or subcultures, law enforcement,[58] criminal justice,[59] corrections,[60] and rehabilitation.

Criminal justice will be joining forces with other professions in projects such as the St. Louis Detoxification and Diagnostic Treatment Center[61] and the New York Narcotic Control Commission[62] in an attempt to deal meaningfully with the "crimes without victims" syndrome.

Both the federal and state governments will accelerate their heretofore lagging interest in law enforcement and the administration of criminal justice.

Justice has been a major concern of man from Paleolithic times through the Hindu Laws of Manu, to the Hebraic Torah and the Christian rule of love, through the Codes of Solon and Draco to the Roman Law of the Twelve Tables, from the magnificent Corpus Juris Civilis of Justinian to the Code Napoleon, and including the Magna Charta and the Constitution and the Bill of Rights. Law and the search for justice are as old as man and as new as the most recently enacted state statute and U.S. Supreme Court decision.

No one society, country, or civilization has ever reached a state of perfect law or perfect justice. But the search for that balance which will provide for a meaningful coexistence between the individual and the society with full and due respect for the rights of both will continue as long as man has the dual desire to live in freedom and within a society.

23. The M'Naghten Rules and Proposed Alternatives*

JEROME HALL

The actual court trial usually follows a generally defined procedure, including arraignment and plea, selection of jury, prosecutor's opening statement, presentation of the state's evidence, presentation of the accused's evidence, the prosecutor's argument to the jury, the accused's argument to the jury, the

58/W. Dienstein, "Sociology of Law Enforcement" (Paper, 2nd National Symposium).

59/W. Herrmann, "Public Order in a Free Society" (Paper, 2nd National Symposium).

60/R. L. Henshel, "Cost Effectiveness in Military Corrections" (Paper, 2nd National Symposium).

61/J. B. Kendis (M.D.), "The St. Louis Experience" (Paper, 2nd National Symposium).

62/D. Glaser, "Research Opportunity Expansion in the Control of Narcotic Addiction in New York" (Paper, 2nd National Symposium).

*Reprinted from *American Bar Association Journal.* Copyright 1963 American Bar Association prosecutor's rebuttal, the judge's instructions upon the law, the rendition of the jury verdict, and the imposition of sentence by the judge, if the verdict is guilty. Many other variables, however, are involved in the determination of guilt or innocence. One of these, of course, is the question of whether the defendant is criminally responsible for the act for which he is charged. The court must determine not only whether the act was intended but also whether the accused possesses the ability to form a rational intent to complete the violation. Because criminal law makes an elementary distinction between those acts which are premeditated or fully intended and those of the opposite extreme which are accidental, it seeks to ascertain whether the accused possessed a *mens rea* (guilty mind) at the time of his act.

Such an attempt to evaluate the accused's state of mental responsibility is tied to the definition of legal insanity. The concept, however, is a legal term which attempts to delineate the behavioral condition of the accused. Consequently, the concept of legal responsibility is open to wide debate because its assumption that human behavior may be clearly delineated into sane-insane forms is not always supported by psychiatric experience (*see* introduction to Article 1).

Under the English M'Naghten rules the British courts assumed that a defense on the ground of insanity must show conclusively that the party accused at the time of commiting the act was laboring under a defect of reason, from a disease of the mind, "as not to know the nature and quality of the act he was doing; or, if he did know it, that he did not know he was doing what was wrong." While the M'Naghten criterion became the basis of insanity judgments in most states in the United States, recent discoveries in psychology and psychiatry have challenged its basic assumptions.

Judge David L. Bazelon believes that M'Naghten is no longer adequate. Recognizing the advanced current understanding of human behavior, Bazelon wrote in the 1954 case of *Durham v. United States* that an accused is not criminally responsible if his act was *the product of mental disease or defect.* Because man is an integrated personality, reason, Bazelon argues, can no longer be viewed as the sole determinant of individual behavior. Criminal law professor Jerome Hall, on the other hand, maintains that M'Naghten needs merely repair rather than replacement.

In the March, 1963, issue of the *American Bar Association Journal,* Justice William J. Brennan, Jr., after stating that he would not even "by the slightest intimation suggest" which insanity test he thought preferable to the M'Naghten Rules, "if indeed it has yet been proved that any one of them is better," proceeds directly to express some very definite preferences on this subject.[1]

1/Brennan, "Law and Psychiatry Must Join in Defending Mentally Ill Criminals," 49 *A.B.A.J.* 239 (March, 1963).

Thus, evidently referring to those who defend the M'Naghten Rules, he asks a startling and illuminating question: "How valid is the assumption that morality and safety require punishment . . . of mentally ill people?" This is startling because it seems to suggest that defenders of the M'Naghten Rules wish to have psychotic persons punished. It is illuminating because it indicates a lack of awareness of the fact that the principal problems in this area concern the meaning of "mentally ill," the "knowledge" by reference to which this is to be determined, and how mental illness can best be decided in a democratic society when the issue is criminal responsibility.[2] One's concern is heightened by the justice's confidence in "medical assessment" as a condition of release from imprisonment and by his evident opinion that there is an obvious answer to the question whether "mentally ill offenders" should be sent to a hospital or a penal institution.

The M'Naghten Rules were propounded by English judges in 1843 in *Daniel M'Naghten's Case,* . . . , in response to inquiries from the House of Lords. They hold that "to establish a defense on the ground of insanity, it must be clearly proved that, at the time of the committing of the act, the party accused was laboring under such a defect of reason, from disease of the mind, as not to know the nature and quality of the act he was doing; or, if he did know it, that he did not know he was doing what was wrong." This test has been and is followed (with some glosses) in almost all American jurisdictions, except New Hampshire, Vermont and perhaps Illinois. In New Hampshire, for instance, in *State v. Pike,* 49 N. H. 399 (1869), the Supreme Court of that state formulated a test holding that an accused is not criminally responsible "if the [unlawful act] was the offspring or product of mental disease . . .".

Durham Case Arouses Interest in Insanity Rules

The present interest in insanity as a defense in trials of criminal responsibility was aroused by the decision of the United States Court of Appeals for the District of Columbia Circuit in 1954 in *Durham v. United States,* 214 F. 2d 862, in which the court held that a defendant was not criminally responsible "if his unlawful act was the product of mental disease or mental defect." The Court of Appeals for the Third Circuit has refused, as have many other courts, to follow the *Durham* rule, stating: "We are of the opinion that the following formula most nearly fulfills the objectives just discussed: The jury must be satisfied that at the time of committing the prohibited act the defendant, as a result of mental disease or defect, lacked substantial capacity to conform his conduct to the requirements of the law which he is alleged to have violated."[3]

Another alternative to the M'Naghten Rules is proposed in the Model Penal Code of the American Law Institute. This provides:

2/These questions are discussed in Hall, *General Principles of Criminal Law* 449-529 (2d ed. 1960).
3/*United States v. Currens,* 290 F. 2d 751 (1961).

(1) A person is not responsible for criminal conduct if at the time of such conduct as a result of mental disease or defect he lacks substantial capacity either to appreciate the criminality [wrongfulness] of his conduct or to conform his conduct to the requirements of law.

(2) As used in this article, the terms "mental disease or defect" do not include an abnormality manifested only by repeated criminal or otherwise antisocial conduct.[4]

.   .   .   .

Justice Douglas Thinks Durham Is Improvement

In a lecture a few years ago to a group of psychiatrists, Justice William O. Douglas hailed the *Durham* rule as a great improvement on the "rigid," the "arbitrary, fixed" M'Naghten Rules.[5] He first attributed the M'Naghten test to political pressure, public clamor and newspaper publicity, but later he said: "The only warrant of the *M'Naghten* rule of insanity was tradition." "To most psychiatrists," he continued, the *Durham* decision "was a break with legal tradition that was long overdue." It has the great advantage of permitting the psychiatrist to "speak to the court and to the jury in the language of his discipline," he declared.

Justice Douglas, in my opinion, was seriously mistaken in every one of these statements. Not the least significant evidence of this is that an overwhelming majority of the judges who have had an opportunity to pass on the question have rejected the *Durham* rule and the psychiatry summoned in support of it. The irony of these implied and expressed criticisms of the McNaghten Rules is that these justices, especially sensitive to the protection of civil liberties, do not realize that if the McNaghten Rules are abandoned, the consequence will probably be a "tyranny of experts."[6] The vaunted "humanitarianism" of some psychiatrists contemplates the long-term incarceration of vast numbers of persons who have violated no law, as well as the detention of thousands of petty offenders for as long a time as the so-called experts withhold their favorable prognosis. . . .

.   .   .   .

Informed Discussion Shouldn't Be Curtailed

Can anything be done to remedy this situation, especially in its relation to issues of the gravest importance that will no doubt be presented in due course to the Supreme Court? Certainly it would be a mistake for judges to refrain from

4/Section 4.01, *Model Penal Code* (Proposed Official Draft) 66 (1962). See also, Schwartz, "The Model Penal Code. An Invitation to Law Reform," 49 *A.B.A.J.* 447, at 449 (May, 1963).

5/Douglas, "The Durham Rule: A Meeting Ground for Lawyers and Psychiatrists," 41 *Iowa L. Rev.* 485 (1956).

6/Wertham, "Psychoauthoritarianism and the Law," 22 *U. Chi. L. Rev.* 337 (1955).

public speaking and printed publication, for then important potential contributions would not be made and the occasional need for further study would be unknown.

It may be suggested, in the first place, that when a judge delivers a public lecture and has it published in a widely read journal, it is both fair and necessary that the views he expresses be subjected to the same sort of searching criticism as the published views of others. But objectivity is very difficult to maintain when a justice of the United States Supreme Court is concerned.

Moreover, one can hardly ignore the fact that although we avow a free market in ideas as the best test of truth, the heads of well-financed psychiatric institutions and powerful officials enjoy strategic positions in the formation of public opinion. The implications are alarming when a justice of the Supreme Court appears to have accepted certain philosophical versions of psychiatry.

It would, of course, be absurd to imply that either Justice Brennan or Justice Douglas would approve any philosophy that depreciated human freedom. What troubles one is their apparent failure to recognize the relationship to human freedom of the thesis that everyone or that every criminal is "mentally ill." What troubles, also, is the apparent acceptance of the extremely broad meaning of "mental illness" propagated by psychiatrists whose philosophy is, quite consistently, the utter repudiation of freedom, responsibility and other basic values of democratic society. It is hardly possible to avoid the conclusion that what is plainly needed is further study of this difficult problem by judges and practicing lawyers so that at least the cogent questions can be raised.

National Seminar Is Proposed

Can anything be done to facilitate this and to assure a fair and informed hearing of these problems? Given competent guidance, it would be possible for an able lawyer or judge to acquire a significant degree of critical competence in this area in a year of carefully planned reading and bimonthly discussions. This could be done in seminars or round-table discussions in which the M'Naghten adherents were given a role and an opportunity equal to that of the critics of the prevailing law. . . .

.   .   .   .

Some Subjects for Discussion

The following program of a seminar or discussion group is suggested as illustrative. No preference is implied as to the order of studying the various problems and their formulation is not wholly neutral since my purpose is, also, to raise questions regarding current criticism of the M'Naghten Rules.

1. What are the principal meanings of "disease"? Is mental illness like physical illness, or is it so different from it that even a very wide analogy is misleading?

2. What is "science"? Is there an intermediate type of knowledge between science, rigorously defined, and common sense? Where should psychiatry be placed, *e.g.,* what of statements by leading psychiatrists to the effect that psychiatry is an art? . . .

3. What is an expert, *e.g.,* does that term imply that there is a body of knowledge with reference to which all or most "experts" agree? . . .

4. Does psychiatry include expert skill in elucidating such terms as "right," "freedom," "justice," "punishment" and "responsibility"? What is the special competence of psychiatrists? . . .

5. The history of legal tests of insanity should be explored to ascertain their relationship to the contemporaneous medical and psychiatric knowledge, moral ideas and views of "human nature" and, also, to evaluate certain recent statements, *e.g.,* that the M'Naghten Rules were merely the product of political pressure, that a "wild beast" test was ever actually a rule of law in England in the implied literal sense, ...

6. Important, also, is a comparative study of American, English and Continental law, especially with reference to the "irresistible impulse" test as a complete alternative to the cognitive (M'Naghten) test. On what grounds has the Report of the Royal Commission, 1949-1953, so highly praised in this country by critics of M'Naghten, been criticized by English judges, for instance, Justice Devlin? . . .

7. In the study of such social problems, the most difficult question often is: What *is* the question or the proposal that is made? . . .

8. The characteristics and requirements of a democratic legal order should be studied especially in relation to the role of unfettered officials, unfettered experts and unfettered juries. Are the prevailing conceptions of human nature, individual responsibility, freedom, right and wrong, as traditionally expressed in the rules of law which guide judges and juries, to be subordinated to the theories of psychiatrists and, if so, to which ones—Freudian, neo-Freudian, anti-Freudian, Jungian, Adlerite, existentialist, organicist, neurologist, Reikian, Frommian, or eclectic?[7] Should the selected experts be permitted to present any theories or opinions to juries who receive no guidance from judges or laws?

9. There are still unsettled questions about "punishment" to be studied; they involve questions of public policy, ethics and free discussion. There are distinctions to be drawn between reforms, utopias and the relation of punishment to freedom and social responsibility. . . .

10. Finally, efforts might be made to formulate conclusions reached at the end of the inquiry, which, presumably, would correctly and precisely reflect the various positions held at that time. . . .

7/"We are forced to conclude that the psychologically minded psychiatrist and his organicist colleague, though often members of the same professional organizations, do not talk the same language and do not have the same interests. It is not surprising, then, that they have nothing good to say to each other, and that when they do communicate it is only to castigate each other's work and point of view." Szasz, *The Myth of Mental Illness* 93 (1961).

Study Has Values Even Without Answers

There is, of course, no certainty that a general agreement will be reached on these difficult questions even after a year's study; it is possible that one's ultimate premises, one's "can't helps," as Holmes put it, will persist to the very end. . . .

For me the existence of a significant degree of human freedom is a "can't help," as it is, no doubt, for Justices Brennan and Douglas and the vast majority of thoughtful Americans. So, too, as regards moral values, *e.g.,* that after thinking about a problem it makes sense to speak of "right" and "wrong" actions. But human freedom and moral values depend upon understanding—they imply the reasoning, generalizing, cognitive functions of the human mind. "Mental illness" in at least some of its meanings deeply affects the validity of these postulates and their implications.

Seen in relation to these basic postulates, the M'Naghten Rules are neither a political contrivance nor a mere tradition. They may be faulty in their formulation, in emphasis on one phase of personality and in connotating the one-sidedness of the supporting psychology of the times. But despite its defects, M'Naghten incorporates the most important function of human personality in terms of criteria with which a civilized body of criminal law must be concerned.

M'Naghten Needs Repairs, Not Abandonment

For that reason, what is relevant is not the abandonment of M'Naghten, but only its repair. . . . This means the avoidance of completely autonomous alternatives such as the Durham rule, the American Law Institute's alternative proposal in terms of lack of "substantial capacity . . . to conform" and other forms of the "irresistible impulse" hypothesis. A test solely in terms of "control of conduct" is ambiguous because it is silent on the crucial question: whether understanding has anything to do with conduct. To preserve the sound core of M'Naghten requires that the rationality of the human mind (understanding, knowledge, appreciation) be *included* in the proposed test, in which case it may, of course, and probably should be, joined to other major functions of the personality.[8]

. . . .

8/Hall, *op. cit. supra* at 521-522.

24. The Practice of Law as Confidence Game*

ABRAHAM S. BLUMBERG

The vast number of American criminal cases are decided on the basis of the defendant's admission of guilt (*see* Bilek, Article 22). Consequently, American justice is less a system of trial and more a procedure for sentencing following the preadmission of guilt. Probably as many as 95 percent of the less serious misdemeanor cases involving drunkenness, disorderly conduct and other nontraffic misdemeanor offenses are adjudicated on the basis of guilty pleas (*see* introduction to Article 4). Because these cases take only a few minutes to process, any major changes in current court procedures or trial processes automatically involve lags in the administration of justice.

While many guilty pleas are based upon a confession which has either been voluntarily offered or procedurally extracted from the alleged offender, others are encouraged by the elaborate system of negotiation among the defense lawyer, the prosecuting attorney, and sometimes the judge, who attempt to bargain for the most advantageous position for their office or client. Tacit or explicit bargaining, therefore, is widespread and often replaces the importance of trial innocence or guilt. Some evidence, for example, suggests that many lawyers encourage the bargaining system because it enables them to defend clients with minimum effort at a stated fee (*see* Blumberg, Article 24). Because the evidence in each case may not guarantee conviction on the charge, negotiation is looked upon by the prosecutor as a means to guarantee a good record, by the defense attorney as a procedure which mitigates the harshness of the system of justice, and by the judge as a means to expedite cases.

While bargaining in civil cases is more easily condoned on the ground that two parties of equal strength are contending before the judge for civil judgment in their favor, action in a criminal case is far more subtle and involves the action of the police officer and prosecuting attorney against the defense attorney and the charged offender. The power of the state in criminal cases exceeds the power of the individual to meet the challenge of the political organization. Because the relative bargaining positions of the participants are unequal, the criminal defense is highly tenuous. Although even a minor shift in the number of cases going to trial necessarily involves a major dislocation of case flow through the court system, the disposition of cases through a plea-bargaining system, Arthur Rosett

*Reprinted from *Law and Society Review*, Volume 1 (June, 1967), pp. 15-39, with the permission of the editors and author.

suggests, tends to be governed by such tactical factors as the court and prosecutor work load, the aggressiveness of case lawyers, personal relationships of court personnel and defense attorneys, general court practices, and other factors which affect the disposition of criminal cases.

The problems of the criminal defense are especially acute in cases involving lower status groups. Dallin H. Oaks and Warren Lehman found in a study of lawyers for the poor that the uncertain economic character of the practice of criminal law leads many lawyers to avoid the full-time practice of criminal defense. In a study of 5,597 indictments representing 4,040 defendants, nearly 40 percent, Oaks and Lehman found, involved cases of indigents served by the Cook County (Illinois) public defender's office. Although nearly 4 percent of the indictments involved indigents defended by members of the Chicago Bar Association's Defense of Prisoner Committee, the remainder (56 percent) were defended by other private attorneys. Not only were private or other appointed counsel more successful in gaining dismissal before trial (29 percent versus 8 percent for public defenders and 6 percent for the Bar Association Committee), but they were less likely to settle for a guilty plea (53 percent versus 75 percent for the public defender and 63 percent for the Bar Association Committee). While many of their differences are undoubtedly due to variations in style as well as the hopefulness of the alleged offender, the public defender obviously works under severe handicaps. Consequently, the continued participation of the private lawyer, Oaks and Lehman conclude, may well be necessary to maintain a continued integrity in the treatment of the poor in the American criminal court.

Although the existence of the right to counsel to all persons charged with criminal violations was designed to enhance the rights of the poor (*see* introduction to Part Five), its extension, Abraham S. Blumberg suggests, may result in an effect which is somewhat different from that desired and anticipated by the Supreme Court.

A recurring theme in the growing dialogue between sociology and law has been the great need for a joint effort of the two disciplines to illuminate urgent social and legal issues. Having uttered fervent public pronouncements in this vein, however, the respective practitioners often go their separate ways. . . . [S]cant attention—apart from explorations of the legal profession itself—has been given to the sociological examination of legal institutions, or their supporting ideological assumptions. Thus, for example, very little sociological effort is expended to ascertain the validity and viability of important court decisions, which may rest on wholly erroneous assumptions about the contextual realities of social structure. A particular decision may rest upon a legally impeccable rationale; at the same time it may be rendered nugatory or self-defeating by contingencies imposed by aspects of social reality of which the lawmakers are themselves unaware.

Within this context, I wish to question the impact of three recent landmark decisions of the United States Supreme Court; each hailed as destined to effect profound changes in the future of criminal law administration and enforcement in America. The first of these, *Gideon v. Wainwright*, . . . required states and localities henceforth to furnish counsel in the case of indigent persons charged with a felony.[1] The Gideon ruling left several major issues unsettled, among them the vital question: What is the precise point in time at which a suspect is entitled to counsel?[2] The answer came relatively quickly in *Escobedo v. Illinois*, . . . , which has aroused a storm of controversy. Danny Escobedo confessed to the murder of his brother-in-law after the police had refused to permit retained counsel to see him, although his lawyer was present in the station house and asked to confer with his client. In a 5-4 decision, the court asserted that the counsel must be permitted when the process of police investigative effort shifts from merely investigatory to that of accusatory: "when its focus is on the accused and its purpose is to elicit a confession—our adversary system begins to operate, and, under the circumstances here, the accused must be permitted to consult with his lawyer."

As a consequence, Escobedo's confession was rendered inadmissible. The decision triggered a national debate among police, district attorneys, judges, lawyers, and other law enforcement officials, which continues unabated, as to the value and propriety of confessions in criminal cases.[3] On June 13, 1966, the Supreme Court in a 5-4 decision underscored the principle enunciated in *Escobedo* in the case of *Miranda v. Arizona*.[4] Police interrogation of any suspect in custody, without his consent, unless a defense attorney is present, is prohibited by the self-incrimination provision of the Fifth Amendment. . . . In all three decisions, the Supreme Court reiterates the traditional legal conception of a defense lawyer based on the ideological perception of a criminal case as an *adversary, combative* proceeding, in which counsel for the defense assiduously musters all the admittedly limited resources at his command to *defend* the accused.[5] The fundamental question remains to be answered: Does the Supreme Court's conception of the role of counsel in a criminal case square with social reality?

. . . This paper is based upon observations made by the writer during many

1/This decision represented the climax of a line of cases which had begun to chip away at the notion that the Sixth Amendment of the Constitution (right to assistance of counsel) applied only to the federal government, and could not be held to run against the states through the Fourteenth Amendment.

2/In the case of federal defendants the issue is clear. In *Mallory v. United States*, 354 U.S. 449 (1957), the Supreme Court unequivocally indicated that a person under federal arrest must be taken "without any unnecessary delay" before a U.S. commissioner where he will receive information as to his rights to remain silent and to assistance of counsel which will be furnished, in the event he is indigent, under the Criminal Justice Act of 1964.

3/See *N.Y. Times*, Nov. 20, 1965, p. 1, for Justice Nathan R. Sobel's statement to the effect that based on his study of 1,000 indictments in Brooklyn, N.Y. from February-April, 1965, fewer than 10% involved confessions.

4/*Miranda v. Arizona*, 384 U.S. 436 (1966).

5/Even under optimal circumstances a criminal case is a very much one-sided affair, the parties to the "contest" being decidedly unequal in strength and resources.

years of legal practice in the criminal courts of a large metropolitan area. No claim is made as to its methodological rigor, although it does reflect a conscious and sustained effort for participant observation.

COURT STRUCTURE DEFINES ROLE OF DEFENSE LAWYER

The overwhelming majority of convictions in criminal cases (usually over 90 per cent) are not the product of a combative, trial-by-jury process at all, but instead merely involve the sentencing of the individual after a negotiated, bargained-for plea of guilty has been entered.[6] . . . [T]he extremely high conviction rate produced without the features of an adversary trial in our courts would tend to suggest that the "trial" becomes a perfunctory reiteration and validation of the pretrial interrogation and investigation.[7]

The institutional setting of the court defines a role for the defense counsel in a criminal case radically different from the one traditionally depicted.[8] Sociologists and others have focused their attention on the deprivations and social disabilities of such variables as race, ethnicity, and social class as being the source of an accused person's defeat in a criminal court. Largely overlooked is the variable of the court organization itself, which possesses a thrust, purpose, and direction of its own. It is grounded in pragmatic values, bureaucratic priorities, and administrative instruments. . . .

Organizational goals and discipline impose a set of demands and conditions of practice on the respective professions in the criminal court, to which they respond by abandoning their ideological and professional commitments to the accused client, in the service of these higher claims of the court organization. All court personnel, including the accused's own lawyer, tend to be coopted to become agent-mediators[9] who help the accused redefine his situation and restructure his perceptions concomitant with a plea of guilty.

Of all the occupational roles in the court the only private individual who is officially recognized as having a special status and concomitant obligations is the lawyer. His legal status is that of "an officer of the court" and he is held to a standard of ethical performance and duty to his client as well as to the court. This obligation is thought to be far higher than that expected of ordinary individuals occupying the various occupational statuses in the court community. However, lawyers, whether privately retained or of the legal-aid, public defender

6/F. J. Davis et al., Society and the Law: New Meanings for an Old Profession 301 (1962); L. Orfield, Criminal Procedure from Arrest to Appeal 297 (1947).
   D. J. Newman, "Pleading Guilty for Considerations: A Study of Bargain Justice," 46 J. Crim. L. C. & P.S. 780-90 (1954).
   7/G. Feifer, Justice in Moscow (1965).
   8/For a concise statement of the constitutional and economic aspects of the right to legal assistance, see M. G. Paulsen, Equal Justice for the Poor Man (1964); for a brief traditional description of the legal profession see P. A. Freund, "The Legal Profession," Daedalus 689-700 (1963).
   9/I use the concept in the general sense that Erving Goffman employed it in his Asylums: Essays on the Social Situation of Mental Patients and Other Inmates (1961).

variety, have close and continuing relations with the prosecuting office and the court itself through discreet relations with the judges via their law secretaries or "confidential" assistants. Indeed, lines of communication, influence and contact with those offices, as well as with the Office of the Clerk of the court, Probation Division, and with the press, are essential to present and prospective requirements of criminal law practice. Similarly, the subtle involvement of the press and other mass media in the court's organizational network is not readily discernible to the casual observer. Accused persons come and go in the court system schema, but the structure and its occupational incumbents remain to carry on their respective career, occupational and organizational enterprises. The individual stridencies, tensions, and conflicts a given accused person's case may present to all the participants are overcome, because the formal and informal relations of all the groups in the court setting require it. The probability of continued future relations and interaction must be preserved at all costs.

This is particularly true of the "lawyer regulars" *i.e.,* those defense lawyers, who by virtue of their continuous appearances in behalf of defendants, tend to represent the bulk of a criminal court's non-indigent case workload, and those lawyers who are not "regulars," who appear almost casually in behalf of an occasional client. Some of the "lawyer regulars" are highly visible as one moves about the major urban centers of the nation, their offices line the back streets of the courthouses, at times sharing space with bondsmen. Their political "visibility" in terms of local club house ties, reaching into the judge's chambers and prosecutor's office, are also deemed essential to successful practitioners. Previous research has indicated that the "lawyer regulars" make no effort to conceal their dependence upon police, bondsmen, jail personnel. Nor do they conceal the necessity for maintaining intimate relations with all levels of personnel in the court setting as a means of obtaining, maintaining, and building their practice. These informal relations are the *sine qua non* not only of retaining a practice, but also in the negotiation of pleas and sentences.[10]

The client . . . is a secondary figure in the court system as in certain other bureaucratic settings.[11] He becomes a means to other ends of the organization's incumbents. He may present doubts, contingencies, and pressures which challenge existing informal arrangements or disrupt them; but these tend to be resolved in favor of the continuance of the organization and its relations as before. . . . In short, the court is a closed community.

This is more than just the case of the usual "secrets" of bureaucracy which are fanatically defended from an outside view. Even all elements of the press are zealously determined to report on that which will not offend the board of judges, the prosecutor, probation, legal-aid, or other officials, in return for privileges and courtesies granted in the past and to be granted in the future.

10/A. L. Wood, "Informal Relations in the Practice of Criminal Law," 62 *Am. J. Soc.* 48-55 (1956); J. E. Carlin, *Lawyers on Their Own* 105-09 (1962); R. Goldfarb, *Ransom—A Critique of the American Bail System* 114-15 (1965).

11/There is a real question to be raised as to whether in certain organizational settings, a complete reversal of the bureaucratic-ideal has not occurred.

Rather than any view of the matter in terms of some variation of a "conspiracy" hypothesis, the simple explanation is one of an ongoing system handling delicate tensions, managing the trauma produced by law enforcement and administration, and requiring almost pathological distrust of "outsiders" bordering on group paranoia.

The hostile attitude toward "outsiders" is in large measure engendered by a defensiveness itself produced by the inherent deficiencies of assembly line justice, so characteristic of our major criminal courts. . . . As a consequence, an almost irreconcilable conflict is posed in terms of intense pressures to process large numbers of cases on the one hand, and the stringent ideological and legal requirements of "due process of law," on the other hand. A rather tenuous resolution of the dilemma has emerged in the shape of a large variety of bureaucratically ordained and controlled "work crimes," short cuts, deviations, and outright rule violations adopted as court practice in order to meet production norms. Fearfully anticipating criticism on ethical as well as legal grounds, all the significant participants in the court's social structure are bound into an organized system of complicity. This consists of a work arrangement in which the patterned, covert, informal breaches, and evasions of "due process" are institutionalized, but are, nevertheless, denied to exist.

These institutionalized evasions will be found to occur to some degree, in all criminal courts. Their nature, scope and complexity are largely determined by the size of the court, and the character of the community in which it is located, e.g., whether it is a large, urban institution, or a relatively small rural county court. In addition, idiosyncratic, local conditions may contribute to a unique flavor in the character and quality of the criminal law's administration in a particular community. . . . A wide variety of coercive devices are employed against an accused-client, couched in a depersonalized, instrumental, bureaucratic version of due process of law, and which are in reality a perfunctory obeisance to the ideology of due process. These include some very explicit pressures which are exerted in some measure by all court personnel, including judges, to plead guilty and avoid trial. In many instances the sanction of a potentially harsh sentence is utilized as the visible alternative to pleading guilty, in the case of recalcitrants. Probation and psychiatric reports are "tailored" to organizational needs, or are at least responsive to the court organization's requirements for the refurbishment of a defendant's social biography, consonant with his new status. A resourceful judge can, through his subtle domination of the proceedings, impose his will on the final outcome of a trial. Stenographers and clerks, in their function as record keepers, are on occasion pressed into service in support of a judicial need to "rewrite" the record of a courtroom event. Bail practices are usually employed for purposes other than simply assuring a defendant's presence on the date of a hearing in connection with his case. Too often, the discretionary power as to bail is part of the arsenal of weapons available to collapse the resistance of an accused person. . . .

The defense attorneys, therefore, whether of the legal-aid, public defender variety, or privately retained, although operating in terms of pressures specific to their respective role and organizational obligations, ultimately are concerned with strategies which tend to lead to a plea. . . . The lawyer "regulars" are frequently former staff members of the prosecutor's office and utilize the prestige, know-how and contacts of their former affiliation as part of their stock in trade. Close and continuing relations between the lawyer "regular" and his former colleagues in the prosecutor's office generally overshadow the relationship between the regular and his client. . . .

FEE COLLECTION AND FIXING

The real key to understanding the role of defense counsel in a criminal case is to be found in the area of the fixing of the fee to be charged and its collection. The problem of fixing and collecting the fee tends to influence to a significant degree the criminal court process itself, and not just the relationship of the lawyer and his client. In essence, a lawyer-client "confidence game" is played. . . .

Legal service lends itself particularly well to confidence games. . . .

. . . Much legal work is intangible either because it is simply a few words of advice, some preventive action, a telephone call, negotiation of some kind, a form filled out and filed, a hurried conference with another attorney or an official of a government agency, a letter or opinion written, or a countless variety of seemingly innocuous, and even prosaic procedures and actions. . . . [M]uch legal activity, whether it is at the lowest or highest "white shoe" law firm levels, is of the brokerage, agent, sales representative, lobbyist type of activity, in which the lawyer acts for someone else in pursuing the latter's interests and designs. The service is intangible.[12]

The large scale law firm may not speak as openly of their "contacts," their "fixing" abilities, as does the lower level lawyer. They trade instead upon a facade of thick carpeting, walnut panelling, genteel low pressure, and superficialities of traditional legal professionalism. There are occasions when even the large firm is on the defensive in connection with the fees they charge because the services rendered or results obtained do not appear to merit the fee asked.[13] . . .

Although the fee at times amounts to what the traffic and the conscience of the lawyer will bear, one further observation must be made with regard to the size of the fee and its collection. The defendant in a criminal case and the material gain he may have acquired during the course of his illicit activities are soon parted. . . . Inexorably, the amount of the fee is a function of the dollar value of the crime committed, and is frequently set with meticulous precision at a sum which bears an uncanny relationship to that of the net proceeds of the

12/C. W. Mills, *White Collar* 121-29 (1951); J. E. Carlin *supra,* note 11.
13/E. O. Smigel, *The Wall Street Lawyer* 309 (1964).

particular offense involved. On occasion, defendants have been known to commit additional offenses while at liberty on bail, in order to secure the requisite funds with which to meet their obligations for payment of legal fees. . . . Lawyers . . . seek to keep their clients in a proper state of tension, and to arouse in them the precise edge of anxiety which is calculated to encourage prompt fee payment. . . .

In varying degrees, as a consequence, all law practice involves a manipulation of the client and a stage management of the lawyer-client relationship so that at least an *appearance* of help and service will be forthcoming. . . . At the outset, the lawyer-professional employs with suitable variation a measure of sales-puff which may range from an air of unbounding self confidence, adequacy, and dominion over events, to that of complete arrogance. This will be supplemented by the affectation of a studied, faultless mode of personal attire. In the larger firms, the furnishings and office trappings will serve as the backdrop to help in impression management and client intimidation. In all firms, solo or large scale, an access to secret knowledge, and to the seats of power and influence is inferred, or presumed to a varying degree as the basic vendible commodity of the practitioners.

The lack of visible end product offers a special complication in the course of the professional life of the criminal court lawyer with respect to his fee and in his relations with his client. The plain fact is that an accused in a criminal case always "loses" even when he has been exonerated by an acquittal, discharge, or dismissal of his case. The hostility of an accused which follows as a consequence of his arrest, incarceration, possible loss of job, expense and other traumas connected with his case is directed, by means of displacement, toward his lawyer. It is in this sense that it may be said that a criminal lawyer never really "wins" a case. . . .

At the outset, because there are great risks of nonpayment of the fee, due to the impecuniousness of his clients, and the fact that a man who is sentenced to jail may be a singularly unappreciative client, the criminal lawyer collects his fee *in advance*. Often, because the lawyer and the accused both have questionable designs of their own upon each other, the confidence game can be played. The criminal lawyer must serve three major functions, or stated another way, he must solve three problems. First, he must arrange for his fee; second, he must prepare and then, if necessary, "cool out" his client in case of defeat [14] (a highly likely contingency); third, he must satisfy the court organization that he has performed adequately in the process of negotiating the plea, so as to preclude the possibility of any sort of embarrassing incident which may serve to invite "outside" scrutiny.

In assuring the attainment of one of his primary objectives, his fee, the criminal lawyer will very often enter into negotiations with the accused's kin,

14/Talcott Parsons indicates that the social role and function of the lawyer can be therapeutic, helping his client psychologically in giving him necessary emotional support at critical times.

including collateral relatives. In many instances, the accused himself is unable to pay any sort of fee or anything more than a token fee. It then becomes important to involve as many of the accused's kin as possible in the situation. This is especially so if the attorney hopes to collect a significant part of a proposed substantial fee. It is not uncommon for several relatives to contribute toward the fee. The larger the group, the greater the possibility that the lawyer will collect a sizable fee by getting contributions from each.

.   .   .   .

DEFENSE LAWYER AS DOUBLE AGENT

The lawyer has often been accused of stirring up unnecessary litigation, especially in the field of negligence. He is said to acquire a vested interest in a cause of action or claim which was initially his client's. The strong incentive of possible fee motivates the lawyer to promote litigation which would otherwise never have developed. However, the criminal lawyer develops a vested interest of an entirely different nature in his client's case: to limit its scope and duration rather than do battle. Only in this way can a case be "profitable." Thus, he enlists the aid of relatives not only to assure payment of his fee, but he will also rely on these persons to help him in his agent-mediator role of convincing the accused to plead guilty, and ultimately to help in "cooling out" the accused if necessary.

It is at this point that an accused-defendant may experience his first sense of "betrayal." While he had perhaps perceived the police and prosecutor to be adversaries, or possibly even the judge, the accused is wholly unprepared for his counsel's role performance as an agent-mediator. In the same vein, it is even less likely to occur to an accused that members of his own family or other kin may become agents, albeit at the behest and urging of other agents or mediators, acting on the principle that they are in reality helping an accused negotiate the best possible plea arrangement under the circumstances. . . .

The fee is often collected in stages, each installment usually payable prior to a necessary court appearance required during the course of an accused's career journey. At each stage, in his interviews and communications with the accused, or in addition, with members of his family, if they are helping with the fee payment, the lawyer employs an air of professional confidence and "inside-dopesterism" in order to assuage anxieties on all sides. He makes the necessary bland assurances, and in effect manipulates his client, who is usually willing to do and say the things, true or not, which will help his attorney extricate him. Since the dimensions of what he is essentially selling, organizational influence and expertise, are not technically and precisely measurable, the lawyer can make extravagant claims of influence and secret knowledge with impunity. Thus, lawyers frequently claim to have inside knowledge in connection with information in the hands of the D.A., police, probation officials or to have access to these functionaries. Factually, they often do, and need only to exaggerate the nature of their relationships with them to obtain the desired effective impression upon the client. But, as in the genuine confidence game, the victim who has participated is loathe to do anything which will upset the lesser plea which his lawyer has "conned" him into accepting.[15]

In effect, in his role as double agent, the criminal lawyer performs an extremely vital and delicate mission for the court organization and the accused. Both principals are anxious to terminate the litigation with a minimum of expense and damage to each other. There is no other personage or role incumbent in the total court structure more strategically located, who by training and in terms of his own requirements, is more ideally suited to do so than the lawyer. In recognition of this, judges will cooperate with attorneys in many important ways. For example, they will adjourn the case of an accused in jail awaiting plea or sentence if the attorney requests such action. While explicitly this may be done for some innocuous and seemingly valid reason, the tacit purpose is that pressure is being applied by the attorney for the collection of his fee, which he knows will probably not be forthcoming if the case is concluded. . . .

The judge will help an accused's lawyer in still another way. He will lend the official aura of his office and courtroom so that a lawyer can stage manage an impression of an "all out" performance for the accused in justification of his fee. The judge and other court personnel will serve as a backdrop for a scene charged with dramatic fire, in which the accused's lawyer makes a stirring appeal in his behalf. . . .

Afterward, there is a hearty exchange of pleasantries between the lawyer and district attorney, wholly out of context in terms of the supposed adversary nature of the preceding events. The fiery passion in defense of his client is gone, and the lawyers for both sides resume their offstage relations, chatting amiably and perhaps including the judge in their restrained banter. No other aspect of their visible conduct so effectively serves to put even a casual observer on notice, that these individuals have claims upon each other. . . .

.   .   .   .

THE CLIENT'S PERCEPTION

The "cop-out" ceremony, in which the court process culminates, is not only invaluable for redefining the accused's perspectives of himself, but also in reiterating publicly in a formally structured ritual the accused person's guilt for the benefit of significant "others" who are observing. The accused not only is made to assert publicly his guilt of a specific crime, but also a complete recital of its details. He is further made to indicate that he is entering his plea of guilt freely, willingly, and voluntarily, and that he is not doing so because of any

15/The question has never been raised as to whether "bargain justice," "copping a plea," or justice by negotiation is a constitutional process.

promises or in consideration of any commitments that may have been made to him by anyone. . . .

However, for the accused, the conception of self as a guilty person is in large measure a temporary role adaptation. His career socialization as an accused, if it is successful, eventuates in his acceptance and redefinition of himself as a guilty person.[16] However, the transformation is ephemeral, in that he will, in private, quickly reassert his innocence. Of importance is that he accept his defeat, publicly proclaim it, and find some measure of pacification in it.[17] Almost immediately after his plea, a defendant will generally be interviewed by a representative of the probation division in connection with a presentence report which is to be prepared. The very first question to be asked of him by the probation officer is: "Are you guilty of the crime to which you pleaded?" This is by way of double affirmation of the defendant's guilt. Should the defendant now begin to make bold assertions of his innocence, despite his plea of guilty, he will be asked to withdraw his plea and stand trial on the original charges. Such a threatened possibility is, in most instances, sufficient to cause an accused to let the plea stand and to request the probation officer to overlook his exclamations of innocence. The table that follows is a breakdown of the categorized responses of a random sample of male defendants in Metropolitan Court[18] during 1962, 1963, and 1964 in connection with their statements during presentence probation interviews following their plea of guilty.

It would be well to observe at the outset, that of the 724 defendants who pleaded guilty before trial, only 43 (5.94 per cent) of the total group had confessed prior to their indictment. . . .

As the data indicate, only a relatively small number (95) out of the total number of defendants actually will even admit their guilt, following the "cop-out" ceremony. However, even though they have affirmed their guilt, many of these defendants felt that they should have been able to negotiate a more favorable plea. The largest aggregate of defendants (373) were those who reasserted their "innocence" following their public profession of guilt during the "cop-out" ceremony. These defendants employed differential degrees of fervor, solemnity and credibility, ranging from really mild, wavering assertions of innocence which were embroidered with a variety of stock explanations and rationalizations, to those of an adamant, "framed" nature. Thus, the "Innocent" group, for the most part, were largely concerned with underscoring for their probation interviewer their essential "goodness" and "worthiness," despite their formal plea of guilty. Assertion of his innocence at the post plea stage resurrects

16/This does not mean that most of those who plead guilty are innocent of any crime. Indeed, in many instances those who have been able to negotiate a lesser plea, have done so willingly and even eagerly.

17/"Any communicative network between persons whereby the public identity of an actor is transformed into something looked on as lower in the local scheme of social types will be called a 'status degradation ceremony.' " H. Garfinkel, "Conditions of Successful Degradation Ceremonies," 61 *Am. J. Soc.* 420-24 (1956).

18/The name is of course fictitious.

a more respectable and acceptable self concept for the accused defendant who has pleaded guilty. A recital of the structural exigencies which precipitated his plea of guilt serves to embellish a newly proffered claim of innocence, which many defendants mistakenly feel will stand them in good stead at the time of sentence, or ultimately with probation or parole authorities.

Relatively few (33) maintained their innocence in terms of having been "framed" by some person or agent-mediator, although a larger number (86) indicated that they had been manipulated or "conned" by an agent-mediator to plead guilty, but as indicated, their assertions of innocence were relatively mild.

A rather substantial group (147) preferred to stress the pragmatic aspects of their plea of guilty. They would only perfunctorily assert their innocence and would in general refer to some adverse aspect of their situation which they believed tended to negatively affect their bargaining leverage, including in some instances a prior criminal record.

One group of defendants (92), while maintaining their innocence, simply

TABLE 1
Defendant Responses as to Guilt or Innocence After Pleading Guilty
(N = 724; years−1962, 1963, 1964)

Nature of Response		N of Defendants
Innocent (Manipulated)	"The lawyer or judge, police or D.A. 'conned me' "	86
Innocent (Pragmatic)	"Wanted to get it over with" "You can't beat the system" "They have you over a barrel when you have a record"	147
Innocent (Advice of counsel)	"Followed my lawyer's advice"	92
Innocent (Defiant)	"Framed"− Betrayed by "Complainant," "Police," "Squealers," "Lawyer," "Friends," "Wife," "Girlfriend"	33
Innocent (Adverse social data)	Blames probation officer or psychiatrist for "Bad Report," in cases where there was prepleading investigation	15
Guilty	"But I should have gotten a better deal" Blames lawyer, D.A., Police, Judge	74
Guilty	Won't say anything further	21
Fatalistic (Doesn't press his "innocence," won't admit "Guilt")	"I did it for convenience" "My lawyer told me it was only thing I could do" "I did it because it was the best way out"	248
No Response		8
Total		724

employed some variation of a theme of following "the advice of counsel" as a covering response, to explain their guilty plea in the light of their new affirmation of innocence.

The largest single group of defendants (248) were basically fatalistic. They often verbalized weak suggestions of their innocence in rather halting terms, wholly without conviction. By the same token, they would not admit guilt readily and were generally evasive as to guilt or innocence, preferring to stress aspects of their stoic submission in their decision to plead. . . .

In order to determine which agent-mediator was most influential in altering the accused's perspectives as to his decision to plead or go to trial (regardless of the proposed basis of the plea), the same sample of defendants were asked to indicate the person who first suggested to them that they plead guilty. They were also asked to indicate which of the persons or officials who made such suggestion was most influential in affecting their final decision to plead.

Table 2 indicates the breakdown of the responses to the two questions.

It is popularly assumed that the police, through forced confessions, and the district attorney, employing still other pressures, are most instrumental in the inducement of an accused to plead guilty.[19] As Table 2 indicates, it is actually the defendant's own counsel who is most effective in this role. Further, this phenomenon tends to reinforce the extremely rational nature of criminal law administration, for an organization could not rely upon the sort of idiosyncratic

TABLE 2
Role of Agent-Mediators in Defendant's Guilty Plea

Person or Official	First Suggested Plea of Guilty	Influenced the Accused Most in His Final Decision to Plead
Judge	4	26
District attorney	67	116
Defense counsel	407	411
Probation officer	14	3
Psychiatrist	8	1
Wife	34	120
Friends and kin	21	14
Police	14	4
Fellow inmates	119	14
Others	28	5
No response	8	10
Total	724	724

19/Failures, shortcomings and oppressive features of our system of criminal justice have been attributed to a variety of sources including "lawless" police, overzealous district attorneys, "hanging" juries, corruption and political connivance, incompetent judges, inadequacy or lack of counsel, and poverty or other social disabilities of the defendant.

measures employed by the police to induce confessions and maintain its efficiency, high production and overall rational-legal character. The defense counsel becomes the ideal agent-mediator since, as "officer of the court" and confidant of the accused and his kin, he lives astride both worlds and can serve the ends of the two as well as his own.[20]

... The defense counsel being a crucial figure in the total organizational scheme in constituting a new set of perspectives for the accused, the same sample of defendants were asked to indicate at which stage of their contact with counsel was the suggestion of a plea made. There are three basic kinds of defense counsel available in Metropolitan Court: Legal-aid, privately retained counsel, and counsel assigned by the court (but may eventually be privately retained by the accused).

The overwhelming majority of accused persons, regardless of type of counsel, related a specific incident which indicated an urging or suggestion, either during the course of the first or second contact, that they plead guilty to a lesser charge if this could be arranged. Of all the agent-mediators, it is the lawyer who is most effective in manipulating an accused's perspectives, notwithstanding pressures that may have been previously applied by police, district attorney, judge or any of the agent-mediators that may have been activated by them. Legal-aid and assigned counsel would apparently be more likely to suggest a possible plea at the point of initial interview as response to pressures of time. In the case of the assigned counsel, the strong possibility that there is no fee involved may be an added impetus to such a suggestion at the first contact.

In addition, there is some further evidence in Table 3 of the perfunctory,

TABLE 3
Stage at Which Counsel Suggested Accused to Plead
(N = 724)

| | Counsel Type | | | | | | | |
| Contact | Privately Retained | | Legal-Aid | | Assigned | | Total | |
	N	%	N	%	N	%	N	%
First	66	35	237	49	28	60	331	46
Second	83	44	142	29	8	17	233	32
Third	29	15	63	13	4	9	96	13
Fourth or more ...	12	6	31	7	5	11	48	7
No response	0	0	14	3	2	4	16	2
Total	190	100	487	101*	47	101*	724	100

*Rounded percentage.

20/Aspects of the lawyer's ambivalences with regard to the expectancies of the various groups who have claims upon him are discussed in H. J. O'Gorman, "The Ambivalence of Lawyers," paper presented at the Eastern Sociological Association meetings, April 10, 1965.

ministerial character of the system in Metropolitan Court and similar criminal courts. There is little real effort to individualize, and the lawyer's role as agent-mediator may be seen as unique in that he is in effect a double agent. Although, as "officer of the court" he mediates between the court organization and the defendant, his roles with respect to each are rent by conflicts of interest. . . .

CONCLUSION

Recent decisions of the Supreme Court, in the area of criminal law administration and defendant's rights, fail to take into account three crucial aspects of social structure which may tend to render the more libertarian rules as nugatory. The decisions overlook (1) the nature of courts as formal organization; (2) the relationship that the lawyer-regular *actually* has with the court organization; and (3) the character of the lawyer-client relationship in the criminal court (the routine relationships, not those unusual ones that are described in "heroic" terms in novels, movies, and TV).

Courts, like many other modern large-scale organizations, possess a monstrous appetite for the cooptation of entire professional groups as well as individuals.[21] Almost all those who come within the ambit of organizational authority find that their definitions, perceptions and values have been refurbished, largely in terms favorable to the particular organization and its goals. As a result, recent Supreme Court decisions may have a long range effect which is radically different from that intended or anticipated. The more libertarian rules will tend to produce the rather ironic end result of augmenting the *existing* organizational arrangements, enriching court organizations with more personnel and elaborate structure, which in turn will maximize organizational goals of "efficiency" and production. Thus, many defendants will find that courts will possess an even more sophisticated apparatus for processing them toward a guilty plea!

21/Some of the resources which have become an integral part of our courts, *e.g.,* psychiatry, social work and probation, were originally intended as part of an ameliorative, therapeutic effort to individualize offenders.

25. The American Jury and the Death Penalty*

HARRY KALVEN, JR., and HANS ZEISEL

Although the secrecy of jury proceedings makes it difficult to gather information on jury decision-making processes, a definitive study on the American jury by Harry Kalven, Jr., and Hans Zeisel offers insight into the role of that body in the crime adjudication process. Studying 3,567 criminal jury cases, the authors found that a jury is sometimes moved to be more lenient and to make distinctions which the law does not make and at other times to be more severe than the presiding judge as it overrides a legal distinction included within the law. Juries have a tendency to implement their own norms and to modify legal statutes as they evaluate the actual facts in a particular criminal case. Approximately three quarters of the time, the jury agrees with the judge, although two thirds of the disagreements with the presiding officer of the court involve some value distinction. The jury, the researchers found, may "hunt for doubts" and recognizes values which fall outside the prescribed rules. Primarily equity-prone, its decisions reflect both the existing state of law and public opinion. Nevertheless, a jury secured at random generally tends to support predominant and nondissenting norms. In some instances, however, if dissidence is sufficiently widespread or localized within a particular area, jury representatives may define a view contrary to existing law. Whatever its decision, however, its final judgment tends to follow the direction of the vote at the beginning of the deliberation process. Through deliberation, the small group, Kalven and Zeisel found, usually forges a consensus out of the initial majority opinion.

The criminal jury is a unique institution designed to ameliorate harsh features in the law and to give expression to the pragmatic public will. Its power to modify and to interpret represents a unique system of checks and balances built into an often impersonal system of social control. As a result, the jury represents flexibility, equity, and representative public discretion, theoretically designed to overcome the coercive aspects of state power. Given the authority to determine the facts of the case, the jury also possesses the potential to bend the law in a discretionary manner without undermining its basic characteristic. While its critics argue that it undermines the intent of criminal legislation, the jury's supporters note that no legislature can take all human contingencies into consideration when it formulates the content of any law. Since laws may often

*Reprinted from *The American Jury*, Chapter 35, pp. 434-49. Copyright by Little, Brown and Company.

reflect the will of the legitimating majority rather than the will of the public, the jury serves a valuable function as it reviews the contemporary context of the law and its import upon community affairs.

Laws change, but they are only slowly repealed from the criminal code. The jury, therefore, may discretionarily anticipate the move toward change in its contemporary judgment procedures. As the death penalty ceased to be mandatory, the jury, Kalven and Zeisel point out in the following selection, has often been empowered to exercise the discretion formally reserved for the legislature. However, the discretionary use of the death penalty, the authors conclude, requires the jury, the judge, or the executive to make a decision which "no human should be called upon to make."

The reversal of civilized opinion on the death penalty during the past century and a half has been truly remarkable. It is an example of law in the process of radical change.

As late as 1825 England had no less than 230 capital crimes on its law books. By the turn of the century legislative inroads had reduced the capital list to murder and treason, and, after an attempt to reduce it still further to certain types of murder, the English evolution has come to completion and the death penalty has now been abolished for all crimes. Although in England the death penalty, wherever applicable by statute, was mandatory on the trial process, the English jury played a major role in its gradual attenuation. On many occasions the jury simply refused to convict a clearly guilty defendant in order to avoid the death penalty, and this nullification had its impact on the legislature.

In the United States the development has been different and more complicated, and the role of the jury even more important. While the number of capital crimes has at no point been as high as in England, a similar legislative process has been making inroads into the death sentence, so that today ten states have abolished it altogether and other states have limited it severely.

In addition, the death penalty has ceased to be mandatory. The legislatures have left it to the discretion of the trial process, and it is now predominantly the jury which is called upon to exercise this discretion, even in states where the jury has no voice in other penalties.

The discretion which the jury in the United States is asked to exercise is, it should be emphasized, striking: there is neither rule nor standard to guide it. For this reason comparison of judge and jury decision must here depart from the standard pattern of analysis which discussed disagreement in terms of why the jury differed from the judge. . . .

We have, in all, 111 cases in which either judge or jury found the defendant guilty of a capital crime and hence *could* have given the death penalty.[1] Table 1 sets forth the pattern of agreement and disagreement.

1/These 111 cases are those in which the defendant was convicted of a crime that permitted a finding for the death penalty and in which the judge agreed with the guilty verdict of the jury. They happen to be all murder cases.

TABLE 1
Frequency of Death Sentence for Defendants Found Guilty of a Crime

Jury Gave

		Prison	Death Penalty
Judge Gave—	Prison	68% 76	6% 7
	Death Penalty	13% 14	13% 14

Number of cases   111

The upper lefthand cell represents the approximately two-thirds of all cases where both judge and jury withhold the death penalty. In only 13% of all cases (lower righthand cell) do both jury and judge agree on the death penalty. When they disagree, the jury is somewhat more lenient, but the imbalance is modest.[2] Neither jury nor judge imposes the death penalty with any great frequency. The jury does so in only (13 + 6 =) 19% of the cases, the judge somewhat more often, in (13 + 13 =) 26% of the cases.

. . . .

The cases in which jury and judge agree that the defendant should pay for his crime with his life are marked for the most part by peculiar heinousness. In many, a clear pattern emerges: there is an aspect of almost gratuitous violence. Five involve multiple victims. In one the defendant kills his wife and her brother. In another the defendant exterminates his entire family, although the trial is limited to the murder of his nine-year-old son. In a third domestic murder case the defendant comes upon his separated wife at her mother's home, kills her, and severely stabs the mother as well.

The theme of multiple murder is at times aggravated by the patent defenselessness of the victim. Thus there is a burglary case in which an old man and his wife are beaten to death with a tire iron:

Victim wounded a dozen times with a metal tool. Asleep in his home when aroused.

2/It is of interest to see the full extent of the disagreement in the 21 cases where only one decider opts for death:

Extent of Disagreement on the Death Penalty

	Judge gives death penalty	Jury gives death penalty
	Jury	*Judge*
Agrees on capital charge but not on death penalty	10	7
Convicts on lesser (non-capital) charge	4	0

Another case adds still other alienating factors to the multiple victim theme: special ugliness in the tools of a murder with sexual overtones:

Defendant, a sex deviate, murdered two girls—one aged 8 years, the other 18 years. Both killings were with a screw driver.

Two other cases pick up the sex element; both are murders committed in the course of rape. In one, a strangulation, the judge adds that this was the defendant's seventh criminal offense of a violent nature, a fact also known to the jury. He says:

This was a violent and brutal killing, a heinous crime by a sadistic defendant.

In a burglary case, after the burglary is complete and almost as an afterthought, the defendant rapes and then stabs to death "with a paring knife" a woman who a few moments before had been secure and asleep.

Then there is perhaps the ugliest of these cases, which the judge describes as follows:

Defendant was charged with the rape and sodomy of a four and a half-year old child who was also his step-child. The penetration of the anal canal resulted in massive hemorrhage which caused shock and ultimately death ensued.

The mark of the beast is perhaps a little less evident in the remaining cases in which judge and jury agree on the death penalty. In one the victim is an elderly truck driver making his last trip prior to retirement. During a stop, his helper in the truck steals his receipts and shoots him while he is asleep, leaving the body in the van on the desert. In a second case the defendant, refused credit by a village merchant, returns with his rifle and shoots the seventy-two-year-old grocer in the back through the window of his office. And in a domestic murder case, where husband and wife have been separated, the judge notes with pungent brevity:

Husband killed wife. Six pistol shots, 2:30 a.m., at wife's home.

Finally, in a robbery-mugging case, the defendant brutally beats an elderly, crippled man, then drags him to a lonely spot in the woods where he strangles him.

These cases in which judge and jury have agreed on the death penalty give, at first impression, a strong sense of unity. Among cases of premeditated killing they seem to stand out as especially vicious. The trouble is that some aspects of this viciousness verge so much on the clearly pathological that the criterion loses some of its usefulness. Moreover, as we shall see, many of the murder cases in which the judge and jury disagree on the death penalty appear no less heinous than those in which they agree.

. . . The cases of disagreement, as may be recalled from Table 1, exceed the agreements 21 to 14.

The first group of cases involves a measure of mental and emotional instability on the part of the defendant, which falls short, however, of insanity. In the first case, where the violence is atrocious, it is the jury which is lenient. A twenty-two-year-old inmate of an institution for defective delinquents kills an aged guard in an unprovoked and ferocious attack. The judge tells us:

Defendant had been in one school or institution after another from the age of ten. His father and mother separated when defendant was approximately two years of age. The defendant had been an inmate of this institution for six years prior to the commission of this crime. I believe the jury reached the conclusion that, even though the defendant knew the difference between right and wrong, and even though he was not insane, nevertheless he did not possess a normal mentality and for this reason I believe the jury concluded not to impose the supreme penalty of capital punishment. . . . This conclusion, coupled with the story of the defendant's hardships during his early life, probably led the jury to conclude that despite the enormity of the crime, the defendant should not be required to suffer penalty of death.

A second case presents the same pattern: a crime of violence, an unsuccessful plea of insanity as the leniency-disposing factor, and the jury as the lenient decider. This is the judge's description:

The defendant in this case beat and broke the neck of a young woman then cut her throat and threw her in a lake. He went to the police, told them what he had done, and asked them to have him executed as soon as possible. His attorneys pleaded insanity. He was examined by the state authorities, and found to be sane. He pleaded insanity through his attorneys on the trial. The insanity plea was submitted to the jury. He did not take the stand, and the jury agreed as to his guilt, but disagreed as to death penalty. I automatically sentenced him to life in the state penitentiary.

The judge notes that he thinks "the defendant feigned insanity" and adds:

This was a very cruel murder. Defendant said he killed her because he loved her.

In these two cases the suggestion is that the jury is responding to a level of insanity or instability not sufficient to preclude a verdict of first degree murder but sufficient to avoid the death penalty. Two other cases, however, show how much judgment may waver when the death penalty is the issue.

In a multiple victim case, we are told:

The defendant stopped at a filling station and because of his conduct was requested to leave. Station owner approached the car owner a second time whereupon the defendant shot him and when his wife ran out defendant shot and killed her.

This time it is the judge who is lenient. He explains:

> I believe the defendant shot the [station owner] because he said "You damn niggers get the hell out of here," and killed the wife because his anger toward the [station owner] was not satisfied when he shot him down.

The judge, who, unlike the jury, did not respond to the touch of insanity in the first two cases, does accept this sudden anger as a sufficient reason for withholding the death penalty. And the jury, sensitive to the marginal responsibility in the previous cases, is deaf to the wild anger in this one.

The final case in this cluster deals with a killing committed in the course of an armed robbery. There are two accomplices, but the defendant is the actual killer; once again there is an unsuccessful plea of insanity, and again it is the judge who is lenient. The circumstance which divides judge and jury is set forth by the judge as follows:

> The conduct of defendant and his counsel was such as to antagonize the jury and in the opinion of the court caused the imposition of death penalty rather than life imprisonment. The defendant indulged in repeated outbursts of vile language and finally was handcuffed to seat and his mouth taped. At one point, defendant jumped up and threw a book at jury. Defense lawyer was entirely incompetent although of defendant's own choice—in fact defendant refused any other counsel. Conduct of defendant and his counsel was such to antagonize jury and in the opinion of the court caused the imposition of death penalty rather than life imprisonment.

It is easy to see what alienated the jury here, but we can only surmise what moved the judge to leniency. Possibly, he distrusted the ability of the trial process to render fair judgment on the issue of death where the circumstances have been made so prejudicial to the defendant, albeit by his own conduct and that of incompetent counsel.

Another group of disagreement cases involves, in differing ways, situations of domestic tension. Here the context tends to belie somewhat any deliberate intent to kill. A husband and wife are charged with the murder of their four-year-old daughter, who died "after the administering of a brutal beating." The jury, which is lenient, finds only second degree murder—thus precluding the death penalty, which the judge would have given. Little background is supplied about the case, but there may be a clue in the fact that the husband pleads insanity as a defense. Presumably there was no literal intent to kill the child. The judge finds first degree murder pursuant to the legal rule which holds the actor liable, as if he intended it, for a death that occurs in the course of a felony.[3] In

---

3/The felony murder doctrine provides in general that if a death occurs in the course of the commission of a felony, or certain felonies, the crime is murder in the first degree, even if the intent was not to kill.

this context the jury will not accept the legal fiction of intent. Further, with respect to the wife, the jury may have been following its special form of chivalry in not imposing the death penalty on a woman; and the husband may accordingly have been the beneficiary of a desire, at least where the death penalty is at issue, to treat partners in crime with an even hand.

In another domestic case the defendant kills his estranged wife, whose reputation was "poor so far as marital relations were concerned." There is a record of prior abuse by the defendant of the victim, "a good looking woman." The jury is lenient, and the judge is explicit as to why:

> Eternal triangle if this is extenuating. Perhaps the so-called unwritten law.

In another version, a man jealous of his paramour because she tried, as the judge puts it, to "quit being familiar with him," stabbed her to death—"in the daytime on a public street while she was running from him." The jury is lenient. The judge adds the following comment to the explanation suggested by the jealousy theme:

> A Negro killing a Negro, that is, the jury did not attach enough importance to the value of a human life due to race.

Perhaps one other case is conveniently placed here. The body of the victim, a woman of poor reputation, is found in the desert. Her boy friend confesses to the killing. On the witness stand he boasts of his criminal reputation. This time it is the judge who is lenient because of the status of the victim. He explains:

> I felt that because the victim was herself an underworld character and was guilty at least of keeping company with a person of defendant's reputation—society because of her wrongful death did not require the supreme penalty of the defendant.

Other disagreement cases pick up a theme touched on in the case of the parents who beat their child to death. In each case there are partners in the crime and the defendant is not the actual killer. The felony murder rule precipitates the disagreement.[4] The jury rebels at imposing the death penalty for the vicarious criminal responsibility of the defendant. One illustration will suffice. Four defendants conspire to rob a seventy-six-year-old woman in a hotel room. In the course of the robbery the victim is gagged and she accidentally strangles. The defendant has been a mere go-between in recruiting accomplices to the crime. Three of the accomplices, the judge reveals, have "been tried, found guilty of first degree murder and given life by the jury." There are two leniency-disposing factors: the defendant did not commit the act of violence and the death penalty had already been withheld for the partners in the crime.

A final source of disagreement is somewhat curious. In two instances the judge, when asked for his hypothetical decision "had he tried the case without a

---

4/We had anticipated that, because of the rigidity of the felony murder rule, the jury's sense of equity would produce a broad area of disagreement.

jury," refers to what he would have done had the defendant in fact waived a jury trial:

> The killing was wanton but on a plea of guilty or a bench trial, I would have spared his life.

> The jury verdict of first degree murder without recommendation of mercy was, in my opinion, justified by the nature of the attempt to escape although I would have imposed a life sentence rather than invoke the death penalty if I had tried the case myself without a jury.

The waiver is apparently regarded as a gesture of cooperation warranting withholding the death penalty.

Table 2 imposes, if for a brief moment, a sense of regularity on the

TABLE 2
Factors Evoking Leniency in Cases Where One Decider
Gives Death Sentence

	Number of Cases
Law	
Diminished responsibility	
Abnormal mentality, though not legally "insane"	2
Provocation, anger, jealousy	
Lovers' triangle	4
Neighborhood fight	1
Child-beating	2
Negro is called "nigger"	1
"Worthless victim"	
Underworld characters	1
Negro kills Negro	1
Felony murder	
Others involved did not get death penalty	7
Defendant not the actual killer	4
Procedural	
Trial process distrusted, because defendant's behavior prejudiced trial against him	1
Guilty plea or jury waiver would have mitigated	2
Defendant	
Defendant a female	2
Father cried on stand	1
Counsel	
Incompetent counsel	1
Evidence	
Prosecution witness—contradiction between first and second trial	1
Unexplained	2
Total cases	21*

*Factors add to more than 21 because of multiple reasons.

discretionary allocation of the death penalty. The leniency categories have a plausible ring. But the brute fact is that each time one of the factors listed was persuasive to one of the deciders, it was unpersuasive to the other. Either the judge or the jury was willing, despite the presence of the leniency-disposing factor, to have the defendant executed.

Having explored in detail the pattern of decision for our two deciders, the judge and the jury, we look now at the record of the third decider, the executive. Although commutations are seldom accompanied by published reasons, we know something about these reasons. In 1949 in the United Kingdom, the Home Office itself submitted an illuminating memorandum to the Royal Commission on Capital Punishment[5] and there is a fine recent study on the variety of commutation procedures in the United States.[6]

It will be convenient to follow the structure of the American study, noting the analogous English materials. The study lists thirteen factors or standards which have influenced clemency.

The Nature of the Crime. "[A] cts which, because of the status of the victim and the viciousness of the crime, most offend the community. The more heinous the crime, the less chance for clemency."

Doubt as to Guilt. This is less frequent basis than one might expect, because the executive is often hesitant to displace the jury as fact-finder.

Fairness of Trial. "[The question] usually arises in a situation where there has been considerable publicity surrounding the trial."

Relative Guilt and Disparity of Sentences. "The principle [in felony murder trials] that the acts of one shall be the acts of all, insofar as it fails to recognize relative degrees of culpability, leaves to the clemency authority the opportunity to inqure into the defendant's personal responsibility and the directness of his participation. . . ."

Geographical Equalization of Sentences. "The acceptance of this standard is rooted in the belief that the locale of the crime should not dictate the severity of the sentence."

Mitigating Circumstances. "The existence or lack of mitigating circumstances accompanying the commission of the crime, such as duress, provocation, intoxication and self-defense, is of some importance. . . ."

Rehabilitation. "Rehabilitation appears to be a standard for commutation only in cases where the defendant has managed through court action to remain alive for a number of years after the original date of execution."

Mental and Physical Condition of the Defendant. "Dissatisfaction with the *M'Naghten* rule and the artificial line between 'legal' and 'medical' insanity has led more than a few clemency authorities to commute a sentence on the basis of medical insanity where the defendant had previously been judged legally sane."

Dissents and Inferences Drawn from the Courts. Certain pardon officials have

5/Royal Commission on Capital Punishment, *Minutes of Evidence* 1-38 (1949).
6/Comment, "Executive Clemency in Capital Cases," 39 *N.Y.U.L. Rev.* 136 (1964).

given special consideration to a case where in the appellate court "one or more judges dissented . . . . Somewhat similar . . . is a written opinion . . . which, while affirming the death penalty, intimates that the case might be appropriate for the exercise of executive clemency."

The Clemency Authorities' Views on Capital Punishment. "[T]he views of a clemency official on the issue of capital punishment will have some influence. . . ."

The Role of Precedent. "There is generally a discernible continuity of policy in the actions of a governor within his administration and in those of a board within its term of office."

The comparison of executive discretion with that of the judge and jury is suggestive. There are, of course, several points—rehabilitation, judicial dissent, political pressure, prosecutor recommendation, geographical equalization—which in the nature of things have no parallel in the judge-jury situation. But for other factors the parallelism is worth noting. Thus heinousness offends both. And provocation, marginal insanity, the rigors of the felony murder rule, and procedural fairness are visible leniency factors in both forums. Somewhat surprisingly, doubt as to guilt is not a salient factor in Table 2.

The empirical data about jury, judge, and the executive, however, do little to upset an a priori conviction that the administration of the death penalty today is singularly agonizing. The jurisdictions that retain it follow the same policies. There is agreement that not all of those convicted of first degree murder should be executed, and also it is a dominant policy that the legislature does not specify by a general rule any category of defendants for whom the death penalty and its execution should be mandatory. As a result, the law can only leave to discretion the decision as to who is to die. The materials just reviewed show how difficult the exercise of this discretion is, whether by the jury, the judge, or the executive.

Procedural changes are being attempted to improve the administration of the discretionary death penalty. Thus, California and New York now require a separate trial on the issue of death, so as to permit the jury access to the broadest possible evidence about the defendant.[7] The new penal code for Illinois requires explicit agreement of jury and judge for the death penalty. . . .

But even these techniques for locating a hard core of capital cases do not put to rest the concern about evenhanded justice. In the end the task is one of deciding who, among those convicted of capital crimes, is to die. Whatever the differences on which this decision hinges, they remain demeaningly trivial compared to the stakes. The discretionary use of the death penalty requires a decision which no human should be called upon to make.

7/See Comment, "The Two-Trial System in Capital Cases," 39 *N.Y.U.L. Rev.* 50 (1964).

26. The Juvenile Court—Quest and Realities*

EDWIN M. LEMERT

The May 15, 1967, *Gault* ruling of the United States Supreme Court, which held that the juvenile court must grant children the criminal procedural protections guaranteed adults, represented a belated recognition of the shortcomings of the system of juvenile adjudication and treatment. Although early evaluators of the court's decision believed that the judgment would have little effect upon the functional operations of the juvenile court, many prosecuting attorneys quickly informed law enforcement personnel that all future juvenile cases should necessarily be prepared with the same thoroughness now demanded in adult prosecutions.

Since the child-adolescent under juvenile court philosophy is extremely vulnerable to the processes of justice, the *Gault* decision presupposed the need to guarantee the juvenile the right to an attorney, to due process, and to full disclosure of the charges against his person. Challenging the doctrine of *parens patriae* (the idea that the state assumes the role of a substitute parent at the direction of the court), the Supreme Court argued that the concept is both murky in meaning and dubious in relevance. Because the constitutional and theoretical basis of the juvenile court system is open to debate, the mere renaming of institutions, the Court argued, is not a sufficient act to alter the reality that the receiving home and industrial school are actually places where juveniles are deprived of their liberty. The substitute parents anticipated in juvenile court philosophy are little more than guards, state employees, or other institutionalized juveniles who have often committed even more serious offenses than many of those sent to the "training" school. Since the system of juvenile justice has fallen quite short of its early hopes and aspirations, the due process clause, the Court directed, must be made applicable to the many aspects of juvenile court proceedings.

While the Court's decision opened the question of juvenile court effectiveness and purpose to full review, it stopped short of granting juveniles all the rights guaranteed adults by the 14th Amendment and the Bill of Rights, especially in procedures or rights related to pre-judicial or post-adjudicative stages of the

*Reprinted from the *Juvenile Delinquency and Youth Crime* Task Force Report of the President's Commission on Law Enforcement and the Administration of Justice.

juvenile court process. Consequently, the rights of the adult criminal suspect, as enunciated in the *Escobedo* and *Miranda* decisions, have not been fully applied to the juvenile suspect. Whether the Fourth Amendment's prohibitions against unreasonable searches and seizures applied to juvenile cases is not yet fully clear. Even the right to grand jury indictment and the prohibition against double jeopardy have not been clarified. Nevertheless, it is clear that the juvenile court will never be the same. Still-admissible heresay evidence will gradually possess less meaning and validity. The greater use of legal counsel in juvenile offender cases will undoubtedly lead to fewer "rehabilitations."

Although the concept of the juvenile court seemed to be a marked advance in the treatment of juvenile offenders, its full potential has never been realized. Because the context of the child's problem, Edwin M. Lemert notes, becomes lost in the volume of urban delinquency cases and must be restructured under artificial circumstances in stereotyped written reports, the commonsense goal of the original juvenile court has been compromised by community pressures to speed judgment. Los Angeles juvenile court cases in 1959, for example, were processed in the larger courts on an average of one every three minutes (*see also* Luger, Article 5; and Empey and Erickson, Article 15), a finding which does little to establish confidence in the nature of juvenile justice. Edwin M. Lemert analyzes the quest and reality for juvenile justice.

Roscoe Pound called the juvenile court one of the great social inventions of the 19th century. But the enthusiasms heralding its birth and early history have dampened considerably with the slow stain of passing time. . . . The occasional early voice of the dissenting judge and of the frustrated lawyer has grown to a heavy swell of modern contention that the juvenile court under the noble guise of humanitarian concern and scientific treatment of the problems of children too often denies them the elements of justice and fair play.

. . . .

THE PHILOSOPHY AND FUNCTION OF THE JUVENILE COURT

Much has been said of the philosophy of the juvenile court and little that is definitive can be added to it, other than to note that the very preoccupation with its philosophy sets it apart from other courts. In general, American courts created for children were given broad grants of power by legislatures to protect and help children, depart from strict rules of legal procedure, and utilize kinds of evidence ordinarily excluded from criminal and civil adjudication. . . .

. . . .

In historical retrospect the juvenile court has the look of an agency of social control directed to raising and maintaining standards of child care, protection, and family morals, a purpose currently reinforced by its close association with social welfare organizations. At the same time the juvenile court by virtue of its inescapable identity as a court of law is an agency of law enforcement seeking to reduce and prevent crime, but also protecting legal rights. Finally, it serves purposes derived from its essentially local nature as an arena of conflict resolution, in which conflicts within and between families, between individuals, and between organizations (not excluding those within the court itself) are aired, dramatized, and sometimes turned into cold war compromises.

Despite their insular character and the cloak of independence given juvenile courts by their connection with the regular courts, they tend to reflect patterns of values and power alinements within the community or areas they service. When this is joined with the fact that there are 50 federated States, these States having from 5 to 58 more or less autonomous juvenile courts each, it is painfully clear that efforts to outline the distinctive philosophy and function of the juvenile court are feckless. . . .

.   .   .   .

STIGMA

Social scientists familiar with the juvenile court and its problems in the main agree that one of the great unwanted consequences of wardship, placement, or commitment to a correctional institution is the imposition of stigma. Such stigma, represented in modern society by a "record," gets translated into effective handicaps by heightened police surveillance, neighborhood isolation, lowered receptivity and tolerance by school officials, and rejections of youth by prospective employers. Large numbers of youth appearing in juvenile court have lower class status or that of disadvantaged minorities, whose limited commitments to education already puts them in difficulties in a society where education increasingly provides access to economic opportunity. Given this, the net effect of juvenile court wardship too often is to add to their handicaps or to multiply problems confronting them and their families.

.   .   .   .

Proposals, laws, and administrative action to preserve the anonymity of juvenile court proceedings through closed hearings, sealing case records, and expunging records are probably worthy moves, but it is vain to expect them to eliminate the stigma of wardship and contacts with the juvenile court. In smaller communities, as one judge observed, "Everyone knows about juvenile court cases anyway." In larger communities strongly organized police departments can be expected to resist rigorous controls over delinquency records detrimental to their efficiency, and will search for ways to circumvent them. Employers denied information from juvenile courts often get the desired facts from the police.

Expunging records is not the simple operation it may seem. In California it requires initiative from the party concerned and usually the assistance of an attorney; the procedure necessitates a hearing, and it may be complicated or impossible if a person has been a juvenile ward in more than one county. Private and public organizations can and do protect themselves by including questions about a juvenile record on application forms for employment or for occupational licenses, indicating that perjured replies will be grounds for rejection. . . .

While the successful management of stigma by individuals is not impossible, the necessary insights and social skills are not given to many people, least of all immature youth or those struggling with other status handicaps. A number of social psychologists, including the author, believe that social rejections provoked by such stigma may reinforce a self-image held by the individual that he is no good or that he can't make it on the outside. . . .

PREVENTING DELINQUENCY

The indiscriminate way in which stigma embraces juvenile court wards raises the most serious questions about an important part of the rationale for state intervention into the lives of youth and parents through the juvenile court. . . . This belief rests upon uncritical conceptions that there are substantive behaviors, isometric in nature, which precede delinquency, much like prodromal signs of the onset of disease. The viability of these ideas probably can be traced to their lineal ties with older, repressive Puritan philosophy; they received new life from early 20th century propaganda of the mental hygiene movement, which helped to birth child guidance clinics, school social work, and establish juvenile courts in many areas. Quaint examples of these views were the 19th century convictions that smoking or drinking by youth, shining shoes, selling newspapers, or frequenting poolrooms insidiously set them on a downward path toward a life of crime. Their contemporary survivals can be seen in unproved concepts like predelinquent personality, or delinquency prone, and in laws of a number of States which make truancy, running away from home, or refusal to obey parents or school officials jurisdictional bases for juvenile court control.

Social science research and current theory in social psychology refute the idea that there are fixed, inevitable sequences in delinquent or criminal careers. As yet no behavior patterns or personality tendencies have been isolated and shown to be the antecedents of delinquency, and it is unlikely that they will be. Furthermore, youthful actions conventionally regarded as delinquent tendencies in a number of jurisdictions, such as truancy, curfew violations, incorrigibility, and running away from home on close examination are found to correspond to no behavior entities, but rather to arbitrary definitions by school authorities, parents, and police. . . .

.   .   .   .

The brave idea that the juvenile court can prevent delinquency is further deflated or even reduced to absurdity by sociological studies of unreported or hidden delinquency. These have brought to light that the majority of high school and college students at some time or another engage in delinquencies, not excluding serious law violations. The main difference which emerged from comparisons of delinquencies by college students and those by youths who had been made wards of juvenile courts was the greater recidivism of the latter group. While these data admit of several interpretations, on their face they demand explanation as to why the large population of youth committing delinquent acts and made court wards commit more rather than fewer delinquencies. The conclusion that the court processing rather than the behaviors in some way helps to fix and perpetuate delinquency in many cases is hard to escape.

There are other data which suggest that formal efforts by the juvenile court to shape the course of childhood and adolescent development away from hypothetically dire directions in the large may be gratuitous or self-defeating. The reference is to facts or common knowledge that most youth pass through epochs in their lives when they engage in activities definable in other than their contexts as delinquency. Children normally play hookey, help themselves to lumber from houses under construction, snitch lipstick or other items from 10-cent stores, swipe some beer, get a little drunk, borrow a car, hell around, learn about sex from an available female or prostitute, or give the old man a taste of his own medicine. . . .

Most youth phase out of their predelinquency, so-called, and their law flaunting; they put away childish things, ordinarily as they become established in society by a job, marriage, further education, or the slow growth of wisdom. . . .

THE 3-MINUTE CHILDREN'S HOUR

The ideology of delinquency prevention is much more urban than rural. Handling problems of youthful disorders and petty crime in rural areas and small towns, characteristically by sheriffs' deputies, town police, the district attorney, and probation officer in the past and even yet today in many places has been largely informal. Sharp distinctions are drawn between less consequential moral and legal infractions—"mickey mouse stuff"—and serious delinquencies, with no implications that one conduces to the other. . . . The juvenile court usually reserves formal action for real problems of families and the community; the functional context of youthful misconduct ordinarily can be realistically gauged and its consequences dealt with in a number of different situations.

A major difficulty in the large bureaucratic urban juvenile court is that the functional context of child problems directed to it easily gets lost; it has to be reconstructed by bits and pieces of information obtained through investigations and inquiries conducted under highly artificial circumstances, and communicated in written reports which easily become stereotyped as they pass from person to person. There is little or no direct community feedback of criticism and reaction which might put individual cases into a commonsense context which would encourage normalization. This plus the rapidity with which cases are heard in large courts (3 minutes per case in Los Angeles circa 1959) explains why the distinction between mild and serious child problems breaks down or disappears. A notorious illustration of the tendency came to light in Orange

County, Calif., in 1957 when a private attorney put his own investigator to work on a case of an 8- and 9-year-old boy and girl accused of a sex crime against a 7-year-old girl. It was discovered that the probation officer presenting the case in court had not even investigated, and the private investigator's report swiftly pared down the charge to an imputed incident witnessed by no one and reported 2 days after it supposedly occurred.

.   .   .   .

POLICE AND COMMUNITY DELINQUENCY PREVENTION

The ideology of delinquency prevention and statutes incorporating special laws for regulating the conduct of children have not been ill adapted to the needs and problems of police in large cities, and to some extent have been their outgrowth. It needs to be emphasized, however, that police generally are less concerned with the prevention of delinquency in individual cases than in its prevention and control as a communitywide problem variously manifested in gang violence, disturbances of public order, a rise in crime rates, or mounting property losses. . . .

Lest a picture be left of police as ruthless manipulators of juveniles of law enforcement ends, be it noted that in a number of areas they have sought to aid juveniles avoid clashes with the law through setting up recreation programs, Big Brother assignments, informal probation, and even police social work. However, such undertakings have declined in recent years and tend to be looked upon as too widely divergent from essential police functions. This also may point to growing disillusionment with more generalized or communitywide delinquency prevention programs. Police in some cities sharply disagree with community organizers of such projects over the issue of maintaining the autonomy of neighborhood gangs; they tend to take a jaundiced view of proposals and attempts to divert such groups from law breaking into more compliant pursuits.

Research assessments of community programs to prevent delinquency, such as the Chicago area project, the Harlem project, and the Cambridge-Somerville youth study, have been disappointing; results either have been negative or inconclusive. . . . [T]hey seem to work best in towns between 2,000 and 15,000 population; it remains unclear whether they can be adapted successfully to large urban areas. Significantly, they work chiefly by exchanging agency information, and referrals of cases to community agencies, with full support and cooperation of the police. In effect they represent concerted action to bypass the juvenile court, and it might be said that their purpose if not function is prevention of delinquency by preventing, wherever possible, the adjudication of cases in the court.

TREATMENT OF CHILD PROBLEMS AND DELINQUENCY

Much of what has already been said about preventing delinquency by means of juvenile court intervention is equally applicable as criticism of intervention by the court to treat youth problems and delinquency by therapeutic means. The ideal of therapeutic treatment found its way into juvenile court philosophy from social work and psychiatry, its pervasiveness measurable by the extent to which persons educated and trained in social work have indirectly influenced the juvenile court or moved into probation and correctional officer positions. An underlying premise of therapeutic treatment of children is that scientific knowledge and techniques exist making possible specific solutions to individual and family problems. It seeks to impose the positivism of hard science upon individual behavior.

... Accent in treatment is laid upon the internal emotional life rather than upon external acts; the social worker or the psychiatrist is a specialist who understands the problems while the client does not; the specialist knows best, studies, analyzes, and treats, much in the manner of the authoritative medical practitioner.

A divergent, competing line of thought in social work repudiates scientific treatment in favor of a more simple conception of its task as essentially a helping process, in which problems are confronted in whatever terms the child or youth presents them; responsible involvement of the client is a sine qua non of success in this process. Needless to say, this conception of the nature of social work is much more compatible with a philosophy of democracy.

Generally speaking, social workers advocate a more curtailed dispositional function for the juvenile court and advocate assigning to other agencies many of the tasks it has assumed. Some social workers seriously doubt whether the helping process can be carried on in an authoritarian setting, and to emphasize their stand refuse as clients children who have been wards of the court. Other social workers believe that judges go beyond their competence, and should use their power solely for adjudication, after which determination of treatment should pass on to social work agencies. A smaller number of social workers hold to a more sanguine view of reconciling personal help and authority within the role of the probation officer. Finally, there are some social workers who are not beyond using juvenile court power as a tool for getting access to clients, or prolonging their contacts with them because they will benefit from treatment. . . .

A long-standing, ubiquitous problem of social workers and psychiatrists of whatever theoretical persuasion has been that of the noninvolvement of their clients or patients. Clients are either disinclined to seek their services or they break off contacts after they have been established, or they respond superficially without showing interest in changing their personal values or life styles. Much of the difficulty stems from the identification of social workers with middle-class values and the invidious moralistic implications of imputing defective personalities to those they try to assist. As a result, barriers to communication often become insurmountable.

Actually, comparatively few juvenile court cases are referred to social workers for treatment and many juvenile court judges and probation officers are inhospitable toward social workers. According to a U.S. Children's Bureau study some years ago, the most frequent disposition of juvenile court cases was dismissal, followed by informal or formal supervision under a probation officer. Dismissals can scarcely be called treatment even though the associated court appearance before an admonitory judge may have a chastening effect upon some youths. At most, such cases have a brief exchange with an intake or investigating officer who asks some questions, issues a stern warning, and says he hopes he will not see the boy again.

The consequences of supervision of delinquents by probation officers either in parental homes or in foster homes have been little studied and the outcome, even when successful, little understood. Probation practices with juveniles have little in common if the Nation is taken as a whole, and often they consist of a bare minimum of office interviews and phone or mail reports. . . .

If the results of probation supervision of delinquents on the whole are disappointing or inconclusive, even less can be said in behalf of the treatment of juvenile offenders undertaken under institutional commitments. Sociological analysis and evaluations of correctional programs in institutional settings tend to be uniformly negative, with some writers taking a position that the goals of correctional programs in prisons and reformatories are inherently self-defeating. . . .

The less-than-sanguine remarks here directed to the ideology of delinquency treatment do not exclude the possibility that clinically trained and humanly wise people cannot help youth solve problems which have brought them athwart the law. Rather the intent is to leaven professional contumely with humility, to place the notion of treatment into a more realistic perspective, and to point out denotative differences between dealing with problems of human relationships and treatment as it has evolved in the practice of medicine. The treatment of delinquency is best regarded as a kind of guidance, special education, and training, much more akin to midwifery than medicine, in which hopeful intervention into an ongoing process of maturation is undertaken. Objective criteria for the use of methods of intervening, and controlled conditions necessary for predictable outcomes are neither present nor likely to be. Hence the actions of a judge, probation officer, correctional counselor, or an institutional psychiatrist at most can be small influences brought to bear among many simultaneously affecting child development and emergence of youth into adulthood. . . .

JUDICIOUS NONINTERVENTION

The aims of preventing delinquency and the expectation of definitively treating a profusion of child and parental problems have laid an impossible burden upon the juvenile court, and they may be seriously considered to have no proper part in its philosophy. If there is a defensible philosophy for the juvenile court it is one of judicious nonintervention. It is properly an agency of last resort for children, holding to a doctrine analogous to that of appeal courts which require that all other remedies be exhausted before a case will be considered. This means that problems accepted for action by the juvenile court will be demonstrably serious by testable evidence ordinarily distinguished by a history of repeated failures at solutions by parents, relatives, schools, and community agencies. The model should be derived from the conservative English and Canadian juvenile courts, which in contrast to the American, receive relatively few cases.

This statement of juvenile court philosophy rests upon the following several propositions:

1. Since the powers of the juvenile court are extraordinary, properly it should deal with extraordinary cases.
2. Large numbers of cases defeat the purposes of the juvenile court by leading to bureaucratic procedures antithetical to individualized treatment (guidance).
3. The juvenile court is primarily a court of law and must accept limitations imposed by the inapplicability of rule and remedy to many important phases of human conduct and to some serious wrongs. Law operates by punishment, injunction against specific acts, specific redress, and substitutional redress. It cannot by such means make a father good, a mother moral, a child obedient, or a youth respectful of authority.
4. When the juvenile court goes beyond legal remedies it must resort to administrative agents, or itself become such an agency, which produces conflicts and confusion of values and objectives. Furthermore, it remains problematical whether child and parental problems can be solved by administrative means.

It may be protested that the conception of the juvenile court adumbrated here is so narrow as to emasculate it or take away any distinctive purpose. However, if it can be accepted that many acts termed delinquent in reality are not equatable with adult crimes, and that many situations called dangerous for youth on close examination turn out to be functions of moral indignation by persons and groups who, to paraphrase Maitland, "Screw up standards of reasonable ethical propriety to unreasonable heights," then organized nonintervention by the juvenile court assumes a definite protective function for youth. It has become equally or more important to protect children from unanticipated and unwanted consequences of organized movements, programs and services in their behalf than from the unorganized, adventitious "evils" which gave birth to the juvenile court. America no longer has any significant number of Fagans, exploiters of child labor, sweatshops, open saloons, houses of prostitution, street trades, an immoral servant class, cruel immigrant fathers, traveling carnivals and circuses, unregulated racetracks, open gambling, nor professional crime as it once existed. The battles for compulsory education have long since been won and technological change has eliminated child labor—perhaps too well. The forms of delinquency have changed as the nature of society has changed; social and personal problems of youth reflect the growth of affluence in one area of society and the growth of hostility and aggression in a nonaffluent sector. Current sociological theories of delinquency stress drift and risktaking as causes on one hand and on the other deprivation and dilapidated opportunity structures.

. . . .

STRUCTURING THE JUVENILE COURT

A philosophy of judicious nonintervention demands more than verbal or written exhortation for implementation. Action is needed to research and redefine the jurisdiction of the court, the nature of the roles assigned to its personnel, and its procedures. Ideally it will be so structured that it will have built-in controls, feedback mechanisms, and social scanning devices which make it self-regulating and adaptive. . . .

It follows that relationships between juvenile courts and policing agencies probably will become more critical with a shrinkage in juvenile court functions. However, it can be hoped that this will be an irritant means whereby more police departments develop juvenile bureaus and upgrade their competence for screening and adjusting cases within their own cognizance. Even now it is common practice for many police departments to dismiss large numbers of juvenile arrests or adjust them within the department. More and better trained juvenile officers and rationalizing of their procedures can greatly decrease referrals to juvenile courts. This does not mean that police should develop their own probation or social work service, but rather will parsimoniously utilize contacts with relatives and referrals to community agencies, or at most, engage in brief, policeman-like counseling with youths where they believe it may do some good. One way to answer the cry of American police for public support is to funnel grants of aid into juvenile officer training and police consultation services.

Since police probably always will to some extent seek to employ the juvenile court for their own special purposes of keeping law and order or preventing crime in the large, the second line of defense protecting jurisdictional boundaries of the juvenile court must be manned by intake workers of the juvenile court or the probation department serving it. These ideally should be organized into an intake, referral, and adjustment division, where the maximum effort of the court is made by its most competent personnel. . . .

. . . .

Jurisdiction

Action to narrow and refine the functions of the juvenile court will need much greater precision than now holds in setting the jurisdictional limits to its authority, explicitly with reference to problem categories and minimum age of cases accepted. Statutes conferring jurisdiction over children on the juvenile court generally differentiate four categories: (1) Those lacking care due to contingencies of family life—death, absence of a parent or parents, or their inability to provide the care, (2) those who are neglected or mistreated, (3) those who disregard, defy, or disobey authority of parents, guardians, custodians, or teachers, (4) those who violate laws. Popularly, administratively, and to some extent legally, these categories are status attributions designating the dependent child, the neglected child, and the delinquent. Although the early and primary aim of the juvenile court was to abolish the stigma of such statutes, this has not occurred, and the pall of moral questionability continues to settle over all children made wards in these categories.

It is difficult or impossible in the face of facts known about modern society to defend the locus of jurisdiction over dependent children in the juvenile court on any grounds other than convenience. . . .

Probation officers are apt to defend juvenile court jurisdiction over dependent children by referring to cases in which a delinquent child and a dependent child are in the same family and to contend that duplicate supervision should be avoided. They also have defended placing dependent children in the same institution with delinquent children on these grounds and the additional one that families should not be broken up. Yet in a number of areas welfare agencies carry a large share of the supervision of dependency cases for the juvenile court, and on the whole they are probably better prepared than probation officers to supervise such cases. Unless a child presents the most serious kind of delinquency or unless welfare agencies refuse to do the job, less delinquent and dependent children in the same family should be under welfare supervision.

The arguments for retaining juvenile court jurisdiction over neglected children are somewhat stronger but still questionable, for if the child's problem is truly the fault of his parents why should he receive the stigma of wardship? The suspicion is strong that juvenile court procedure has been invoked to gain control over children where it would be troublesome or impossible to prove neglect in an adult criminal court, borne out by the fact that statutes in some States allow such cases to be tried in juvenile courts. . . .

A less obvious but more pervasive reason why juvenile court people wish to retain jurisdiction over dependent and neglected children lies in persistent beliefs that the roots of delinquency and crime are discoverable in dependency and parental neglect. . . .

Sociological research has discovered little durable evidence to support the contention that poverty, broken homes, and many of the charges of parental unfitness—alcoholism, sexual immorality, or cruelty—are in themselves causes of delinquency. Most delinquents come from intact homes, and various studies comparing the incidence of delinquents with broken and with unbroken homes show differences to range from 7 to 24 percent. Furthermore, for every child in a broken home who is delinquent there are on the average two or more brothers or sisters who are nondelinquent. . . . The rationale for bringing dependent and neglected children under juvenile court aegis to prevent delinquency rests upon small statistical pluralities which are categorical or group differences, not predictable individual differences.

Delinquent Tendencies

Truancy, runaways, and incorrigibility [are] diffuse categories whose conversion into statutory foundation for jurisdiction by the juvenile court is made superficially plausible by unexamined assumptions that they are precursors to delinquency. If the juvenile court is to proceed with approximate uniformity which is a central attribute of law, the weakness of such statutes either as substantive law or as legislative directives for the development of administrative rules is patent. The reasons may be summarized as follows: (1) They lack common meaning from one jurisdiction to another, or between different judge's rulings in the same jurisdiction, (2) they are not derived from any fixed criteria, (3) they assign criminal responsibility to children in many instances where blame or responsibility cannot be determined or where closer investigation would reveal their actions to have been reasonably normal responses to highly provocative or intolerable situations.

If the image of the juvenile court is to be changed from that of a multifarious problem-solving agency, and its functions circumscribed to be more consistent with available means, then its statutory jurisdiction cannot be allowed to rest upon subjective definitions. Furthermore, if it is to avoid the risk of making delinquents by a labeling process, statutes whose vagueness in some localities allow almost any child, given compromising circumstances, to be caught up in the jurisdictional net of the court, must be altered.

Highly important is the fact that when such specious legal grounds as incorrigibility and associated terms are written into statutes as warrants for juvenile court action they invite its use for extraneous conflict resolution. They allow parents, neighbors, school officials, and police—even the youth themselves—to solve their problems by passing them on to the court. . . .

. . . .

A depressing sidelight is that the juvenile court itself can be a cause of incorrigibility when in effect it holds a child in contempt. Thus failure to obey an order of the court can be an official reason for a more severe disposition—even commitment to an institution. . . .

A net conclusion is that incorrigibility, truancy, and running away should not in themselves be causes for assuming juvenile court jurisdiction over children. There is much reason to believe that the bulk of such problems can be handled successfully by referrals, demonstrated by an inquiry in the District of Columbia where it was found that noncourt agencies took responsibility for 98 percent of the total identifiable or reported runaways, 95 percent of truancies, 76 percent of sex offenses, and 46 percent of youth termed ungovernable. If disobedience, truancy, and running away are retained as bases for juvenile court jurisdiction, statutes should be rigorously drawn to require a showing of their material relevance to serious law violations, or a showing that other agencies have been incapable of containing the problems.

Traffic

The heavy rise in the volume of juvenile traffic offenses in past decades and the large portion of total juvenile arrests for which they account have produced much confusion of procedures and stirred hot debates over the subject of jurisdiction. There are those who contend that ordinary traffic violations of juveniles are no different from those of adults, and since the State in licensing juveniles assumes them capable of ordinary care and caution in operating automobiles, their violations should be processed by regular courts. Opposition to removing jurisdiction over juvenile traffic offenses from the juvenile court has been strong, even fervent, among judges and others who see such proposals as part of a militant campaign to cripple or eliminate the juvenile court. Some of their arguments have validity, namely that juveniles under regular traffic courts would be liable for large, and for them, excessive fines, and that they could be sentenced to jails or road camps in the company of petty criminals and drunkenness offenders. The further claim that juveniles should not be exposed to the routinized, "cash register" justice of adult traffic courts is less convincing, and the argument that the end justifies the means—adjudication in the juvenile court of traffic offenses allows more serious problems to be detected and treated—is from the point of view here presented least defensible of all.

While separate juvenile traffic courts with limited punitive and administrative powers are well enough justified, safeguards are needed to preclude their use as formal or informal catch places to funnel youth into juvenile courts. Organization along the lines of 1959 Minnesota legislation, which spells out that traffic offenses are not to be construed as delinquency, is preferable to placing them within jurisdiction of the juvenile courts. The strongest sanction which juvenile traffic courts can apply is revocation of drivers licenses, which they must share with State motor vehicle departments. . . .

Age

Discussion of the minimum age for juvenile court jurisdiction is muddied by the fact that a specialized, technologically geared society generates functional concepts of age rather than chronological. Thus, in our society, persons as young as 15 years can be licensed to drive automobiles in some States, leave school for adult employment by the time they reach 17 years, yet be unable to marry without parental permission until they are 21. As civilians persons may be unable to purchase alcoholic beverages until past their 21st birthdays yet as members of the Armed Forces may enjoy the right at 18. . . .

From such facts it must be concluded that setting a sociologically realistic minimum age for bringing youth under authority of the juvenile court is difficult or impossible if its substantive jurisdiction is pushed too far beyond law violations. Hence any discussion of age limits of jurisdiction must return to the question of the age at which responsibility for criminal actions can be assumed. Most States have settled on age 18 as the minimum below which children cannot be tried in criminal courts. However, this is qualified by statutory exceptions covering such offenses as murder or armed robbery. In highly punitive States the list of such offenses may be quite long.

Any age limit for juvenile court jurisdiction has to be arbitrary because maturation is an uneven process and varies from individual to individual. Furthermore, violation of laws symbolizing highly important social values of life, person and property are likely to arouse public demands for formal demonstration trials and punishment even though the offender involved is below the age limit. . . .

The problems of jurisdiction and age to some extent are met by establishing concurrent jurisdiction in which offenses committed by youth in marginal age categories may be tried in either juvenile or criminal courts. California, for example, establishes 16 years as the minimum age for exclusive jurisdiction by the juvenile court, but shares jurisdiction over 17- through 21-year-old offenders with the superior court. In practice few 18-year-olds are retained by the juvenile court and very rarely those of 19 and 20. Considering that youth of 17 years coming before the courts usually have committed more serious violations and are more likely to have a lengthy juvenile court record, their retention in juvenile court in most cases is immaterial.

As a matter of fact, a youth in these borderline age groups may receive a more lenient disposition as a first time offender in an adult court than as a last resort offender in juvenile court. The most important requirement in concurrent jurisdictions is statutory safeguards to insure that the decision as to where cases in concurrent age categories get heard be made by the juvenile court. This guarantees that the occasional immature youth of 18 or 19 years will not get lost in routine processing by prosecutors and judges in adult courts, who have less experience to make such decisions.

If age is to be an effective means of limiting the authority of the juvenile court it may be as important to tie it to dispositions as jurisdiction. This should be observed closely for children of younger ages, whose offenses while chargeable as law violations qualitatively are seldom comparable to crimes. . . .

Procedures

.   .   .   .

Narrowing the scope of juvenile court functions to avoid what have been its less desirable features calls for new procedures designed to modify and better fix the roles of judges and probation officers, to augment the probabilities of dismissals of cases where indicated, and to change the order of values dominant in dispositions. First and foremost are hard rules governing the number, forms, and timing of hearings, which in many courts have tended to become attenuated, ex parte or even nonexistent. The minimum essential can be no less than provision for hearings in every instance in which the freedom of children is abridged, curtailed by detention or commitment, changed from lesser to greater restraint or custody renewed according to law. . . .

Significant changes in the direction of greater conservatism in juvenile courtwork can be achieved by introducing bifurcated or split hearings, in which adjudication is sharply set apart from dispositions. The first hearing should be devoted to findings of fact rich enough to authorize court jurisdiction, the second to ascertain what should be done with the child, equally rigorous in procedure, but admitting the soft data and evaluations which customarily make up the so-called social report.

.   .   .   .

The aim of bifurcated hearings in juvenile cases is to make certain that impressionistic, diagnostic, purely recorded, heresay type evidence will not be received by the court at the time of adjudication. However, the introduction of such hearings alone may go wide of their target if rules concerning admissibility of social reports are not also clarified. . . .

.   .   .   .

If the contents of the social report continue to be admitted during adjudication hearings or are part of the materials on which the judge makes a finding, then the social report should be open to scrutiny by persons who are its subjects or to their representatives. Authors of statements contained therein should on request be summoned as witnesses to cross-examination in either jurisdictional or dispositional hearing if they are separated in time. As the tenor of the language here implies, the knowledge and skills of competent counsel are prerequisites to the fullest exploitation of such procedural rights and controls.

The Right to Counsel

.   .   .   .

A more generic issue underlying the legal debates revolves about the compatibility of the presence of counsel with the special philosophy of the juvenile court, which ideologically has charged the judge and the probation officer with protection of the child's interests. Rhetorical questions are posed as to whether the presence of counsel will not rob the court of its informality and open it to the possibility of regular adversary proceedings, and whether such a change does not risk converting the juvenile court into little more than a miniaturized criminal court.

The arguments that children as well as adults are entitled to full protection of constitutional rights are quite powerful when considered in the context of a society radically changed since the juvenile court was born. However, it must be heeded that the nature of law has been changing rapidly, hence it may be more informative to examine immediate questions, such as how and to what extent traditional advocacy and adversary interaction can be synthesized with a court which, although more circumscribed in function, must remain a children's court. . . .

Research on the presence of counsel in the juvenile court has barely begun, so that any conclusions must be tentative. Research by the author in California juvenile courts has shown that advising juveniles and their parents of their right to counsel, as ordered by 1961 legislation, has indeed increased the use of counsel, but that the rate of increase and of current use varies tremendously from county to county. For all counties of the State the gain has been from about 3 percent of the cases to 15 percent. In some counties appearance of attorneys in court has risen from 0 to 1 or 2 percent, in others from a low of 15 percent to highs of 70 or even 90 percent. Generally speaking, the factors found to affect the use of counsel are the existence of a public defender's office and the attitudes of judges and probation officers at the time they advise juveniles and parents of their rights. In assigning counsel, courts tend to favor dependent and neglected children and those in which serious offenses are alleged, likely to be followed by commitment to the California Youth Authority. Thus far there is no evidence of any discrimination in assignment of counsel on the basis of social class or race.

Problems have emerged because private attorneys without experience or knowledge of the juvenile court are unsure as to what their roles should be, and often do little for their clients. Moreover public defenders tend to be co-opted by the court and may simply stipulate to the allegations by the probation officer in order not to make his workload excessive, or even because they think a youth needs some chastening experience or punishment by the court. . . .

Another kind of problem develops where youth deny the allegations of the petition and transform hearings into adversary proceedings. The burden of presenting the case or protecting the interests of the public tends to fall most heavily on the probation officer, who is neither legally trained nor temperamentally inclined to play what is in essence a prosecutor's role. Often he resents the assignment because it alienates the youth or parents he is expected to help subsequently—often impossible. . . .

. . . .

Despite the problems coming with the appearance of attorneys in juvenile court and a trend toward more formal, adversary-type hearings, the author's research on one intensively studied California juvenile court indicates that attorneys do their clients some good. A comparison of cases with and without attorneys showed that the former had a higher percentage of dismissals, fewer wardships declared, and more sentences to the California Youth Authority suspended. However, dismissals were not proportionately numerous, and moreover they clustered among cases alleging neglect by parents or unfit homes. Hence the main conclusion reached was that the major contribution of attorneys in the juvenile court lay in their ability to mitigate the severity of dispositions rather than disproving allegations of the petitions.

Attorneys often successfully challenged the precision of allegations in the jurisdictional hearings, causing them to be reduced in number and seriousness. This then became grounds to argue for a more lenient disposition of the cases. Specific dispositions were influenced when attorneys found relatives to take a child in preference to a foster home placement, or when they proposed psychiatric treatment or psychological counseling as an alternative to commitment to a ranch school. Sometimes they gave emphasis to reasons why a boy should be given another chance at home, and swayed an otherwise uncertain judge. Finally, attorneys sometimes protected the client, especially a parent, against himself, by persuading him to accept a condition of probation in order to avoid a more draconic order by the court.

Not all of the good work of attorneys was reflected in the outcomes of hearings; some of it was done before and after the court sessions, through convincing probation officers to change a recommendation or make some administrative modification of an order. If California findings are indicative, the adversary function of the emerging role of the attorney in juvenile court is likely to be marginal; more important is his role as a negotiator, interpreter of court decisions to child and parents, and as a source of psychic support in a new kind of court where there is greater social distance between probation officers and juveniles. Finally, the very presence of an attorney or the possibility of his entry into cases has a monitory value reinforcing the new consciousness of judges and probation officers of rights of juveniles. For this reason it may be that the New York State concept of the attorney in juvenile court as a law guardian is a most fitting description of his role.

Commentaries on the New York system for bringing counsel into family courts have been sensitive to the problem of his possible cooptation by the court, and the need to preserve his independence of action. To make him an agent of the court raises a real question as to where his loyalties would lay. Yet total independence may mean disruption and loss of informality in the court proceedings. A recent proposal seeks to solve this dilemma by moving delinquency hearings from the juvenile court into the probation department where defense officers would be assigned to juveniles, leaving the court in a supervisory or appellate position. However, administrative justice has its own unsolved problems in which the use or function of adversary contention is clouded by uncertainties as to where and how findings are made. Loyal opposition is the desideratum, but opposition remains the social mechanism which compels total and critical assessment of facts.

Levels of Proof

. . . .

Many California judges have met the thorny problem of hearsay evidence in juvenile court hearings by admitting everything, on the assumption that they can cull out that which is not competent. This tack has some support from law scholars who argue that the heresay rule was intended for gullible juries rather than judges. However, this misses an important point, that much juvenile court evidence is in the form of reports which often are little more than compilations of professional heresay. Whether the ordinary run of judges and referees are qualified to sift this kind of evidence is questionable; many juvenile court judges appear remarkably naive about psychiatric diagnoses and the true nature of that which is easily called psychiatric treatment. Their knowledge of social science and its critical evaluations of psychiatry and social work at best are rudimentary.

.   .   .   .

For the most grievous juvenile law violations, in which protection of public interests becomes a dominant value, the canons of criminal proof should prevail. However, their seriousness can be defined more meaningfully in operational terms by making them contingent upon legally possible dispositions rather than on formal allegations that the offense is analogous to a felony. . . .

One difficulty with this kind of proposal is that judges, subjected to heavy public pressures or confronted with difficulties due to lack of resources for dispositions, may simply find that for the purposes at hand a given institution is noncorrectional or otherwise meets statutory requirements. If appellate courts are unwilling to look behind such findings and evaluate the evidence rather than merely determining that the judge's finding was based on evidence, other remedies, perhaps administrative, would be necessary.

SOCIAL ACTION TO CHANGE THE JUVENILE COURT

Juvenile courts evolve and change in several ways: by legislation, rulings on appeals, administrative policy formation by regulatory agencies, and the cumulative, day-to-day actions of judges, probation officers, and correctional workers. Because the court is either a local or ecologically contained institution, the interaction within the court and between the court and the community is the most important area for studying the processes by which it changes. Legislation, appellate decisions, and administrative programs for this reason need formulation with recognition that the corpus of juvenile court practice to be changed is highly diverse and that outcomes of intervention will not be so much the result of selected causes as products of interaction.

While law represents a striving for uniformity, it must be heeded that similar ends may be reached by a variety of means, administrative as well as legislative. The juvenile court is a prime example of an agency in which the connection between legal action and administrative action, traditionally neglected in American jurisprudence, must be coordinated. . . .

On the whole, appellate court decisions have not been effective means for shaping the course of juvenile court evolution, although they may become more so with passing time. One recent exception was the supreme court decision in Utah which removed juvenile courts from control by the department of public welfare and gave them status as an independent judiciary. The history and background of this action throws considerable light on the weaknesses of vesting administrative control over juvenile courts in a State welfare agency, which in this instance had made some notable improvements but had stirred strong dissatisfaction among judges by more or less pre-empting their right of judicial review.

. . . .

Ordinarily bar associations may be expected to take the lead or strongly support others seeking to better adapt the juvenile court to its contemporary social setting, and this has been true for New York State and to a degree in other States. However, the California State bar has shown a singular lack of interest in problems of the juvenile court. Obviously, then, action to legislate change in the juvenile court will have to work through limitations imposed by the nature of the values or commitments of elite groups in professional associations and State power structures.

An issue which complicates any action to modify juvenile court procedures is the old one as to whether the legislature or the courts should make rules for courts to follow. Since the juvenile court is a peculiar type of court, with direct policy implications, the scales get weighted in favor of legislative action. However, legislative action pushed without a sense of full participation by judges and their probation officers risks subversion of changes by judicial indifference or noncompliance, and judges are a notoriously hard lot to discipline by direct means.

Modifying the structure and procedures of the juvenile court through legislative channels in such a way to make it part of the living law, the implicit as well as the explicit rules of the game, is contingent on complementary communication and opinion change among judges. . . . Changes which make the fate of the juvenile courts the proprietary interests of judges should be avoided, because the police, probation officers, prosecutors, public defenders, and social workers all have solid stakes in the workings of the juvenile court.

The most important objective, so far as administrative action is concerned, is that some State body exist to continuously oversee juvenile court operations, to promote the organic growth and advise application of legal procedures, to accumulate data, and contract for research on the court as needed. Such an agency could not review the decisions of juvenile court judges but it might conceivably be given some power to review the acts of administrative officials in juvenile correctional institutions or some inquisitorial and injunctive power to compel them to desist from practices inconsistent with juvenile court objectives. Hopefully this might begin to establish long-needed liaison between work of the juvenile court and ministrations of State institutions for juveniles. Even more, its very existence might discourage commitments to State institutions and speed a trend toward community centered forms of guidance and training of errant juveniles, not unlike the shifts which are occurring in treatment of mentally disordered persons.

THE PLACE OF RESEARCH

Although there is a great volume of impressions, opinions, and speculative discussion published about the juvenile court, the amount of carefully designed, relevant empirical research is pitifully small.... There is a pressing need for some basic ethnographic or descriptive studies to discover in greater depth what are the patterns of actions in juvenile courts, and then proceeding from these, to make more comprehensive studies of the modalities and dispersions in its patterns.

Our society now has both the surplus energy and trained social science personnel to do this job; the problem is one of their reallocation. Whether this will or can occur through the research funding methods and policies of the National Institutes of Mental Health is debatable. Research into juvenile delinquency and the program innovation for juvenile courts are of sufficient importance to merit their separate husbandry by the Federal Government. Furthermore, it does not appear that the strong appeal of health or mental health auspices is a prerequisite to securing needed research funds, for Congress already has shown its willingness to support special research and developmental programs on delinquency and the juvenile court.

The Federal Government is in a much better position than State governments to stimulate and fund the independent type of inquiry needed to clarify the nature of the anomaly which has been the juvenile court. Whatever mechanisms it devises for this purpose should be sufficiently flexible to catch up the marginal, lone wolf investigators whose detachment from organizations and wariness towards their values may be especially fitting for studying the problems of the juvenile court in modern society.

In concluding, the author freely admits to his omission of any other than incidental discussion of the kinds of adaptations in the fields of public welfare, private social work, special education and community organization which a more conservative construction of the juvenile court would entail. The changes taking place in these areas are many and rapid but their overall directions are not easy to make out in a more general atmosphere of conflict and confusion of goals. New ways of looking at things are badly needed by social workers and educators, with a recognition that differentiation and flexibility are collateral requirements of organizational advances towards common ends.

Meantime sufficient consensus on new goals for the juvenile court has accumulated to make the times propitious for its change through social action.

SOURCES

1. The California Juvenile Court. *Stanford Law Review,* 1958, *10,* 471-524.
2. Richard Cloward. *Social Control in Prison,* "Theoretical Studies in Social

Organization of the Prison." Social Science Research Council, New York, 1960, 20-48.

3. *Comparative Survey of Juvenile Delinquency*—Part I. North America. United Nations, N.Y., 1958.

4. Bernard Fisher, "Juvenile Court: Purpose, Promise, and Problems." *Social Service Review, 34*, 1960, 75-82.

5. Margaret Greenfield, *Juvenile Traffic Offenders and Court Jurisdiction.* Bureau of Public Administration, University of California, Berkeley, 1951.

6. Tadeuz Grygier, "The Concept of a State of Delinquency—an Obituary." *J. Legal Education, 18*, 1965, 131-141.

7. Joel Handler, "The Juvenile Court and the Adversary System: Problems of Function and Form." *Wisconsin Law Review, 54*, 1965, 7-51.

8. Jacob Isaacs, "The Role of the Lawyer in Representing Minors in the New Family Court." *Buffalo Law Review, 12*, 1962, 501-521.

9. Alfred Kahn, *A Court for Children*, Columbia University Press, 1953.

10. Orman Ketcham, "Legal Renaissance in the Juvenile Court," *Northwestern University Law Review, 60*, 1965, 585-598.

11. Edwin Lemert, "Legislating Change in the Juvenile Court, MNS." Center for the Study of Law and Society, Berkeley, Calif., 1966.

12. ————, "Revisionism and the Juvenile Court Law, MNS." Center for the Study of Law and Society, Berkeley, Calif., 1964.

13. David Matza, *Delinquency and Drift.* John Wiley & Sons, Inc., 1964.

14. Henry Nunberg, "Problems in the Structure of the Juvenile Court." *J. Criminal Law and Criminology, 48*, 1957, 500-515.

15. Lloyd Ohlin, *Conflicting Interests in Correctional Objectives,* "Theoretical Studies in Social Organization of the Prison." Social Science Research Council, New York, 1960, 111-129.

16. Maynard Pirsig, "Juvenile Delinquency and Crime: Achievements of the 1959 Minnesota Legislation." *Minnesota Law Review, 44*, 1959, 363-410.

17. Austin L. Porterfield, *Youth in Trouble.* The Leo Potishman Foundation, Fort Worth, 1946.

18. Roscoe Pound, "The Limits of Effective Legal Action, 22nd Annual Report of the Pennsylvania Bar Association," Bedford Springs, Pa., XXII, 1916, 221-239.

19. "Report of the Governor's Special Study Commission on Juvenile Justice," I, II. By I. J. Shain and Walter Burkhart, Sacramento, 1960.

20. "Report of the Minnesota Legislative Interim Commission on Public Welfare Laws." Minneapolis, 1959.

21. "Report of the New York Joint Legislative Committee on Court Reorganization," II. The Family Court Act, Albany, N.Y., 1962.

22. "Report of the Special Committee on Juvenile Courts of the Utah State Bar." Salt Lake City, May 1962.

23. "Report of the Wisconsin Legislative Council, Conclusions and Recom-

mendations of the Child Welfare Committee," vol. VI, part I. Madison, 1955.

24. Margaret Rosenheim (ed.). *Justice for the Child,* Free Press of Glencoe, New York, 1962.

25. William H. Sheridan, "Juvenile Court Intake." *J. of Family Law, 2,* 1962, 139-156.

26. James Short, Jr., and F. Ivan Nye, "Extent of Unrecorded Juvenile Delinquency." *J. Criminal Law and Criminology, 49,* 1958, 296-302.

27. Eugene E. Siler, Jr., "The Need for Defense Counsel in Juvenile Court," *Crime and Delinquency, 11,* 1965, 45-58.

28. Paul Tappan, *Delinquent Girls in Court.* Columbia University Press, New York, 1947.

29. R. Weiss, "The Illinois Family Court Act." *University of Illinois Law Forum,* 1962, 533-549.

30. Glenn Winters, "The Utah Juvenile Court Act of 1965." *Utah Law Review, 9,* 1965, 509-517.

part SEVEN

Crime and
Contemporary Corrections

The American correctional system, the world's largest, is diverse and multifaceted. Composed of city and county jails, state training or penal institutions, and federal penitentiaries or allied institutions, the system is a product of the historic American commitment to correctional institutions. Currently, somewhat more than 1.3 million offenders are maintained within this correctional system on any given day. During one year, more than 2.5 million admissions, costing over a billion dollars, take place within the system. Born of the idea that the correction of the offender is best accomplished in an isolated and controlled punishment setting, the prison has become a testimony to the weakness of earlier penal philosophy.

Prisons not only fail to correct but they also advance the amateur offender's knowledge of the criminal process. Bringing vast numbers of criminal types together, they serve as graduate schools in crime. Not only does the prison fail to offer adequate treatment facilities but it often tends to degrade and dehumanize the already deficient offender. Because the imprisoned offender represents only a minority of all crime participants, he is often incarcerated in institutions which emphasize security and isolation with limited, if any, treatment programs (*see* Berk, Article 29). Existing facilities, programs, and personnel usually are badly overtaxed; the continuation of present arrest, conviction, and imprisonment trends only aggravates an already heightened problem. And yet, while adult institutional commitments have become more stable in recent decades, the increase of juvenile commitments continues (*see* Lemert, Article 26).

Because criminal violators represent all shapes, sizes, emotional types, and personality needs, their correction is difficult. Since the prison houses violent, emotionally disturbed, mentally retarded, and sexually deviant inmates (*see* Gagnon and Simon, Article 30), many less serious offenders are immediately exposed to a wider range of criminality than they would normally have in day-to-day contact within the community. While the greatest majority of the incarcerated offenders is male, mostly between 16 and 30, more than 80 percent

311

have failed to complete four years of high school (*see* Elliott, Article 10). Consequently, the unskilled or marginally skilled laborer, service worker, operative, or craftsman-foreman is disproportionately represented among the prisoner population.

The typical offender enters the correctional system at the level of the city or county jail and receives minimal treatment upon entrance. The reason is apparent when one realizes that only 24,000 (20 percent) of the 121,000 persons working in correctional institutions in 1965 were employed in probation, parole, educational, social, psychological, or psychiatric services. Of the total manpower in corrections, approximately 80 percent simply maintained institutional facilities or supervised prisoner custody (*see* National Profile, Article 28). However, the more recent emphasis upon an individualized treatment approach has challenged the former prison philosophy—one method of corrections for all inmates—which allowed this failure to emphasize treatment (*see* Stark, Article 31). The recognition that current methods are 10 times more costly than supervised probation or parole within the offender's own community has reenforced the community concept of individualized treatment. Most studies of probation success, for example, reveal that between 60 to 90 percent of all probationers complete their terms without revocation. This discovery that a variety of actively administered community probation services can play a dramatic role in leading the offender to "normal" social behavior has stimulated a whole new trend toward the greater use of more flexible sentencing alternatives (*see* Toby, Article 32).

Evaluating the context of existing correctional systems, the President's Commission on Law Enforcement and Administration of Justice found a need for greater juvenile, adult misdemeanant, and felon probation and parole services. Every state, the Commission concluded, should provide programs for the societal reentry of prisoners, even if they are not paroled under supervision but receive an outright release upon the completion of their sentence (*see* Bennett, Article 27). Recognizing that current probation case responsibilities are excessive, the Commission recommended that probation and parole loads should average 35 offenders per officer, a goal which can only be accomplished through a greater recruitment and financing of probation and parole officers. The use of volunteers and subprofessionals, it reasoned, should also be explored further as a means of bringing about better prisoner-community adjustments. Therefore, correctional authorities, the Commission recommended, should develop more flexible and community-oriented treatment programs in order to offer both juvenile and adult offenders an alternative to institutionalization (*see* Stark, Article 31). Not only must existing centralized penal institutions give way to community-oriented treatment programs, but traditional guard, administrator, and prisoner antagonisms must be lessened in order to develop a joint staff and inmate responsibility for institutional rehabilitation programs. While educational and vocational training within the corrections program should be upgraded, effective industrial and training programs, the Commission held, can only be created through the modification or repeal of state and federal laws restricting the sale of prison-made products, despite labor and management opposition. Not only should graduated release and furlough programs be expanded in order to ease the reentry and adjustment of the offender to the community, but they should also be accompanied by guidance programs which are coordinated with other community treatment services.

The current lack of coordination between state correctional systems and local jails and misdemeanor institutions must be overcome. Enforcement agencies, the Commission recommended, should withdraw from the operation of the local institutions in order that the state may integrate rehabilitative programs and enact other correctional reforms. Not only should separate juvenile detention facilities be provided, but all jurisdictions should maintain shelter facilities for abandoned, neglected, or runaway children. Recognizing that a high proportion of alleged offenders may never be judged guilty, the Commission recommended that persons awaiting trial should be housed and handled separately from convicted offenders. Greater individualized efforts should be made to screen and diagnose problems and to devise treatment programs. Competent parole board members should be appointed and trained to assume their responsibility. Because the greatest number of all offenders will ultimately return to the community, meaningful programs of treatment, the Commission concluded, must replace existing indifference.

Additional facets of the correctional problem are reviewed in Part Seven, Crime and Contemporary Corrections. James V. Bennett reviews the procedures involved in the sentence and treatment of offenders. In the second article, entitled "The National Profile of Correction," a broad overview of the existing correctional system is established. B. B. Berk turns to an examination of the barriers to correctional and institutional goals raised by the inmates' social system. John Gagnon and William Simon analyze the implications of prison homosexuality, and Heman G. Stark discusses contemporary alternatives to institutionalization.

27. The Sentence and Treatment of Offenders*

JAMES V. BENNETT

Any attempt to develop a treatment or rehabilitation program within a correctional institution must eventually confront the problem of punishment (see Toby, Article 32). Although the correctional or penal institution represents a composite of the multiple goals of punishment, deterrence, offender isolation,

*Reprinted from the *Annals,* Volume 339 (January, 1962), pp. 142-56, with permission of the author and the publishers, The American Academy of Political and Social Science.

prevention, and remotivation-rehabilitation, the punishment ideal still holds prominence.

In its early form punishment was initiated and inflicted by the aggrieved person or family against the violator or his kin. As such retribution was eventually institutionalized within the existing social structure, social rules were defined in order to minimize public conflict and yet accomplish social control. In these early years the benefits which accrued from punitive action were directly transmitted to the offended party in order to redress the moral violation which had occurred earlier. As society became more complex, however, the power of punishment passed from the general social group to the hands of sovereign heads of the territorial states. During and following the period of Western European political disintegration and the establishment of feudalism, the power of the feudal lord reached a new high. However, the political concepts of feudalism and absolute monarchy involved an abdication of personal rights in return for guarantees of personal and social security from the reigning lord or monarch. While the feudal or monarchical ruler assumed increasing control of the destiny of his subjects, he also assumed obligations designed to enhance the public interest.

Similar changes also occurred in criminal law during the Middle Ages. Only in the 17th and 18th centuries did the structure of criminal justice, often administered with excessive harshness, become clear. Challenges to the concept of the divine right of kings were issued in parallel 18th-century disputes concerning the right of lords and monarchs to act unilaterally without review in criminal matters. As the peasants and serfs regained some control over the criminal system, the harshness of punishment was reduced.

Corporal punishment has largely disappeared. Prison life has been progressively ameliorated as the general standard of living has continued to rise (see National Profile, Article 28). Probation and parole, alternate sentencing systems designed to treat various forms of criminal deviance more effectively, have gained favor. At the same time that law enforcement agencies have been developed and extended throughout much of the Western world (see Dienstein, Article 19), the administration of justice has become more humane and purposeful (see Stark, Article 31). The rise of social sciences has undoubtedly played a large role in the development of these humane practices (see Hall, Article 23; and Gibbs, Article 33). However, the public has not always accepted the value of these new approaches, because of its lack of understanding of the problem or its solution.

The old doctrine of retributive punishment, James V. Bennett writes, is, however, progressively falling into disuse in most Western countries. Instead, the attempt to blend deterrent and protective factors with the self-sustaining goal of effective restoration of the offender to the community has received added support. Probation, indeterminate sentence, and parole, Bennett argues, offer three more basic and more valuable correctional alternatives which recognize the socioenvironmental context of the offender (also see Stark, Article 31; and Toby, Article 32).

What a society does with its convicted law-breakers reflects in large measure the philosophical underpinnings of its criminal law. In the United States, as in most other Western countries, the old doctrine that the purpose of the criminal law is to exact from the criminal a retributive suffering proportionate to the heinousness of the offense, if not completely discarded, has been fairly successfully dissipated. In its place, the administration of criminal justice has been searching for a more rational approach to the disposition of the convicted offender in an effort to combine the principles of deterrence and public protection with the objective of restoring the offender to a more self-sustaining status in the community.

... [T]he increasing use of probation is providing the courts with a constructive alternative to imprisonment; parole and the indeterminate sentence are mitigating the inflexibility of statutory penalties; and the more recent proposals for separate sentencing tribunals offer the promise of more individualization in the disposition of the offender and, at the same time, of reducing the harmful effects of wide disparity of sentences.

Thus, the current trend in the United States with respect to the disposition of the offender is unmistakably in the direction of an individualized penal treatment administered within the framework of a flexible criminal code. . . .

Since the purpose of this article is to present in some detail the current trends and practices in the United States with respect to prison administration, sentencing, probation, and parole, it is necessary at the beginning to point out that there are in the United States fifty separate state systems and the District of Columbia in addition to a federal system which enforces criminal laws dealing with crimes of an interstate character as well as those relating to matters exclusively granted the federal government by the Constitution. . . .

INDIVIDUALIZING THE SENTENCE

Despite the complexity of American criminal laws everywhere in the United States, a sentence implies a term of imprisonment or its equivalent in terms of restricted freedom, with the exception of those few cases where the death penalty is prescribed. Originally all sentences were fixed and definite, deriving from the classical principle of equality of punishment according to the seriousness of the crime committed. This principle was perhaps best exemplified in the French Penal Code of 1791, which soon found the rigidity of such a formula impractical and had to be modified allowing a wider degree of judicial discretion in adapting a sentence to certain mitigating circumstances.

The rigidity of the sentence was first modified by so-called good-time or good-conduct laws which reduced sentences of prisoners in American prisons by credits or marks earned by prisoners for good conduct. The real departure, however, from the rigid, definite sentence came with the introduction of the indeterminate sentence and parole. Historically, these two concepts developed contemporaneously and are closely related to the correctional or treatment theory of the function of the sentence. Today, except for certain types of offenses which require the imposition of a mandatory term without the privilege of parole, practically all sentences in the United States are, in effect, indefinite sentences with the possibility of parole or mandatory release after reduction of the maximum by good-conduct allowances.

. . . .

The indeterminate sentence as used in the various states is expressed in several ways: both the minimum and maximum sentence may be specified or the maximum may be specified and the minimum not specified. A definite sentence is always expressed as a single specified term of years. Prisoners committed under the indeterminate type of sentence ordinarily become eligible for parole consideration after serving the minimum term imposed, and those sentenced to definite terms become eligible after serving one third, one fourth, or some other specific portion of the sentence. Twenty-seven of the states and the District of Columbia have predominantly indeterminate sentences, and twenty-one states retain predominantly definite-sentence systems.

Although the indeterminate sentence was founded on the concept of individualized treatment of the offender, it has never quite achieved its early promise, chiefly because of insistence that a considerable measure of deterrence and punishment be preserved in the imposition of sentence. The major criticisms directed against the present complicated sentencing systems in the United States are two: one is that the wide disparity of sentences which now exist, not only from one state to another but within the same state for the same type of offense, reflect differences in attitudes of legislative bodies and judges rather than actual differences between offenders or their acts; and the other is that the times served by prisoners on various sentences are excessive and vary too much in duration.

. . . .

Obviously, the use of parole, probation, or any other device cannot solve the basic problem of unequal sentences which all legal systems face in one form or another. While many other countries have provided by statute for appellate review of sentences, this is not the situation in the United States, where appeals in criminal cases are based on questions of law alone and the sentence imposed by the trial court is immune from any review. Only very recently, however, have any serious attempts been made to eliminate disparity of sentence by legislative action. . . .

FEDERAL SENTENCING PROCEDURES

Until very recently, practically all persons convicted of violation of federal laws could be sentenced only to definite sentences with eligibility for parole after serving one third of the sentence. In 1950 the federal government made the first important reform of the definite sentence by the adoption of the Youth Corrections Act which affected youthful offenders between the ages of eighteen and twenty-two.

The federal courts now have several alternatives for the disposition of this age group. Unless the offender is placed on probation, the court may sentence the offender under the provisions of the conventional definite sentence. If, however, a judge is uncertain as to the disposition which will most appropriately meet the needs of a youthful offender, he may commit him prior to sentence to the custody of the Attorney General for study, diagnosis, and a recommendation as to the treatment needed. On the other hand, the judge may commit the youth for a term not to exceed six years. In some extreme cases, the commitment may be for an indefinite period not to exceed the maximum provided by statute for the substantive offense. The determination of the proper time when the youth shall be released from the institution rests with the Youth Correction Division of the United States Board of Parole, which may release him conditionally at any time but must do so not later than two years before the expiration of the maximum period of commitment, which in most cases would be four years.

An even greater flexibility in sentencing for all federal offenders was the introduction in 1958 of a new federal sentencing law. Under the provisions of this legislation, the federal courts may use now one of three types of sentences: (1) one with a minimum term which is less than one third of the statutory maximum sentence, at which time the prisoner shall be eligible for parole; (2) a maximum term within the limits prescribed by law but leaving to the discretion of the United States Board of Parole the determination of the time at which the prisoner shall become eligible for parole consideration; and (3) a maximum sentence prescribed by law for the offense but commit the offender for a diagnostic study to the Director of the Bureau of Prisons. Under this last type of sentence, a full report on the individual together with any pertinent recommendations are submitted to the court within ninety days. The court may then reaffirm the original sentence or reduce it, or it may impose a sentence under any applicable provision of the law; or the court may place the offender on probation. In addition to these three choices, the judge may use the older more definite type of sentence which imposes a prescribed sentence. In such a case, the prisoner becomes eligible for parole after serving one third of the sentence.

The new sentencing law also extends the Youth Corrections Act to persons under the age of twenty-six. . . .

Although these new sentencing procedures for the federal courts are in themselves a significant and forward step, just as important is a parallel law passed by Congress at the same time which authorizes the Judicial Conference of the United States to establish institutes and joint councils on sentencing for the purpose of "Studying, discussing, and formulating the objectives, policies, standards, and criteria for sentencing those convicted of crimes and offenses in the courts of the United States." Some of the objectives which these institutes are intended to achieve are also stated in the law:

(1) The development of standards for the content and utilization of presentence reports.

(2) The establishment of factors to be used in selecting cases for special study and observation in prescribed diagnostic clinics.

(3) The determination of the importance of psychiatric, emotional, sociological and physiological factors involved in crime and their bearing upon sentences.

(4) The discussion of special sentencing problems in unusual cases such as treason, violation of public trust, subversion, or involving abnormal sex behavior, addiction to drugs or alcohol, mental and physical handicaps.

(5) The formulation of sentencing principles and criteria which will assist in promoting the equitable administration of criminal laws of the United States.

.   .   .   .

CALIFORNIA CORRECTIONAL SYSTEM

Among the state correctional systems in the United States, that of California stands out as unique in its pattern of organization and in the degree of integration achieved between the indeterminate sentence, correctional treatment, and parole. In 1944 the California legislature reorganized its prisons, reformatories, and sentencing methods. A centralized Department of Corrections was established with responsibility for the administration of all its institutions, now housing about 20,000. When first established, the Department of Corrections also included the Youth Institutions, but, by legislative action in 1953, this agency became a separate department. The act also lodged all responsibility for determining how long a prisoner was to serve in independent tribunals called an Adult Authority and a Youth Authority.

The Adult Authority has the major responsibility for setting the term of imprisonment in each case in co-ordination with the programs of classification, treatment, and training. Under the California program, all sentenced offenders are first received at one of several reception-diagnostic centers where diagnostic and classification studies are conducted and recommendations made as to the most suitable type of institution and individual program. Members of the Adult Authority meet at each institution as often as necessary to review each case and to determine the term of imprisonment in relation to the information developed at the reception-diagnostic centers. They also meet at the institution to which the individual is sent to consider release plans for each prisoner and to set a tentative and final release date and supervision plans.

.   .   .   .

The California correctional system, in its basic organization and program development since its establishment about fifteen years ago, stands out as embodying the most modern in theory and practice of present-day attempts to solve basic sentencing problems and the co-ordination of individualized treatment programs with the judicial guilt-finding process.

CHARACTERISTICS OF CORRECTIONAL INSTITUTIONS

Because of the wide diversity between the states, it is difficult to generalize about American penal and correctional institutions. Some which date back to the early nineteenth century have changed very little over the years. Some are comparatively new and have put into practice the most advanced practices and correctional programs. Between is a great variety of institutions differing widely in administration and program. . . .

Perhaps the most outstanding characteristic of the developing pattern of the American correctional system is its increasing specialization. Historically, the prison and, later, the reformatory constituted the core of the prison system. . . .

With the introduction of the concept of classification, which has as its purpose the individualization of the correctional process based on detailed medical, psychiatric, educational, and sociological examinations, the diversification of institutions became increasingly important in American penology. As a result, separate institutions have been established for males and females, felons, misdemeanants, adults and youthful offenders, the sane and the insane, and institutions for those requiring maximum, medium, and minimum security type of imprisonment.

Another characteristic of the American correctional system is that it is becoming increasingly centralized. . . . A third important feature of American institutions is the general improvement in living conditions. Aside from the fact that these institutions are generally cleaner, better ventilated, and better lighted than at any time in their history, more attention is being paid to adequate medical care and the preparation and serving of food. . . . Of central importance, of course, is the correctional program itself which, because of the impact of classification, is becoming more and more individualized. . . . And, finally, there is an increased recognition that the effective implementation of a program of correctional treatment is impossible without high personnel standards and a continuous program of personnel training.

. . . There are many obstacles to be overcome, however, before American institutions as a whole can be said to have achieved these goals. Many institutions throughout the country are old and antiquated, and others are too large and overcrowded. Unemployment and idleness is still a major problem in many state prison systems. Although the number of professionally trained persons engaged in correctional work is increasing, the number of psychiatrists, psychologists, and social workers is not sufficient to meet the needs. And, in many institutions, low salaries, lack of tenure, and long hours make the task of raising personnel standards extremely difficult.

PAROLE PRACTICES VARIATIONS

The principle of parole, which is in essence the conditional release of an offender who has already served a portion of his sentence in a penal or correctional institution, is now almost universally accepted as an integral part of the sentence. In the United States, the first systematic use of parole is associated with the beginnings of the reformatory type of institution with its indeterminate sentence in New York about 1869. However, it was not until 1910 that the federal government adopted parole and not until 1944 that all of the states had adopted some form of a parole law. But, despite this general acceptance of parole in principle, wide variations exist in organization, administration, and the use of parole.

First, with respect to organization and administration, three types of parole boards are found in the United States: one type of parole board, which is rapidly disappearing, is that composed of the staff of an individual institution; a second type of paroling authority is a state board of parole which is part of a state department of correction and which may authorize release on parole from any of the state institutions; and, third, there is the independent state board of parole which has both the authority to release on parole and to administer the supervision of all persons on parole. However, the trend is toward the centralization of independent paroling authorities composed of qualified, full-time members as the standard organizational pattern in the United States.

Although practically all paroling authorities agree that parole should be used for all prisoners, only a few jurisdictions in the United States approximate this result in practice. In the selection of parolees, the paroling agency must operate within the limitations of the criminal code of each state and of the sentence imposed in each case. . . . Furthermore, eligibility for parole usually depends on completion of a portion of any definite sentence or upon completion of the minimum period of an indefinite sentence. For life sentences, eligibility also varies from a minimum of seven years in three states to twenty years in four states, twenty-five years in four states, and as much as thirty-five years in one state.

Consequently, the use of parole becomes a very complex and diverse system in practice. . . .

Because of the differences in statutory sentences and sentencing structures among the states, there is also as much diversity in the statutory provisions regulating the discharge from parole supervision as there is in release on parole. In most states, a parolee is discharged from supervision only after completing the maximum term of his sentence. In a few states, however, the parolee may be discharged from parole supervision in not less than six months and, in other states, not less than one year.

POTENTIALITIES OF PROBATION

Although probation in principle and in practice, especially for juveniles and petty offenders, antedates both the indeterminate sentence and parole by more than fifty years, it lacks as much, or more, in uniformity of practice as sentencing and parole. Nevertheless, probation as an alternative method to imprisonment is used extensively in the United States. Moreover, probation as a method of individualized treatment is being steadily divorced from its original concept as a legal device for granting leniency through the suspension of sentence. With very few exceptions, all states and the federal government have legislation authorizing the use of probation for adults. Legislation providing for probation for juveniles had been in force many years before its extension to adults. However, the implementation of such authorizing legislation rests almost entirely with the courts, and the contrasts in the administration and use of probation among the various geographic localities are too intricate to map out in detail here.

. . . Some states leave the selection of offenders to be placed on probation to the discretion of the court, while many other states list many particular exceptions with respect to offense and to the type of offender. In several states, probation cannot be used in cases of serious offenses or offenses punishable by more than five or ten years of imprisonment; some states make only first offenders eligible for probation; in others, only certain types of courts or courts in political subdivisions with a specified population may use probation. Also, even though the basic legislation for probation is available, rural areas tend to lag behind urban areas in establishing probation services, and many urban communities fail to develop probation because of lack of financial resources, disinterest on the part of the public, or even opposition to probation by some judges.

. . . .

GROWTH TOWARD GREATER UNIFORMITY

In a country as politically complex as the United States, a wide diversity of practice in most areas of public administration is inevitable. . . . But the gap between principle and general practice is slowly but steadily being closed, and the trend is definitely in the direction of greater uniformity, at least in the areas of organization and administration which hopefully will result in more uniformity of practice.

One of the devices being used to achieve this universality of philosophy and uniformity in administration is the development of the Standard or Model Act which the state legislatures may adopt or adapt to their own conditions, needs, and financial capabilities. . . .

Another device to achieve not only uniformity of practice but the upgrading of correctional services as well is the formulation of standards which are applicable to the whole gamut of correction from detention for those awaiting trial, to sentence, probation, institutional commitment, parole, and parole supervision. . . .

And, finally, a third major development of fundamental importance in the

United States is the growing recognition of the need for a redefinition and codification of substantive crimes in terms of contemporary social and economic conditions. . . . While many states have attempted a form of codification by a more systematic arrangement or classification of offenses, only a few states so far have attempted to rewrite their criminal codes.

. . . The American Law Institute has for more than twenty-five years been interested in the field of criminal law reform, but it was only [recently] that the American Law Institute has been able to concentrate on the project of formulating a Model Penal Code.

Among the many problem areas dealt with in the development of the Model Penal Code are questions of disposition of the offender, types of disposition, and the criteria to be considered in imposing sentences; the classification of offenses; the complex problems of competency; and the organization and administration of a department of correction, parole, probation, and related agencies.

MODEL PENAL CODE

A number of important innovations proposed by the Model Penal Code . . . deal with sentencing and treatment of offenders.

There is a classification of offenses into six categories of seriousness, each carrying a standard sentence:

Category	Maximum	Minimum
Felony of the First Degree	Life	1 to 10 years
Felony of the Second Degree	10 years	1 to 3 years
Felony of the Third Degree	5 years	1 to 2 years
Misdemeanor	1 year	None
Petty Misdemeanor	3 months	None
Violation	Fine only	

This scheme is intended to introduce some order and rationality into the anarchy of existing statutory penalties individually prescribed by the legislature for particular crimes.

The judge's discretion as to minimum sentence is restricted, . . . , on the theory that the proper date of release can best be determined by the parole board on the basis of the prisoner's development subsequent to sentencing. Some discretion remains, however, in deference to the view that it is sometimes necessary to make a sentence sufficiently reflect the gravity of the offense, lest the deterrent efficacy of the law be dissipated. In addition, the Model Penal Code authorizes the judge to reduce the degree of a conviction one step where the ordinary sentence would be "unduly harsh."

The Code provides for probation as a possibility in every conviction where the judge deems that "imprisonment is unnecessary for protection of the public." The criteria on which this judgment is to be based are specified in the statute, and include the following:

(a) The defendant does not have a history of prior delinquency or criminal activity, or, having such a history, has led a law abiding life for a substantial period of time before the commission of the present crime;

(b) The defendant's criminal conduct neither caused nor threatened serious harm;

(c) The defendant did not contemplate that his criminal conduct would cause or threaten serious harm;

(d) The defendant's criminal conduct was the result of circumstances unlikely to recur;

(e) The defendant acted under the stress of a strong provocation;

(f) The victim of the defendant's criminal conduct consented to its commission or was largely instrumental in its perpetration;

(g) The imprisonment of the defendant would entail excessive hardship because of his advanced age or physical condition;

(h) The character and attitudes of the defendant indicate that he is unlikely to commit another crime.

Some have contended that there should be a presumption in favor of probation for first offenders.

The Model Penal Code makes provision against one of the worst abuses of current sentencing, namely, the power of the judge to aggregate sentences for multiple offenses. Thus, under present law, a thief or burglar who has been involved in half a dozen crimes may be sentenced to a maximum that is six times as long as the statutory maximum for one offense. The Model Penal Code deals with this and some other situations by means of the "extended sentence." In effect, the ordinary sentence may be prolonged by not more than 100 per cent in the case of multiple offenders, habitual offenders, professional criminals, and mentally abnormal persons.

Parole becomes part of every penitentiary sentence under the Model Penal Code. This differs from the present situation inasmuch as an offender who serves his full term in prison—presumably because the parole authorities regard him as most dangerous—now emerges with no time remaining to be served "on parole." Obviously, the most dangerous, who are confined longest, should also have the most careful parole supervision. Accordingly, the Code relates the period of parole to the period of actual detention rather than to the unexpired portion of the original sentence.

The Model Penal Code ... developed by the American Law Institute is not designed to be adopted uniformly by all states. The principal objective is to examine and make more explicit the problems of the criminal law, to bring into the forum of discussion alternative solutions, and to express conclusions in clear statutory language. . . .

.   .   .   .

28. The National Profile of Correction*

NATIONAL COUNCIL ON CRIME AND DELINQUENCY

Although one may date the beginnings of modern penal philosophy from about 1787, when a small band of Quakers and freethinkers met at the home of Benjamin Franklin, it took many years to realize the aims of this original discussion, which supported the classification of prisoner housing, a rational system of prison labor, indeterminate sentences, and individualized treatment of offenders according to the nature of the crime. By 1790, the Walnut Street jail in Philadelphia was remodeled to carry out the rudimentary demands of this reform philosophy. However, the weaknesses of the experiment were soon apparent, leading the reformers by 1820 to anticipate a new approach to the crime problem. Only the work of Elam Lynds, who established the system of discipline at the Auburn State Prison (New York) with the help of the architect John Cray, and John Haviland, who created the Pennsylvania system at Eastern Penitentiary in Philadelphia, saved the penitentiary approach to corrections. Beginning with the assumption that correction cannot take place until the criminal spirit is broken, the three leading figures articulated a penal philosophy of austerity and strict discipline. Not only should the offenders, they argued, do time as penance for their misconduct but they should also refrain from any communication with their fellow prisoners. Consequently, prisoners under the Auburn system were housed in cells within the prison buildings and worked silently in congregate work locations. However, inmates within the Pennsylvania system, working and living in solitary confinement, were quartered in cells providing outside access.

Not until 1930 did these approaches undergo any major modification. When Thomas Mott Osborn allowed prisoners to share in staff discussions on prisoner problems in 1916, he stimulated the development of a new penal and correctional philosophy. Under its ensuing provisions a concept of individualized treatment replaced the earlier presupposition that all prisoners must be classified and treated alike regardless of their need or crime. Progressive correctional philosophy has since expanded Osborn's concepts and introduced even more striking changes into the functioning penal system. The value of the prison as a treatment location has received increased scrutiny. Halfway houses and work

*Reprinted from *Crime and Delinquency*, Volume 13, Number 1 (January, 1967), pp. 227-62, with the permission of the editors.

release programs (*see* Stark, Article 31) have been introduced as alternatives to institutionalization. However, modern penal philosophy still represents an ambiguous and confusing fusion of deterrent, correctional, and punishment goals. Five simple concepts, Howard Gill believes, distinguish existing penal philosophy:

1. Security must be assured in order to keep prisoners in their proper place.
2. Prisoners can be classified into four basic groups of new, intractable, tractable, and defective.
3. Primary attention must be given to the solving of the problems of the tractable or treatable prisoners; secondary concern to the acculturation of these prisoners to society.
4. Correctional staffs will operate in five areas of executive, administrative (including fiscal and clerical), professional, security and treatment.
5. Prison architecture must meet these four needs.

The functional American correctional system is diverse and decentralized. A conglomerate of local, county, state and federal institutions, it suffers from the lack of funds, personnel, equipment, and facilities. The following article, a product of The National Council on Crime and Delinquency, describes the scope of modern corrections in the United States.

I. INTRODUCTION

The main systems of correction dealt with here are juvenile probation, juvenile detention, juvenile aftercare, juvenile correctional institutions, adult probation, adult correctional institutions, and adult parole. Because services for adult misdemeanants are generally operated independently, two additional categories—misdemeanant probation and local correctional institutions and jails—were also included in the survey.

Historically, ... each of these systems in the United States developed independently of the others, as autonomous systems and not as divisions of some existing service. With few exceptions, they continue to operate as separate entities today. Each system has its own set of standards and goals, and generally its personnel identify their careers with the special system rather than with correction as a whole. Indeed, until recently the term "correction" for all practical purposes denoted adult correctional institutions only; to many personnel in all services, this is still what it means. Many juvenile probation and aftercare workers tend to regard child welfare as their field rather than correction. As a result of these separations, each system has become exclusive.

Though these several systems have separate roles and are administered at different levels of government within states, they are, in fact, interdependent, and it is in the public interest that they all be of good quality and that there be no gaps in meeting correctional needs. . . .

.   .   .   .

Because the purpose of the survey was to view correction *nationally*, this report has not emphasized the *intrastate* relationship of services. It can be noted here, however, that disparities in correctional services *within* a state are often as great as differences found among the states. . . . In most states not more than two or three of the nine correctional services are consolidated under one correctional administration. Few states still have any administrative arrangement or other mechanism to enable joint planning and evaluation of services in the interest of achieving a better balanced correctional program. Voluntary efforts by correctional administrators have been sparse. . . .

. . . .

II. SURVEY FINDINGS

On any one day in the U.S., about 1¼ million persons—more than the population reported for 16 states—are under the jurisdiction of state and local correctional agencies and institutions. In addition, many thousands more are serving from a few days to a few weeks in a variety of local lockups and jails not included in this survey.

Of the total volume reported, 28 per cent are juveniles and 72 per cent are adults (according to the definitions of each category, which vary from state to state). The number of adults under probation and parole supervision and in correctional institutions (876,412) is more than the number of enlisted personnel (846,684) reported in the U.S. Army for 1965. (See Table 25.)

A. Does It Make a Difference Where the Offender Is?

One-third (more than 400,000) of all offenders reported, juvenile and adult, were found in institutions; two-thirds (over 800,000) were in communities under probation or parole supervision. (See Table 1.) However, about 20 per cent of

TABLE 1
Average Daily Population of Offenders in Correctional Systems

	Juvenile		Adult		Total	
	No.	%	No.	%	No.	%
In the community . . .	283,491	82.16	533,889	60.92	817,380	66.92
In institutions	61,526	17.84	342,523	39.08	404,049	33.08
Total	345,017	100.00	876,412	100.00	1,221,429	100.00

the latter are on either parole or aftercare status, having first served time in an institution. Judges and juries evidently place a high degree of reliance on institutional commitment.

FIGURE 1

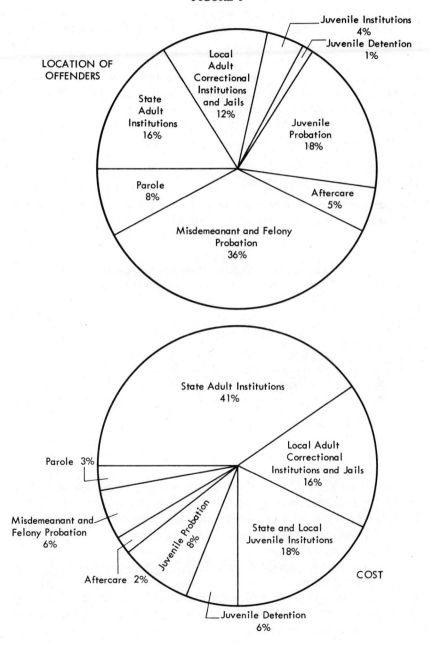

Agencies and institutions receive, during the course of a year, more than 2.5 million persons, whose status as inmate, probationer, or parolee directly affects, in addition, 5,825,000 members of their families.[1] One may well speculate on the number affected over a 10- or 20-year period and the percentage of the entire population this would represent.

The question of *where* an offender is—in the community (on probation or parole) or in an institution—makes a profound difference to his family's economic condition and the welfare resources of his community. Although the total commitment rate for the nation cannot be estimated accurately, it would appear that (excluding those sentenced to fines) about two-thirds of all offenders are committed to institutions. (See Table 25.) . . .

B. How Much Does Correction Cost?

The estimated cost of operating state and local correctional services in 1965 (see Table 2) was almost $1 billion ($940,467,494).

TABLE 2
Annual Expenditures for Correctional Systems

	Juvenile		*Adult*		*Total*	
	No. $	*%*	*No. $*	*%*	*No. $*	*%*
In the						
community ...	93,159,382	29.9	93,122,837	14.9	186,282,219	19.9
In institutions ...	221,410,413	70.1	532,774,862	85.1	754,185,275	80.1
Total	314,569,795	100.0	625,897,699	100.0	940,467,494	100.0

About 80 per cent of the total operating cost is allocated for institutions. Of that allocation, more than half goes to support state adult correctional institutions. (See Table 25.) Local institutions and jails account for about 16 per cent of all expenditures; juvenile detention accounts for about 6 per cent of the total. Only 14.4 per cent of correctional costs are allocated for probation services, including supervision of offenders and preparation of social studies to aid courts in making dispositions.

Of the total cost, one-third ($314,569,795) is for juvenile detention, institutions, and aftercare.

Costs for local services for misdemeanant offenders account for 18.7 per cent of the total, with only 3 per cent going for probation services and 15.7 per cent on confinement of misdemeanants.

1/According to the U.S. Bureau of the Census (March 1964), the average number of persons per household is 3.33.

1. *Per Capita Cost.* The figures for per capita cost of all correctional expenditures according to per capita income are not available for all states, but they undoubtedly would show wide variations, with some of the poorer states paying proportionately more than some of the wealthier states. Table 3 compares, regionally, per capita expenditures for state-operated adult and juvenile institutions and parole.

Table 4 illustrates the wide variations in per capita expenditure for these services in the ten largest states, where the average is $2.95 but the range is from $1.75 to $5.31. The average total expenditure is 0.10 per cent of per capita income, but the range extends from 0.06 per cent to 0.17 per cent.

TABLE 3

Per Capita Expenditures for State-operated Institutions, Aftercare, and Parole, by Regions

	Expenditures		Average Income	Per Cent of Per Capita Income
	Total	Per Capita		
East*	$176,412,231	$3.46	$2,836	0.12%
Midwest†	140,770,260	2.40	2,381	0.10%
South‡	106,961,398	2.16	1,904	0.12%
West§	146,950,278	4.81	2,482	0.19%
Insular‖........	9,824,473	2.65	2,189	0.12%
Total	$580,918,640	$3.00	$2,386	0.13%

*Connecticut, Delaware, Washington, D.C., Maine, Maryland, Massachusetts, New Hampshire, New Jersey, New York, Pennsylvania, Rhode Island, Vermont.

†Illinois, Indiana, Iowa, Kansas, Kentucky, Michigan, Minnesota, Missouri, Nebraska, North Dakota, Ohio, South Dakota, West Virginia, Wisconsin.

‡Alabama, Arkansas, Florida, Georgia, Louisiana, Mississippi, North Carolina, Oklahoma, Tennessee, Texas, South Carolina, Virginia.

§Arizona, California, Colorado, Idaho, Montana, Nevada, New Mexico, Oregon, Utah, Washington, Wyoming.

‖ Alaska, Hawaii, Puerto Rico.

TABLE 4

Per Capita Expenditures for State-operated Institutions, Aftercare, and Parole, in the Ten Largest States

State	Per Capita Expenditure	Per Cent of Per Capita Income
A	$1.75	0.08%
B	1.89	0.06%
C	2.37	0.09%
D	2.46	0.09%
E	2.56	0.08%
F	2.69	0.10%
G	3.03	0.13%
H	3.16	0.11%
I	4.29	0.14%
J	5.31	0.17%

TABLE 5
Per Capita Expenditures for Selected Correctional Services, by State Populations*

States†	Adult Institutions	Parole	Juvenile Institutions	Aftercare‡
Group I §				
A	$1.10	$.15	$ .26	$...
B	1.14	.07	.90	...
C	1.16	.06	.48	.05
D	1.24	.17	.34	.93
E	1.24	.13	.49	.03
F	1.38	.07	.97	.14
G	1.40	.11	.84	.11
H	1.56	.07	.79	.06
I	1.58	.11	.32	.06
J	1.69	.14	.44	...
K	1.72	.13	.91	.12
L	1.91	.13	.63	.02
M	2.04	.20	.61	...
N	2.30	.21	.49	...
O	2.36	.12	.61	.07
P	2.96	.14	.72	...
Q	3.24	.34	.66	.05
R	3.46	.44	1.14	.27
Group II ‖				
AA	$ .26	$.25	$ .22	$...
BB	.62	.01	.23	...
CC	.63	.02	.35	.03
DD	1.07	.07	.19	...
EE	1.13	.12	.77	.07
FF	1.14	.12	.49	.07
GG	1.14	.20	.44	...
HH	1.25	.05	.81	.10
II	1.48	.07	.45	.04
JJ	1.52	.15	.72	...
KK	1.58	.06	.54	...
LL	1.83	.07	.68	.07
MM	2.04	.09	1.71	...
NN	2.09	.09	.52	.09
OO	2.18	.07	.58	...
PP	2.36	.11	2.02	.17
QQ	2.56	.08	1.85	.36
RR	2.98	.29	1.33	.13
SS	3.11	.30	1.41	...
Group III ¶				
AAA	$ .71	$.05	$ .95	$.02
BBB	1.07	.07	.19	.03
CCC	1.19	.14	.90	...
DDD	1.38	.02	1.52	.25

*Population figures based on July 1, 1964, estimate.
†Includes Puerto Rico.
‡Includes only states operating special statewide programs.
§States having populations over 3.5 million.
‖States having populations between 1 and 3.5 million.
¶States having populations under 1 million.

TABLE 5 (Continued)

States	Adult Institutions	Parole	Juvenile Institutions	Aftercare
EEE	1.45	.07	1.05	.03
FFF	1.61	.13	1.13	.02
GGG	1.64	.24	.68	.19
HHH	1.68	.93	.74	.07
III	2.00	.09	1.32	.04
JJJ	2.13	.06	1.11	...
KKK	2.28	.17	.87	.10
LLL	2.61	.08	1.54	.11
MMM	2.82	.04	.90	.03
NNN	2.98	.08	3.05	...

Variations in expenditures for some of the services within each state are shown in Table 5.

Greater expenditures in use of probation services could account in some states—not all—for smaller expenditures for institutions and parole. Probation is known to be undeveloped in many states that appropriate either much less or much more than the average percentage of per capita income.

. . . .

2. *Daily Cost per Case.* The overall daily cost for a juvenile in an institution is 10 times more than the cost of juvenile probation or aftercare. For adults, state institutional cost is about six times that of parole and about 14 times that of probation. (See Table 6.)

The low cost of probation can be attributed in part to excessively heavy caseloads and low salaries. The average cost per case should be more than doubled to enable probation nationally to become more effective.

The "half-starved" condition of probation services may be one reason why commitment rates are so high. Many judges interviewed during the course of NCCD's state and community surveys report their reluctance to add more offenders to the burdens of an already overburdened probation service. On the other hand, where probation services have been improved, judges have made greater use of them.

. . . .

TABLE 6
Average Daily Costs per Case

	Juvenile	Adult
Detention	$11.15	$ ...
State institutions	9.35	5.24
Local institutions (including jails)	10.66	2.86
Probation	.92	.38
Parole or aftercare	.84	.88

TABLE 7

Current and Planned Construction of Correctional Institutions in the U.S.

	Type of Facility					
	Adult			Juvenile		
	Local Institutions	Jails‡	Correctional Institutions	Institutions	Detention (inc. Jails)	Total
1. Current Estimated Capacity*	192,197†	(see 1st col.)	213,558	43,027	25,932	474,714
2. Construction:						
a) In process	3,196	4,240	6,360	4,164	1,711	19,671
b) Authorized	2,683	9,824	18,107	7,090	2,247	39,951
c) Total line a and b	5,879	14,064	24,467	11,254	3,958	59,622
d) Planned by end of 1975 ...	9,982	17,247	16,909	6,606	3,136	58,880
Total	15,861	31,311	41,376	17,860	7,094	113,502
3. Estimated cost ($000)§	158,610	313,110	413,760	178,760	70,940	1,135,020

*Number of beds.
†Includes prorated capacity for jails which receive inmates for 30 days or longer.
‡Jail construction is for persons awaiting trial or serving time.
§Cost estimated at $10,000 a bed.

3. *Are Expenditures for More Institutions Really Needed?* ... The total bed capacity of new construction in process or authorized is about 60,000. (See Table 7.) [Rearranged for clarity in this format.] Construction currently being planned for completion by 1975 would add over 50,000 more beds, for a total of almost 114,000 new beds by that date. Some of the new construction will replace obsolete facilities, but probably most of it will add to the present capacity. If all of the units being planned are added, the present capacity of correctional institutions will be increased by 24 per cent. If the cost of correctional institution construction is estimated conservatively at an average of $10,000 a bed, the cost of these added facilities will be over $1 billion ($1,135,020,000). The added capacity will, of course, increase the operating expense. When fully occupied, the new space will add, on the basis of current per capita costs, over $200 million annually to the operating cost of the institutions. That amount alone is about equal to the total amount now being spent on all probation and parole services, both juvenile and adult.

This trend can be reversed by more adequate staffing of conventional field services and by the development of new and more effective approaches within existing programs.

C. How Is Correctional Manpower Being Used?

1. *Distribution.* The overall distribution of personnel in correction is featured by disparity; specifically, a disproportionate allocation to institutions. The ratio of institutional personnel to probation and parole personnel is 4:1 in juvenile correction and 10:1 in adult correction. Institutional personnel make up almost 90 per cent of the entire correctional force. (See Table 8.) State institution personnel alone constitute 42 per cent of all correctional personnel. (See Table 25.)

Within the institutions themselves, 62.7 per cent of all employees are custodial staff. (See Table 25.) Treatment staff, including caseworkers, psychologists, and psychiatrists, are only 3.6 per cent; educational staff,

TABLE 8
Distribution of Correctional Personnel*

	Juvenile		Adult		Total	
	No.	*%*	*No.*	*%*	*No.*	*%*
Detention	7,898	20.32	...	...	7,898	7.10
State institutions	21,247	54.77	46,680	64.50	67,927	61.10
Local institutions and jails	2,004	5.16	19,195	26.52	21,199	19.05
Probation	6,320	16.26	4,501	6.22	10,821	9.73
Parole	1,359	3.50	1,999	2.76	3,358	3.02
Total	38,828	100.00	72,375	100.00	111,203	100.00

*Part-time personnel are prorated. For detention, probation, and local institutions and jails, estimates were made. For parole and state institutions, actual figures are used.

TABLE 9a
Personnel in Correctional Institutions by Position and Type of Institution

| | Selected Institutional Staff | | | | |
| | Treatment | | | Educational | |
Type of Program	Social Worker	Psychol-ogist	Psychi-atrist	Academic Teacher	Vocational Teacher
Juvenile institutions	926	182	46	1,770	725
Local juvenile institutions	272	28	9	359	51
Local institutions and jails	167	33	58	106	137
Adult institutions	800	203	121	893	761
Totals..............	2,165	446	234	3,128	1,674

TABLE 9b
Percentage Distribution of Institutional Personnel, by Classification and System

Type of System	Treatment*	Educational†	Custodial‡	Other	Total
Juvenile institutions...........	5.6	11.8	40.7	41.9	100%
Local institutions and jails	1.3	1.3	78.1	19.3	100%
Adult institutions...........	2.4	3.6	66.0	28.0	100%

*Includes social workers, counselors, psychologists, and psychiatrists.
†Both academic and vocational.
‡Includes guards, houseparents, and correctional officers.

including both academic and vocational teachers, account for 5.9 per cent. All other personnel account for 27.8 per cent. . . .

. . . Another way to see how correctional personnel are distributed is to examine their number in relation to the number of persons in their charge. In this way, we can gain some notion at least of their possible influence on the offender population. Table 10 shows how great the difference is between the custodial personnel ratio, on one hand, and, on the other, the treatment and educational personnel ratio. Also, note that the custodial personnel ratio doesn't vary much according to type of institution, in contrast to the sharp fluctuations found for the treatment and educational ratios. The figures in Table 10 are averages; there are state correctional institutions where the treatment personnel ratio is as high as 1:2,406, and in many jails there are no treatment personnel at all.

TABLE 10
Ratio of Institutional Staff to Institutional Population

	Institutional Staff		
	Treatment*	Educational	Custodial
Juvenile detention	1:14	1:14	1:11†
Juvenile institutions	1:36	1:17	1:5
Local juvenile institutions	1:20	1:22	1:5
Adult institutions..................	1:179	1:121	1:7
Local institutions and jails...........	1:548	1:581	1:9

*Includes social workers, counselors, psychologists, and psychiatrists.
†Includes group supervisors.

Since 4.8 custodial personnel are required to staff a three-shift post, fewer are available at any one time than the ratio indicates.

2. *Caseloads.* Caseload sizes of field personnel also vary according to systems. Generally, parole officers and juvenile aftercare workers carry smaller caseloads than probation officers. Since caseloads are frequently mixed—combinations of probation and parole, or aftercare and juvenile probation, or juvenile probation and child neglect, etc.—the survey asked for the total average caseload being carried by correctional personnel. Table 11 shows the percentages of persons being supervised in various ranges of caseload size. (In some counties, however, there were no services and some persons were not in a caseload. Aftercare cases in child welfare and public welfare caseloads are not included.)

More than three-fourths of the persons on misdemeanant probation and more than two-thirds of those under felony probation supervision are in caseloads of over 100. Since personnel in these two systems are responsible also for presentence investigations (each counted as equivalent to five supervision units),

TABLE 11
Average Caseload in Probation and Parole

Size of Caseload*	Juvenile		Misdemeanant Probation	Adult	
	Probation	Aftercare		Probation	Parole
Under 40	3.66%	19.10%	.68%	.78%	3.08%
41-50	8.10	9.06	.18	2.32	4.81
51-60	11.60	4.68	4.26	2.65	25.38
61-70	19.55	48.81	3.86	6.51	20.74
71-80	29.71	5.73	2.38	7.64	23.22
81-90	5.65	4.45	1.39	6.64	3.66
91-100	11.05	5.75	10.91	6.41	14.70
Over 100	10.68	2.42	76.34	67.05	4.41
Total	100.00%	100.00%	100.00%	100.00%	100.00%

*During a "recent month."

a caseload of "over 100" is several times larger than the 50-unit caseload recommended by the standard. Not quite 1 per cent of the misdemeanants, only 3 per cent of adult probationers, and only 8 per cent of parolees were found in supervision loads of 50 or under. The situation is a little better in the two other services: about 12 per cent of juvenile probationers and 28 per cent of juveniles under aftercare supervision are in caseloads of 50 or less. The median caseload range is 61-70 in juvenile aftercare and parole, and 71-80 in juvenile probation. As noted above, the median caseload range in both misdemeanant and adult probation is "over 100." The majority of offenders under supervision, taken as a whole (420,903, or 51.5 per cent) are in caseloads above 90.

.   .   .   .

3. *The Manpower Shortage.* Addition of 16,583 field and institutional personnel (excluding detention) to the staff now employed is needed to bring ratios of professional, social, and psychological treatment services up to recommended standards. Of the total additional force, 12,532 are required in probation and parole (see Table 12) and 4,051 in institutions (see Table 13). Total staff needs of institutions cannot be estimated as there are no standard ratios for custodial personnel.

4. *Personnel Policies.* Standards for correctional personnel call for merit system or civil service coverage, appropriate educational qualifications, and adequate salaries and working conditions. Much variation in personnel policies is found among the systems.

a) Merit Systems. Civil service covers juvenile aftercare officers in 72.5 per cent of the states and adult parole officers in only 32 per cent of the states. (See Table 14.) Coverage for institutional superintendents is not as good as it is for their custodial staffs. Part of the difference may be explained by the location of the service in government. The superintendent is more likely to be covered if the service is part of a larger agency and he is relatively low in the administrative hierarchy.

TABLE 12

Estimated Selected Personnel Needs of Probation and Parole Programs
(based on task force standards)

	Officers and Supervisors Employed	Officers and Supervisors Needed	Additional Officers and Supervisors Required
Juvenile probation*	6,320	8,136	1,816
Aftercare	1,359	1,737	378
Misdemeanant probation	1,944	6,657†	4,713†
Adult probation	2,557	7,555	4,998
Parole	1,999	2,626	627
Total	14,179	26,711	12,532

*Including intake, based on NCCD standards (one intake officer for each 450 to 500 cases referred annually).

†About 11,000 more than this number would be needed if standards were applied to presentence investigations in all misdemeanant cases.

TABLE 13
Estimated Selected Personnel Needs of Correctional Institution Programs
(based on task force standards)

	Juvenile Institutions	Local Juvenile Institutions	Jails and Local Institutions	Adult Institutions	Total
Social workers needed	1,413	201	942	1,341	3,897
Social workers employed	926	272	167	800	2,165
Additional social workers needed	487	. . .	775	541	1,803
Psychologists needed	282	40	707	1,006	2,035
Psychologists employed	182	28	33	203	446
Additional psychologists needed	100	12	674	803	1,589
Psychiatrists needed	282	40	236	335	893
Psychiatrists employed	46	9	58	121	234
Additional psychistrists needed	236	31	178	214	659
Total additional needed					4,051

TABLE 14
Merit System Coverage for Key Personnel, by System

A. Community-based Services

	Director	Probation or Parole Officer
Juvenile probation	44.0%	44.0%
Juvenile aftercare	63.8%	72.5%
Misdemeanant probation	46.0%	46.0%
Adult probation	51.0%	51.0%
Adult parole	32.0%	32.0%

B. Institutional Services

	Superintendent	Professional Staff in Institutions	Custodial Staff
Juvenile detention	43.0%	43.0%	39.0%
State-operated juvenile institutions	42.3%	63.5%	59.6%
Local institutions and jails	44.0%	44.0%	86.0%
Adult institutions	46.0%	72.0%	74.0%

b) Educational Qualifications. Starting educational qualifications also reflect a wide variety of practice among the services and for the same types of personnel within a service. About 53 per cent of local jails and institutions but less than 5 per cent of the juvenile aftercare programs have no educational requirements. (See Table 15.) Probation agencies are more apt than parole agencies to require

TABLE 15
**Percentage of Agencies Requiring Educational Qualifications for Staff
by Type of Agency, Qualification, and Position**

A. Qualifications Required of Directors and Superintendents

Agency	None	High School	College Graduate	Graduate Degree
Juvenile detention	18.0%	19.0%	47.0%	16.0%
Juvenile probation	10.0%	12.0%	63.0%	15.0%
Juvenile institutions	19.7%	1.9%	54.9%	23.5%
Misdemeanant probation	17.0%	9.0%	68.0%	6.0%
Adult probation	22.6%	12.8%	57.3%	7.3%
Local institutions and jails	52.9%	39.5%	7.6%	. . .
Adult institutions	48.0%	28.0%	24.0%	. . .
Adult parole	34.0%	8.0%	52.0%	6.0%

B. Qualifications Required of Probation and Parole Supervisors

Agency	None	High School	College Graduate	Graduate Degree
Aftercare	2.5%	10.0%	60.0%	27.5%
Misdemeanant probation	7.0%	4.0%	85.0%	4.0%
Adult probation	9.6%	14.7%	71.3%	4.4%
Adult parole	21.6%	17.6%	56.9%	3.9%

C. Qualifications Required of Probation and Parole Officers

Agency	None	High School	College Graduate	Graduate Degree
Juvenile probation	8.0%	14.0%	74.0%	4.0%
Aftercare	5.0%	10.0%	82.5%	2.5%
Misdemeanant probation	11.0%	13.0%	74.0%	2.0%
Adult probation	15.5%	21.3%	62.3%	0.9%
Adult parole	21.6%	19.6%	58.8%	. . .

D. Qualifications Required of Custodial Staff

Agency	None	High School	College Graduate	Graduate Degree
Juvenile detention	25.0%	61.0%	14.0%	. . .
Juvenile institutions	49.0%	51.0%	. . .	. . .
Local institutions and jails	53.0%	46.0%	1.0%	. . .
Adult institutions	41.1%	58.9%	. . .	. . .

college graduation. Graduate degrees are more frequently required by juvenile agencies than by agencies serving adults. Generally, personnel qualifications for work in institutions fall below those required by probation and parole agencies.

c) Salaries. The Task Force standards call for salaries to be "adequate and commensurate with the high trust and responsibility involved." Starting salaries vary considerably within each of the nine correctional systems and among the systems as a whole, but most of them have one thing in common: they fall below the recommended standard.

The median range of starting salaries for superintendents of state adult institutions is higher than for superintendents in juvenile institutions and directors of probation and parole agencies. However, the starting range for social workers is higher in juvenile institutions than in adult institutions. Starting salaries for supervisory and field staff personnel are fairly consistent throughout the services and are also, however, consistently low; the median for field staff is in the $5,000-6,000 range. The lowest median range—$3,000-4,000—is for custodial personnel in juvenile institutions. (See Table 16.)

Because salaries are low throughout the correctional field, the turnover of personnel is heavy and many positions go unfilled, with resultant increases in caseloads. A better balance between commitment and probation would, because of the difference in daily cost, make funds available for field services; part of the money saved could be used to establish a higher salary structure generally for correctional personnel.

d) Work Week. Working conditions are frequently poor in correctional agencies. A work week of more than 40 hours is required of juvenile institutional personnel in 16 states and adult institution personnel in 17 states. (See Table 17.) The nature of probation and parole work demands that personnel frequently work nights and weekends. Payment for overtime is rare and, because

TABLE 16
Median Ranges of Starting Salaries for Personnel in Correctional Services and Facilities

	Superintendent	Social Worker	Custodial Staff
Juvenile detention	$ 7,000- 8,000		$4,000-5,000
Juvenile institutions	9,000-10,000	$6,000-7,000	3,000-4,000
Local institutions and jails	7,000- 8,000		4,000-5,000
Adult institutions	10,000-11,000	5,000-6,000	4,000-5,000

	Director or CPO	Supervisor	Field Staff
Juvenile probation	$8,000- 9,000	$7,000-8,000	$5,000-6,000
Aftercare	9,000-10,000	7,000-8,000	5,000-6,000
Misdemeanant probation	8,000- 9,000	7,000-8,000	5,000-6,000
Adult probation	8,000- 9,000	7,000-8,000	5,000-6,000
Parole	9,000-10,000	7,000-8,000	5,000-6,000

of caseload pressures and court schedules, compensation by way of compensatory time is usually impracticable.

e) Staff Development. Generic standards call for staff development programs for all agencies, with funds budgeted and staff assigned for the purpose.

TABLE 17
Work Week in Correctional Institutions

	40 Hours or Under	*Over 40 Hours*
Juvenile institutions	36 states	16 states
Adult institutions	35 states	17 states

Because outside educational training for correctional personnel is unsatisfactory, in-service training is especially necessary. The survey found that provisions for in-service training programs vary widely among the services. (See Table 18.) Most of the juvenile aftercare agencies and state adult institutions

TABLE 18
**Percentage of Agencies Having Regular
In-Service Training Programs**

	Yes	*No*
Juvenile detention	39.0%	61.0%
Juvenile probation	48.0%	52.0%
Aftercare	80.0%	20.0%
Misdemeanant probation	56.0%	44.0%
Adult probation	51.0%	49.0%
Local institutions and jails	58.5%	41.5%
Adult institutions	78.8%	21.2%
Adult parole	54.9%	45.1%

reported having an in-service training program, but only half of the probation agencies and a little more than a third of the juvenile detention homes reported that they had one.

Quality of the training could not be assessed, but information was obtained on the frequency of training sessions. The training session is usually held once a month. Many adult probation and parole agencies report having annual sessions only. (See Table 19.)

TABLE 19
Frequency of In-Service Training Programs, by Period and Agency*

	Frequency				
	Weekly	Monthly	Quarterly	Annually	Other
Juvenile detention	33.0%	46.0%	8.0%	4.0%	9.0%
Aftercare	12.5%	43.8%	28.1%	9.4%	6.2%
Adult probation	7.6%	29.8%	26.0%	30.8%	6.2%
Juvenile probation	23.0%	35.0%	22.0%·	7.0%	13.0%
Adult parole	3.6%	21.4%	7.1%	28.6%	39.3%

*Limited to agencies where frequency was requested.

D. What Is the State Responsible For?

Because of the interdependence of correctional services and the need for statewide coverage, standards call for state governments to have responsibility for the quality of all correctional systems, including those operated by local city and county jurisdictions.

1. *Types of Assistance.* The state's responsibility for local service is understood to include consultation, standard setting, recruitment, and subsidy. In practice, however, the state government's role seems to vary with each type of correctional service.... (See Table 20.)

Where states do provide standards and subsidy, there are marked differences

TABLE 20
Role of State in Providing Direct Services or Setting Standards
for Community-based Programs

	States Providing Direct Service		States Setting Standards for Local Service		Total		States Providing Neither	
System	No.	%	No.	%	No.	%	No.	%
Juvenile detention	8	15.7	10	19.6	18	35.3	33	64.7
Juvenile probation	19	37.3	13	25.4	32	62.7	19	37.3
Aftercare	40	78.4	...	...	40	78.4	11	21.6
Misdemeanant probation	22	43.1	9	17.7	31	60.8	20	39.2
Adult probation	37	72.5	8	15.7	45	88.2	6	11.8
Jails*	4	7.8	19	37.2	23	45.0	28	55.0
Local adult institutions	...	...	12	23.6	12	23.6	39	76.4

*For purposes of this table, jails were separated from other local institutions.

according to the correctional service (see Table 21). For example, 40 per cent of the states inspect jails but only 25 per cent inspect local correctional institutions. About half of the states (45.5 per cent) subsidize local probation services, yet only 14 per cent subsidize juvenile detention, only 4.5 per cent subsidize local misdemeanant probation services, and only 4 per cent subsidize local correctional institutions. Consultation is given in 61 per cent of the states to juvenile probation and in 57 per cent to adult probation, but in only 32 per cent to misdemeanant probation. . . .

.   .   .   .

TABLE 21
Percentage of States Offering Assistance Other than Direct Service*

Agencies Providing Direct Service	Services Rendered by States to Improve Local Services				
	Standards	Inspection	License	Subsidies	Consultation
Juvenile detention	23.8%	33.3%	9.5%	14.3%	47.6%
Jails	40.4%	40.4%	...	12.8%	34.0%
Local institutions	27.3%	25.0%	...	4.3%	27.7%
Juvenile probation	40.6%	...	...	45.5%	60.6%
Misdemeanant probation ..	40.9%	...	...	4.5%	31.8%
Adult probation	57.1%	...	...	21.4%	57.1%

*Excludes states providing the given service at the state level.

2. *Research and Statistics.* The standards call for a central state agency to collect statistical data and to provide for research on the planning and evaluation of correctional programs. . . . The survey found . . . that few states have a central source of correctional information and that no state has a central information agency for all its correctional systems. (See Table 22.)

Without going into the quality of the statistical information collected by the states, the survey found that only 25 per cent of the states collect statistics on jails and local institutions, only 36 per cent do so on misdemeanant probation, 57 per cent on aftercare programs, and 75 per cent on probation services. In over one-fourth of the states, information on juvenile and adult institutions is available only from each institution.

The agencies responsible for collecting some information and statistics include public welfare departments, correctional agencies, health departments, administrative offices of courts, bureaus of research, boards of control, departments of public safety, and "others." In not a single state is there any *one* agency responsible for collecting information from all the correctional services or capable of presenting a statistical profile of correction for the state as a whole.

TABLE 22
State's Role in Collection of Statistics

	Percentage of States Routinely Collecting Statistics	Agencies Responsible for Collecting Statistics			
		Department of Public Welfare	Correction Agency	Bureau of Research	Others
Juvenile detention	56.0%	46.4%	28.6%	...	25.0%
Juvenile probation	74.5%	31.1%	44.8%	...	24.1%
Juvenile institutions	73.5%	31.1%	46.9%	6.3%	15.7%
Aftercare	56.9%	23.2%	66.4%	...	11.4%
Misdemeanant probation	35.9%	14.3%	78.6%	...	7.1%
Local institutions and jails....................	25.5%	42.9%	57.1%	...	...
Adult probation	74.5%	12.0%	80.0%	...	8.0%
Adult institutions	70.6%	7.7%	77.0%	3.8%	11.5%

3. *Sensible Administration.* In only one state (Alaska) are all nine correctional services organized in a single correctional department; in two states, seven functions are administered by a single correctional agency. At the other extreme, each juvenile institution in five states and each adult institution in three states has a separate board. Between these extremes, we find only six states in which more than three functions are administered by a single state correctional agency. (See Table 23.)

In a number of states, correctional services are administered by departments that also have other responsibilities, such as welfare, mental health, hospitals, public safety, etc. In all, there are 41 state departments whose primary function is not correction but which administer several correctional services. This does not mean that the services are consolidated since seldom is more than one correctional service placed under one correctional administrator. The total number of state departments having correctional functions is 131.

. . . .

E. What's New?

The survey included a request to each state and local agency to describe any unusual and imaginative program it was conducting. . . . Perhaps the most significant finding is that most correctional agencies reported having *no* unusual or imaginative program under way. (See Table 24.)

Juvenile institutions reported more innovative programs than any other state agency; parole agencies reported the fewest.

Of the programs reported by all agencies, the most prevalent type was group counseling and group therapy for offenders or their parents. Other popular

TABLE 23
Parent Agency Responsible for Administering Services,* by States

States	Juvenile Detention	Juvenile Probation	Juvenile Institutions	Juvenile Aftercare
Alabama .... local		Dept. of Pensions & Security & local	3 separate & independent boards	Dept. of Pensic & Security & local
Alaska .... Div. of Youth & Adult Authority		Div. of Youth & Adult Authority	Div. of Youth & Adult Authority	Div. of Youth & Adult Author
Arizona .... local		local	Bd. of Dir. of State Insts. for Juveniles	Bd. of Dir. of State Insts. fo Juveniles
Arkansas .... local		State DPW & local	4 independent boards	State DPW & local
California........ local		local	Youth & Adult Correc. Agency	Youth & Adult Correc. Agenc
Colorado .... local		local	Dept. of Insts.	Dept. of Insts.
Connecticut ...... State Juvenile Courts		State Juvenile Courts	2 independent boards of trustees	2 independent boards of trustees
Delaware .... Youth Serv. Comm.		local	Youth Serv. Comm.	Youth Serv. Comm.
Florida .... local		local	Div. of Child Training Schools	Div. of Child Training Schools
Georgia .... Dept. of Family & Child Serv. & local		Dept. of Family & Child Serv. & local	Dept. of Family & Child Serv.	Dept. of Family & Child Serv.
Hawaii .... local		local	Dept. of Soc. Serv.	Dept. of Soc. S
Idaho .... local		Dept. of Health & local	Dept. of Educ.	Dept. of Educ.
Illinois .... local		local	Youth Comm.	Youth Comm.
Indiana .... local		local	Bd. of Correc.	Bd. of Correc.
Iowa .... local		local	Bd. of Control	Bd. of Control
Kansas .... local		local	Dept. of Soc. Wel.	Dept. of Soc. Wel.
Kentucky........ local		Dept. of Child Wel. & local	Dept. of Child Wel.	Dept. of Child Wel.
Louisiana .... local		State DPW & local	Dept. of Insts.	State DPW
Maine........... local		Dept. of Mental Health & Correc.	Dept. of Mental Health & Correc.	Dept. of Menta Health & Correc.

*Some states also have some local services in addition to state services.

Misdemeanant Probation	Adult Probation	Local Adult Institutions and Jails	Adult Institutions	Parole
Bd. of Pardons & Paroles & local	Bd. of Pardons & Paroles	local	Bd. of Correc.	Bd. of Pardons & Paroles
Div. of Youth & Adult Authority	Div. of Youth & Adult Authority	Div. of Youth & Adult Authority	Div. of Youth & Adult Authority	Div. of Youth & Adult Authority
none	local	local	Supt. of State Prison	Parole Bd.
none	Bd. of Pardons, Paroles & Prob.	local	Penitentiary Comm.	Bd. of Pardons, Paroles & Prob.
local	local	local	Youth & Adult Correc. Agency	Youth & Adult Correc. Agency
local	Parole Div. & local	local	Dept. of Insts.	Parole Div.
Comm. on Adult Prob.	Comm. on Adult Prob.	State Jail Administration	3 separate & independent boards	3 separate & independent boards
Dept. of Correc.	Dept. of Correc.	local	Dept. of Correc.	Dept. of Correc.
Prob. & Parole Comm.	Prob. & Parole Comm. & local	local	Dept. of Correc.	Prob. & Parole Comm.
Bd. of Prob. & local	Bd. of Prob. & local	local	Bd. of Correc.	Parole Bd.
local	local	local	Dept. of Soc. Serv.	Dept. of Soc. Serv.
none	Bd. of Correc.	local	Bd. of Correc.	Bd. of Correc.
local	local	local	Dept. of Pub. Safety	Dept. of Pub. Safety
local	local	local	Bd. of Correc.	Bd. of Correc.
none	Bd. of Parole	local	Bd. of Control	Bd. of Parole
local	Bd. of Prob. & Parole	local	Office of Dir. of Mental Inst.	Bd. of Prob. & Parole
Dept. of Correc.	Dept. of Correc.	local	Dept. of Correc.	Dept. of Correc.
none	Dept. of Insts.	local	Dept. of Insts.	Dept. of Insts.
Dept. of Mental Health & Correc.	Dept. of Mental Health & Correc.	local	Dept. of Mental Health & Correc.	Dept. of Mental Health & Correc.

TABLE 23 (Continued)

States	Juvenile Detention	Juvenile Probation	Juvenile Institutions	Juvenile Aftercare
Maryland	State DPW & local	Dept. of Parole & Prob. & local	DPW	Dept. of Parole & Prob. & DPW & local
Massachusetts	Youth Serv. Bd.	Prob. Comm. & local	Youth Serv. Bd.	Youth Serv. Bd.
Michigan	local	local	Dept. of Soc. Serv.	Dept. of Soc. Serv.
Minnesota.	local	Dept. of Correc. & local	Dept. of Correc.	Dept. of Correc.
Mississippi	local	local	Bd. of Trustees	State DPW & local
Missouri	local	local	Bd. of Training Schools	Bd. of Training Schools
Montana	local	local	Dept. of Insts.	Dept. of Insts.
Nebraska	local	local	Dept. of Public Insts.	Dept. of Public Insts.
Nevada	local	local	Dept. of Health & Wel.	Dept. of Health & Wel.
New Hampshire . . .	Bd. of Trustees	Dept. of Prob. & local	Bd. of Trustees	Bd. of Trustees
New Jersey	local	local	Dept. of Insts. & Agencies	Dept. of Insts. & Agencies
New Mexico	local	local	4 separate boards	local
New York	local	local	Dept. of Soc. Wel.	Dept. of Soc. Wel.
North Carolina . . .	local	local	Bd. of Juv. Correc.	local
North Dakota.	local	DPW & local	Board of Administration	local
Ohio	local	local	Youth Comm.	Youth Comm.
Oklahoma	local	local	DPW	DPW
Oregon	local	local	Bd. of Control	Bd. of Control
Pennsylvania	local	local	DPW	local
Rhode Island	Dept. of Soc. Wel.	Dept. of Soc. Wel.	Dept. of Soc. Wel.	Dept. of Soc. Wel.
South Carolina	local	local	Bd. of State Indus. Schools	Bd. of State Indus. Schools

Misdemeanant Probation	Adult Probation	Local Adult Institutions and Jails	Adult Institutions	Parole
Dept. of Parole & Prob. & local	Dept. of Parole & Prob.	local	Dept. of Correc.	Bd. of Parole & Prob.
Prob. Comm. & local	Comm. on Prob.	local	Dept. of Correc.	Dept. of Correc. & local
local	Dept. of Correc. & local	local	Dept. of Correc.	Dept. of Correc.
Dept. of Correc. & local	Dept. of Correc. & local	local	Dept. of Correc.	Dept. of Correc.
none	Bd. of Prob. & Parole	local	independent board	Bd. of Prob. & Parole
Bd. of Prob. & Parole & local	Bd. of Prob. & Parole	local	Dept. of Correc.	Bd. of Prob. & Parole
none	Bd. of Pardons	local	Dept. of Insts.	Bd. of Pardons
local	District Judges Assn.	local	Dept. of Public Insts.	Bd. of Pardons
Dept. of Parole & Prob.	Dept. of Parole & Prob.	local	Bd. of Prison Commissioners	Dept. of Parole & Prob.
Dept. of Prob. & local	Dept. of Prob. & local	(not applicable)	Bd. of Trustees of state prison	Bd. of Trustees of state prison
local	local	local	Dept. of Insts. & Agencies	Dept. of Insts. & Agencies
Bd. of Prob. & Parole & local	Bd. of Prob. & Parole	local	Bd. of Dir. of state prison	Bd. of Prob. & Parole
local	local	local	Dept. of Correc.	Div. of Parole
Prob. Comm.	Prob. Comm.	local	Prison Dept.	Bd. of Parole
Dept. of Parole & Prob.	Dept. of Parole & Prob.	local	Board of Administration	Dept. of Parole & Prob.
local	local	local	Dept. of Mental Hyg. & Correc.	Dept. of Mental Hyg. & Correc.
none	local	local	Bd. of Public Affairs	Pardon & Parole Dept.
Bd. of Parole & Prob. & local	Bd. of Parole & Prob. & local	local	Bd. of Control	Bd. of Parole & Prob.
none	local	local	Dept. of Justice	Bd. of Parole
Dept. of Soc. Wel.	Dept. of Soc. Wel.	Dept. of Soc. Wel.	Dept. of Soc. Wel.	Dept. of Soc. Wel.
Prob., Parole & Pardon Bd.	Prob., Parole & Pardon Bd.	local	Dept. of Correc.	Prob., Parole & Pardon Bd.

TABLE 23 (Concluded)

States	Juvenile Detention	Juvenile Probation	Juvenile Institutions	Juvenile Aftercare
South Dakota .... local	local	Bd. of Charities & Correc.	Bd. of Pardons & Paroles
Tennessee .... local	Dept. of Correc. & local	Dept. of Correc.	Dept. of Correc.
Texas .... local	local	Youth Council	Youth Council
Utah .... local	State Juv. Ct.	DPW	DPW
Vermont .... Dept. of Soc. Wel.	Dept. of Soc. Wel.	Dept. of Insts.	Dept. of Insts.
Virginia .... local	local	Dept. of Wel. & Insts.	local
Washington ...... local	local	Dept. of Insts.	Dept. of Insts.
West Virginia ..... local	Dept. of Public Assistance	Commissioner of Public Insts.	DPW
Wisconsin........ local	DPW	DPW	DPW
Wyoming .... local	local	Bd. of Charities & Reform	Dept. of Prob. & Parole
Puerto Rico ...... Dept. of Health	Adm. Office of Courts	Dept. of Health	Dept. of Health

projects included special vocational counseling or training, special education, work release, and special projects for alcoholics and for narcotics law violators.

Perhaps the limited number of new and existing projects can be explained by the widespread deficiencies in basic services. Administrators are not encouraged to establish new programs when their energies are directed primarily toward securing basic program needs. . . .

TABLE 24
Unusual and Imaginative Programs

Agencies in 250-County Sample	% Reporting No Unusual Program	State Agencies	% Reporting No Unusual Program
Juvenile detention	82%	Juvenile aftercare	67%
Juvenile probation	58%	Juvenile institutions	43%
Misdemeanant probation	62%	Adult institutions	51%
Adult probation	73%	Parole	82%
Local institutions and jails	53%		

Misdemeanant Probation	Adult Probation	Local Adult Institutions and Jails	Adult Institutions	Parole
none	Bd. of Pardons & Paroles	local	Bd. of Charities & Correc.	Bd. of Pardons & Paroles
Dept. of Correc.	Dept. of Correc.	local	Dept. of Correc.	Dept. of Correc.
local	local	local	Dept. of Correc.	Bd. of Pardons & Paroles
Bd. of Correc.	Bd. of Correc.	local	Bd. of Correc.	Bd. of Correc.
Dept. of Insts.	Dept. of Insts.	local	Dept. of Insts.	Dept. of Insts.
Dept. of Wel. & Insts.	Dept. of Wel. & Insts.	local	Dept. of Wel. & Insts.	Dept. of Wel. & Insts.
local	Bd. of Prison Terms & Paroles	local	Dept. of Insts.	Bd. of Prison Terms & Paroles
DPW	DPW	local	Commissioner of Public Insts.	DPW
DPW	DPW	local	DPW	DPW
Dept. of Prob. & Parole	Dept. of Prob. & Parole	local	Bd. of Charities & Reforms	Bd. of Charities & Reforms
none	Adm. Office of Courts	Dept. of Justice	Dept. of Justice	Dept. of Justice

III. THE VOICE OF THE FIELD

Any attempt to understand the needs, problems, and possibilities of correction in the United States would be incomplete without knowledge of the opinions, attitudes, and hopes of those who operate the correctional agencies and are concerned with the problems of correction in states and communities day by day.

To tap this huge reservoir of experience, NCCD issued invitations to key correctional officials and others familiar with correctional problems in each state to attend a one-day meeting as part of the survey process.

. . . .

Correctional administrators from both statewide and local agencies were present. Some of the groups included university faculty members and interested laymen influential in correctional affairs. Leaders of state correctional organizations also attended. . . . The correctional issues cited at the meetings can be arranged into three categories:

1. Problems whose solution may require long-term efforts—for example: public understanding of correction, improvement in administration of justice, etc.

TABLE 25
Some National Characteristics of Correction

| | Received in 1965 | Average Daily Population | | Cost of Operating, 1965 | | Number of Personnel | | | | | | | | | |
| | | | | | | Treatment* | | Educational† | | Custodial | | Other | | Total | |
		No.	%	No.	%	No.	%	No.	%	No.	%	No.	%	No.	%
Juvenile detention	409,218	13,113	1.0	$ 53,353,507	5.7	671	3.8	917	16.0	5,108‡	8.4	1,202	4.5	7,898	7.1
Juvenile probation	189,878	223,805	18.3	74,750,727	8.0	6,320	35.7	...	...	...	...	...	...	6,320	5.7
State juvenile institutions	...	42,389	3.5	144,596,618	15.4	1,154	6.5	2,495	43.6	8,666	14.3	8,932	33.1	21,247	19.1
Local juvenile institutions§	...	6,024	.5	23,460,288	2.5	309	1.7	410	7.1	1,235‡	2.0	50	.2	2,004	1.8
Juvenile aftercare‖	...	59,686	4.9	18,408,655	1.9	1,359	7.7	...	...	...	...	...	...	1,359	1.2
Misdemeanant probation	300,440	201,385	16.5	28,682,914	3.0	1,944	11.0	...	...	...	...	...	...	1,944	1.7
Adult probation	144,199	230,468	18.9	31,507,204	3.4	2,557	14.5	...	...	...	...	...	...	2,557	2.3
Local institutions and jails	1,016,748	141,303	11.6	147,794,214	15.7	258	1.5	243	4.3	14,993	24.7	3,701	13.7	19,195	17.3
State adult institutions	125,647¶	201,220	16.5	384,980,648	40.9	1,124	6.3	1,654	29.0	30,809	50.6	13,093	48.5	46,680	42.0
Adult parole	62,513	102,036	8.3	32,932,719	3.5	1,999	11.3	...	...	...	...	...	...	1,999◇	1.8
Totals		1,221,429	100%	$940,467,494	100%	17,695	100%	5,719	100%	60,811	100%	26,978	100%	111,203	100%

*Includes social workers, counselors, psychologists, and psychiatrists in institutions; supervisors, intake personnel, and field personnel prorated for probation, parole, and aftercare.

† Academic and vocational.

‡ Includes group supervisors in detention homes and personnel with custodial as well as other duties in local training schools.

§ Total for 83 institutions, and estimated for 28 institutions unreported.

‖ For 40 states, and estimated for 10 states and Puerto Rico.

¶ Includes 45,901 misdemeanants.

◇ Does not include 32 parole employment specialists.

2. Problems that may be ameliorated in the near future—for example: training and education of probation officers, more diagnostic services, etc.

3. Possible federal roles for helping solve state and local correctional problems.

A. General Issues

Seven broad categories of correctional issues emerge as an overall characteristic of the state meetings.

1. The need for *across-the-board strengthening of probation and parole.* . . .

2. The need for *greater, broader funding of correctional services.* . . .

3. The need for *a clearer correctional philosophy.* . . .

4. The need for *better public understanding of the correctional task.* . . .

5. The need for *more manpower with which to handle crime and delinquency.* . . .

6. The need for *increased state-level coordination of correctional services.* . . .

7. The need for *general improvement in the administration of justice.* . . .

B. Specific Issues

The seven categories above were seen as "built in" problems which are likely to pervade correction indefinitely and which may require long-term planning for their solution. On the other hand, several other well-defined problems are regarded as capable of solution now or in the near future. . . .

1. *Training and Education.*—Though the correctional field acknowledges quite frankly that it needs more knowledge and skills, the question remains—where are they to be obtained? In-service training emerged as a top priority. Some participants called for a national academy for correction, others for regional workshops. Many expressed interest in programs that would provide opportunities for graduate and undergraduate education, though admittedly much current training seems to be unrelated to any specific correctional rationale. . . .

2. *Diagnostic Services.*—The number of professional personnel available for testing, evaluation, and psychiatric and psychological consultation to courts, parole agencies, and institutions is insufficient. Diagnostic services need to be accompanied by expanded treatment resources.

3. *Detention.*—The conferences generalized a need for more and better juvenile detention centers. Many children are still jailed; where detention homes exist, there is often a lack of adequate programing, with undue emphasis on custody. This was consistently traced to lack of funds and trained staff. Detention centers frequently are not constructed according to modern standards; few are available regionally. . . .

4. *Special Services.*—All meetings voiced the need for more alternatives for control and treatment of the offender. Most frequently mentioned were vocational rehabilitation, group services, halfway houses, foster homes, work

release, and camps—all of them well publicized but few of them available for the mass of offenders.

5. *Diversification.*—The groups pointed up the need for special kinds of physical facilities and programs to meet different needs. The retarded or marginally defective offender and the criminally insane were most frequently mentioned in this regard. . . .

6. *Statistical System.*—There was general agreement that more coordinated, centralized statistical programs are needed for accurate information on volume, costs, personnel, etc., for planning and interpretation.

7. *Regionalization.*—Many of the administrators deplored the location of correctional facilities in isolated rural communities, often built and retained there because of political influences. A number of participants argued that state institutions should be relocated to serve regional and local needs better.

8. *Presentence Reports.*—The meetings reported that many decisions affecting offenders are being made without benefit of social psychological data, because of an insufficient number of probation staff, no staff at all, untrained staff, or an attitude that such reports are not important. It was generally thought that more and better use of presentence and diagnostic reports would be an important step toward a more effective system of correction.

9. *Research.*—Generally, the groups called for more research on causes of deviant behavior and on ways to measure the effectiveness of existing as well as experimental treatment programs. A strong role was seen for the federal government in meeting this kind of need.

10. *Adult Services.*—Additional issues related to adult programs only included (a) legislation and services needed for the *misdemeanant offender;* (b) disparities in *sentencing practices;* (c) broader development of services for *addicts and alcoholics;* (d) increased need for *jail standards* relative to construction, maintenance, and program.

11. *Miscellaneous.*—Among other matters considered important but not mentioned as frequently as those noted above are the following: (a) the need for more uniformity in legal codes; (b) creation of family district courts; (c) creation of youth authorities modeled on the California plan and similar plans; (d) legislation permitting youthful offender programs; (e) establishing and improving police juvenile bureaus; (f) elimination of political influences in appointments; (g) creation of commissions for planning in adult correction; and (h) state citizen action programs to bring nonpartisan interest to bear on planning.

C. Relationship to Current Federal Programs

In addressing issues related to current federal programs, the conference came to remarkably similar conclusions on some major points: (a) the alliance between correction and these projects should be far closer than it is, and (b) at least three means are at hand to narrow the gap:

1. While the field needs a great deal of help in developing new techniques, support should also be made available to those traditional or conventional

methods which have been demonstrated to be effective but have not yet "had a chance" at full-scale operation. Innovation for the sake of innovation itself is not desirable, and it should not be allowed to discourage development of basic treatment services.

2. Offenders are excluded from the Job Corps, the Neighborhood Youth Corps, and other OEO projects, by administrative policy. This exclusionary rule should be amended to allow for their controlled participation in these programs, and correctional leaders should be included in the early planning for this change.

3. Federally funded programs should now be developed from a correctional focus. A common objection to current procedure was that, to qualify for federal help, correctional officials had to tailor their work to fit some other point of view, like mental health, vocational rehabilitation, education, etc. . . .

D. Suggested Federal Role

As viewed by the more than 700 persons at the state conferences, the federal role is to *prompt* and *initiate* the plans and *provide the means* to carry them out; the state role is to *design* and *execute* the plans. The state meetings suggested the following as most appropriate to the federal role:

1. *Education and Training.*—The federal government should subsidize formal and informal education for correction—long-term graduate and undergraduate education and short-term in-service training.

2. *Leadership.*—Federal leadership is required in setting standards, encouraging growth, providing opportunities, assessing needs, etc.

3. *Research.*—The federal role here stems from the conviction that the kinds of special skills required are not generally available at the local level.

4. *Statistical System.*—A uniform national statistical system is suggested.

5. *Grantsmanship Information.*—Local leaders need authoritative advice and information on how to qualify for federal grants.

6. *Permanency and Coordination of Federal Programs.*—The Neighborhood Youth Corps, the Job Corps, and other similar federal programs related to delinquency prevention should become permanent and should be coordinated in a centralized structure including all federal agencies concerned with crime and delinquency. . . .

7. *Construction Subsidies.*—Through the Hill-Burton Act, the federal government should provide the means for construction of detention homes, diagnostic centers, halfway houses, and facilities for group living.

IV. IMPLICATIONS OF THE SURVEY

The outstanding characteristic of this survey's findings is that they locate and measure the wide gap between correctional standards and correctional practices.

As these gaps are closed, correctional agencies will become better managed; costs will be better distributed; correctional methods will become more effective through greater use of research, evaluation, and statistical reporting; treatment techniques will become more appropriate to the needs of offenders and the safety of the community, and the public will become better informed of correctional goals and accomplishments.

.   .   .   .

If correction is to make the most of its unique capacity for helping the offender relate positively and constructively to community life, it must become a continuous process operating within the framework of a common philosophy. Realization of this goal has implications for organization, coordination, and methods.

The effects of fragmentation of correctional services and the consequent breaks in continuity must be overcome, if not by merger then at least by joint formulation and better communication of policies. Generic training for key personnel may be one way to surmount the language barriers, resolve the problems of identity within correction, and reinforce a common philosophy.

The shifting of population from rural to urban centers, which, in turn, spread far beyond county lines, poses special problems for the organization and location of correctional services. New administrative patterns must be developed to effectively serve the correctional needs of sprawling urban areas without, at the same time, neglecting the rural population. Achievement of adequate systems of correction for large urban regions may well depend on replacing, with regional administration, the present stratification under which some correctional services are operated separately by the counties and cities in the region and others are operated by the state.

Differential treatment of offenders according to their individual needs is fundamental to the correctional task. Diagnostic services must be made available at every major decision point along the correctional continuum. This is now impossible because of the proliferation of local agencies and locally based state services, and it will continue to be impossible unless the state assumes greater responsibility for providing, developing, and stimulating the use of professional staff and clinical services.

Differential treatment of offenders implies a variety of treatment resources and alternatives. Group methods in all correctional settings, intensive counseling in small caseloads, prerelease centers, halfway houses, skill training based on job market needs, use of volunteers to bridge the community-correction gap—these are but a few of many varied devices for helping the offender achieve a satisfactory social adjustment.

Undoubtedly, many offenders—especially those whose problems are more social than criminal—can be screened out of the correctional system without danger to the community, especially a community where remedies for their problems can be obtained through existing noncorrectional resources. The juvenile court intake and referral methods have proved the value of this policy of diversion. Application of a similar system to adult cases could reduce court dockets and correctional caseloads. Criteria for the diversion of adult offenders from the correctional process need to be developed, and, to support the policy and practice of diversion, community agencies must cooperate by extending their services to offenders.

If correction is to reach its potential, the quality of its decisions and services must be improved. Unless better means for evaluation and assessment of what works and what doesn't work are developed, much correctional planning will depend on blind chance. Computerization of data for monitoring and assessing a state's correctional systems and methods offers much promise. Its greatest contribution, perhaps, may be the incontrovertible conclusion that correctional funds ought to be allocated according to correctional effectiveness.

. .   .   .

29. Organizational Goals and Inmate Organization*

B. B. BERK

The condition of the nation's jails and prisons as well as the failure of all counties and states to provide juvenile and adult probation and/or parole services, received heavy attack in the 1967 report of the President's Crime Commission. Although a study of the National Council on Crime and Delinquency completed for the Commission revealed that 3,047 counties operate one or more types of correctional activities or institutions, they found that each level of government tends to act independently of the other (*see* introduction to Article 28). The lack of coordination of juvenile and adult correctional programs and the absence of concern for misdemeanant jail or workhouse treatment consequently make any coherent correctional program largely impossible. Not only does the correctional program reveal wide gaps in services but, the Council reported, it also supervises poorly the nearly 700 thousand offenders under treatment in the community on any given day. Even in correctional institutions 80 percent of employed personnel engage primarily in custodial and maintenance functions. A maximum of 20 percent participate in programs designed to encourage the institutional rehabilitation of the offender (*see* National Profile, Article 28).

While society still demands the punishment and isolation of the offender (*see* Toby, Article 32), growing personnel and maintenance costs, a greater number of prisoner incarcerations, and the increase of data verifying the effectiveness of other correctional approaches have hastened the development of treatment

*Reprinted from the *American Journal of Sociology*, Volume 71, Number 5 (March, 1966), pp. 522-34, by permission of the publisher, The University of Chicago Press, and the author.

alternatives (*see* Stark, Article 31). But not all sentenced prisoners can meaningfully participate in these more flexible and nontraditional correctional forms. The prison, therefore, continues to occupy its central place in corrections because the reorientation of the violator from criminal to conforming conduct is not readily accomplished in an unstructured situation.

Mere imprisonment, however, may offer no solution either. Prisons vary in effectiveness, program offerings, and correctional intent. Administrative procedure and inmate attitudes may often conflict. Consequently, prison incarceration may actually produce major discontinuities in prisoner resocialization (*see* Gagnon and Simon, Article 30) and undermine correctional goals. This is illustrated in the following study by B. B. Berk, who probes the relationship between organizational goals and the inmate social system. Examining relationships at three institutions, Berk finds a wide variance in treatment-punishment orientations and inmate response to organizational goals.

While sociological interest in informal organization dates back to the time of Cooley, there has been little exploration of the relationships between formal and informal organization. Earlier research efforts have been more concerned with documenting the existence of informal organization and demonstrating that it had an impact upon organizational functioning than in trying to establish relationships between it and the organizational context. Different conclusions have been reached in regard to its contribution to the formal organization's ability to achieve its goals, with Roethlisberger and Dickson highlighting its subversive aspect in limiting productivity in economic organizations, while Shils and Janowitz suggest it can facilitate the goals of military organizations by developing social cohesion.[1] . . .

Specifically, this paper examines relationships between organizational goals and informal organization in a variety of correctional institutional settings. The study had major objectives. First, we sought to replicate Grusky's study of the consequences of treatment goals for the informal organization of prison inmates.[2] Second, we were concerned with extending existing formulations concerning the relationship between the formal and informal structure of total institutions and, in particular, the conditions which generate informal organizations that are fundamentally opposed to the existing administration.

DESCRIPTION OF RESEARCH SITES

The three institutions selected for study were minimum-security prisons which differed in their emphasis of treatment goals. The criteria used to

1/F. J. Roethlisberger and W. J. Dickson, *Management and the Worker* (Cambridge, Mass.: Harvard University Press, 1939); Edward A. Shils and Morris Janowitz, "Cohesion and Disintegration of the Wehrmacht in World War II," *Public Opinion Quarterly*, XII (1948), 280-315.

2/The replicated study was: Oscar Grusky, "Organizational Goals and the Behavior of Informal Leaders," *American Journal of Sociology*, LXV, No. 1 (July, 1959), 59-67.

determine the extent to which treatment goals were dominant were: (1) the presence of a full time counselor or of treatment personnel; (2) the existence of a rehabilitative program; and (3) the active implementation of educational, vocational, or other auxiliary-type programs. The three prisons (to be called Benign, Partial, and Lock) were ranked on a continuum ranging from a strong treatment orientation to a strong custodial orientation.[3]

Camp Benign ranked as the most treatment-oriented institution, as all three criteria were present. In addition, it was the smallest, containing only ninety-seven inmates. This prison was characterized by considerable staff-inmate interaction, maximal opportunities for counseling and guidance,[4] and a sincere effort directed at changing the inmate. Camp Partial was slightly larger (127 inmates) and had both a full-time counselor and a limited educational program. However, it did not have an official treatment program. Treatment techniques employed in this institution tended to be subverted to custodial ends, such as securing inmate conformity. Camp Lock, which had 157 inmates, was the most custodially oriented institution, the sole rehabilitative program being an Alcoholics Anonymous group. Its primary goal was containment, and there was little official pretense or concern about treatment or rehabilitation. The officials sought to run an institution which attracted as little attention as possible from the community.

THE FINDINGS

Inmate Attitudes. The first area investigated was the differences in attitudes of inmates of the treatment and custodial prisons. . . .

. . . .

As in the original study, inmate attitudes in three areas were examined: attitudes toward the prison, staff, and treatment program. Table 1 demonstrates a positive relationship between favorable inmate response toward the prison and the degree of development of its treatment goals. Where about six out of ten of Benign's inmates were positively oriented toward the prison (63 per cent), not quite five of ten of Partial's inmates (48 per cent) and less than four of ten of the inmates at Lock (39 per cent), the most custodially oriented prison of the three, had positive feelings toward their institutions. A similar pattern is revealed concerning attitudes toward the staff. At Benign, 44 per cent of the men had favorable attitudes toward the staff, whereas only 29 per cent at Partial and 23 per cent at Lock were as positively oriented toward the staff. The third area of inmate attitudes investigated was those toward existing programs. These attitudes were also found, as expected, to be related to the goals of the prison. At Benign, 89 per cent of the men felt that the program had helped them, as compared with 82 per cent of the men at Partial, and 75 per cent of the men at

3/It is important to keep in mind that all three prison camps would be located on the treatment end of the continuum if compared with maximum-security institutions.

4/The fact that Benign almost doubled in size between the original study and the replication, while inmate attitudes remained relatively unchanged, casts some doubt on its usefulness in accounting for our findings.

TABLE 1
Inmate Attitudes toward the Prison, Staff, and Program

	Benign (Per Cent)	Partial (Per Cent)	Lock (Per Cent)
Attitudes toward the prison:*			
Favorable (Scale Types I-II)	63.1	48.2	39.1
Attitudes toward the staff:†			
Favorable (Scale Types I-II)	44.3	29.2	23.4
Attitudes toward the program:‡			
Favorable (Item response "yes")	88.8	81.9	74.8
N = ...	(95)	(124)	(138)

*For a description of scale see O. Grusky, "Treatment Goals and Organizational Behavior" (unpublished Ph.D. dissertation [University of Michigan, 1958]), p. 141. The coefficients of reproducibility for this scale were Benign .91, Partial .90, and Lock .93. The coefficients of scalability were .54, .77, and .81, respectively. A difference of over 12.5 per cent between the camps is significant at the .05 level by a difference-of-proportions test.

†The coefficients of reproducibility for this scale were Benign .88, Partial .91, and Lock .92; for scalability, they were .53, .75, and .77, respectively.

‡Only a single item, "Do you feel (the program) has helped you in any way?" was available. No answer: Benign 2, Partial 3, Lock 19.

Lock who expressed similar views. Attitudes toward the programs were the most positive and reflected, in part, the salience of the program which, in turn, was due to the official support for treatment goals. In short, Grusky's original hypothesis was strongly confirmed.[5] Significant differences were found between the prison which was most custodially oriented and the one most treatment-oriented.

The Effects of Socialization. . . . It would be expected that the longer the inmate was exposed to the values and programs of the prison, the more likely he would be influenced by them; that is, inmates who have spent a long time in the prison should most clearly reflect the impact of the prison on their attitudes, and those who have been there only a short time should be least affected.

The data presented in Figure 1 show a strong relationship between attitude toward the staff and length of time spent in the prison. Inmates who had spent longer time in the custodially oriented prison were more likely to hold negative attitudes than those who had only been there a few months, whereas the reverse was true at the treatment-oriented prison where inmates who had spent a long time in the prison were more likely to hold positive attitudes than negative ones.[6] When those inmates at Benign who had spent fewer than three months in the prison were compared with those who had spent more than eight months there, we found that only about one of three (35 per cent) of the former, as contrasted with about half (56 per cent) of the latter, fell into the most favorable scale type. At Camp Lock the reverse was found true. The proportion

5/In comparing Grusky's results with our own, there was remarkable agreement in the percentages of positive responses.

6/See Stanton Wheeler, "Socialization in Correctional Communities," *American Sociological Review*, XXVI (October, 1961), 697-712.

FIGURE 1
Relationship of Attitudes toward Staff to Length of Time Spent
in Prison

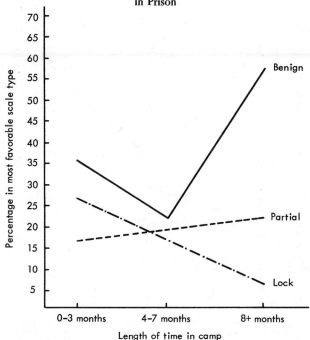

Length of time in camp

The *N*'s from which percentages were based for the 0-3
month period were: Benign 26, Partial 33, and Lock 55. For the
4-7 month period, they were 36, 35, and 44, respectively. And
for the 8+ month period, they were 30, 59, and 35.

of positive responses dropped sharply from 27 per cent of the inmates who had
been there less than three months to less than 9 per cent of those who had been
there eight or more months. Camp Partial exhibited a mild positive influence,
reflecting its intermediate position.[7]

In Figure 2, the same general relationship is revealed with respect to attitudes
toward the prison, but not quite as clearly. The proportion of inmates at Lock
who were favorably oriented decreased slightly from 36 per cent of those whose
stay was short-term to 31 per cent of those having a longer-term stay in the
prison. In contrast, the percentage of favorable responses increased at Benign
from 50 per cent of those having less than three months' experience to 64 per
cent of those who had eight or more months in prison. However, in both prisons,
inmates with four to seven months' experience were most negative.[8]

7/It should be pointed out that a smaller proportion of fairly recent (0-3 months)
inmates of Partial than those from the more custodial Lock demonstrated favorable
attitudes toward the staff. However, the percentage of favorable responses increased steadily
with experience in the former institution, and decreased steadily in the latter.

8/Wheeler, *op. cit.,* found a similar U-shaped pattern in regard to conforming attitudes
held by inmates and attributed this to the stage of the inmate's institutional career.

FIGURE 2
Relationship of Attitudes toward Prison and Length of Time
Spent in Prison

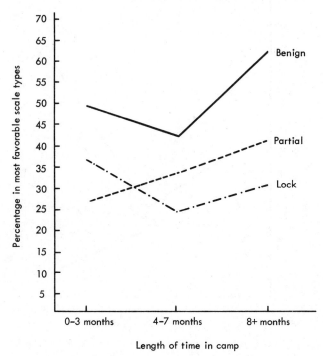

The *N*'s from which percentages were based are the same as
for Figure 1.

Influence of Other Variables. Before any conclusions could be drawn from
these findings, it was necessary to control for other relevant variables, since an
important obstacle to studies of this nature is that inmates are not usually
randomly assigned to treatment institutions. This was true of this study as well,
in that inmates at Benign were younger and likely to have been less serious
offenders. However, this type of selectivity does not appear to have accounted
for the results obtained in this study. *Age:* Initially, it might have been argued
that the older age of the inmates at Lock and Partial would be sufficient to
account for the more negative attitudes found there. Our findings, on the
contrary, show age to be inversely related to negative attitude at both Lock and
Benign, with the younger inmates in both camps more likely to hold negative
attitudes. No difference was found at Partial. Furthermore, young inmates were
more positive at Benign than their counterparts at Lock. The same was true for
older inmates. This would suggest that selectivity in regard to age would operate
against the hypothesis. *Type of offender:* It similarly could have been argued
that inmates at Partial and Lock were more experienced and hardened criminals,
well indoctrinated in the ways of crime and would, therefore, exhibit more

negative attitudes. . . . Again, the findings show, in contradiction to what is commonly believed, that the more serious offenders, by a variety of measures, did not have more negative attitudes. On the contrary, these two variables were generally unrelated. In the few cases where differences were found, they were small and variable. Furthermore, the direction of this relationship was reversed in the treatment institution, where the more serious offenders were more likely to hold more positive attitudes than the less serious offenders. And, finally, when comparable groups of types of offenders were compared in the various camps, they were more positive in their attitudes at Benign than at Lock.[9]

It would appear (see Table 2) that the selectivity in regard to age and type of offender would not be sufficient to account for the differences obtained in this study, and certainly could not account for the differences between Partial and Lock, since there was little difference in the types of inmates sent to those two camps. . . . [W]hatever differences existed in the nature of the inmates in the organization initially as a result of differential recruitment procedures, inmates became more positive over time in the treatment institution and more negative in the custodial one, reflecting the differential impact of the organization upon its members.

. . . .

Informal Organization. These attitudinal differences between prisons reflected major differences in the nature of the informal organization among prison inmates. . . .

. . . .

TABLE 2
Inmate Attitudes toward the Prison by Age and Type of Offender
(per cent in most favorable scale type)

	Benign (Per Cent)	N	Partial (Per Cent)	N	Lock (Per Cent)	N
Age						
25 years and under	47.6	(86)	36.3	(11)	11.1	(18)
26+	77.7	(9)	35.4	(111)	35.9	(114)
Number of prison sentences						
1	48.6	(70)	37.1	(62)	34.2	(76)
2 or more	56.0	(25)	35.1	(61)	29.3	(58)
Number of charged crimes						
1-3	45.9	(61)	31.9	(47)	35.5	(45)
4+	65.3	(26)	39.6	(63)	33.3	(70)
Seriousness of crimes*						
Less serious crimes	50.0	(18)	47.5	(59)	30.8	(39)
More serious crimes	50.0	(74)	34.7	(59)	31.6	(76)

*When more than one crime was charged, the most serious was coded. Serious crimes were regarded as murder, rape, and assault. The less serious crimes consisted in robbery, burglary, larceny, etc.

9/The total time spent by the inmate in confinement in any institution was also found to be related to negative attitudes; the longer the time spent in custodial institutions, the more negative the attitude.

Involvement and participation in the [inmate] subculture was measured by the number of friendship choices the inmate received from other inmates. Three types of inmates were distinguished: the uninvolved or isolate who received no choices, the moderately involved who received from one to three choices, and the highly involved who received four or more friendship choices. Table 3 shows

TABLE 3
Degree of Involvement in Informal System and Attitudes toward the Prison*
(per cent in most favorable scale type)

	Benign (Per Cent)	N	Partial (Per Cent)	N	Lock (Per Cent)	N
Isolates (received no choices)	33.3	(15)	32.4	(37)	33.3	(75)
Moderately involved (received 1-3 choices)	50.6	(63)	38.5	(78)	30.2	(59)
Highly involved (received 4+ choices)	64.6	(17)	25.0	(12)	20.0	(5)

*Involvement measured by the number of friendship choices received by the inmate.

that at Benign isolates were the most negative and the highly involved inmates the most positive in their attitudes toward the prison. At Lock, the reverse was true with the highly involved inmates the most negative and the uninvolved inmates the most positive in their attitudes. At Partial, negative attitudes were related to both high and low involvement in the subculture. It is not immediately clear why moderately involved inmates at Partial were more positive than isolates. In all three prisons, however, favorableness of attitude was related to degree of involvement with the informal organization.[10]

Informal Leadership. Further evidence of the impact of custodial and treatment goals on informal organization among prison inmates was found in the kinds of attitudes held by informal leaders in the various prisons.

. . . Grusky hypothesized that orientation of the leader would vary with the type of total institution; specifically, informal leaders in treatment institutions were seen as more likely to be co-operative than their counterparts in custodially oriented prisons.

Consistent with Grusky's hypothesis, leaders at Benign were more positive in their attitudes than were leaders at Partial who, in turn, were more positive than those at Lock.[11] However, this might have been true for any sample of inmates, because inmates were, as a whole, more positive at Benign than at Lock. By

10/Wheeler's study, *op. cit.,* also demonstrated a relationship between the speed and degree of "prisonization" and involvement in informal inmate organization.

11/Leaders were designated in accordance with Grusky's (*op. cit.*) and Schrag's studies. (Clarence Schrag, "Leadership among Prison Inmates," *American Sociological Review,* XIX (February, 1954), 37-42.)

comparing the leaders with the non-leaders within each prison, a more precise test of this relationship was obtained. Tables 4 and 5 show leaders were more positive than the non-leaders at Benign, while the reverse was true at Lock where the leaders were more negative than the non-leaders. This relationship was found to hold both for attitudes toward the prison and the institution's programs.

TABLE 4
Leadership and Attitudes toward Prison
(per cent in most favorable scale type)

	Benign (Per Cent)	N	Partial (Per Cent)	N	Lock (Per Cent)	N
Leaders	61.3	(31)	47.5	(50)	23.3	(37)
Non-leaders	45.3	(66)	35.5	(77)	34.3	(97)

TABLE 5
Leadership and Attitudes toward Program*
(per cent favorable)

	Benign (Per Cent)	N	Partial (Per Cent)	N	Lock (Per Cent)	N
Leaders	74.2	(31)	47.6	(50)	39.3	(37)
Non-leaders	62.5	(66)	48.0	(77)	63.5	(97)

*The particular item asked if they thought the programs in the camp were a good idea.

OBSERVATIONS ABOUT INFORMAL ORGANIZATION

The Function of Informal Organization in Total Institutions. Having replicated Grusky's study and substantiated the hypothesis, we sought to develop a fuller explanation of the findings. Inmate attitudes reflect the nature of inmate subculture and informal organization which, in turn, is conditioned by formal organizational characteristics, such as the formal structure and the official objectives.

Informal organization develops in prison because: (1) inmates are isolated from society; (2) institutionalization generates common problems of adjustment[12] which require co-operation for their solution while simultaneously providing a situation with opportunity for effective interaction with others similarly situated;[13] and (3) inmates are members of a formal organization

12/In the typical custodial prison, social rejection; pervasive and rigid social control; and loss of liberty, autonomy, respect, affection, heterosexual relationships, security, and self-esteem have been identified as problems which inmates experience.

13/Cf. Albert K. Cohen, *Delinquent Boys* (Glencoe, Ill.: Free Press, 1956), chap. iii, for a penetrating analysis of the formation of subcultures.

which, by its very nature as a system of action, can never fully anticipate or co-ordinate all behavior through the formal system alone; hence, informal organization serves to close the gaps of the formal organization.

Two kinds of informal organization have been identified in the prisons studied—one supportive of the official structure and the other in opposition to it. We submit that the goal of treatment encourages the development of the former, and the goal of custody the latter.

Inmate subcultures develop as solutions to the problems and deprivations experienced by inmates in the prison situation. They would, therefore, differ in their form and content as the nature of the problems experienced by inmates, particularly those created by the institutional experience itself, differ. The two different types of informal organization developed because the inmate subsystem performed contrasting functions in the treatment and custodial institutions.

Two reasons may be suggested to explain the character of the inmate subculture in the custodial institution; first, the problems faced by inmates tend to be more severe there; in addition, inmates perceive the custodial institution itself to be responsible for their problems. As a result, they band together in opposition to the prison and its administration, which they see as the source of their frustrations. Consequently, inmate subcultures tend to become more and more dominated by the values of professional criminals which already emphasize a strict demarcation between the guards and inmates, since these groups are seen as fundamentally in opposition to one another.

The emergence of this subculture compounds an already difficult problem—a central concern, in fact, of the custodial institution—that of maintaining social control within the prison. Since techniques for insuring conformity are inadequate, guards resort to various methods of accommodation and bargain for conformity with the means available to them. One method, as Sykes points out, is to "buy compliance at the cost of tolerating deviance." In return for the guards overlooking selected infractions of the rules, inmates are expected to comply with the rest. . . . In this manner, inmates are able to gain some degree of freedom from the demands and pressures of the formal organization, thereby increasing the relative amount of control they can exercise over the conditions of their existence. This newly gained mastery over their environmental conditions is, however, illusory. It would appear that they have merely traded their previous situation and its attendant deprivations for subjugation to an even more despotic ruling group—other inmates who have less compunctions and fewer limitations about the use of force and violence to gain compliance with their ends. . . .

In contrast to this picture of informal organization in custodial institutions, we can view the development of informal organization in treatment institutions. While inmate organization can also be found in treatment institutions, it does not generally take on an oppositional character. It does not simply because many of the psychological deprivations of imprisonment have been reduced, and a shift in patterns of control has occurred. Inmates are treated with more respect by the organization and, as a result, the institution is not perceived by inmates to be totally against them or antithetical to their interests. In addition, the treatment institution is more flexible in regard to its rules, and treatment needs of inmates are considered in its demands for conformity. Furthermore, in its attempt to regulate behavior, formal methods of controls are replaced by more informal ones, thus reducing resentment and hostility. This leads to a greater tolerance in the range of inmate conformity and, concomitantly, "control" becomes less important in the hierarchy of organization objectives. Accordingly, there is little payoff from the administration for inmates' regulation of their own behavior.

Selected aspects of the formal organization's structure also have an impact on informal organization. Particularly in total institutions, the formal authority structure serves as a model for the informal. The custodially oriented prison, which is usually highly centralized, tends to produce a similar type of informal inmate leadership; for such an adaptation serves, on the one hand, to strengthen official control and administration of the prison and, on the other, to stabilize inmate relations by focusing attention on the deprivations inflicted by the authorities. Because inmate subculture there is dominated by criminal values emphasizing a strict demarcation between guards and inmates, informal leadership must thereby justify itself by securing special concessions from the oppressors, the "screws," in return for which the leaders prevent their men from stepping too far out of line. . . .

.   .   .   .

These speculations led to a new hypothesis about the structure and functioning of informal leadership in the different types of prisons. As we have pointed out, one of the techniques for maintaining order in the custodial prison was the *centralization of control* by informal leadership. Because this function was less important for the inmate subsystem in the treatment institution, it was hypothesized that the more treatment-oriented the prison, the less centralized the informal leadership structure would be and the proportionately greater number of inmates who would emerge as top leaders.

The data supported this hypothesis. At Benign, 9.3 per cent of the inmates were chosen as top leaders (that is, received nine or more choices), while at Partial 6.3 per cent were chosen, compared with only 1.3 per cent of the inmates at Lock. When inmates were asked: "Who were leaders?" similar results were obtained. Forty-three per cent of the inmates at Benign were named, compared with 38 per cent at Partial and 23 per cent at Lock.[14] Both measures indicated greater concentration of power and centralization of control in the custodial prison.

A second technique, adopted by inmate leaders in the custodial prison to

14/In part, some of the differences between camps in the proportions of top leaders was a function of the numbers of nominations made by respondents in the different camps.

control inmate behavior, was the use of coercion to secure conformity and to maintain power. This led to a hypothesis dealing with types of persons likely to rise to positions of leadership or influence in the two types of prisons. Because *control* was an important function of the inmate leaders in the custodial prison, individuals disposed toward such behavior would be more likely to rise to positions of leadership there than would be true of treatment prisons where a more charismatic, socioemotional, or consensus-oriented type of leader would be expected to develop. Therefore, it was hypothesized that leaders in the custodial institution would be more authoritarian, reflecting their "tough-minded" orientation toward the use of power, and would be "less well liked," due to their reliance upon coercion and emphasis upon control than leaders in treatment institutions. Support for this hypothesis comes from the finding that leaders were selected from the most authoritarian inmates at Lock, whereas the reverse was true at Benign, where leaders were selected from the least authoritarian inmates.[15] Not only was the leadership structure more decentralized at Benign, but the leadership positions were occupied there, as well, by less authoritarian persons. Furthermore, leaders at Benign were less authoritarian than those at Partial who, in turn, were less authoritarian than the leaders found at Lock. No difference in authoritarianism was found between the general population of inmates at the three prisons. In addition to their being less authoritarian, the leaders at Benign were liked better, friendlier, and more approachable by other inmates than was true of the leaders at Lock.[16]. . .

SUMMARY AND CONCLUSIONS

The purpose of this study was twofold: (1) to replicate a study conducted by Grusky; and (2) to examine the consequences of treatment and custodial goals upon the inmate subsystem within correctional institutions, with particular emphasis on the conditions generating oppositional informal organization. Three areas of concern were inmate attitudes, the effect of socialization, and the development of informal leadership.

1. The findings on the whole supported Grusky's major hypothesis: Inmates were more positive in their attitudes toward the institution, staff, and programs in the treatment institution than those in the custodial one. Furthermore, they became more positive or negative with the length of time they spent in the prison, depending upon the type of organizational goal, thereby suggesting that it was the prison experience which was primarily responsible for the development of negative attitudes.

2. Differences between prisons were found to be related to differences in inmate organization. Two facts suggested this: First, attitudes were found to be

15/Leaders were more authoritarian than non-leaders at Lock and less authoritarian than non-leaders at Benign.

16Leaders were also less well liked and more socially distant from non-leaders in the custodial institution.

related to degree of involvement with inmate organization, and second, leaders' attitudes were found to vary systematically with the prison's goals, being more positive in the treatment institution and more negative in the custodial one.

3. The informal leadership structure was also found to be more centralized in the custodial institution in an attempt to maintain more effective control over inmate behavior. The informal leaders among the inmates played different roles, depending upon organizational goals and contexts; and these roles were directly linked to the function of the inmate subculture within the prison. Leaders in the custodial prison were also found to be more authoritarian and less well liked than leaders in the treatment prison, reflecting the differences in their roles.

The goal of "custody," with its concomitant centralized- and formal-authority structure and increased deprivations for inmates, contributed significantly to the development of the hostile informal organization in the custodial prison. The disenfranchisement of inmates from possible rewards of the institution encouraged the development of negative attitudes and a hostile informal leadership.

30. The Social Meaning of Prison Homosexuality*

JOHN GAGNON and WILLIAM SIMON

Prison homosexuality, like community homosexuality, is more pervasive than the public believes. The Kinsey reports, for example, disclosed that 33 percent of the male population admitted engaging in some homosexual experience and that approximately 6 percent actually committed sodomy or some other criminal sexual offense with another male. Although data concerning prison homosexuality are difficult to gather, the prison, like other one-sex communities, tends to encourage such conduct. While most prison homosexual relationships seem to be transitory, occurring infrequently once or twice a year, exact information concerning actual prison practice is highly limited.

The sexual problems of incarcerated offenders have largely been ignored by penal administrators and social reformers. However, their existence can no longer be neglected. Former San Quentin Warden Clinton Duffy, for example, argues that nearly all prison riots have their origins in sexual frustrations. While prison administrators admit that prison life blocks the prisoner's aspirational fulfillment and severely challenges his ego-ideal, they are slow to admit the sexual implications (homosexual and heterosexual) of prison incarceration.

*Reprinted from *Federal Probation,* Volume 32, Number 1 (March, 1968), pp. 23-29, with the permission of the authors and editors.

Nevertheless, the existence of the sexual problem can no longer be denied. Many inmates are first introduced to such practices while incarcerated. Prison overcrowding and early-evening lockups encourage their continuance.

The Mississippi State Prison at Parchman has attempted to overcome some of these sexual frustrations by allowing the conjugal visiting of wives in huts on the prison grounds in exchange for good behavior. While many other countries allow similar practices, the generalized adoption of this practice in the United States, Richard D. Knudten believes, is unlikely, due to the added problems of custody and security which it entails, the potential of increased welfare costs inherent in added pregnancies, the continuing dominance of a punishment philosophy, and a puritanical attitude which discourages discussion of the basic problem. The American public, therefore, piously punishes both the prisoner and his family while ignoring the implications of prison homosexuality for personality development and family unity. Consequently, the prison administrator, John H. Gagnon and William Simon believe, is faced with a fundamental dilemma which he is unable to resolve easily. While aware of the sexual needs of the prison population, he also recognizes that any attempt to meet the problem of sexual adjustment will receive little public support and may result in legislative repercussions.

The last half century has seen marked, if uneven, progress in most areas of prison management and perhaps even more marked progress in the creation of a new ideology of prison management. However, despite evidence of progress, there still remains a major area of behavior with which prison systems have been unable to cope. This is the problem of sexual adjustment that occurs in all institutions where one sex is deprived of social or sexual access to the other. It is in the area of sexuality that the prison is perhaps more limited than it is in other areas of activity, partially because of its very single-sex nature and partially because the society rarely provides clear guidelines for sexual behavior even outside the penal institution.

In the midst of the confusion about sexual standards and sexual behavior, the prison exists as the major single-sex institution in the society that has (unlike the mental hospital and other closed institutions) within its walls a population that is physically and, for the most part, psychologically, intact and is, at the same time, sexually experienced. The prison administrator is faced with a fundamental dilemma: He is aware of the sexual needs of the population that he is charged with holding and retraining, but he is also aware that he is not going to get much support or even a sympathetic hearing from the larger society if he focuses upon the problem of the sexual adjustment of his population.

SOME MAJOR CONSIDERATIONS

There are two major areas that require clarification before one can proceed to discuss the actual patterns of sexual adjustment among prison populations. The first is an unfortunate tendency to view the sexual adjustment of prisoners as arising exclusively from the contexts of prison life. It is frequently assumed that any group of people who were incarcerated for any period of time would react sexually in the same way as those who are presently in prison. This is a major oversimplification brought about primarily because of a lack of information about the prior sexual and nonsexual lives of those who are imprisoned and the way in which this prior experience conditions person's responses not only to sexual deprivation, but also to a general loss of liberty.

The second element that is important to specify is the range of sexual responses that are available to those imprisoned. With the exception of the small number of prisons that allow conjugal visits, there are only three forms of sexual behavior that are generally available to a prison population (except for animal contact for those males on prison farms). These are nocturnal sex dreams, self-masturbation, and sexual contact with other inmates of the same sex. The meaning, amount, and the character of these adjustments will be strongly dependent on the meaning that these same behaviors had for the inmate before he or she was incarcerated. Thus, the problem for the inmate is not merely the release of sexual tension, but the social and psychological meaning that such release has and the motives and beliefs that it expresses for him. The source of this set of values does not reside in the prison experience, but outside the prison in the community at large. Thus, the prison provides a situation to which prior sexual and social styles and motives must be adapted and shaped.

There are two major dimensions on which most sexual activity is based. One is that of age, with the primary break occurring between adolescence and adulthood. The other, perhaps of greater significance, is the differential meaning of sexuality to the two sexes. Thus, the striking differences between the sexual orientations of men and women noted in the Kinsey volumes offer the best starting point for a discussion of sex in prison.[1] The discussion that follows focuses on the responses of adult male and female inmates to the prison experience, with only passing reference to institutions for adolescents as they represent continuities to the adult institutions.

MALE RESPONSES TO IMPRISONMENT

Male prison populations are not random selections from the larger society and do not reflect the usual distributions of the population in terms of education, income, ethnicity, occupation, social class, and general life style. The men who make up the bulk of the imprisoned populations tend to be drawn from deprived sections of the society or from families imbedded in what we have now come to call the culture of poverty. As a consequence, the sexual experiences of these men and the meaning that sex has for them differs in significant ways from other portions of the population that are less likely to be imprisoned.

A number of dimensions of these differences may be found in the work of

1/Alfred C. Kinsey, et al., Sexual Behavior in the Human Female. Philadelphia: W. B. Saunders Company, 1953, pp. 642-689.

Kinsey and his colleagues in which they report the substantial differences to be found in the sexual activity and attitudes of men who have differing amounts of education.[2] These findings are further amplified in the volume *Sex Offenders,* where a comparison of imprisoned men and men of the same social origins without delinquent histories showed that the men with prison histories generally have wider sexual experience of all kinds than do men leading conventional and nondelinquent lives.[3] These variables suggest that at least the modal male prison population enters institutions with differing commitments to sexuality than would a middle-class or working-class population. We can therefore suggest that the response of these latter groups to institutionalization will differ as well.

Prior Sexual Adjustment a Factor. Drawing on what we know about the dimensions of the prior sexual adjustments of men who go to prison, our first major sense of the experience is actually how little sexual activity of any sort occurs within the prison.[4] Thus, even after the shock of imprisonment has worn off (and often for the recidivist this occurs quickly), there is no sudden burst of sexual activity of any type. Confirming these impressions is the low order of complaint one hears about sexual deprivation, even when prisoners are presenting a list of grievances after a riot or outbreak of some sort. Part of this is surely due to the closeness of custody in the institution and the fact that men move and live in close proximity, and, except for certain moments of the day, there is very little privacy—not so much from the custodial staff as from the inmates.

However, another cause of this reduction is that sexual activity is potentiated by or channeled through an existing set of social frameworks that do not exist in prison. The man in prison finds himself without the appropriate stimuli which suggest opportunities for sexual activity or situations that are appropriate for such activity. Without the existence of these social cues, the biological imperative of sexual arousal is never even elicited.[5] The absence of females, the sheer sensory monotony of the prison environment, the absence of those social situations that call for sexual responses (being out on the town, going drinking, etc.) serve as effective inhibitors of sexual responsiveness. The most successful aphrodisiacs seem to be an absence of anxiety, the presence of available sexual

2/*Ibid., Sexual Behavior in the Human Male.* Philadelphia: W. B. Saunders Company, 1948, pp. 327-393.

3/Paul H. Gebhard, *et al., Sex Offenders.* New York: Harper & Row, 1965.

4/From a preliminary analysis of the differences between the preinstitutional and the institutional sexual outlet of adult male prisoners interviewed by the Institute for Sex Research, the institutional rates are only one-tenth to one-fifth of noninstitutional rates. For some males the institutional rates are nearly zero.

5/For a discussion of the necessity of socially facilitating cues for sexual arousal and performance, see John H. Gagnon and William Simon, "Pornography: Raging Menace or Paper Tiger," *Trans-Action* (Vol. 4, No. 8, July-August 1967), pp. 41-48; and William Simon and John H. Gagnon, "Pornography: The Social Sources of Sexual Scripts," a paper presented at the 17th Annual Meeting of the Society for the Study of Social Problems (San Francisco, August 1967).

cues, an adequate diet, and plenty of rest. Of these, only the latter two are commonly in the prison environment and in some cases only the last is.

The other source of sexual cues is fantasy, those remembered or desired sexual experiences that commonly serve as the basis for masturbation. However, as a result of the social origins of the bulk of the prison population, there is a major taboo against masturbation and a paucity of complex fantasies that would sustain a commitment to sexual experience.[6] Thus, unlike the middle-class male who learns and rehearses sexual styles in the context of masturbation, the usual prisoner is drawn from a population in which sexual experience is concrete and not symbolic; in which there is a taboo on masturbation; and, finally, in which much of heterosexual experience is structured around the need to have sexual encounters that validate his masculinity among other men. In this environment it might be said that men have sex in order to be able to talk about it.

The Kinsey evidence is that even among lower-class men who do masturbate there is often no conscious fantasy accompanying the behavior, and it serves primarily as a mechanical release of felt physical tension. This is quite unlike the middle-class situation in which masturbation occurs at relatively high rates accompanied by fantasies of sexual experience. These fantasies then begin to facilitate further masturbation and a continuing commitment to this sexual outlet. This adjustment rarely happens in the lower-class environment and, along with the sensory poverty of the prison environment, accounts for the ease with which strong commitments to sexuality are abandoned. Thus, prisoners may complain about sexual deprivation in terms such as "I would really like to have a piece," but often this is a continuation of lower-class male talk about sex, not a passionately felt drive that will eventuate in sexual activity.

Male Homosexuality More Than Outcome of Sexual Desire or Need for Physical Release. Since most prisoners do not seem to feel an overwhelming sexual need, male homosexuality in this context must be seen as something more complex than merely the outcome of sexual desire or the need for physical release. There are varying estimates of the number of males who have homosexual contact during their periods of imprisonment, but the range is probably somewhere between 30 and 45 percent, depending upon the intensity of custody in the institution, the social origins of the population, and the duration of the individual sentence.[7] It seems quite clear that the frequency of homosexual contact is usually quite low, even among cellmates; and in no sense does it approach the rates of heterosexual or homosexual behavior of these same

6/Alfred C. Kinsey, *et al., Sexual Behavior in the Human Male.* Philadelphia: W. B. Saunders Company, 1948, pp. 497-509.

7/Estimates may be found in the following sources: Joseph Fishman, *Sex in Prison* (New York: National Library Press, 1934), 30-40 percent; Gresham Sykes, *Society of Captives* (Princeton: Princeton University Press, 1957), 35 percent; Donald Clemmer, "Some Aspects of Sexual Behavior in the Prison Community," Proceedings of the American Correctional Association (1958), 40 percent. Preliminary estimates from the Institute for Sex Research data are 35-45 percent.

prisoners on the outside, except possibly for those prisoners who come into the institutions with well-developed homosexual commitments and who become the "passive" partners in homosexual liaisons. In some prisons, usually those with a very low order of custody inside the walls, high rates of homosexual behavior may be achieved; however, these are not the prevalent conditions in most prison systems.

It must be pointed out that homosexuality in prison is quite a different phenomenon than homosexual experience in the outside community. Thus, the image of homosexuality as consisting of masculine-seeming men who are always "active" and feminine men who are always "passive" in the sexual performance derives primarily from both journalists and scientists observing homosexuality in prisons and then extending their observations unchecked to the outside world.[8]

Homosexuality in the prison context is partly a parody of heterosexuality, with the very sexual activity suggesting masculine and feminine role components. We now know that this is a basic oversimplification not only of homosexuality in general, but heterosexuality as well. It is, however, in the prison environment where this parody is most likely to occur, for the crucial variable is that many of the men who take part in the homosexual performances conceive of themselves, and wish others to conceive of them, as purely heterosexual.

Thus those prisoners known in prison parlance as "jockers" or "wolves" think of themselves as heterosexual; and, as long as there is no reciprocity in the sexual performance (aiding in the ejaculation of the other male), or the penis is not inserted in their mouth or anus, other inmates will continue to conceive of them in the same way. Thus the homosexual world of the prison is roughly divisible into aggressive "active" males (jockers, wolves) and "passive" males. The latter group commonly includes males who are heterosexual on the outside but who are coerced, either by fear or debt, to be homosexual (usually labeled "punks") and males who have already well-developed preferences for males from their outside experience and who enter prison as homosexuals.[9] The relationships of these males is usually highly stylized both socially and sexually, the aggressor providing protection, a measure of affection and perhaps gifts (in the case of

8/The notions of "active" and "passive" in homosexual relationships are more obscuring of the actual conditions of the behavior than they are enlightening. The psychiatrist Irving Bieber has suggested the words "insertor" and "insertee" be substituted for active and passive, since these latter words assume that role behavior in sexual act has major meaning in psychological personality terms. (*Homosexuality,* New York: Basic Books, 1962, pp. 238-254.) For an attempt at clarification of this confusion, see William Simon and John H. Gagnon, "Homosexuality: The Formulation of a Sociological Perspective," *The Journal of Health and Social Behavior,* Vol. 8, No. 3, September 1967, pp. 177-185.

9/Robert Lindner, "Sexual Behavior in Penal Institutions," in Albert Deutsch, *Sex Habits of American Men,* New York: Prentice Hall, 1948, pp. 201-215; Arthur Huffman, "Sex Deviation in a Prison Community," *Journal of Social Therapy,* Vol. 6, No. 3, 1955, pp. 170-181; George Devereaux and M. C. Moss, "The Social Structure of Prisons and the Organic Tensions," *Journal of Criminal Psychopathology,* Vol. 4, No. 2, October 1942, pp. 306-324.

older inmates), and the passive inmate providing sexual access, affection, and other, pseudo-feminine services. In the cases of long-term inmates these relationships may be conceived of as pseudo-marriages, resulting sometimes in a greater degree of sexual reciprocity; however, such reciprocity results in a decline in other inmates' estimates of the aggressive male's masculinity.

Search for Meaningful Relationships. The sources of this homosexual activity for the predominantly heterosexual and aggressive male seem to be twofold. One element is certainly a search for meaningful emotional relationships that have some durability and which serve as a minimal substitute for affective relationships that they normally have on the outside. This is not unlike the chance homosexual contact between men during combat or in other situations of all-male communities under circumstances of fear and crisis. It represents an attempt to counter the effort of the prison to atomize the inmate community in order to reduce the potential for collusion, which could result either in conniving for goods and services or in attempting escape.

One of the collective responses to this attempt is the development of a resistant inmate community, and at the individual level one of the responses is the establishment of homosexual liaisons.

A second motivation underlying many of these relationships transcends the level of affectional need and essentially becomes a source for the continued validation of masculinity needs and a symbol of resistance to the prison environment. The male whose primary source of masculine validation in the outside community has been his sexual success (rather than work, family, etc.) and who has conceived of himself as aggressive and controlling in his responses to his world finds himself in prison deprived of these central supports for his own masculinity. In reaction to this he enters into homosexual relationships in which he can be conceived as the masculine, controlling partner and which for him and for other males in the system validate continued claims to masculine status. A complicating factor here is that some men suffer a profound psychological crisis when the supports for their masculine identity are removed. In these cases both severe homosexual panics or falling into "passive" homosexual roles are likely to result.

In general, these homosexual relationships are developed not through force, though there is evidence of homosexual rape, especially in poorly controlled detention institutions where the powerful threat of imprisonment to masculinity is first felt, in penal institutions that are inadequately controlled, and in juvenile institutions where the sexual impulse is less well-ordered and tends to be confused with aggression by the adolescent male. In most cases the "passive" partner drifts into the relationship through falling into debt, being afraid of the environment, and feeling that he requires protection, or because he already has a well-developed commitment to homosexuality that he cannot or does not want to conceal. Once an inmate has fallen into this role it is extremely difficult to shift out of it, and, if a current relationship breaks up, there will be pressure to form a new one. Even in a reincarceration there will be a memory of his role from prior institutionalization and there will be pressure to continue. It is as if the prison required as one of its role types the "passive" homosexual, and, if a number of them are removed, there is pressure to restore to equilibrium the relationship between those playing aggressive-masculine roles and those playing passive-feminine roles.

Problems Facing the Prison Administrator. This conceptualization of the pattern of homosexuality in the prison for men suggests a number of problems that face the prison administrator in dealing with sexuality. It means that as long as the prison is an environment which is largely devoid of situations where legitimate affectional ties can be established there will be a tendency for the formation of homosexual relationships, especially among those men serving long sentences who have concomitantly lost contact with meaningful persons in the free community. If in addition the prison does not allow legitimate attempts of the inmates to control their own lives and does not give an opportunity for expressions of masculinity and self-assertion that are meaningful among men at this social level, there will be homosexual relationships created to fulfill this need. The proposal for conjugal visits does not meet this problem, in part because it is available for only the very small number of inmates who have intact families. There is little evidence that the society will tolerate sexual relationships for prisoners when these relationships are not sheltered under the umbrella of a marriage.

What is clear is that the prison is not a seething volcano of sexual passions, and that as a matter of fact most males survive the deprivation of the sexual outlet and usually even survive transitory homosexual commitments to return to relatively conventional heterosexual lives on the outside.

What the sexual problem in the male prison does represent is a series of land mines, some for the administration, more for the inmates. In the case of the inmates, men get into relationships which have some potential for shaping their future commitments to sexuality; relationships which leave them open to exploitation; and, especially for those who take the passive role, the possibility of distortion of their self-conceptions. Further, there is some tendency for these relationships to create problems of sexual jealousy. When a relationship deteriorates or when a transfer of affection takes place, there is a distinct possibility of violence. The violence that does occur often is extreme, and at this point becomes a serious matter for prison management.

The dilemma for the prison manager is that often he is not aware of the relationships until they erupt into violence. Attempts at intervention in this process through getting inmates to aid in the identification of those involved may result in serious scapegoating of these persons out of the sexual anxieties of the other prisoners. The segregation of these prisoners has also been attempted. However, one major difficulty with this measure seems to be that when the most obvious homosexuals are removed from the situation there is a tendency to co-opt other persons to take their place. This tendency is also noted when the aggressive male is removed, though the policy has usually been to remove only those men who are conventionally obvious, that is, who are excessively effeminate.

Probably the only long-term solution is to adopt the policy of home visits at intervals during incarceration and to provide alternative modes of self-expression for those social and psychological needs which, because of the current structure of the male prison, result in homosexuality.

FEMALE RESPONSES TO IMPRISONMENT

As we have noted before, the major dimension which differentiates between the sexual adjustment of persons in the larger society is gender; that is, men and women differ fundamentally in their sexual commitments. While this is obvious, the consequences for the differential sexual adaptation of the males and females in prison are not.

By and large, there is in society a bias against committing females to prison, especially when any alternative is available. Thus the women's prison often has within it women who have either committed major crimes (most commonly homicide) or had long careers in crime and who have been strongly recidivistic. Thus in a certain sense the female institution is composed of some women who have had no prior link to delinquent life-styles and a larger number who had long-term ties with such a life.

Women Have Fewer Problems Than Men in Managing Sexual Deprivation. However, the sexual adjustment of these women to imprisonment is strongly linked to the general goals to which most women are socialized in the larger society. Probably the most significant difference between men and women in this regard is that women are socialized in the language of love before they learn about sex, while men are socialized in the language of sex before they learn about love. The consequence of this is that women commonly show considerably fewer problems managing sexual deprivation than do men, and while there is little evidence, one might expect that the frequencies of any sexually ameliorative behaviors, such as masturbation and homosexuality, are considerably less frequent for women than for men in prison. There is considerable evidence that such behaviors are less frequent among women in the free society than among men, and one should not be surprised that such continuity would be found inside the prison. In addition, women seem to tolerate the absence of overt sexual activity far better than do men, and thus the rates of overt sexual behavior in the female institutions should be considerably lower than those found in male institutions.

Women Tend to Establish Family Systems. The typical response of women to the depersonalizing and alienating environment of the penal institution differs substantially from that of males. Nearly universally in juvenile institutions, and in some observed cases in institutions for adult females, female prisoners appear to form into pseudofamilies with articulated roles of husband and wife, and then, especially in juvenile institutions, extend the family to include father, mother, and children, and aunts, uncles, and cousins.[10] These family systems seem to arise from three sources. One source is a process of compensation; the majority of females in these institutions are from severely disordered homes, and the creation of the pseudofamily often compensates for this lack. A second source results from the socialization of women who, unlike males who form gangs in self-defense, tend to form families, the basic institution in the society in which they have stable and legitimate roles. Finally there is the fact that the pseudofamily operates to stabilize relationships in the institution and to establish orders of dominance and submission, the primary model for which women have in family relationships with fathers, husbands, and children. Since all social systems require some form of articulation which is hierarchical in nature, it is not odd that women model their experience on the institution that they know best in the outside community. There is some evidence that the pseudofamily is not as prevalent in institutions with older females, and it is possible to speculate that in these institutions dyadic friendship patterns are more frequent and may be more similar to those in male institutions.

Inside the context of these familial structures there is the potential for and the acting out of overt homosexual contacts. In the two most recent studies of female prisons there are varying estimates of the number of women who are involved in homosexual practices, but this variation is probably a function of differing definitions, with one limiting the estimate to overt physical contact (yielding a rate of about one-half) and the other probably referring to the proportion of the population who are currently involved in roles in pseudofamily structures (yielding a rate of about 85 percent).[11]

Deprivation of Emotionally Satisfying, Stable, Predictable Relationships with Males. A minor part of the overt female homosexual contacts may arise from deprivation of sexuality, but the primary source is the deprivation of the emotionally satisfying relationships with members of the opposite sex and the desire to create the basis for a community of relationships that are stable and predictable. The overt homosexuality derives somewhat from the conventional sexual content role definitions of husband and wife, but also partially from the fact that a certain proportion of females who come into these institutions may well have experience with lesbian relationships through experience with prostitution in the free community. This is not to say that female homosexuals become prostitutes, but rather that among prostitutes homosexual relationships

10/See Seymour L. Halleck and Marvin Hersko, "Homosexual Behavior in a Correctional School for Adolescent Girls," *American Journal of Orthopsychiatry,* Vol. 32, No. 5, 1962, pp. 911-917; Rose Giallombardo, *Society of Women: A Study of a Women's Prison,* New York: John Wiley & Sons, 1966; David Ward and Gene Kassebaum, *Women's Prison: Sex and Social Structure,* Chicago: Aldine, 1965; Sidney Kosofsky and Albert Ellis, "Illegal Communications Among Institutionalized Female Delinquents," *The Journal of Social Psychology,* Vol. 48, August 1958, pp. 155-160.

11/The two volumes are Ward and Kassebaum, *op. cit.,* and Giallombardo, *op. cit.* For an excellent comparative discussion, see the joint review of these volumes by Sheldon Messinger, *The American Sociological Review,* Vol. 32, No. 1, February 1967, pp. 143-146.

are sought because of the degraded conditions of contacts with men. The processes of induction into homosexual activity in the women's prison are often based on the same principles that one observes in male institutions as part of a search for affection and stability in personal relationships. The homosexual relationship offers protection from the exigencies of the environment and the physical homosexual contacts are less sought for the physical release that they afford than for the validation of emotionally binding and significant relationships.

CONCLUSION

From the arguments posed above it is suggested that what is occurring in the prison situation for both males and females is not a problem of sexual release, but rather the use of sexual relationships in the service of creating a community of relationships for satisfying needs for which the prison fails to provide in any other form. For the male prisoner homosexuality serves as a source of affection, a source of the validation of masculinity, or a source of protection from the problems of institutional life.

In a like manner, the females tend to create family structures in an attempt to ward off the alienating and disorganizing experience of imprisonment; the homosexual relationships are merely part of the binding forces of these relationships.

The problem for the prison administrator then becomes considerably more complex than merely the suppression of sexual activity—it becomes a problem of providing those activities for which the homosexual contacts are serving as substitutes. The inmates are acting out their needs for self-expression, control over their own behavior, affection, and stability of human relationships. The homosexual relationship provides one of the few powerful ways of expressing and gratifying these needs. Unless these needs are met in some other way, there is little opportunity for adequate control of homosexual activity in the prison environment. It might be hypothesized that any attempt to become more coercive and controlling of inmate behavior in order to reduce homosexual contacts may result not in a decrease in activity, but perhaps in an increase. By increasing coercion one increases the pressure to divide inmates from one another, and one decreases their capacity for self-expression and self-control. As the pressure builds there may well be a tendency for homosexual relationships to increase in importance to the inmate population as a reaction to the intensity of the pressure.

Imprisonment and the concomitant sexual deprivation of inmates obviously has some serious consequences, at least during imprisonment, and has a minor potential for complicating postinstitutional life. Little systematic research exists that links the prior nonprison experience of the prisoner, both sexual and nonsexual; methods of institutional management; and the consequences of the interaction of these two elements for the inmate's future functioning. The fact that many inmates adjust easily to the climate of deprivation in the prison may be a measure of their pathology and inability to get along in the outside community rather than a measure of healthy functioning. Just because we manage to make people conform to a climate of deprivation, both sexual and nonsexual, it is no reason that we should.

31. Alternatives to Institutionalization*

HEMAN G. STARK

Although modern society has become highly complex and sophisticated, attempts to humanize the enforcement and corrections process have created social tensions and a demand for both a greater and a lessened punishment of offenders (see Bennett, Article 27). Consequently, the use of probation and parole, increasing in recent decades, has not been without its critics. While opponents of probation and parole, J. Edgar Hoover notes, are often slurred as reactionaries, their advocates have periodically been denounced as impractical visionaries who turn loose hardened criminals to prey upon local citizens. Neither viewpoint is correct. In some cases probation and parole have obviously failed; in others they have fulfilled their design. Both probation and parole, however, represent a philosophy that crime control is best accomplished when the offender is resocialized and is able to exert his own self-control. Although the individualized handling of convicted offenders is designed to lessen the problem of recidivism (subsequent criminal violations), the tensions between critics and supporters of the probation and parole system reflect determinist-indeterminist and punishment versus rehabilitation tensions (see introduction to Article 1).

Many citizens believe that probation and parole are forms of criminal coddling, but, rather, they represent only moderate modifications of historic judicial and punishment procedures. Both involve offender supervision. Both require the offender to prove his ability to engage in normatively acceptable behavior. Probation, however, is essentially community oriented, while the parole has been developed as an attempt to overcome the shortcomings of the prison. Although probation remains a judicial matter, parole, technically part of the indeterminate sentencing system, is administered by a representative state or federal board which determines the conditions for early release under supervision. However, probation and parole prediction, refined from previous decades and generations, still lacks preciseness. The more than 600 completed

*Reprinted from Crime and Delinquency, Volume 13, Number 2 (April, 1967), pp. 323-29, with the permission of the editors.

prediction studies have not appreciably increased the existing prediction capability, a failure possibly due to the general inability of researchers to relate prediction theory to their investigations.

Of the many experimental and operational programs designed as *alternatives to institutionalization,* guided group interaction programs, foster and group homes, prerelease guidance centers, intensive treatment programs, and reception-center parole offer the greatest potential value. *Guided group interaction programs* presume that delinquent behavior is a common group experience which is subject to control only when the delinquent group faces its problems, develops a common culture, and encourages members to act responsibly. The use of *foster and group homes,* a second alternative designed to maintain offenders without institutional confinement, is less stigmatizing and less expensive. Used largely for juveniles, it involves the temporary rupture of family ties in the attempt to create an adequate treatment locale. The creation of *prerelease guidance centers,* such as a half-way house, a third altèrnative, takes the two forms of "half-way in" between probation and institutional commitment and "half-way out" between prison incarceration and parole or outright release. Offering the offender institutional supports during pre- or postinstitutionalization reentry, the prerelease guidance center overcomes many of the shortcomings of actual prison incarceration.

Intensive community treatment programs, a fourth alternative, combine the best in testing with the full use of community facilities and treatment resources. The frequent use of short-term detention at an agency reception center "encourages" compliance with program aims and helps to define the limits of participant behavior. Under the provisions of the *reception-center parole* and *short-term treatment program,* similar to several of the foregoing programs, all juvenile court commitments are referred to a diagnostic reception center for determination of parole eligibility. Conceived as a means by which to overcome acute population pressures in treatment institutions, the diagnostic parole concept has evidenced special success in New York, California, and Washington. While these program alternatives offer high success potentials, the greater bulk of existing correctional programs involves either traditional confinement or semiflexible community probation or parole.

The Community Treatment and the Community Delinquency Control projects of the California Youth Authority, Heman G. Stark notes in the following article, suggest new directions for young offender treatment in the future. The success of these experimental programs encouraged the passage of a state law granting subsidies to counties placing offenders in special treatment programs rather than in state institutions, a move which holds high promise for meaningful offender treatment.

.   .   .   .

Over the past ten years, there has been a definite change in the attitudes of people in the correctional field as well as people in general toward community-based programs sponsored by agencies which have traditionally provided institutional treatment. This paper will deal primarily with such programs that have been or are being developed in the Youth Authority. . . .

The Highfields Project in New Jersey, established in 1950, was one of the first correctional programs in this country to use intensive treatment and short residential stay as a means of getting young offenders, as a group, to examine the problems that led to their delinquencies. All boys are involved in a single program with two principal elements—one, a daily work program; the other, a daily guided-group interaction meeting led by a staff member.

The Essexfields Group Rehabilitation Project in New Jersey, started in 1959, developed as an extension of the Highfields Project. This program follows the pattern established at Highfields, with the important exception that it is nonresidential. Young offenders, assigned to the program by the Essex County Juvenile Court, live at home and come to the program daily.

A second example of a community-based program for delinquent boys—also started in 1959—is the Provo Experiment in Provo, Utah. Like Essexfields, it is a daily program that includes a full day's work and group sessions.

.   .   .   .

COMMUNITY TREATMENT PROJECT

The [California] Youth Authority's Community Treatment Project, started in 1961, is a combined experimental and demonstration project designed to study the feasibility of substituting intensive programs in the community, with selected wards, for traditional programs within an institution. . . .

Boys and girls first committed from the juvenile courts of three California counties are screened for eligibility by the Youth Authority Board, and those who are considered serious threats to the community are excluded. The remainder (about 75 per cent of the boys and 90 per cent of the girls) are randomly assigned to Community Treatment or to the regular Youth Authority program.

The project began with one unit serving two counties (Sacramento and San Joaquin), and consisted of six treatment agents, a treatment supervisor, an administrator, and research staff. After diagnosis according to a maturity-level typology, a ward perceived as needing a certain type of treatment was matched with the agent particularly adept in it. Each agent supervised an average of eight wards.

Phase I

The goals set during the first three years of operation (Phase I) were as follows:

1. To determine the feasibility of releasing selected Youth Authority wards directly from a reception center to a treatment-control program in the community and to determine whether communities would be willing to

accept, under special treatment conditions, the return of wards who had just been committed to the Youth Authority.

2. To compare the effectiveness of a period of treatment in the community with treatment in the regular Youth Authority program, as measured by parole performance and attitudinal and behavioral changes.
3. To develop hypotheses regarding particular treatment plans for specific types of delinquents in specified settings.

During Phase I, all of the goals mentioned above were met. First, the program was found to be feasible in the community. . . . Second, the overall success rate of the project participants was significantly higher than that of their counterparts in the regular Youth Authority program. This was true for both boys and girls, with the success ratio of girls in the project particularly high. Finally, certain types of youngsters did particularly well under the given treatment conditions, while others appeared to do about the same as if they had been institutionalized and released on parole.

Phase II

In the second phase, designed to last for five years, the size of the Community Treatment Project has increased and new goals have been set. Caseloads have been raised from eight to twelve. In 1964 the unit serving two counties was doubled in size and divided, with one full unit assigned to Sacramento and one to San Joaquin. In 1965, two units were added in another county (San Francisco). One of these is a differential treatment unit, based on the model of the other Community Treatment units; the other is a guided-group interaction unit, modeled after LaMar Empey's Provo Experiment. Random assignment is practiced in all units, but in San Francisco a three-way design has been introduced, with eligibles randomly assigned to the differential treatment unit, the guided-group interaction unit, and the regular Youth Authority program.

The goals of Phase II of the project are as follows:

1. To describe in detail the program elements of the Community Treatment Program and to continue the follow-up of wards from Phase I.
2. To detail the differential treatment model, describing the operation of treatment strategies for all delinquent subtypes.
3. To compare the effectiveness of a community-located program based on the differential treatment model to a community-located program modeled after the Provo Experiment.

.   .   .   .

COMMUNITY DELINQUENCY CONTROL PROJECT

In 1963 and 1964 the Youth Authority's institutions were overcrowded. As a result of the experience gained from the Community Treatment Project, the

Department was able to quickly inaugurate a new community-based treatment program. . . . [T]he Community Delinquency Control Project was begun in 1964. Two units were opened in 1964, one in 1965, and a fourth in 1966. A unit consists of eight parole agents and a parole supervisor, plus supportive services. Each unit is designed to provide intensive service to one hundred youngsters for an average of twelve months, in addition to about fifty wards in less intensive supervision until termination of parole. Wards receiving intensive service are supervised in caseloads of fifteen. One of the major differences from Community Treatment is that no formal maturity-level typology is systematically employed in the Community Delinquency Control Project, although differential treatment is provided for wards.

The goals of the program are as follows:

1. To reduce overcrowding in Youth Authority institutions through the immediate release of selected wards to an intensive parole treatment program.
2. To determine the feasibility of such a program in the community.
3. To determine whether such a program will result in better parole performance than would regular parole services.
4. To effect significant and lasting behavioral changes in a nondelinquent direction.

At this point, the first two goals have been achieved. The units have accepted their established quotas of releasees and have thereby reduced the institutional overcrowding. Community officials have been willing to accept a sufficient number of wards to maintain the program and, in many cases, regard this program as more desirable than the regular program. The immediate responses that agents can make to law enforcement officials, probation officers, and school personnel regarding the wards' community problems have "sold" the program to many who were at first skeptical.

. . . .

The wards in the Community Delinquency Control Project are performing considerably better on parole than are other parolees throughout the state. However, because of the selection process, as well as other considerations, the effectiveness of this program has not yet been scientifically demonstrated. . . .

PROGRAM ELEMENTS AND SERVICES

Both the Community Treatment Project and the Community Delinquency Control Project provide more intensive services and have more resources available to them than traditional parole operations. All units are housed in community centers, which are generally located in high delinquency areas and are close to the center of the caseloads. In addition to office space for the agents, the centers have room and facilities for group counseling, school tutoring, arts and crafts, and a general recreation area. The centers greatly facilitate the use of the following regularly employed treatment resources:

Regularly Scheduled Case Conferences. Each case is periodically reviewed by the agent and his supervisor and, in some cases, other resource persons. These conferences establish the initial treatment plan, review progress toward goals, and modify plans where indicated.

Increased Out-of-Home Placement. The proportion of out-of-home placements, including the traditional foster homes and recently developed group homes, is larger than in regular parole. Because of smaller caseloads, agents are better able both to recruit homes and to provide supportive services to the foster parents.

Individual Counseling. The agents are able to provide more intensive individual counseling and are able to maintain a higher level of surveillance and control than in regular parole.

Group Counseling. ... Various types of group counseling are being attempted and evaluated, with the majority of youngsters participating.

Family Counseling. Both scheduled and informal counseling are employed. Since many of the wards are either emancipated from their families or in the process, however, this approach is not appropriate in all cases.

School Tutoring. Tutoring and remedial services are provided for a number of youths. In most cases, these services are used to retain them in public schools or to assist in their re-entry into school. . . .

Activity Groups, Arts and Crafts, Recreation. Within each center there are arts and crafts facilities and both organized and casual recreation. In addition, activity groups have been formed for beach parties, camping trips, ball games, and a variety of other recreational activities that most of these youths would otherwise not experience.

Transportation of Wards. Personnel are provided to drive wards to and from group meetings, relieving the agents for more productive activity.

Consultation. Both projects have regularly scheduled psychiatric and group counseling consultation. In addition, other consultants may be used for specific purposes.

IMPACT OF NEW PROGRAMS

These two programs have influenced the development of other experimental parole programs, the regular parole operation, agency relationships within the communities, and, to some extent, the general public attitude.

First, with reference to the development of other experimental programs, the Youth Authority is also embarking on new parole programs that will *follow* a period of institutionalization rather than *replace* it. A number of youthful offenders are committed to state facilities for crimes sufficiently serious to keep the community from accepting their early release. Other wards may be in need of particular institutional treatment and not yet be ready for any type of community-based program. We do not expect that there will ever be a time when all institutions will be closed. Yet, since our traditional institutional programs have convincingly demonstrated that they are not effective for a large proportion of offenders, more effective treatment must constantly be sought.

The department is now providing special parole programs for wards released from institutions. Two special units—called Violence Control Demonstration Units—have recently been established in San Diego. They are directed toward controlling or reducing violence among all parolees, using all of the treatment techniques and most of the program elements developed and used in the two projects described above. The department is also planning a number of community parole centers, to be located in especially depressed, high-delinquency urban areas in the state. These, too, will employ all of the program elements and treatment techniques of the older programs.

Second, the emergence of experimental programs has had ramifications in the regular parole operation. The new and creative ways of working with youthful offenders in these programs have stirred the imagination of many formerly tradition-bound workers. There is a growing acceptance of experimentation. Such resources as group foster homes, long discussed, are now used in the regular program.

Third, the activities of the agents in the communities have generally improved the relationship between the Youth Authority and local agencies that also work with our wards. Traditionally, this department has striven to maintain close contact and good working relationships with local workers with whom we share responsibility. However, a regular parole agent supervising more than seventy parolees, perhaps geographically scattered, has not always been able to respond immediately to requests for conferences or services. Project agents, on the other hand, are usually immediately available, and are generally able to offer a wider range of services in addition to having more resources to draw from. . . .

Finally, the success of these projects has contributed to the growing public acceptance of community-based treatment programs for youthful offenders who would otherwise be placed in institutions. . . .

FURTHER EFFORTS

With institutional costs about $22,000 a bed and with the cost of maintaining and treating a ward in an institution about $400 a month, the savings of a community-based program in lieu of institutionalization are obvious. . . . For the wards placed in these programs, the rehabilitative influences have proved to be more beneficial than the regular Youth Authority program. Another advantage is that the marginal offenders are removed from the institutions and from the possible negative effects of forced association with more delinquent wards, while the institutions are freed to work more intensively with the hard-core offenders.

We are not suggesting that we view these new programs as the final answer. It is too soon to know what their overall effects will be. We do know, however, on the basis of our current experience, that an institutional stay is not necessary for all commitments and that response to these experimental programs is promising enough for us to develop and expand them further. . . .

part EIGHT

Social Control and
Social Change

The control of crime is a complex problem. Current crime increases are related not only to population growth but also to the lack of public response to the demand for change in modern society. While business organizations have modified their basic practices to keep pace with social inventions and emerging techniques, the systems of law enforcement, justice, and corrections have been unable, due to limited funds, inadequate personnel, and political limitations, to enact corresponding modifications. Part of this failure is due to the community's unwillingness to change, to pay higher taxes, or to give police more power. Government leaders must accept their responsibility for their failure to plan and provide for efficient enforcement, judicial, and correctional systems (*see* Bilek, Article 22; Bennett, Article 27). Because criminal apprehension depends upon an immediate response to a call for police aid, the matter of communications technology exerts a primary influence upon crime control. Effective administration of justice, too, plays a central role. When prompt court and trial procedures give way to delays in adjudication, confidence in the effectiveness of public institutions of social control is lessened. However, even the public's unwillingness to attempt the rehabilitation of incarcerated criminals through personalized treatment methods cannot be dismissed as a factor in the growing crime rate.

Crime continues for many because it is profitable and allows immediate satisfaction. The person who "hangs paper" (passes a bad check) receives immediate rewards. The man who steals does so with approximately one in five chances of being caught. Although many crimes are not profitable but are motivated by maliciousness, hedonistic impulses, boredom, excessive sexuality, and a desire for revenge, the greater volume of crimes centers on the acquisition of some property through stealing, burglary, embezzlement, robbery, or the like. While the criminal takes many risks of apprehension, the greater number of crimes, it is believed, remain either undetected or uncleared by arrest.

Although many citizens demand crime control through police coercion, they fail to see the greater scope of the problem. Crime control is extremely costly; its effectiveness is hard to measure. Of the total estimated costs involved in the maintenance of the criminal justice system, police costs, for example, are estimated at 67 percent, corrections at 20 percent, juvenile processing at 11 percent, and court at 2 percent. The need to evaluate the proficiency of existing delinquency and crime prevention programs, the adequacy of mental health personnel and facilities for treatment of personal problems, the relationship of existing social conditions and deviant behavior, and the effectiveness of enforcement and court procedures are also included within the scope of the problem. The public's attitude of "more of the same," therefore, must be replaced by a conscientious awareness of the need to integrate social changes into more meaningful social control systems (see Lohman, Article 35). The greater use of computer systems in police patrol, crime investigation, police deployment, sentencing, or correctional decisions, correctional program planning, protection of individual rights, governmental budgeting, and law enforcement research and development must be encouraged. Especially critical is the absence of adequate research and planning organizations within the local or state systems of justice (see Bilek, Article 22).

However, the mere use of computer technology cannot overcome previous program deficiencies. While many of these enforcement or correctional techniques were designed to control the few obvious community deviants who could not be controlled through more localized informal control methods, they are no longer adequate for the needs of the greater and more impersonal mass population. Recognizing this change, the President's Crime Commission proposes that federal support be granted for eight major justice areas, including state and local planning, education and training of criminal justice personnel, surveys and advisory services concerning organization and operation of criminal justice agencies, development of coordinated national information systems, development of a limited number of demonstration programs and agencies of justice, scientific and technological research and development, institutes for research and training personnel, and grants-in-aid for operational innovations.

Even these remedies, however, are inadequate. The problem is far greater and ultimately encompasses the whole system of enforcement, adjudication, and corrections. In this concluding part, four authors examine these several dimensions which touch upon the problem of social control and social change. Jackson Toby probes the meaning, purpose, and value of punishment as a means of social control. Jack P. Gibbs delineates the potential contribution of the sociology of law to problems of social change and social control. The selection from the Walker Report on the emotional contagion, police-protestor confrontation, and community response during the Democratic National Convention Week in Chicago (August-September, 1968) gives insight into the contemporary tensions which challenge current social structures. And in conclusion, Joseph D. Lohman examines the crises which arise when a society is in ferment.

32. Is Punishment Necessary?*

JACKSON TOBY

Law enforcement, the courts, and correctional institutions are faced with many basic dilemmas. But nowhere is the character and nature of the dilemma more apparent than in the problems posed by narcotic addiction and alcoholism. Both involve dimensions of control, adjudication, and corrections which are tied to philosophical assumptions about the nature of each question. The correctional problem, however, is most acute because the goal of behavioral change in such instances involves more than a mere change in the person's will (see Kadish, Article 1). The drug addict and the alcoholic are also physically dependent upon the use of drugs and alcohol. While most crimes involve both psychological alienation and socioinstitutional inadequacy, narcotic and alcohol violations are more heavily oriented to physiological and personality needs. And yet both the control of these crime forms and the treatment of the addictive offenders depend upon the discovery of a solution to this basic dilemma, which is so highly integrated into the social system. More than 50 percent of the yearly crime volume, for example, is related in some way to the use of alcohol. The sale of narcotics to retailers and pushers, which produces major income for organized crime, is also closely related to the processes of urbanization. Of necessity, any treatment of the alcoholic or narcotic addict, therefore, involves both personality and sociostructural dimensions.

The nature of drug addiction and treatment is commonly misunderstood. Not only is the treatment of the addict rather complex but meaningful treatment programs are often socially controversial. Consequently, a wide chasm often exists between modern medical science and the political units' response to medicine's new treatment discoveries. In several instances the lower courts have militated against revised treatment procedures which stress the early treatment of narcotic addicts in state institutions by failing to sentence offenders to these treatment institutions in their early addictive career. While the state of California, for example, anticipated that 40 percent of all civil commitments for narcotic addiction would involve cases originating in the municipal courts, only 14 percent were processed from this locus. Many courts, Richard Nahrendorf discovered, tended to impose minor county jail sentences without reference to the narcotic rehabilitation program at the California Rehabilitation Center in Norco, because of the belief that civil commitment is too severe a punishment

*Reprinted with special permission from the *Journal of Criminal Law, Criminology and Police Science*, Copyright © 1964 by the Northwestern University School of Law, Volume 55, No. 3.

for the nature of the offense. Other preliminary data, Nahrendorf also found, likewise suggest that the goal of early treatment of the narcotic offender is undermined by public attitudes and the court's failure to understand the character of the treatment process.

Similar confusion surrounds the issue of public drunkenness. One third of all arrests involve this single crime category. The commonness of the offense has led many courts to establish a revolving-door policy under which drunks are rounded up during the day, allowed to sleep it off during the night in jail, and released again in the morning. Not unexpectedly, therefore, due process guarantees are often lacking or minimized in such a context. Consequently, the President's Crime Commission concluded that drunkenness should be processed as a public health problem rather than a crime, although a 1968 Supreme Court decision upholding existing procedures undermined the proposal, noting that inadequate treatment facilities made the differential handling of drunkenness offenders impractical.

The treatment of alcoholism through punishment is only one phase of the punishment-rehabilitation problem. Although punishment continues to dominate court sentencing and penal treatment procedures, an ever-growing number of voices is asking: Is punishment really necessary? Jackson Toby both poses and answers this question.

Of 11 contemporary textbooks in criminology written by sociologists, ten have one or more chapters devoted to the punishment of offenders.[1] . . . Several textbook writers express their opposition to punishment, especially to cruel punishment. This opposition is alleged to be based on an incompatibility of punishment with scientific considerations. . . . Most of the textbook writers note with satisfaction that "the trend in modern countries has been toward humanizing punishment and toward the reduction of brutalities."[2] They point to the decreased use of capital punishment, the introduction of amenities into the modern prison by enlightened penology, and the increasing emphasis on nonpunitive and individualized methods of dealing with offenders, e.g., probation, parole, psychotherapy. In short, students reading these textbooks might infer that punishment is a vestigial carryover of a barbaric past and will disappear as humanitarianism and rationality spread. Let us examine this inference in terms of the motives underlying punishment and the necessities of social control.

1/Barnes & Teeters, *New Horizons in Criminology* (3d ed. 1959); Caldwell, *Criminology* (1956); Cavan, *Criminology* (1955); Elliot, *Crime in Modern Society* (1952); Korn & McCorkle, *Criminology and Penology* (1959); Reckless, *The Crime Problem* (2d ed. 1955); Sutherland & Cressey, *Principles of Criminology* (5th ed. 1955); Taft, *Criminology* (3d ed. 1956); Tappan, *Crime, Justice and Correction* (1960); von Hentig, *Crime: Causes and Conditions* (1947); Wood & Waite, *Crime and Its Treatment* (1941).

2/Reckless, *op. cit. supra* note 1, at 450.

THE URGE TO PUNISH

Many crimes have identifiable victims. In the case of crimes against the person, physical or psychic injuries have been visited upon the victim. In the case of crimes against property, someone's property has been stolen or destroyed. In pressing charges against the offender, the victim may express hostility against the person who injured him in a socially acceptable way. Those who identify with the victim—not only his friends and family but those who can imagine the same injury being done to them—may join with him in clamoring for the punishment of the offender. If, as has been argued, the norm of reciprocity is fundamental to human interaction, this hostility of the victim constituency toward offenders is an obstacle to the elimination of punishment from social life.[3] . . . [However,] it is possible that nearly everyone identifies with the victim of a murderer but relatively few people with the victim of a blackmailer. The greater the size of the victim constituency, the greater the opposition to a nonpunitive reaction to the offender.

It would be interesting indeed to measure the size and the composition of the victim constituencies for various crimes. Take rape as an illustration. Since the victims of rape are females, we might hypothesize that *women* would express greater punitiveness toward rapists than *men* and that degrees of hostility would correspond to real or imaginary exposure to rape. Thus, pretty young girls might express more punitiveness toward rapists than homely women. Among males, we might predict that greater punitiveness would be expressed by those with more reason to identify with the victims. Thus, males having sisters or daughters in the late teens or early twenties might express more punitiveness toward rapists than males lacking vulnerable "hostages to fortune."

Such a study might throw considerable light on the wellsprings of punitive motivation, particularly if victimization reactions were distinguished from other reasons for punitiveness. One way to explore such motivation would be to ask the same respondents to express their punitive predispositions toward offenses which do not involve victims at all, e.g., gambling, or which involve victims of a quite different kind. Thus, rape might be balanced by an offense the victims of which are largely male. . . .

THE SOCIAL CONTROL FUNCTIONS OF PUNISHMENT

Conformists who identify with the *victim* are motivated to punish the offender out of some combination of rage and fear. Conformists who identify with the *offender,* albeit unconsciously, may wish to punish him for quite different reasons. Whatever the basis for the motivation to punish, the existence of punitive reactions to deviance is an obstacle to the abolition of punishment.

3/Gouldner, "The Norm of Reciprocity: A Preliminary Statement," 25 *Am. Soc. Rev.* 161 (1960).

However, it is by no means the sole obstacle. Even though a negligible segment of society felt punitive toward offenders, it might still not be feasible to eliminate punishment if the social control of deviance depended on it. Let us consider, therefore, the consequences of punishing offenders for (a) preventing crime, (b) sustaining the morale of conformists, and (c) rehabilitating offenders.

Punishment as a Means of Crime Prevention

Durkheim defined punishment as an act of vengeance. "What we avenge, what the criminal expiates, is the outrage to morality."[4] But why is vengeance necessary? Not because of the need to deter the bulk of the population from doing likewise. The socialization process prevents most deviant behavior. Those who have introjected the moral norms of their society cannot commit crimes because their self-concepts will not permit them to do so. Only the unsocialized (and therefore amoral) individual fits the model of classical criminology and is deterred from expressing deviant impulses by a nice calculation of pleasures and punishments.[5] Other things being equal, the anticipation of punishment would seem to have more deterrent value for inadequately socialized members of the group. . . . [T]he deterrent effect of anticipated punishments is a complex empirical problem, and Durkheim was not interested in it. Feeling as he did that *some* crime is normal in every society, he apparently decided that the crime prevention function of punishment is not crucial. He pointed out that minute gradation in punishment would not be necessary if punishment were simply a means of deterring the potential offender (crime prevention). "Robbers are as strongly inclined to rob as murderers are to murder; the resistance offered by the former is not less than that of the latter, and consequently, to control it, we would have recourse to the same means."[6] Durkheim was factually correct; the offenses punished most severely are not necessarily the ones which present the greatest problem of social defense. Thus, quantitatively speaking, murder is an unimportant cause of death; in the United States it claims only half as many lives annually as does suicide and only one-fifth the toll of automobile accidents. Furthermore, criminologists have been unable to demonstrate a relationship between the murder rate of a community and its use or lack of use of capital punishment.

Most contemporary sociologists would agree with Durkheim that the anticipation of punishment is not the first line of defense against crime. The socialization process keeps most people law-abiding, not the police—if for no other reason than the police are not able to catch every offender. This does not mean, however, that the police could be disbanded. . . . Even though punishment is uncertain, especially under contemporary urban conditions, the possibility of

4/Durkheim, *The Division of Labor in Society* 89 (1947).
5/Parsons, *The Structure of Social Action* 402-03 (1949).
6/*Op. cit. supra* note 4, at 88.

punishment keeps some conformists law-abiding. The empirical question is: *How many* conformists would become deviants if they did not fear punishment?

Punishment as a Means of Sustaining the Morale of Conformists

Durkheim considered punishment indispensable as a means of containing the demoralizing consequences of the crimes that could not be prevented. Punishment was not for Durkheim mere vindictiveness. Without punishment Durkheim anticipated the demoralization of "upright people" in the face of defiance of the collective conscience. He believed that unpunished deviance tends to demoralize the conformist and therefore he talked about punishment as a means of repairing "the wounds made upon collective sentiments."[7] . . .

Durkheim anticipated psychoanalytic thinking, as the following reformulation of his argument shows: One who resists the temptation to do what the group prohibits, to drive his car at 80 miles per hour, to beat up an enemy, to take what he wants without paying for it, would like to feel that these self-imposed abnegations have some meaning. When he sees others defy rules without untoward consequences, he needs some reassurance that his sacrifices were made in a good cause. . . . The social significance of punishing offenders is that deviance is thereby defined as unsuccessful in the eyes of conformists, thus making inhibition or repression of their own deviant impulses seem worthwhile. Righteous indignation is collectively sanctioned reaction formation. The law-abiding person who unconsciously resents restraining his desire to steal and murder has an opportunity, by identifying with the police and the courts, to affect the precarious balance within his own personality between internal controls and the temptation to deviate. . . . No doubt, some of the persons involved in the administration of punishment are sadistically motivated. But Durkheim hypothesized that the psychic equilibrium of the *ordinary* member of the group may be threatened by violation of norms; Durkheim was not concerned about psychopathological punitiveness.

Whatever the practical difficulties, Durkheim's hypothesis is, in principle, testable. It should be possible to estimate the demoralizing impact of nonconformity on conformists. Clearly, though, this is no simple matter. The extent of demoralization resulting from the failure to punish may vary with type of crime. . . .

Once the facts on the rate and the incidence of moral indignation are known, it will become possible to determine whether something must be done to the offender in order to prevent the demoralization of conformists. Suppose that research revealed that a very large proportion of conformists react with moral indignation to *most* violations of the criminal laws. Does this imply that punishment is a functional necessity? Durkheim apparently thought so, but he

7/Durkheim, *op. cit. supra* note 4, at 108.

might have been less dogmatic in his approach to punishment had he specified the functional problem more clearly: making the nonconformist unattractive as a role model. If the norm violation can be defined as unenviable through some other process than by inflicting suffering upon him, punishment is not required by the exigencies of social control.

Punishment can be discussed on three distinct levels: (a) in terms of the motivations of the societal agents administering it, (b) in terms of the definition of the situation on the part of the person being punished, and (c) in terms of its impact on conformists. At this point I am chiefly concerned with the third level, the impact on conformists. Note that punishment of offenders sustains the morale of conformists only under certain conditions. The first has already been discussed, namely that conformists unconsciously wish to violate the rules themselves. The second is that conformists implicitly assume that the nonconformity is a result of *deliberate defiance* of society's norms. For some conformists, this second condition is not met. Under the guidance of psychiatric thinking, some conformists assume that norm violation is the result of illness rather than wickedness.[8] For such conformists, punishment of the offender does not contribute to their morale. Since they assume that the nonconformity is an involuntary symptom of a disordered personality, the offender is automatically unenviable because illness is (by definition) undesirable. Of course, it is an empirical question as to the relative proportions of the conforming members of society who make the "wicked" or the "sick" assumption about the motivation of the offender, but this can be discovered by investigation.

In Western industrial societies, there is increasing tendency to call contemporary methods of dealing with offenders "treatment" rather than "punishment." Perhaps this means that increasing proportions of the population are willing to accept the "sick" theory of nonconformity. Note, however, that the emphasis on "treatment" may be more a matter of symbolism than of substance. . . . [I] t would be an error to suppose that punishment is invariably experienced as painful by the criminal whereas treatment is always experienced as pleasant by the psychopathological offender. Some gang delinquents consider a reformatory sentence an opportunity to renew old acquaintances and to learn new delinquent skills; they resist fiercely the degrading suggestion that they need the services of the "nut doctor." Some mental patients are terrified by shock treatment and embarrassed by group therapy.

What then is the significance of the increasing emphasis on "treatment"? Why call an institution for the criminally insane a "hospital" although it bears a closer resemblance to a prison than to a hospital for the physically ill? In my opinion, the increased emphasis on treatment in penological thinking and practice reflects the existence of a large group of conformists who are undecided as between the "wicked" and the "sick" theories of nonconformity. When they observe that the

8/Talcott Parsons has repeatedly suggested the analogy between illness and criminality. See also Aubert & Messinger, "The Criminal and the Sick," 1 *Inquiry* 137 (1958), and Wootton, *Social Science and Social Pathology* 203-67 (1959).

offender is placed in "treatment," their provisional diagnosis of illness is confirmed, and therefore they do not feel that he has "gotten away with it." Note that "treatment" has the capacity to make the offender unenviable to conformists whether or not it is effective in rehabilitating him and whether or not he experiences it as pleasant. . . .

Punishment as a Means of Reforming the Offender

Rehabilitation of offenders swells the number of conformists and therefore is regarded both by humanitarians and by scientifically minded penologists as more constructive than punishment. Most of the arguments against the imprisonment and other forms of punishment in the correctional literature boil down to the assertion that punishment is incompatible with rehabilitation. The high rate of recidivism for prisons and reformatories is cited as evidence of the irrationality of punishment.[9] What sense is there in subjecting offenders to the frustrations of incarceration? If rehabilitative programs are designed to help the offender cope with frustrations in his life situation, which presumably were responsible for his nonconformity, imprisoning him hardly seems a good way to begin. To generalize the argument, the status degradation inherent in punishment makes it more difficult to induce the offender to play a legitimate role instead of a nonconforming one. Whatever the offender's original motivations for nonconformity, punishment adds to them by neutralizing his fear of losing the respect of the community; he has already lost it.

Plausible though this argument is, empirical research has not yet verified it. The superior rehabilitative efficacy of "enlightened" prisons is a humanitarian assumption, but brutal correctional systems have, so far as is known, comparable recidivism rates to "enlightened" systems. True, the recidivism rate of offenders who are fined or placed on probation is less than the recidivism rate of offenders who are incarcerated, but this comparison is not merely one of varying degrees of punishment. . . .

Even on theoretical grounds, however, the incompatibility of punishment and rehabilitation can be questioned once it is recognized that one may precede the other. Perhaps, as Lloyd McCorkle and Richard Korn think, some types of deviants become willing to change only if the bankruptcy of their way of life is conclusively demonstrated to them.[10] On this assumption, punishment may be a necessary preliminary to a rehabilitative program in much the same way that shock treatment makes certain types of psychotics accessible to psychotherapy.

It seems to me that the compatibility of punishment and rehabilitation could be clarified (although not settled) if it were considered from the point of view of the *meaning* of punishment to the offender. Those offenders who regard punishment as a deserved deprivation resulting from their own misbehavior are qualitatively different from offenders who regard punishment as a misfortune

9/Vold, "Does the Prison Reform?" 293 *Annals* 42 (1954).
10/McCorkle & Korn, "Resocialization Within Walls," 293 *Annals* 88 1954).

bearing no relationship to morality. Thus, a child who is spanked by his father and the member of a bopping gang who is jailed for carrying concealed weapons are both "punished." But one accepts the deprivation as legitimate, and the other bows before superior force. I would hypothesize that punishment has rehabilitative significance only for the former. If this is so, correctional officials must convince the prisoner that his punishment is just before they can motivate him to change. This is no simple task. It is difficult for several reasons:

1. It is obvious to convicted offenders, if not to correctional officials, that *some* so-called "criminals" are being punished disproportionately for trifling offenses whereas *some* predatory businessmen and politicians enjoy prosperity and freedom. To deny that injustices occur confirms the cynical in their belief that "legitimate" people are not only as predatory as criminals but hypocritical to boot. . . .

2. Of course, the more cases of injustice known to offenders, the harder it is to argue that the contemporary approximation of justice is the best that can be managed. It is difficult to persuade Negro inmates that their incarceration has moral significance if their life experience has demonstrated to them that the police and the courts are less scrupulous of *their* rights than of the rights of white persons. It is difficult to persuade an indigent inmate that his incarceration has moral significance if his poverty resulted in inadequate legal representation.[11]

3. Finally, the major form of punishment for serious offenders (imprisonment) tends to generate a contraculture which denies that justice has anything to do with legal penalties.[12] That is to say, it is too costly to confine large numbers of people in isolation from one another, yet congregate confinement results in the mutual reinforcement of self-justifications. . . .

In view of the foregoing considerations, I hypothesize that punishment—as it is now practiced in Western societies—is usually an obstacle to rehabilitation. Some exceptions to this generalization should be noted. A few small treatment institutions have not only prevented the development of a self-righteous contraculture but have managed to establish an inmate climate supportive of changed values.[13] In such institutions punishment has rehabilitative significance for the same reason it has educational significance in the normal family: it is legitimate.

To sum up: The social control functions of punishment include crime prevention, sustaining the morale of conformists, and the rehabilitation of offenders. All of the empirical evidence is not in, but it is quite possible that punishment contributes to some of these and interferes with others. Suppose, for example, that punishment is necessary for crime prevention and to maintain

---

11/Trebach, "The Indigent Defendant," 11 *Rutgers L. Rev.* 625 (1957).

12/For a discussion of the concept of contraculture, see Yinger, "Contraculture and Subculture," 25 *Am. Soc. Rev.* 625 (1960).

13/McCorkle, Elias & Bixby, *The Highfields Story* (1958), and Empey & Rabow, "Experiment in Delinquency Rehabilitation," 26 *Am. Soc. Rev.* 679 (1961).

the morale of conformists but is generally an obstacle to the rehabilitation of offenders. Since the proportion of deviants is small in any viable system as compared with the proportion of conformists, the failure to rehabilitate them will not jeopardize the social order. Therefore, under these assumptions, sociological counsel would favor the continued employment of punishment.

CONCLUSION

A member of a social system who violates its cherished rules threatens the stability of that system. Conformists who identify with the victim are motivated to punish the criminal in order to feel safe. Conformists who unconsciously identify with the criminal fear their own ambivalence. If norm violation is defined by conformists as willful, visiting upon the offender some injury or degradation will make him unenviable. If his behavior is defined by conformists as a symptom of pathology they are delighted not to share, putting him into treatment validates their diagnosis of undesirable illness. Whether he is "punished" or "treated," however, the disruptive consequence of his deviance is contained. Thus, from the viewpoint of social control, the alternative outcomes of the punishment or treatment processes, rehabilitation or recidivism, are less important than the deviant's neutralization as a possible role model. Whether punishment is or is not necessary rests ultimately on empirical questions: (1) the extent to which identification with the victim occurs, (2) the extent to which nonconformity is prevented by the anticipation of punishment, (3) what the consequences are for the morale of conformists of punishing the deviant or of treating his imputed pathology, and (4) the compatibility between punishment and rehabilitation.

33. Crime and the Sociology of Law*

JACK P. GIBBS

Reasoned attempts to solve the apparent inadequacies in the criminal process necessarily demand evaluations of manpower, equipment, facilities, and programs. Each is related to the other and together they form a related, but sometimes incoherent, whole. Modifications in one element, therefore, may lead to modifications in others. Ultimately, effective social control in a mass society depends upon greater self-control, associational and community social control

*Reprinted from *Sociology and Social Research*, Volume 51, Number 1 (October, 1966), pp. 23-38, with the permission of the editors.

and more efficient enforcement, court, and correctional capabilities. Such diverse elements as schools, families, community organizations, political governments, and social control agencies share in this process (*see* Elliott, Article 10; Dienstein, Article 19; and Lemert, Article 26).

While personnel inadequacies may be overcome by providing opportunity for skill development and continuing education, increased monetary commitments to enforcement and corrections, too, must be provided. But because the public sees so few quick positive results, it is slow to accept major changes in the current approach. The maintenance of social control is no easy matter (*see* Toby, Article 32). Delinquency and crime are largely symptoms of earlier social deviance, often encouraged by the dysfunctions brought about by social change. What, for example, are the relationships among inflation, working mothers, and delinquency? Or between masculine and feminine role redefinitions? The results of one decade are not immediately measured, however. Even modifications in correctional philosophy or policy are not quickly apparent. On the other hand, the enactment of new laws which define formerly undefined behavior as violations of the criminal code immediately result in an increase in the total number of incarcerated offenders (*see* Kadish, Article 1).

The enforcement, judicial, and penal systems need competent personnel supported by the necessary financial resources. The system of criminal justice, especially, the President's Commission on Law Enforcement and Administration of Justice notes, cannot operate fairly or in the interest of the society unless its personnel are competent and fair. Swift justice depends upon efficient and well-informed personnel. Court case backlogs (*see* Bilek, Article 22), which are often encouraged by the absence of adequate court facilities or court personnel, are likewise due to the lack of trained criminal lawyers. Because the system of criminal justice has too often been content merely to process cases within its jurisdiction rather than to realize the theoretical implications of the idea of justice, the criminal courts have often fallen victim to the problems of urban growth. The lack of information in the current system of justice concerning court procedures and the influence of court sentences upon the eventual behavior of the convicted offender is similar to flying blind without adequate navigational equipment. The ideals of law enforcement, swift justice, and personalized corrections have never been completely realized. While some changes may take place in the future, the transitions caused by urban growth, world wars, population expansion, and the knowledge explosion continue to influence all areas of the criminal system without a clear public understanding of the directions and costs of such change.

Consequently, Jack P. Gibbs argues in the following selection that neither a statutory nor a nonlegal conception of crime offers an adequate foundation for understanding the processes of social control. An adequate sociology of law, necessary for the development of a coherent scientific approach to the problems inherent in the criminal justice systems, can only emerge if one studies the universals of social control through research into other societies and cultures.

STATEMENT OF THE PROBLEM

Since most research on crime is conducted in societies with codified laws, criminologists tend to employ a statutory criterion of criminality. However, the idea that a crime is an act so designated by a statute can be criticized on several grounds. First of all, if one uses statutory designations, criminal acts can be defined only enumeratively or denotatively in a finite universe, meaning a particular society at a given point in time. Further, since a penal code may not, and in fact typically does not, include a generic definition of criminal behavior, statutes leave the common attributes of crime unspecified, i.e., legislators or other sovereigns designate certain acts as criminal, but they may not define crime apart from the individual proscriptions in the code. . . . A statute may be viewed as nothing more than the specification of a sanction which supposedly applies if a person is found guilty of committing a designated act; and, as such, one can only impute criminal law and proscriptions to the statute. Moreover, whatever the wording of codes, a statutory conception of crime is always relative to a particular language. For example, we should not say without qualification that a given act was a crime in ancient Babylonia, because the word obviously does not appear in Hammurabi's code. . . . Finally, apart from the problem of language translation, a statutory criterion of crime virtually excludes the phenomenon from non-literate societies, which is, from the perspective of the sociology of law, a sufficient reason to reject the criterion.

Difficulties in Defining Crime. However inadequate the statutory conception of crime may be, alternative definitions are not easily formulated, largely because many of the attributes commonly ascribed to crimes are dubious. Witness, for example, the notion that criminal laws are sanctioned. But not all sanctioned norms are laws. Moreover, it does not appear feasible to define criminal law in terms of specific kinds of sanctions. A variety of sanctions may be attached to the statutes in one penal code—fines, incarceration, banishment, loss of status, death, whipping, branding, etc.—and the use of suspended sentences and probation further complicates the picture.

The variety of sanctions also makes it difficult to distinguish criminal from "civil law." Torts and breaches of contract may result in loss of money or property, just as may certain types of "crime." Further, the notion that the person damaged receives compensation in civil but not criminal actions is false. While rare, restitution is provided for in the criminal proceedings of certain common law jurisdictions, including at least some of the United States,[1] and it is even more prevalent in other legal systems.[2] Equally important, the addition of restitution to purely penal sanctions, or even the substitution of the former for

1/Sol Rubin, *et al., The Law of Criminal Correction* (St. Paul, Minnesota: West Publishing Co., 1963), 260-61.

2/A. S. Diamond, *Primitive Law,* 2nd ed. (London: Watts and Co., 1960), 278. The picture is further complicated by Diamond's observation: "In . . . actions of tort . . . the defendant may be punished, for 'vindictive' as well as compensatory damages can be given to the plaintiff. . . ."

the latter, would not result necessarily in an alteration of the penal code. Also, apart from statutory considerations, it is doubtful that a change from purely penal sanctions to restitution would alter the public conception of a criminal act, as imagine the consequence of a change from imprisonment of the offender to monetary compensation for the victim of rape.

Another difficulty is that a definition may be couched in terms that introduce a subjective element, as when one attempts to distinguish criminal from civil actions in terms of the "intent" of the adjudication or the perception of the outcome by the participants. The loss of property or money in a civil action may be perceived as punishment regardless of the intention of the law, which in itself is difficult to establish.[3] The subjective element is only less apparent in definitions which describe crimes as acts "against the welfare of society," "which offend the community," etc. . . .

Finally, a definition of crime which refers to the "state" is objectionable, not only in that it may fail to distinguish criminal laws from other types of law but also because the concept is most nebulous in a cross-cultural context. The same objection applies only somewhat less to such terms as legislature, court, and officials. These terms are not only difficult to apply cross-culturally but also tend to reflect an ethnocentric view of law.

SOME ALTERNATIVE SOLUTIONS

Despite the widespread reliance on statutory designations of crime, the definitional problem has not gone unrecognized. Thorsten Sellin has declared it to be *the* problem in criminology;[4] and the debate over the legal status of "white-collar" crime[5] has generated an awareness that the issue is not peculiar to cross-cultural research. However, although the problem has not been ignored, the proposed solutions are far from adequate.

A Non-legal Conception of Crime. Perhaps the most radical solution is that set forth by Sellin. He proposes, in effect, that criminology abandon the concept criminal law and study violations of conduct norms rather than crime in a legal sense.[6] Sellin's argument is that laws may be, and in fact often are, contrary to conduct norms; and, from a scientific perspective, the legal designation of acts as criminal is arbitrary.

Whatever the merits of Sellin's solution for purposes of criminology, it is clearly inadequate for the sociology of law. The latter loses its identity without a focus on legal norms, however arbitrary these norms may appear to criminologists who seek a "social" definition of crime. . . .

3/". . . who is to say that a complainant may not feel just as much compensated when the accused is incarcerated or fined, as when he himself wreaks a violent revenge on him or receives damages from him?" *Ibid.,* 278.

4/Thorsten Sellin, *Culture Conflict and Crime* (New York: Social Science Research Council, Bulletin 41, 1938), 20.

5/See George B. Vold, *Theoretical Criminology* (New York: Oxford University Press, 1958), 243-53.

6/Sellin, *op. cit.,* 21-39.

Social Evaluation of Crime. While recognition of cultural relativity cautions against an attempt to compile a list of specific acts that are crimes in all societies, several investigators have sought to define crime by identifying what purports to be a universal social evaluation of acts as criminal, i.e., the acts are distinguished by the character of public reaction to them. This approach differs from a strictly non-legal conception in that it may differentiate crimes from norm violations in general.

Garofalo's concept "natural crime"[7] represents one of the earliest and certainly the most well known attempt to identify crime in terms of social evaluations. The idea is that a "natural crime" is an act which violates prevailing sentiments of probity and/or pity.

An appraisal of Garofalo's concept is made difficult, of course, by the fact that any definition of crime is neither right nor wrong. However, if one grants that a definition cannot be (or at least should not be) entirely divorced from statutory designations of criminal acts, Garofalo's criterion of crime is most debatable. . . .

.   .   .   .

The Analytical Approach. Rather than abandon the concept altogether or look outside the law for the distinguishing characteristics of crime, one may seek a generic definition in the common features of acts statutorily designated as crimes and in laws of criminal procedure.

This analytical approach is illustrated in the following list of the differentiae of crime, as compiled by Sutherland and Cressey: (1) an external consequence amounting to a "harm," (2) the harm is legally forbidden, (3) intentional or reckless action, (4) *mens rea* or "criminal intent," (5) a fusion of *mens rea* and conduct, (6) a "causal" connection between the legally forbidden harm and the voluntary misconduct, and (7) legally prescribed punishment.[8]

The merit of the analytic approach is that it does not confuse laws with other types of norms; but there is a problem in that one tends to focus on those differentiae of crime as it is known in his own political unit. More serious, it is extremely doubtful if any list of differentiae is valid for even one penal code. . . .

Rather than focus on the differentiae of criminal acts, one may define crime as any conduct which is contrary to criminal law and then formulate an analytic definition of the latter. Sutherland and Cressey again provide an illustration: "The criminal law . . . is defined conventionally as a body of specific rules regarding human conduct which have been promulgated by political authority, which apply uniformly to all members of the classes to which the rules refer, and which are enforced by punishment administered by the state."[9]

Of the four essential characteristics of crime singled out in the above definition—politicality, penal sanction, specificity, uniformity—the first two are incorporated in most other "analytic" definitions. However, even if one grants

7/Raffaele Garofalo, *Criminology* (Boston: Little, Brown, and Co., 1914), Chapter I.

8/Edwin H. Sutherland and Donald R. Cressey, *Principles of Criminology,* 6th ed. (Chicago: J. B. Lippincott, 1960), 11-14.

9/Sutherland and Cressey, *op. cit.,* 4.

that politicality and penal sanctions are in some way essential characteristics of criminal laws, the two concepts do not yield to a definition which is applicable cross-culturally. The notion of politicality is closely wedded to the concept state, which is, as suggested earlier, more vague and more subject to ethnocentric connotations than is criminal law itself; and the problem of distinguishing "penal" from "non-penal" sanctions in a cross-cultural context borders on the impossible. Further, it is not clear how politicality and penal sanctions (or uniformity and specificity for that matter) distinguish criminal from tort law.

A DEFINITION OF LAW

Any definition should recognize not only that crimes are acts contrary to law but also that, at least in some societies, not all such acts are crimes. Stated otherwise, crimes are acts contrary to criminal law and not laws in general. Accordingly, before one can formulate a definition of criminal law, it is necessary to first define "law" in its generic sense; and, when attempting to do so, it becomes obvious that the term is most ambiguous. The literature on the subject leads to one inescapable conclusion—authorities on jurisprudence do not agree in their conceptions of law,[10] not even positive law—and the situation is further complicated by the difficulties of extending any commonly accepted definition to non-Western societies, non-literate ones in particular.

In terms of cross-cultural applicability, Max Weber's definition of law deserves special consideration.

> An order will be called *law* if it is externally guaranteed by the probability that coercion (physical or psychological), to bring about conformity or avenge violation, will be applied by a *staff* of people holding specially ready for that purpose.[11]

Weber's definition is consistent with the opinions of two authorities on comparative law, Hoebel and Diamond,[12] but it needs extension and clarification.

Observe first of all that the term "order" is a very abstract notion, and one that is left vague in Weber's treatment of legal phenomena. The term "norm" could be substituted, but it has a general meaning not entirely consistent with a particular feature of laws. . . . The point is that while a law is an evaluation of conduct,[13] it is not always a collective evaluation. It is necessary only that one or more persons in a social unit hold the evaluation, as long as there is a certain kind of reaction to contrary behavior.

10/See H. L. A. Hart, *The Concept of Law* (Oxford: Clarendon Press, 1961), for an excellent summary of the various conceptions of law.

11/Max Rheinstein, *Max Weber on Law in Economy and Society* (Cambridge: Harvard University Press, 1954), 5.

12/E. Adamson Hoebel, *The Law of Primitive Man* (Cambridge: Harvard University Press, 1954), 26-28; and Diamond, *op. cit.*, Chapter XXV.

13/For an extended discussion of the "evaluative" character of law, see A. Vilhelm Lundstedt, *Legal Thinking Revised* (Stockholm: Almquist and Wiksell, 1956).

Although not made explicit, reaction to deviant behavior is a crucial element in Weber's definition. Note at the outset, however, that there may be a reaction to violation or norms other than laws, as, for example, acts contrary to the mores, which means that "legal procedure" is a particular kind of reaction. Contrary to popular opinion, the reaction is not necessarily distinguished by violence or a special kind of punishment, i.e., it is not the content of the sanction which distinguishes legal reactions. Violence and severe punishment may characterize reactions to behavior which is contrary to norms other than laws, and the sanctions applied in legal reactions are too varied to differentiate laws from other norms. The essential characteristic of a legal reaction is that it is made by, to quote Weber again, "a staff of people holding themselves specially ready for that purpose." Stated in terms more commonly employed in contemporary sociology, "legal reactors" are persons in special statuses.

Since the notion of a special status for legal reactors is crucial in distinguishing laws from other types of norms additional observations on the subject are necessary. Further clarification can be achieved by considering a hypothetical situation. Suppose that in a given social unit only "fathers" are expected to react to the rape of their unmarried daughters. Is the norm proscribing rape a law? Certainly "father" represents a status, and in this context only the persons in that status are expected to react. However, while the designation of a particular status definitely means that reaction to deviant behavior is socially organized, it does not follow that the related norm is a law. Reaction to law violations is also organized, but one should recognize that the emergence of legal phenomena means the appearance of a special kind of social organization. The essence of this kind of organization is that the reactors are persons in statuses which do not entail a distinctive social relation to the parties involved in the norm violation (i.e., the deviant and or the person damaged by the norm violation). Thus, in the United States such reactor statuses as sheriff, judge, and prison warden do not entail a distinctive social relation to violators of laws, or the victims; but this is not so where the reactors to deviant conduct represent the husband, father, brother, or master (to mention a few possibilities) of the deviant or the injured person. . . .

Another variable is the content of a legal reaction. Weber's definition makes it clear that the content is not distinctive, beyond the fact that it *may* involve physical force. The point is that any kind of an attempt (including something as mild as an admonition) to secure conformity to or to avenge violation of the evaluation qualifies. But there must be a high probability that such an attempt will be made, a criterion which excludes "dead laws" (unenforced statutes). Further, while in some instances the majority of the violators of the law may not be detected or successfully prosecuted, it is the attempt to avenge violation or otherwise secure conformity that is crucial and not the actual success achieved.[14]

14/The requirement of a high degree of success in the administration of sanctions probably would eliminate a large number of laws in urban societies, such as the United States, where the majority of certain types of crimes known to police are not cleared by an arrest, much less successful prosecution.

Still another essential characteristic of legal reactions is that they are not followed regularly by retaliation on the part of persons other than the individual at whom the reaction is directed. . . .

Finally, one crucial point is ignored entirely in Weber's definition of law. The probability of reaction must be considered separately for two different conditions. As we shall see, violation of some laws results in action by a legal reactor only at the request or with the implied permission of the person damaged by the violation; but reaction to the violation of another type of law may take place with *or* without such a request or implied permission. A statement as to exactly what constitutes a high probability of reaction (or retaliation for reaction) in either condition must await systematic research; nonetheless, one must recognize that the probability of reaction is relative to types of laws.

To summarize, a law is:

1. an evaluation of conduct held by at least one person in a social unit, and
2. a high probability that, on their own initiative or at the request of others, persons in a special status will attempt by coercive or noncoercive means to revenge, rectify, or prevent behavior that is contrary to the evaluation, with
3. a low probability of retaliation by persons other than the individual or individuals at whom the reaction is directed.

SOME COMPARATIVE OBSERVATIONS

. . . .

Of the six societies surveyed in this study,[15] some Eskimo communities probably represented the nearest approximation to a "lawless" social unit. It is doubtful that there was any status among the Eskimo in which the occupants regularly attempted to avenge the violation of a norm by a person who did not stand in any distinctive social relation to them. This conclusion stems not only from accounts of the outcome of deviant acts among the Eskimo but also from the absence of special names for reactors. The only possible legal reactors among the Eskimo were the shamans and persons who executed homicidal recidivists. Shamans did react to deviant conduct, but the regularity of their reaction and whether or not it included the use of force with a law probability of retaliation are open to question. Eskimos who executed homicidal recidivists with "public

15/Cheyenne, Comanche, Eskimo, Ifugao, Kapauku Papuans, and Nuer. Primary sources: K. N. Llewellyn and E. Adamson Hoebel, *The Cheyenne Way* (Norman: University of Oklahoma Press, 1941); E. Adamson Hoebel, *The Political Organization and Law-Ways of the Comanche Indians* (Menasha, Wisconsin: American Anthropological Association, Memoirs, No. 54, 1940); Hoebel, *op. cit.,* Chapter 5 (a survey of reports on the Eskimo); R. F. Barton, *Ifugao Law* (Berkeley: University of California Publications in American Archaeology and Ethnology, Vol. 15, No. 1 (February, 1919); Leopold Pospisil, *Kapauku Papuans and Their Law* (New Haven: Yale University Publications in Anthropology, No. 54, 1958); E. E. Evans-Pritchard, *The Nuer* (Oxford: Clarendon Press, 1940).

approval" did not face retaliation, but often such persons stood in a distinctive social relation (e.g., kinsman) to the deviant and were selected because that relation reduced the probability of retaliation.

Reactor statuses may have existed among the Comanche, Nuer, and Ifugao; but it is questionable if they were "legal reactors" as defined above. The Comanche "champion-at-law" attempted to avenge violations of a norm through force, but such reaction evidently was highly irregular. The reaction of a Nuer "leopard-skin chief" and the Ifugao *monkalun* to deviant behavior may have been fairly regular; but the leopard-skin chief's response did not include the use of physical force, and the coercive quality of reaction by a *monkalun* is debatable. All that can be said with certainty is that persons in these statuses primarily played the role of "go-between" in cases of disputes.

Only among the Cheyenne and the Ijaaj-Pigome confederacy of New Guinea do we have rather clear-cut evidence of laws. Members of the Cheyenne "military associations" regularly enforced certain norms (most of them relating to hunting) even when the deviant did not stand in any special relationship to the association. Further, the reaction frequently involved the use of force, and instances of retaliation evidently were uncommon. What has been said of the Cheyenne military associations also applies to the status of the *tonowi* in the Ijaaj-Pigome confederacy, except the range of reaction to deviant behavior was much greater for the latter.

The above brief survey suggests two conclusions. First, in no case can it be said *without any doubt* that law, as defined above, was absent. Second, it is most probable that a few of the norms in at least some non-literate societies are laws. Consequently, the perennial debate in jurisprudence over the presence of law in non-literate societies is a misdirected polemic. . . . From a cultural perspective, the prevalence of law can be reckoned in terms of the proportion or norms which are laws; but perhaps a more meaningful measure, particularly as far as social organization is concerned, would express the presence of the following: (1) statuses in which the occupants attempt to react to deviant conduct and do so independently of a special social relationship to the persons involved in the norm violations, (2) the regularity of such reactions, and (3) whether or not reaction may involve the use of force with a low probability of retaliation.

CRIMINAL LAW

Even if the above conception of law be accepted, it does not provide a solution to the problem of defining crime. As noted earlier, in some societies not all behavior contrary to law constitutes a crime, and therefore it is necessary to distinguish criminal law from other types of law.[16] Such a distinction can be accomplished in terms of the two major variables which enter into the above

16/Although a variety of different types of law are recognized in jurisprudence, the central problem in this connection appears to be the distinction between criminal and "civil" law.

generic definition of law—(1) evaluations of conduct and (2) the character of reactions to behavior which is contrary to such evaluations.

Like all types of norms, a law is an evaluation of conduct but it need not be a collectively shared evaluation. Further, a particular evaluation may apply to the behavior of only one person, as in the case where two individuals enter into an agreement (express or implied) to perform certain acts or to refrain from committing certain acts. This agreement is an evaluation of conduct, that is, ego believes that alter ought to behave in a certain way, consistent with their agreement. . . .

Criminal law differs from contract law in two respects. First, as an evaluation of conduct, criminal law applies not to particular individuals but rather to an infinite number of individuals in the social unit. Second, whereas a breach of contract results in action by a legal reactor only at the request or with the implied permission of an interested party, a legal reactor may take action when a crime is detected with or without the request of another person.

The possibility of independent action on the part of a legal reactor also distinguishes a crime from a tort. Unlike contract law, both criminal and tort law represent evaluations of conduct which apply to an infinite number of persons;[17] but in the case of tort law a legal reactor will not take action unless requested to do so by the person or persons who claimed to have suffered a damage from the violation of an evaluation of conduct.

The distinctions among contract, tort, and criminal law are organized in a way of a property-space arrangement in Table 1. Observe that the distinctions are drawn in terms of only two differentiae—(1) whether or not a legal reactor may initiate the reaction process and (2) whether the evaluation of conduct applies to particular persons or to an infinite number of persons in the social unit.

The cross-classification of the two dichotomized differentiae yields four classes, one of which is identified as a possible null class. Stated briefly, the rationale for anticipating an empty class is related to the notion of discretion in a legal system. In no society are all acts regulated by law. Whatever the reason, a wide range of behavior is permissive, meaning that actors are free to govern their conduct by their own discretion. One aspect of discretion is to allow persons to enter into an agreement with other persons as to their mutual conduct. While the enforcement of contracts serves to further reciprocity in social relations, the law implicitly recognizes that whether or not a given contract should be enforced is an integral element in such reciprocity. Just as the future goal to be achieved by a contract is a matter of discretion, so is the actual achievement of that goal or its equivalent through enforcement of the contract.

Ethnocentric Criticism of the Taxonomy. Since criticism of analytical definitions of law and related distinctions tends to take a certain direction, some objections to the taxonomy in Table 1 can be anticipated. The most prevalent

17/Consequently, the classical distinction in jurisprudence between rights and duties *in personam* versus *in rem* does not differentiate criminal from tort law.

TABLE 1
A Taxonomy of Laws

	A Legal Reaction* to a Violation of the Evaluation of Conduct Occurs Only at the Request or with the Implied Permission of an Interested Party†	A Legal Reaction to a Violation of the Evaluation of Conduct May Occur without the Request or Implied Permission of an Interested Party
The Evaluation of Conduct‡ Applies to an Infinite Number of Persons in the Social Unit with or without Their Acceptance of the Obligation.	Tort Law	Criminal Law
The Evaluation of Conduct Applies Only to Those Persons in the Social Unit Who Have by Agreement Accepted the Obligation.	Contract Law	Possible Empirical Null Class

*See text for a description of a legal reaction.
†Any person who claims damages as a consequence of the violation or someone who stands in a special social relation (e.g., kinsman) to such a person.
‡The belief that one *ought* or ought not behave in a certain way.

criticism, and certainly the most relevant one in this case, is that analytical definitions must "fit" the legal system which the critic takes as his point of reference, typically that of his own country. Thus, if a particular statute, legal procedure, cause of action, etc., is identified as "criminal law" in the analytical scheme but not so in the critic's own legal system, then the scheme is judged invalid.

A more ethnocentric evaluation of a definition or a taxonomy scarcely could be imagined. The whole purpose of an analytical approach is to avoid *ad hoc,* particularistic conceptions of legal phenomena. Even the words crime, tort, contract, etc., can be and perhaps should be abandoned, because they are found only in Anglo-American law. Indeed, speculation as to why some legal phenomenon is identified as tort rather than criminal or contract law cannot possibly extend beyond English-speaking nations. . . .

ADDITIONAL COMPARATIVE OBSERVATIONS

Although the quality of the data again precludes any definite conclusions, it appears highly probable that criminal law did not exist among the Comanche, Eskimo, Ifugao, or Nuer. This judgment stems in part from evidence that these four societies, and the Eskimo in particular, may not have had any type of law, criminal or otherwise. Even if one grants the existence of law in the other three cases, there is little evidence of criminal law. Specifically, whatever may have been the typical reaction of a Comanche champion-at-law, an Ifugao *monkalun*, and a Nuer leopard-skin chief to norm violations, it took place only at the request or with the implied permission of the injured party. Accordingly, insofar as these three societies had any law at all, it was restricted to contracts and torts.

Just as laws definitely prevailed in the Ijaaj-Pigome confederacy and among the Cheyenne, so it is equally certain that at least some criminal laws were present in both societies. However, there is one very important difference between the two. There appears to have been only a few criminal laws in the confederacy, i.e., in most instances of norm violation a *tonowi* reacted only if an interested party requested it.[18] This is consistent with the theory that criminal law emerged from tort law, but observations on the Cheyenne cast doubt on the idea. There were "mediator" statuses among the Cheyenne in which persons reacted to deviant conduct at the request of an interested party; but a reaction which included the use of coercion with a low probability of retaliation probably was peculiar to the military associations, whose major function apparently was the enforcement of criminal law as defined above. Stated generally, what we have in the case of the Cheyenne is a limited number of definite criminal laws but few if any tort laws, which is contrary to the theory that the former evolved from the latter. Also relevant, tort law was far more conspicuous in the Ijaaj-Pigome confederacy than it was among the Cheyennes; but the members of the confederacy were agriculturalists and the Cheyenne were predominantly hunters. The criminal laws among the Cheyenne may have been due to the circumstance activities (i.e., the need to maintain strict control of hunting); but if so, the absence of criminal law among the Comanche is clearly contrary to the explanation. In any event, it appears that the presence or prevalence of criminal law in a society is not easily explained in terms of conventional evolutionary notions. There may be some very general evolutionary patterns in legal phenomena, such as those recently reported by Schwartz and Miller,[19] but the present findings suggest that numerous societies may not conform.[20] As a matter of research strategy, the search for patterns should await achievement of greater conceptual precision in the sociology of law and detailed studies of those societies for which we have reasonably good data.

18/In his description of norms and reaction to deviant behavior in the Ijaaj-Pigome confederacy, Pospisil (*op. cit.*) does not state explicitly that a *tonowi* may react without the request or implied permission of the injured party, but some of his observations suggest that such reaction does apply for a few norms.

19/Richard D. Schwartz and James C. Miller, "Legal evolution and Societal Complexity," *American Journal of Sociology*, LXX (September, 1964), 159-69.

20/Significantly, the Crow Indians, who were very similar socially and culturally to the Cheyenne, appear as an exception to the pattern found by Schwartz and Miller.

34. Violence in Chicago: Rights in Conflict*

THE WALKER REPORT

Democratic National Convention Week in Chicago (1968) represented a microcosm of social, political, and international tensions. It brought war antagonists, police representatives, legitimate delegates, political dissidents, social critics, suppressed minorities, and poverty group representatives, among others, together in a political forum influenced simultaneously by hope and despair (*see* Lohman, Article 35). Consequently, the events surrounding the convention were no ordinary events, for they included all the frustrations and pent-up emotions produced by the struggle between those who would define new alternatives and restructure society and those who would minimize major changes in political and social structures. The shock of the Vietnam Tet offensive, the assassinations of the black and white leaders of social change (Martin Luther King, Jr., and Robert F. Kennedy), the frustrations brought due to unresponsive political leaders, the earlier police use of force against Chicago peace marchers, the provocative news releases by establishment and dissident leaders preceding the convention, and the despair encouraged by the inability of political units to solve questions of poverty came to a head in the Chicago violence.

Although the Walker Report lacks scientific preciseness, it offers a valuable insight into the consequences of interactional and emotional contagion. Both establishment and dissident representatives admit that the number bent on confrontation with the police was a definite minority of the total group which gathered to protest real or imagined injustices. Nevertheless, the Chicago events vividly illustrate how the goal of police-protestor confrontation, planned by a revolutionary minority, may be realized when both antagonists are manipulated through collective behavior to irresponsible actions. When emotion obscured reasoned discipline, both camps engaged in irresponsible conduct. Normative leaders lost control to leaders representing the extremes. General conduct norms were subsequently neutralized; the norms of confrontation took their place. And yet, the majority of the police and the dissidents maintained a level of restraint which prevented bloodshed.

Although the following selection from the report, entitled *Rights in Conflict,* reportedly written by Chicago Investigating Commission Director Daniel Walker,

*The Violent Confrontation of Demonstrators and Police in Parks and Streets of Chicago during the Week of the Democratic National Convention of 1968—for National Commission on the Causes and Prevention of Violence. Walker Report—Foreword and Summary.

a recognized member of the Chicago establishment, describes the context of the basic conflict, students of emotional contagion and social change should review the complete document. Chicago, the director claims, witnessed a police riot. The mace and club attacks by policemen on peaceful demonstrators, innocent bystanders, newsmen, photographers, and Chicago residents, he finds, were largely senseless and malicious. If the police are not held accountable for their actions, the fundamental order of society is in question.

Police-community tensions, especially toward minorities, have been common (*see* Reiss, Article 21). But Chicago brought a new dimension of the individual rights-police power struggle to public attention. Suddenly, middle class youth and dissidents were engrossed in confrontation with the police for the whole world to see. If nothing else, the events in Chicago suggest that the use of excessive force by the police merely escalates the level of police-protestor confrontation, undermines the enforcement's societal maintenance responsibilities, and still is unable to guarantee social peace in the long run. The confrontation at Chicago ceased when its reason for being, the Democratic National Convention, was terminated by adjournment.

FOREWORD

The right to dissent is fundamental to democracy. But the expression of that right has become one of the most serious problems in contemporary democratic government. That dilemma was dramatized in Chicago during the Democratic National Convention of 1968—the dilemma of a city coping with the expression of dissent.

Unlike other recent big city riots, including those in Chicago itself, the events of convention week did not consist of looting and burning, followed by mass arrests. To a shocking extent they consisted of crowd-police battles in the parks as well as the streets. And the shock was intensified by the presence in the crowds (which included some anarchists and revolutionaries) of large numbers of innocent dissenting citizens.

The initial response, precipitated by dramatic television coverage, was a horrified condemnation of city and police. When demonstrators compared the Chicago police to the Soviet troops then occupying Prague, news commentators sympathetically relayed that comparison to the world. Not since Birmingham and Selma had there been so heated a mood of public outrage.

An immediate counterresponse, however, expressed the feeling that the demonstrators got what they deserved, and the thinking that the city had no alternative. Many observers thought that, in view of the provocation and the circumstances, police had performed admirably and with restraint.

The commentary far outlasted the convention. Major writers in some of the world's most respected periodicals denounced the city, the police, and the Democratic leaders. For its part, the City of Chicago issued "The Strategy of Confrontation," a paper detailing the threat to the city, itemizing provocations, describing a battery of bizarre weapons allegedly intended for use against law enforcement officers, and charging the American news media with biased coverage. The city also prepared a one-hour film shown nationally on television.

These conflicting responses, and the nature of the dilemma imposed upon Chicago, make this study necessary. Our purpose is to present the facts so that thoughtful readers can decide what lessons come out of them; for it is urgent that any such lessons be speedily incorporated into American public life. The *Chicago Tribune* began its special report on convention week with the line, "Not everyone wins." They might have added that there are circumstances in which *no one* wins, in which everyone loses. Such circumstances make up this report.

We have addressed ourselves to questions like the following. What were the objectives of the planned demonstrations, and who planned them? How did the city prepare itself? What types of people made up the crowds in the parks? Were physical and verbal attacks typical of demonstrator behavior? And did they precipitate police violence or follow it? Was the clubbing done by a few tired policemen goaded into "over-reacting," or was there large-scale police brutality? Is there evidence that newsmen were singled out for assault? Was Chicago itself conducive to violence, or was it merely where the convention, and the cameras, happened to be?

We believe we have laid a factual foundation for meaningful answers to those questions.

Our charge was not to decide what ought to have been done, or to balance the rights and wrongs, or to recommend a course of action for the future. Having sought out the facts, we intend to let them speak for themselves. But we urge the reader, in assessing these facts, to bear in mind that the physical confrontations in Chicago will be repeated elsewhere until we learn to deal with the dilemma they represent.

In principle at least, most Americans acknowledge the right to dissent. And, in principle at least, most dissenters acknowledge the right of a city to protect its citizens and its property. But what happens when these undeniable rights are brought—deliberately by some—into conflict?

Convention week in Chicago is what happens, and the challenge it brings is plain: to keep *peaceful assembly* from becoming a contradiction in terms.

. . . .

SUMMARY

During the week of the Democratic National Convention, the Chicago police were the targets of mounting provocation by both word and act. It took the form of obscene epithets, and of rocks, sticks, bathroom tiles and even human feces hurled at police by demonstrators. Some of these acts had been planned; others were spontaneous or were themselves provoked by police action. Furthermore, the police had been put on edge by widely published threats of attempts to disrupt both the city and the convention.

That was the nature of the provocation. The nature of the response was unrestrained and indiscriminate police violence on many occasions, particularly at night.

That violence was made all the more shocking by the fact that it was often inflicted upon persons who had broken no law, disobeyed no order, made no threat. These included peaceful demonstrators, onlookers, and large numbers of residents who were simply passing through, or happened to live in, the areas where confrontations were occurring.

Newsmen and photographers were singled out for assault, and their equipment deliberately damaged. Fundamental police training was ignored; and officers, when on the scene, were often unable to control their men. As one police officer put it: "What happened didn't have anything to do with police work."

The violence reached its culmination on Wednesday night.

A report prepared by an inspector from the Los Angeles Police Department, present as an official observer, while generally praising the police restraint he had observed in the parks during the week, said this about the events that night:

> There is no question but that many officers acted without restraint and exerted force beyond that necessary under the circumstances. The leadership at the point of conflict did little to prevent such conduct and the direct control of officers by first line supervisors was virtually non-existent.

He is referring to the police-crowd confrontation in front of the Conrad Hilton Hotel. Most Americans know about it, having seen the 17-minute sequence played and replayed on their television screens.

But most Americans do not know that the confrontation was followed by even more brutal incidents in the Loop side streets. Or that it had been preceded by comparable instances of indiscriminate police attacks on the North Side a few nights earlier when demonstrators were cleared from Lincoln Park and pushed into the streets and alleys of Old Town.

How did it start? With the emergence long before convention week of three factors which figured significantly in the outbreak of violence. These were: threats to the city; the city's response; and the conditioning of Chicago police to expect that violence against demonstrators, as against rioters, would be condoned by city officials.

The threats to the city were varied. Provocative and inflammatory statements, made in connection with activities planned for convention week, were published and widely disseminated. There were also intelligence reports from informants.

Some of this information was absurd, like the reported plan to contaminate the city's water supply with LSD. But some were serious; and both were strengthened by the authorities' lack of any mechanism for distinguishing one from the other.

The second factor—the city's response—matched, in numbers and logistics at least, the demonstrators' threats.

The city, fearful that the "leaders" would not be able to control their followers, attempted to discourage an inundation of demonstrators by not granting permits for marches and rallies and by making it quite clear that the "law" would be enforced.

Government—federal, state and local—moved to defend itself from the threats, both imaginary and real. The preparations were detailed and far ranging: from stationing firemen at each alarm box within a six block radius of the Ampitheatre to staging U.S. Army armored personnel carriers in Soldier Field under Secret Service control. Six thousand Regular Army troops in full field gear, equipped with rifles, flame throwers, and bazookas were airlifted to Chicago on Monday, August 26. About 6,000 Illinois National Guard troops had already been activated to assist the 12,000 member Chicago Police Force.

Of course, the Secret Service could never afford to ignore threats of assassination of Presidential candidates. Neither could the city, against the background of riots in 1967 and 1968, ignore the ever-present threat of ghetto riots, possibly sparked by large numbers of demonstrators, during convention week.

The third factor emerged in the city's position regarding the riots following the death of Dr. Martin Luther King and the April 27th peace march to the Civic Center in Chicago.

The police were generally credited with restraint in handling the first riots—but Mayor Daley rebuked the Superintendent of Police. While it was later modified, his widely disseminated "shoot to kill arsonists and shoot to maim looters" order undoubtedly had an effect.

The effect on police became apparent several weeks later, when they attacked demonstrators, bystanders and media representatives at a Civic Center peace march. There were published criticisms—but the city's response was to ignore the police violence.

That was the background. On August 18, 1968, the advance contingent of demonstrators arrived in Chicago and established their base, as planned, in Lincoln Park on the city's Near North Side. Throughout the week, they were joined by others—some from the Chicago area, some from states as far away as New York and California. On the weekend before the convention began, there were about 2,000 demonstrators in Lincoln Park; the crowd grew to about 10,000 by Wednesday.

There were, of course, the hippies—the long hair and love beads, the calculated unwashedness, the flagrant banners, the open lovemaking and disdain for the constraints of conventional society. In dramatic effect, both visual and vocal, these dominated a crowd whose members actually differed widely in physical appearance, in motivation, in political affiliation, in philosophy. The crowd included Yippies come to "do their thing," youngsters working for a political candidate, professional people with dissenting political views, anarchists and determined revolutionaries, motorcycle gangs, black activists, young thugs, police and secret service undercover agents. There were demonstrators waving the Viet Cong flag and the red flag of revolution and there were the simply curious who came to watch and, in many cases, became willing or unwilling participants.

To characterize the crowd, then, as entirely hippy-Yippie, entirely "New Left," entirely anarchist, or entirely youthful political dissenters is both wrong and dangerous. The stereotyping that did occur helps to explain the emotional reaction of both police and public during and after the violence that occurred.

Despite the presence of some revolutionaries, the vast majority of the demonstrators were intent on expressing by peaceful means their dissent either from society generally or from the administration's policies in Vietnam.

Most of those intending to join the major protest demonstrations scheduled during convention week did not plan to enter the Ampitheatre and disrupt the proceedings of the Democratic convention, did not plan aggressive acts of physical provocation against the authorities, and did not plan to use rallies of demonstrators to stage an assault against any person, institution, or place of business. But while it is clear that most of the protesters in Chicago had no intention of initiating violence, this is not to say that they did not expect it to develop.

It was the clearing of the demonstrators from Lincoln Park that led directly to the violence: symbolically, it expressed the city's opposition to the protesters; literally, it forced the protesters into confrontation with police in Old Town and the adjacent residential neighborhoods.

The Old Town area near Lincoln Park was a scene of police ferocity exceeding that shown on television on Wednesday night. From Sunday night through Tuesday night, incidents of intense and indiscriminate violence occurred in the streets after police had swept the park clear of demonstrators.

Demonstrators attacked too. And they posed difficult problems for police as they persisted in marching through the streets, blocking traffic and intersections. But it was the police who forced them out of the park and into the neighborhood. And on the part of the police there was enough wild club swinging, enough cries of hatred, enough gratuitous beating to make the conclusion inescapable that individual policemen, and lots of them, committed violent acts far in excess of the requisite force for crowd dispersal or arrest. To read dispassionately the hundreds of statements describing at firsthand the events of Sunday and Monday nights is to become convinced of the presence of what can only be called a police riot.

Here is an eyewitness talking about Monday night:

> The demonstrators were forced out onto Clark Street and once again a traffic jam developed. Cars were stopped, the horns began to honk, people

couldn't move, people got gassed inside their cars, people got stoned inside their cars, police were the objects of stones, and taunts, mostly taunts. As you must understand, most of the taunting of the police was verbal. There were stones thrown of course, but for the most part it was verbal. But there were stones being thrown and of course the police were responding with tear gas and clubs and everytime they could get near enough to a demonstrator they hit him.

But again you had this police problem within—this really turned into a police problem. They pushed everybody out of the park, but this night there were a lot more people in the park than there had been during the previous night and Clark Street was just full of people and in addition now was full of gas because the police were using gas on a much larger scale this night. So the police were faced with the task, which took them about an hour or so, of hitting people over the head and gassing them enough to get them out of Clark Street, which they did.

But police action was not confined to the necessary force, even in clearing the park:

A young man and his girl friend were both grabbed by officers. He screamed, "We're going, we're going," but they threw him into the pond. The officers grabbed the girl, knocked her to the ground, dragged her along the embankment and hit her with their batons on her head, arms, back and legs. The boy tried to scramble up the embankment to her, but police shoved him back in the water at least twice. He finally got to her and tried to pull her in the water, away from the police. He was clubbed on the head five or six times. An officer shouted, "Let's get the fucking bastards!" but the boy pulled her in the water and the police left.

Like the incident described above, much of the violence witnessed in Old Town that night seems malicious or mindless:

There were pedestrians. People who were not part of the demonstration were coming out of a tavern to see what the demonstration was . . . and the officers indiscriminately started beating everybody on the street who was not a policeman.

Another scene:

There was a group of about six police officers that moved in and started beating two youths. When one of the officers pulled back his nightstick to swing, one of the youths grabbed it from behind and started beating on the officer. At this point about ten officers left everybody else and ran after this youth, who turned down Wells and ran to the left.

But the officers went to the right, picked up another youth, assuming he was the one they were chasing, and took him into an empty lot and beat him. And when they got him to the ground, they just kicked him ten times—the wrong youth, the innocent youth who had been standing there.

A federal legal official relates an experience of Tuesday evening.

> I then walked one block north where I met a group of 12 to 15 policemen. I showed them my identification and they permitted me to walk with them. The police walked one block west. Numerous people were watching us from their windows and balconies. The police yelled profanities at them, taunting them to come down where the police would beat them up. The police stopped a number of people on the street demanding identification. They verbally abused each pedestrian and pushed one or two without hurting them. We walked back to Clark Street and began to walk north where the police stopped a number of people who appeared to be protesters, and ordered them out of the area in a very abusive way. One protester who was walking in the opposite direction was kneed in the groin by a policeman who was walking towards him. The boy fell to the ground and swore at the policeman who picked him up and threw him to the ground. We continued to walk toward the command post. A derelict who appeared to be very intoxicated, walked up to the policeman and mumbled something that was incoherent. The policeman pulled from his belt a tin container and sprayed its contents into the eyes of the derelict, who stumbled around and fell on his face.

It was on these nights that the police violence against media representatives reached its peak. Much of it was plainly deliberate. A newsman was pulled aside on Monday by a detective acquaintance of his who said: "The word is being passed to get newsmen." Individual newsmen were warned, "You take my picture tonight and I'm going to get you." Cries of "get the camera" preceded individual attacks on photographers.

A newspaper photographer describes Old Town on Monday at about 9:00 P.M.:

> When the people arrived at the intersection of Wells and Division, they were not standing in the streets. Suddenly a column of policemen ran out from the alley. They were reinforcements. They were under control but there seemed to be no direction. One man was yelling, "Get them up on the sidewalks, turn them around." Very suddenly the police charged the people on the sidewalks and began beating their heads. A line of cameramen was "trapped" along with the crowd along the sidewalks, and the police went down the line chopping away at the cameras.

A network cameraman reports that on the same night:

> I just saw this guy coming at me with his nightstick and I had the camera up. The tip of his stick hit me right in the mouth, then I put my tongue up there and I noticed that my tooth was gone. I turned around then to try to leave and then this cop came up behind me with his stick and he jabbed me in the back.

All of a sudden these cops jumped out of the police cars and started just beating the hell out of people. And before anything else happened to me, I saw a man holding a Bell & Howell camera with big wide letters on it, saying "CBS." He apparently had been hit by a cop. And cops were standing around and there was blood streaming down his face. Another policeman was running after me and saying, "Get the fuck out of here." And I heard another guy scream, "Get their fucking cameras." And the next thing I know I was being hit on the head, and I think on the back, and I was just forced down on the ground at the corner of Division and Wells.

If the intent was to discourage coverage, it was successful in at least one case. A photographer from a news magazine says that finally, "I just stopped shooting, because every time you push the flash, they look at you and they are screaming about, 'Get the fucking photographers and get the film.' "

There is some explanation for the media-directed violence. Camera crews on at least two occasions did stage violence and fake injuries. Demonstrators did sometimes step up their activities for the benefit of TV cameras. Newsmen and photographers' blinding lights did get in the way of police clearing streets, sweeping the park and dispersing demonstrators. Newsmen did, on occasion, disobey legitimate police orders to "move" or "clear the streets." News reporting of events did seem to the police to be anti-Chicago and anti-police.

But was the response appropriate to the provocation?

Out of 300 newsmen assigned to cover the parks and streets of Chicago during convention week, more than 60 (about 20%) were involved in incidents resulting in injury to themselves, damage to their equipment, or their arrest. Sixty-three newsmen were physically attacked by police; in 13 of these instances, photographic or recording equipment was intentionally damaged.

The violence did not end with either demonstrators or newsmen on the North Side on Sunday, Monday and Tuesday. It continued in Grant Park on Wednesday. It occurred on Michigan Avenue in front of the Conrad Hilton Hotel, as already described. A high-ranking Chicago police commander admits that on that occasion the police "got out of control." This same commander appears in one of the most vivid scenes of the entire week, trying desperately to keep individual policemen from beating demonstrators as he screams, "For Christ's sake, stop it!"

Thereafter, the violence continued on Michigan Avenue and on the side streets running into Chicago's Loop. A federal official describes how it began:

I heard a 10-1 call [policeman in trouble] on either my radio or one of the other hand sets carried by men with me and then heard "Car 100—sweep." With a roar of motors, squads, vans and three-wheelers came from east, west and north into the block north of Jackson. The crowd scattered. A big group ran west on Jackson, with a group of blue shirted policemen in pursuit, beating at them with clubs. Some of the crowd would jump into doorways and the police would rout them out. The action was very tough. In my judgment, unnecessarily so. The police were hitting with a vengeance and quite obviously with relish. . . .

What followed was a club-swinging melee. Police ranged the streets striking anyone they could catch. To be sure, demonstrators threw things at policemen and at police cars; but the weight of violence was overwhelmingly on the side of the police. A few examples will give the flavor of that night in Chicago:

"At the corner of Congress Plaza and Michigan," states a doctor, "was gathered a group of people, numbering between thirty and forty. They were trapped against a railing [along a ramp leading down from Michigan Avenue to an underground parking garage] by several policemen on motorcycles. The police charged the people on motorcycles and struck about a dozen of them, knocking several of them down. About twenty standing there jumped over the railing. On the other side of the railing was a three-to-four-foot drop. None of the people who were struck by the motorcycles appeared to be seriously injured. However, several of them were limping as if they had been run over on their feet."

A UPI reporter witnessed these attacks, too. He relates in his statement that one officer, "with a smile on his face and a fanatical look in his eyes, was standing on a three-wheel cycle, shouting, 'Wahoo, wahoo,' and trying to run down people on the sidewalk." The reporter says he was chased thirty feet by the cycle.

A priest who was in the crowd says he saw a "boy, about fourteen or fifteen, white, standing on top of an automobile yelling something which was unidentifiable. Suddenly a policeman pulled him down from the car and beat him to the ground by striking him three or four times with a nightstick. Other police joined in . . . and they eventually shoved him to a police van.

"A well-dressed woman saw this incident and spoke angrily to a nearby police captain. As she spoke, another policeman came up from behind her and sprayed something in her face with an aerosol can. He then clubbed her to the ground. He and two other policemen then dragged her along the ground to the same paddy wagon and threw her in."

"I ran west on Jackson," a witness states. "West of Wabash, a line of police stretching across both sidewalks and the street charged after a small group I was in. Many people were clubbed and maced as they ran. Some weren't demonstrators at all, but were just pedestrians who didn't know how to react to the charging officers yelling 'Police!' "

"A wave of police charged down Jackson," another witness relates. "Fleeing demonstrators were beaten indiscriminately and a temporary, makeshift first aid station was set up on the corner of State and Jackson. Two men lay in pools of blood, their heads severely cut by clubs. A minister moved amongst the crowd, quieting them, brushing aside curious onlookers, and finally asked a policeman to call an ambulance, which he agreed to do. . . ."

An Assistant U.S. Attorney later reported that "the demonstrators were running as fast as they could but were unable to get out of the way because of the crowds in front of them. I observed the police striking numerous individuals, perhaps 20 to 30. I saw three fall down and then overrun by the police. I observed two demonstrators who had multiple cuts on their heads. We assisted one who was in shock into a passer-by's car."

Police violence was a fact of convention week. Were the policemen who committed it a minority? It appears certain that they were—but one which has imposed some of the consequences of its actions on the majority, and certainly on their commanders. There has been no public condemnation of these violators of sound police procedures and common decency by either their commanding officers or city officials. Nor (at the time this Report is being completed—almost three months after the convention) has any disciplinary action been taken against most of them. That some policemen lost control of themselves under exceedingly provocative circumstances can perhaps be understood; but not condoned. If no action is taken against them, the effect can only be to discourage the majority of policemen who acted responsibly, and further weaken the bond between police and community.

Although the crowds were finally dispelled on the nights of violence in Chicago, the problems they represent have not been. Surely this is not the last time that a violent dissenting group will clash head-on with those whose duty it is to enforce the law. And the next time the whole world will still be watching.

35. Crises of a Society in Ferment*

JOSEPH D. LOHMAN

In the decades following World War II and the Korean War, a variety of local, national, and international protest movements have created headlines. As several movements moved their protest beyond the bounds of constitutional legitimacy and into areas of excessive disturbance and even criminal violation, negative public and government response began to coalesce. When the focus changed from an attack upon an alleged unjust law to overt antisocial behavior, the population tended to polarize between definitive extremes. Because issues of race, morality of war, civil liberties, personal freedom, and individual achievement were intermixed, the ensuing polarization took place on several different levels simultaneously. On one dimension, polarization occurred in black and white attitudes; on another in liberal-conservative tensions; on still a

*Reprinted from *Crime and Delinquency*, Volume 14, Number 1 (January, 1968), pp. 31-41, with the permission of the editors.

third in police-student hostility. The black-white polarization, for example, took the form of a white racist appeal to join in the forceful establishment of "law and order" and a "Wallace line" against black intrusion, on the one extreme, and a black extremist demand for a ghetto revolt and a burning of "white" America on the other. Meanwhile, the moderate position was buffeted and compromised by the hate and emotion which such attitudes generate. But this is only one example.

Whether in this form or in the form discussed rather unscientifically in the previous selection (*see* Article 34) from the Walker Report on the Chicago disorders during the week of the Democratic National Convention (1968), polarization continues. However, extremist antagonisms, on the right or on the left, are primarily symptoms of the diverse problems brought about by social change. Because a mass society is a composite of diverse political, theoretical, self, humanitarian, or other interests, competing and often conflicting groups work to maximize their vested interests by influencing power-legitimating agencies. However, no extremist group has yet been able to convince the American population that its polar position should become the public's position, since responsible political and community leadership has moved with variable speed to find solutions to ghetto existence, police abuse of power, protestor attempts to restructure institutions, or governmental intransigence. However, these problems are not quickly solved. The reallocation of resources, the retraining of law enforcement officials, the modification of public attitudes, and the education of minority members, among other needs, often involve generational and attitudinal modifications which transcend the potential changes brought about by the inauguration of immediate or short-term programs.

Because the system of criminal justice is designed to maintain the existing social structure and system, it is inevitably under attack by protestors. Of necessity, it supports those in power in order that they might maintain the structure and stability of society. Consequently, the legislature, enforcement agencies, and the courts tend to support the status quo rather than assume the leadership of social change. The fact that the U.S. Supreme Court has expanded its historic maintenance function to include a change-initiating responsibility has predictably added to its criticism.

Modern crises, the late criminologist and former sheriff Joseph D. Lohman suggests, will not be resolved successfully until the organization and administration of all agencies involved in criminal justice are revised (*see* Bilek, Article 22; and Lemert, Article 26). Law enforcement, correction, welfare and other "helping and service agency" tensions imply that traditional services often have little meaning to that segment of the population to which they are offered and only serve to estrange large sections of the public from their intended functions and goals (*see* Bennett, Article 27; National Profile, Article 28; and Toby, Article 32). Protest, like violence (*see* introduction to Article 7), is a social mechanism which is often used to point out existing social dysfunctions that need correction.

Our institutions are too frequently alienated and estranged from people rather than necessarily the reverse. Our traditional public services do not reflect the changing social scene. So, we have a crisis in education, a crisis in welfare, a crisis in law enforcement, and a crisis in correction. The dilemma of our institutions, such as the school, welfare, criminal justice, is expressed—loud and clear—in the protests of the day, any day, day to day. Along with the *revolt of the Negro* and the *revolt of youth,* we have a whole series of more specific protests expressed in petitions for new legislation, for a new philosophy and orientation on the part of the organized society and its instrumentalities. We face the *revolt of the clients,* which we see reported in the daily press as the request by the poor for a role in the decisions affecting them. . . .

. . . The revolt of the clients is manifest in the attitude they take toward the school, toward welfare, toward police, toward correctional agencies. And we also have the *revolt of the aged.* The newly emergent power of our "senior citizenry" made Medicare a reality. The widespread incidence of new institutional methods at local community levels to deal with this subgroup indicates that there has emerged a recognizable voice and revolt of these elements. They are a new power, to be reckoned with, even in the most conservative legislative chambers. Then, we have a *revolt of the blue-collar workers* out of the deprivation and desperation brought on by changing technology-automation. We face not only a revolution in education because of inadequacy of educational organization and structure, but a *revolt of the teachers.* Many of the teachers are on the side of the pupils because they see that they cannot effectively reach them in the traditional setup. So we have the spectacle of the embattled school system throughout the United States, along with the crisis of civil rights and of the welfare institutions.

We have a general *revolt of our urban population,* protesting against traditional structures. Cities are demanding the reconstitution of legislatures so that they can solve their problems through representative assemblies responsive to their needs and conditions. They are demanding recognition of their disproportionately increasing influence in the social order. The cities are taking on the traditional rural electorate in the legislatures, and the Supreme Court has sided with them in asking for reapportionment. However, all the Supreme Court has done is to follow the election returns. It has recognized the emergence of a new center of power.

OUR VIEW OF OUR VIEW

What relationship does all this have to delinquency and crime? It confronts us bluntly with the crux of the matter: the need for a critical examination of the institutionalized means by which we view and address our problems. Our social organizations and institutions are not things external to us—*they are the way in which we see our problems, work at our tasks, and address the world. They are our view of our view of the problem.* Yes, our view of our view of the problem.

Here is the root of the crisis. This is why it becomes so important that, in training individuals for new tasks and with new techniques, we train them *in context*. We must make it possible for them to act according to their new insights and their new directives and possibilities. . . .

Our view of our view of the problem of delinquency and crime is the condition of our work and of our addressing the problem, and the way we look at this condition of addressing the problem. Richard McGee, agency administrator for correction in California, speaking before a Senate subcommittee in support of a federal commission to deal with the crisis in manpower in the field of correctional administration, urged recognition of a few basic facts:

> First, crime and delinquency rates throughout the country are increasing faster than the population. Second, we are spending great sums of money on old procedures which appear to be poorly adapted to our changing society. With increasing industrialization of our production processes, our population is becoming more and more concentrated in great metropolitan contexts, thus creating social and economic conditions which make the management of the crime and delinquency problem increasingly difficult. Many thousands of young people in their middle teens are being badly damaged by criminal activity and the way in which it is being addressed. The problem of meeting the educational needs of thousands of youth who drop out of school before they have reached their achievement potential has become one of the great challenges of our time. Our correctional schools and prisons are crowded to the breaking point. Local probation services for offenders not institutionalized are scandalously undermanned. Our institutions of higher learning, while literally bulging with students, are producing a woefully inadequate supply of professional workers trained and motivated to carry out the correctional mission. The entire establishment for dealing with the prevention, control, and correction of offenders against the law must be re-examined in the light of new knowledge and the demands of the changing society we live in today.

If he had been a person from the ranks of those who frown upon prevention and rehabilitation and subscribe to the use of punitive sanctions in dealing with offenders, he could not have laid down a more damning indictment than the language he employed. For he suggested, as indicated in his final words, that we must re-examine, in the light of new knowledge and the demands of a changing society, our *entire establishment* of dealing with the prevention, control, and correction of offenders against the law. The re-examination he bespeaks is a challenge to all centers of research and education, to all colleges and institutions of higher learning generally, with reference to the production, on the basis of our developing knowledge of the behavioral sciences, of a point of view, procedures, and methods more relevant to our task than those currently in use.

We give service to many myths in the very character of our institutional preparation of personnel and the tasks to which we assign them. We service myths inbred in most of the population of the United States. We on the firing line, by the way we nurture these myths, are party to them.

The foremost myth says we handle crime with all the techniques developed by our most advanced knowledge. Most of us are happy that in our individual programs, we are experimenting with new methods such as halfway houses or group therapies. We borrow from neighboring colleges and universities research methodologies and an occasional experimental design. The fact is that when one looks at law enforcement and the correctional system in the United States, the most one can say is that it is a massive program of law enforcement and correctional housekeeping. For all practical purposes we are only *warehousing* the problem. . . .

The character of our law enforcement and correctional systems is produced mainly by sheer numbers, with no corresponding expansion of facilities in relation to the enormous increase in crime and our failure to receive commitments from the community to keep abreast of it. We struggle desperately to keep our ancient and failing institutions abreast of crime, while we make limited gestures in the direction of a few innovations and experiments. . . .

HOSTILITY OF PHILOSOPHIES

We all subscribe to another myth we know to be untrue: that the criminal and the delinquent are treated in singular perspective in American society. We have only to inspect the antithetical views of the crime problem entertained by the professionals in the field—the crime preventers, the crime catchers, the crime disposers, the crime keepers, and the crime treaters. . . .

Crime catchers are concerned with apprehending the offender. That is their function and responsibility, but their view of the offender is more largely a function of their mission and their task than a reflection of a common fund of knowledge or generalizations derived from the behavioral sciences. The crime preventers and the crime catchers, each in some measure exposed to pre-service education, even collegiate in character, do not come to their tasks with a *common commitment,* with reference to the nature of crime and the offender, to guard against the views that may develop as a result of the roles they are called upon to play. These problems must be faced and handled. We have not faced up to them squarely enough to offset the consequence of the functional differences which arise.

Unevenness in Sentencing

The dilemma of the crime disposers is reflected in the ambivalent philosophies in sentencing practice. It is not so much a fault of the judge as of the confusion and ambivalence of our society reflected in the law itself. The statutes, at one and the same time, call upon the judge to provide deterrence, retribution, rehabilitation, and incapacitation, all in the same sentence. The judge attempts this by individualizing the sentence, and the result is an unevenness in sentences reflecting an uneven consideration of cases. The problem is more complicated than mere inequality of sentences, for judges arrive at their sentences by measures that demonstrate unequal consideration of such notions as deterrence, rehabilitation, retribution, and incapacitation, and the personal discretion of the judge turns out to be a host of ill-defined and inexplicit variables, hidden by his discretionary power. Our task is to find ways and means by which we can put on tap the fruits of the behavioral sciences so that the sentences imposed by the judge can afford us a condition for building a relevant system of correctional practice. . . .

The correctional system stands divided between custody and treatment. The crime keepers are, on one hand, the custodians; the crime treaters are the professionals. How often do the treatment personnel complain of their problems with custody? As often as not, psychiatrists and other professionals shun correctional work. They tell us they feel like the inmates themselves in the hands of custody; psychiatrists have said they do not like to work in penitentiaries because they do not like to be inmates along with the inmates. In Illinois, not so long ago, the psychiatrists and sociologists were more suspect than the inmates! They were frisked regularly going in and out of the institution.

A Fundamental Error

Our approach to this problem has been fundamentally in error. The current formula is to sensitize custody people to treatment and sensitize treatment people to custody. We will not resolve the issue this way, for we only compound the continuing polarity of these groups under these circumstances. The answer is a critical approach to the problem by way of job analysis and job breakdown. We must break down the tasks and put them back together to achieve a true and genuine differentiation of function within the institution so that all members of the correctional apparatus are seen as fostering a *common* purpose and a *common* objective. They are not opposed each against the other. This will require innovation, imagination, invention in the sense of analyzing and putting things together in new ways. . . . We maintain the arbitrary division between the juvenile officer and those who patrol the rest of the city in the face of the fact that today most of the serious crime is committed, according to police records, by persons eighteen years of age and under. Over three-fifths of Part I crimes are committed by persons eighteen and under. Most will have confrontations with police—not juvenile officers—and yet, for the most part, our approach is in terms of sensitizing the police to providing a specialized function within the police—namely, the juvenile department.

Separate Theories

We have the crime treaters, the crime keepers, the crime disposers, the crime catchers, the crime preventers, and one cannot in good conscience say they view the criminal the same way. They have their *own* theories on crime. They attack any problem with their set theory. Any overall guidelines or new programs of action become fancy paperwork as far as the police are concerned, paperwork as far as the judges are concerned, paperwork as far as the tradition-bound established framework of criminal justice is concerned.

Another myth, while diminishing among professionals, still looms large and remains a challenge to research and to training. In the past decade behavioral science has increasingly emphasized latent functions of our systems in criminal justice. The police, correction, and the courts may indeed, in unintended ways, generate the very tendencies they are set up to repress. These agencies must become concerned about any process inside their structures that produces a product very like the one they originally received and which they assume, in terms of their declared and overt purpose, will become different. Norms and views hostile to the community may be generated through *material* deprivation; however, one may also create a situation where individuals are *psychologically* deprived so that they are driven to antithetical values and notions inside the very institutions designed to breed respect for the law. While in custody, men may be driven to means and practices which are, of themselves, evasions of law.

Rule-breaking tendencies and dispositions are developed within the cover of the rule-making and enforcing institutions themselves. Awareness of this process is not a condition of operation, not a condition of understanding of the institutionalized agencies and services of the land in law enforcement, correction, prosecution, and defense. Lawyers, judges, police may be concerned about the consequences for an individual and be concerned about being human, but they do not generalize this into systems. We all need to know the sense in which these agencies operate as systems, and we need to develop strategies to cope with the problems generated by these social systems.

Group Nature of Delinquency

Still another myth is the idea that we can deal with delinquents as *individuals.* It takes the form: "If only one could give a man enough attention, enough service as an individual. . . ." This myth makes light of social structure and social organization, group circumstances and associations inside of which he must adjust and to which he must reconcile himself. We ought to face squarely the fact that the one-to-one worker-client relationship is not an effective means of dealing with a delinquent. We must, at long last, face the *group nature* of delinquency as the real challenge. . . .

The Metropolitan Community

Then, there is the myth of the *local community* and here some real soul-searching is in order. In recent years we have become increasingly pessimistic about efforts focused on dealing with crime at points remote from the local community. We turned from the state back to the local community so we could deal with delinquency realistically in community terms. However, if in a spirit of political expedience, we accept a definition of local community which reflects the citizenry's mythology as to its nature, we will only perpetuate a self-defeating myth. The *metropolitan* community is the new *local* community. It is the new community context in which crime is generated and to which it returns. It is the case *par excellence* of crime and the community. Although we must see correction and law enforcement in a community context, we must at the same time recognize that the dimensions of the community have changed. . . . Middle-class youngsters do not steal as many cars as lower-class youngsters, but they do all the things in their parents' car that lower-class youth do in stolen cars. They are a similar problem to the police; this has become increasingly apparent to students of the deviance patterns of middle-class youth, particularly those studies addressing the youthful subcultures of metropolitan areas. We must recognize the necessity for looking at the crime problem in terms of the newly emergent community.

The Police Function

Yet another myth is the belief that the single most important variable affecting the kind and amount of crime is the *police* function. This mythology rests upon the persistence among us of doctrinaire views concerning deterrence. Deep within our legal structure rests the notion that sanctions effectively administered will deter the evildoer. Suspect as this notion may be among students of criminal responsibility, it is *not* suspect in the American community; it is not suspect among the agencies of criminal justice; it is not suspect among the mass media. We must come to grips with the notion of deterrence and the myths which have flowered from its uncritical and unqualified acceptance as legal doctrine. . . .

Failure in Education

If we look at the American law enforcement and correctional systems as a challenge, we cannot fail to note that fully a third of the persons in police and correction, presently paid agents of the community in discharging a professional or occupational task, are without any education or training in law enforcement or correction. This is a conservative statement. This should be coupled with the crisis in education. It has been observed that as many as a third of the pupils fed into the school systems of the twelve largest cities in the United States have such limited backgrounds that the systems' traditional methods are incapable of reaching them effectively. . . .

It is more than a coincidence that a third to as much as a half of the law enforcement and correctional personnel (even more in some states) are without any formal education or training in their chosen occupations. This situation cannot be remedied by simply offering a few courses in those states or cities.

Our approach to their educational and training needs must be in terms of the operating systems themselves. This will require adjustments by colleges and universities as drastic as those within the correctional and law-enforcement systems themselves.

Not many people are specifically trained in the widely publicized techniques newly developing in correction and police work in the United States. For example, group therapies, counseling programs, and halfway houses are staffed by people without specific training in the techniques appropriate to these programs. The result is that untrained personnel cheapen the quality of new and progressive programs, even as the relatively few effective methods of our traditional programs of law enforcement and correction are being swallowed up and engulfed by antiquated and obsolescent systems of law enforcement and corrections.

Casework Concept

Casework orientation, traditionally regarded as a condition of entry into correctional and police systems, is no longer an appropriate concept. The traditional and operational definition of casework has not found its counterpart in these systems. Persons trained in casework techniques find it almost universally impossible to practice their profession within the framework of the developing law-enforcement and correctional systems. The result is that agencies other than those in law enforcement and correction absorb the people the social-work schools provide.

QUALITY OF JUSTICE

The increase of crime and delinquency, in terms of official records and official detention, has created the problems attendant upon a large-scale bureaucratic structure. We have an immense new organization which suddenly is upon us without having developed at the same time the conditions for development of middle-management personnel. The qualification of persons who go up the scale to middle-management and supervisory assignments consists entirely of line-function experience. They are, for the most part, persons without policy orientation and without capacity for leadership in restructing and reorganizing our excessively traditional and outmoded systems. A major problem and challenge to centers of law enforcement and correction is the education and training of a whole new class of middle-management and supervisory personnel to cope with the emergent bureaucracies of law enforcement and correction. The urgent need for imaginative programs in this area involves curriculum preparation and the direct servicing of operational systems.

Our municipal courts represent an enormous challenge and, for the most part, are the *terra incognita* of the judicial system. Most of the justice in the United States continues to be dispensed by two agencies with the lowest status in the system of criminal justice—the police and the municipal courts. For the masses of persons, criminal justice is dispensed at the police level. The police are the greatest quasi-judicial element in the experience of the public. Second only to police are the municipal judges, whose low status is both a challenge and an opportunity. In their desire to improve their status they are most amenable to being approached by means of research, experimentation, and innovation. Their involvement in research and training programs can help them improve their status. We must address judicial and quasi-judicial problems at police and municipal court levels with a calculated program of collaborative, institutional-ized education and service. Little, if any, work has been undertaken in this area where a marriage of law and behavioral science is a promising answer.

The increasing polarity between the police and the courts is a major feature of the current crisis. The rapidly heightening police-versus-Constitution controversy poses a dangerous threat to American society. We must end the present maze of individual case precedents by providing broad, positive guidelines for policemen in their daily work. The courts and the police must devise a definition of the limits of police action.

The judiciary could help end the present jungle of individual negative case precedents by formulating broad positive guidelines for police use in their daily work. . . .

. . . The steady stream of Supreme Court decisions and other appellate rules on search and seizure, due process, and other aspects of police investigation has created a situation of ambivalence and anarchy for much of this work. Most of these decisions are limited to a particular set of circumstances, judged after their occurrence. Nearly all the many publicized cases have involved the spectacle of a Kafka-like, powerless individual confronted by the majesty and force of the law. These decisions reflect a very fundamental change in the character of our society. Power has emerged from what were formerly powerless groups, which are bringing these cases before the courts.

The current controversy over "police brutality" is a reflection of the changing power structure. We must explore the problems of police conduct or explain it as a natural phenomenon, even as we explain other natural phenomena. The growing controversy does not mean that the general level of police work has deteriorated; in fact, it has enormously improved. Individual instances of excess and abuse are cause for public concern and protest. Police methods are, in short, not a reflection of ignorance or insensitivity but a collective formula for discharging responsibility colored by the power complex of the society. This is the context of our problem. We must develop education and training in accordance with these considerations.

OUR HYPHENATED SOCIETY

Throughout the nineteenth century America was a complex of hyphenated Americans who came to our melting-pot society and attempted to effect a transition, through institutions tailored to their condition, from their Old World tradition to the American scene. The settlement house taught them English; vocational schools gave them skills to use in the economic interdependence of the new society. Much has happened to such institutions as the settlement house and vocational education since that day. Today, the traditional vocational education is regarded as obsolescent and even pointless in the light of technological change. The settlement house is held ill adapted to the transition of the immigrant populations. Its methods are not appropriate to their condition as they come to the city and metropolitan areas of the North in present times. . . .

The social process is elaborating a complex of subcultures driving us apart in local communities and groups interacting among themselves and producing their own distinctive norms and values. These are the current subcultures of youth, of race, of suburbia, and of income, high and low. The emergence of these subcultures confounds our established institutional structures. We have such a plurality of subcultures that the problem of the individual's adjustment to commonly accepted norms is compounded and deviance is generated as a matter of course. Crime and delinquency are its logical accompaniment. We must develop means for modifying and preparing personnel to play new and meaningful roles.

The paradox of the new metropolitan development means we are constantly moving toward self-defeating extremes in desperate and uninformed efforts to keep abreast of the changing community. The heartlands of our great metropolitan centers are becoming the provinces of the new minorities. These groups are a potential threat that may express themselves in the traditional patterns of organized crime. They have come out of a segregated discriminatory experience, in search of freedom and opportunity, in to a social environment which in many respects is as restrictive as the older pattern. It is not only crime that becomes the abortive fruit of our failure to understand this changing community.

The unwitting processes of the middle-class "suburban drift" and the transformation of vast areas of the central city into an enormous racial slum have profound political implications. In many major cities the balance of political power is changing. We must recognize the coincidence of the development of racial blocs with the traditional organization and location of the urban political machines. The traditional alliances between crime and politics have focused on the immigrant community and the slum. We may be ushering in a new era of unprecedented political conflict between the cities and their suburbs with aggravating overtones of race tension and conflict as an additional feature of organized crime. To ignore the social, economic, and cultural disabilities under which these populations labor and to try to contain their volcanic eruptions by the expedient of repressive and antiquated police measures can only have the effect of force-feeding the fires smoldering in the core of our metropolitan communities.

Many of the problems which confront us stem from the failure of the public to know and to understand the new dimensions and ramifications of community life. Our success in controlling the crime problem, in general, and organized crime, in particular, will depend upon our understanding of the complexities of the newly emerging communal life and the problems it has engendered. An effective law-enforcement function must be familiar with, and equal to, its target.

The changing patterns of crime are a projection of the far-reaching changes in American community life. The police, the courts, the machinery of punishment and correction are also projections of the community. We cannot be successful in controlling crime without seriously changing the organization and administration of criminal justice. The ultimate answer is to see crime not simply as a problem in law enforcement but as a problem in education, family organization, employment opportunity, and housing. These are the structures inside of which deviance and hence crime and delinquency incubate. Man's behavior can be changed only by altering the conditions which underlie that behavior. We must learn to treat causes, not only effects, of crime.

We are at a critical juncture in the history of American community development. The emergence of the metropolitan community is not merely a change in the size of our population or in its geographic location. It implies something of far greater importance—namely, the creation of a whole new set of human values and relations.

Index

Name Index

*This book has been set in 10 point Press
Roman, leaded 2 points. Part numbers and
reading numbers and titles are in Univers Bold.
Part titles are in Univers Medium. The size of
the type page is 27 by 45½ picas.*

D

(